Mathematical Methods and Applications for Artificial Intelligence and Computer Vision

Mathematical Methods and Applications for Artificial Intelligence and Computer Vision

Editors

Ezequiel López-Rubio
Esteban J. Palomo
Enrique Domínguez

Basel • Beijing • Wuhan • Barcelona • Belgrade • Novi Sad • Cluj • Manchester

Editors

Ezequiel López-Rubio
University of Málaga
Málaga
Spain

Esteban J. Palomo
University of Málaga
Málaga
Spain

Enrique Domínguez
University of Málaga
Málaga
Spain

Editorial Office
MDPI
St. Alban-Anlage 66
4052 Basel, Switzerland

This is a reprint of articles from the Special Issue published online in the open access journal *Mathematics* (ISSN 2227-7390) (available at: https://www.mdpi.com/si/mathematics/Mathematical_Methods_Applications_Artificia_Intelligence_Computer_Vision).

For citation purposes, cite each article independently as indicated on the article page online and as indicated below:

Lastname, A.A.; Lastname, B.B. Article Title. *Journal Name* **Year**, *Volume Number*, Page Range.

ISBN 978-3-7258-0061-2 (Hbk)
ISBN 978-3-7258-0062-9 (PDF)
doi.org/10.3390/books978-3-7258-0062-9

© 2024 by the authors. Articles in this book are Open Access and distributed under the Creative Commons Attribution (CC BY) license. The book as a whole is distributed by MDPI under the terms and conditions of the Creative Commons Attribution-NonCommercial-NoDerivs (CC BY-NC-ND) license.

Contents

About the Editors . . . . **vii**

Hyewon Yoon, Shuyu Li and Yunsick Sung
Style Transformation Method of Stage Background Images by Emotion Words of Lyrics
Reprinted from: *Mathematics* **2021**, *9*, 1831, doi:10.3390/math9151831 . . . . **1**

**Jorge Munoz-Minjares, Osbaldo Vite-Chavez, Jorge Flores-Troncoso
and Jorge M. Cruz-Duarte**
Alternative Thresholding Technique for Image Segmentation Based on Cuckoo Search and
Generalized Gaussians
Reprinted from: *Mathematics* **2021**, *9*, 2287, doi:10.3390/math9182287 . . . . **21**

Ganbayar Batchuluun, Na Rae Baek and Kang Ryoung Park
Enlargement of the Field of View Based on Image Region Prediction Using Thermal Videos
Reprinted from: *Mathematics* **2021**, *9*, 2379, doi:10.3390/math9192379 . . . . **40**

Sung-Jin Lee and Seok Bong Yoo
Super- Resolved Recognition of License Plate Characters
Reprinted from: *Mathematics* **2021**, *9*, 2494, doi:10.3390/math9192494 . . . . **69**

Jun-Seok Yun and Seok-Bong Yoo
Single Image Super-Resolution with Arbitrary Magnification Based on High-Frequency
Attention Network
Reprinted from: *Mathematics* **2022**, *10*, 275, doi:10.3390/math10020275 . . . . **88**

**Umesh Kumar Lilhore, Agbotiname Lucky Imoize, Cheng-Chi Lee, Sarita Simaiya,
Subhendu Kumar Pani, Nitin Goyal, et al.**
Enhanced Convolutional Neural Network Model for Cassava Leaf Disease Identification
and Classification
Reprinted from: *Mathematics* **2022**, *10*, 580, doi:10.3390/math10040580 . . . . **107**

Magdiel Jiménez-Guarneros and Roberto Alejo-Eleuterio
A Class- Incremental Learning Method Based on Preserving the Learned Feature Space for
EEG-Based Emotion Recognition
Reprinted from: *Mathematics* **2022**, *10*, 598, doi:10.3390/math10040598 . . . . **126**

**Sur Singh Rawat, Saleh Alghamdi, Gyanendra Kumar, Youseef Alotaibi,
Osamah Ibrahim Khalaf and Lal Pratap Verma**
Infrared Small Target Detection Based on Partial Sum Minimization and Total Variation
Reprinted from: *Mathematics* **2022**, *10*, 671, doi:10.3390/math10040671 . . . . **147**

**Syed Furqan Qadri, Linlin Shen, Mubashir Ahmad, Salman Qadri, Syeda Shamaila Zareen
and Muhammad Azeem Akbar**
SVseg: Stacked Sparse Autoencoder-Based Patch Classification Modeling for
Vertebrae Segmentation
Reprinted from: *Mathematics* **2022**, *10*, 796, doi:10.3390/math10050796 . . . . **166**

**Valerio Varano, Stefano Gabriele, Franco Milicchio, Stefan Schlager, Ian Dryden
and Paolo Piras**
Geodesics in the TPS Space
Reprinted from: *Mathematics* **2022**, *10*, 1562, doi:10.3390/math10091562 . . . . **185**

Sur Singh Rawat, Sukhendra Singh, Youseef Alotaibi, Saleh Alghamdi and Gyanendra Kumar
Infrared Target-Background Separation Based on Weighted Nuclear Norm Minimization and Robust Principal Component Analysis
Reprinted from: *Mathematics* **2022**, *10*, 2829, doi:10.3390/math10162829 205

Mohammad AlElaiwi, Mugahed A. Al-antari, Hafiz Farooq Ahmad, Areeba Azhar, Badar Almarri and Jamil Hussain
VPP: Visual Pollution Prediction Framework Based on a Deep Active Learning Approach Using Public Road Images
Reprinted from: *Mathematics* **2023**, *11*, 186, doi:10.3390/math11010186 227

Noor Ain Syazwani Mohd Ghani, Abdul Kadir Jumaat, Rozi Mahmud, Mohd Azdi Maasar, Farizuwana Akma Zulkifle and Aisyah Mat Jasin
Breast Abnormality Boundary Extraction in Mammography Image Using Variational Level Set and Self-Organizing Map (SOM)
Reprinted from: *Mathematics* **2023**, *11*, 976, doi:10.3390/math11040976 253

Diego Teran-Pineda, Karl Thurnhofer-Hemsi and Enrique Dominguez
Analysis and Recognition of Human Gait Activity BASED on Multimodal Sensors
Reprinted from: *Mathematics* **2023**, *11*, 1538, doi:10.3390/math11061538 273

Shuangshuang Chen and Wei Guo
Auto-Encoders in Deep Learning—A Review with New Perspectives
Reprinted from: *Mathematics* **2023**, *11*, 1777, doi:10.3390/math11081777 290

About the Editors

Ezequiel López-Rubio

Ezequiel López-Rubio is a full professor of Computer Science and Artificial Intelligence at the Department of Computer Languages and Computer Science at the University of Málaga, Spain. He received his M.Sc. and Ph.D. (honors) in Computer Engineering from the University of Málaga, Spain, in 1999 and 2002, respectively, and received his M.Sc. in Social and Cultural Anthropology and M.Sc. in Logic, History and Philosophy of Science from the Spanish National Distance University, Madrid, Spain, in 2010 and 2016, respectively. He received another Ph.D. in Philosophy of Science in 2020. He joined the Department of Computer Languages and Computer Science, University of Málaga, in 2000. His research interests include machine learning, pattern recognition, image processing, and computer vision.

Esteban J. Palomo

Esteban J. Palomo is an associate professor in the Department of Computer Languages and Computer Science at the University of Málaga, Spain. He received his M.Sc. and Ph.D. (with honors) in Computer Engineering from the University of Málaga, Spain, in 2008 and 2013, respectively. For his Ph.D. thesis, he was given the Extraordinary Doctorate Award from the same university. He joined the Department of Computer Languages and Computer Science at the University of Málaga in 2007. In 2015, he joined the School of Mathematical Science and Information Technology at the University of Yachay Tech in Ecuador. He was appointed as adjunct faculty at the Simon A. Levin Mathematical, Computational and Modeling Sciences Center (MCMSC) at Arizona State University (USA) in 2017. That same year, he joined the Department of Computer Languages and Computer Science at the University of Málaga. His current research interests include unsupervised learning, self-organization, data mining, image/video processing, network security, and deep learning.

Enrique Domínguez

Enrique Domínguez is a full professor of Computer Science and Artificial Intelligence in the Department of Computer Languages and Computer Science at the University of Málaga, Spain. He received his B.Sc, MSc, and Ph.D. in Computer Science from the University of Málaga in 1999, 2000, and 2007, respectively. He joined the Department of Computer Science of the University of Málaga in 2000. He has participated as a member of the program committee of prestigious international conferences and journals. He is a member of the European Association for Artificial Intelligence (EurAI), the Spanish Association for Artificial Intelligence (AEPIA), the Spanish Society of Statistics and Operational Research (SEIO), the International Federation of Operational Research Societies (IFORS), the Association of European Operational Research Societies (EURO), and the Euro-Working Group on Locational Analysis (EWGLA). His research areas include neurocomputation, optimization, image/video processing and computer vision, machine/deep learning, and intelligent logistics systems.

Article

Style Transformation Method of Stage Background Images by Emotion Words of Lyrics

Hyewon Yoon, Shuyu Li and Yunsick Sung *

Department of Multimedia Engineering, Dongguk University-Seoul, Seoul 04620, Korea; hyewon@dongguk.edu (H.Y.); lishuyu@dongguk.edu (S.L.)
* Correspondence: sung@dongguk.edu

Citation: Yoon, H.; Li, S.; Sung, Y. Style Transformation Method of Stage Background Images by Emotion Words of Lyrics. *Mathematics* **2021**, *9*, 1831. https://doi.org/10.3390/math9151831

Academic Editors: Ezequiel López-Rubio, Esteban Palomo and Enrique Domínguez

Received: 20 May 2021
Accepted: 30 July 2021
Published: 3 August 2021

Publisher's Note: MDPI stays neutral with regard to jurisdictional claims in published maps and institutional affiliations.

Copyright: © 2021 by the authors. Licensee MDPI, Basel, Switzerland. This article is an open access article distributed under the terms and conditions of the Creative Commons Attribution (CC BY) license (https:// creativecommons.org/licenses/by/ 4.0/).

Abstract: Recently, with the development of computer technology, deep learning has expanded to the field of art, which requires creativity, which is a unique ability of humans, and an understanding of the human emotions expressed in art to process them as data. The field of art is integrating with various industrial fields, among which artificial intelligence (AI) is being used in stage art, to create visual images. As it is difficult for a computer to process emotions expressed in songs as data, existing stage background images for song performances are human designed. Recently, research has been conducted to enable AI to design stage background images on behalf of humans. However, there is no research on reflecting emotions contained in song lyrics to stage background images. This paper proposes a style transformation method to reflect emotions in stage background images. First, multiple verses and choruses are derived from song lyrics, one at a time, and emotion words included in each verse and chorus are extracted. Second, the probability distribution of the emotion words is calculated for each verse and chorus, and the image with the most similar probability distribution from an image dataset with emotion word tags in advance is selected for each verse and chorus. Finally, for each verse and chorus, the stage background images with the transferred style are outputted. Through an experiment, the similarity between the stage background and the image transferred to the style of the image with similar emotion words probability distribution was 38%, and the similarity between the stage background image and the image transferred to the style of the image with completely different emotion word probability distribution was 8%. The proposed method reduced the total variation loss of change from 1.0777 to 0.1597. The total variation loss is the sum of content loss and style loss based on weights. This shows that the style transferred image is close to edge information about the content of the input image, and the style is close to the target style image.

Keywords: image style transformation; lyrics to image style; emotion; deep learning; style transfer

1. Introduction

Advances in computer technology have led to technological innovations such as information revolution, big data processing, and active use of networks. These innovations have increased interest in AI [1,2]. In recent years, AI has been researched in the field of art, which requires creativity, an inherent ability of humans. The field of art has been integrated with various industrial fields, such as AI, which is used in stage art in combination with stage effects. When a singer dances and sings, the audience views the singer's stage performance in combination with stage effects. Stage effects determine the stage mood using several important elements, such as lighting, music, acting, and stage background, which visually convey emotions associated with the songs to the audience. Among stage effects, stage background has been transitioning from the expression method of using props to the expression method of media performance that uses images through large light-emitting diode (LED) screens or projectors [3]. In general, background stage images used in media performances are selected in advance by professional stage designers at the planning stage. Stage background images of the singing performance represent the emotions expressed in song lyrics. It is difficult for computers to represent emotions that humans have been manually designing for stage background images. Recently, research was conducted to enable AI to design stage background images in place of humans. In this approach, a stage background image recommendation system is used to automatically compose stage background images according to dance styles without professional stage designers. However, the limitation of the stage background images selected through conventional recommendation systems is that the emotions to be represented in the song lyrics are not reflected in the stage performance. It would be ideal to represent emotions represented in song lyrics through stage background images during stage performances. Research regarding the reflection of emotions contained in song lyrics in a stage background are scarce; however, it is possible to use research that transforms background images according to their meanings or purpose by synthesizing background images with text or images containing the meaning to be represented. There is research that partially transforms images using the content contained in text [4–6] and transfers the style such as color, line, and texture of image to another image [7–11]. The existing stage background image recommendation system recommends images for dancers, but this does not include the characteristics of the song lyrics.

This paper proposes a method to transform the multiple styles of stage background images based on the emotion words contained in each verse and chorus of song lyrics. First, the lyrics selected by the user are divided into sentences. Multiple verses and choruses are derived from the lyrics, one at a time and compared to the emotion word dictionary to extract emotion words included in each verse and chorus. Second, the probability distributions of the emotion words are calculated for each verse and chorus and the image with the most similar probability distribution from the image dataset with the emotion word tags in advance is selected for each verse and chorus. Finally, for each verse and chorus, the stage background images with the transferred style are outputted for each verse and chorus. The advantages of the proposed method are as follows.

- It uses emotion words contained in song lyrics to transform the style of stage background images. Audience immersion can be increased by using stage background images to represent emotions expressed in the song lyrics used for singing in stage performances. Emotions that are complex to represent using computers can be represented.
- Certain emotions that are difficult for humans to determine intuitively can be represented because the proposed method can transform the style of images based on an image with a high correlation with the emotion represented using lyrics.

The remainder of this paper is organized as follows. Section 2 introduces the stage background recommendation system, methods of extracting the visual features of emotion words, and image style transformation methods reported in related work, and examines their limitations and technical constraints. Section 3 describes the method proposed to derive emotion words contained in the verses and choruses of song lyrics to reflect the emotions in stage background images and apply the style that is directly related to the derived emotion words to the stage background images. Section 4 verifies whether the stage background images are transformed according to the probability distribution of emotion words represented for each verse and chorus. Section 5 summarizes the findings and describes the limitations of this research and future research directions.

2. Related Work

In this section, we introduce the existing stage background recommendation system, methods of extracting the visual features of emotion words and image style transformation methods. Song lyric-based style transformation methods are compared, and their limitations and technical constraints are examined.

2.1. Stage Background Image Recommendation System

A stage background image recommendation system recommends stage background images by reflecting the dancer's preferences and dance styles such as ballet, belly dance, street dance, modern dance, tango, and waltz [3]. Dancers choose familiar or favorite stage background images. Therefore, the stage background images can be artistic images or actual photographs that the dancers prefer. Reference [3] proposed a model that predicts users' preferred images through social media. The proposed model predicts the K number of images that the dancer (user) is most likely to use as stage background images via three procedures. First, the features of the images shared by the dancer on social media (Pinterest) are extracted. Second, the profile of the dancer is learned based on the features of the shared images. Third, the interest level of the dancer in each candidate image is predicted, and the candidate images are ranked according to the dancer's predicted interest level. However, because only dances are reflected, the stage background images from the stage background recommendation system cannot represent the emotions that a stage performance aims to express through lyrics.

2.2. Emotion Classification

To express emotions using images that are difficult to process using computers, research was conducted recently to improve the accuracy of the sentimental understanding of human emotions [12–18].

Human emotions are visualized and used in psychotherapy, image search, etc. In general, models for representing emotions are divided into two types: categorical emotion states (CES) models, which classify emotions into several basic categories such as fear, amusement, and sadness, and dimensional emotion space (DES) models, which use three-dimensional emotion space such as arousal, time, and harmony. As it is difficult to construct a multidimensional emotion space using information about time included in song lyrics, we used the CES method to consider images as a basic category of emotions. The CES method is easy for users to understand and convenient for emotion classification of images. The research in [12] used the CES method to extract principles-of-art-based emotion features (PAEF) to classify features of emotions included in images to understand the relationship between artistic principles and emotions. PAEF are a combination of representation features derived from the principles of balance, emphasis, harmony, variety, gradation, and movement. PAEF are used to classify the basic emotion words evoked in humans through images. A psychological research classified common basic emotion words into eight categories based on images through facial electromyography, heart rate, finger temperature, etc. That is, emotions contained in images are classified into eight categories, which define anger, disgust, fear and sadness as negative emotions and amusement, awe, contentment, and excitement as positive emotions [13]. These are called images of emotional levels, whereby an image of emotional level refers to the relationship between the style, such as color, saturation, brightness, and contrast, and the emotional effect derived from art theory [17]. The level of basic emotion words defined in the eight categories is classified for images. To evaluate this, the participants looked at the images, selected the most appropriate basic emotion category, and evaluated the emotional labels of the images. However, because it is not possible to visualize the features of images classified with the level of basic emotion words, there is no way of knowing the images that are appropriate for the stage background. Therefore, it is necessary to derive a method of visualizing the features of each basic emotion to find its relationship with the song lyrics and reflect them in the stage background images.

2.3. Style Transfer

Style is transferred to reflect the features of each basic emotion word in the stage background images. Usually, style transfer is used to transfer the image style. Style transfer consists of content image and style image. Content image refers to an image that has information such as an object or a common landscape that people can usually recognize, and style image refers to an image that has information such as color or texture that will be combined with the content image. Style transfer transfers the style based on a convolutional neural network (CNN) [10,11] and a generative adversarial network (GAN) [5–7]. Style transfer based on the CNN model extracts features by separating content and style in an image. Training is performed to extract content features from deep layers and extract style features from middle layers through the CNN model. The GAN model is used to change the content in detail, but in this research, the CNN model is used because it changes the overall image style.

2.4. Comparison of Methods for Image Style Transformation

Table 1 presents the difference between the existing methods of transforming image style and the proposed method. The research in Zhao et al. [12] investigates the concept of the principle of art and its effect on emotion and classifies emotion images into eight basic emotion words. However, because many images are classified for each basic emotion word, it is difficult to find an appropriate image for the stage background image.

Table 1. Comparison of the proposed method and image synthesis methods.

	Zhao et al. [12]	Machajdik et al. [13]	Zhao et al. [17]	The Proposed Method
Training data	IAPS, Art photo, Abstract painting	IAPS, Art photo, abstract painting	User's metadata, IAPS, Abstract painting, Flickr	Song lyrics, Flickr
Encoding	Image-based	Image-based	User's metadata-based	One-hot encoding, Texture-based
Model	SVM	Waterfall segmentation algorithm	Multi-Task Hypergraph learning	CNN

3. Method of Transferring Image Style Based on Song Lyrics

This section presents the proposed method to transfer stage background images using the emotion words contained in song lyrics. The proposed method consists of the lyrics preprocessing stage, which extracts the probability distribution of emotion words for each verse and chorus from selected lyrics and the emotion image processing stage, which transfers the styles of each verse and chorus images related to the extracted probability distribution of emotion words. The proposed method transfers the stage background image using styles of images related to emotion words extracted from each verse and chorus. The number of images with representative emotion image styles applied is equal to the sum of the number of verses and choruses from selected lyrics.

3.1. Overview

Figure 1 is the overview of the proposed method. The proposed method is composed of the lyrics preprocessing stage and the emotion image processing stage. Table 2 is the description of all stages. In the lyrics preprocessing stage, the selected lyrics by a user are extracted into verses and choruses, and the probability distribution of emotion words contained in each verse and chorus is extracted separately. In the emotion image processing stage, the emotion images with tags, where the tags are matched to the corresponding emotion images in advance, are selected from the extracted emotion words of each verse and chorus and the stage background image is transferred to the different styles of the selected emotion image according to each verse and chorus.

Table 2. Process for transforming stage background image style based on song lyrics.

Stage	Description
Lyric preprocessing	User's selected lyrics are divided into verses and choruses, and a probability distribution of emotion words is extracted for each verse and chorus.
Emotion image processing	From emotion images with tags, the appropriate images are selected for each verse and chorus, and styles of selected images transferred to stage background image.

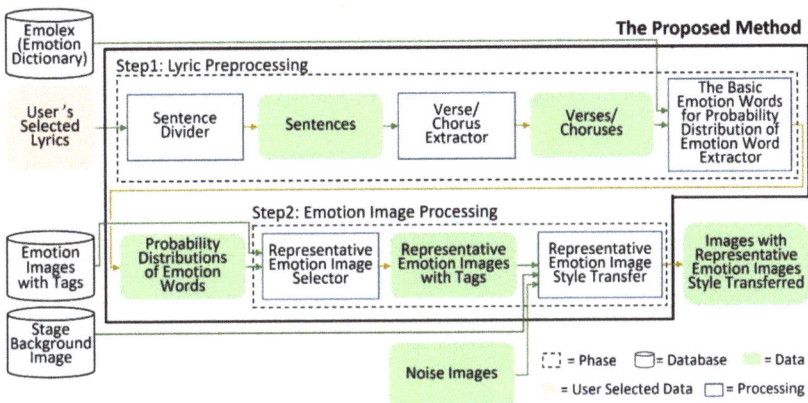

Figure 1. Process of applying emotions of song lyrics to stage background images.

3.2. Step 1: Lyric Preprocessing

The lyric preprocessing step is composed of a sentence divider, verse/chorus extractor and the basic emotion words for the emotion word extractor. The sentence divider divides the lyrics into sentences. The verse/chorus extractor extracts the selected lyrics into verses and choruses. The basic emotion words for the emotion word extractor extracts the probability distribution of emotion words contained in each verse and chorus. Figure 2 is an overview of step 1.

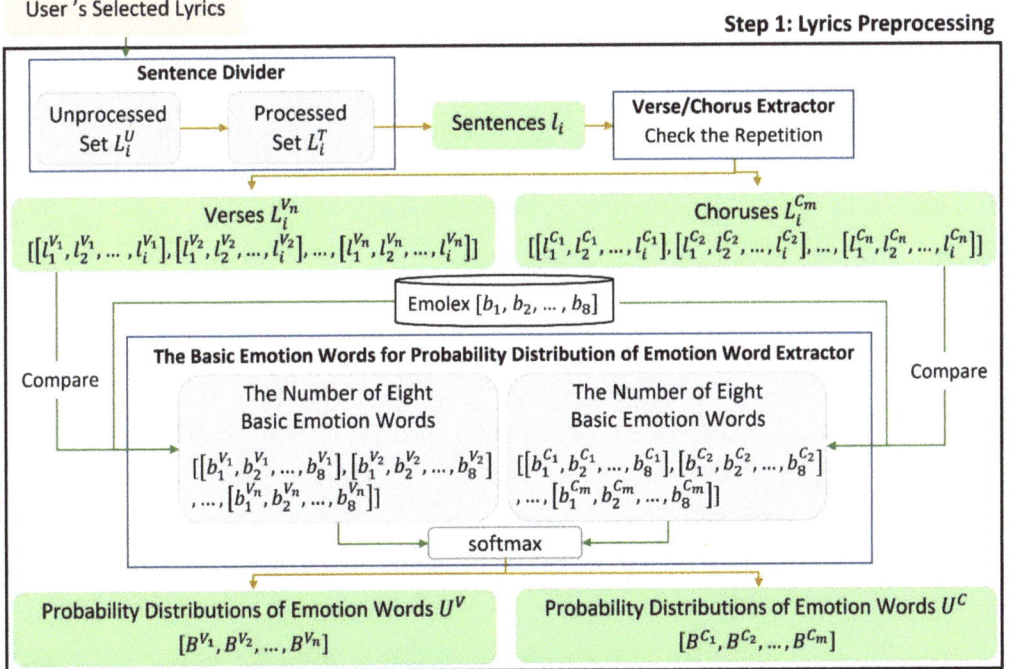

Figure 2. Step 1: Lyric preprocessing.

The sentence divider divides the lyrics into a set of sentences considering capital letters. The set of sentences in the lyrics is defined as the unprocessed set L_i^U. All sentences in L_i^U are processed as a set L_i^T, which is classified as verses and choruses through the classification process. This is repeated until there are no sentences left in L_i^U and all sentences in L_i^T are processed.

The verse/chorus extractor executes the following processes. The user's selected lyrics consist of n verses and m choruses. The ith sentence inputted in L_i^T is compared to the sentences in L_i^U, and the frequency is repeatedly checked. The set of sentences with no repetition in the lyrics as verse $L^{V_n} = \left[\left[l_1^{V_1}, l_2^{V_1}, \ldots, l_i^{V_1}\right], \left[l_1^{V_2}, l_2^{V_2}, \ldots, l_i^{V_2}\right], \ldots, \left[l_1^{V_n}, l_2^{V_n}, \ldots, l_i^{V_n}\right]\right]$ and the set of sentences that are repeated in the lyrics are classified as chorus $L^{C_n} = \left[\left[l_1^{C_1}, l_2^{C_1}, \ldots, l_i^{C_1}\right], \left[l_1^{C_2}, l_2^{C_2}, \ldots, l_i^{C_2}\right], \ldots, \left[l_1^{C_m}, l_2^{C_m}, \ldots, l_i^{C_m}\right]\right]$.

The basic emotion words for probability distribution of the emotion word extractor compares the L^{V_n}, L^{C_m} with an Emolex (Emotion Dictionary) [19] and finds the matching emotion words. The Emolex consists of a total of 14,182 words classified into the basic emotion words, as shown in Figure 3, and information on whether they are positive emotion or negative emotion is also included. All basic emotion words are expressed by eight emotions, categorized into the positive emotions of anticipation, joy, surprise and trust, and the negative emotions of anger, disgust, fear and sadness, as proposed by Plutchik [20] to provide a high-dimensional emotion lexicon [19]. The extracted emotion words in each verse and chorus are replaced with the classified basic emotion words. Each basic emotion word is counted by the corresponding numbers, the number of anticipation b_1, that of joy b_2, that of trust b_3, that of surprise b_4, that of anger b_5, that of fear b_6, that of sadness b_7, and that of disgust b_8. The probability distribution of the basic emotion words is calculated. The set that counts the number of eight basic emotion words contained in L_i^T is defined as B. The number of eight basic emotion words included in the nth verse from L^{V_n} is stored in $B^{V_n} = \left[\left[b_1^{V_1}, b_2^{V_1}, \ldots, b_8^{V_1}\right], \left[b_1^{V_2}, b_2^{V_2}, \ldots, b_8^{V_2}\right], \ldots, \left[b_1^{V_n}, b_2^{V_n}, \ldots, b_8^{V_n}\right]\right]$ and the number of eight basic emotion words included in the mth chorus from L^{C_m} is stored in $B^{C_m} = \left[\left[b_1^{C_1}, b_2^{C_1}, \ldots, b_8^{C_1}\right], \left[b_1^{C_2}, b_2^{C_2}, \ldots, b_8^{C_2}\right], \ldots, \left[b_1^{C_m}, b_2^{C_m}, \ldots, b_8^{C_m}\right]\right]$. The probability distributions of the basic emotion words included in verses and choruses are defined as $U^V = softmax(B^{V_n})$, $U^C = softmax(B^{C_m})$, and calculated as Equation (1).

$$U^V = Softmax\left(B^{V_n}\right) = \frac{e^{b_i^{V_n}}}{\sum_{j=1}^{8} e^{b_j^{V_n}}}, \ i \in (1, 2, \ldots, 8) \quad U^C = Softmax\left(B^{C_m}\right) = \frac{e^{b_i^{C_m}}}{\sum_{j=1}^{8} e^{b_j^{C_m}}}, \ i \in (1, 2, \ldots, 8) \quad (1)$$

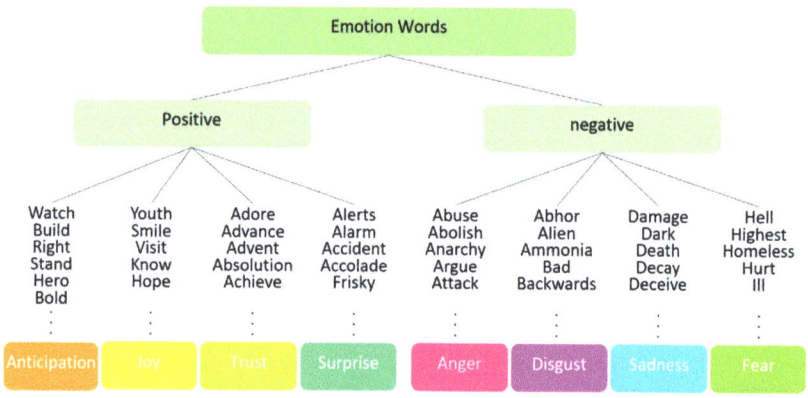

Figure 3. Classification of the emotion lexicon.

3.3. Step 2: Emotion Image Processing

The emotion image processing step is composed of a representative emotion images selector and representative emotion images style transfer. The representative emotion images selector searches and selects images with a probability distribution similar to the U^V, U^C of the emotion images with tags. The representative emotion images style transfer transfers stage background images into the styles of the selected emotion images with tags. Figure 4 shows an overview of step 2.

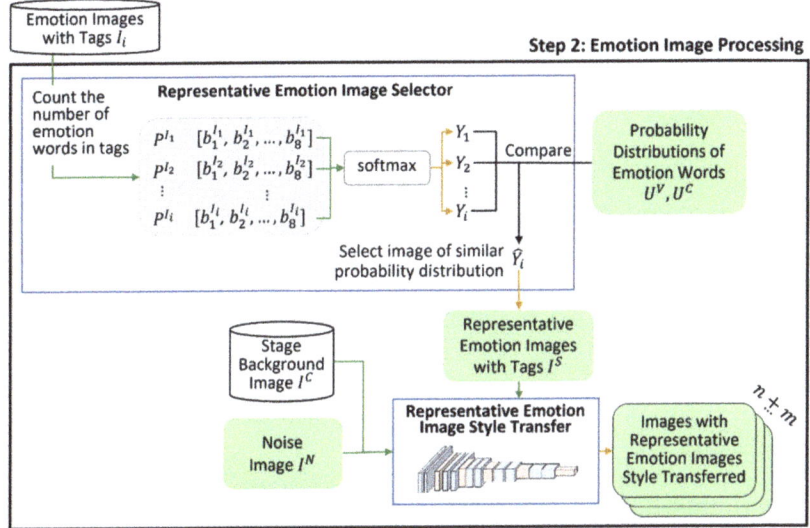

Figure 4. Step 2: Emotion image processing.

The representative emotion images selector selects emotion images with tags similar to probability distributions U^V, U^C contained in each verse and chorus in the lyric preprocessing step. In total, 1000 emotion images with tags were downloaded from Flickr and defined as I_i. P^{l_i} is defined as a set that counts the number of eight basic emotion words contained in I_i. P^{l_i} is the set of the number of basic emotion words in which the ith image was classified through peer evaluation. The probability distribution of the basic emotion words included in the ith image is Y_i and is calculated as Equation (2).

$$Y_i = softmax\left(P^{l_i}\right) = \frac{e^{b_k^{l_i}}}{\sum_{u=1}^{8} e^{b_u}}, \quad k \in (1, 2, \ldots, 8) \qquad (2)$$

Finally, to select the emotion images with tags associated with the user's selected lyrics, the representative emotion images selector finds $\hat{Y}_i$, which has a probability distribution that is most similar to that of U, included in U^V, U^C. The index i of $\hat{Y}_i$ where the difference in the probability distribution is the minimum, as defined in Equation (3).

$$\hat{i} = \underset{i}{argmin}(U - V_i)^2, \quad i \in (1, 2, \ldots, 1000) \qquad (3)$$

The representative emotion images style transfer transfers the styles of $(n + m)$ emotion images with tags derived from the representative emotion images selector through a CNN model-based style transfer algorithm to the stage background image. Style is features such as color, saturation, brightness, contrast, stroke, and texture. Figure 5 shows the method of outputting an image with a transferred style through a CNN that extracts the image features of content related to the stage background image and a CNN that extracts the features of style from emotion images with tags. The CNN model normalized the weight of the network using the VGG-16 network, and average pooling was used instead of max pooling. Style characteristics are based on the Gram matrix, ignoring spatial information, and extracting features such as texture and color. Since the correlation of the feature maps of multiple layers, not a single layer, is viewed at the same time, static information, not layout information that the image has globally, is obtained in consideration of multiple scales.

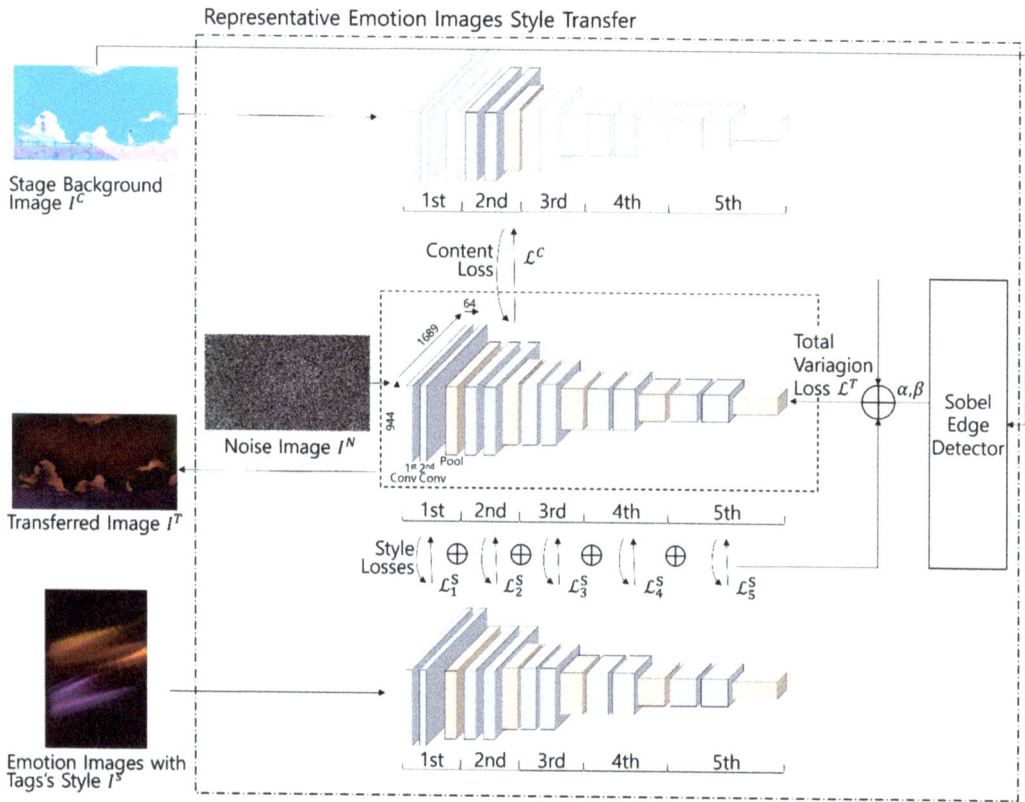

Figure 5. Representative emotion image style transfer process.

Style transfer [9–11] is applied to the representative emotion images style transfer as shown below. There are three types of input images: Stage background image related to the selected lyrics is defined as content image I^C, I_i selected from the representative emotion images selector is defined as style image I^S, and noise image is defined as noise image I^N. A noise image is a random variation of brightness or color information in images. This paper synthesizes content of I^C and style of I^S on I^N. The CNN model is composed of a total of five blocks, $B_{1,...,5}$ and one block B consists of two convolution layers and one pooling layer. After going through one block, each content feature and style feature are extracted. When the input is I^C, the output from the second block is defined as the content features, and when the input is I^S, the output at each block is defined as the style features. Content features should have location information of objects included in I^C and edge information of the object, and the style feature is the correlation of feature maps. The content features of I^C and the style features of I^S jointly minimize the distance from the features of I^N. Content loss $\mathcal{L}^c$ is calculated by comparing the content of features of I^C with I^N as in Equation (4).

$$\mathcal{L}^C = \left(B_2\left(I^N\right) - B_2\left(I^C\right)\right)^2 \tag{4}$$

I^C is feed forward through the network. Style loss $\mathcal{L}^S$, is calculated by comparing the style features of I^S with I^N as in Equation (5).

$$\mathcal{L}^S = \sum_{n=1}^{5} \left(B_n\left(I^N\right) - B_n\left(I^S\right)\right)^2 \tag{5}$$

The pixel-level information disappears as the layer deepens, but the semantic information of I^C remains the same. Style features should be independent of spatial features. Low-level convolution layers represent low-level features such as edges. This feature maintains a higher resolution. The deeper the layer, the more difficult it is to visualize and interpret features such as edges because they are not directly connected to I^C. High-level convolution layers capture semantic and less granular spatial information. Style features can get information that considers multiple magnifications of the image globally. However, artifacts occur while transferring I^C into styles. This implies that I^N, which is output through the model, loses content information, including the edge information of the objects in I^C. The deformed error value of the image should be minimized with the transferred style. Edge information of I^C is recovered through the sobel edge detector [21]. The sobel edge detector is used to reduce the generation of artifacts without losing content features, and then α, β is calculated. α controls the preservation of the content image, and β controls the preservation of the style image. It detects the content features of I^C, making the content features of I^T even stronger. The content feature difference between I^C and I^T is defined as $\mathcal{L}^V$ and optimization is performed. In 2D images, sobel edge detection is performed in two directions, vertical and horizontal. The total variation loss $\mathcal{L}^T$ is calculated based on α, β, $\mathcal{L}^C$, $\mathcal{L}^S$ as in Equation (6). The noise image I^N is updated through back propagation based on the total variation loss $\mathcal{L}^T$.

$$\mathcal{L}^T = \alpha \mathcal{L}^C + \beta \mathcal{L}^S \tag{6}$$

Optimization proceeds with the limited-memory Broyden–Fletcher–Goldfarb–Shanno (L-BFGS) algorithm [22] to find the minimum of $\mathcal{L}^T$.

4. Experiments

The probability distribution accuracy verification experiment and the style variation quality verification experiment were performed. It is important that the style of the stage background image is well transformed according to the distribution of emotion words included in the lyrics. This paper verified whether the styles of the stage background image change according to the probability distribution of emotion words included in each verse and chorus and verified the CNN-based style transfer performance.

4.1. Dataset and Experimental Environment

The datasets used to verify the proposed method are the NRC Word-Emotion Association Lexicon (Emolex) and images from Unsplash. The Emolex dataset is a list of English words and their associations with eight basic emotion words (anger, fear, anticipation, trust, surprise, sadness, joy, and disgust) and two sentiments (negative and positive). The annotations were performed manually. It includes 6475 English words, and 281 English words were used in the experiment. Table 3 presents the number and distribution of emotion words for each English word to facilitate the use of the Emolex dataset in this experiment. Unsplash is a high-quality open-access image dataset that can be used for further research on machine learning, image quality and search engines. We downloaded 1000 abstract images from Unsplash, and seven colleagues classified them into anger, disgust, fear, sadness, amusement, awe, content, and excitement. Table 3 presents the classified results.

Amusement is a compound emotion of anger and joy, awe is of fear and surprise, content is of joy and trust and excitement is of surprise and joy. The user's selected lyrics used in the experiment was "Forgotten heroes" as shown in Figure 6. The Figure 6 is input to the experiment. The experiments included Windows 10, Intel i7–7700, Nvidia Titan RTX 24 GB graphics card and DDR4 40 GB RAM. The proposed system was developed using Python, and the CNN model was implemented using a deep learning library called Tensorflow.

Table 3. Emotion words distribution of Emolex.

	Anger	Disgust	Fear	Sadness	Anticipation	Joy	Surprise	Trust
Quantity	3428 (16%)	3414 (15%)	3572 (17%)	3449 (15%)	2312 (6%)	2325 (10%)	2625 (10%)	2692 (11%)

User's selected lyrics – "Forgotten heroes"

Her alarm goes off And she gets up to watch the morning news Doesn't work no more But tells a lot of stories 'bout her youth Drinks more lately And got pills in many different colors too Morning light is showing She moves the chair to look out at her view But a shop was built right across the street And it stands were the sunrise used to be In the afternoons on the couch to read Goes through old pictures and memories Our heroes have been forgotten Our heroes so brave and bold Our heroes have been forgotten Our heroes oh they got old Our heroes have been forgotten Our heroes so brave and bold Our heroes have been forgotten Our heroes oh they got old Our heroes oh they got old Our heroes oh they got old Smiles they fade because Her daughter only visits once a month Since she got a family of her own It's kept the two apart Used to have so many visitors But now the only one Is the nurse that helps her Move the chair to look out at the sun But a shop was built right across the street And it stands were the sunrise used to be In the afternoons on the couch to read Goes through old pictures and memories Our heroes have been forgotten Our heroes so brave and bold Our heroes have been forgotten Our heroes oh they got old Our heroes have been forgotten Our heroes so brave and bold Our heroes have been forgotten Our heroes oh they got old People don't stay the same you know I just hope their stories will still be told

Figure 6. User's selected lyrics.

4.2. Experiment Results

Figure 7 shows the result of extracting verses and choruses from Figure 6 using the verse/chorus extractor. Figure 6 consists of 44 sentences, and each word in each sentence was compared to all the words in entire sentence. A total of 12 consecutive sentences that were repeated twice were extracted as chorus and 20 non-repeated sentences were extracted as verses. Since 44 sentences should be compared with emotion words, the sentences are split into multiple words.

Using the basic emotion words for probability distribution of the emotion word extractor, we compared the emotion words in the lyrics to those in Emolex, as shown in Figure 8. When the words matched, the words in the lyrics were replaced with the basic emotion words. As shown in Figure 8, a total of seven emotion words (alarm, watch, youth, lately, pill, different, and show) were matched in Verse 1; a total of eight emotion words (build, right, stand, couch, hero, old, forgot and bold) in the chorus; a total of five emotion words (hero, old, smile, fade and visit) in Verse 2; and a total of two emotion words (know and hope) in Verse 3. The emotion words were matched a total of 199 times in the song lyrics including duplicates, and the searched emotion words were replaced with the Emolex-based basic emotion words. The probability distributions of the emotion words extractor count the total number of replaced basic emotion words and calculate the probability distribution of each basic emotion word for each verse and chorus.

Figure 7. Verse/chorus extractor.

Verses/Choruses	The Basic Emotion Words for Probability Distribution of Emotion Word Extractor	Probability Distributions of Emotion Words
Verse1 Her, alarm, goes, off, And, she, gets, up, to, watch, the, morning, news, Doesn't, work, no, more, But, tells, a, lot, of, stories, 'bout, her, youth, Drinks, more, lately, And, got, pills, in, many, different, colors, too, Morning, light, is, showing, She, moves, the, chair, to, look, out, at, her, view	Alarm → Fear, Surprise Watch → Anticip, Fear Youth → Anger, Anticip, Fear, Joy, Surprise lately → Sadness Pill → Trust Different → Surprise Show → Trust	**Verse1** Total Emotion Words: 14 Anger : 1 / 14 7.7% Anticip : 2 / 14 15.4% Fear : 3 / 14 23.1% Joy : 1 / 14 7.7% Sadness : 1 / 14 7.7% Surprise : 3 / 14 23.1% Trust : 2 / 14 15.4%
Chorus1 But, a, shop, was, built, right, across, the, street, And, it, stands, were, the, sunrise, used, to, be, In, the, afternoons, on, the, couch, to, read, Goes, through, old, pictures, and, memories, Our, heroes, have, been, forgotten, Our, heroes, so, brave, and, bold, Our, heroes, have, been, forgotten, Our, heroes, oh, they, got, old, Our, heroes, have, been, forgotten, Our, heroes, so, brave, and, bold, Our, heroes, have, been, forgotten, Our, heroes, oh, they, got, old	Build → Anticip, Joy, Surprise, Trust Right → Anticip, Joy, Surprise, Trust Stand → Anticip, Joy, Surprise, Trust Couch → Sadness Hero → Anticip, Joy, Surprise, Trust Old → Sadness Forgot → Fear, Sadness Bold → Anticip, Joy, Surprise, Trust	**Chorus1** Total Emotion Words: 75 Anticip : 15 / 75 20.0% Fear : 5 / 75 6.7% Joy : 15 / 75 20.0% Sadness : 10 / 75 13.3% Surprise : 15 / 75 20.0% Trust : 15 / 75 20.0%
Verse2 Our, heroes, oh, they, got, old, Our, heroes, oh, they, got, old, Smiles, they, fade, because, Her, daughter, only, visits, once, a, month, Since, she, got, a, family, of, her, own, It's, kept, the, two, apart, Used, to, have, so, many, visitors, But, now, the, only, one, Is, the, nurse, that, helps, her, Move, the, chair, to, look, out, at, the, sun	Hero → Anticip, Joy, Surprise, Trust Old → Sadness Smile → Joy, Surprise, Trust Fade → Anger, Disgust, Fear, Sadness Visit → Anticip, Joy, Surprise, Trust	**Verse2** Total Emotion Words: 27 Anger : 1 / 27 3.7% Anticip : 4 / 27 14.8% Disgust : 1 / 27 3.7% Fear : 1 / 27 3.7% Joy : 6 / 27 22.2% Sadness : 3 / 27 11.1% Surprise : 5 / 27 18.5% Trust : 6 / 27 22.2%
Chorus2 But, a, shop, was, built, right, across, the, street, And, it, stands, were, the, sunrise, used, to, be, In, the, afternoons, on, the, couch, to, read, Goes, through, old, pictures, and, memories, Our, heroes, have, been, forgotten, Our, heroes, so, brave, and, bold, Our, heroes, have, been, forgotten, Our, heroes, oh, they, got, old, Our, heroes, have, been, forgotten, Our, heroes, so, brave, and, bold, Our, heroes, have, been, forgotten, Our, heroes, oh, they, got, old	Build → Anticip, Joy, Surprise, Trust Right → Anticip, Joy, Surprise, Trust Stand → Anticip, Joy, Surprise, Trust Couch → Sadness Hero → Anticip, Joy, Surprise, Trust Old → Sadness Forgot → Fear, Sadness Bold → Anticip, Joy, Surprise, Trust	**Chorus2** Total Emotion Words: 75 Anticip : 15 / 75 20.0% Fear : 5 / 75 6.7% Joy : 15 / 75 20.0% Sadness : 10 / 75 13.3% Surprise : 15 / 75 20.0% Trust : 15 / 75 20.0%
Verse3 People, don't, stay, the, same, you, know, I, just, hope, their, stories, will, still, be, told	Know → Anticip, Joy, Surprise, Trust Hope → Anticip, Joy, Surprise, Trust	**Verse3** Total Emotion Words: 8 Anticip : 2 / 8 25.0% Joy : 2 / 8 25.0% Surprise 2 / 8 25.0% Trust 2 / 8 25.0%

Figure 8. The basic emotion words for probability distribution emotion word extractor input/output.

The representative emotion image selector compares the similarity with the probability distributions of emotion words extracted through step 1 and probability distributions of the emotion images tags and selects the images for each verse and chorus, as shown in Figure 9. The probability distribution that is similar to the corresponding probability distribution is searched in the dataset of emotion images with tags. Verse 1 has the most similar probability distribution to the probability distribution of (A) and Chorus 1 has the most similar probability distribution to the probability distribution of (B).

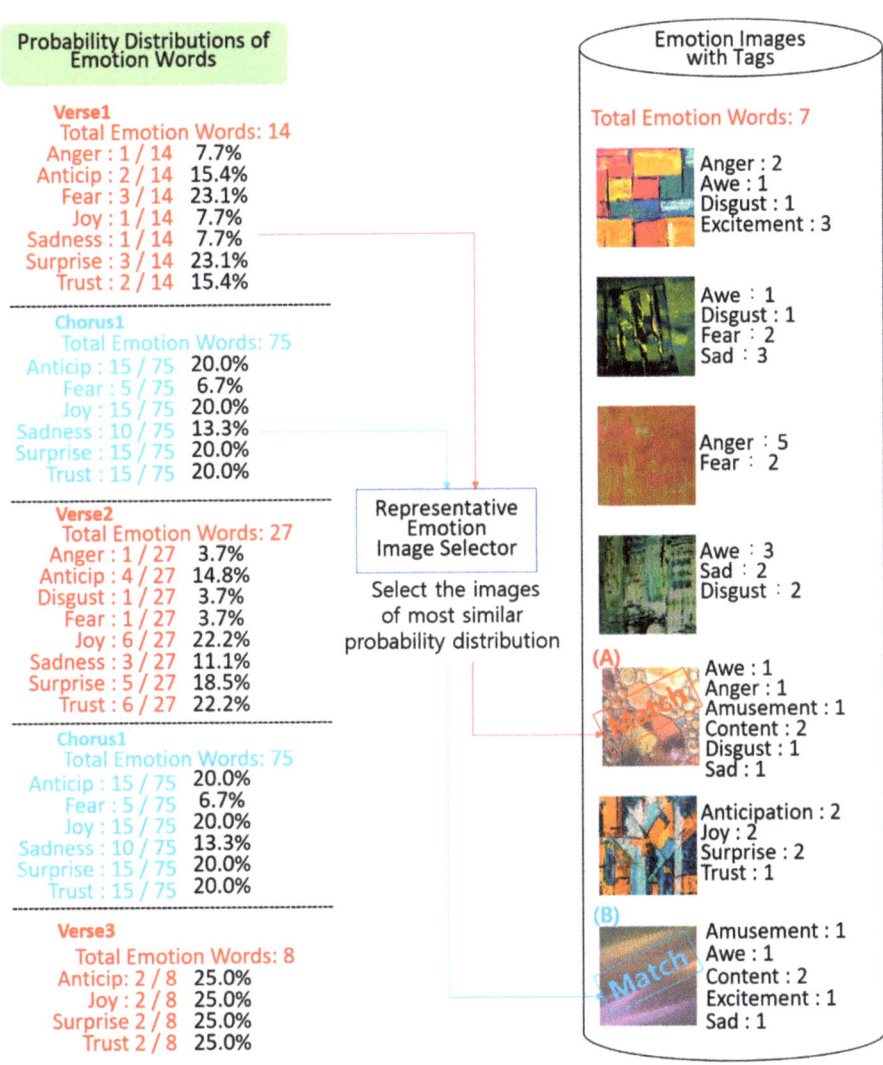

Figure 9. Representative emotion images selector input/output.

However, the disadvantage of this style transfer method is that many high-frequency artifacts occur. The sobel edge detector extracts the edge features of content in the horizontal and the vertical directions because the image is 2 dimension, and edge features of content strengthen. In Figure 10a,b, the edge features of the content are extracted, and it maintains the content edge information well. Figure 10c,d show the high-frequency composition of the image to which the style is applied, but the content edge information is lost as the style is transferred. Figure 11a,b maintain the content feature even when the style is transferred by strengthening the edge feature through the sobel edge detector. As a result, representative emotion image style transfer was output as Table 4, optimization was performed by minimizing style loss and content loss. Figure 12 shows that the total variation loss is minimized from 1.0777 to 0.1597.

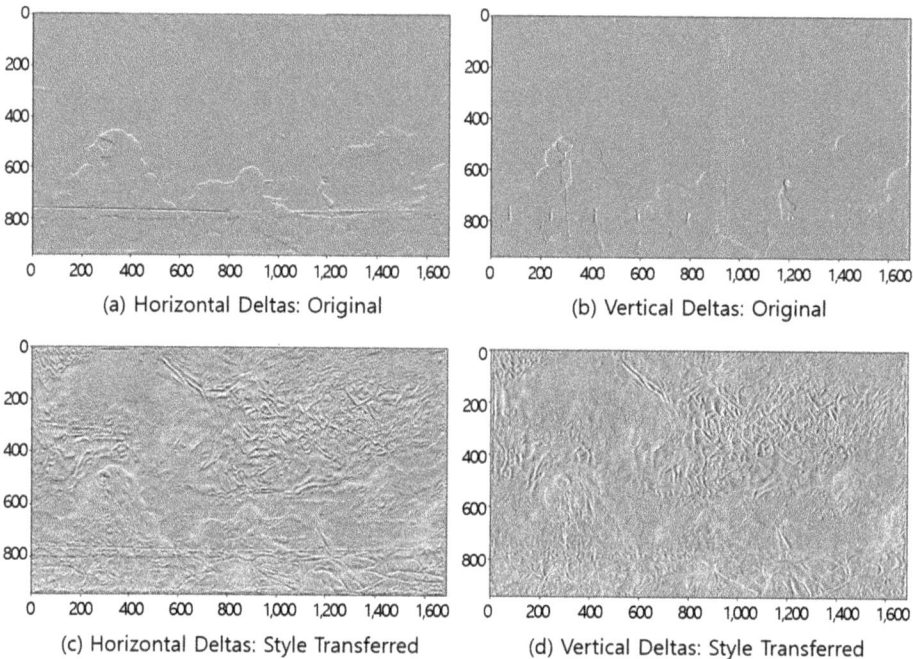

Figure 10. Results of losing content features problem.

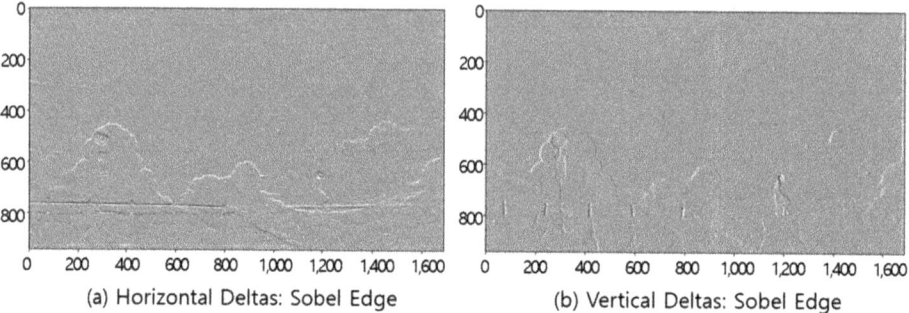

Figure 11. Results of preserving the content features from sobel edge detector.

Table 4. Comparison of edges.

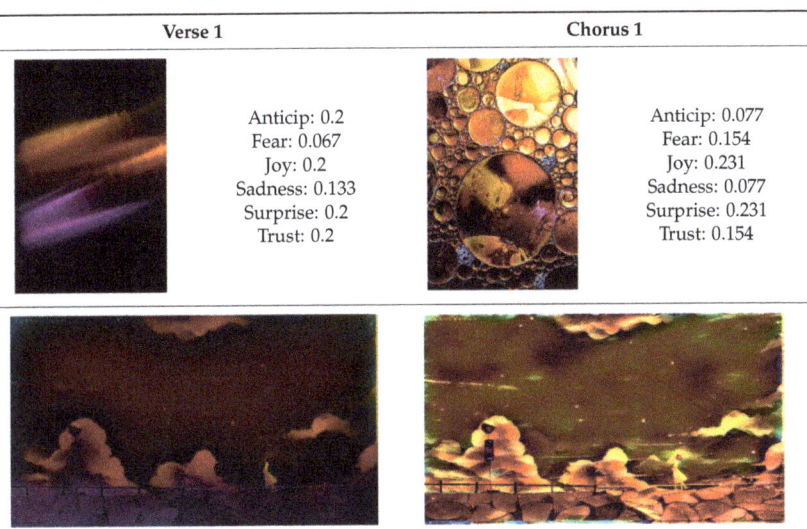

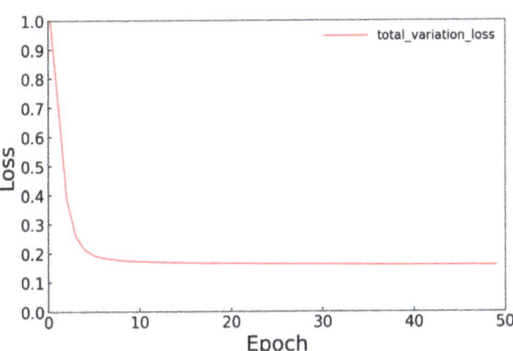

Figure 12. Total variation loss.

Table 5 shows the result of comparing the histogram distributions using compareHist function. The styles of images (a), (b) with similar probability distributions of emotion words and an image (c) with a different probability distribution of emotion words were transferred to the stage background image, and the similarity of the images was compared. When the distributions of the pixels of images are similar, the similarity of the images is high, and vice versa. The similarity of images is compared using the compareHist function. The compareHist function allows comparison of image features such as image contrast, color distribution and brightness. (a), (b) and (c) images are compared with the target image for similarity comparison. HISTCMP_CORREL (correlation) [23] is a correlation expressed by calculating pixels having the same value and is calculated as in Equation (7). The closer the value is to 1, the more similar the images are. H is a histogram, and N is the total number of histogram bins.

$$d(H_1, H_2) = \frac{\sum_J (H_1(J) - \overline{H_1})(H_2(J) - \overline{H_2})}{\sqrt{\sum_J (H_1(J) - \overline{H_1})^2}\sqrt{\sum_J (H_2(J) - \overline{H_2})^2}} \text{ where, } \overline{H_k} = \frac{1}{N}\sum_T H_k(T) \quad (7)$$

Table 5. Result of histogram comparison using compareHist function.

	Target image	Image with a similar distribution (a)	Image with a similar distribution (b)	Image with a different distribution (c)

Emotion probability distribution	Amusement: 0.14 Awe: 0.14 Content: 0.29 Excitement: 0.29 Sad: 0.14	Amusement: 0.14 Awe: 0.29 Content: 0.29 Excitement: 0.14 Sad: 0.14	Amusement: 0.29 Awe: 0.14 Content: 0.29 Excitement: 0.29	Anger: 1.00
HISTCMP_CORREL	1.00	0.12	0.22	0.1
HISTCMP_CHISQR	0.00	7665.83	7443.83	17,372.30
HISTCMP_INTERSECT	1.00	0.38	0.28	0.05
HISTCMP_BHATTACHARYYA	0.00	0.62	0.62	0.92

HISTCMP_CHISQR (Chi-squared distribution) [23] is the distribution of the spread of pixel values. It is calculated as in Equation (8) and the closer it is to 0, the more similar the images are.

$$d(H_1, H_2) = \sum_J \frac{(H_1(J) - H_2(J))^2}{H_1(J)} \quad (8)$$

HISTCMP_INTERSECT (intersection) [23] computes the similarity of two discrete probability distributions, as in Equation (9), using the possible values of the intersection between 0 and 1. The closer to 1, the more similar the images are.

$$d(H_1, H_2) = \sum_J \min(H_1(J), H_2(J)) \quad (9)$$

HISTCMP_BHATTACHARYYA [24] calculates the degree of overlap of two probability distributions as in Equation (10). The closer to 0, the more similar images are.

$$d(H_1, H_2) = \sqrt{1 - \frac{1}{\sqrt{\overline{H_1 H_2} N^2}} \sum_J \sqrt{H_1(J) \cdot H_2(J)}} \quad (10)$$

Table 6 shows histogram graph according to RGB distribution, hue, and value. The horizontal axis of the graph represents the change in color tone from 0 to 255, with the left side representing the dark area and the right side representing the bright area. The vertical axis of the graph represents the size of the area captured in each horizontal area, that is, the total number of pixels. This is the number of pixels in an image over a range of 256 pixel values.

Table 6. Results of histogram graph according to RGB distribution, hue, and value.

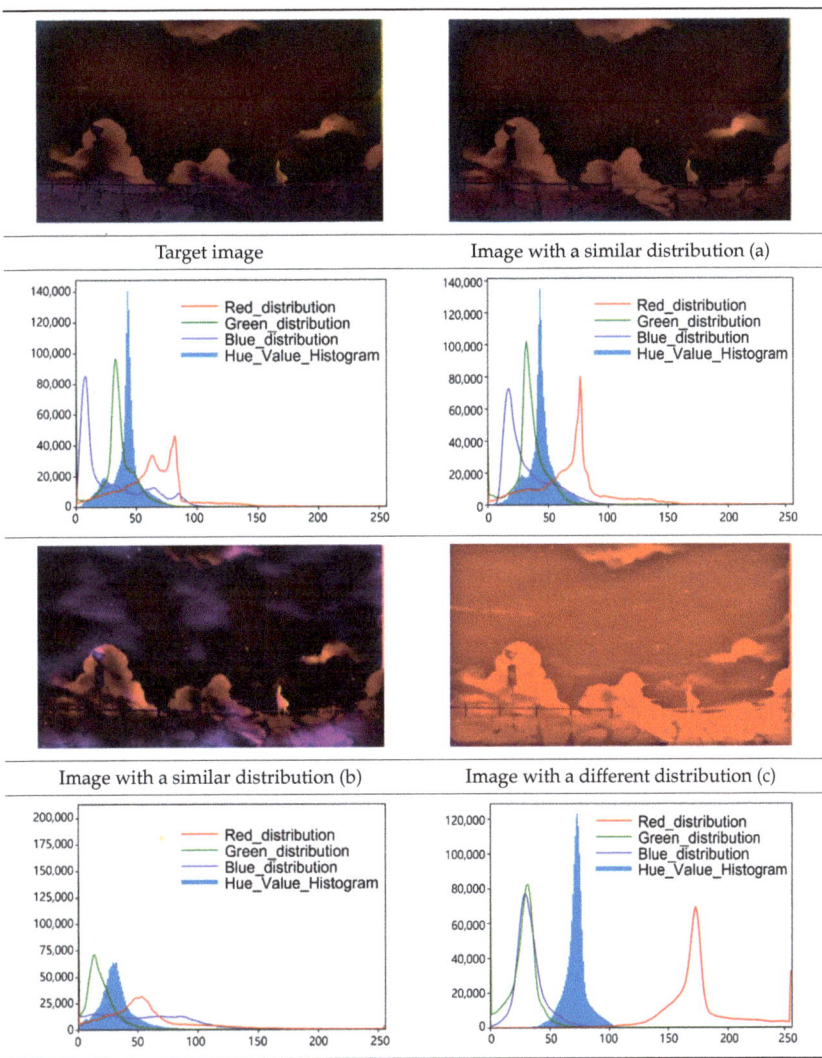

Table 7 shows the results of inputting various lyrics. By inputting the song lyrics of "Meant to be this way", "Sax is my cardio" and "Heart of lion (Leo)", the stage background images were transformed according to the proposed method for each verse and chorus.

Table 7. Results of inputting various lyrics.

Lyrics	Verse 1	Chorus	Verse 2	
Forgotten hero				
Meant to be this way				
Sax is my cardio				
Heart of a lion (Leo)	Verse 1	Chorus	Verse 2	Verse 3

The song lyrics "Meant to be this way" is consisted of two verses and two choruses, and a total of 12 emotion words were extracted. In this song's lyrics, 4 emotion words out of 14 sentences in verse, 5 emotion words out of 14 sentences in chorus, and 3 emotion words out of 14 sentences in verse 2 were extracted. The song lyrics to "Sax is my cardio" is consisted of two verses and two choruses, 28 emotion words were extracted. In this song's lyrics, 14 emotion words out of 12 sentences in verse 1, 7 emotion words out of 8 sentences in chorus, and 7 emotion words out of 12 sentences were extracted in verse 2. The song lyrics "Heart of a lion (Leo)" is consisted of three verses and two choruses, and a total of 32 emotion words were extracted. In this song's lyrics, 5 emotion words out of 8 sentences in verse 1, 10 emotion words out of 13 sentences in chorus, 3 emotion words out of 8 sentences in verse 2 and 9 emotion words out of 8 sentences in verse 3 were extracted. The styles were transferred by selecting the images with the most similar probability distributions for each verse and chorus through the emotion words extracted from each song lyrics. We confirmed through the results in Table 7 that the styles are well transformed even from complex stage background images.

5. Conclusions

This paper proposed a method to transfer stage background images into styles based on the emotion words contained in each verse and chorus from lyrics selected by a user. First, multiple verses and choruses were derived from the lyrics, one at a time, and compared with the emotion word dictionary to extract the emotion words included in each verse and chorus. Next, the image with the most similar probability distribution to the corresponding probability distribution was selected based on the probability distribution of emotion words included in the lyrics, and the styles were transferred to the stage background image for each verse and chorus. In the experiment, the performance of the style transfer was verified, and the probability distribution of the emotion words in the transformed stage background image was verified as similar to the probability distributions of the song lyrics. Experimental results showed that the proposed method reduced total variation loss from 1.0777 to 0.1597. This result shows that the style transferred image is close to edge information about the content of the input image, and the style is close to the target style image. In addition, stage background image and images of transferred styles with similar emotion words probability distributions were 38% similar, and stage background image and image of transferred styles with completely different probability distributions were 8% similar.

Due to the limitations of lexicon-based approaches, several aspects related to the design of relevant emotion analysis models need to design a model in future works. The input of the models that extract emotions by considering full sentences is sentence, but the lyrics do not follow the complete sentence structure. It is difficult to use each structure as an input to the previous models. In the case of a full sentence, there is a limit to the accuracy because there is uncertainty of specifying all emotions corresponding to the words of each sentence. Therefore, in this paper, limited emotion words were selected and utilized.

Author Contributions: Conceptualization, H.Y., S.L. and Y.S.; methodology, H.Y., S.L. and Y.S.; software, H.Y., S.L. and Y.S.; validation, H.Y., S.L. and Y.S. All authors have read and agreed to the published version of the manuscript.

Funding: This research was funded by the Ministry of Science, ICT (MSIT), Korea, under the High-Potential Individuals Global Training Program, grant number 2019-0-01585 and 2020-0-01576 supervised by the IITP (Institute for Information & Communications Technology Planning & Evaluation), and the APC was funded by 2019-0-01585 and 2020-0-01576.

Institutional Review Board Statement: Not applicable.

Informed Consent Statement: Informed consent was obtained from all subjects involved in the study.

Data Availability Statement: Not applicable.

Acknowledgments: This manuscript is one of the results by the project funded by the Ministry of Science, ICT (MSIT), Korea under the High-Potential Individuals Global Training Program, grant number 2019-0-01585 and 2020-0-01576 supervised by the IITP (Institute for Information & Communications Technology Planning & Evaluation).

Conflicts of Interest: The authors declare no conflict of interest.

References

1. Li, S.; Jang, S.; Sung, Y. Melody Extraction and Encoding Method for Generating Healthcare Music Automatically. *Electronics* **2019**, *8*, 1250. [CrossRef]
2. Li, S.; Jang, S.; Sung, Y. Automatic Melody Composition Using Enhanced GAN. *Mathematics* **2019**, *7*, 883. [CrossRef]
3. Wen, J.; She, J.; Li, X.; Mao, H. Visual Background Recommendation for Dance Performances Using Deep Matrix Factorization. *ACM Trans. Multimed. Comput. Commun. Appl. (TOMM)* **2018**, *14*, 1–19. [CrossRef]
4. Xu, T.; Zhang, P.; Huang, Q.; Zhang, H.; Gan, Z.; Huang1, X.; He, X. AttnGAN: Fine-Grained Text to Image Generation with Attentional Generative Adversarial Networks. In Proceedings of the IEEE Conference on Computer Vision and Pattern Recognition (CVPR), Salt Lake City, UT, USA, 18–22 June 2018.
5. Zhang, H.; Xu, T.; Li, H.; Zhang, S.; Wang, X.; Huang, X.; Metaxas, D.N. Stackgan++: Realistic Image Synthesis with Stacked Generative Adversarial Networks. *IEEE Trans. Pattern Anal. Mach. Intell.* **2019**, *41*, 1947–1962. [CrossRef] [PubMed]
6. Hu, X.; Downie, J.S.; Ehmann, A.F. Lyric Text Mining in Music Mood Classification. In Proceedings of the 10th International Society for Music Information Retrieval(ISMIR), Kobe, Japan, 26–30 October 2009.
7. Karras, T.; Laine, S.; Aila, T. A Style-Based Generator Architecture for Generative Adversarial Networks. In Proceedings of the IEEE/CVF Conference on Computer Vision and Pattern Recognition, Long Beach, CA, USA, 16–20 June 2019.
8. Hori, G. Color Extraction from Lyrics. In Proceedings of the 2019 4th International Conference on Automation, Control and Robotics Engineering (CACRE), Shenzhen, China, 19–21 July 2019.
9. Isola, P.; Zhu, J.; Zhou, T.; Efros, A.A. Image-to-Image Translation with Conditional Adversarial Networks. In Proceedings of the IEEE Conference on Computer Vision and Pattern Recognition, Honolulu, HI, USA, 21–26 July 2017.
10. Sung, Y.; Jin, Y.; Kwak, J.; Lee, S.; Cho, K. Advanced Camera Image Cropping Approach for CNN-Based End-to-End Controls on Sustainable Computing. *Sustainability* **2018**, *10*, 816. [CrossRef]
11. Gatys, L.A.; Ecker, A.S.; Bethge, M. Image Style Transfer Using Convolutional Neural Networks. In Proceedings of the IEEE Conference on Computer Vision and Pattern Recognition, Las Vegas, NV, USA, 26 June–1 July 2016.
12. Zhao, S.; Gao, Y.; Jiang, X.; Yao, H.; Chua, T.; Sun, X. Exploring Principles-of-Art Features For Image Emotion Recognition. In Proceedings of the 22nd ACM International Conference on Multimedia, Orlando, FL, USA, 3–7 November 2014.

13. Machajdik, J.; Hanbury, A. Affective image classification using features inspired by psychology and art theory. In Proceedings of the 18th ACM International Conference on Multimedia, Florence, Italy, 25–29 October 2010.
14. Han, E.; Cha, H. Extraction of Critical Low-Level Image Features for Effective Emotion Analysis. *Inst. Control. Robot. Syst.* **2019**, *25*, 319–326. [CrossRef]
15. Wei, Z.; Zhang, J.; Lin, Z.; Lee, J.; Balasubramanian, N.; Hoai, M.; Samaras, D. Learning Visual Emotion Representations from Web Data. In Proceedings of the IEEE/CVF Conference on Computer Vision and Pattern Recognition, Seattle, WA, USA, 16–18 June 2020.
16. Yang, D.; Lee, W. Music Emotion Identification from Lyrics. In Proceedings of the IEEE International Symposium on Multimedia (ISM), San Diego, CA, USA, 14–16 December 2009.
17. Zhao, S.; Yao, H.; Gao, Y.; Ding, G.; Chua, T. Predicting Personalized Image Emotion Perceptions in Social Networks. *IEEE Trans. Affect. Comput.* **2018**, *9*, 526–540. [CrossRef]
18. Lee, J.; Lim, H.; Kim, H. Similarity Evaluation of Popular Music based on Emotion and Structure of Lyrics. *KIISE Trans. Comput. Pract.* **2016**, *22*, 479–487. [CrossRef]
19. NRC Word-Emotion Association Lexicon. Available online: http://saifmohammad.com/WebPages/NRC-Emotion-Lexicon.htm (accessed on 31 December 2020).
20. Mohammad, S.M.; Turney, P.D. Emotions evoked by common words and phrases: Using Mechanical Turk to create an emotion lexicon. In Proceedings of the Computational Approaches to Analysis and Generation of Emotion in Text(CAAGET), Los Angeles, CA, USA, 13–19 June 2010.
21. Gao, W.; Zhang, X.; Yang, L.; Liu, H. An improved Sobel edge detection. In Proceedings of the 2010 3rd International Conference on Computer Science and Information Technology, Chengdu, China, 9–11 July 2010; Volume 5, pp. 67–71.
22. Zhu, C.; Richard, H.B.; Lu, P. Algorithm 778: L-BFGS-B: Fortran subroutines for large-scale bound-constrained optimization. *ACM Trans. Math. Softw. (TOMS)* **1997**, *23*, 550–560. [CrossRef]
23. Ogul, H.; Celik, N. A Web Application for Content based Geographic Image Retrieval. In Proceedings of the 2017 25th Signal Processing and Communications Applications Conference (SIU), Antalya, Tulkey, 15–18 May 2017; pp. 1–4.
24. Choi, E.; Lee, C. Feature extraction based on the Bhattacharyya distance. In *Pattern Recognition*; Elsvier: Amsterdam, The Netherland, 2003; Volume 36, pp. 1703–1709.

Article

Alternative Thresholding Technique for Image Segmentation Based on Cuckoo Search and Generalized Gaussians

Jorge Munoz-Minjares [1], Osbaldo Vite-Chavez [2], Jorge Flores-Troncoso [2] and Jorge M. Cruz-Duarte [3],*

[1] Department of Electrical Engineering, Universidad Autónoma de Zacatecas "Campus Jalpa", Libramiento Jalpa Km. 156+380, Zacatecas 99601, Mexico; ju.munoz@uaz.edu.mx
[2] Department of Electrical Engineering, Universidad Autónoma de Zacatecas, Av. Ramón López Velarde 801, Zacatecas 98000, Mexico; osvichz@uaz.edu.mx (O.V.-C.); jflorest@uaz.edu.mx (J.F.-T.)
[3] Tecnologico de Monterrey, School of Engineering and Sciences, Av. Eugenio Garza Sada 2501 Sur, Monterrey 64849, Mexico
* Correspondence: jorge.cruz@tec.mx

Abstract: Object segmentation is a widely studied topic in digital image processing, as to it can be used for countless applications in several fields. This process is traditionally achieved by computing an optimal threshold from the image intensity histogram. Several algorithms have been proposed to find this threshold based on different statistical principles. However, the results generated via these algorithms contradict one another due to the many variables that can disturb an image. An accepted strategy to achieve the optimal histogram threshold, to distinguish between the object and the background, is to estimate two data distributions and find their intersection. This work proposes a strategy based on the Cuckoo Search Algorithm (CSA) and the Generalized Gaussian (GG) distribution to assess the optimal threshold. To test this methodology, we carried out several experiments in synthetic and practical scenarios and compared our results against other well-known algorithms from the literature. These practical cases comprise a medical image database and our own generated database. The results in a simulated environment show an evident advantage of the proposed strategy against other algorithms. In a real environment, this ranks among the best algorithms, making it a reliable alternative.

Keywords: image segmentation; thresholding; cuckoo search; generalized Gaussian distribution

1. Introduction

Despite considerable advances in computer vision, object detection is still an active topic of study [1–4]. This process is used in many fields, such as biomedical imaging, biometry, video surveillance, vehicle navigation, visual inspection, robot navigation, and remote sensing [1–5], to mention a few. Object identification has been considered an essential task and one of the biggest challenges in image processing [1–3,6–8]. Several object recognition problems are solved utilizing digital image processing techniques, where segmentation methods are essential procedures [9–14]. Hence, optimal image segmentation is a crucial step in image preconditioning for further analysis because it precedes processing stages such as object extraction, parameter measurement, and object recognition [9,15]. Specifically, the thresholding methods are the most widely utilized in image segmentation due to their simplicity and effectiveness [9,11,15–17]. In layman's terms, these methods aim to separate the image foreground from its background by finding a limit or threshold in the image histogram. The challenge is, therefore, finding such a limit.

Many works in the literature have proposed a colorful palette of procedures and metrics to tackle such a challenge [9,10,18,19]. One of the most relevant, which is also considered a traditional technique, is the Otsu algorithm that aims to maximize the difference between the pixels belonging to the left and right sides of the threshold [20]. Other strategies that are worth mentioning are the Minimum Error method [21] and the Maximum

Citation: Munoz-Minjares, J.; Vite-Chavez, O.; Flores-Troncoso, J.; Cruz-Duarte, J.M. Alternative Thresholding Technique for Image Segmentation Based on Cuckoo Search and Generalized Gaussians. *Mathematics* 2021, 9, 2287. https://doi.org/10.3390/math9182287

Academic Editors: Ezequiel López-Rubio, Esteban Palomo and Enrique Domínguez

Received: 16 June 2021
Accepted: 14 August 2021
Published: 17 September 2021

Publisher's Note: MDPI stays neutral with regard to jurisdictional claims in published maps and institutional affiliations.

Copyright: © 2021 by the authors. Licensee MDPI, Basel, Switzerland. This article is an open access article distributed under the terms and conditions of the Creative Commons Attribution (CC BY) license (https://creativecommons.org/licenses/by/4.0/).

Entropy algorithm [22–24]. As usual, in the healthy development of computer science procedures, these techniques have disadvantages, so improved versions have appeared. For example, those that enhance the Otsu algorithm performance include e.g., the Valley Emphasis [17,25], Fan-Lei [26] and Xing-Yang methods [27]. These algorithms are suitable when the gray level histogram exhibits an evident bimodal behavior, and the optimal threshold is located at the valley bottom [28]. However, in several image processing works, the thresholds given by different algorithms are considered inaccurate. This is mostly due to the histogram distributions, which represent the background and object, and are not normal or seem to be quasi-unimodal functions [17,25–27,29,30].

To solve this inconvenience, an accepted methodology to discriminate the background and object is to estimate the data distributions and compute their intersection [31–34]. These works present a parametric image histogram threshold method based on an approximation f the statistical parameters of the object and background classes via estimation methods, such as Expectation-Maximization (EM), Particle Swarm Optimization (PSO), and Maximize Likelihood (ML). Even some improvements in these methods were proposed as in [35]. However, these algorithms have some disadvantages, such as slow or premature convergence and high sensibility in terms of the initial conditions. Additionally, these works omitted the near-unimodal histogram testing, which is a challenging task.

This work proposes a threshold algorithm based on a mixture of General Gaussian Distribution (GGD) functions to fit the image histogram. To do this, we implement the Cuckoo Search Algorithm (CSA) as a solver to assess the distribution parameters' optimal configuration. We carried out several experiments to prove the benefits of using the proposed methodology, and compared the results with those obtained with other thresholding methods from the literature. Furthermore, we implemented the methodology in two practical segmentation problems in a publicly available medical images database and our collection of organic and inorganic products.

The rest of this manuscript is organized as follows. We begin with a brief description of image segmentation and an introduction to the basic concepts employed in this work in Section 2. Section 3 describes the proposed methodology based on the GG function and the metaheuristic solver CSA. The experimental details are explained in Section 4. Subsequently, Section 5 presents and discusses the experiment and the obtained results. Then, Section 6 highlights the most relevant conclusions obtained from the experiments and comments on future work.

2. Theoretical Foundations

This section starts by describing the image segmentation process; then, it overviews the most common thresholding methods, such as the Otsu, Maximum Entropy, and Kittler–Illingworth.

2.1. Image Segmentation

Image segmentation is the process of partitioning a digital image into multiple parts, which are pixel sets, known as image objects [11]. The goal is to represent an image as something more meaningful and straightforward to analyze [9]. For that reason, many researchers define image segmentation as the process of labeling every image pixel according to certain characteristics [9,16]. Several general-purpose image segmentation methods have been developed; the simplest ones are the thresholding strategies [9,11,15,16]. The histogram techniques are incredibly efficient compared to other image segmentation methods because they typically require only one sweep over the image pixels. In these routines, a histogram is computed, employing the intensity values from all pixels, and its landscape (peaks and valleys) serves to locate the possible clusters [17,25].

2.2. Thresholding Methods

These techniques are based on a threshold value to transform a gray-scale image $I_g \in \mathbb{Z}_G^{M \times N}$ into a binary image $I_B \in \mathbb{Z}_2^{M \times N}$. The gray-scale image I_g is defined with elements (pixels) $I_{x,y}$, such as $I_g \ni I_{x,y} \in \{0, \ldots, G-1\}$, where G is the number of distinct intensities of gray (256), and $M \times N$ is the size, given by the number of rows times the number of columns. Some standard thresholding methods are described below.

2.2.1. Otsu Method

The Otsu method, proposed by Nobuyuki Otsu in 1979, is one of the best known and most applied for image segmentation. This automatically selects the optimal threshold by maximizing the between-class variance in the segmented image [20]. Consider the gray-scale image I_g and the occurrence probability $p(g): \mathbb{Z}_G \mapsto [0,1]$ for a specific gray level g in the image is determined as

$$p(g) = \frac{n_g}{n} = \frac{1}{NM} \sum_{x=1}^{M} \sum_{y=1}^{N} \delta_{g, I_{x,y}}, \qquad (1)$$

where $\delta_{\{\},\{\}}$ is the well-known Kronecker delta, n_g is the number of pixels with the same gray level, and n is the total number of pixels in the image. These pixels are divided into two classes, D_0 and D_1, based on a threshold t. Therefore, D_0 and D_1 consist of pixels with levels between $[0, t]$ and $[t+1, G-1]$, respectively. The cumulative probabilities $P_0(t)$ and $P_1(t)$ of D_0 and D_1, respectively, can be defined as follows,

$$P_0(t) = \Pr(D_0) = \sum_{g=0}^{t} p(g), \qquad (2)$$

$$P_1(t) = \Pr(D_1) = \sum_{g=t+1}^{G-1} p(g) = 1 - P_0(t). \qquad (3)$$

In the same way, the mean levels $\mu_0(t)$ and $\mu_1(t)$ can be computed as

$$\mu_0(t) = \sum_{g=0}^{t} \frac{g \cdot p(g)}{P_0(t)}, \qquad (4)$$

$$\mu_1(t) = \sum_{g=t+1}^{G-1} \frac{g \cdot p(g)}{P_1(t)}. \qquad (5)$$

For both classes, minimizing the within-class variance is equivalent to maximizing the between-class variance [18,20]. Accordingly, the between-class variance maximization criterion is used, and is obtained with the following equation:

$$\sigma_b^2(t) = P_0(t) P_1(t) (\mu_1(t) - \mu_0(t))^2. \qquad (6)$$

According to the Otsu method, this expression serves as a metric for evaluation of a given threshold. Therefore, the optimal threshold t^* guarantees the greatest distinction between the two classes D_0 and D_1, t^* maximizes $\sigma_b^2(t)$, as shown,

$$t^* = \underset{0 < t < G-1}{\operatorname{argmax}} \left\{ \sigma_b^2(t) \right\}. \qquad (7)$$

In the simplest scenario, when a single threshold is required, the Otsu method has an astonishing performance, with histograms of a bimodal distribution [17,18]. This is chiefly because the method assumes that the object and background's gray level presents a Gaussian distribution with equal variances [17]. However, the threshold achieved with this method is inaccurate when the histogram distribution shows unimodal or quasi-unimodal distribution characteristics [11,17,18].

To implement the Otsu method, it is only necessary to sweep the different gray levels and pick one that satisfies (7). Note that no optimization method is needed. Naturally, one must take several additional conditions into account for practical cases, so the "brute-force" strategy may not be the best alternative. However, the Otsu method is incorporated in almost all digital image processing software. One of the most popular methods is the Matlab's function, called `graythresh`, based on the Otsu method [20] used in this work. Nonetheless, this function can use the histogram data or the image as input, with the latter being the most used.

2.2.2. Maximum Entropy Method

The Maximum Entropy (MxE) method is a different and novel criterion function, used to select an appropriate threshold. This alternative to searching an optimal threshold was proposed using the Shannon's entropy definition in [22–24]. According to their idea, the histogram and the Probability Mass Function (PMF) of a gray-scale image I_g can be represented by $h(g)$ and $p(g)$, respectively, for g from 0 to $G-1$. In several particular applications, it is possible to define g between a narrower range, given by $g_{min} \leq g \leq g_{max}$. However, if these extrema are not explicitly indicated, it is assumed that $0 \leq g \leq G-1$. Thence, the cumulative probability function is defined as

$$P(g) = \sum_{g=0}^{G-1} p(g), \tag{8}$$

Assuming that $p(g)$ is calculated from the histogram of the image $h(g)$, normalizing it by the total number of samples. In the context of image segmentation, $\mathbb{Z}_f^{M \times N} \ni I_g \leq t$ and $\mathbb{Z}_b^{M \times N} \ni I_g > t$, where f could represent the foreground and b the background or vice-versa. Therefore, when an object appears to be brighter than the background, the set of pixels with gray intensities greater than t would be defined as the foreground. $P_f(g)$ and $P_b(g)$ are the probabilities of two distribution classes (D_0 and D_1), separated by a threshold t, in the image histogram. Therefore, $P_f(g)$ represents the foreground and $P_b(g)$ the background for the ranges $0 < g \leq t$ and $t+1 \leq g \leq G-1$, respectively. Foreground and background area probabilities are calculated as follows:

$$P_f(t) = \sum_{g=1}^{t} p_f(g), \text{ and } P_b(t) = \sum_{g=t+1}^{G-1} p_b(g). \tag{9}$$

Now, it is possible to calculate t based on the entropy for both the foreground and background, such that:

$$H_f(t) = -\sum_{g=1}^{t} p_f(g) \log p_f(g), \text{ and } H_b(t) = -\sum_{g=t+1}^{G-1} p_b(g) \log p_b(g). \tag{10}$$

The total entropy $H(t)$ for the image distribution $p(g)$ is obtained by

$$H(t) = H_f(t) + H_b(t). \tag{11}$$

The maximum H then corresponds to the optimal threshold value for the separation between background and foreground, i.e.,

$$t^* = \operatorname*{argmax}_{0 < t < G-1} \{H(t)\}. \tag{12}$$

With this reference threshold and the histogram of the image $h(g)$, the binarization can be carried out to separate the object from the background.

2.2.3. Kittler-Illingworth Method

The Kittler–Illingworth method, founded on the mixture of distributions, corresponds to a more realistic approach to practical image segmentation implementations. This is the main reason that we selected it as the foundation of our proposed algorithm. The mixture comprises two Normal distributions with different means and variances, $\mathcal{N}(\mu_1, \sigma_1^2)$ and $\mathcal{N}(\mu_2, \sigma_2^2)$, and the proportions q_1 and q_2 [21]. Therefore, the mixture distribution $f(g) : \mathbb{Z}_G \mapsto [0,1]$ described in the histogram takes the form

$$f(g) = \frac{q_1}{\sqrt{2\pi}\sigma_1} \exp\left(-\frac{(g-\mu_1)^2}{2\sigma_1^2}\right) + \frac{q_2}{\sqrt{2\pi}\sigma_2} \exp\left(-\frac{(g-\mu_2)^2}{2\sigma_2^2}\right) \qquad (13)$$

Consider a trial threshold t is given by a brightness level; then, two pixel populations are modeled, such as $p_1(g)$ and $p_2(g)$. Similarly to the methods described above, the brightness level g in $p_1(g)$ is less than or equal to the threshold t, whilst in $p_2(g)$, g is greater than or equal to the threshold t. These two populations are modeled by the Normal distributions $\mathcal{N}(\mu_1(t), \sigma_1^2(t))$ and $\mathcal{N}(\mu_2(t), \sigma_2^2(t))$. For the general case, when the image has a brightness level of up to g, it is successively tested with different threshold values. Therefore, by considering the histogram frequencies $P(0), P(1), \ldots, P(G-1)$ for the observed brightness values $0, 1, \ldots, G-1$, a fitting criterion $J(t)$ can be determined for each value t, such as:

$$J(t) = 1 + 2\left(p_1(t) \log \frac{\sigma_1(t)}{p_1(t)} + p_2(t) \log \frac{\sigma_2(t)}{p_2(t)}\right), \qquad (14)$$

since

$$p_1(t) = \sum_{g=0}^{t} P(g) \text{ and } p_2(t) = \sum_{g=t+1}^{G-1} P(g). \qquad (15)$$

It is worth noting that the better the models fit the data, the smaller the criterion $J(t)$. Therefore, the optimal threshold value t^* value minimizes the criterion function $J(t)$ as

$$t^* = \underset{0 < t < G-1}{\operatorname{argmin}} \{J(t)\}. \qquad (16)$$

Therefore, solving the problem in (16), one can estimate the optimal threshold without requiring additional solution methods.

3. Proposed Method

The proposed methodology employs two main procedures. The first one comprises the fitting problem of a metamodel $f_m(\vec{z}; g)$ based on the Generalized Gaussian (GG) function and the histogram data $(\vec{g}_e, \vec{f}_e)$ from a gray image. This minimization problem is given by

$$\vec{z}^* = \underset{\vec{z} \in 3^D}{\operatorname{argmin}} \left\| \vec{f}_e - \vec{f}_m(\vec{z}; \vec{g}_e) \right\|_2^2, \qquad (17)$$

since $\vec{z}$ stands the metamodel parameters. A metaheuristic solver such as the Cuckoo Search Algorithm (CSA) is implemented to deal with such a problem. The second procedure then utilizes the information from the optimal parameters $\vec{z}^*$ and the histogram data to identify the threshold. Figure 1 illustrates the aforementioned proposed methodology. The remainder of this section details the metamodel, the optimization algorithm, and the threshold identification.

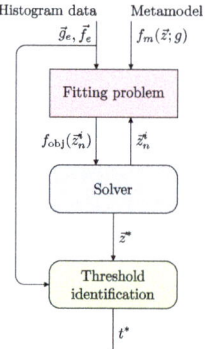

Figure 1. Proposed method based on the Generalized Gaussian function as the metamodel and the Cuckoo Search Algorithm as the optimizer.

3.1. Generalized Gaussian Function

The sum of Generalized Gaussian Distributions (GGDs) is proposed as a metamodel according to [36]. The major feature of a GGD is its ability to approach several statistical distributions by only varying a parameter α, such as the Impulsive ($\alpha \to 0$), sub-Laplacian ($\alpha < 1$), Laplacian ($\alpha = 1$), Gaussian ($\alpha = 2$), and uniform ($\alpha \to \infty$) ones. Given this flexibility, we considered that GGDs are excellent candidates to describe the statistical characteristics presented in an image histogram as a meta-distribution.

We assumed that the histogram for the background and object shows two principal lobes (bimodal histogram); based on (13), it is proposed $f_m(g) : \mathbb{Z}_G \mapsto [0,1]$ to approximate two probability density functions, such as

$$f_m(\vec{z};g) = f_1(\vec{z};g) + f_2(\vec{z};g). \tag{18}$$

In this distribution model, $f_k(\vec{z};g) : \mathbb{Z}_G \mapsto [0,1]$ is given by

$$f_k(g) = G_k \exp\left(-\left|\frac{g - \mu_k}{\sigma_k}\right|^{\alpha_k}\right), \quad \forall\, k \in \{1,2\}, \tag{19}$$

where $g \in \mathbb{Z}_G$, $\mu_k \in \mathbb{R}$, $\sigma_k \in \mathbb{R}_+$, and $\alpha_k \in \mathbb{R}_+$ are the intensity of the gray level, its mean, scale, and shape, respectively. Moreover, $\vec{z}$ is the parameter vector and $G_k \in \mathbb{R}_+$ is the normalizing constant defined by

$$G_k = \frac{\alpha_k}{2\sigma_k \Gamma(1/\alpha_k)}, \quad \forall\, k \in \{1,2\}. \tag{20}$$

We consider G_1 and G_2 as two global constants to avoid the use of the $\Gamma(\cdot)$ function and thus to reduce the computational complexity; i.e., they are specified in parameter vector $\vec{z} = (G_1, \mu_1, \sigma_1, \alpha_1, G_2, \mu_2, \sigma_2, \alpha_2)^\mathsf{T}$. Furthermore, we set a simple constraint to this model to facilitate its analysis, such as $\mu_1 < \mu_2$.

3.2. Cuckoo Search Algorithm

Cuckoo Search Algorithm (CSA) is a metaheuristic optimization method based on a population, and Lévy flights [37]. CSA mimics the brood parasitism behavior of certain cuckoo species, which hide their eggs inside alien nests. The general scientific community has widely accepted this method in numerous variants and applications [38–40]. CSA can be implemented to tackle a given minimization problem, such as

$$\vec{z}^* = \underset{\vec{z} \in \mathfrak{Z}^D}{\arg\min}\, f_{\text{obj}}(\vec{z}), \tag{21}$$

where $\vec{z}^*$ is the optimal solution and $f_{\text{obj}}(\vec{z})$ is the objective function. For maximization problems, such as those mentioned in Section 2.2, this objective function is just the negated threshold metric.

In CSA, the population is defined as $Z^t = \{\vec{z}_1(t), \ldots, \vec{z}_N(t)\} \in \mathfrak{Z}$, since i is the time step, N is the number of agents, and D implies the dimensionality of the problem. Thus, $\vec{z}_n(t) \in Z(t)$ is the n-th agent's position in the feasible domain $\mathfrak{Z} \subseteq \mathbb{R}^D$ at the step i. For most problems, such a domain $\mathfrak{Z}$ is defined as shown,

$$\mathfrak{Z} = \left\{\vec{z} \in \mathbb{R}^D : \left(\exists \vec{l}, \vec{u} \in \mathbb{R}^D\right)\left[\vec{l} \preceq \vec{z} \preceq \vec{u}\right]\right\} \tag{22}$$

since $\vec{l}$ and $\vec{u}$ are the lower and upper boundary vectors, respectively.

As first step, the population is initialized at random within the problem domain, i.e., $Z^0 \ni \vec{z}_n^0 \ni z_{d,n} \sim \mathcal{U}(l_d, u_d) \, \forall \, l_d \in \vec{l}, u_d \in \vec{u}$, and the fitness value for each agent is evaluated such that $f_n^0 = f_{\text{obj}}(\vec{z}_n^0), \forall \vec{z}_n^0 \in Z^0$. Then, the initial best position $\vec{z}^{0,*}$ and its fitness value $f^{0,*}$ are found, $\vec{z}^{0,*} = \text{argmin}\{f(Z^0)\}$, and the iteration counter is increased as $i \leftarrow i+1$. CSA employs the Lévy flight and local random walk as its primary two search mechanisms, which are applied iteratively until a convergence criterion, which was defined previously, is met. Some examples of the criteria are the maximum number of steps $i \geq i_{\max}$ and the best-fitness change tolerance $f^{i,*} - f^{i-1,*} \leq \varepsilon$.

Thence, the Lévy flight for the n-th agent ($\vec{z}_n^i \in Z^i$) is given by

$$\vec{z}_n^i = \vec{z}_n^i + \zeta \vec{\eta} \odot (\vec{z}_n^{i-1} - \vec{z}^{i-1,*}), \tag{23}$$

where $\zeta > 0$ is the spatial step size, $\vec{\eta}$ is a vector of i.i.d. random numbers obtained from the Mantegna–Stanley's algorithm [41] using the symmetric Lévy stable distribution, and $\odot$ is the Hadamard–Schur's product.

Likewise, the second procedure, namely, local random walk, is defined as

$$\vec{z}_n^i = \vec{z}_n^i + \vec{r} \odot H(\vec{r} - p) \odot (\vec{z}_{q_1}^i - \vec{z}_{q_2}^i), \tag{24}$$

where $\vec{r}$ is a vector of i.i.d. random variables with $\mathcal{U}(0,1)$, $p \in [0,1]$ is the probability of change, and $H : \mathbb{R}^D \to \mathbb{Z}_2^D$ is the element-wise Heaviside step function with $H(0) = 1$. Indices q_1 and q_2 are mutually exclusive integers randomly selected from the population range $[1, N]$.

After applying each of these search mechanisms, all agents are evaluated in the objective function, and only the new positions $\vec{z}_n^i$ better than the previous ones $\vec{z}_n^{i-1}$ are preserved, i.e., $\vec{z}_n^i = \vec{z}_n^{i-1}$ if $f_n^i > f_n^{i-1}, \forall n \in \{1, \ldots, N\}$. Furthermore, once the local random walk is performed and the population is updated, the best position $\vec{z}^{i,*}$ and its fitness value $f^{i,*}$ are found as they were before with the initial population. Thus, the convergence criteria are checked. If any are satisfied, the iterative procedure concludes. Otherwise, the step counter is increased $i = i + 1$, and the search mechanisms are applied again.

3.3. Threshold Identification

The threshold identification procedure is somewhat similar to those described in Section 2. The main differences are that instead of using the histogram data (g_e, f_e), we evaluate a subset of gray-scale levels $T \subset G$ over the fitted GGD model $f_m(\vec{z}^*; t)$. We stress that we do not employ the direct histogram data but the fitted curves. Thus, his subset T is obtained as follows

$$T = \{g \in \vec{g}_e : (\lfloor \mu_1^* + \sigma_1^*/2 \rfloor < g < \lceil \mu_2^* - \sigma_2^*/2 \rceil)[\lfloor \mu_1^* + \sigma_1^*/2 \rfloor < \lceil \mu_2^* - \sigma_2^*/2 \rceil]\}, \tag{25}$$

where $\mu_1^*, \sigma_1^*, \mu_2^*$, and σ_2^* are from the optimal parameter values $\vec{z}^*$ achieved in the optimization procedure. The rounding operators $\lfloor \cdot \rfloor$ and $\lceil \cdot \rceil$ stand the floor and ceil, respectively. This subset will be nonempty, at least in the context of the segmentation problem tackled in this work. Hence, the optimal threshold value using the proposed method is found as shown

$$t^* = \underset{t \in T}{\mathrm{argmin}}\{f_m(\vec{z}^*; t)\}. \qquad (26)$$

4. Methodology

We carried out a three-fold experiment procedure to study the proposed method ThCSA and also to compare it against those methods described in Section 2.2. These methods are Otsu, Matlab's Otsu implementation (GrayThresh), Maximum Entropy (MxE), Kittler–Illingworth (KI), and ThCSA. The graythresh method is omitted for simulated comparison because it requires an image as input. We tested the methods using simulated distributions in the preliminary experiment, which correspond to bimodal histograms with the optimal threshold t_{r1}^* as a reference. The optimal threshold is obtained with the intersection of two well-known distributions. In this work, the sum of distributions was designated as a global histogram. For this experiment, the synthetic histogram was considered as the sum of two distributions, not a histogram in the strict sense. Synthetic histograms have constant parameters to simulate two distributions. Table 1 describes the five cases that comprise this experiment. In the first experiment, we simulated a bimodal histogram corresponding to an image with one object and a well-defined background with two known thresholds.

Table 1. Simulated histograms utilized as study cases for the preliminary experiment. Parameters α_k, σ_k, and μ_k, $\forall k = \{1, 2\}$, correspond to the distribution model in (19).

Simulation	α_1	α_2	σ_1	σ_2	μ_1	μ_2
s_{01}	1	1.62	30.61	43.60	58	183
s_{02}	2	1.42	40.62	33.06	78	163
s_{03}	2	1.71	46.17	48.12	56	187
s_{04}	1	1.38	42.05	38.85	64	195
s_{05}	2	0.97	32.58	33.81	68	175

The remainder experiments were performed following the procedure depicted in Figure 2. First, the original image is read as an RGB image $I \in \mathbb{Z}_G^{M \times N \times 3}$ and then transformed to gray-scale $I_g \in \mathbb{Z}_G^{M \times N}$. The gray-scale image serves to obtain the histogram $f(g)$, as commented in Section 2, except for the GrayThresh method, which utilizes the image I_g directly. Therefore, the thresholding methods are applied to achieve the binary image $I_{b_1} \in \mathbb{Z}_2^{M \times N}$. Lastly, the object perimeter P_I is detected by locating the isolines of the processed I_{b_1} image. The general methodology is summarized in Pseudocode 1.

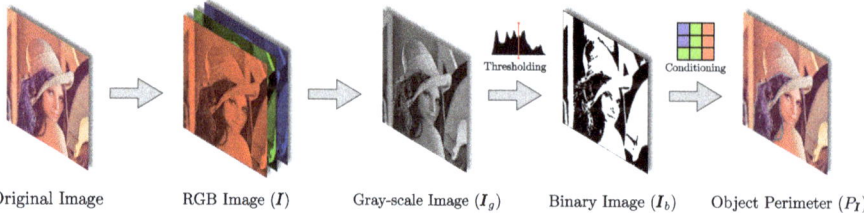

Figure 2. General diagram of image segmentation based on background and object.

The second set of experiments consisted of segmenting samples of melanoma images collected from the PH2 Dermoscopic Image Database [42]. We selected this particular image database mainly because the reference images of the melanoma area are provided and supported by expert dermatologists. In addition, these images present histograms with diversity in their statistical parameters and the distances and amplitudes of the histogram's main lobes. It is worth mentioning that these samples required a special consideration to compute the perimeter of skin lesion; this fact is detailed in the next section. The final experiments comprised the segmentation of organic and inorganic products with a non-uniform background. To do this, we implemented the procedure mentioned above with three images acquired for this work.

Pseudocode 1 Proposed procedure for image segmentation and contour computing

Input: Original image I and thresholding method THRESHOLDINGMETHOD

Output: Processed binary image I_{b_1} and perimeter P_I

1: $I_g \leftarrow$ GRAYSCALE(I)   ▷ Transform from RGB to gray-scale
2: $t \leftarrow$ THRESHOLDINGMETHOD(I_g)   ▷ Threshold t computed with a given method
3: $I_{b_1} \leftarrow$ BINARIZE(I_g, t)   ▷ Binarization according to t
4: $P_I \leftarrow$ CONTOUR(I_{b_1})   ▷ Draws a contour of I_{b_1}

The methodology described in Figure 2 was designed to apply a traditional thresholding procedure and the basic image form (a binary image) to identify the object perimeter. The object perimeter for the second and third experiments is determined for different reasons. The melanoma perimeter helps to provide a view of the morphological structure of skin lesions, which can be used to support a clinic diagnosis [42]. Meanwhile, the methodology proposed for the second experiment can be employed to distinguish between organic and inorganic objects. This is due to the number of centroids of the identified object perimeters.

Moreover, all the experiments were run on a machine with an Intel Core i5 @ 1.6 GHz CPU, 4.00 GB @ 1600 MHz RAM, using the numerical platforms Matlab R2018a and R v4.0.3. We implemented Cuckoo Search Algorithm (CSA) with a population size N of 200, a step size ζ of 1.0, a probability change p of 0.5, a best-fitness change tolerance ε of 10^{-15}, and a maximum number of stagnating iterations of 2000. These values were obtained after performing a preliminary study, which is out of this work's scope but can be consulted in [43].

5. Results and Discussion

The first experiment consists of implementing the proposed method and the others from the literature (ThCSA, Otsu, MxE, and KI) on synthetic histograms (cf. Section 4). Table 2 presents the resulting thresholds from this simulation comparison, where the symbols ↓ and ↑ indicate the worst and the best thresholds, respectively. This is based on the optimal threshold. In the first simulation s_{01}, Otsu yields the closest values to the optimal threshold. Meanwhile, ThCSA achieved a threshold value with a difference of four gray intensity values from the optimal reference. Finally, the worst result was attained by MxE. From the results achieved in simulation s_{02}, it is easy to notice that Otsu, KI and ThCSA had the same performance, closely followed by MxE. In s_{02}, it is worth noticing that Otsu, KI and ThCSA computed a threshold near to the optimal threshold with a difference of two gray intensity levels, respectively. Moreover, the thresholds attained for the simulation s_{03} are diverse. For this simulation, MxE outperforms the other methods according to the optimal reference. It is noticeable that Kittler and ThCSA share the the same threshold, with a difference of two gray intensity values from t_{r1}^*. The worst algorithm to assess the reference threshold was found to be Otsu, with a minimal difference of three gray levels. Now, based on the results shown in Table 2 for simulation s_{04}, we observe that MxE exhibits an advantage over other algorithms for the optimal threshold. Here, Otsu and ThCSA obtained the same level and reached second place with a difference of six gray intensity levels. The last simulation, s_{05}, yields interesting results. In this scenario, ThCSA render the best threshold concerning the optimal threshold. Meanwhile, MxE and Kittler rank at an intermediate level according to the reference threshold. In this simulation, the algorithm Otsu obtained the lowest performance.

Table 2. Comparison of threshold values obtained by different methods in a simulated environment. Based on the optimal threshold t_{r1}^*, the symbols ↓ and ↑ indicate the worst and the best threshold respectively.

Simulation	t_{r1}^*	Otsu	MxE	KI	ThCSA
s_{01}	120	121 ↑	128 ↓	113	116
s_{02}	122	120 ↑	119 ↓	120 ↑	120 ↑
s_{03}	119	122 ↓	118 ↑	121	121
s_{04}	135	129	140 ↑	127 ↓	129
s_{05}	114	125 ↓	119	119	118 ↑

Figure 3 illustrates the cases of those simulated distributions, the optimal threshold and estimated histograms obtained by using ThCSA. In these plots, the fitted histograms (in black solid lines) evidence an outstanding description of the global histogram, especially regarding the reference threshold (in red dashed line). Nevertheless, we observe two issues in these resulting histograms: In the first one in Figure 3a, the right-hand side distribution is lower than the simulated data. Plus, in the second one in Figure 3b, an unsatisfactory fitting of the right and left hand side peaks is evident. In Figure 3c the right-hand and left-hand side distributions are narrower and lower than simulated histogram, respectively.

Subsequently, Table 3 shows the thresholds comparison obtained with the algorithms implemented for segmenting four dermoscopic images, i.e., IMD002, IMD004, IMD015, IMD021, and IMD041. As we mentioned in Section 4, we chose these figures to illustrate histograms with different patterns. The optimal variables achieved by CSA for the GG distributions are also presented. Recall that the α_1 and α_2 values describe abnormal distributions when $\alpha_k \neq 2 \ \forall k \in \{1,2\}$. It is worth noting that the thresholds estimated by ThCSA and Otsu for the IMD002 sample are close. Hence, the histogram of IMD002 is enveloped with a sum of non-Gaussian distribution because $\alpha_1^* = 3$ and $\alpha_2^* = 3$. In the second test, using IMD004, ThCSA estimates a classification edge with an average variation of ca. 29 intensities w.r.t. the other algorithms. The distributions computed have the shape parameters $\alpha_1^* = 1.6$ and $\alpha_2^* = 0.6$, which correspond to sub-Gaussian and sub-Laplacian distributions, respectively. For IMD015 and IMD021, ThCSA and GrayThresh achieve similar thresholds. It can also be observed in Table 3 that the shape parameters to this sample are located at $1 \leq \alpha_1^*, \alpha_2^* < 2$, i.e., between Laplacian and Gaussian distributions. For this experiment, the estimated characteristics can be described with the following ranges $0.1 \leq G_1^*, G_2^* \leq 0.98$, $74 \leq \mu_1^*, \mu_2^* \leq 192$, $10.34 < \sigma_1^*, \sigma_2^* < 25.69$, and $1 < \alpha_1^*, \alpha_2^* < 2$. Finally, the proposed algorithm and GrayThresh obtained the same threshold for IMD041. These results can corroborate the flexibility of the proposed algorithm to estimate several parameters at the same time on a different scale.

Complementing the information achieved in this experiment, as described in Figure 2, we determine the contours P_I for the medical images IMD002, IMD004, IMD015, and IMD021. The segmentation of medical samples generates extra white corners following the procedure depicted in Figure 2 and Pseudocode 1. For this particular case, it is required to remove the contour located in the corner of each image. Figure 4a,c,e,g show the resulting contours P_I in RGB images, which is computed with the isolines of processed I_{b_1} image and depicted with a solid line. Therefore, the contour P_I helps to determine the dark area of melanoma samples.

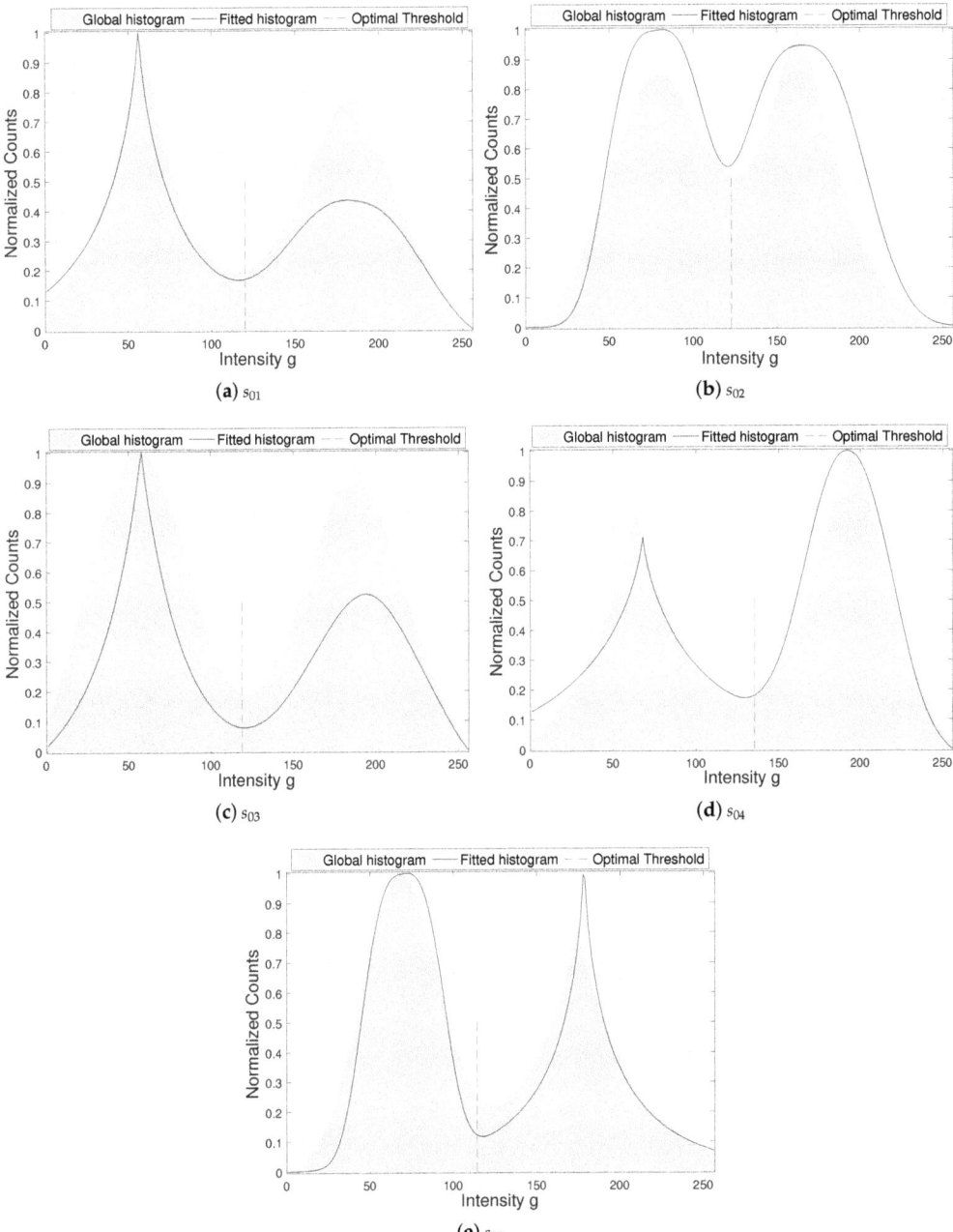

Figure 3. Cases of fitted histograms utilizing the thresholding method based on Cuckoo Search Algorithm. The reference distribution is depicted with a red dashed line.

Table 3. Thresholds detected in medical Images with different methods and variables identified by Cuckoo Search Algorithm.

Image	Thresholds of Medical Images					Optimal Variables Identified via CSA							
	Otsu	GrayThresh	KI	MxE	ThCSA	G_1^*	G_2^*	μ_1^*	μ_2^*	σ_1^*	σ_2^*	α_1^*	α_2^*
IMD002	136	127	132	146	138	0.23	0.92	96	180	31.46	26.71	3.0	3.0
IMD004	162	127	177	169	139	0.10	1.05	91	229	35.73	17.84	1.6	0.6
IMD015	143	127	143	159	125	0.69	0.98	93	192	10.34	25.69	1.4	1.5
IMD021	120	119	123	133	112	0.1	0.84	74	158	24.29	11.85	1.6	1.0
IMD041	157	156	158	169	156	0.36	0.9	97	215	30.71	31.51	1.1	2.3

Figure 4b,d,f,h illustrate the image histogram (gray patch), fitted histogram (black solid line), and estimated threshold (red dashed line) with ThCSA. In these images, one can observe two principal lobes and a valley between them, where the threshold achieved with ThCSA is located. It is also possible to appreciate the estimated distributions with several shape parameters, which are denoted with α_1^* and α_2^* to the first and second lobes, respectively. Additionally, we can notice some discrepancies between the estimated distributions and the histograms in Figure 4b,d,f,h. However, the parameters estimated using ThCSA are able to determine a threshold that achieves the segmentation of the melanoma area.

To complement the previous results, we focus on the visual and numeric comparison of the segmentation outcomes for the medical samples. The segmentation results of IMD004 and IMD015 using the studied algorithms in the are shown in Figure 5. Here, the Otsu methods in Figure 5b, GrayThresh in Figure 5c, Kittler in Figure 5d, MxE in Figure 5e, and ThCSA in Figure 5f obtained similar results for the sample IMD004 in Figure 5a. These images display white corners in the background, i.e., additional white pixels as a component of the skin lesion, which could be removed with additional processing. Some additional white pixels in the segmented background can also be observed using the Kittler, Figure 5d, and MxE, Figure 5e, methods. Based on the same algorithms, the sample IMD015, shown in Figure 5g, is segmented. By using this sample, the algorithms obtained an equivalent segmentation. This can be corroborated for Otsu, GrayThresh, Kittler, MxE, and ThCSA in Figure 5h–l, respectively. Here, the segmented skin lesion is more uniform, without extra white pixels in the background, independent of the corner area. For this sample, all segmentations illustrated in Figure 5h–l, recognize a line of black pixels in the bottom as background components. This error is caused by extra white pixels immersed in the original RGB image.

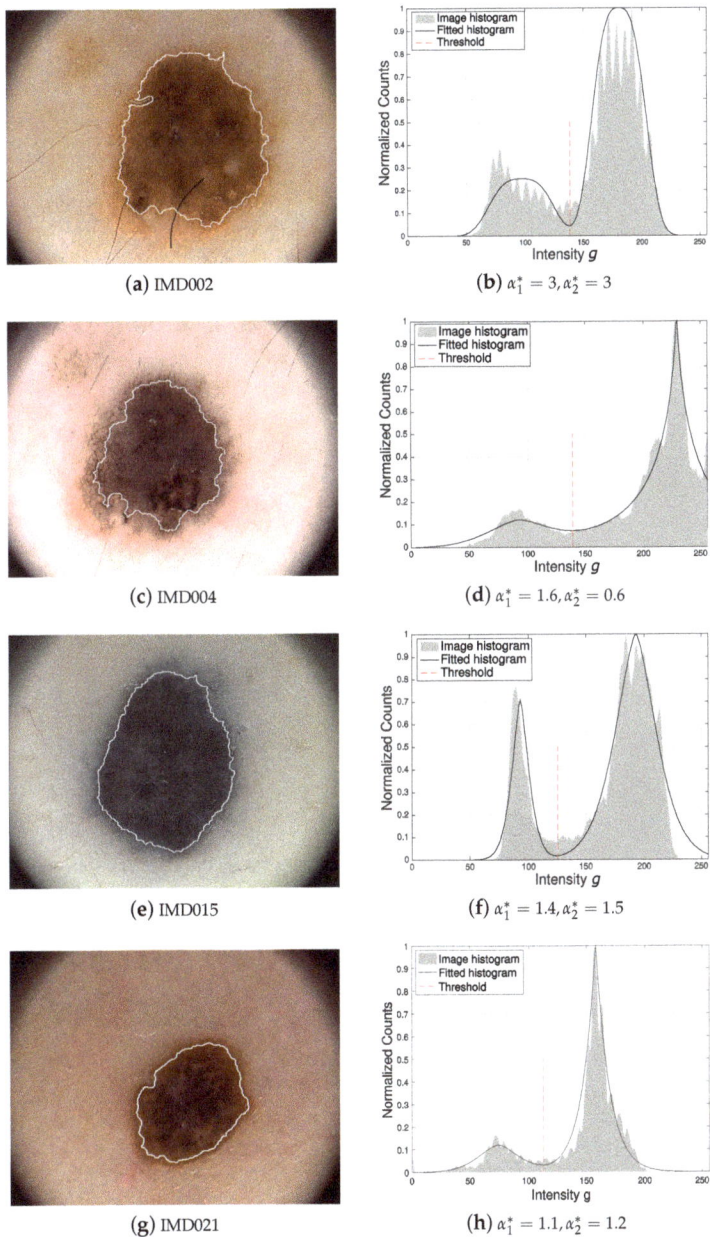

Figure 4. Contours and histograms estimated using the ThCSA algorithm. In the first column, the contour P_I is represented with a solid white line. In the second column, the image histogram, fitted histogram, and optimal threshold are displayed with a gray patch, a black solid line, and a red dashed line.

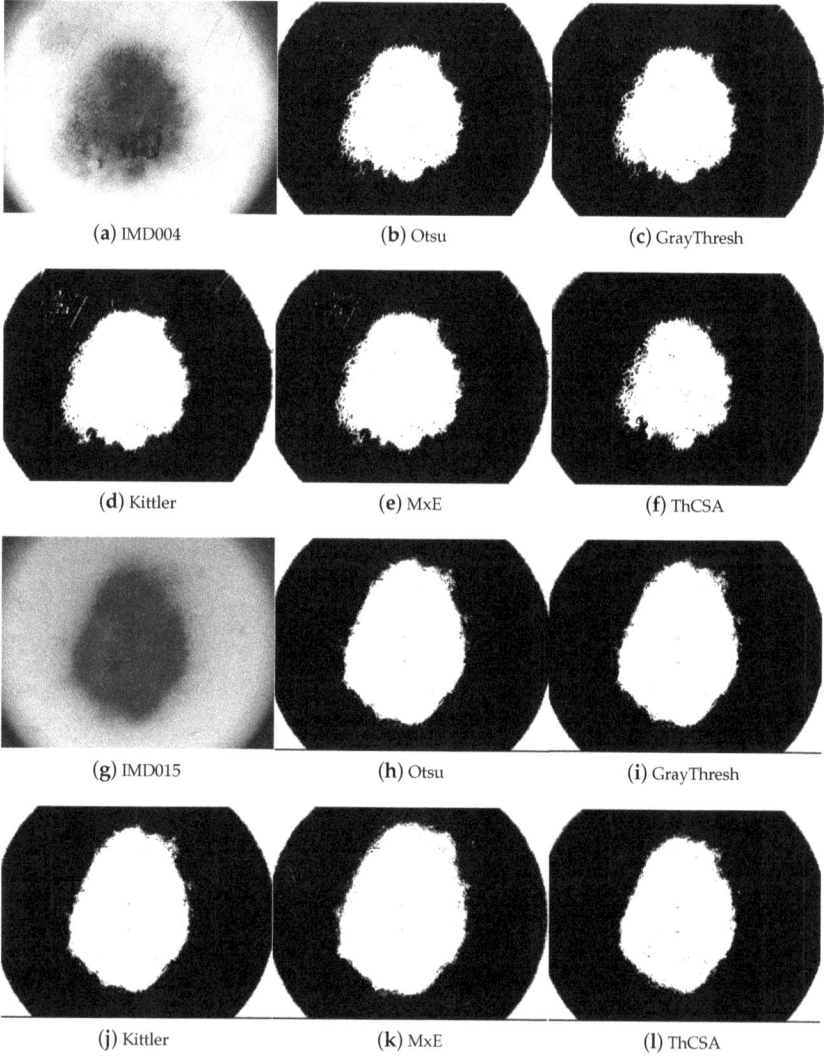

Figure 5. Gray-scale and processed images for IMD004 and IMD015 using the thresholding methods Otsu, GrayThresh, Kittler, MxE, and ThCSA, respectively.

Naturally, the visual comparison is insufficient to determine the best algorithm. For this reason, the reference images of melanomas or ground-truth images are required. Such images are provided by an expert dermatologist in [42], which are represented as $I_{b_r} \in \mathbb{Z}_2^{M \times N}$. $I_{b_r} \in \mathbb{Z}_2^{M \times N}$. Table 4 shows the Jaccard index and the False Negative (FN) pixels for all the methods. The Jaccard index is used to evaluate the image segmentation because it measures the intersection of an obtained binary image (I_{b_1} or I_{b_2}) and the reference image (I_{b_r}) divided by the union of both images [44]. The FN points are the unmatched pixels of the segmented image and the area labeled as object I_{O_r} in the reference image, where $I_{O_r} \subset I_{B_r}$. Employing the FN metric, it is possible to identify which method locates fewer wrong pixels in the object. In Table 4, the FN values are divided by the total number of pixels of I_{O_r} to avoid large numbers. These metrics are obtained for different melanoma images IMD002, IMD004, IMD015, IMD021, and IMD041. Table 4 displays the best Jaccard index in bold font. According to the Jaccard index, we can appreciate that, for IMD002, the best algorithm is MxE. This generates fewer inaccuracies regarding the FN values. Additionally, ThCSA ranks second according to the Jaccard index. For IMD004, the GrayThresh method is the best one. The ThCSA showed the maximal number in the FN column, but this method is in third place. Moreover, we notice that ThCSA is better for the sample IMD015 according to the Jaccard index, although the proposed algorithm obtained the worst values in FN measurements. For the sample IMD021, ThCSA was better than the other algorithms. However, the proposed algorithm obtained a low performance for FN values. The last sample analyzed was the image IMD041. Here, the algorithms GrayThresh and ThCSA were the best options, with the same Jaccard index and FN measures.

It is worth noting that the Jaccard indices are quite low, in the range of 0.6–0.8. This poor performance is due to the extra white pixels located in the corners of the images. However, the Jaccard index is adequate to rank the proposed algorithm. Furthermore, Table 5 shows the computing time comparison between the implemented algorithms. From these data, we can recognize the high computing time as a drawback of the proposed algorithm. Nevertheless, we suggest that this comparison is unfair because all the algorithms studied in this work were employed on different numerical platforms.

Table 4. Jaccard index and False Negative (FN) values obtained via different methods for medical samples. The best Jaccard index is in bold font. Symbols ↑ and ↓ represent the worst and best values, respectively.

Method	IMD002 Jaccard	IMD002 FN	IMD004 Jaccard	IMD004 FN	IMD015 Jaccard	IMD015 FN	IMD021 Jaccard	IMD021 FN	IMD041 Jaccard	IMD041 FN
Otsu	0.6889	0.1296	0.6645	0.0421	0.7117	0.0070	0.6149	0.0206	0.6818	0.0746
GrayThresh	0.6868	0.1362	**0.6664**	0.0447	0.7157	0.0080	0.6176	0.0242	**0.6822**	0.0779 ↑
Kittler	0.6780	0.1577↑	0.6167	0.0143↓	0.7117	0.0070	0.6062	0.0140	0.6816	0.0707
MxE	**0.6939**	0.0786↓	0.6471	0.0263	0.6244	0.0007↓	0.5555	0.0036↓	0.6669	0.0362↓
ThCSA	0.6917	0.1189	0.6601	0.1428↑	**0.7551**	0.0496↑	**0.6256**	0.0558↑	**0.6822**	0.0779↑

Table 5. Computing time required to find the threshold for medical images with different methods.

Method	Computing Time [s]				
	IMD002	IMD004	IMD015	IMD021	IMD041
Otsu	0.03	0.04	0.02	0.03	0.4
GrayThresh	0.02	0.02	0.02	0.03	0.2
Kittler	0.01	0.02	0.01	0.02	0.2
MxE	0.04	0.04	0.03	0.04	0.04
ThCSA	1.5	1.2	1.3	1.4	1.1

Furthermore, we extend the scope of application of the proposed algorithm by studying other kinds of images. To do this, we considered those with a background covering a greater area than the object. Sometimes the objects share pixels with the background in the gray-scale image. Figure 6 depicts three examples of this problem: one organic product and two inorganic products. The organic one is illustrated in Figure 6a, and its histogram is plotted in Figure 6b. The image in gray-scale, see Figure 6a, illustrates a background with different shades of gray and a darker area, representing the organic object. The histogram in Figure 6b shows two no uniform lobes that corroborate the color variability of the object and background. These lobes are approximately $G = 90$ to $G = 130$ for the object, and from $G = 140$ to $G = 175$ for the foreground. Despite fluctuations in the histogram, depicted in

Figure 6b, the algorithm ThCSA computed a good threshold to segment the organic object, which is bounded with a white line in Figure 6a.

Moreover, the two inorganic, which possess transparent areas, are shown in Figure 6c,e, and their histograms in Figure 6d,f, respectively. In Figure 6c, a white line delineates partially incomplete area of an inorganic product. This is because some object pixels are mixed with the background; i.e., they have the same intensity level. Figure 6d shows the threshold achieved by the ThCSA-based methodology. This threshold helps to delimit a large part of the object, although the object's outline is incomplete. Finally, in Figure 6e,f, we observe the most challenging example of this proposed work. To this inorganic object, the bottom, the label, and the screw cap are identified. The histograms (see Figure 6f) evidence where there is little information about the object. However, the proposed methodology can compute the corresponding thresholds to identify parts of this object.

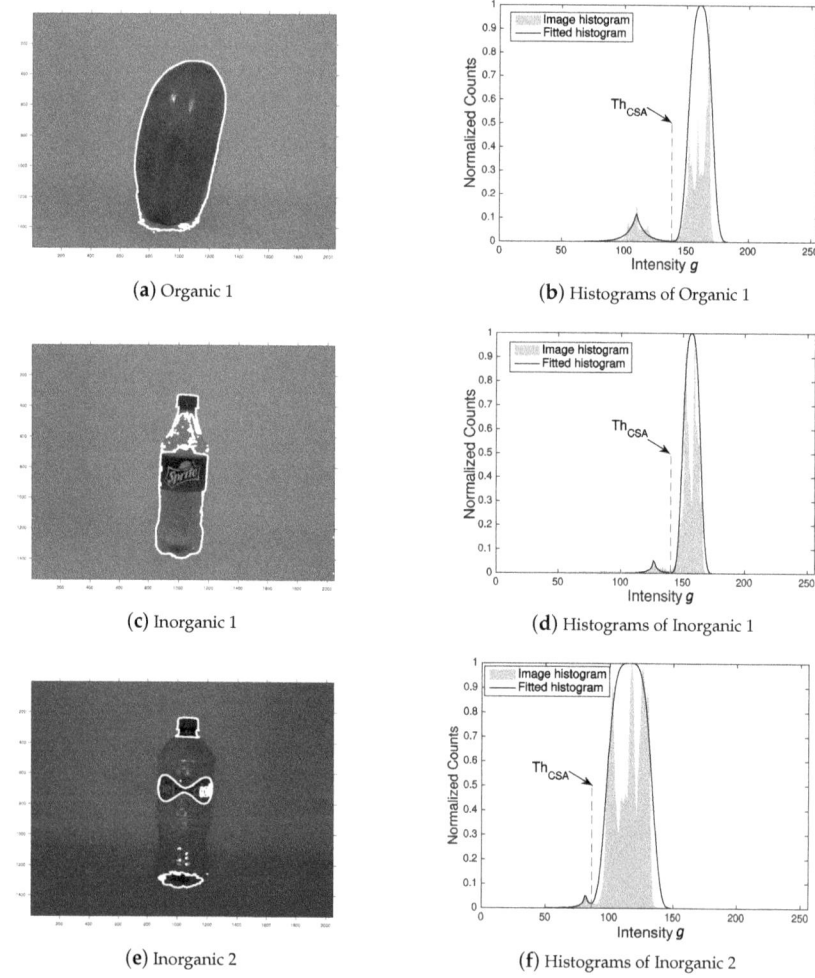

Figure 6. Illustrative example of the proposed algorithm implemented on three images, with quasi-modal histograms, containing either organic or inorganic products. Left column: gray-scale images and achieved detected outlines. Right column: image and fitted histograms and detected threshold.

6. Conclusions

In this work, we proposed ThCSA, a thresholding technique based on the Generalized Gaussian (GG) distributions and Cuckoo Search Algorithm. We implemented this methodology to tackle several image segmentation cases with different conditions and compared its results with some well-known algorithms. We showed that ThCSA, Otsu, and MxE obtain acceptable results when estimating the optimal threshold in simulated histograms. However, Otsu and MxE achieved the worst mark in at least one simulation, and GrayThresh was the worst at estimating the reference threshold. According to the comparison, the proposed algorithm obtained good performances by computing thresholds with a minimal difference and values very close to the optimal reference in most cases. These results are closely followed by the Kittler–Illingworth (KI).

ThCSA achieved the GG function variables in real medical image-processing to determine a threshold that segments the melanoma samples. The skin lesions were bounded with a certain precision based on the proposed methodology. Compared with the manual segmentation (ground-truth), evaluated by an expert dermatologist, the best segmentations were rendered by ThCSA , closely followed by GrayThresh. We corroborated this affirmation through the Jaccard indices, which can be improved with additional processing to avoid the corners induced by the capture instrument.

Furthermore, we noticed a remarkable potential when applying ThCSA to identify objects with no-uniform backgrounds and shared pixels. However, we found some issues while delimiting the complete object by the proposed method, especially when the background and object pixels have the same gray levels. Notwithstanding, ThCSA can detect strategic points to locate parts of the object. This issue should be analyzed and solved with an additional processing step. The principal disadvantage of the proposed methodology is that it requires more processing time than the other methods. Nevertheless, naturally, this work addressed the prototyping of an algorithm that could be enhanced and optimized in future implementations. Therefore, considering the advantages and disadvantages mentioned above, we finally conclude that the proposed methodology is an excellent option to compute optimal thresholds and segment objects from its quasi-uniform environment. This work presented an alternative thresholding tool, based on a global optimization algorithm, to help practitioners in diverse applications, e.g., dermatologic ones. Moreover, we plan to compare ThCSA with different image databases and employ several metrics to measure the segmentation quality for future work. We will also optimize the ThCSA implementation in a particular numerical platform to provide a competitive alternative to thresholding in any practical application.

Author Contributions: Conceptualization, J.F.-T., O.V.-C. and J.M.-M.; methodology, J.F.-T., O.V.-C., J.M.-M. and J.M.C.-D.; software, J.M.-M. and J.M.C.-D.; validation, J.F.-T., O.V.-C., J.M.-M. and J.M.C.-D.; formal analysis, J.M.-M. and J.M.C.-D.; investigation, J.M.-M. and J.M.C.-D.; resources, J.M.-M. and J.M.C.-D.; data curation, J.M.-M. and J.M.C.-D.; writing—original draft preparation, J.F.-T., O.V.-C. and J.M.-M.; writing—review and editing, J.F.-T., O.V.-C., J.M.-M. and J.M.C.-D.; visualization, J.M.-M. and J.M.C.-D.; supervision, J.M.-M. and J.M.C.-D.; project administration, J.M.-M.; funding acquisition, J.M.C.-D. All authors have read and agreed to the published version of the manuscript.

Funding: The research was supported by the Tecnológico de Monterrey (México), under the Program "FAC: Fondo para el financiamiento para la publicación de Artículos Científicos 2020–2021," Grant FAP-1157.

Conflicts of Interest: The authors declare no conflict of interest.

References

1. Lu, S.; Wang, B.; Wang, H.; Chen, L.; Linjian, M.; Zhang, X. A real-time object detection algorithm for video. *Comput. Electr. Eng.* **2019**, *77*, 398–408. [CrossRef]
2. Balaji, S.; Karthikeyan, S.; Manikandan, R. Object detection using Metaheuristic algorithm for volley ball sports application. *J. Ambient. Intell. Humaniz. Comput.* **2020**, *12*, 375–385. [CrossRef]
3. Sharma, V.; Mir, R. Saliency guided faster-RCNN (SGFr-RCNN) model for object detection and recognition. *J. King Saud Univ. Comput. Inf. Sci.* **2019**. [CrossRef]

4. Gollapudi, S. Object Detection and Recognition. In *Learn Computer Vision Using OpenCV*; Apress: New York, NY, USA, 2019; pp. 97–117.
5. Jiang, B.; Li, X.; Yin, L.; Yue, W.; Wang, S. Object Recognition in Remote Sensing Images Using Combined Deep Features. In Proceedings of the 2019 IEEE 3rd Information Technology, Networking, Electronic and Automation Control Conference (ITNEC), Chengdu, China, 15–17 March 2019; pp. 606–610.
6. Khryashchev, V.; Ostrovskaya, A.; Pavlov, V.; Semenov, A. Optimization of convolutional neural network for object recognition on satellite images. In Proceedings of the Systems of Signal Synchronization, Generating and Processing in Telecommunications (SYNCHROINFO), Minsk, Belarus, 4–5 July 2018; pp. 1–5.
7. Wang, L.; Shi, J.; Song, G.; Shen, I.F. Object detection combining recognition and segmentation. In Proceedings of the Asian Conference on Computer Vision, Tokyo, Japan, 18–22 November 2007; pp. 189–199.
8. Kumar, S.; Balyan, A.; Chawla, M. Object Detection and Recognition in Images. *Int. J. Eng. Dev. Res.* **2017**, *5*, 1029–1034.
9. Goh, T.Y.; Basah, S.N.; Yazid, H.; Safar, M.J.A.; Saad, F.S.A. Performance analysis of image thresholding: Otsu technique. *Measurement* **2018**, *114*, 298–307. [CrossRef]
10. Liang, J.; Xue, Y.; Wang, J. Genetic programming based feature construction methods for foreground object segmentation. *Eng. Appl. Artif. Intell.* **2020**, *89*, 103334. [CrossRef]
11. Song, S.B.; Liu, J.F.; Ni, H.Y.; Cao, X.L.; Pu, H.; Huang, B.X. A new automatic thresholding algorithm for unimodal gray-level distribution images by using the gray gradient information. *J. Pet. Sci. Eng.* **2020**, *190*, 107074. [CrossRef]
12. Golpardaz, M.; Helfroush, M.S.; Danyali, H. Nonsubsampled contourlet transform-based conditional random field for SAR images segmentation. *Signal Process.* **2020**, *174*, 107623. [CrossRef]
13. Li, Q.; Ma, Y.; Smarandache, F.; Zhu, S. Single-valued neutrosophic clustering algorithm based on Tsallis entropy maximization. *Axioms* **2018**, *7*, 57. [CrossRef]
14. Chan, K.C.; Chan, R.H.; Nikolova, M. A convex model for edge-histogram specification with applications to edge-preserving smoothing. *Axioms* **2018**, *7*, 53. [CrossRef]
15. Resma, K.B.; Nair, M.S. Multilevel thresholding for image segmentation using Krill Herd Optimization algorithm. *J. King Saud Univ. Comput. Inf. Sci.* **2018**. [CrossRef]
16. Lei, B.; Fan, J. Image thresholding segmentation method based on minimum square rough entropy. *Appl. Soft Comput.* **2019**, *84*, 105687. [CrossRef]
17. Ng, H.F.; Jargalsaikhan, D.; Tsai, H.C.; Lin, C.Y. An improved method for image thresholding based on the valley-emphasis method. In Proceedings of the 2013 Asia-Pacific Signal and Information Processing Association Annual Summit and Conference, Kaohsiung, Taiwan, 29 October–1 November 2013; pp. 1–4.
18. Yuan, X.C.; Wu, L.S.; Peng, Q. An improved Otsu method using the weighted object variance for defect detection. *Appl. Surf. Sci.* **2015**, *349*, 472–484. [CrossRef]
19. Li, J.; Tang, W.; Wang, J.; Zhang, X. Multilevel thresholding selection based on variational mode decomposition for image segmentation. *Signal Process.* **2018**, *147*, 80–91. [CrossRef]
20. Otsu, N. A Threshold Selection Method from Gray-Level Histograms. *IEEE Trans. Syst. Man Cybern.* **1979**, *9*, 62–66. [CrossRef]
21. Kittler, J.; Illingworth, J. Minimum error thresholding. *Pattern Recognit.* **1986**, *19*, 41–47. [CrossRef]
22. Kapur, J.N.; Sahoo, P.K.; Wong, A.K. A new method for gray-level picture thresholding using the entropy of the histogram. *Comput. Vis. Graph. Image Process.* **1985**, *29*, 273–285. [CrossRef]
23. Pun, T. A new method for grey-level picture thresholding using the entropy of the histogram. *Signal Process.* **1980**, *2*, 223–237. [CrossRef]
24. Pun, T. Entropic thresholding, a new approach. *Comput. Graph. Image Process.* **1981**, *16*, 210–239. [CrossRef]
25. Ng, H.F. Automatic Thresholding for Defect Detection. *Pattern Recogn. Lett.* **2006**, *27*, 1644–1649. [CrossRef]
26. Fan, J.L.; Lei, B. A modified valley-emphasis method for automatic thresholding. *Pattern Recognit. Lett.* **2012**, *33*, 703–708. [CrossRef]
27. Xing, J.; Yang, P.; Qingge, L. Automatic thresholding using a modified valley emphasis. *IET Image Process.* **2020**, *14*, 536–544. [CrossRef]
28. Belkasim, S.; Ghazal, A.; Basir, O.A. Phase-based optimal image thresholding. *Digit. Signal Process.* **2003**, *13*, 636–655. [CrossRef]
29. Truong, M.T.N.; Kim, S. Automatic image thresholding using Otsu's method and entropy weighting scheme for surface defect detection. *Soft Comput.* **2018**, *22*, 4197–4203. [CrossRef]
30. Xu, X.; Xu, S.; Jin, L.; Song, E. Characteristic analysis of Otsu threshold and its applications. *Pattern Recognit. Lett.* **2011**, *32*, 956–961. [CrossRef]
31. Bazi, Y.; Bruzzone, L.; Melgani, F. Image thresholding based on the EM algorithm and the generalized Gaussian distribution. *Pattern Recognit.* **2007**, *40*, 619–634. [CrossRef]
32. Boulmerka, A.; Allili, M.S.; Ait-Aoudia, S. A generalized multiclass histogram thresholding approach based on mixture modelling. *Pattern Recognit.* **2014**, *47*, 1330–1348. [CrossRef]
33. Fan, S.K.S.; Lin, Y.; Wu, C.C. Image thresholding using a novel estimation method in generalized Gaussian distribution mixture modeling. *Neurocomputing* **2008**, *72*, 500–512. [CrossRef]
34. Fan, S.K.S.; Lin, Y. A fast estimation method for the generalized Gaussian mixture distribution on complex images. *Comput. Vis. Image Underst.* **2009**, *113*, 839–853. [CrossRef]

35. Yanxia, C.; Yanyan, X.; Tierui, Z.; Dandan, L. Threshold image target segmentation technology based on intelligent algorithms. *Comput. Opt.* **2020**, *44*, 137–141.
36. Nadarajah, S. A generalized normal distribution. *J. Appl. Stat.* **2005**, *32*, 685–694. [CrossRef]
37. Yang, X.S.; Deb, S. Cuckoo search via Lévy flights. In Proceedings of the 2009 World Congress on Nature & Biologically Inspired Computing (NaBIC), Coimbatore, India, 9–11 December 2009; pp. 210–214.
38. Cruz-Duarte, J.M.; Guía-Calderón, M.; Rosales-García, J.J.; Correa, R. Determination of a physically correct fractional-order model for electrolytic computer-grade capacitors. *Math. Methods Appl. Sci.* **2020**, *44*, 4366–4380. [CrossRef]
39. Shehab, M. Cuckoo Search Algorithm. In *Artificial Intelligence in Diffusion MRI*; Springer Nature Switzerland AG: Cham, Switzerland, 2020; pp. 31–59.
40. Shehab, M.; Khader, A.T.; Al-Betar, M.A. A survey on applications and variants of the cuckoo search algorithm. *Appl. Soft Comput. J.* **2017**, *61*, 1041–1059. [CrossRef]
41. Mantegna, R.N.; Stanley, H.E. Stochastic process with ultraslow convergence to a Gaussian: The truncated Lévy flight. *Phys. Rev. Lett.* **1994**, *73*, 2946. [CrossRef]
42. Mendonça, T.; Ferreira, P.M.; Marques, J.S.; Marcal, A.R.S.; Rozeira, J. PH2—A dermoscopic image database for research and benchmarking. In Proceedings of the 2013 35th Annual International Conference of the IEEE Engineering in Medicine and Biology Society (EMBC), Osaka, Japan, 3–7 July 2013; pp. 5437–5440.
43. Cruz-Duarte, J.M.; Garcia-Perez, A.; Amaya-Contreras, I.M.; Correa-Cely, C.R.; Romero-Troncoso, R.J.; Avina-Cervantes, J.G. Design of Microelectronic Cooling Systems Using a Thermodynamic Optimization Strategy Based on Cuckoo Search. *IEEE Trans. Components Packag. Manuf. Technol.* **2017**, *7*, 1804–1812. [CrossRef]
44. Jaccard, P. The distribution of the flora in the alpine zone. 1. *New Phytol.* **1912**, *11*, 37–50. [CrossRef]

Article

Enlargement of the Field of View Based on Image Region Prediction Using Thermal Videos

Ganbayar Batchuluun, Na Rae Baek and Kang Ryoung Park *

Division of Electronics and Electrical Engineering, Dongguk University, 30 Pildong-ro, 1-gil, Jung-gu, Seoul 04620, Korea; ganabata87@dongguk.edu (G.B.); naris27@dgu.ac.kr (N.R.B.)
* Correspondence: parkgr@dgu.edu

Abstract: Various studies have been conducted for detecting humans in images. However, there are the cases where a part of human body disappears in the input image and leaves the camera field of view (FOV). Moreover, there are the cases where a pedestrian comes into the FOV as a part of the body slowly appears. In these cases, human detection and tracking fail by existing methods. Therefore, we propose the method for predicting a wider region than the FOV of a thermal camera based on the image prediction generative adversarial network version 2 (IPGAN-2). When an experiment was conducted using the marathon subdataset of the Boston University-thermal infrared video benchmark open dataset, the proposed method showed higher image prediction (structural similarity index measure (SSIM) of 0.9437) and object detection (F1 score of 0.866, accuracy of 0.914, and intersection over union (IoU) of 0.730) accuracies than state-of-the-art methods.

Keywords: image prediction; thermal videos; deep learning; IPGAN-2

Citation: Batchuluun, G.; Baek, N.R.; Park, K.R. Enlargement of the Field of View Based on Image Region Prediction Using Thermal Videos. *Mathematics* **2021**, *9*, 2379. https://doi.org/10.3390/math9192379

Academic Editors: Ezequiel López-Rubio, Esteban Palomo and Enrique Domínguez

Received: 17 August 2021
Accepted: 22 September 2021
Published: 25 September 2021

Publisher's Note: MDPI stays neutral with regard to jurisdictional claims in published maps and institutional affiliations.

Copyright: © 2021 by the authors. Licensee MDPI, Basel, Switzerland. This article is an open access article distributed under the terms and conditions of the Creative Commons Attribution (CC BY) license (https://creativecommons.org/licenses/by/4.0/).

1. Introduction

Extensive research has been conducted on objection detection [1–4], tracking [5–9], and action recognition [10–13] using conventional camera-based detection systems. However, there are frames where a part of body of a pedestrian disappears because the part of the body of the pedestrian is outside a camera's field of view (FOV) when walking or running. Moreover, there are cases in which a pedestrian comes into the FOV as a part of the body slowly appears. These cases cause the person to be detected or not detected inconsistently. An error also occurs in human tracking and action recognition. In a previous study, the issue in which a part of human body disappears was examined [14], but only a small region within an input image could be predicted. To overcome such an issue, in this study, for the first time, an image restoration was performed, as shown in Figure 1, by predicting the wide region outside the FOV not included in the current image (t) as in image t' for restoring the disappeared part of the body of a pedestrian in a thermal image. The proposed method predicts wider regions on both sides of the FOV in a current image using an image prediction generative adversarial network version 2 (IPGAN-2)-based method, the preceding sequential frame, and the current frame. In this study, various experiments were performed using the marathon subdataset [15] of the Boston University-thermal infrared video (BU-TIV) benchmark open dataset.

In addition, this study is novel in the following four ways compared with the previous studies.

- For thermal camera images, in this study, image prediction was performed in which, for the first time, the occurrence of noise was minimized while wide regions to left and right sides of the FOV in the current image were accurately generated.
- In this study, IPGAN-2 is proposed for performing image prediction.
- For improving the accuracy of image prediction, binary images corresponding to sequential input thermal images were used as input for IPGAN-2.

- The IPGAN-2 model proposed has been disclosed [16] for a fair performance evaluation by other researchers.

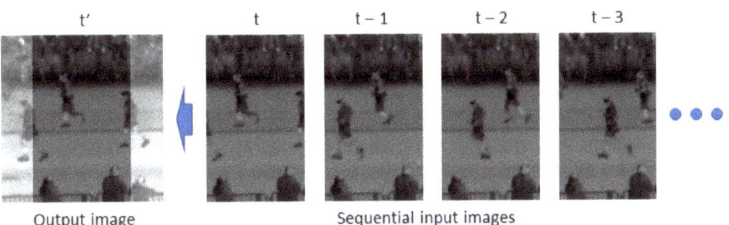

Figure 1. Example of thermal image prediction.

The remainder of this study is organized as follows. In Section 2, previous studies are reviewed. In Section 3, the proposed method is explained in detail. Experimental results and analysis are provided in Section 4. Finally, a discussion and the conclusions are provided in Sections 5 and 6, respectively.

2. Related Works

Previous studies on image prediction that generate the current frame or next frame can be largely divided into five categories, as explained in Sections 2.1 and 2.2.3.

2.1. Not Using Previous Frames but Using Current Frame (Image Inpainting)

Studies (image inpainting) have been conducted on the restoration of part of a current image by using only the current frame [17–22]. In [17], a fine deep-generative-model-based approach with a novel coherent semantic attention (CSA) layer was used to restore a visible light image. In [18], a visible light image was restored based on gated convolution and SN-PatchGAN. In [19], a visible light image was restored based on the parallel extended-decoder path for semantic inpainting network (PEPSI). In [20], a visible light image was restored using a context encoder method based on a channel-wise fully connected layer. A visible light image was restored in [21] using a method based on edge prediction and image completion based on the predicted edge map. Finally, in [22], the sequential-based, convolutional neural network (CNN)-based, and generative adversarial network (GAN)-based image restoration methods and the datasets used were explained.

2.2. Using Current and Previous Frames
2.2.1. Prediction of Next Frame

In some earlier studies [23–25], a next frame was predicted using the current frame and previous sequential frames. A dual-motion GAN model (ConvLSTMGAN) was proposed [23], and image prediction was performed using a visible light image. This method involves encoding sequential input frames using a probabilistic motion encoder (encoder CNN). The encoder CNN consists of four convolutional layers, one intermediate ConvLSTM layer, and two ConvLSTM layers. Furthermore, the next frame and next flow images are generated through future-image and future-flow generators. In [24], a method was proposed for generating the next optical flow image and next frame using a visible light image and encoder and decoder CNN (OptCNN-Hybrid). In this method, the proposed network was trained in a hybrid way using real and synthetic videos. In [25], a method for generating the next frame using a visible light image and ConvLSTM was proposed. In this study, the depth image is predicted using a current image and camera trajectory. Moreover, the next frame is generated using depth information by creating a depth image based on the advantages of camera scene geometry.

2.2.2. Prediction of Next Sequential Frames

In earlier studies [26–30], the next sequential frames were predicted using the current frame and previous sequential frames. In [26], image prediction was performed using a visible light image and the encoder and decoder model based on long short-term memory (LSTM) and a 3D convolution layer. In [27], the image was predicted using a visible light image, the newly proposed PhyCell, and PhyDNet based on LSTM. In [28], image prediction was performed using a visible light image, LSTM, and a CNN. In [29], the image was predicted using a visible light image and the encoder and decoder model. Image prediction was performed in [30] using a visible light image and a stochastic variational video prediction (SV2P) method. In a review study [31], the datasets from 2004 to 2019 used in image prediction were compared with the image prediction models that were released between 2014 and 2020. In the survey in [32], studies on and datasets for image prediction were explained.

2.2.3. Prediction of Small Left Region of Current Frame

In the following study, a region out of the FOV of a current frame was generated using the current frame and previous sequential frames. In [14], image prediction was performed in which a region out of the FOV was generated using a thermal video and GAN. The regions outside the FOV were predicted using the image obtained from a thermal camera that measured the heat of a human body rather than the image obtained from a general visible light camera. However, this method created a wide image by predicting a small region to the left of the FOV. Noise also occurred in the prediction region in the generated image, and the region includes more noise as the size of the region being predicted increased. Therefore, there is a limitation in the size of the region being predicted.

Table 1 provides comparisons between the proposed method and previous studies.

Table 1. Summaries of comparisons between the proposed method and previous image prediction studies.

Category	Not Using Previous Frames but Using Current Frame (Prediction of Removed Part in Current Frame (Image in painting))	Using Current and Previous Frames			
		Prediction of Next Frame	Prediction of Next Sequential Frames	Prediction of Small Left Region of Current Frame	Prediction of Large Right and Left Regions of Current Frame
Methods	CSA layer [17], gated convolution + SN-PatchGAN [18], PEPSI [19], context encoder [20], edge prediction and image completion [21], and review [22]	ConvLSTMGAN [23], OptCNN-Hybrid [24], ConvLSTM [25]	Encoder–decoder model [26,29], PhyDNet [27], CNN + LSTM [28], SV2P [30], and review & survey [31,32]	IPGAN [14]	IPGAN-2 (Proposed method)
Input	High-quality and high-resolution RGB visible light image			Low-quality and low-resolution grayscale thermal image	Low-quality and low-resolution grayscale thermal image and binary image
Output	RGB visible light image			An RGB thermal image	A grayscale thermal image
Advantages	High performance is achieved by restoring the information deleted in the current image by using the remaining information of the current image.	High performance is obtained when generating the next image by using the current image and previous sequential images.		- Considers image prediction besides FOV - Uses low-resolution, low-quality thermal image	- A wide image of left and right of the FOV is generated for image prediction - Noise does not occur in the predicted image outside the FOV
Disadvantages	- Does not consider image prediction outside the FOV - Does not use low-resolution, low-quality thermal image			- The size of predicted image is limited. - Noise occurs in the predicted image - Only the region to the left of the FOV is generated for image prediction.	Low processing speed

3. Materials and Methods

3.1. Overall Procedure of Proposed Method

In this section, the proposed method is explained in detail. Image region prediction is performed in this method based on sequential thermal images using IPGAN-2. In Sections 3.2–3.5, the IPGAN-2 architecture, postprocessing, differences between IPGAN and the proposed IPGAN-2, and dataset with experimental setup for image prediction are explained in detail. Figure 2a shows the overall flowchart of the proposed method and Figure 2b shows the overall procedure of the proposed method with image examples. The length of the sequential input images is 20 frames (t − 0, t − 1, . . . t − 19), the size of each image is 120 × 160 pixels, and the size the output image is 200 × 160 pixels. Specifically, the part connecting a disappeared part of a person not in the camera FOV (left region of the FOV) and the background in the current image is generated, while simultaneously generating a disappeared part of a person coming into the camera FOV (right region of the FOV) to generate the output image. As shown in Figure 2b, sequential thermal images for input and the corresponding sequential binary images are used as input for IPGAN-2. Input images for image prediction are horizontally flipped, and IPGAN-2 is applied one more time, during which the same model is used. In Figure 2b, red arrows represent a horizontal concatenate operation of the three images. In Table 2, the detailed procedure of the proposed algorithm is explained step by step.

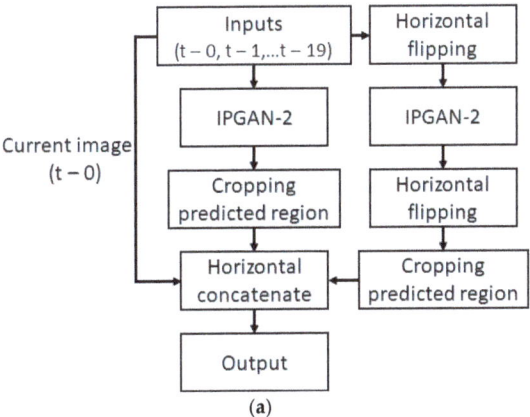

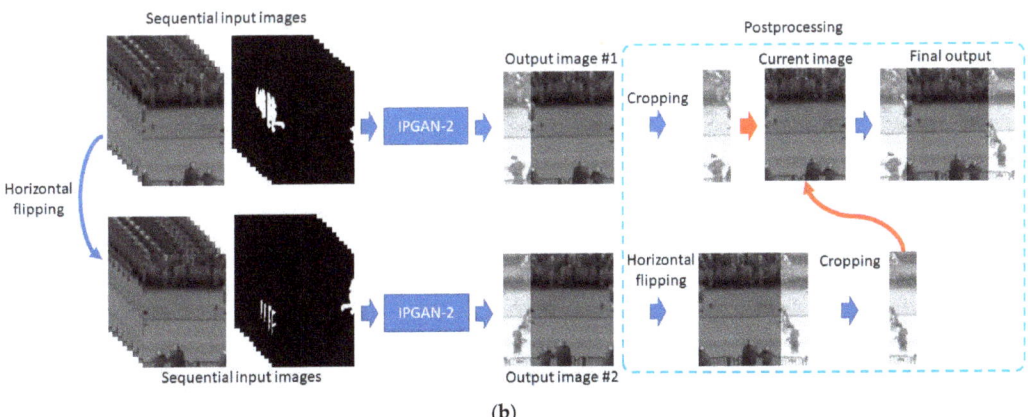

Figure 2. Flowchart of the proposed method. (**a**) Overall flowchart; (**b**) overall procedure with image examples.

Table 2. The proposed method detailed by using pseudo code.

Input thermal image with size of $(120 \times 160 \times 1) = X_{t-0}$
Input binary image with size of $(120 \times 160 \times 1) = Y_{t-0}$
Output thermal image with size of $(160 \times 160 \times 1) = O_{t-0}$
Final output thermal image with size of $(200 \times 160 \times 1) = Z_{t-0}$
IPGAN-2 model = $model$
Horizontal image flipping = $flip$
Image cropping = $crop$

Algorithm procedure	Output shape/dimension
$A = [X_{t-0}, X_{t-1}, \ldots X_{t-19,}]$	$120 \times 160 \times 20$
$B = [Y_{t-0}, Y_{t-1}, \ldots Y_{t-19,}]$	$120 \times 160 \times 20$
$A' = flip(A)$	$120 \times 160 \times 20$
$B' = flip(B)$	$120 \times 160 \times 20$
$C = concatenate(A, B, axis = channel)$	$120 \times 160 \times 40$
$C' = concatenate(A', B', axis = channel)$	$120 \times 160 \times 40$
$O_{t-0} = model(C)$	$160 \times 160 \times 1$
$O'_{t-0} = model(C')$	$160 \times 160 \times 1$
$O''_{t-0} = flip(O'_{t-0})$	$160 \times 160 \times 1$
$R_{t-0} = crop(O_{t-0}, [0:39, 0:159])$	$40 \times 160 \times 1$
$R'_{t-0} = crop(O''_{t-0}, [120:159, 0:159])$	$40 \times 160 \times 1$
$C'' = concatenate(R_{t-0}, X_{t-0}, axis = horizontal)$	$200 \times 160 \times 1$
$Z_{t-0} = concatenate(C'', R'_{t-0}, axis = horizontal)$	$200 \times 160 \times 1$

3.2. Proposed IPGAN-2 Model

As shown in Figure 2b, sequential thermal images ($120 \times 160 \times 20$ pixels) and sequential binary images ($120 \times 160 \times 20$ pixels) are used as input for the proposed IPGAN-2. The IPGAN-2 architecture is shown in Figure 3. The generator in Figure 3 includes the concatenate layer (L2 and L31), convolution blocks (L9, L22, and L26), encoder blocks (L3, L4, L5, L14, L15, and L16), residual blocks (L6–L8, L10–L13, L23–25, and L27–30), and convolution layers (L17, L20, L21, L32, and L33) in order. In the concatenate layer (L2), sequential images are applied with depth-wise concatenation to generate a multichannel single image ($120 \times 160 \times 40$), while in the concatenate layer (L31), feature maps are combined in the horizontal direction to generate a wide image. Furthermore, the discriminator includes convolution blocks (L1–L6) and a fully connected layer (L7) in order.

Specific details of the IPGAN-2 architecture are presented in Tables 3–8. In Tables 3–6, the filter size, stride, and padding are (3×3), (1×1), and (1×1), respectively. In Table 3, two filter numbers, 128 and 64, are used in conv_block_1–conv_block_3. In Table 7, the filter size, stride, and padding in conv_block_1–conv_block_3 are (3×3), (1×1), and (0×0), while the filter size, stride, and padding in conv_block_4–conv_block_6 are (3×3), (2×2), and (0×0), respectively. The layer types of Tables 3–8 are prelu (parametric rectified linear unit (relu)), lrelu (leaky relu), maxpool (max pooling operation), tanh (hyperbolic tangent activation function), res_block (residual block), encod_block (encoder block), conv2d (two-dimensional convolution layer), add (addition operation), conv_block (convolution block), dense (fully connected layer), concat (concatenate layer), and sigmoid (sigmoid activation function). Furthermore, reshape (L19) of Table 3 is a layer that reshapes input tensors into the given shape. As the input in Table 3, 20 sequential thermal images ($120 \times 160 \times 1$) and 20 sequential binary images ($120 \times 160 \times 1$) were used, as in Figure 3, and the output image was one image ($160 \times 160 \times 1$).

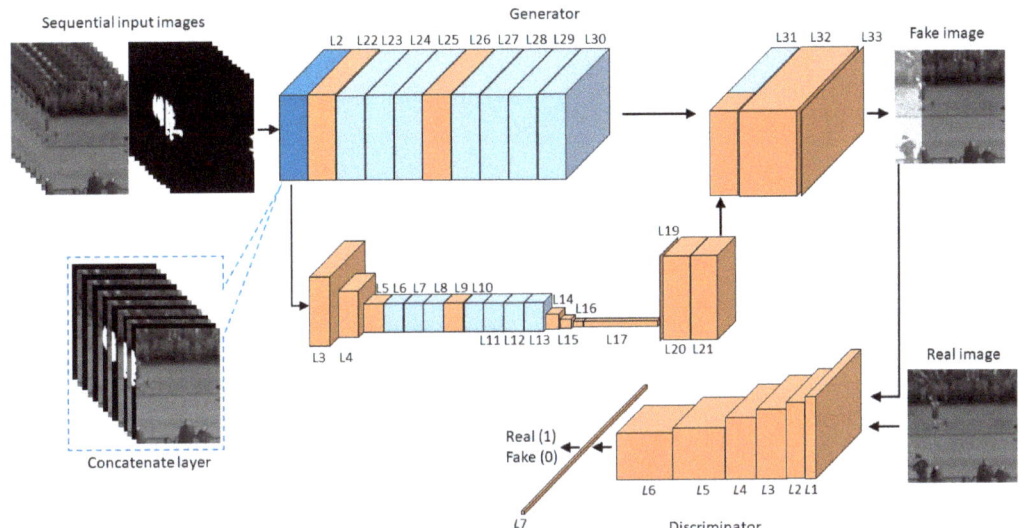

Figure 3. Example of the structure of proposed IPGAN-2.

Table 3. Description of the generator of IPGAN-2.

Layer Number	Layer Type	Number of Filters	Number of Parameters	Layer Connection (Connected to)
0	input_layers_1–20		0	input_1–20
1	input_layers_21–40		0	input_21–40
2	concat_1		0	input_layers_1–20 & input_layers_21–40
3	encod_block_1	64	48,640	concat_1
4	encod_block_2	64	73,984	encod_block_1
5	encod_block_3	64	73,984	encod_block_2
6	res_block_1	64	73,920	encod_block_3
7	res_block_2	64	73,920	res_block_1
8	res_block_3	64	73,920	res_block_2
9	conv_block_1	128/64	147,840	res_block_3
10	res_block_4	64	73,920	conv_block_1
11	res_block_5	64	73,920	res_block_4
12	res_block_6	64	73,920	res_block_5
13	res_block_7	64	73,920	res_block_6
14	encod_block_4	64	73,984	res_block_7
15	encod_block_5	64	73,984	encod_block_4
16	encod_block_6	64	73,984	encod_block_5
17	conv2d_1	3200	1,846,400	encod_block_6
18	prelu_1	3200	3200	
19	reshape		0	conv2d_1
20	conv2d_2	64	640	reshape
21	conv2d_3	64	36,928	conv2d_2
22	conv_block_2	128/64	97,152	concat_1
23	res_block_8	64	73,920	conv_block_2
24	res_block_9	64	73,920	res_block_8
25	res_block_10	64	73,920	res_block_9
26	conv_block_3	128/64	147,840	res_block_10
27	res_block_11	64	73,920	conv_block_3
28	res_block_12	64	73,920	res_block_11

Table 3. Cont.

Layer Number	Layer Type	Number of Filters	Number of Parameters	Layer Connection (Connected to)
29	res_block_13	64	73,920	res_block_12
30	res_block_14	64	73,920	res_block_13
31	concat_2		0	conv2d_3 & res_block_14
32	conv2d_4	256	147,712	concat_2
33	conv2d_5	1	2305	conv2d_4
34	tanh		0	conv2d_5
Total number of trainable parameters: 3,883,457				

Table 4. Description of an encoder block of the generator.

Layer Number	Layer Type	Number of Filters	Layer Connection (Connected to)
1	conv2d_1	64	input
2	prelu_1	64	conv2d_1
3	conv2d_2	64	prelu_1
4	prelu_2	64	conv2d_2
5	maxpool		prelu_2

Table 5. Description of a convolution block of the generator.

Layer Number	Layer Type	Number of Filters	Layer Connection (Connected to)
1	conv2d_1	128	input
2	prelu_1	128	conv2d_1
3	conv2d_2	64	prelu_1
4	prelu_2	64	conv2d_2

Table 6. Description of a residual block of the generator.

Layer Number	Layer Type	Number of Filters	Layer Connection (Connected to)
1	conv2d_1	64	input
2	prelu	64	conv2d_1
3	conv2d_2	64	prelu
4	add		conv2d_2 & input

Table 7. Description of the discriminator of IPGAN-2.

Layer Number	Layer Type	Number of Filters	Number of Parameters	Layer Connection (Connected to)
0	input layer		0	input
1	conv_block_1	32	896	input layer
2	conv_block_2	64	18,496	conv_block_1
3	conv_block_3	128	73,856	conv_block_2
4	conv_block_4	128	147,584	conv_block_3
5	conv_block_5	256	295,168	conv_block_4
6	conv_block_6	256	590,080	conv_block_5
7	dense		92,417	conv_block_6
8	sigmoid		0	dense
Total number of trainable parameters: 1,218,497				

Table 8. Description of a convolution block of the discriminator.

Layer Number	Layer Type	Layer Connection (Connected to)
1	conv2d	input
2	lrelu	conv2d

3.3. Postprocessing

The postprocessing method shown in Figure 4 was used in this study. As shown in Figure 3, the final output shown in Figure 4 is obtained by cropping and combining the predicted regions outside the FOV from the first output image obtained using IPGAN-2 and the second output image obtained by horizontally flipping sequential input images and using IPGAN-2. The reason for using the method in Figure 4, instead of performing image prediction for both sides of the FOV of the current image, is explained in Section 4.2 based on experimental results.

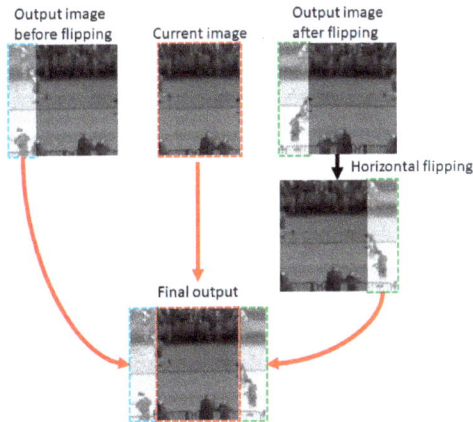

Figure 4. Example of the postprocessing.

3.4. Differences between IPGAN and Proposed IPGAN-2

In this section, the difference between the proposed method and a previous method [14] is explained in detail. These two methods have different architectures overall. In particular, the region in the image being predicted is different, and each step is designed differently. Table 9 shows the overall structure of the two methods in steps. Table 10 presents the advantage and disadvantage of the two methods.

Table 9. Comparison of overall structure of previous method [14] and proposed method.

Steps	Previous Method [14] (IPGAN)	Proposed Method (IPGAN-2)
Input	Original thermal image (85 × 170 × 1)	Original thermal image (120 × 160 × 1)
Preprocessing	Conversion of original thermal image to three-channel color thermal image with zero padding	Image binarization by using background subtraction and horizontal flipping
Network input	Three-channel color thermal image (170 × 170 × 3)	Original thermal image (120 × 160 × 1) and binary image (120 × 160 × 1)
Network output	Three-channel color thermal image (170 × 170 × 3)	One-channel thermal image (160 × 160 × 1)

Table 9. Cont.

Steps	Previous Method [14] (IPGAN)	Proposed Method (IPGAN-2)
Postprocessing	Image cropping (crop a small part of predicted region) and combining	Image cropping (crop the entire predicted region), horizontal flipping, and combining
Output	Three-channel color thermal image (105 × 170 × 3)	One-channel thermal image (200 × 160 × 1)

Table 10. Comparison of advantage and disadvantage of previous method [14] and proposed method.

Factors	Previous Method [14] (IPGAN)	Proposed Method (IPGAN-2)
Predicted region	Only left side	Left and right sides
Size of predicted region	Smaller (input of 85 × 170 to output of 105 × 170)	Larger (input of 120 × 160 to output of 200 × 160)
Error	Gray noise occurs over predicted region	No gray noise
Processing speed	Higher	Lower

3.5. Dataset and Experimental Setup

The experiment in this study was conducted using the marathon subdataset of the BU-TIV benchmark open thermal dataset [15]. The marathon subdataset was created for the purpose of multi-object tracking and includes various objects, such as pedestrians, cars, motorcycles, and bicycles. This dataset also consists of four videos (image sequences) with different sizes. Images in the dataset are provided in the image format of portable network graphics (PNG). Annotations for the object detection for the four sequences are provided. An FLIR SC800 camera (FLIR Systems, Inc., Wilsonville, OR, USA) was used to collect the dataset. The pixel value of a thermal image ranges between 3000 and 7000 units of uncalibrated temperature [15]. In this study, image sequences 1 and 2 of the marathon sub-dataset were used, and 3999 images (size of 1024 × 512 × 1, and pixel depth of 16 bits) were used. When training the proposed model, 3999 original images are cropped to create 19,995 images in a dataset (image size of 160 × 160 × 1, and pixel depth of 8 bits) to perform training and testing. The region in which pedestrians are running (region of interest (ROI) of the red boxes in Figure 5) in the original image was cropped. A ground-truth (*GT*) image (green boxes) and input images (blue boxes) were generated, as shown in Figure 5, by cropping the ROI into 160 × 160.

Our network is not aware of the scenes of testing cases. Various scenes have been used in our experiments. In the below Figure 5d,e, example images used in training and testing phases are presented. As shown in this figure, the images used in training phase are completely different from those in testing phase, and they were not cropped from same scene.

The experiment was conducted as two-fold cross validation. More specifically, half the total data were used for training, while the other half were used for testing (10% of the testing data were used as validation data, while the remaining 90% were used as testing data). The two datasets were switched for performing training and testing once again, and the average of the two testing accuracy values was set as the final accuracy.

Training and testing of the proposed algorithm were performed using a desktop computer. The desktop computer was equipped with Intel core i7-6700 CPU@3.40GHz, a Nvidia GeForce GTX TITAN X graphics processing unit (GPU) card [33], and random-access memory (RAM) of 32 GB. The proposed model and algorithm were implemented with OpenCV library (version 4.3.0) [34], Python (version 3.5.4) [35], and the Keras application programming interface (API) (version 2.1.6-tf) with a TensorFlow backend engine (version 1.9.0) [36].

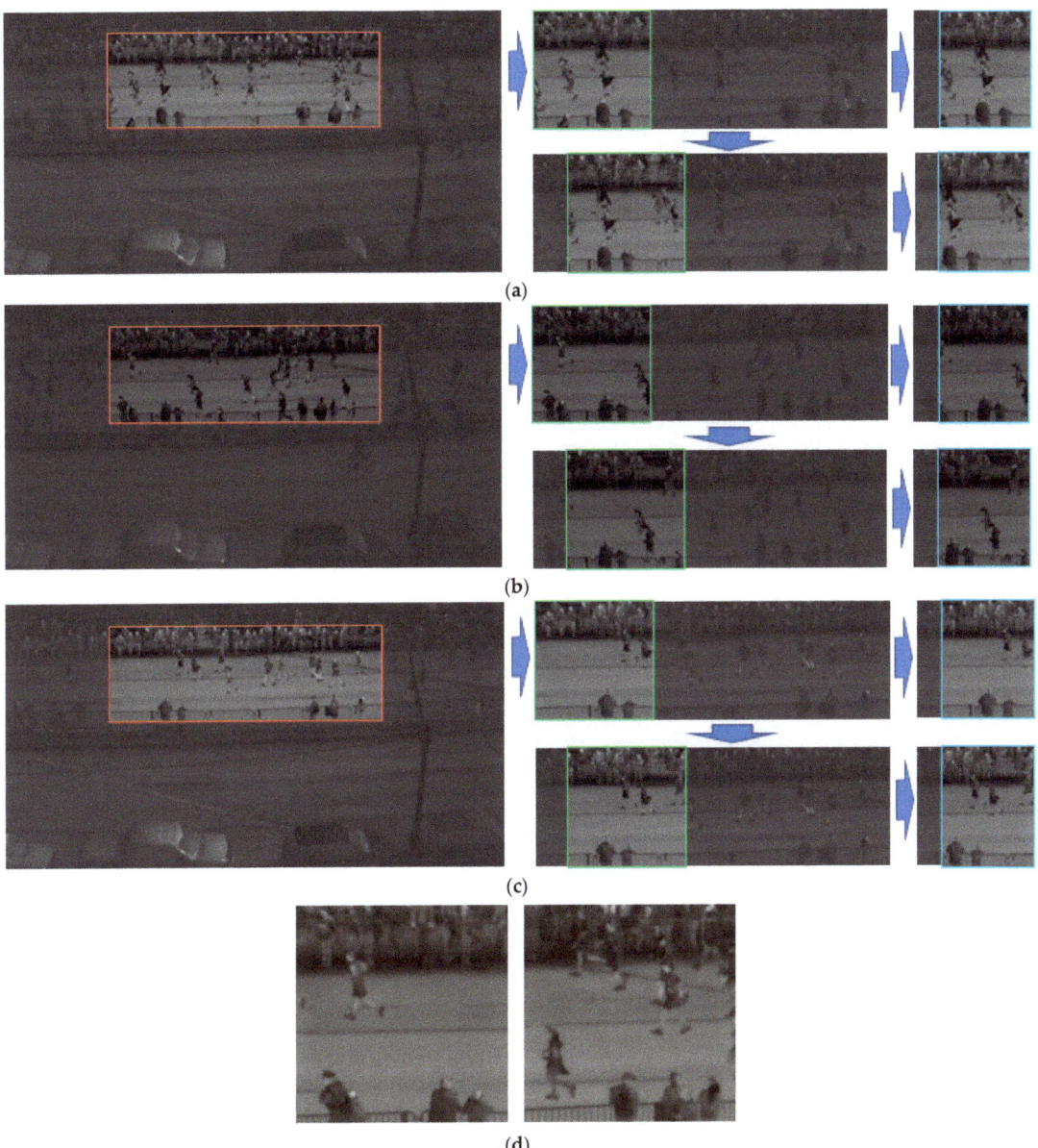

Figure 5. *Cont.*

(e)

Figure 5. Example images of dataset: the left images in red boxes show the cropped ROI, the middle images in green boxes represent the *GT* images, and the right images in blue boxes show the input images to model for image prediction. (**a**–**c**) the procedure of making the dataset; (**d**) example images used in training phase; (**e**) example images used in testing phase.

4. Results

This section is divided into four subsections on training, testing, comparisons, and processing time to explain the experimental results. In Section 4.1, the hyperparameters and training loss used in the training step are explained. In Section 4.2, the results obtained through the ablation study are compared. In Section 4.3, the results obtained using the proposed method and the state-of-the-art methods are compared. In Section 4.4, additional experiments using different datasets (Casia thermal image dataset C and BU-TIV marathon thermal image dataset) for training and testing are conducted. Finally, in Section 4.5, the processing time was measured for each component.

4.1. Training

The proposed IPGAN-2 was trained as follows. The batch size, training iteration, and learning rate in IPGAN-2 were 1, 483,581, and 0.001, respectively. Moreover, binary cross-entropy loss was used as generator loss and discriminator loss, and adaptive moment estimation (Adam) [37] was used as an optimizer. More detailed information about the search space and selected hyperparameter values is provided in Table 11. Hyperparameters were selected based on the best accuracies of human segmentation explained in Section 4.3 using the training data. Forty sequential images (20 thermal images and 20 binary images) of $120 \times 160 \times 1$ pixels were used for all training and testing methods. Figure 6a shows the training loss curves of IPGAN-2 per iteration, while Figure 6b shows the validation loss curves of IPGAN-2 per iteration. All results converged as the iterations increased; in particular, Figure 6b shows that IPGAN-2 was sufficiently trained without being overfitted by the training data.

Table 11. Search space and selected values of hyperparameters.

Parameters	Weight Decay (Weight Regularization L2)	Loss	Kernel Initializer	Bias Initializer	Optimizer	Learning Rate	Beta_1	Beta_2	Epsilon	Iterations	Batch Size
Search Space	[0.001, 0.01, 0.1]	["binary cross-entropy loss", "mse","VGG-19 loss"]	"glorot uniform"	"zeros"	["SGD", "adam"]	[0.0001, 0.001, 0.01, 0.1]	[0.7, 0.8, 0.9]	[0.8, 0.9, 0.999]	[1×10^{-9}, 1×10^{-8}, 1×10^{-7}]	[1~500 K]	[1,4,8]
Selected Value	0.01	"binary cross-entropy loss"	"glorot uniform"	"zeros"	"adam"	0.001	0.9	0.999	1×10^{-8}	483,581	1

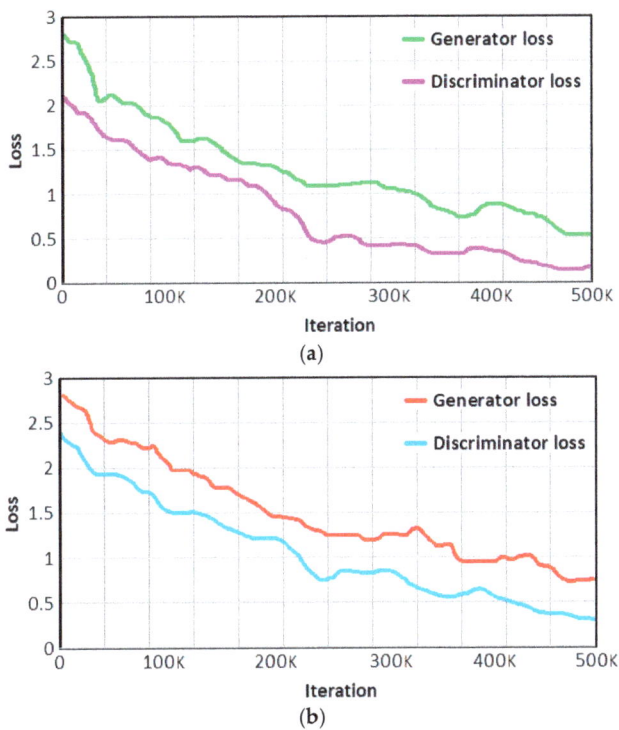

Figure 6. Loss curves of IPGAN-2 with (**a**) training data and (**b**) validation data.

4.2. Testing (Ablation Study)

In this subsection, the results of several ablation studies using the proposed method are explained. Identical datasets and six GAN structures were used for the experiment. The accuracy of image prediction was measured in terms of the similarity between the output image and the *GT* image. The accuracy of image prediction was measured using three types of metric in Equations (1)–(3). In Equation (1), *R* and *C* represent the number of rows (height) and columns (width) of the image matrix, respectively. In Equations (1) and (3), *Res* and *GT* refer to result image and *GT* image, respectively. In Equation (2), PSNR is the peak signal-to-noise ratio [38]. In the structural similarity index measure (SSIM) [39] equation, m_{GT} and S_{GT} are the mean and standard deviation of the pixel values of a *GT* image, respectively, m_{Res} and S_{Res} are the mean and standard deviation of the pixel values of the result image, respectively, S_{ResGT} is the covariance of the two images, and $St1$ and $St2$ represent positive constants to make the denominator nonzero.

$$\text{MSE} = \frac{\left(\sqrt{\sum_{i=1}^{R}\sum_{j=1}^{C}(GT(j,i)-Res(j,i))^2}\right)^2}{RC} \quad (1)$$

$$\text{PSNR} = 10\log_{10}\left(\frac{255^2}{\text{MSE}}\right) \quad (2)$$

$$\text{SSIM} = \frac{(2m_{Res}m_{GT}+St1)(2S_{ResGT}+St2)}{(m_{Res}^2+m_{GT}^2+St1)(S_{Res}^2+S_{GT}^2+St2)} \quad (3)$$

In addition, the accuracy of human detection was measured based on true positive rate (TPR) (#TP/(#TP+#FN)) and positive predictive value (PPV) (#TP/(#TP+#FP)) [40] and using accuracy (ACC) [40], F1 score (F1) [41], and intersection over union (IoU) [40], which are expressed in Equations (4)–(6). Here, TP, FP, FN, and TN refer to true positive, false positive, false negative, and true negative, respectively. Positive and negative signify the pixels detected in the GT image and the pixels not detected in the GT image. TP refers to a case where positive pixels were accurately detected, while TN refers to a case where negative pixels were inaccurately detected. FP refers to a case where negative pixels were falsely detected as positive pixels, while FN refers to a case where positive pixels were falsely detected as negative pixels. Here, the symbol # indicates "the number of".

$$\text{ACC} = \frac{\#TP + \#TN}{\#TP + \#TN + \#FP + \#FN} \quad (4)$$

$$F1 = 2 \cdot \frac{PPV \cdot TPR}{PPV + TPR} \quad (5)$$

$$\text{IoU}(X, Y) = \frac{|X \cap Y|}{|X \cup Y|} = \frac{\#TP}{\#TP + \#FP + \#FN} \quad (6)$$

Six methods were comparatively examined through ablation studies. In Figure 7, the t-th image I_t was set as the input image (at the far left) among the 20 sequential input thermal images.

In Figure 7a, the GT image (at the far right) included the images on both sides (left and right of the I_t image) of the I_t image (left image). Specifically, the images on both sides (40 × 160 × 1 and 40 × 160 × 1) of the I_t image (80 × 160 × 1) were predicted (pred2reg), as shown in Figure 7a. After the images on both sides of the I_t image are predicted, the regions predicted as the last are cropped to be combined with the current image I_t, as shown in Figure 1. In this experiment, sequential original images (80 × 160 × 20) and sequential binary images (80 × 160 × 20) were used for prediction. However, the output image obtained thereby (160 × 160 × 1) differs significantly from the GT image as in the output image O_t (middle image) in Figure 7a.

Unlike pred2reg in Figure 7b, the experiment was conducted to predict the entire O_t image (160 × 160 × 1) (predWholeIm) from sequential input images (thermal image (80 × 160 × 20) and binary image (80 × 160 × 20)).

In Figure 7c, after extracting feature maps from sequential binary images (80 × 160 × 20) and sequential thermal images (80 × 160 × 20) through a two-channel convolution structure, the feature maps (160 × 160 × 64 and 160 × 160 × 64) obtained from sequential binary images and original sequential images were combined along the depth axis (2-chanPred) in the last convolution layer.

The following three methods were utilized as follows to improve the accuracy. In Figure 7d, two images (40 × 160 × 1 and 40 × 160 × 1) on both sides of the current image were predicted (singImPred) using one thermal image (80 × 160 × 1) and one binary image (80 × 160 × 1) rather than sequential images. The output image (160 × 160 × 1) obtained through singImPred had a clearer background than the images obtained through previously mentioned methods but had a poorer performance in human prediction.

In Figure 7e, a method (seq&sing) was utilized where sequential images (thermal images (80 × 160 × 20) and binary images (80 × 160 × 20)) were used to predict the image on the left of the current image, while a current image (thermal image (80 × 160 × 1) and binary image (80 × 160 × 1)) was used to predict the image on the right of the current image. A two-channel convolution structure was applied in the experiment, but the predicted images on both sides were combined with the current image, as in pred2reg in the last concatenate layer. In this method, the left predicted image (using sequential images) has a higher result than the right predicted image (using a single image).

Figure 7f shows the result obtained through a method using a three-channel image (pred3-chan [14]). The final result of this method has the removed part that was not predicted well in the image generated through the GAN structure. For comparing the output images with the GT image, as with other methods, Figure 7f shows the result before removing the parts that were not predicted well for the comparison. However, as explained in pred3-chan [14], it is difficult to obtain a result similar to the *GT* because of gray noise.

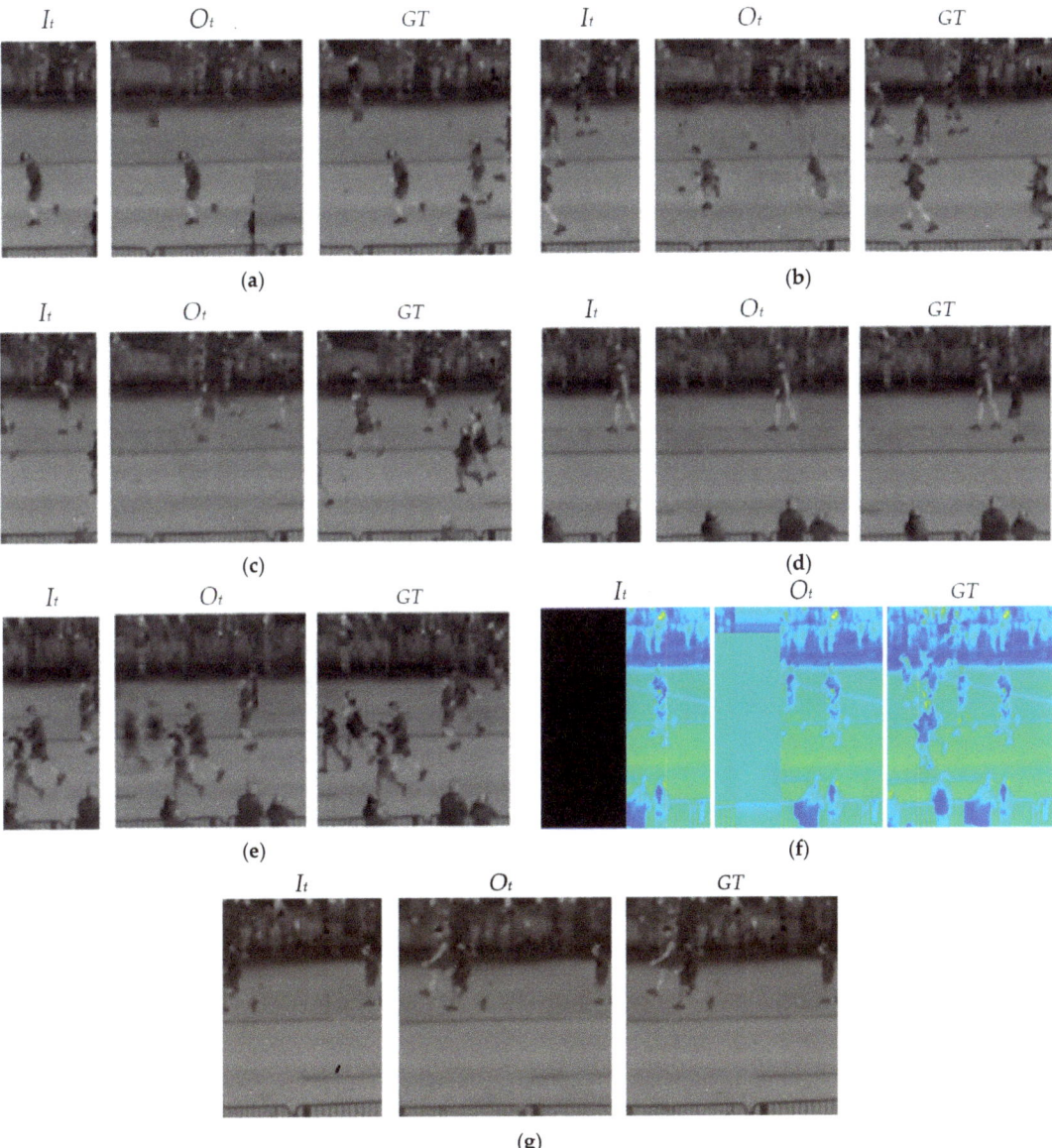

Figure 7. Examples of result images obtained by various methods: from left to right, input, output, and *GT* images obtained by (**a**) pred2reg, (**b**) predWholeIm, (**c**) 2-chanPred, (**d**) singImPred, (**e**) seq&sing, (**f**) pred3-chan [14], and (**g**) predLreg.

Therefore, only the left image (40 × 160 × 1) was predicted (predLreg) among the sequential input images (thermal images (120 × 160 × 20) and binary images (120 × 160 × 20)) in Figure 7g. When conducting this experiment, the feature maps (40 × 160 × 64) that were extracted similarly to L31 in Figure 3 were combined with the feature maps (120 ×

160 × 64) along the horizontal axis to obtain the feature maps (160 × 160 × 128), and the final output image (160 × 160 × 1) is obtained.

In the next experiment, the PSNR and SSIM of the GT image and the output image generated by each method were compared, as shown in Table 12. As Figure 7 and Table 12 show, predLreg had the highest PSNR and SSIM accuracy among the methods. Therefore, this study used predLreg to generate the images on both sides of the current image through flipping, cropping, and combining operations, as shown Figures 2 and 4. Figure 8a shows the image generated by predLreg, while Figure 8b shows the image generated by predLRreg (proposed method). Figure 9 shows the examples of various images generated by predLRreg (proposed method).

Table 12. Comparisons of various image prediction methods.

Methods	PSNR	SSIM
pred2reg	19.450	0.8156
predWholeIm	14.501	0.6395
2-chanPred	15.261	0.6121
singImPred	19.214	0.8132
seq&sing	21.340	0.8413
pred3-chan [14]	24.927	0.8403
predLreg	26.592	0.9581

Figure 8. Examples of result images obtained by predLreg and predLRreg (proposed method): from left to right, input, GT, and output images obtained by (**a**) predLreg and (**b**) predLRreg (proposed method).

Figure 9. Examples of result images obtained by predLRreg (proposed method): in (a–c), from left to right, original images, *GT* images, and predicted (output) images.

In the next experiment, the results of detecting humans in the original input image and *GT* image were compared with the result of detecting humans in the image predicted by the proposed method for examining the efficiency of the proposed method. For a fair experiment, an identical Mask R-CNN [42] was used for the two methods during human seg-mentation. Figure 10 shows the result of human segmentation using Mask R-CNN as mask images. As shown in Figure 10, the result of human segmentation in the *GT* image and the result of human segmentation in the image predicted by the proposed method are quite similar. The segmentation result in the predicted image is closer to the segmentation result in the *GT* image than in the original input image. In Table 13, the detection accuracies measured between the result images of object segmentation with original images (or-detect) and the result images of object segmentation with *GT* images are shown. Furthermore, the detection accuracies were measured and compared between the resulting images of object segmentation with images predicted by the proposed method (pred-detect) and the resulting images of object segmentation with *GT* images. As shown in Table 13, pred-detect was more accurate than or-detect, indicating that the result is closer to the segmentation in the *GT* image when the image predicted by the proposed method was used than when the original input image was used.

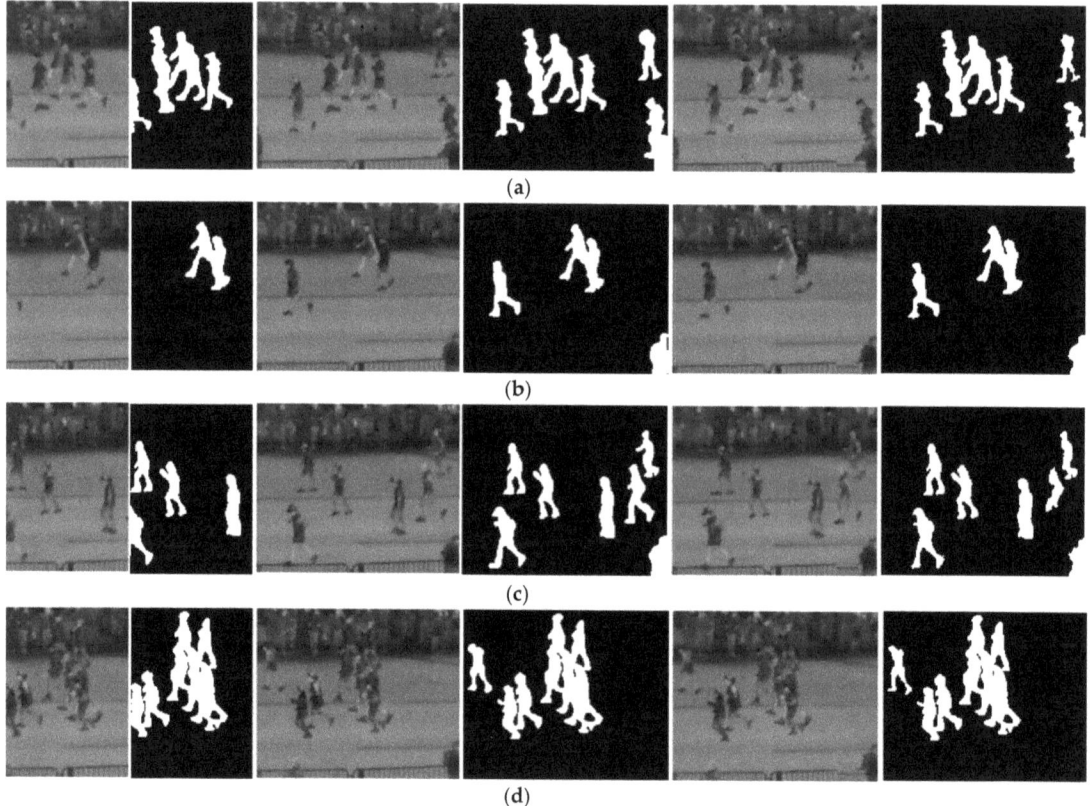

Figure 10. Examples of segmentation results before and after image prediction. (**a–d**) From left to right, the original input images, results with original input images, *GT* images, results with *GT* images, images predicted by the proposed method, and results with predicted images.

Table 13. Comparisons of segmentation accuracies with original images (or-detect) and with images predicted by the proposed method (pred-detect).

Methods	TPR	PPV	F1	ACC	IoU
or-detect	0.601	0.613	0.606	0.71	0.483
pred-detect (proposed)	0.887	0.847	0.866	0.914	0.730

4.3. Comparisons of Proposed Method with the State-of-the-Art Methods

In this subsection, the proposed method is compared with state-of-the-art methods. When measuring accuracy, the output image obtained by the proposed method is compared based on the similarity to the *GT* image. In Table 14, the conventional image prediction [26], image region prediction [14], and inpainting [17,19,21] methods were compared with the proposed IPGAN-2-based image prediction method. Figures 11–13 show the comparisons of the images obtained by all the methods. For a fair performance evaluation, previous methods [17,19,21], which typically use one image, were applied with sequential images (thermal images (120 × 160 × 20) and binary images (120 × 160 × 20)), as in the proposed method; accordingly, the input layers of these methods [17,19,21] were changed to the layers 0, 1, and 2 of the proposed method shown in Table 3. To evaluate the performance of pred3-chan [14] against other methods fairly, the result before removing the parts that were not predicted well was used for the comparison, as explained in Section 4.2—see Figure 7f. Flipping, cropping, and combining were performed, as in Figure 2b, to predict the images on both sides, and an image of 200 × 160 × 1 was generated for comparison. As shown in Figures 11–13 and Table 14, the proposed method produced superior results to those of the state-of-the-art methods. The proposed predLreg method in Table 12 generated only the image to the left of the current image, while it generated left and right region images in Table 14; thus, the PSNR and SSIM values of the proposed method in Table 14 differ from the PSNR and SSIM values of the proposed predLreg in Table 12.

Table 14. Comparisons of accuracies of image prediction and human segmentation by the proposed method with those of the state-of-the-art methods.

Methods	Image Prediction		Mask R-CNN				
	PSNR	SSIM	TPR	PPV	F1	ACC	IoU
Haziq et al. [26]	22.843	0.8917	0.801	0.654	0.720	0.904	0.521
Liu et al. [17]	20.557	0.8454	0.638	0.626	0.631	0.864	0.432
Shin et al. [19]	22.181	0.8781	0.687	0.631	0.657	0.866	0.502
Nazeri et al. [21]	22.112	0.8724	0.651	0.672	0.661	0.890	0.514
pred3-chan [14]	25.146	0.8711	0.792	0.714	0.753	0.901	0.536
Proposed method	26.018	0.9437	0.887	0.847	0.866	0.914	0.730

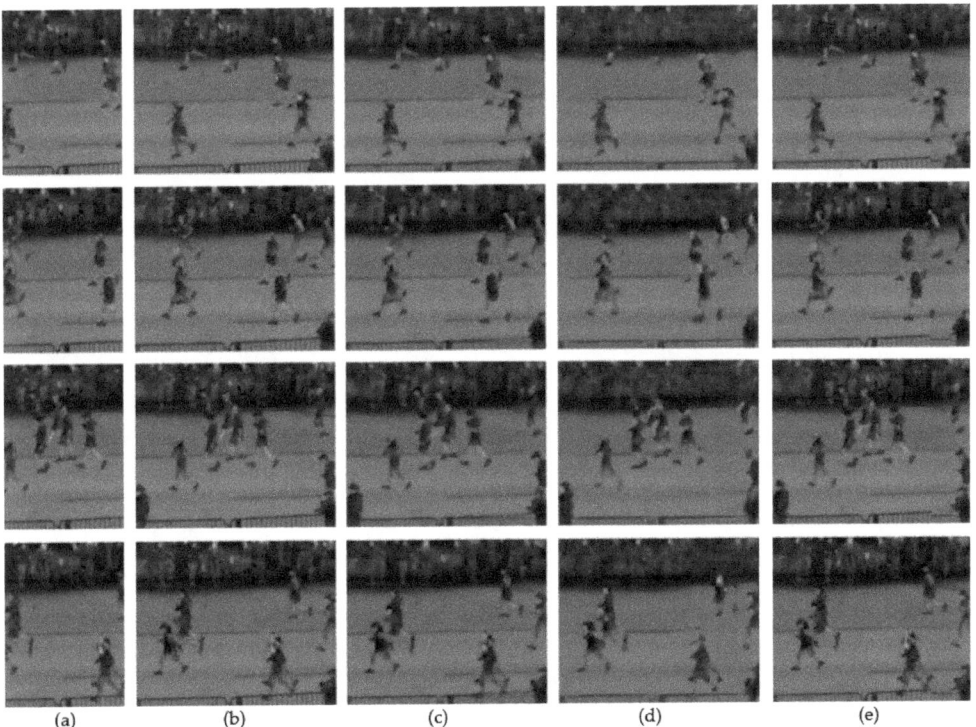

Figure 11. Comparisons of original images, *GT* images, the prediction results obtained by the state-of-the-art methods, and the proposed method: (**a**) original images, (**b**) *GT* images, and images predicted by (**c**) Haziq et al. [26], (**d**) Liu et al. [17], and (**e**) the proposed method.

Figure 12. Comparisons of original images, *GT* images, and the prediction results obtained by the state-of-the-art methods and the proposed method: (**a**) original images, (**b**) *GT* images, and images predicted by (**c**) Shin et al. [19], (**d**) Nazeri et al. [21], and (**e**) the proposed method.

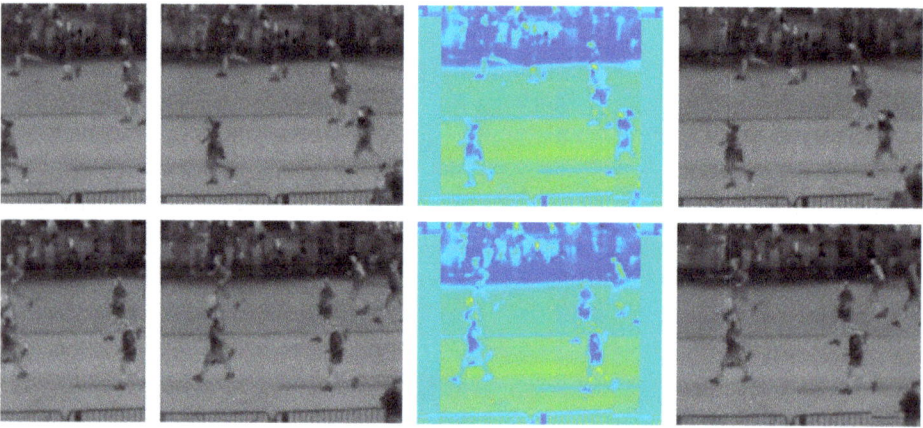

Figure 13. *Cont.*

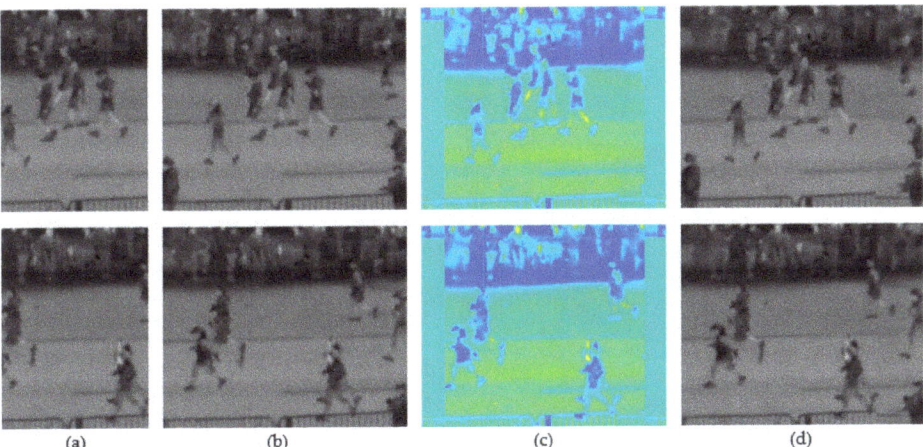

Figure 13. Comparisons of original images, *GT* images, and the prediction results obtained by the state-of-the-art methods and the proposed method: (**a**) original images, (**b**) *GT* images, and images predicted by (**c**) pred3-chan [14] and (**d**) the proposed method.

For the subsequent experiment, the performance was compared with Mask R-CNN human segmentation. The segmentation accuracy and output images are compared in Table 14 and Figures 14–16. Identical Mask R-CNN [42] based human segmentation was applied for all methods for a fair evaluation. As shown in Table 14 and Figures 14–16, the human segmentation performance was superior when the images obtained by the proposed method were used than when the images obtained by the state-of-the-art methods were used.

Figure 14. Comparisons of detection results using original images, *GT* images, and the predicted images obtained by the state-of-the-art methods and the proposed method: (**a**) original images; detection results using (**b**) original images and (**c**) *GT* images of Figures 11b, 12b and 13b; and the images predicted by (**d**) Haziq et al. [26], (**e**) Liu et al. [17], and (**f**) the proposed method.

Figure 15. Comparisons of detection results using original images, GT images, and the predicted images obtained by the state-of-the-art methods and the proposed method: (**a**) original images; detection results using (**b**) original images and (**c**) GT images of Figures 11b, 12b and 13b; and the images predicted by (**d**) Shin et al. [19], (**e**) Nazeri et al. [21], and (**f**) the proposed method.

Figure 16. *Cont.*

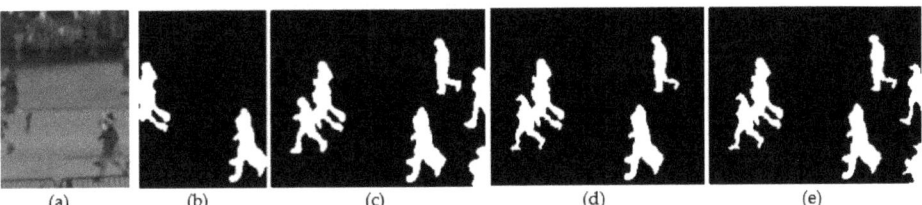

Figure 16. Comparisons of detection results using original images, GT images, and the predicted images obtained by the state-of-the-art methods and the proposed method: (**a**) original images; detection results using (**b**) original images and (**c**) GT images of Figures 11b, 12b and 13b; and the images predicted by (**d**) pred3-chan [14] and (**e**) the proposed method.

4.4. Experiments Using Different Datasets (Casia Dataset C and BU-TIV Marathon Dataset) for Training and Testing

In this section, additional experiments were conducted using Casia thermal image dataset C [43] and BU-TIV marathon dataset [15]. These two databases were acquired from different cameras, and they include different angle images with totally different backgrounds and foregrounds. The Casia dataset C includes thermal videos captured in outdoor environment using a thermal camera during nighttime. In addition, the Casia dataset C was captured under four walking conditions, namely slow, normal, fast walking, and normal walking with a bag. In the dataset, data of various humans including men and women are included. The total number of subjects and image sequences in this dataset are 153 and 1530, respectively. The pixel value of a thermal image ranges between 0 and 255. In this experiment, 2000 images (size of 320 × 240 × 1, and pixel depth of 8 bits) were used. For experiments, 2000 images of Casia dataset C and 2000 images of BU-TIV marathon dataset were used for training and testing. In addition, because the size of humans (height = 115 and width = 45 pixels) in images of Casia dataset C is much greater than that (height = 50 and width = 15 pixels) in images of BU-TIV marathon dataset, the images of Casia dataset C and images of BU-TIV marathon dataset were resized to make the size of humans in both datasets similar as shown in Figure 17. The experiments were conducted by two-fold cross validation. More specifically, the Casia dataset C was used for training, while the BU-TIV marathon dataset was used for testing in the fold-1 as shown in Figure 17. Then, the two datasets were switched for performing training and testing once again to perform two-fold cross validation. In Table 15, the results of fold-1 (train data = Casia dataset C, test data = BU-TIV dataset), fold-2 (train data = BU-TIV dataset, test data = Casia dataset C), and the average of fold-1 and fold-2 are presented. In addition, image prediction and human segmentation results are presented in Figures 18 and 19, and Figures 20 and 21, respectively. As shown in Table 15 and Figures 18–21, we confirm that our method can be adopted to the case of using two different databases for training and testing.

Figure 17. Example images of datasets in fold-1. (**a**) Example images used in training phase; (**b**) example images used in testing phase.

Table 15. Accuracies of image prediction and human segmentation by the proposed method using two different datasets.

Results	Image Prediction		Mask R-CNN				
	PSNR	SSIM	TPR	PPV	F1	ACC	IoU
Fold-1	24.984	0.9211	0.851	0.821	0.835	0.895	0.725
Fold-2	24.028	0.9064	0.835	0.802	0.818	0.889	0.705
Average	24.506	0.9137	0.843	0.811	0.826	0.892	0.715

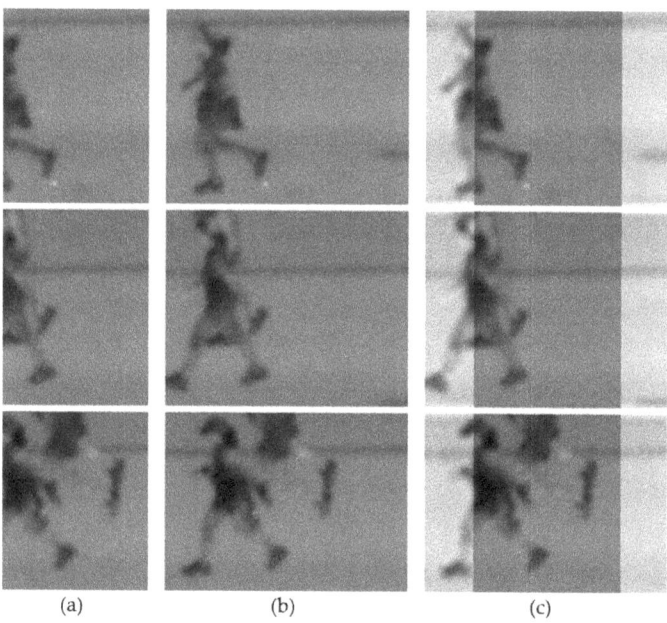

Figure 18. Example images of image prediction from fold-1: (**a**) original images; (**b**) *GT* images; (**c**) images predicted by the proposed method.

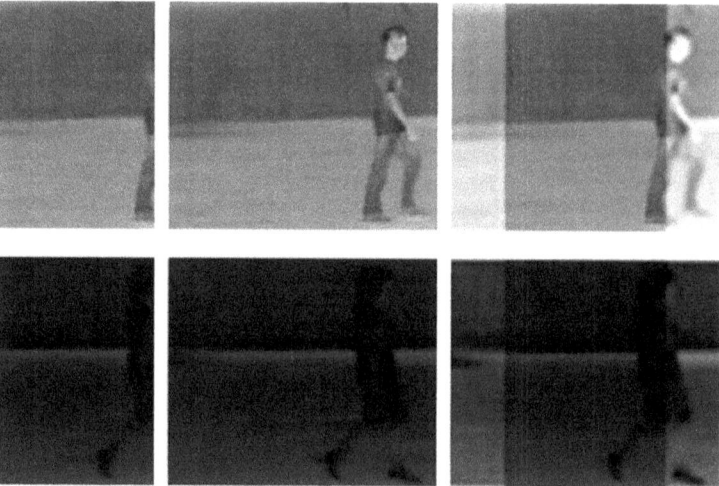

Figure 19. *Cont.*

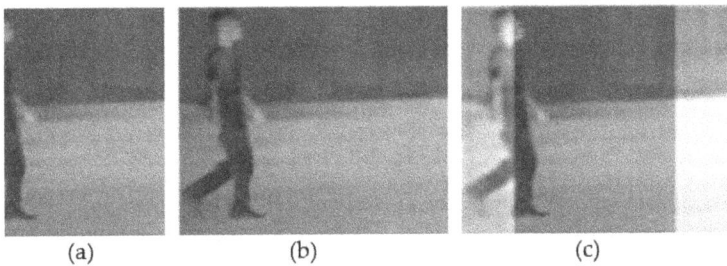

Figure 19. Example images of image prediction from fold-2: (**a**) original images; (**b**) *GT* images; (**c**) images predicted by the proposed method.

Figure 20. Example images of human segmentation from fold-1: (**a**) original images; segmentation results using (**b**) original images and (**c**) *GT* images; and the images predicted by (**d**) the proposed method.

Figure 21. *Cont.*

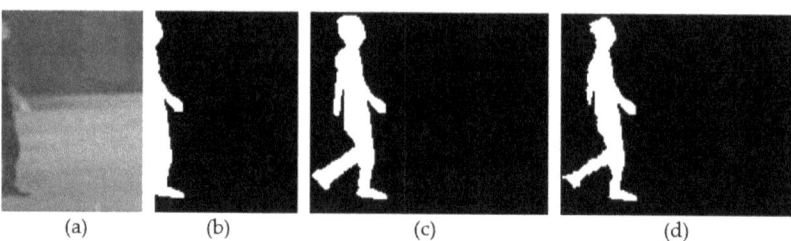

Figure 21. Example images by human segmentation from fold-2: (**a**) original images; segmentation results using (**b**) original images and (**c**) *GT* images; and the images predicted by (**d**) the proposed method.

4.5. Processing Time

The processing times of the proposed image prediction method and the human segmentation method are shown in Table 16. Each component of the proposed method (as shown in Figure 2b) is shown in Table 16 as well. The processing time was measured in the environments described in Section 3.5.

Table 16. Processing time of the proposed method per image (unit: ms).

Methods	Component	Processing Time
Image prediction	IPGAN-2 (before flipping)	48.4
	IPGAN-2 (after flipping)	48.4
	Postprocessing	0.01
Human segmentation	Mask R-CNN	54.1
Total		150.91

As shown in Table 16, the processing time of the Mask R-CNN is higher than other components. The frame rate of the proposed image prediction method is approximately 10.33 frames per second (fps) (1000/(48.4 + 48.4 + 0.01)). The total frame rate including both image prediction and the human segmentation method is approximately 6.63 fps (1000/150.91). The time and space complexities of the proposed method are $O(2^n)$ and $O(n)$ in training phase, respectively. They are $O(n)$ and $O(1)$ in testing phase, respectively.

5. Discussion

As shown in Figures 11–13, the persons in the predicted region of an image may be poorly segmented compared with the persons in the *GT* image. For example, it is difficult to detect a human body part with the proposed method when the pixel values corresponding to a human body part in the input image are similar to the pixel values corresponding to the background. In addition, the low-resolution thermal images used in this study have less spatial pattern information than the general visible light images, which may have contributed to the error.

Proposed IPGAN-2 predicts images on the left side not because the movement of humans is towards the left side. As shown in Figure 22a, IPGAN-2 predicts the left side of the current image at t-0 when the movement is towards the left side. In addition, as shown in Figure 22b, IPGAN-2 predicts the left side of the current image at t-0 after flipping images when the movement is towards the right side. Finally, we combine the two predicted regions with the current image at t-0. Thus, the prediction does not rely on the movement direction. By predicting both left and right sides of current image, we can increase the FOV of current image. In addition, the reason why we do not predict the left and right-side regions outside FOV at the same time using a single IPGAN is owing to experimental results as shown in Figure 7 in Section 4.2 (Ablation study). As shown in Figure 7, the performance of predicting the left and right sides of the current image at the same time (Figure 7a–d) is lower than predicting only one side of the image (Figure 7g).

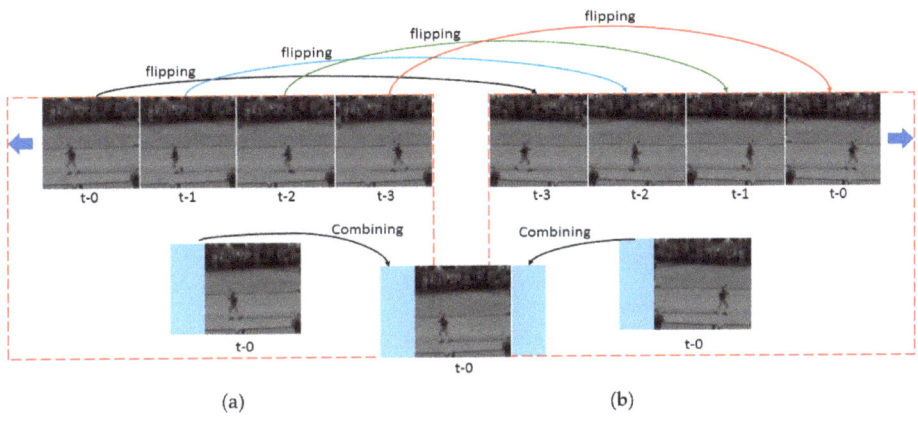

Figure 22. Example of our image prediction method.

Figure 23 shows examples of gradient-weighted class activation mapping (Grad-CAM) [44] images extracted from Conv2, Conv3, and Conv8, which are the layers in Mask R-CNN, which uses the images generated by IPGAN-2 as input.

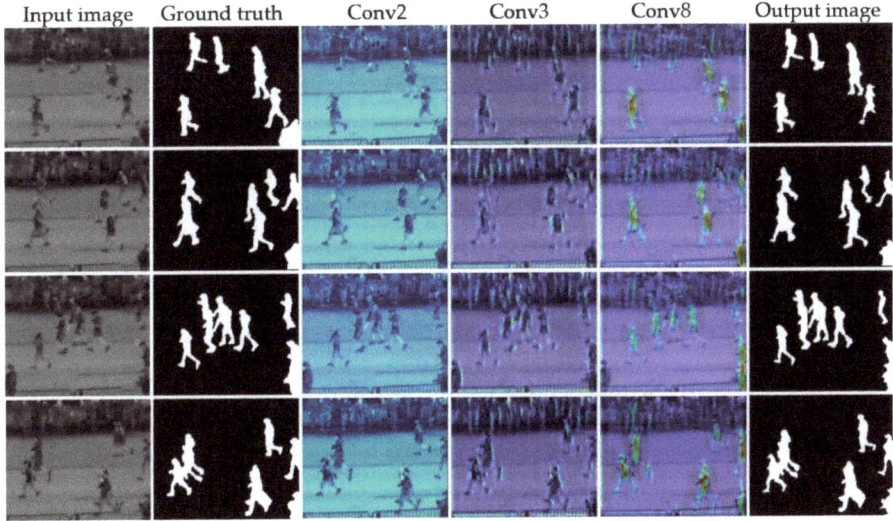

Figure 23. Example images extracted from Mask R-CNN layers by using Grad-CAM.

As shown in Figure 23, the Grad-CAM images extracted from the convolution layer (Conv2) of Mask R-CNN had almost no high activation regions. As convolution proceeded, activation regions were observed in the legs and head of a person and in the edge region of the front and back torso in the Grad-CAM images extracted from the convolution layer (Conv3). Figure 23 confirms that activation regions were observed in a more global region, including the torso, starting from the Conv8 layer, which signifies that more-accurate human segmentation is possible in the output image.

In this study, we proposed a method to predict image region outside FOV to restore a part of human body which has disappeared when a pedestrian leaves the camera FOV. There are several reasons that we started this study. For example, in case of tracking a suspect in the CCTV camera system, our method helps to generate a body of the suspect after he or she has left the FOV of camera. In addition, the proposed method helps to track suspects continuously without losing them when a camera changes the view direction to a suspect who left the FOV.

Moreover, we conducted various experiments (Table 12 and Figure 7) in our ablation study to achieve good results. To validate the predicted images by the proposed method, we conducted human segmentation using the predicted images (Tables 13 and 14, and Figures 10 and 14–16). We measured the predicted images using SSIM and PSNR, and measured segmentation results using TPR, PPV, ACC, F1 score, and IoU, which confirms that the performance of our method is better than those of the state-of-the-art methods.

6. Conclusions

The IPGAN-2 method was proposed for image prediction for thermal images where the occurrence of noise is minimized while the wide regions to the left and right sides of the FOV in the current image are accurately generated. For improving the accuracy of image prediction, binary images corresponding to sequential input thermal images were used as input for IPGAN-2. For evaluating the performance of the proposed method, various ablation studies using original one-channel thermal images and comparative experiments using state-of-the-art methods were performed. The experimental results using an open database showed that the proposed IPGAN-2-based method had higher image prediction accuracy than other methods, including the state-of-the-art methods. The TPR, PPV, F1, ACC, and IoU of human segmentation using the proposed method were 0.887, 0.847, 0.866, 0.914, and 0.730, respectively, which are better results than those of the state-of-the-art methods. In the experimental results, the persons in the predicted region of an image may be more poorly segmented than the persons in the GT image. This could be because the pixel values corresponding to the human are similar to the pixel values corresponding to the background, which hindered the distinction between the human body part and background. Moreover, thermal images with less spatial pattern information and the factors in low-resolution images obtained from long distance may be affected the error.

In future work, image prediction using thermal and visible light images combined is planned to resolve such issues. For the proposed method, experiments were only conducted in a fixed-camera setting and not in a moving-camera setting; therefore, further experiments should be conducted to determine whether the proposed method is applicable in a moving-camera setting. In addition, further research is planned on image prediction in which the FOV of a visible light camera in a vehicle is expanded in four directions.

Author Contributions: Methodology, G.B.; validation, N.R.B.; supervision, K.R.P.; writing—original draft, G.B.; writing—review and editing, K.R.P. All authors have read and agreed to the published version of the manuscript.

Funding: This work was supported in part by the National Research Foundation of Korea (NRF) funded by the Ministry of Science and ICT (MSIT) through the Basic Science Research Program (NRF-2019R1F1A1041123), in part by the NRF funded by the MSIT through the Basic Science Research Program (NRF-2021R1F1A1045587), and in part by the MSIT, Korea, under the ITRC (Information Technology Research Center) support program (IITP-2021-2020-0-01789) supervised by the IITP (Institute for Information & Communications Technology Planning & Evaluation).

Institutional Review Board Statement: Not applicable.

Informed Consent Statement: Not applicable.

Data Availability Statement: Not applicable.

Conflicts of Interest: The authors declare no conflict of interest.

References

1. Gong, J.; Zhao, J.; Li, F.; Zhang, H. Vehicle detection in thermal images with an improved yolov3-tiny. In Proceedings of the IEEE International Conference on Power, Intelligent Computing and Systems, Shenyang, China, 28–30 July 2020.
2. Batchuluun, G.; Kang, J.K.; Nguyen, D.T.; Pham, T.D.; Muhammad, A.; Park, K.R. Deep learning-based thermal image reconstruction and object detection. *IEEE Access* **2021**, *9*, 5951–5971. [CrossRef]
3. Batchuluun, G.; Yoon, H.S.; Nguyen, D.T.; Pham, T.D.; Park, K.R. A study on the elimination of thermal reflections. *IEEE Access* **2019**, *7*, 174597–174611. [CrossRef]
4. Batchuluun, G.; Baek, N.R.; Nguyen, D.T.; Pham, T.D.; Park, K.R. Region-based removal of thermal reflection using pruned fully convolutional network. *IEEE Access* **2020**, *8*, 75741–75760. [CrossRef]
5. Zhang, X.; Chen, R.; Liu, G.; Li, X.; Luo, S.; Fan, X. Thermal infrared tracking using multi-stages deep features fusion. In Proceedings of the Chinese Control and Decision Conference, Hefei, China, 22–24 August 2020.
6. Svanström, F.; Englund, C.; Alonso-Fernandez, F. Real-time drone detection and tracking with visible, thermal and acoustic sensors. In Proceedings of the 25th International Conference on Pattern Recognition, Milan, Italy, 10–15 January 2021.
7. Liu, Q.; Li, X.; He, Z.; Fan, N.; Yuan, D.; Wang, H. Learning deep multi-level similarity for thermal infrared object tracking. *IEEE Trans. Multimed.* **2021**, *23*, 2114–2126. [CrossRef]
8. Liu, Q.; He, Z.; Li, X.; Zheng, Y. PTB-TIR: A thermal infrared pedestrian tracking benchmark. *IEEE Trans. Multimed.* **2020**, *22*, 666–675. [CrossRef]
9. Kang, B.; Liang, D.; Ding, W.; Zhou, H.; Zhu, W.-P. Grayscale-thermal tracking via inverse sparse representation-based collaborative encoding. *IEEE Trans. Image Process.* **2020**, *29*, 3401–3415. [CrossRef] [PubMed]
10. Batchuluun, G.; Kim, Y.G.; Kim, J.H.; Hong, H.G.; Park, K.R. Robust behavior recognition in intelligent surveillance environments. *Sensors* **2016**, *16*, 1010. [CrossRef] [PubMed]
11. Batchuluun, G.; Kim, J.H.; Hong, H.G.; Kang, J.K.; Park, K.R. Fuzzy system based human behavior recognition by combining behavior prediction and recognition. *Expert Syst. Appl.* **2017**, *81*, 108–133. [CrossRef]
12. Batchuluun, G.; Nguyen, D.T.; Pham, T.D.; Park, C.; Park, K.R. Action recognition from thermal videos. *IEEE Access* **2019**, *7*, 103893–103917. [CrossRef]
13. Batchuluun, G.; Kang, J.K.; Nguyen, D.T.; Pham, T.D.; Arsalan, M.; Park, K.R. Action recognition from thermal videos using joint and skeleton information. *IEEE Access* **2021**, *9*, 11716–11733. [CrossRef]
14. Batchuluun, G.; Koo, J.H.; Kim, Y.H.; Park, K.R. Image region prediction from thermal videos based on image prediction generative adversarial network. *Mathematics* **2021**, *9*, 1053. [CrossRef]
15. Wu, Z.; Fuller, N.; Theriault, D.; Betke, M. A thermal infrared video benchmark for visual analysis. In Proceedings of the IEEE Conference on Computer Vision and Pattern Recognition Workshops, Columbus, OH, USA, 23–28 June 2014.
16. Image Prediction Generative Adversarial Network v2 (IPGAN-2). Available online: http://dm.dgu.edu/link.html (accessed on 25 March 2021).
17. Liu, H.; Jiang, B.; Xiao, Y.; Yang, C. Coherent semantic attention for image inpainting. In Proceedings of the IEEE/CVF International Conference on Computer Vision Workshop, Seoul, Korea, 27 October–2 November 2019.
18. Yu, J.; Lin, Z.; Yang, J.; Shen, X.; Lu, X.; Huang, T. Free-form image inpainting with gated convolution. In Proceedings of the IEEE/CVF International Conference on Computer Vision Workshop, Seoul, Korea, 27 October–2 November 2019.
19. Shin, Y.-G.; Sagong, M.-C.; Yeo, Y.-J.; Kim, S.-W.; Ko, S.-J. PEPSI++: Fast and lightweight network for image inpainting. *IEEE Trans. Neural Netw. Learn. Syst.* **2021**, *32*, 252–265. [CrossRef] [PubMed]
20. Pathak, D.; Krähenbühl, P.; Donahue, J.; Darrell, T.; Efros, A.A. Context encoders: Feature learning by inpainting. In Proceedings of the IEEE Conference on Computer Vision and Pattern Recognition, Las Vegas, NV, USA, 27–30 June 2016.
21. Nazeri, K.; Ng, E.; Joseph, T.; Qureshi, F.; Ebrahimi, M. EdgeConnect: Structure guided image inpainting using edge prediction. In Proceedings of the IEEE/CVF International Conference on Computer Vision Workshop, Seoul, Korea, 27 October–2 November 2019.
22. Elharrouss, O.; Almaadeed, N.; Al-Maadeed, S.; Akbari, Y. Image inpainting: A review. *Neural Process. Lett.* **2020**, *51*, 2007–2028. [CrossRef]
23. Liang, X.; Lee, L.; Dai, W.; Xing, E.P. Dual motion GAN for future-flow embedded video prediction. In Proceedings of the IEEE International Conference on Computer Vision (ICCV), Venice, Italy, 22–29 October 2017.
24. Sedaghat, N.; Zolfaghari, M.; Brox, T. Hybrid learning of optical flow and next frame prediction to boost optical flow in the wild. *arXiv* **2017**, arXiv:1612.03777v2.
25. Mahjourian, R.; Wicke, M.; Angelova, A. Geometry-based next frame prediction from monocular video. *arXiv* **2017**, arXiv:1609.06377v2.
26. Haziq, R.; Basura, F. A log-likelihood regularized KL divergence for video prediction with a 3D convolutional variational recurrent network. In Proceedings of the IEEE/CVF Winter Conference on Applications of Computer Vision Workshops, Virtual, Waikola, HI, USA, 5–9 January 2021.
27. Guen, V.L.; Thome, N. Disentangling physical dynamics from unknown factors for unsupervised video prediction. In Proceedings of the IEEE Conference on Computer Vision and Pattern Recognition, Virtual, Seattle, WA, USA, 14–19 June 2020.
28. Finn, C.; Goodfellow, I.; Levine, S. Unsupervised learning for physical interaction through video prediction. In Proceedings of the Advances in Neural Information Processing Systems 29, Barcelona, Spain, 5–10 December 2016.

29. Xu, J.; Xu, H.; Ni, B.; Yang, X.; Darrell, T. Video prediction via example guidance. In Proceedings of the 37th International Conference on Machine Learning, Online, 13–18 July 2020.
30. Babaeizadeh, M.; Finn, C.; Erhan, D.; Campbell, R.H.; Levine, S. Stochastic variational video prediction. In Proceedings of the 6th International Conference on Learning Representations, Vancouver, BC, Canada, 30 April–3 May 2018.
31. Oprea, S.; Martinez-Gonzalez, P.; Garcia-Garcia, A.; Castro-Vargas, J.A.; Orts-Escolano, S.; Garcia-Rodriguez, J.; Argyros, A. A review on deep learning techniques for video prediction. *IEEE Trans. Pattern Anal. Mach. Intell* **2020**. [CrossRef]
32. Rasouli, A. Deep learning for vision-based prediction: A survey. *arXiv* **2020**, arXiv:2007.00095v2.
33. Nvidia GeForce GTX TITAN X. Available online: https://www.nvidia.com/en-us/geforce/products/10series/titan-x-pascal/ (accessed on 25 March 2021).
34. OpenCV. Available online: http://opencv.org/ (accessed on 25 March 2021).
35. Python. Available online: https://www.python.org/download/releases/ (accessed on 25 March 2021).
36. Keras. Available online: https://keras.io/ (accessed on 25 March 2021).
37. Kingma, D.P.; Ba, J.L. Adam: A method for stochastic optimization. *arXiv* **2014**, arXiv:1412.6980.
38. Peak Signal-to-Noise Ratio. Available online: https://en.wikipedia.org/wiki/Peak_signal-to-noise_ratio (accessed on 29 April 2021).
39. Wang, Z.; Bovik, A.C.; Sheikh, H.R.; Simoncelli, E.P. Image quality assessment: From error visibility to structural similarity. *IEEE Trans. Image Process.* **2004**, *13*, 600–612. [CrossRef]
40. Powers, D.M.W. Evaluation: From precision, recall and f-measure to ROC, informedness, markedness & correlation. *Mach. Learn. Technol.* **2011**, *2*, 37–63.
41. Derczynski, L. Complementarity, f-score, and NLP evaluation. In Proceedings of the International Conference on Language Resources and Evaluation, Portorož, Slovenia, 23–28 May 2016.
42. He, K.; Gkioxari, G.; Dollár, P.; Girshick, R. Mask R-CNN. In Proceedings of the IEEE International Conference on Computer Vision, Venice, Italy, 22–29 October 2017.
43. Tan, D.; Huang, K.; Yu, S.; Tan, T. Efficient night gait recognition based on template matching. In Proceedings of the 18th International Conference on Pattern Recognition, Hong Kong, China, 20–24 August 2006.
44. Selvaraju, R.R.; Cogswell, M.; Das, A.; Vedantam, R.; Parikh, D.; Batra, D. Grad-CAM: Visual explanations from deep networks via gradient-based localization. *arXiv* **2016**, arXiv:1610.02391v4.

Article
Super-Resolved Recognition of License Plate Characters

Sung-Jin Lee and Seok Bong Yoo *

Department of Artificial Intelligence Convergence, Chonnam National University, Gwangju 11866, Korea; sungjin8191@gmail.com
* Correspondence: sbyoo@jnu.ac.kr; Tel.: +82-625303437

Abstract: Object detection and recognition are crucial in the field of computer vision and are an active area of research. However, in actual object recognition processes, recognition accuracy is often degraded due to resolution mismatches between training and test image data. To solve this problem, we designed and developed an integrated object recognition and super-resolution framework by proposing an image super-resolution technique that improves object recognition accuracy. In detail, we collected a number of license plate training images through web-crawling and artificial data generation, and the image super-resolution artificial neural network was trained by defining an objective function to be robust to image flips. To verify the performance of the proposed algorithm, we experimented with the trained image super-resolution and recognition on representative test images and confirmed that the proposed super-resolution technique improves the accuracy of character recognition. For character recognition with the 4× magnification, the proposed method remarkably increased the mean average precision by 49.94% compared to the existing state-of-the-art method.

Keywords: super-resolved recognition; license plate characters; data augmentation; flip loss function

Citation: Lee, S.-J.; Yoo, S.B. Super-Resolved Recognition of License Plate Characters. *Mathematics* **2021**, *9*, 2494. https://doi.org/10.3390/math9192494

Academic Editors: Ezequiel López-Rubio, Esteban Palomo and Enrique Domínguez

Received: 18 September 2021
Accepted: 29 September 2021
Published: 5 October 2021

Publisher's Note: MDPI stays neutral with regard to jurisdictional claims in published maps and institutional affiliations.

Copyright: © 2021 by the authors. Licensee MDPI, Basel, Switzerland. This article is an open access article distributed under the terms and conditions of the Creative Commons Attribution (CC BY) license (https://creativecommons.org/licenses/by/4.0/).

1. Introduction

Object recognition is a field of computer vision focused on recognizing information, such as a particular object area, type, or size, from a single image. The objects being detected can vary widely, and common applications are concerned with objects such as people or vehicles. The accurate detection of an object of interest from a single image is the vital element of object recognition. To recognize an object of interest in a single image, it is essential to detect a relevant object region in the image using an object detection neural network, and then adjust the size of the detected region appropriately to match the input size of the object attribute recognition.

However, in the process of resizing the image to match the input size of the object recognition neural network, the input image resolution degrades, which causes a discrepancy in resolution between the input images and training images used for the training of the object recognition neural network. This problem brings about the poor performance of the object recognition neural network because of the distortion of input images of object recognition neural network. In order to solve this problem, domestic and foreign researchers focused on improving the recognition rate of the object recognition neural network with a preprocessing method that improves the quality of the low-resolution image, which is the input of the object recognition neural network.

Although there have been various studies aimed at improving the accuracy and speed of object detection neural networks and object attribute recognition neural net-works themselves, studies on techniques for upscaling low-resolution (LR) image inputs in object recognition are still lacking. Therefore, in this paper, to address this problem of object recognition degradation, we develop techniques for image super-resolution (SR) and object recognition studies to transform LR images into high-resolution (HR) images through SR techniques as a means of achieving higher recognition rates. Research using image SR technology to improve object recognition accuracy will produce higher recognition rates in future real-world object recognition applications, such as a smart parking system that can manage parking lots without a person, an intelligent transportation system that can administrate the traffic situation efficiently, and text-to-speech.

Our contributions in this paper are summarized threefold as follows:

1. We proposed the new loss function that can augment data without the addition of data capacity by using the flip function. It trains the parameters of the SR neural network so that the SR result is robust to left-right reversal.
2. We proposed simple yet advanced methods of collecting data. The proposed web-crawling method would be helpful to collect the ready-made datasets which are available on the website. Another one is the proposed artificial license plate image generation that will be helpful in new fields such as scene text recognition research for data augmentation.
3. We integrated the SR network and character recognition neural network, and derived the optimized result by learning the proposed model with self-collected training data.

2. Related Works

2.1. Super-Resolution (SR)

SR technology, which converts LR images into HR images, is a major computer vision field. The SR method designates the original high resolution (HR) as the ground truth that needs to be restored, improves the resolution of the LR, and makes the restored image equal to the original HR image.

The typical criteria for measuring the quality of an SR image is the ratio of noise power to the maximum power a signal can have. That is, the peak signal to noise ratio (PSNR) and structural similarity (SSIM) used to evaluate the distortion of structural information. Recently, with the growing interest in convolutional neural networks (CNNs), CNNs have been utilized in several computer vision fields, and techniques using CNNs have been proposed in SR fields [1–15].

CNN-based SR technology is a method of restoring LR images through multiple convolutional layers into which LR images are inputted. Based on the loss function, it is possible to train the CNNs to minimize their values by defining the sum (L1 loss) of the difference between the original and predicted values, and the sum (L2 loss) of the difference between the original and predicted values can also be minimized. SRCNN [1] was the first method to utilize a CNN for high resolution conversion problems, outperforming example-based learning methods (example-based SR [2]) and sparse coding methods (sparse coding-based SR [3]) using LR–HR image pairs. At the time, the SRCNN showed the highest performance among any high resolution conversion method. However, SRCNN scaled LR images via linear interpolation, passing enlarged images through CNNs to obtain a resilient image, which required substantial computing power due to the HR-domain CNNs and had limitations in accuracy because it used only three layers of CNNs.

Accordingly, deep neural network utilization and various neural network lightening techniques have been proposed to improve performance. Subsequently, methods such as FSRCNN [4] and ESPCN [5] improved performance by reducing computing power and increasing the number of CNN layers using LR images as CNN inputs and by expanding the size of the output layers. However, as the CNN layer deepens, there is a gradual loss of information from the front layer through each subsequent layer. Thus, several methods have been proposed in subsequent studies to address this problem. An EDSR [6] technique using skip connection-based residual learning (ResNet [7]) was proposed. This technique demonstrated that batch regularization had little effect on HR image restoration problems and eliminates them; the input images were connected directly to output terminals. Additional methods have been proposed, such as VDSR [8], which utilizes both ResNet and VGGNet [9] structures, and DBPN [10] and RDN [11], which utilize DenseNet [12], to connect all networks. DBPN undergoes repeated up-sampling and down-sampling during the learning process and learns by calculating the difference from the source at each layer and providing feedback to reduce the reconstruction error at the next learning stage.

In addition, even newer CNN techniques, such as DRN [13], USRNet [14], and MZSR [15], were proposed. Unlike conventional models that typically use a single loss value, DRN adds a double regression loss to the existing loss and combines the two loss values to use as its loss function. Double regression loss limits the down-sampling of images restored from LR to resemble the input LR images. The USRNet and MZSR methods, unlike other models that typically train using only the bicubic kernel, were proposed to perform robust SR in various kernel environments. USRNet is a method of restoring images by setting and adjusting the noise level and kernel type as hyper parameters, whereas MZSR is a method of restoring images that is more flexible under actual blue conditions by training on various kernels.

2.2. Object Recognition

Among the various object recognition technologies, character recognition technology uses computer vision to detect vehicle license plate locations and recognize the vehicle numbers, and this application is widely used for real-life services, such as smart transportation and smart parking. The goal of this technology is to correct traffic regulations by recognizing the number of vehicles that are speeding or violating signals and to accurately recognize the number of vehicle plates that are geometrically distorted or unrecognizably damaged. In this context, character recognition consists of a license plate detector, which detects the area of a license plate in a vehicle image by passing the vehicle image to a CNN, and a character recognizer, which recognizes the internal letters from the detected license plate. Intersection over union (IoU) and mean average precision (mAP) can be used as criteria for measuring the performance of license plate detectors and character recognizers. IoU is a metric of evaluating a model by calculating the ratio of the intersection and aggregation between the detection results predicted by the model and the location of the actual object. In general, if the IoU value exceeds 0.5, then the speculative model has properly detected the position of the object. mAP is a calculation that evaluates the accuracy of object recognition CNNs, which is defined as the proportion of information recognized through the CNN that matches the label of the actual object.

A wide range of research has been conducted on vehicle license plate detection and character recognition techniques [16–20]. In Korea, a license plate database was constructed by virtually generating an artificial license plate similar to an actual vehicle license plate and applying six data expansion methods to the generated license plate. Accordingly, a method was proposed to solve problems of data shortage, which is a major challenge in training CNNs [16]. Traditional artificial data generation methods often result in models that do not recognize license plates at various angles because they only generate images of front-facing license plates. Therefore, a method for building a three-dimensional, rotation-based artificial license plate database has been proposed to address this problem [17]. We previously proposed a method to merge license plate detection and license plate recognition into a single network to improve local binary pattern (LBP)-based cascaded detector quality using minimal CNNs [18]. SSD [19] is a method of object recognition using a single deep neural network, wherein the bounding box in the output space is separated using a base space with various aspect ratios and scales, and then the final bounding box is generated. CCPD [20] has collected more than 250,000 license plates to help address the inadequacy of a license plate database and to address the low recognition problem and has built large datasets that are approximately 30GB in size, providing 100,000 learning datasets and 150,000 test datasets. This is significant in addressing the problem of data scarcity in future license plate recognition studies through the establishment of large license plate databases.

3. Proposed Method

3.1. Training SR Networks

For SR neural network training, we collected a total of 13,230 license plate images from web crawl and by synthetic generation and divided them into a training set and a validation set. The training set is 11,231 HR license plate images and the validation set is

1999 HR license plate images. LR images were acquired by reducing the size of the HR images collected through biological interpolation. Neural network parameters were trained to restore the images via SR artificial neural networks to make them look similar to the original. In this work, the DBPN [10] method was benchmarked, modified, and improved for license plate image SR. The proposed method, as presented in Figure 1, underwent repeated up-blocks and down-blocks through multiple CNN layers in the learning process.

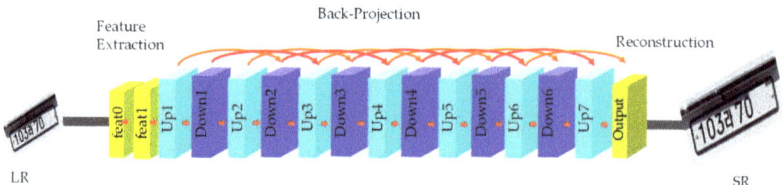

Figure 1. Iterative up and down blocks for SR framework. Two characters were masked due to privacy policies.

In this paper, various data extensions, such as rotations, perspective transformations, and crops, were used for training the SR artificial neural networks. In addition, hyper parameters were set and used (as shown in Table 1) to expand various magnifications, such as $2\times$, $3\times$, and $4\times$.

Table 1. Hyper parameters of the SR framework.

Scale	$2\times$	$3\times$	$4\times$
Kernel size	6	5	8
Stride	2	3	4
Padding	2	1	2

The proposed method consists of SR and character recognition. The computational time of the proposed SR method for different scale factors of $2\times$, $3\times$, and $4\times$ is as follows. Given the ground-truth HR image with 144×96 pixels, the proposed SR method takes 0.9 ms for a LR image with 72×48 pixels and $2\times$ scale factor, 1.0 ms for a LR image with 48×32 pixels and $3\times$ scale factor, and 1.1ms for a LR image with 36×24 pixels and $4\times$ scale factor. The computational time of the proposed character recognition model takes 2.1 ms for a input image with 128×128 pixels.

Figure 2 shows the changes in the mean PSNR and mean SSIM according to the proposed SR artificial neural network checkpoint. A total of 1999 license plate images were used as data sets for verification. Overall, it can be seen that the value gradually increases, then increases significantly around checkpoint 1000, and then no longer changes and is saturated. The blue graph represents $2\times$ SR results, the black graph represents $3\times$ SR results, and the purple graph represents $4\times$ SR results.

In this work, we propose a new loss function for improving the performance of the SR network, as depicted in Figure 3. The loss function is defined as

$$Loss_{total} = Loss_{SR} + Loss_{flip} \qquad (1)$$

$$Loss_{SR} = \sum_{i=1}^{N} |y_i - f(x_i)| \qquad (2)$$

$$Loss_{flip} = \sum_{i=1}^{N} \{f(x_i), flip(f(flip(x_i)))\} \qquad (3)$$

where n denotes the number of training images, x_i denotes the i-th LR training image, $f(x_i)$ denotes the SR result of x_i, and y_i denotes the i-th HR training image corresponding to the

SR image $f(x_i)$. In addition, $flip(\cdot)$ denotes the function that inverts left and right sides from the input image. The flip loss function $Loss_{flip}$ enables us to train the parameters of the SR neural network so that the SR result is robust to left–right reversal. As shown in Figure 3, for flip loss calculations, the left–right inverted LR image was passed through the SR artificial neural network to obtain an additional flipped SR. Then, we obtained a re-flipped SR that originally reversed the restore image back to its original side and calculated the sum of the absolute values of the original SR image and the re-flipped SR image to obtain flip loss. Additionally, the original loss was obtained by applying the input LR image to the SR artificial neural network and by calculating the sum of the obtained restored image and the absolute value of the difference between it and the HR image. Finally, the total loss was calculated by combining the flip loss and original loss. Our image SR model was trained in the direction of reducing this total loss.

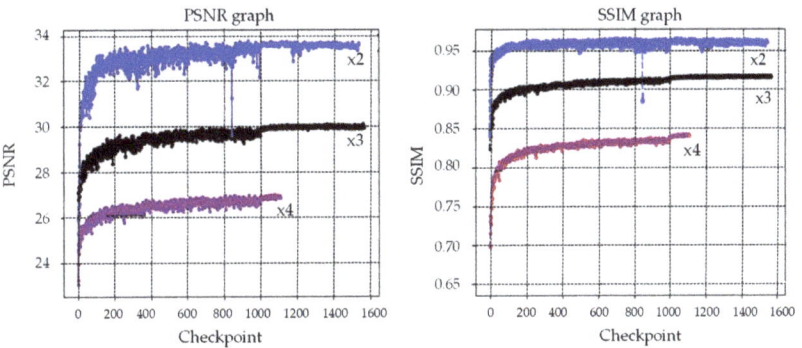

Figure 2. Trends of the average PSNR and SSIM results, according to the checkpoint.

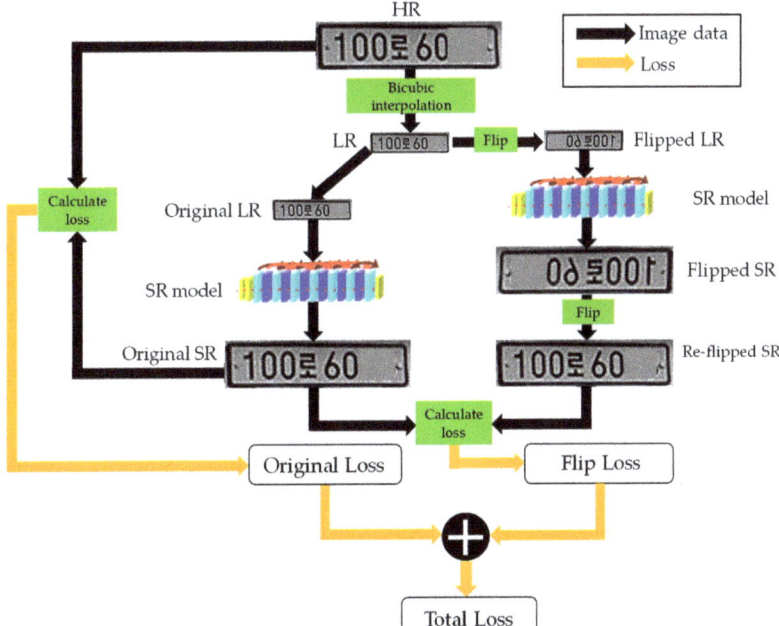

Figure 3. Proposed loss function for the SR framework. Two characters were masked due to privacy policies.

3.2. Chracter Recognition Networks

In this study, vehicle image data was collected through a web crawl using the BeautifulSoup Library. BeautifulSoup is a Python-based library that can load and store desired data from HTML or XML web pages, allowing data to be extracted to fit a specific format. The web crawler is a module that facilitates the viewing of all the information posted on the browser, as well as the storage of that information locally in an easy-to-use manner, As shown in Algorithm 1, the pseudocode capable for performing web crawl was implemented to collect the necessary data.

Algorithm 1. Web-crawling code

1. N: number of pages that should be crawled
2. M: the length of the html tags that were stripped
3. For k from 1 to N do
4. try:
   a. obtain uniform resource locator of page and gather all html tags of page.
   b. strip all html tags and obtain car image tags of pages.
   c. obtain car license plate character tags.
   d. for (i = 0 to i < M):
      i. if(length of car license plate character tags = 8):
      ii. save car images that have 8-digit license plate.
      iii. else:
      iv. continue
5. except:
   a. continue

During the process of collecting real-world data through web crawl, we encountered a shortage in the Korean character data. We implemented the source code for generating synthetic license plates using OpenCV-based traditional methods [21] to compensate for the lack of data, as shown in Algorithm 2. Figure 4 presents an example of artificially generated 8-digit license plates.

Algorithm 2. Artificial license plate image generation code

1. N: number of artificial license plate images that should be generated
2. **L**: license plate image which is empty
3. For i = 1 to N do:
4. resize the plate image **L** and define the character that should be generated.
5. obtain the number list and character list to be inserted in empty license plate image.
6. for j = 1 to 8 do:
   a. if j = 4 do:
      i. Char = character list[random(0, length of character list)]
      ii. draw the Char on the empty plate image on the third position
   b. else do:
      i. Num = number list[random(0, length of number list)]
7. draw the Num on the empty plate image on the j-th position on the image.

Figure 4. Examples of artificial license plate images.

To perform character recognition with the developed database, we designed and trained a two-step CNN model for vehicle character recognition. The first CNN model is intended to detect the license plate region within the input image. This model outputs the character region coordinates of the license plate region when passed through a neural network. The second CNN model is for character recognition, which receives cropped license plate images and outputs the characters, types, and locations of Korean characters in the license plate. We designed a two-step neural network model using the Darkflow [22] open source module with real-time character recognition, and individually trained two neural network parameters using the data we collected through web crawl and artificial data generation. For training the character recognition network, 122 classes were defined as presented in Table 2. We trained the character recognition network with 11,231 HR license plate images, which are the same in the training of the SR network, and we tested the character recognition network with 200 HR license plate images. Among 1999 validation images for the SR network, we selected 200 representative images as the validation set of the character recognition and labeled each character for 200 images by ourselves to validate the performance of the character recognition.

3.3. Integrated Framework for Improving the Recognition Accuracy

The general process of character recognition can be described as follows. The license plate area is cropped and extracted from the entire image. The extracted license plate image acts as input for the neural network, and the trained neural network recognizes the positions and labels of each character. Although interpolation methods, such as bicubic interpolation, can be used to resize the license plate to the input size of the neural network, these methods reduce clarity during the image magnification process. To address such problems, this work proposes a restoration preprocessing technique for images using SR. As shown in Figure 5, the license plate image, which is an LR image, is cropped from the car image. SR network extracts the feature of cropped license plate image, and improve the resolution of image with iterative up and down blocks. The character recognition network input the SR image to backbone model of character recognition neural network. The backbone model of character recognition neural network, Focus layer and CSP1 layer, extracts feature of input image by combining and shaping image features at different granularities. The neck model of character recognition neural network, CSP2 layer, and PANet aggregate image features to deliver them forward to character prediction of image. And finally, the head model predicts the box and the class of input image. The recognition rate can be improved by improving the clarity of the character through the proposed SR technique before the license plates that are extracted from the vehicle image enter the input of the character recognition neural network. Without the SR process, some characters can become degraded and difficult to recognize when recognizing vehicle characters in images. The proposed technique enables such characters to have high-definition clarity. The recognizer's character recognition rate can be improved with characters having high brightness, with their resolution close to that of the characters learned by the recognition neural network. By utilizing neural network weights trained separately using only vehicle license plate image data, which is the character class of interest, we can obtain highly accurate vehicle license plate restoration results compared to universal SR neural networks that cover various character classes at once.

Table 2. 122 classes for character recognition.

Class	Character	Class	Character	Class	Character	Class	Character
0	0	31	강원	62	두	93	차
1	1	32	경기	63	드	94	처
2	2	33	경남	64	라	95	초
3	3	34	경북	65	러	96	추
4	4	35	광주	66	로	97	츠
5	5	36	대구	67	루	98	카
6	6	37	대전	68	르	99	커
7	7	38	부산	69	마	100	코
8	8	39	서울	70	머	101	쿠
9	9	40	세종	71	모	102	크
10	강	41	울산	72	무	103	타
11	경	42	인천	73	므	104	터
12	광	43	전남	74	바	105	토
13	대	44	전북	75	배	106	투
14	부	45	제주	76	버	107	트
15	서	46	충남	77	보	108	파
16	세	47	충북	78	브	109	퍼
17	울	48	가	79	사	110	포
18	인	49	거	80	소	111	푸
19	전	50	고	81	수	112	하
20	제	51	공	82	스	113	프
21	충	52	그	83	아	114	호
22	구	53	국	84	어	115	허
23	기	54	나	85	오	116	해
24	남	55	너	86	우	117	후
25	북	56	노	87	육	118	흐
26	산	57	누	88	자	119	합
27	원	58	느	89	저	120	영
28	종	59	다	90	조	121	-
29	주	60	더	91	주		
30	천	61	도	92	즈		

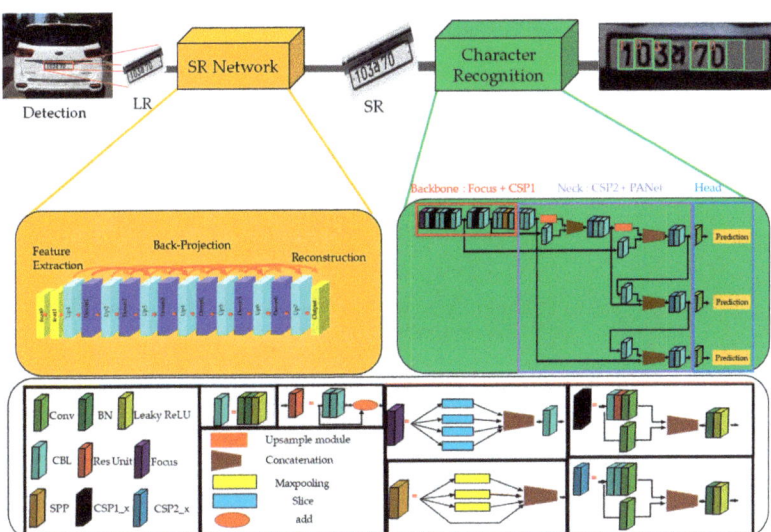

Figure 5. Flowchart of the integrated SR and character recognition. Two characters were masked due to privacy policies.

4. Results

4.1. Results of SR

To verify the performance of the SR neural networks trained in Section 3.1, we measured the PSNR and SSIM and compared the restored SR images after SR restoration and the original HR images using 1999 cropped license plate images. The proposed SR method has superior performance in restoring the quality of license plates compared to the conventional method, as demonstrated in Figures 6–8 and Table 3. For example, Figure 6 compares the results of existing SR techniques and the proposed SR method. Since the shapes of Korean letters tend to be more complex than that of the numbers in the license plate image, Korean letters can be more blurred than the numbers in the LR license plate image. As in Figure 6b which is the input of the SR network, when the LR bicubic image's quality is low and the character is heavily blurred, the LR character is hard to restore. In Figure 6g, while the numbers in the image are clear, other shapes are still unclear. Nevertheless, we note that the proposed image restoration performance is superior to or equivalent to existing state-of-the-art SR methods, and the proposed method provides much clearer results in the boundary edge area of other characters or numbers in the license plate image. These results allow us to qualitatively confirm that the proposed SR method has superior resolution improvements over conventional methods. Table 3 presents the performance of several SR techniques using the PSNR and SSIM. This quantitatively demonstrates the effectiveness of the proposed SR method.

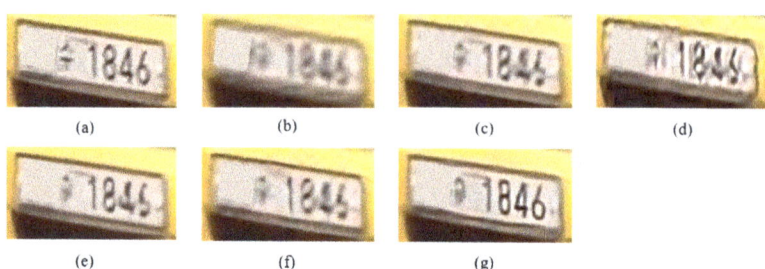

Figure 6. SR results of the first plate image (4×). (**a**) HR (128 × 64), (**b**) Bicubic, (**c**) DRN, (**d**) MZSR, (**e**) USRNet, (**f**) DBPN, (**g**) Proposed. Two characters were masked due to privacy policies.

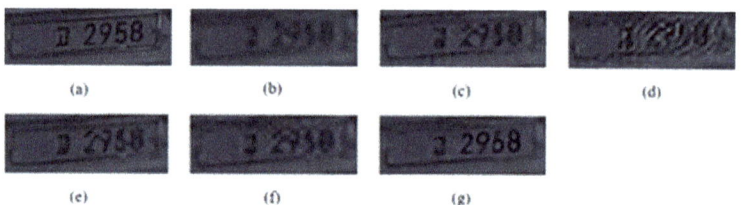

Figure 7. SR results of the second plate image (4×). (**a**) HR (140 × 48), (**b**) Bicubic, (**c**) DRN, (**d**) MZSR, (**e**) USRNet, (**f**) DBPN, (**g**) Proposed. Two characters were masked due to privacy policies.

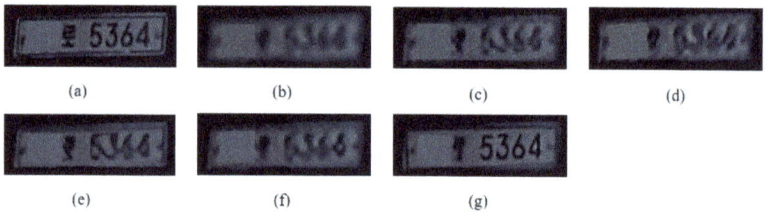

Figure 8. SR results of the third plate image (4×). (**a**) HR (144 × 40), (**b**) Bicubic, (**c**) DRN, (**d**) MZSR, (**e**) USRNet, (**f**) DBPN, (**g**) Proposed. Two characters were masked due to privacy policies.

Table 3. Average PSNR/SSIM of license plates for validation.

Scale	2×		3×		4×	
Bicubic	30.85	0.9297	26.09	0.7960	23.68	0.6516
MZSR	21.15	0.7056	21.27	0.5942	19.53	0.3788
DRN	-	-	-	-	25.80	0.6945
DBPN	33.72	0.9616	-	-	25.41	0.7739
Proposed	33.75	0.9632	30.09	0.9181	26.99	0.8430

4.2. Results of Character Recognition

Figure 9 presents the mAP results for 200 test sets (150 new 8-digit license plates and 50 electric vehicle license plates) measured using a two-stage character recognition neural network model. As shown in Figure 9a, due to insufficient Korean license plate data, for some characters, such as 113(하), 115(호), and 116(허), the character recognition neural network did not recognize Korean letter classes, and achieved an mAP score of 87.14%. To improve this, the additional building and training using the data obtained through web crawl and synthetic data generation achieved an mAP score of 95.30%. This was obtained by gradually improving the character recognition rates for other classes and by recognizing all of the problematic Korean letter classes, as shown in Figure 9b.

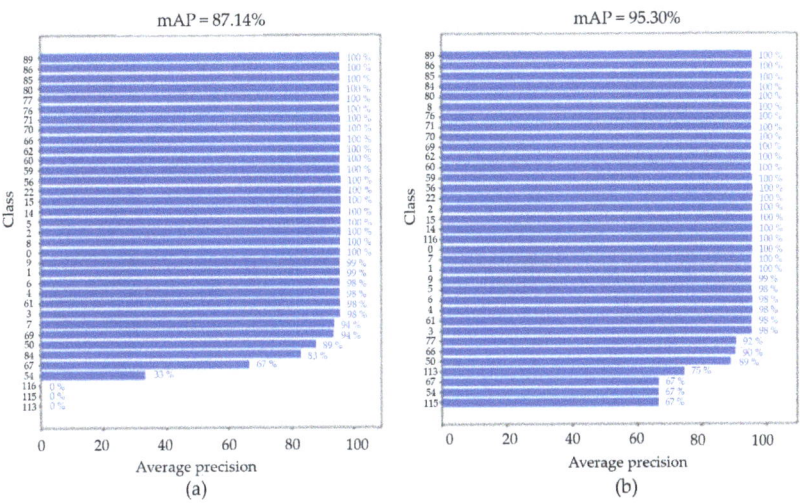

Figure 9. Results of character recognition (**a**) without and (**b**) with artificial license plate generation.

Figures 10 and 11 present the results of detection and text recognition of the new 8 digits and the electric vehicle license plates, respectively. Figure 10 shows the license plate area detection and character recognition results from the vehicle image together, whereas Figure 11 shows the results of the character region detection and label information recognition from the cropped license plate images. For reference, the number plate recognition processing speed in the video was approximately 30 fps or higher, thus achieving real-time processing.

In addition, the character recognition algorithm proposed in this study can be extended to the recognition of vehicle license plate characters in other countries through re-the training of neural networks without any change to our algorithm. Unfortunately, however, there are few open license plate datasets due to issues such as personal information privacy, so it cannot be applied immediately. If other foreign license plate data is available in the future, our character recognition algorithm can be extended and applied to other foreign characters.

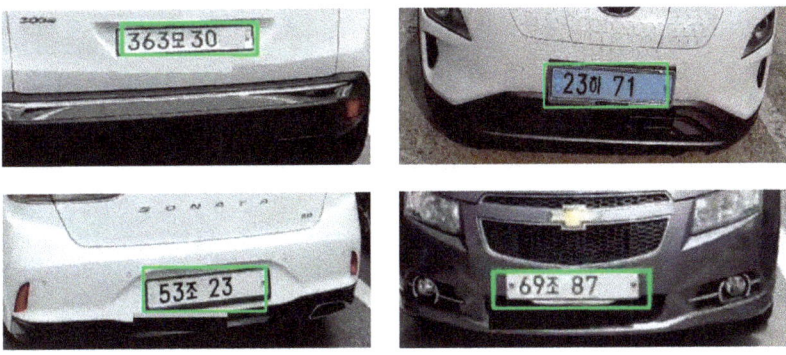

Figure 10. Examples of plate detection results. Two characters were masked due to privacy policies.

Figure 11. Examples of character recognition results. Two characters were masked due to privacy policies.

4.3. Integrated Results of SR and Character Recognition

This section presents the performance improvements in character recognition from using SR techniques. Image quality was improved using the proposed SR technique after converting the original license plate image into 2×, 3×, and 4× LR images, which were degraded by bicubic interpolation. As can be seen in Table 3, the images were improved through SR. These images possessed higher PSNR values than the LR images. However, the higher PSNR values cannot guarantee image quality, because higher PSNR values do not necessarily mean that our proposed SR technique was effective with respect to character recognition. This is because comparing the similarities between HR and SR images can result in a high PSNR calculation due to superficial similarities, such as in color or the position of letters, even if their shape is distorted in the process of improving the quality of letters or numbers. Therefore, we aimed to verify whether the proposed SR technique could improve the performance of character recognition by utilizing the character recognition neural network. When measuring the recognition rate from the license plate images in Figures 12 and 13, we observed that the data were detected by the license plate recognizer only when the confidence of the data was over 50%. Although the perceived confidence of images, with improved quality owing to the SR techniques, was similar to that of the original HR images, the degree of image quality improvement was not significant in the case of double magnification. However, with enhancement in the image quality owing to the 3× and 4× magnification SR techniques, the recognition rate was significantly improved, as the letters not recognized in the LR image were newly recognized in the SR image, as observable in Figures 12 and 13. Meanwhile, in the case of bad weather conditions (nighttime, heavy rain, heavy snow, etc.) or the angle of the license plate in the video is rotated a lot, the proposed algorithm often gives wrong results. The several wrong results from bad conditions such as nighttime and rotation situations are shown in Figure 14. For example, there are some missing and false recognition results in Figure 14b. The proposed algorithm often provides a failure case when there is a bad weather environment or when the angle of the license plate in the image is rotated too much. This is considered a limitation of the current algorithm, and the limitation is expected to be resolved via the application of an additional data augmentation technique.

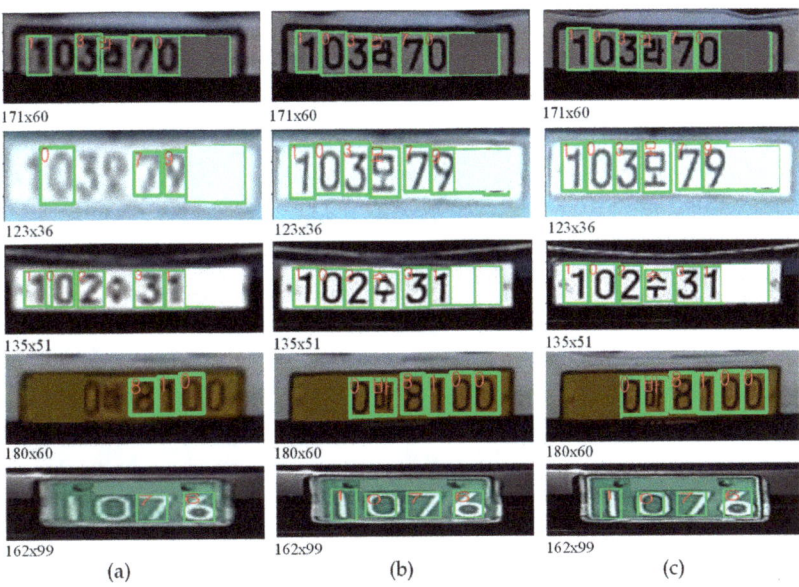

Figure 12. Examples of character recognition results. Recognition results on (**a**) bicubic results (3×), (**b**) proposed SR results (3×), and (**c**) HR images. Two characters were masked due to privacy policies.

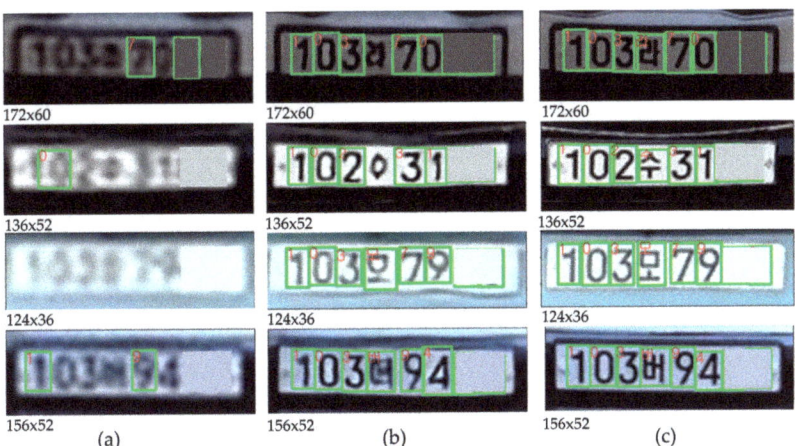

Figure 13. Examples of character recognition results. Recognition results on (**a**) bicubic results (4×), (**b**) proposed SR results (4×), and (**c**) HR images. Two characters were masked due to privacy policies.

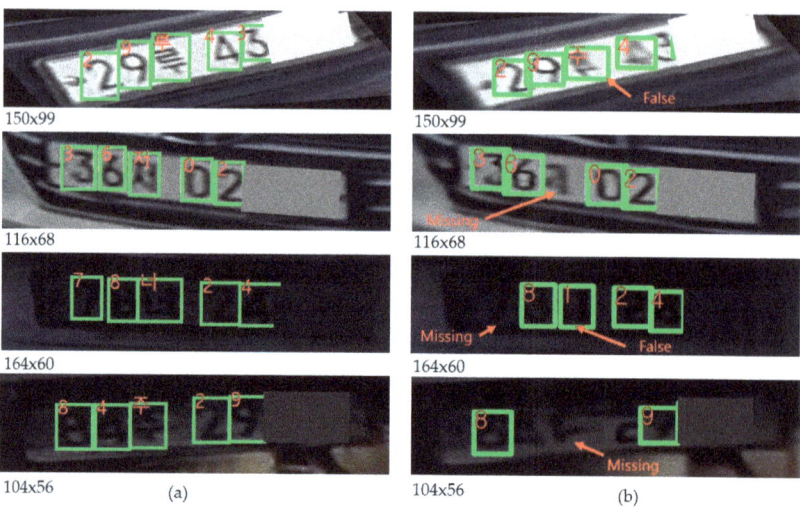

Figure 14. Failure examples of character recognition results. (**a**) Ground-truth labels on HR images and (**b**) the proposed SR (4×) and character recognition results obtained from LR images. Two characters were masked due to privacy policies.

The evaluation was conducted using mAP to quantitatively verify how many license plate numbers and letters recognized in this manner were accurate. By scaling 1999 LR license plate images through biological interpolation, mAP was measured by applying proposed SR technology instead of biological interpolation. Comparisons were made with the results in Figures 15–18. This demonstrates that the character recognition accuracy for LR images was significantly lower than that for HR images.

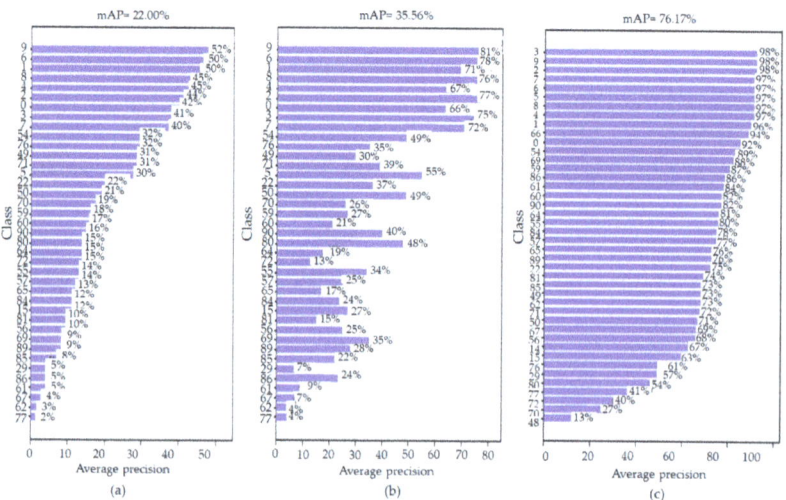

Figure 15. mAP comparison results. (**a**–**c**) represent the mAP results on bicubic results (3×), proposed SR results (3×), and HR images, respectively.

The mAP did not exhibit a significant improvement for SR images because the performance of the original image was not significantly different from the quality of the 2× LR images. Meanwhile, Figure 15 shows the character recognition mAP results for 3× LR, SR, and HR images, from left to right. From this, we can observe that all of the class (0–121)-specific mAPs (35.56%) for the SR image results were 13.56% higher than the mAP (22.00%) calculated for the LR images, which was closer to the mAP results (96.7%) of the HR images. This result shows that SR is a technology that has a positive impact on the performance of character recognition software. In addition, Figure 16 shows the mAP results for a numeric class (0–9) for LR, SR, and HR images. The numerical class for SR image results (0–9) mAP (71.80%) was increased by 27.90% when compared to the mAP (43.90%) for LR images.

Figure 17 presents the results of the 4× magnification LR, DBPN, the proposed SR, and the number recognition mAP for HR images, starting from the upper left. All class (0–121)-specific mAPs (25.13%) for the SR image results were 20.30% higher than the mAP (4.83%) for the LR images, and 11.55% points higher than the mAP (13.58%) for the existing DBPN SR images. This shows that the proposed SR image was closer to the mAP result (76.17%) from the HR image than the LR and DBPN SR images. Additionally, Figure 18 shows the mAP results for a numeric class (0–9) for LR, DBPN, proposed SR, and HR images. The numerical class for the SR image results (0–9) mAP (61.30%) was 49.94% points higher than that of the mAP (11.36%) for the LR images, and 41.5% points higher than that the mAP (19.80%) for the existing DBPN SR images. Tables 4 and 5 present a comparison of the results of character recognition of several SR techniques using mAP. Tables 4 and 5 show the mAP comparison of various SR methods for the whole 122 classes and for 10 classes only, respectively. The proposed method outperforms other methods of character recognition. This quantitatively demonstrates the effectiveness of the proposed SR method in character recognition.

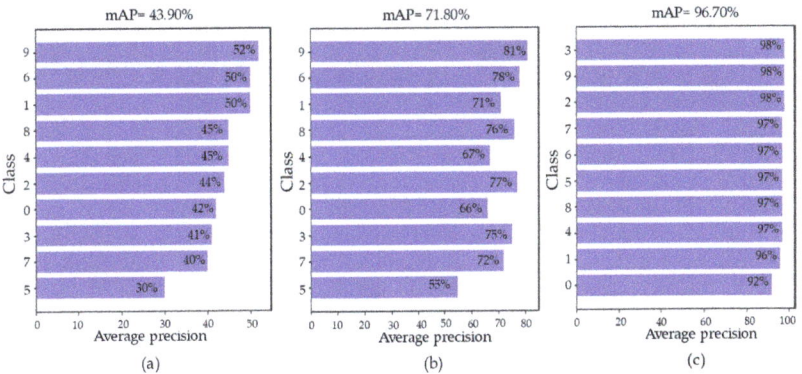

Figure 16. mAP comparison results for only numbers (0–9). (**a**–**c**) represent the mAP results on bicubic results (3×), proposed SR results (3×), and HR images, respectively.

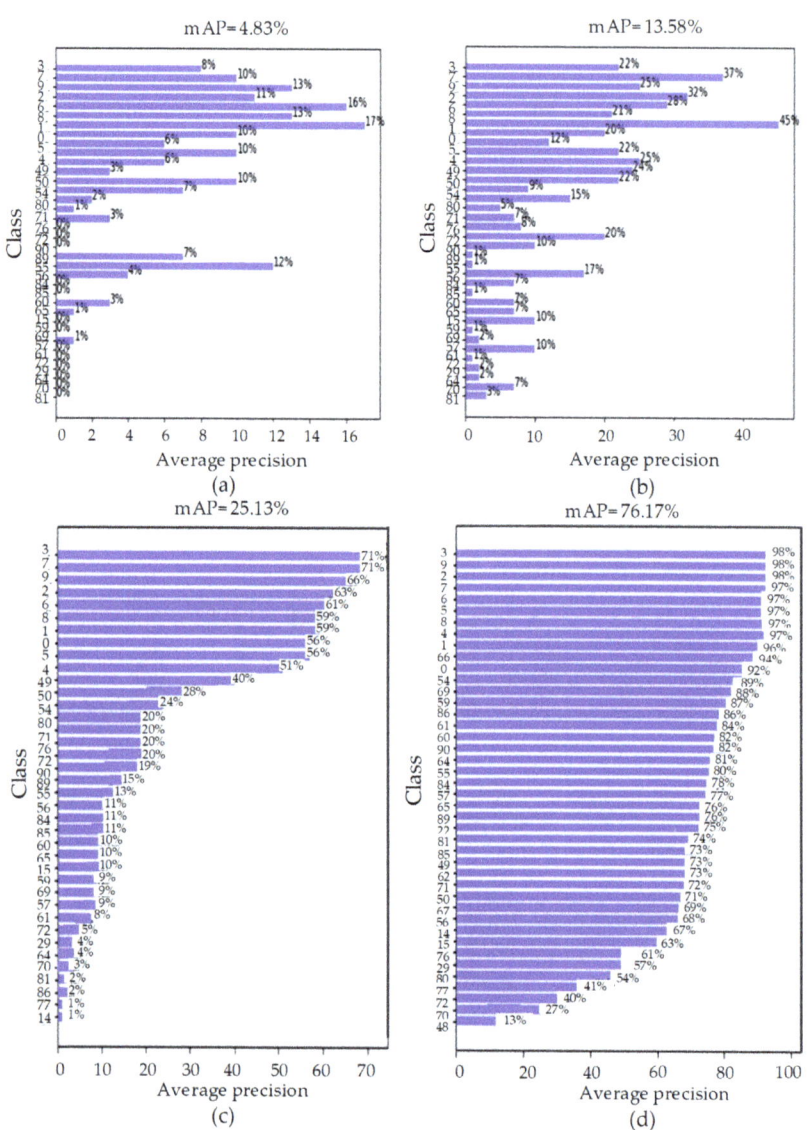

Figure 17. mAP comparison results. (**a**–**d**) represent the mAP results on bicubic results (×4), DBPN results (×4), proposed SR results (×4), and HR images, respectively.

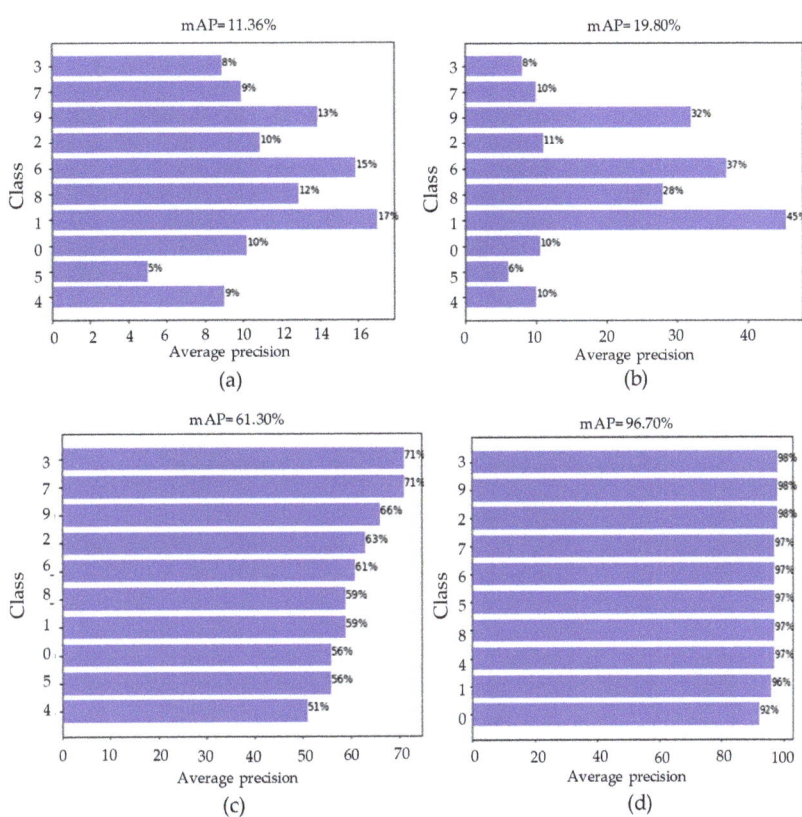

Figure 18. mAP comparison results for only numbers (0–9). (**a–d**) represent the mAP results on bicubic results (×4), DBPN results (×4), proposed SR results (×4), and HR images, respectively.

Table 4. Average mAP (%) comparison of LR license plates for validation of 122 classes (0–121).

Scale	2×	3×	4×
Bicubic	62.61	22.00	4.83
MZSR	18.24	18.53	7.65
DRN	-	-	14.60
DBPN	57.49	-	13.58
Proposed	64.78	35.56	25.13

Table 5. Average mAP (%) comparison of LR license plates for validation of 10 classes (0–9).

Scale	2×	3×	4×
Bicubic	85.13	43.90	11.36
MZSR	58.37	58.86	30.86
DRN	-	-	48.40
DBPN	85.85	-	19.80
Proposed	91.70	71.80	61.30

5. Discussion

In this section, we discuss the strengths and weaknesses of the proposed structure in detail. Our results show that the proposed integrated framework, super-resolved character recognition, improves character recognition performance. For example, the proposed method remarkably increased the mAP by 49.94% points compared to the existing state-of-the-art method for character recognition with the $4\times$ magnification. However, failure cases in bad environments such as nighttime and rotation situations of our proposed framework can be generated. This is considered a weakness of our proposed algorithm and these shortcomings can be overcome through the data augmentation technique.

Meanwhile, image quality factors that should be considered important to recognize characters well include sharpness, contrast ratio, color, and noise. In general, the sharper the image, the higher the contrast ratio, the higher the color saturation, and the lower the noise, the better the character can be recognized. An integrated criterion can be proposed by comprehensively considering these quality factors. Additionally, the loss function (localization loss, confidence loss, and classification loss) used for character recognition can be simultaneously applied to the SR neural network training. As a future study, the end-to-end training of SR and character recognition can be considered.

6. Conclusions

In this paper, we analyzed the problem of reduced character recognition caused by differences in resolution between the test and learning image data. Both these data were trained by character recognizers and the proposed SR technique, which can improve character recognition in LR test input environments. To verify the performance of the proposed method, we implemented and experimented with SR and character recognition integration systems using Darkflow-based implemented license plate recognizers, confirming that SR techniques can help to innovatively improve license plate recognition rates. Additionally, we confirmed that data expansion using web crawl and artificial data generation methods can improve the performance of license plate recognizers. The license plate data set secured through this study and the SR artificial neural network weights can be widely utilized in areas such as smart transportation and smart parking, or any domain wherein text recognition of LR input images can be utilized. In the future, in addition to integer magnifications, such as $2\times$, $3\times$, and $4\times$, further intensification studies examining minority magnification (1.1 to 3.9) and network memory compression through the parameter sharing of weights by magnification can be performed.

Author Contributions: Conceptualization, S.B.Y.; methodology, S.-J.L. and S.B.Y.; software, S.-J.L.; validation, S.-J.L.; formal analysis, S.-J.L. and S.B.Y.; investigation, S.-J.L. and S.B.Y.; resources, S.-J.L. and S.B.Y.; data curation, S.-J.L. and S.B.Y.; writing—original draft preparation, S.-J.L. and S.B.Y.; writing—review and editing, S.-J.L. and S.B.Y.; visualization, S.B.Y.; supervision, S.B.Y.; project administration, S.B.Y.; funding acquisition, S.B.Y. Both authors have read and agreed to the published version of the manuscript.

Funding: This work was supported by the Institute of Information & Communications Technology Planning & Evaluation (IITP) grant funded by the Korea government (MSIT) (No. 2020-0-00004, Development of Previsional Intelligence based on Long-term Visual Memory Network) and the National Research Foundation of Korea (NRF) grant funded by the Korea government (MSIT) (NRF-2020R1G1A1100798).

Institutional Review Board Statement: Not applicable.

Informed Consent Statement: Not applicable.

Data Availability Statement: Not applicable.

Conflicts of Interest: The authors declare no conflict of interest.

References

1. Dong, C.; Loy, C.C.; He, K.; Tang, X. Image super-resolution using deep convolutional networks. *IEEE Trans. Pattern Anal. Mach. Intell.* **2015**, *38*, 295–307. [CrossRef] [PubMed]
2. Freeman, W.T.; Jones, T.R.; Pasztor, E.C. Example-based super-resolution. *IEEE Comput. Graph.* **2002**, *22*, 56–65. [CrossRef]
3. Yang, J.; Wright, J.; Huang, T.; Ma, Y. Image super-resolution as sparse representation of raw image patches. In Proceedings of the IEEE Conference on Computer Vision and Pattern Recognition, Anchorage, AK, USA, 23–28 June 2008; pp. 1–8.
4. Dong, C.; Loy, C.C.; Tang, X. Accelerating the super-resolution convolutional neural network. In Proceedings of the European Conference on Computer Vision, Amsterdam, The Netherlands; 2016; pp. 391–407.
5. Shi, W.; Caballero, J.; Huszár, F.; Totz, J.; Aitken, A.P.; Bishop, R.; Rueckert, D.; Wang, Z. Real-time single image and video super-resolution using an efficient sub-pixel convolutional neural networks. In Proceedings of the IEEE Conference on Computer Vision and Pattern Recognition, Las Vegas, NV, USA, 27–30 June 2016; pp. 1874–1883.
6. He, K.; Zhang, X.; Ren, S.; Sun, J. Deep residual learning for image recognition. In Proceedings of the IEEE Conference on Computer Vision and Pattern Recognition, Las Vegas, NV, USA, 27–30 June 2016; pp. 770–778.
7. Lim, B.; Son, S.; Kim, H.; Nah, S.; Lee, K.M. Enhanced deep residual networks for single image super-resolution. In Proceedings of the IEEE Conference on Computer Vision and Pattern Recognition Workshops, Honolulu, HI, USA, 21–26 July 2017; pp. 136–144.
8. Simonyan, K.; Zisserman, A. Very deep convolutional networks for large-scale image recognition. *arXiv* **2014**, arXiv:1409.1556.
9. Kim, J.W.; Lee, J.K.; Lee, K.M. Accurate image super-resolution using very deep convolutional networks. In Proceedings of the IEEE Conference on Computer Vision and Pattern Recognition, Las Vegas, NV, USA, 27–30 June 2016; pp. 1646–1654.
10. Huang, G.; Liu, Z.; Maaten, L.; Weinberger, K.Q. Densely connected convolutional networks. In Proceedings of the IEEE Conference on Computer Vision and Pattern Recognition Workshops, Honolulu, HI, USA, 21–26 July 2017; pp. 2261–2269.
11. Haris, M.; Shakhnarovich, G.; Ukita, N. Deep back-projection networks for super-resolution. In Proceedings of the IEEE Conference on Computer Vision and Pattern Recognition, Salt Lake City, UT, USA, 18–22 June 2018; pp. 1664–1673.
12. Zhang, Y.; Tian, Y.; Kong, Y.; Zhong, B.; Fu, Y. Residual dense network for image super-resolution. In Proceedings of the IEEE Conference on Computer Vision and Pattern Recognition, Salt Lake City, UT, USA, 18–22 June 2018; pp. 2472–2481.
13. Guo, Y.; Chen, J.; Wang, J.; Chen, Q.; Cao, J.; Deng, Z.; Xu, Y.; Tan, M. Closed-loop matters: Dual regression networks for single image super-resolution. In Proceedings of the IEEE/CVF Conference on Computer Vision and Pattern Recognition, Virtual, 14–19 June 2020; pp. 5407–5416.
14. Zhang, K.; Gool, L.V.; Timofte, R. Deep unfolding network for image super-resolution. In Proceedings of the IEEE/CVF Conference on Computer Vision and Pattern Recognition, Virtual, Seattle, WA, USA, 14–19 June 2020; pp. 3217–3226.
15. Soh, J.W.; Cho, S.; Cho, N.I. Meta-transfer learning for zero-shot super-resolution. In Proceedings of the IEEE/CVF Conference on Computer Vision and Pattern Recognition, Virtual, Seattle, WA, USA, 14–19 June 2020; pp. 3516–3525.
16. Lee, J.H.; Cho, S.M.; Lee, S.J.; Kim, C.H. License plate recognition system using synthetic data. *IEIE J.* **2020**, *57*, 107–115.
17. Lee, Y.J.; Kim, S.J.; Park, K.M.; Park, K.M. Comparison of number plate recognition performance of Synthetic number plate generator using 2D and 3D rotation. In Proceedings of the Korean Institute of Broadcast and Media Engineers Summer Conference, Virtual, 13–15 July 2020; pp. 141–144.
18. Sergey, Z.; Alexey, G. LPRNet: License plate recognition via deep neural networks. *arXiv* **2018**, arXiv:1806.10447.
19. Liu, W.; Anguelov, D.; Derhan, D.; Szegedy, C.; Reed, S.; Fu, C.Y.; Berg, A.C. SSD: Single shot multibox detector. In Proceedings of the European Conference on Computer Vision, Amsterdam, The Netherlands; 2016; pp. 21–37.
20. Xu, Z.; Yang, W.; Meng, A.; Lu, N.; Hunag, H.; Ying, C.; Huang, L. Towards end-to-end license plate detection and recognition: A large dataset and baseline. In Proceedings of the European Conference on Computer Vision, Munich, Germany, 8–14 September 2018; pp. 261–277.
21. Lee, H.C. Design and implementation of efficient place number region detecting system in vehicle number plate image. *KSCI J.* **2005**, *10*, 87–93.
22. Translate Darknet to Tensorflow. Available online: https://github.com/thtrieu/darkflow (accessed on 15 September 2021).

Article

Single Image Super-Resolution with Arbitrary Magnification Based on High-Frequency Attention Network

Jun-Seok Yun and Seok-Bong Yoo *

Department of Artificial Intelligence Convergence, Chonnam National University, Gwangju 61186, Korea; 218062@jnu.ac.kr
* Correspondence: sbyoo@jnu.ac.kr; Tel.: +82-625303437

Abstract: Among various developments in the field of computer vision, single image super-resolution of images is one of the most essential tasks. However, compared to the integer magnification model for super-resolution, research on arbitrary magnification has been overlooked. In addition, the importance of single image super-resolution at arbitrary magnification is emphasized for tasks such as object recognition and satellite image magnification. In this study, we propose a model that performs arbitrary magnification while retaining the advantages of integer magnification. The proposed model extends the integer magnification image to the target magnification in the discrete cosine transform (DCT) spectral domain. The broadening of the DCT spectral domain results in a lack of high-frequency components. To solve this problem, we propose a high-frequency attention network for arbitrary magnification so that high-frequency information can be restored. In addition, only high-frequency components are extracted from the image with a mask generated by a hyperparameter in the DCT domain. Therefore, the high-frequency components that have a substantial impact on image quality are recovered by this procedure. The proposed framework achieves the performance of an integer magnification and correctly retrieves the high-frequency components lost between the arbitrary magnifications. We experimentally validated our model's superiority over state-of-the-art models.

Keywords: image super-resolution; arbitrary magnification; high-frequency attention; DCT spectral domain

Citation: Yun, J.-S.; Yoo, S.-B. Single Image Super-Resolution with Arbitrary Magnification Based on High-Frequency Attention Network. *Mathematics* **2022**, *10*, 275. https://doi.org/10.3390/math10020275

Academic Editors: Esteban Palomo, Ezequiel López-Rubio and Enrique Domínguez

Received: 8 December 2021
Accepted: 12 January 2022
Published: 16 January 2022

Publisher's Note: MDPI stays neutral with regard to jurisdictional claims in published maps and institutional affiliations.

Copyright: © 2022 by the authors. Licensee MDPI, Basel, Switzerland. This article is an open access article distributed under the terms and conditions of the Creative Commons Attribution (CC BY) license (https://creativecommons.org/licenses/by/4.0/).

1. Introduction

Owing to convolutional neural networks (CNNs), image super-resolution shows excellent high-resolution reconstruction from low-resolution images. In addition, research is being conducted to improve the performance of various computer vision applications by converting low-resolution images into high-resolution images using super-resolution.

For example, in object detection, regions of interest are detected in an image through an object detection neural network. Subsequently, it is essential to adjust the detection region to the size of the object attribute recognition neural network. However, real-world images taken using CCTV cameras, black boxes, drones, etc., have small object areas, and when the image is resized by general interpolation, it causes blur and lowers the performance of object recognition. To solve this problem, Lee et al. [1] applied the super-resolution approach to an image that has a small object area. By applying this approach, object recognition accuracy was improved compared to the existing interpolation method. However, small object areas of various sizes cannot be converted into target sizes utilizing existing super-resolution methods. Conventional super-resolution methods restore only integer magnifications ($\times 2$, $\times 4$). Alternatively, the input image is enlarged or reduced by a decimal (floating-point) magnification using the interpolation method, and then an arbitrary magnification is performed through a super-resolution neural network. This method causes a loss of restoration capability and an increase in computing cost due to the deformation of the input image. Therefore, a super-resolution neural network capable of arbitrary magnification is required for the task at hand. Figure 1 is an example application of arbitrary magnification super-resolution in object recognition tasks. Object detection results taken by CCTV cameras can have arbitrary resolutions. There is a problem when using detection results for object recognition because most recognition models have a fixed input size. To resolve this problem, bicubic interpolation can be considered. However, it causes blur then lowers the performance of object recognition. Therefore, an arbitrary magnification super-resolution is required to upscale the image with an arbitrary resolution while preserving image quality, as shown in Figure 1. When applying our method to the application in Figure 1, it can perform the arbitrary magnification super-resolution with a single weight of an integer magnification model and small capacity weights for each decimal magnification model. To this end, weights for the decimal magnification candidates should be stored in the memory in advance.

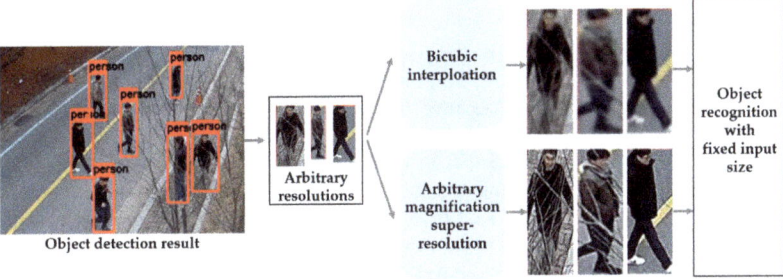

Figure 1. Example application of arbitrary magnification super-resolution in object recognition task.

In addition, the necessity of arbitrary magnification super-resolution for other tasks is described in the related works section. When constructing an arbitrary magnification super-resolution, it should be magnified to the target size through the decimal magnification by interpolation. In this case, various interpolation methods can be applied, but existing interpolation methods expand to a state in which many low-frequency components are not preserved. Applying this to a super-resolution model causes a decrease in image restoration capability. Therefore, for arbitrary super-resolution, a method capable of expanding to a target magnification while preserving the preservation of low-frequency components is essential. We propose a method using DCT to solve this problem. We utilized the principle that in the DCT spectrum domain, low-frequency components are concentrated in the upper-left direction, and high-frequency components are concentrated in the lower-right direction. In this case, while preserving a low-frequency component that greatly affects performance, it expands in the lower-right direction, which is a high-frequency component. Using this, we can preserve the low-frequency components and obtain an image magnified at an arbitrary magnification in which only the high-frequency component is insufficient. From the acquired image, we use DCT to more delicately extract high-frequency components through the mask generated using hyperparameters. The extracted high-frequency component is amplified through a high-frequency attention network. The amplified high-frequency component is added to the input image, and the arbitrary magnification is completed. The proposed high-frequency attention network gives the network a definite purpose of high-frequency restoration by receiving high-frequency components as input. This leads to good performance as the network is more focused on purpose.

In this study, a super-resolution network capable of arbitrary magnification is proposed as follows: Integer scaling is performed through a super-resolution neural network, and the space for residual scaling is expanded in the DCT spectral domain. In this case, the expanded DCT spaces were part of the high-frequency region. Therefore, arbitrary magnification is performed by filling in the insufficient high-frequency space in the spatial domain through the high-frequency attention network. The arbitrary magnification model proposed in this study has better restoration performance than other arbitrary magnification methods by retaining the advantages of the integer magnification model and proceeding with additional arbitrary magnification.

The highlights of this study are summarized as follows:

- The image is enlarged to target resolution in the DCT spectral domain.
- The high frequency, which is insufficient owing to the DCT spectral domain spatial expansion, is restored through the spatial domain high-frequency concentration network.
- The proposed model preserves the superiority of the existing integer super-resolution model. By simply adding the hybrid-domain high-frequency model without modifying and additionally training on the existing integer super-resolution model, our model's arbitrary magnification restoration performance is better than that of state-of-the-art models.

2. Related Works

2.1. Conventional Single Image Super-Resolution

The purpose of super-resolution is to use a low-resolution image as input and predict a corresponding high-resolution image. However, this is an ill-posed problem to solve because various degradations occur while reducing the image quality from high resolution to low resolution. Various studies have been conducted to address this problem. Super-resolution convolutional neural network (SRCNN) [2] showed innovative restoration performance using a super-resolution CNN for the first time. Based on this, studies on better super-resolution performance were conducted. A very deep convolutional network (VDSR) [3] designed the model more deeply through a residual learning strategy. An efficient sub-pixel convolutional neural network (ESPCNN) [4] overcomes the limitation of inputting an image with a target magnification as input by implementing a pixel-shuffling layer that can be learned with an upsampling module. Computing overhead is reduced because the input images do not need to be enlarged by interpolation, and a deeper network can be built using small-sized filters. Deep back-projection networks (DBPN) [5] created a structure that repeatedly stacks the image upscaling and downscaling layers. It showed better performance by repeatedly reducing and enlarging the size of the input image. Residual channel attention network (RCAN) [6] introduced a channel attention mechanism to create a deep model. Dual regression networks (DRN) [7] improved the restoration ability by constructing a closed circuit inside the model and adding a low-resolution domain loss function that calculates the difference from the input image by downscaling the super-resolution result image, in addition to the existing high-resolution domain loss function. Residual dense network (RDN) [8] learned the hierarchical representation of all feature maps through the residual density structure. Second-order attention network (SAN) [9] showed good performance by strongly improving the representation of image feature maps and learning the interdependencies between feature maps. SRGAN [10] used adversarial learning to improve super-resolution performance. This model consists of a generator and a discriminator network, and the generator aims to create a super-resolution output that the discriminator cannot differentiate from a sample input. Recently, SRFlow [11], which uses a normalizing flow to predict a complex probability distribution from a normal distribution, has been attracting attention. SRFlow transforms a high-resolution image into a complex probability distribution and gradually differentiates the probability distribution into a normal distribution of a low-resolution image by using the Jacobian matrix. In addition, there is an affine coupling layer in SRFlow, which divides the dimension of the input value into two, leaving one dimension unchanged and performing shift and affine transformations on the other dimension. This transform makes it easy to compute the inverse transform and the Jacobian determinant. This differentiation process is learned, and when a normal distribution of a low-resolution image is processed, it can be transformed into a complex probability distribution. Complex probability distributions generate images from probability distributions using a flow-based generative model. The advantage of SRFlow is that it has enhanced diversity to create high-resolution images from fewer low-resolution images than a generative adversarial network (GAN). In addition, the log-likelihood loss is used to prevent divergence during learning to ensure stability, and it is easier to learn than the generator and discriminator of the GAN separately. SRFlow-DA [12] showed improved performance by adding six more convolution layers to extend the receptive field of the SRFlow model and removing the normalization layer that does not fit the super-resolution structure. Noise conditional SRFlow (NCSR) [13] inserts noise into low-resolution and high-resolution images during training and removes artifacts caused by noise. SwinIR [14] proposed a strong baseline model for image restoration based on the swin transformer [15]. SwinIR is composed of several residual swin transformer blocks, each of which has several swin transformer layers together with a residual connection. Through this, SwinIR showed excellent image restoration ability. A cross-scale non-local network (CSNLN) [16] proposed the first cross-scale non-local (CS-NL) attention module with integration into a recurrent neural network. Additionally, they combine the new CS-NL prior with local and non-local priors. These methods present good quality image results and have a lot of advantages, as shown in Table 1. However, due to the various resolutions of taken images in the real world, the need for arbitrary magnification is emerging. Despite the development of the latest super-resolution as above, these methods have shortcomings, as shown in Table 1. To perform the arbitrary magnification super-resolution, existing methods should utilize interpolation methods such as bicubic, bilinear, etc. Due to this limitation, the interpolation results show poor image quality. Therefore, to deal with this problem, we propose a super-resolution network capable of arbitrary magnification.

Table 1. Conventional single image super-resolution methods' advantages and shortcomings.

Method	Advantages (Characteristics)	Shortcomings
SRCNN	Uses only three convolutional layers and enhances the performance of super-resolution.	
VDSR	Cascades small filters many times; information over an image is exploited in an efficient way.	
ESPCNN	Effectively replacing the bicubic filter, computing cost is reduced.	
DBPN	Concatenates the features of the repeated upsampling and downsampling, super-solution performance improved.	
RCAN	Bypasses multiple skip connections and focuses on learning high-frequency information.	
DRN	Estimates kernel and utilizes it to restore low-resolution images.	Perform integer super-resolution only and should utilize interpolation methods to perform the arbitrary magnification super-resolution.
RDN	Learns hierarchical representation and stabilizes the training process.	
SAN	Rescales the features adaptively and learns feature expressions and feature correlation.	
SRGAN	Uses adversarial learning and recovers heavily downsampled images.	
SRFlow-DA	Enlarges the receptive field and takes more expressive power.	
NCSR	Adds the noise conditional layer and extends diversity.	
SwinIR	Applies a Swin transformer and utilizes interactions between image content and attention weights.	
CSNLN	Finds and utilizes more cross-scale feature correlations.	

2.2. Arbitrary Magnification Single Image Super-Resolution

Most of the super-resolution rely on non-learning-based interpolation when scaling low-resolution images to decimal magnifications. ESPCNN proposed a magnification method capable of learning by proposing a pixel-shuffling layer. Using this, VDSR can magnify a low-resolution image to a target resolution and put it into a super-resolution model for arbitrary magnification. However, if the image is enlarged and passed through a neural network, it requires significant computing resources, and it has to have a large model weight for each magnification; thereby, its performance is more specialized for integer magnification. Meta-SR [17] can perform arbitrary magnification with only one model by replacing the enlarged part of the existing super-resolution model with an upscale module. Meta-SR has a weight prediction layer that can be trained to predict weights expanded by an integer magnification. This weight is applied to the upscale module and magnifies the image by an integer magnification. In the image enlarged by an integer multiple, a pixel value is selected according to the size suitable for arbitrary magnification by using a suitable pixel mask. This overcomes the limitations of existing algorithms by applying the k-neighborhood algorithm to deep learning. SRWarp [18] receives images warped by enlargement, reduction, distortion, etc., as input values. For the input image, the backbone extracts a feature map for each magnification ($\times 1$, $\times 2$, $\times 4$), and the adaptive warping layer predicts a transform function that can restore the feature map image to its original shape. Thereafter, multiscale blending combines the feature maps for each magnification, which are restored to a non-warping form, using the rich information possessed by each magnification ($\times 1$, $\times 2$, $\times 4$). Thus, SRWarp proposed a neural network that allows arbitrary magnification through the multiscale blending of an image. Wang et al. [19] proposed a plug-in module for existing super-resolution networks to perform arbitrary magnification, which consists of multiple scale-aware feature adaption blocks and a scale-aware upsampling layer. These methods have a lot of advantages, as shown in Table 2. However, these arbitrary magnification methods have shortcomings that cannot preserve the integer super-resolution performance. It is because these arbitrary magnification models replaced the upscale module of the existing integer magnification super-resolution models with the proposed arbitrary upscale module. Due to the replacement of the upscale module, the restoration capability of the integer magnification super-resolution model is not maintained, resulting in poor performance. There is a need for a method that preserves the performance of the integer magnification model as much as possible in the arbitrary magnification model and enables arbitrary magnification. Therefore, in order to maintain the performance of the model, this paper proposes a high-frequency attention network capable of arbitrary magnification without modifying the structure of the integer magnification model.

Table 2. Arbitrary magnification single image super-resolution methods' advantages and shortcomings.

Method	Advantages (Characteristics)	Shortcomings
Meta-SR	Upscales images with arbitrary scale factors through a single model.	Cannot preserve the integer super-resolution performance due to the replacement of the upscale module.
SRWarp	Uses a multiscale blending and handles numerous possible deformations.	Focuses on the warp of the image and is similar to Meta-SR performance.
Wang et al.'s	Uses multiple scale-aware feature adaption blocks and a scale-aware upsampling layer.	Needs additional training of integer super-resolution model due to the replacement of the existing module.

2.3. Frequency Domain Super-Resolution

Images can be transformed into various frequency domains, and studies have been conducted to predict various frequency information that can express high-resolution images through CNNs. Kumar et al. [20] proposed convolutional neural networks for wavelet domain super-resolution (CNNWSR) to predict wavelet coefficients of high-resolution images. The predicted wavelet coefficients are used to reconstruct a high-resolution image using a two-dimensional inverse discrete wavelet transform (DWT). Frequency domain neural network for fast image super-resolution (FNNSR) [21] and improved frequency domain neural networks super-resolution (IFNNSR) [22] solve the super-resolution problem in the Fourier domain. FNNSR formulated a neural network that parameterizes with pointwise multiplication in the spectral domain using a single convolutional layer to approximate the Rectified Linear Unit (ReLU) activation function. IFNNSR uses Hartley transform instead of Fourier transform and multiple convolutional layers to approximate the ReLU activation function well. It also emphasizes the error of high-frequency components by proposing a new weighted Euclidean loss. Aydin et al. [23] predict DCT coefficients that can reconstruct a high-resolution image through a fully connected (FC) layer in the DCT spectral domain after extending the input image to a target magnification through interpolation. The loss is defined as the mean square error with the DCT coefficient for the corresponding high-resolution image, which showed the possibility of CNN learning in the DCT spectral domain. These methods have a lot of advantages, as shown in Table 3. Although it is a super-resolution model that uses the frequency domain, it shows lower performance than other spatial domain super-resolution models despite the fast speed. It is because these frequency domain-based models do not properly consider spatial domain information. In this paper, frequency and spatial domain are used as a hybrid to utilize the advantages of each domain. In the frequency domain, a high-frequency component is extracted using the principle of the DCT spectral domain. In the spatial domain, an amplified high-frequency component can be obtained by using the extracted high-frequency component through a high-frequency attention network. These advantages can lead to excellent performance when performing arbitrary magnification.

Table 3. Frequency domain super-resolution methods' advantages and shortcomings.

Method	Advantages (Characteristics)	Shortcomings
CNNWSR	Predicts the wavelet coefficients of three images that can be used for image restoration.	Provide lower performance than other spatial domain super-resolution models despite the fast speed.
FNNSR	Applies Fourier transform to super-resolution and is faster than the alternatives.	
IFNNSR	Learns the basic features in transformed images.	
Aydin et al.'s	Predicts DCT coefficients and reconstruct an image in the DCT spectral domain.	

2.4. State-of-the-Art Task-Driven Arbitrary Magnification Super-Resolution

Previous studies on single image super-resolution cannot deal with arbitrary magnification super-resolution. To perform the arbitrary magnification super-resolution, it should be resized by interpolation after passing through the integer super-resolution network. However, these results do not show acceptable performance for each task. To deal with this, recent studies were conducted in each task by adapting arbitrary magnification super-resolution.

According to Zhu et al. [24], high-quality medical images with various resolutions are important in the current clinical process. To acquire magnetic resonance (MR) images for each magnification, they should scan each scale, as shown in Figure 2a. However, scanning all medical images with arbitrary magnifying factors requires enormous acquisition time and equipment constraints. On the other hand, as shown in Figure 2b, an arbitrary super-resolution model can upscale to various target resolutions while preserving the high image quality without multiple scans. Consequently, they devised an approach for medical image arbitrary-scale super-resolution (MIASSR), in which they combined a meta-learning method with GAN to super-resolve medical images at any scale of magnification.

According to Zhi et al. [25], it is a common requirement to zoom the image arbitrarily by rolling the mouse wheel, as shown in Figure 3. It can be used for identifying the object detail in the satellite image. To meet the requirement, they proposed arbitrary scale super-resolution (ASSR) that consists of a feature learning module and an arbitrary upscale module.

According to Truong et al. [26], a depth map allows for structural information to be utilized in various applications, such as view synthesis or 3D reconstruction. However, the resolution of depth maps is often much lower than the resolution of RGB images due to the limitations of depth sensors. To solve this problem, the low-resolution depth image can be upscaled to target resolution through the depth image super-resolution with arbitrary scale factors, as shown in Figure 4.

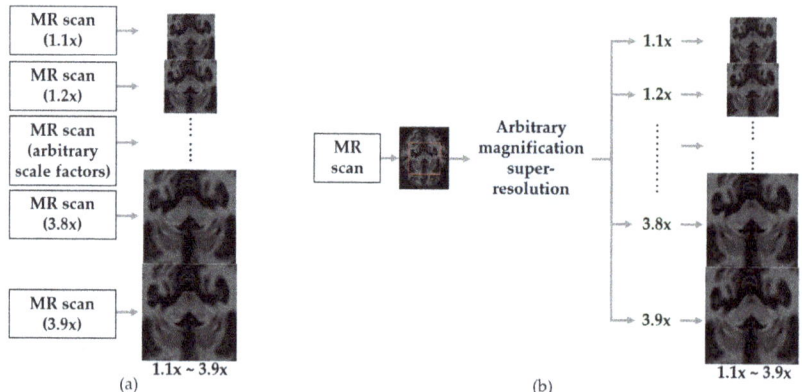

Figure 2. Example application of arbitrary magnification super-resolution in medical image processing task. (**a**) Conventional approach to obtain arbitrary magnification MR images. (**b**) Arbitrary magnification super-resolution approach to obtain arbitrary magnification MR images.

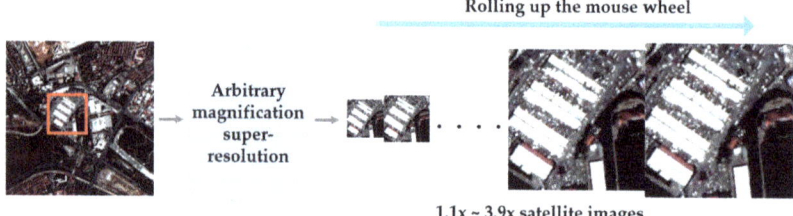

Figure 3. Example application of arbitrary magnification super-resolution in satellite image processing task.

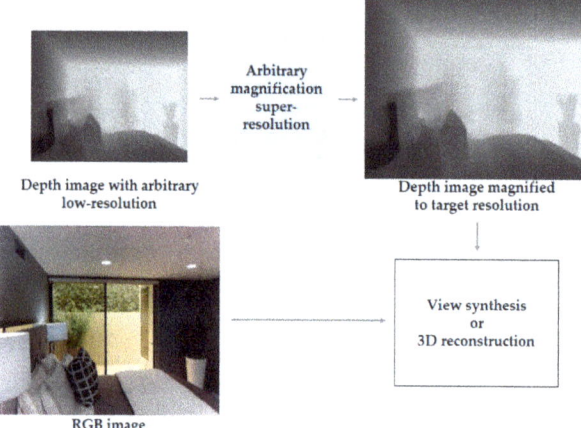

Figure 4. Example application of arbitrary magnification super-resolution in camera sensor depth image processing task.

Lee et al. [1] presented a high character recognition accuracy via integer magnification super-resolution in low-resolution conditions. However, in the real world, detected object areas may have arbitrary resolutions depending on the distance between the camera and the subject, as shown in Figure 5. It is mentioned that applying an arbitrary magnification in low-resolution conditions would provide a higher character recognition performance than applying bicubic interpolation.

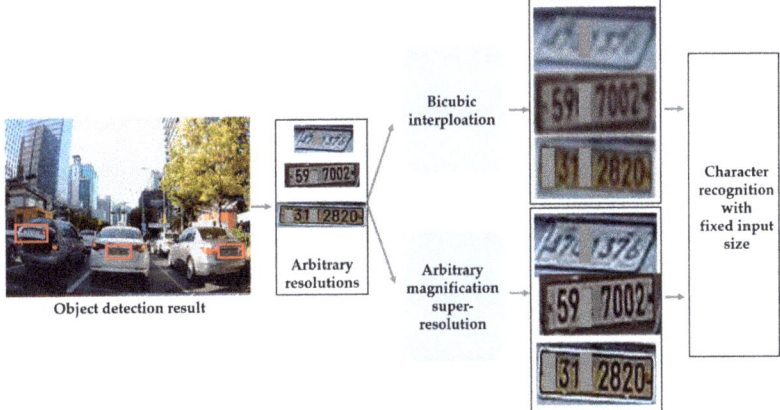

Figure 5. Example application of arbitrary magnification super-resolution in license plate character recognition task. One or two characters were masked due to privacy policies.

The above studies proposed arbitrary magnification super-resolution models to solve the limit of integer magnification and suggested the application of arbitrary magnification super-resolution. These studies also indicate that the arbitrary magnification super-resolution works well for the object recognition task, medical image processing, satellite image processing, depth image processing, and character recognition task. In conclusion, we note that arbitrary magnification super-resolution is required for various real-world tasks.

3. Proposed Method

This section describes the method proposed in this study for an arbitrary magnification super-resolution. In Section 3.1, the DCT overview is first described, the proposed hybrid-domain high-frequency attention network is described in Section 3.2, and the loss function defined in this network is described in Section 3.3.

3.1. Discrete Cosine Transform (DCT)

A spatial domain signal can be transformed into a spectral domain signal, and the converse also holds through. The most commonly used transform for this procedure is the discrete Fourier transform (DFT). In DFT, even if the input signal is a real number, the conversion result includes a complex number. A complex number can be calculated, but computational overhead is an issue. Therefore, DCT, which decomposes a signal into a cosine function and produces only real values from its spectral representation, is widely used in low-cost devices. A two-dimensional spatial domain discrete signal input of size $N \times M$ can be expressed in the frequency domain through DCT as given below.

$$\mathbf{F}(u,v) = \alpha(u)\beta(v) \sum_{x=0}^{N} \sum_{y=0}^{M} \mathbf{f}(x,y)\gamma(x,y,u,v) \qquad (1)$$

$$\gamma(x,y,u,v) = \cos\left(\frac{\pi(2x+1)u}{2N}\right)\cos\left(\frac{\pi(2y+1)v}{2M}\right) \qquad (2)$$

$$\alpha(u) = \begin{cases} \sqrt{\frac{1}{N}}, & u = 0 \\ \sqrt{\frac{2}{N}}, & u \neq 0 \end{cases} \quad (3)$$

$$\beta(v) = \begin{cases} \sqrt{\frac{1}{M}}, & v = 0 \\ \sqrt{\frac{2}{M}}, & v \neq 0 \end{cases} \quad (4)$$

$$\mathbf{f}(x,y) = \sum_{u=0}^{N} \sum_{v=0}^{M} \alpha(u)\beta(v)\mathbf{F}(u,v)\gamma(x,y,u,v) \quad (5)$$

In Equation (1), $\mathbf{f}(x,y)$ is the pixel value of the (x,y) position of the input image, and $\mathbf{F}(u,v)$ is the DCT coefficient value at the (u,v) position. Equations (2)–(4) show the definitions of the cosine basis function and regularization constant, respectively. In contrast, the signal transformed into the frequency domain can be transformed into the spatial domain using a two-dimensional inverse DCT (IDCT), as shown in Equation (5). Figure 6a shows a sample image and the results of the two-dimensional DCT on the image. It is easy to observe the frequency information of various components, although not intuitively because of the deformation of the spatial structure. Figure 6b shows the 64 8 × 8 cosine basis functions. After expanding the image space in the DCT spectrum domain, IDCT can be performed to generate the resulting image with the target size. In this case, when expanding the DCT spectrum, the image may be extended in the upper-left or lower-right direction. Because many low-frequency components are concentrated in the upper-left direction and high-frequency components are concentrated in the lower-right direction, depending on the area to be enlarged, the image has insufficient frequency information. The goal of image super-resolution is to improve a blurry image into a sharp image, which can be seen as restoring the high-frequency components that make the image sharp. In this study, we propose a hybrid-domain high-frequency attention network for arbitrary magnification super-resolution (H^2A^2-SR). First, we expand the image in the DCT spectrum domain to the target magnification. Second, frequency bands are divided according to hyperparameters to extract the high-frequency components. Finally, the high-frequency attention network restores the lost high-frequency.

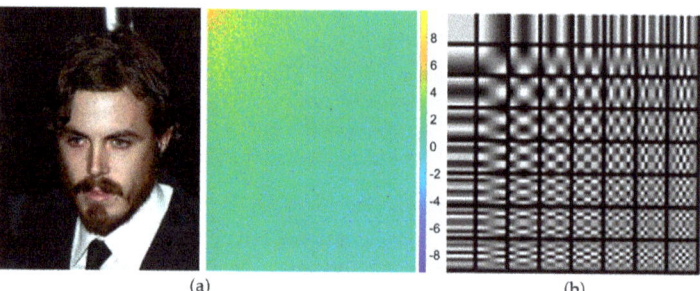

Figure 6. (a) 2D DCT example; (b) 8 × 8 cosine basis functions.

3.2. Hybrid-Domain High-Frequency Attention Network

In this section, the H^2A^2-SR framework is described. The architecture of the proposed model is shown in Figure 7. The low-resolution image received as input is magnified by an integer magnification close to the target magnification through the integer super-resolution network. For example, when the target magnification is ×2.5, the integer magnification network performs ×2 magnification, and when the target magnification is ×3.5, ×3 magnification is performed. The image magnified by an integer magnification was converted from the spatial domain to the spectral domain through DCT. We use the characteristics of DCT, in which the low-frequency in the upper left and the high frequency in the lower-right direction are concentrated and expand the spatial area by the residual decimal magnification in the lower-right direction. According to the principle that the spatial domain extended in the DCT spectrum has the same spatial size in the spatial domain, the resultant image adjusted to the target magnification can be obtained when it is re-converted to the spatial domain through IDCT. Because the high-frequency region is arbitrarily expanded, the image acquired through this process lacks high-frequency components. DCT follows the principle of energy conservation. When the image is expanded or reduced in the DCT domain, the brightness of the image is restored by multiplying it by the corresponding coefficient value. However, there is still a lack of high-frequency components. To overcome this problem, we designed a model that focuses on the accurate reconstruction of high-frequency components. The high-frequency attention network uses a channel attention layer that can learn the correlation between RGB channels to create high-frequency information and deepens the model through the residual learning structure. As shown in Figure 8, a block unit channel attention called the residual channel attention block (RCAB) [6] is configured. The proposed model is constructed by stacking five RCABs in layers, and residual learning is applied to each block to determine the correlation between each block.

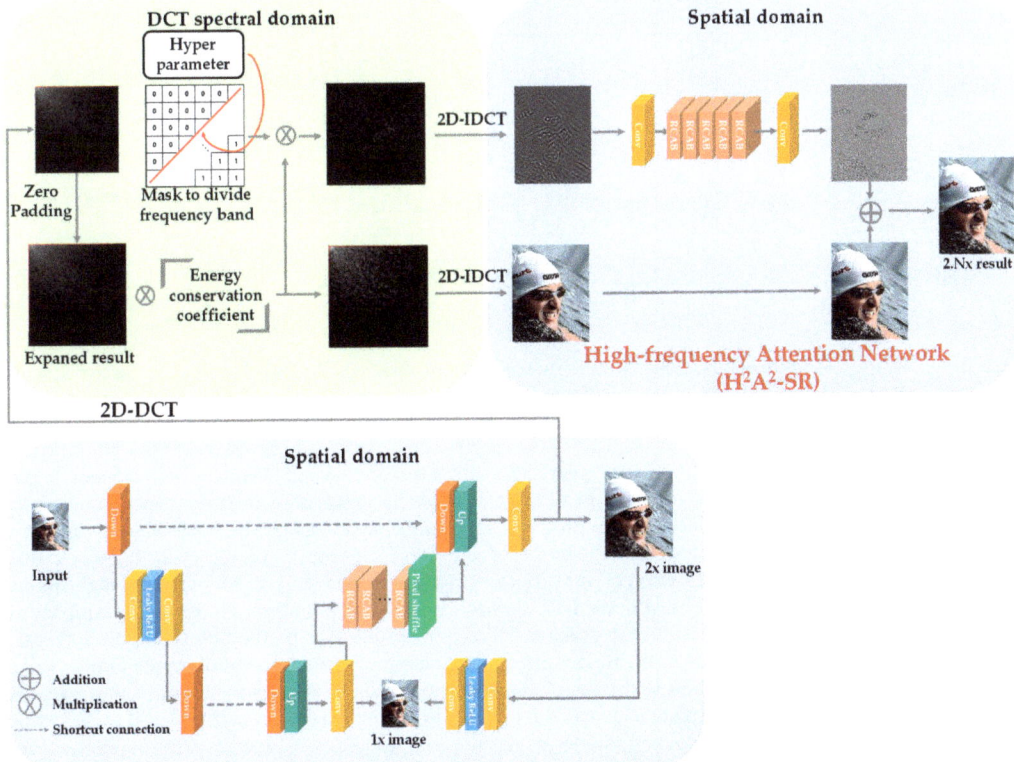

Figure 7. Overall organization of the proposed H^2A^2-SR model.

To focus the network on high-frequency reconstruction, we extract high frequencies by dividing the frequency domain according to the hyperparameters in the DCT domain. As shown in Figure 9a, **D** denotes the index of the zig-zag scan for 10 × 10 pixels. If the hyperparameter λ is set to 15, it is possible to extract high-frequency components except for components up to 15, as shown in Figure 9b. To this end, we determine a mask $\mathcal{M}$ by using λ as

$$\mathcal{M}(x,y) = \begin{cases} 0, & \mathbf{D}(x,y) \leq \lambda \\ 1, & \text{otherwise} \end{cases} \quad (6)$$

where x and y denote horizontal and vertical coordinates, respectively.

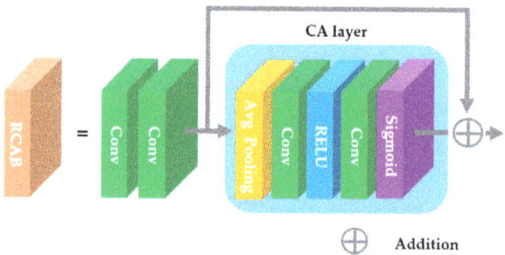

Figure 8. Configuration of RCAB [6] structure.

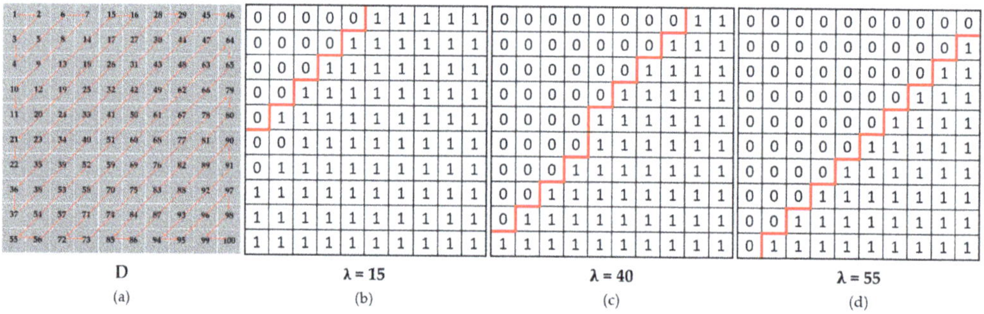

Figure 9. (a) Index of zig-zag scan for 10×10 pixels. (b) A mask obtained from the hyperparameter λ of 15. (c) A mask obtained from the hyperparameter λ of 40. (d) A mask obtained from the hyperparameter λ of 55.

Then, an image constructed with the extracted high-frequency components is passed through the network. In addition, to focus the network on high-frequency reconstructions, an expanded image with many low-frequency components is added to the result. The overall procedure of the proposed algorithm is also given in Algorithm 1. We note that the main contribution of our proposed method is not using RCAB but using high-frequency images obtained in the DCT domain as inputs to pass through the high-frequency attention network. In the existing arbitrary magnification method, the computation cost and the capacity of the model increase by passing the super-resolution neural network after magnification to the target magnification through the bicubic interpolation method. In addition, in actual use cases, all super-resolution networks must be trained at each arbitrary magnification and, therefore, require a large capacity of memory. In contrast, our model preserves the integer magnification performance by preserving its weight as it is and can achieve high-performance arbitrary magnification by adding a relatively small capacity network. In addition, unlike conventional methods of restoring the entire frequency band of an image at once, better performance can be achieved by intensively restoring a target high-frequency component.

Algorithm 1 H^2A^2-SR model

INPUT: low-resolution image (L), target magnification factor (s).
OUTPUT: arbitrary magnification image result (O).
Step 1: Obtain integer magnification image (I) from L by using the baseline SR model.
Step 2: Transform I into the DCT domain.
Step 3: Expand to residual decimal magnification ($r = s/(s - \text{floor}(s))$) in the DCT domain.
Step 4: Multiply the energy conservation factor (r^2) to the expanded image (E).
Step 5: Generate a mask (M) according to Equation (6).
Step 6: Multiply E and M for high-frequency (H) extraction.
Step 7: Convert E and H into the spatial domain through IDCT.
Step 8: Make H into 64 channels through the conv layer.
Step 9: Recover high-frequency (H_r) through 64 channels and 5 RCAB layers.
Step 10: Make H_r into 3 channels through the conv layer.
Step 11: Obtain O by adding E and the attention network's result.

3.3. Loss Function for High-Frequency Attention Network

In the proposed model, a loss function is L defined as in Equation (7) to restore the high-frequency component in the region extended by the DCT.

$$L = \frac{1}{N} \|\mathbf{F}_{H^2A^2-SR}(\mathbf{F}_{SR}(x^{lr})) - x^{hr}\|^2 \tag{7}$$

where N denotes the image batch size, $\mathbf{F}_{sr}(x^{lr})$ denotes a model that enlarges a low-resolution image by an integer magnification through a super-resolution network, and $\mathbf{F}_{H^2A^2-SR}$ denotes a residual decimal magnification model. A loss function for network learning is calculated using the mean square error between the arbitrary magnification super-resolution model results and the corresponding high-resolution image.

4. Experimental Results

4.1. Network Training

In traditional super-resolution learning, each patch unit is obtained from a low-resolution image, i.e., an input image, and a high-resolution image, i.e., a target image, and it is learned through comparison. For example, with respect to a 60 × 60 high-resolution patch, in the ×2 magnification model, a low-resolution input patch of 30 × 30 size was used, and network training was performed. However, performing an arbitrary magnification is an issue. If a pixel value is a decimal when performing an arbitrary magnification, a pixel shift phenomenon occurs as the decimal value is discarded from the image. Therefore, we have to cut the high-resolution image according to the arbitrary magnification and construct the low-resolution image individually. Because this is very time-consuming, we used the torch.nnf.interpolate function from Pytorch 1.8.0, an open-source machine learning library in Python, to create low-resolution images inside the code. We used PyTorch 1.8.0 to implement our model and use python 3.8.8, CUDA 11.2, and cuDNN 8.2.0. In addition, 2D-DCT and 2D-IDCT were implemented using the built-in functions of torch.fft.rfft and torch.fft.irfft, respectively. Our experiment was performed with AMD Ryzen 5 5600X 6-Core Processor CPU, 32GB memory, and NVIDIA RTX 3070 GPU. Our model was trained by Adam optimizer with $\beta_1 = 0.9$, $\beta_2 = 0.999$. β_1, β_2 denote exponential decay rates of the estimated moments, as the previous value is successively multiplied by the value less than 1 in each iteration. We set the training batch size to 16, the number of epochs to 200, and the learning rate to 10^{-4}. Note that the optimized values were determined experimentally.

4.2. Performance Comparison of Meta-SR and the Proposed Method

In this section, we compare the performance of the proposed H^2A^2-SR with Meta-SR, a model that can arbitrarily magnify images. Since Meta-SR can perform arbitrary magnification with a single weight, Meta-SR does not require training for each magnification factor. However, Meta-SR has limitations in image restoration performance because this method does not use a specialized weighting model according to the magnification factor. We note that there is a trade-off between weight capacity and image restoration performance. By focusing on improving image restoration performance, individual training for each magnification factor can be considered so that arbitrary magnification super-resolution models provide the optimized image restoration performance. Therefore, we trained the Meta-SR network and H^2A^2-SR for each magnification factor. We denote the Meta-SR network trained for each magnification factor as Meta-SR*. In addition, the results of the original Meta-SR that have a single weight are presented in Table 4 to compare it with H^2A^2-SR. Since a model that proceeds with integer magnification is required for an arbitrary magnification model, in this study, DRN is learned for $\times 2$ and $\times 3$ magnifications and used as an integer magnification model. The peak signal-to-noise ratio (PSNR) of the DRN $\times 2$ model was 35.87 dB, and the PSNR of the DRN $\times 3$ model was 32.22 dB. CelebA [27] was used as the dataset, with 40,920 and 5060 samples for training and validation, respectively. While Meta-SR selects pixel values according to the appropriate size for an arbitrary magnification from an image enlarged by an integer multiple, H^2A^2-SR concentrates the purpose of high-frequency restoration on the network to further enhance the edges and textures related to high-frequency components. It can be seen from the images in Figure 10 that the proposed model performs well on the dataset. We additionally present the expanded results in DCT to provide step-wise results of our method, as shown in Figure 10. It can be seen that H^2A^2-SR has less image noise than any other arbitrary magnification model. As shown in the enlarged image in Figure 10, the proposed model is restoring the eye area such as the eyelid, iris, and pupil more clearly. In addition, in the quantitative evaluation, H^2A^2-SR showed a higher PSNR value and a higher SSIM value than the existing method, as shown in Table 4. The inference time of our model was measured from $\times 2$ to 19 ms and $\times 3$ to 23 ms. The size of the image passed through the model is 178×218, and the input is an image reduced according to the corresponding magnification. At this time, the high-resolution image was cropped by 1 to 2 pixels depending on the scale.

Table 4. Comparison of the quantitative quality arbitrary super-resolution models in terms of PSNR (dB) and SSIM.

Method	Metric	PSNR (dB)/SSIM on CelebA with Arbitrary Scale Factors					
		$\times 2.2$	$\times 2.5$	$\times 2.8$	$\times 3.2$	$\times 3.5$	$\times 3.8$
DRN + Meta-SR	PSNR	29.02	31.37	31.33	27.51	28.14	28.00
	SSIM	0.7268	0.7665	0.7696	0.6494	0.6533	0.6437
DRN + Meta-SR*	PSNR	33.80	32.91	31.80	31.94	31.41	30.20
	SSIM	0.8462	0.8142	0.7787	0.7618	0.7487	0.7024
DRN + H^2A^2-SR (ours)	PSNR	**35.23**	**33.98**	**32.98**	**32.22**	**31.52**	**30.77**
	SSIM	**0.8766**	**0.8476**	**0.8201**	**0.7978**	**0.7788**	**0.7543**

Meta-SR* denotes the Meta-SR network trained for each magnification factor. The bold represents the best scores.

4.3. Performance Comparison of the Existing Arbitrary Magnification Method and the Proposed Method

For additional performance comparison with the existing arbitrary magnification methods, the experiment was conducted using the training dataset and the test dataset used in the existing arbitrary magnification method [17], as in the proposed method. The proposed network was trained using the DIV2K [28] dataset, and B100 [29] was used as the dataset for testing the trained model. To generate arbitrary magnification input images, it was reduced using bicubic interpolation n of torch.nnf for each arbitrary magnification. To compare with the existing state-of-the-art network capable of integer magnification, the input image was expanded to bicubic for decimal magnification, and the image for each arbitrary magnification was passed through our model without any modifications. For the arbitrary magnification model, the RDN model was set as the base model for an equal comparison. The PSNR of the RDN $\times 2$ model is 31.22 dB, and the PSNR of the RDN $\times 3$ model is 27.49 dB. The base model freezes training when learning arbitrary magnification weights. For reference, SRWarp could not be tested because the source code for the arbitrary magnification test is not currently available. Because there is no other arbitrary magnification model, we magnified the low-resolution image as an input to the state-of-the-art model in a bicubic format to match the magnification and used it as an input value. The PSNR of the HAN [30] ×2 model is 31.39 dB, and the PSNR of the HAN ×3 model is 27.70 dB. The PSNR of the SwinIR [14] ×2 model is 32.45 dB, and the PSNR of the SwinIR ×3 model is 29.39 dB. The PSNR of the CSNLN [16] ×2 model is 32.40 dB, and the PSNR of the CSNLN ×3 model is 29.34 dB. As can be seen in Table 5, even a small range in the image, such as ×2.2 and ×3.2 magnifications, is expanded, but the PSNR value is greatly lost. However, our proposed model is robust against scaling for decimal magnification, so it shows an advantage of approximately 1.5 dB in terms of average PSNR and 0.1013 in terms of average SSIM. Figure 11 also shows the comparison of the subjective visual quality on B100 for different scale factors. In Figure 11, red arrows were used to emphasize the improved part. We note in the figure that the proposed model outperforms the existing algorithms in many edge regions such as the whiskers, the window, the tree, and the statue.

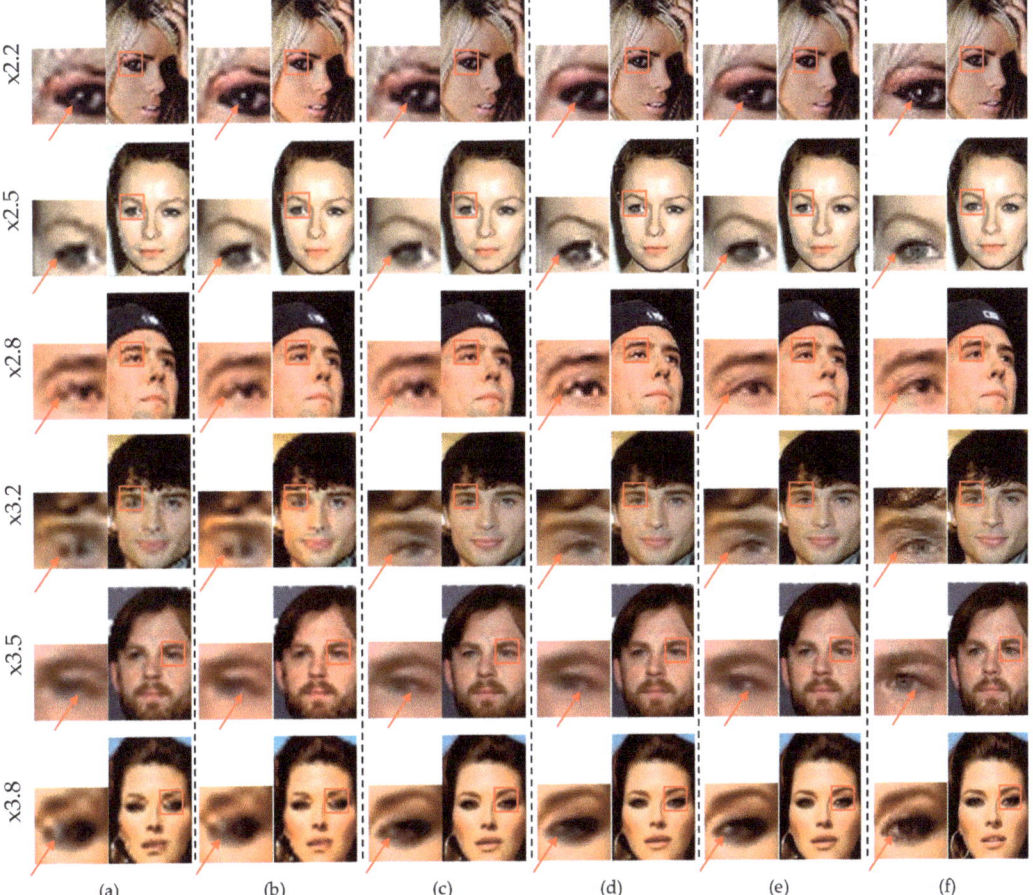

Figure 10. Comparison between our H²A²-SR results and Meta-SR results: (**a**) bicubic results; (**b**) DRN + Meta-SR results; (**c**) DRN + Meta-SR* results; (**d**) DRN + expanded results in DCT; (**e**) DRN + H²A²-SR results; (**f**) high-resolution image.

Table 5. Quantitative comparison of the state-of-the-art SR methods.

		PSNR (dB)/SSIM on B100 with Arbitrary Scale Factors					
Method	Metric	×2.2	×2.5	x2.8	×3.2	×3.5	×3.8
RDN + bicubic	PSNR	27.34	26.87	26.25	25.88	25.33	24.86
	SSIM	0.8087	0.7849	0.7586	0.7086	0.6906	0.6728
HAN + bicubic	PSNR	28.39	27.42	26.51	25.88	25.26	24.77
	SSIM	0.8180	0.7852	0.7563	0.7102	0.6914	0.6731
CSNLN + bicubic	PSNR	29.52	28.21	26.28	24.89	24.377	24.28
	SSIM	0.8471	0.8072	0.7221	0.6739	0.6639	0.6543
SwinIR + bicubic	PSNR	28.50	27.28	26.75	25.86	25.40	24.47
	SSIM	0.8162	0.7954	**0.7866**	0.6973	0.6961	0.6639
RDN + Meta-SR*	PSNR	28.51	28.19	27.41	27.01	26.50	25.95
	SSIM	0.8262	0.8063	0.7801	0.7530	0.7315	0.7075
RDN + H^2A^2-SR	PSNR	**29.52**	**28.31**	**27.63**	**27.34**	**26.81**	**26.32**
	SSIM	**0.8473**	**0.8097**	0.7819	**0.7638**	**0.7433**	**0.7237**

Meta-SR* denotes the Meta-SR network trained for each magnification factor. The bold represents the best scores.

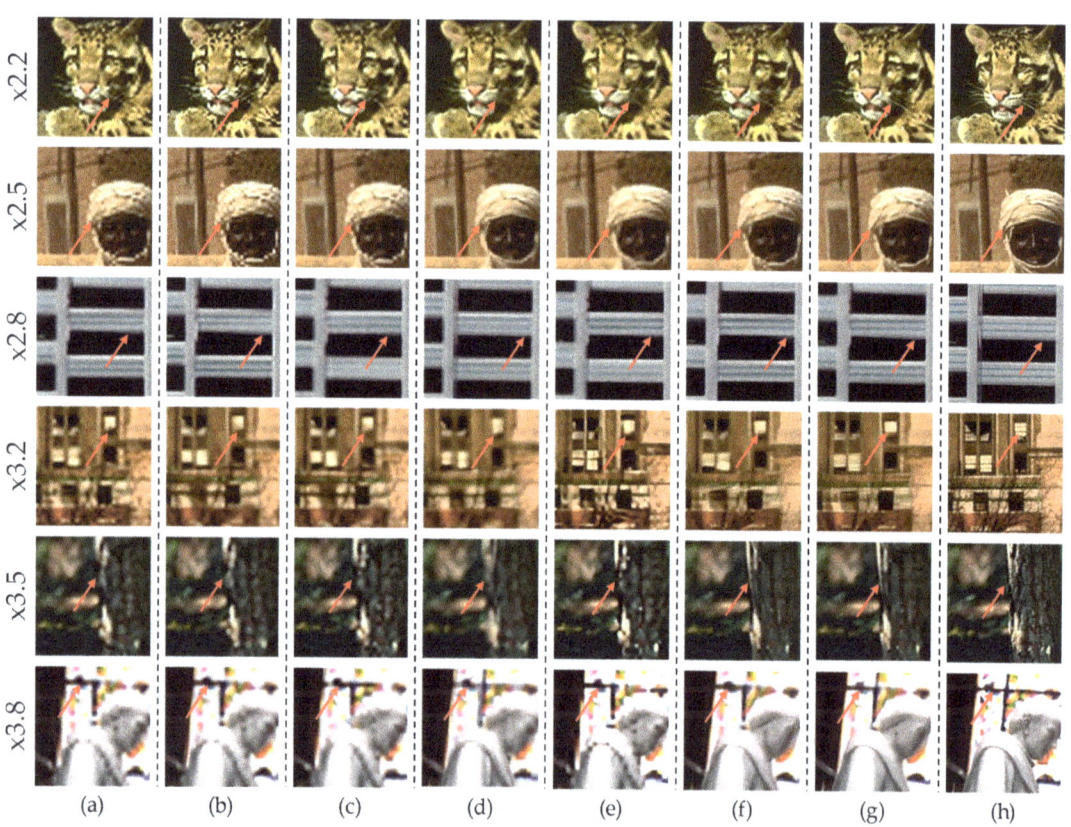

Figure 11. Super-resolution reconstruction results: (**a**) bicubic results; (**b**) RDN results; (**c**) HAN results; (**d**) SwinIR results; (**e**) CSNLN results; (**f**) RDN + META-SR results; (**g**) RDN + H^2A^2-SR results; (**h**) high-resolution images.

4.4. Ablation Study

For the ablation study, we compare the network with H^2A^2-SR and without H^2A^2-SR. In Table 6, it can be seen H^2A^2-SR is effective as much as 4.5 dB and as low as 0.6 dB. In

Figure 12, the results are numbered step-by-step inside the model for a better understanding. Figure 13 shows the results of the step-by-step images. Step 1 refers to an image using the base SR model for integer magnification. Step 2 is the result of multiplying the integer magnification image by the energy conservation factor after extending it to the target magnification in the DCT spectral domain. In the Step 2 image of Figure 13, it can be seen that the image is well expanded to the target magnification by multiplying the energy conservation coefficient. However, it can also be seen that the expression of textures or lines, which are high-frequency components, is insufficient owing to excessive expansion. Step 3 extracts high-frequency components from the result of step 2 with a mask generated through a hyperparameter. Step 4 is the result of the high-frequency components extracted in Step 3 through the high-frequency attention network. As shown in the Step 4 image of Figure 13, it can be seen that our network effectively reconstructs the high-frequency components of lines and textures well. In Step 5, by adding the results of Steps 4 and 2, the model is used to reconstruct the high-frequency component well. It can be seen that the jagged between the swimming cap and the face is eliminated, and the arbitrary magnification is clear by effectively removing the noise around the logo of the swimming cap. It can be seen that our H^2A^2-SR is effective not only at arbitrary magnification but also in making the image clearer by restoring high-frequency components well.

Meanwhile, our method may have limitations. First, since our model is an add-on algorithm, it depends on the performance of the adopted integer super-resolution model. Therefore, it is important to adopt the appropriate integer super-resolution model. Second, our H^2A^2-SR model requires the training process for each magnification to obtain better image restoration performance. Therefore, our model needs memory capacity for storing weights for each decimal magnification factor in practical applications. We note that there is a trade-off between weight capacity and image restoration performance. To address this trade-off issue, optimization techniques such as network weight compression or weight sharing can be further applied.

Table 6. Quantitative comparison between our H^2A^2-SR with and without high-frequency attention model.

	PSNR (dB) on CelebA with Arbitrary Scale Factors						
Method	Metric	×2.2	×2.5	×2.8	×3.2	×3.5	×3.8
Without high-frequency attention model	PSNR	30.89	29.62	28.48	31.73	30.90	30.15
DRN + H^2A^2-SR (ours)	PSNR	**35.23**	**33.98**	**32.98**	**32.22**	**31.52**	**30.77**

The bold represents the best scores.

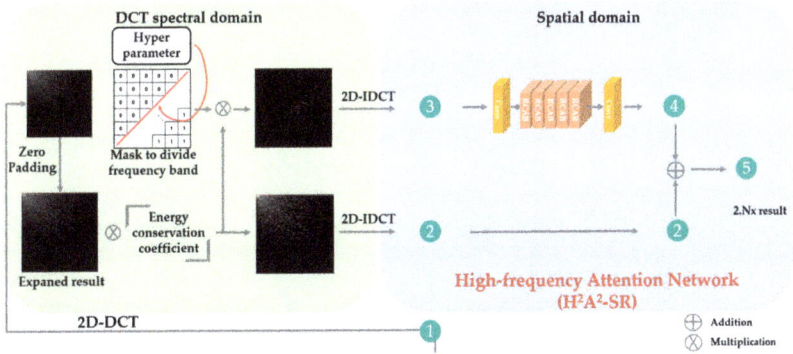

Figure 12. Flowchart of H^2A^2-SR's steps. Each number represents a step in H^2A^2-SR.

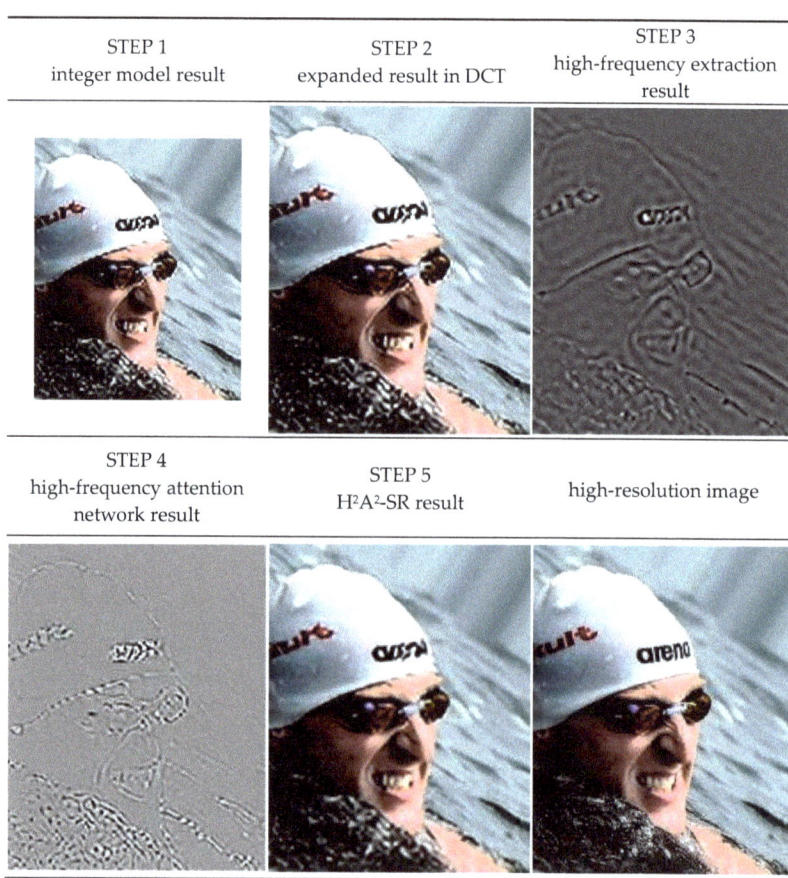

Figure 13. Result examples of H^2A^2-SR's steps.

5. Conclusions

In this paper, we propose an arbitrary magnification super-resolution method to reconstruct high-frequency components using spatial and spectral hybrid domains. Through spatial expansion in the DCT spectral domain, an image can be flexibly expanded to a target resolution, and it is restored through a high-frequency attention network that supplements the insufficient high-frequency components of the expanded image. Thus, the accuracy of the existing integer magnification super-resolution model is preserved even at arbitrary magnification, and high-performance decimal magnification results can be obtained by adding the proposed arbitrary magnification model without modifying or re-learning the existing model. Experimental results show that the proposed method has excellent restoration performance, both quantitatively and qualitatively, compared to the existing arbitrary magnification super-resolution methods. As a future study, it will be possible to lighten the network by appropriately combining the weight sharing method between integer multipliers and the knowledge distillation technique. In addition, research to improve the object recognition rate for low-resolution images by integrating an arbitrary magnification super-resolution network and an object recognition network can be conducted.

Author Contributions: Conceptualization, S.-B.Y.; methodology, J.-S.Y. and S.-B.Y.; software, J.-S.Y.; validation, J.-S.Y.; formal analysis, J.-S.Y. and S.-B.Y.; investigation, J.-S.Y. and S.-B.Y.; resources, J.-S.Y. and S.-B.Y.; data curation, J.-S.Y. and S.-B.Y.; writing—original draft preparation, J.-S.Y. and S.-B.Y.; writing—review and editing, J.-S.Y. and S.-B.Y.; visualization, S.-B.Y.; supervision, S.-B.Y.; project administration, S.-B.Y.; funding acquisition, S.-B.Y. All authors have read and agreed to the published version of the manuscript.

Funding: This work was supported by the Institute of Information & Communications Technology Planning & Evaluation (IITP) grant funded by the Korea government (MSIT) (No.2020-0-00004, Development of Previsional Intelligence based on Long-term Visual Memory Network, 2022-0-02068, Artificial Intelligence Innovation Hub) and the National Research Foundation of Korea (NRF) grant funded by the Korea government (MSIT) (NRF-2020R1A4A1019191).

Institutional Review Board Statement: Not applicable.

Informed Consent Statement: Not applicable.

Data Availability Statement: Not applicable.

Conflicts of Interest: The authors declare no conflict of interest.

References

1. Lee, S.-J.; Yoo, S.B. Super-resolved recognition of license plate characters. *Mathematics* **2021**, *9*, 2494. [CrossRef]
2. Dong, C.; Loy, C.C.; Tang, X. Accelerating the super-resolution convolutional neural network. In Proceedings of the European Conference on Computer Vision, Amsterdam, The Netherlands, 8–16 October 2016; pp. 391–407.
3. Kim, J.W.; Lee, J.K.; Lee, K.M. Accurate image super-resolution using very deep convolutional networks. In Proceedings of the IEEE Conference on Computer Vision and Pattern Recognition, Las Vegas, NV, USA, 27–30 June 2016; pp. 1646–1654.
4. Shi, W.; Caballero, J.; Huszár, F.; Totz, J.; Aitken, A.P.; Bishop, R.; Rueckert, D.; Wang, Z. Real-time single image and video super-resolution using an efficient sub-pixel convolutional neural networks. In Proceedings of the IEEE Conference on Computer Vision and Pattern Recognition, Las Vegas, NV, USA, 27–30 June 2016; pp. 1874–1883.
5. Haris, M.; Shakhnarovich, G.; Ukita, N. Deep back-projection networks for super-resolution. In Proceedings of the IEEE Conference on Computer Vision and Pattern Recognition, Salt Lake City, UT, USA, 18–22 June 2018; pp. 1664–1673.
6. Zhang, Y.; Li, K.; Li, K.; Wang, L.; Zhong, B.; Fu, Y. Image super-resolution using very deep residual channel attention networks. In Proceedings of the European Conference on Computer Vision, Munich, Germany, 8–14 September 2018; pp. 286–301.
7. Guo, Y.; Chen, J.; Wang, J.; Chen, Q.; Cao, J.; Deng, Z.; Xu, Y.; Tan, M. Closed-loop matters: Dual regression networks for single image super-resolution. In Proceedings of the IEEE Conference on Computer Vision and Pattern Recognition, Seattle, WA, USA, 14–19 June 2020; pp. 5407–5416.
8. Zhang, Y.; Tian, Y.; Kong, Y.; Zhong, B.; Fu, Y. Residual dense network for image super-resolution. In Proceedings of the IEEE Conference on Computer Vision and Pattern Recognition, Salt Lake City, UT, USA, 18–22 June 2018; pp. 2472–2481.
9. Dai, T.; Cai, J.; Zhang, Y.; Xia, S.T.; Zhang, L. Second-order attention network for single image super-resolution. In Proceedings of the IEEE Conference on Computer Vision and Pattern Recognition, Long Beach, CA, USA, 16–20 June 2019; pp. 11065–11074.
10. Ledig, C.; Theis, L.; Huszar, F.; Caballero, J.; Cunningham, A.; Acosta, A.; Aitken, A.; Tejani, A.; Totz, J.; Wang, Z. Photo-realistic single image super-resolution using a generative adversarial network. In Proceedings of the IEEE Conference on Computer Vision and Pattern Recognition Workshops, Honolulu, HI, USA, 21–26 July 2017; pp. 4681–4690.
11. Lugmayr, A.; Danelljan, M.; Gool, L.V.; Timofte, R. Srflow: Learning the super-resolution space with normalizing flow. In Proceedings of the IEEE Conference on Computer Vision and Pattern Recognition, Seattle, WA, USA, 14–19 June 2020; pp. 715–732.
12. Jo, Y.H.; Yang, S.J.; Kim, S.J. Srflow-da: Super-resolution using normalizing flow with deep convolutional block. In Proceedings of the IEEE Conference on Computer Vision and Pattern Recognition Workshops, Nashville, TN, USA, 19–25 June 2021; pp. 364–372.
13. Kim, Y.G.; Son, D.H. Noise conditional flow model for learning the super-resolution. In Proceedings of the IEEE Conference on Computer Vision and Pattern Recognition Workshops, Nashville, TN, USA, 19–25 June 2021; pp. 424–432.
14. Liang, J.; Cao, J.; Sun, G.; Zhang, K.; Van, G.; Timofte, R. SwinIR: Image restoration using swin transformer. In Proceedings of the IEEE International Conference on Computer Vision, Montréal, QC, Canada, 11–17 October 2021; pp. 1833–1844.
15. Liu, Z.; Lin, Y.; Cao, Y.; Hu, H.; Wei, Y.; Zhang, Z.; Stephen, L.; Guo, B. Swin Transformer: Hierarchical Vision Transformer Using Shifted Windows. *arXiv* **2021**, arXiv:2103.14030. Available online: https://arxiv.org/abs/2103.14030 (accessed on 6 November 2021).
16. Mei, Y.; Fan, Y.; Zhou, Y.; Huang, L.; Huang, T.S.; Shi, H. Image super-resolution with cross-scale non-local attention and exhaustive self-exemplars mining. In Proceedings of the IEEE Conference on Computer Vision and Pattern Recognition, Seattle, WA, USA, 14–19 June 2020; pp. 5690–5699.
17. Hu, X.; Mu, H.; Zhang, X.; Wang, Z.; Tan, T.; Sun, J. Meta-SR: A magnification-arbitrary network for super-resolution. In Proceedings of the IEEE Conference on Computer Vision and Pattern Recognition, Long Beach, CA, USA, 16–20 June 2019; pp. 1575–1584.

18. Son, S.H.; Lee, K.M. SRWarp: Generalized image super-resolution under arbitrary transformation. In Proceedings of the IEEE Conference on Computer Vision and Pattern Recognition, Nashville, TN, USA, 19–25 June 2021; pp. 7782–7791.
19. Wang, L.; Wang, Y.; Lin, Z.; Yang, J.; An, W.; Guo, Y. Learning a single network for scale-arbitrary super-resolution. In Proceedings of the IEEE International Conference on Computer Vision, Montréal, QC, Canada, 11–17 October 2021; pp. 4801–4810.
20. Kumar, N.; Verma, R.; Sethi, A. Convolutional neural networks for wavelet domain super resolution. *Pattern Recognit. Lett.* **2017**, *90*, 65–71. [CrossRef]
21. Li, J.; You, S.; Kelly, A.R. A frequency domain neural network for fast image super-resolution. In Proceedings of the International Joint Conference on Neural Networks, Rio de Janeiro, Brazil, 8–13 July 2018; pp. 1–8.
22. Xue, S.; Qiu, W.; Liu, F.; Jin, X. Faster image super-resolution by improved frequency-domain neural networks. *Signal Image Video Process.* **2019**, *14*, 257–265. [CrossRef]
23. Aydin, O.; Cinbiş, R.G. Single-image super-resolution analysis in DCT spectral domain. *Balk. J. Electr. Comput. Eng.* **2020**, *8*, 209–217. [CrossRef]
24. Zhu, J.; Tan, C.; Yang, J.; Yang, G.; Lio, P. Arbitrary Scale Super-Resolution for Medical Images. *Int. J. Neural Syst.* **2021**, *31*, 2150037. [CrossRef] [PubMed]
25. He, Z.; He, D. A unified network for arbitrary scale super-resolution of video satellite images. *IEEE Trans. Geosci. Remote Sens.* **2020**, *59*, 8812–8825. [CrossRef]
26. Truong, A.M.; Philips, W.; Veelaert, P. Depth Completion and Super-Resolution with Arbitrary Scale Factors for Indoor Scenes. *Sensors* **2021**, *21*, 4892. [CrossRef] [PubMed]
27. Liu, Z.; Luo, P.; Wang, X.; Tang, X. Large-Scale CelebFaces Attributes (CelebA) Dataset. p. 11. Available online: https://mmlab.ie.cuhk.edu.hk/projects/CelebA.html (accessed on 15 August 2018).
28. Timofte, R.; Agustsson, E.; Gool, L.V.; Yang, M.H.; Zhang, L.; Lim, B.; Son, S.; Kim, H.; Nah, S.; Lee, K.M. Ntire 2017 challenge on single image super-resolution: Methods and results. In Proceedings of the IEEE Conference on Computer Vision and Pattern Recognition Workshops, Honolulu, HI, USA, 21–26 July 2017; pp. 114–125.
29. Martin, D.; Fowlkes, C.; Tal, D.; Malik, J. A database of human segmented natural images and its application to evaluating segmentation algorithms and measuring ecological statistics. In Proceedings of the Eighth IEEE International Conference on Computer Vision, Vancouver, BC, Canada, 7–14 July 2001; pp. 416–423.
30. Niu, B.; Wen, W.; Ren, W.; Zhang, X.; Yang, L.; Wang, S.; Zhang, K.; Cao, X.; Shen, H. Single image super-resolution via a holistic attention network. In Proceedings of the European Conference on Computer Vision, Glasgow, Scotland, 23–28 August 2020; pp. 191–207.

Article

Enhanced Convolutional Neural Network Model for Cassava Leaf Disease Identification and Classification

Umesh Kumar Lilhore [1], Agbotiname Lucky Imoize [2,3], Cheng-Chi Lee [4,5,*], Sarita Simaiya [1], Subhendu Kumar Pani [6], Nitin Goyal [1], Arun Kumar [7] and Chun-Ta Li [8]

1. Chitkara University Institute of Engineering and Technology, Chitkara University, Rajpura 140401, India; umesh.lilhore@chitkara.edu.in (U.K.L.); sarita.simaiya@chitkara.edu.in (S.S.); nitin.goyal@chitkara.edu.in (N.G.)
2. Department of Electrical and Electronics Engineering, Faculty of Engineering, University of Lagos, Akoka, Lagos 100213, Nigeria; aimoize@unilag.edu.ng
3. Department of Electrical Engineering and Information Technology, Institute of Digital Communication, Ruhr University, 44801 Bochum, Germany
4. Research and Development Center for Physical Education, Health, and Information Technology, Department of Library and Information Science, Fu Jen Catholic Univesity, New Taipei 24205, Taiwan
5. Department of Computer Science and Information Engineering, Asia University, Taichung 41354, Taiwan
6. Krupajal Engineering College, Biju Patnaik University of Technology (BPUT), Rourkela 751002, India; pani.subhendu@gmail.com
7. Panipat Institute of Engineering and Technology, Panipat, Samalkha 132102, India; ranaarun1.ece@piet.co.in
8. Department of Information Management, Tainan University of Technology, 529 Zhongzheng Road, Tainan 710302, Taiwan; th0040@mail.tut.edu.tw
* Correspondence: cclee@mail.fju.edu.tw

Abstract: Cassava is a crucial food and nutrition security crop cultivated by small-scale farmers and it can survive in a brutal environment. It is a significant source of carbohydrates in African countries. Sometimes, Cassava crops can be infected by leaf diseases, affecting the overall production and reducing farmers' income. The existing Cassava disease research encounters several challenges, such as poor detection rate, higher processing time, and poor accuracy. This research provides a comprehensive learning strategy for real-time Cassava leaf disease identification based on enhanced CNN models (ECNN). The existing Standard CNN model utilizes extensive data processing features, increasing the computational overhead. A depth-wise separable convolution layer is utilized to resolve CNN issues in the proposed ECNN model. This feature minimizes the feature count and computational overhead. The proposed ECNN model utilizes a distinct block processing feature to process the imbalanced images. To resolve the color segregation issue, the proposed ECNN model uses a Gamma correction feature. To decrease the variable selection process and increase the computational efficiency, the proposed ECNN model uses global average election polling with batch normalization. An experimental analysis is performed over an online Cassava image dataset containing 6256 images of Cassava leaves with five disease classes. The dataset classes are as follows: class 0: "Cassava Bacterial Blight (CBB)"; class 1: "Cassava Brown Streak Disease (CBSD)"; class 2: "Cassava Green Mottle (CGM)"; class 3: "Cassava Mosaic Disease (CMD)"; and class 4: "Healthy". Various performance measuring parameters, i.e., precision, recall, measure, and accuracy, are calculated for existing Standard CNN and the proposed ECNN model. The proposed ECNN classifier significantly outperforms and achieves 99.3% accuracy for the balanced dataset. The test findings prove that applying a balanced database of images improves classification performance.

Keywords: convolutional neural network model; ECNN; deep neural network; cassava leaf disease identification; global average election polling layer

Citation: Lilhore, U.K.; Imoize, A.L.; Lee, C.-C.; Simaiya, S.; Pani, S.K.; Goyal, N.; Kumar, A.; Li, C.-T. Enhanced Convolutional Neural Network Model for Cassava Leaf Disease Identification and Classification. *Mathematics* **2022**, *10*, 580. https://doi.org/10.3390/math10040580

Academic Editors: Ezequiel López-Rubio, Esteban Palomo and Enrique Domínguez

Received: 17 January 2022
Accepted: 11 February 2022
Published: 13 February 2022

Publisher's Note: MDPI stays neutral with regard to jurisdictional claims in published maps and institutional affiliations.

Copyright: © 2022 by the authors. Licensee MDPI, Basel, Switzerland. This article is an open access article distributed under the terms and conditions of the Creative Commons Attribution (CC BY) license (https://creativecommons.org/licenses/by/4.0/).

1. Introduction

Cassava is the main crop in Africa and many other nations. Africa is the largest producer of Cassava crops. Cassava can be cultivated successfully in any climate, including drought and unproductive soil. Cassava crops encounter several challenges during production, i.e., leaf diseases and poor quality. Cassava leaf diseases are the principal cause of production reduction, and they can directly affect farmers' revenue [1].

Cassava leaf disease identification must be treated on a priority basis to improve production capacity. The automatic detection of crop diseases focused on crop leaves is critical in crop production. Furthermore, effective and accurate detection of leaf diseases significantly affects crop productivity improvement. Cassava leaf diseases are similar to Maize leaf diseases [2].

Early recognition of leaf disease facilitates the rescue of cultivars well before the plant can be infected permanently [3]. A few researchers focused on building fusion plants resistant to pathogenic organisms and created a system to recognize and anticipate crop disease formation from leaf images [4].

Farm owners can significantly raise farm yields by using smart farming. Farmers spend a lot of time, money, and effort in the manual identification of plant diseases, and the results are still inaccurate. Research [5] has developed an intelligent system based on image classification and deep-learning methods.

A deep-learning and machine-learning-based model is discussed in research [6] for leaf disease detection. The automated machine-learning model for detecting and treating Cassava crop diseases enables farmers and experts to increase system throughput and accuracy. Deep-learning-based CNN classifiers can enhance leaf disease detection in all the possible situations where image-based diagnostics with advanced training are involved. Various portable devices are also used in leaf disease detection.

In all the instances where an intelligent classifier is installed on portable devices and contains a novel disease, datasets can enhance detection accuracy. Portable devices, i.e., smartphones, drones, and laptops, can be easily tested in realistic scenarios [7].

Researchers have considered various novel techniques to resolve leaf disease detection issues, i.e., image classification, AI, machine learning, and deep learning [8]. Data pre-processing is an essential phase in image analysis, which includes various processes, i.e., image optimization, color adjustment, reshaping, and feature extraction. An image classification method must be applied with an image enhancement technique for better outcomes [9].

A hybrid deep-learning and image-classification-based model for leaf disease detection is discussed in [10]. However, these existing research works have several challenges, which need immediate attention. This motivates researchers to work on Cassava leaf disease detection [11]. These factors also encourage researchers to develop a more robust and reliable Cassava leaf disease detection system.

This research aims to fill the gaps by presenting a better overview of leaf disease detection and analysis in Cassava plants. This research provides a comprehensive learning strategy for real-time Cassava leaf disease identification based on enhanced CNN models (ECNN). The main contributions of this research are as follows:

- This research presents a complete overview of Cassava leaf diseases.
- This research presents a detailed overview of the CNN model and describes how the CNN model can improve Cassava leaf disease detection.
- The existing Standard CNN models [12] utilize a complex set of features and a massive computational overhead. To overcome these issues, in the proposed model, we upgraded the traditional convolution network model by adding new features.
- The proposed ECNN model utilizes a depth-wise separable convolution, which minimizes the feature count and computational overhead.
- The proposed ECNN also utilizes a distinct block processing feature to process imbalanced images.

- Furthermore, the proposed ECNN model utilizes de-correlation stretching with Gamma correction. It enhances the image color segregation feature and provides a higher band-to-band correlation.
- The proposed model utilizes a global average election polling layer to replace the fully connected layer to decrease the number of variables. After that, ECNN utilizes a batch normalization layer that enhances the overall computational efficiency [13].
- The proposed ECNN method is validated by calculating the standard performance measuring parameters, and the results are compared with the existing Standard CNN method.

The research article is organized as follows. Section 1 covers introductory work related to the research; Section 2 covers related positions in Cassava leaf disease identification and classification. Next, Section 3 covers materials and methods related to research. Section 4 covers the proposed ECNN model's implementation, results, and discussion. Section 5 covers the conclusion and future work.

2. Related Work

Cassava is the most popular commercial and industrial crop in Africa and Thailand. Due to the apparent pleasant environment and soil, it is primarily produced in these countries. Cassava crop encounters several issues, i.e., leaf disease and fungal infection, thus reducing production and increasing cost. Early and accurate detection of Cassava leaf disease is a promising research area for researchers. Various research articles suggest different methods and models to improve Cassava leaf disease detection. Existing research has also tried to determine effective methods for improving Cassava crop production. This section covers the existing research on Cassava leaf disease detection.

2.1. Machine Learning Based

ResNet-50- and SVM-classifier-based Cassava leaf disease model is presented in [14]. The proposed model first extracts all the relevant features and then classifies the image dataset using an SVM classifier in the next phase. The outcomes show better accuracy and performance by incorporating ResNet-50 and SVM classifiers.

A digital image processing model uses a hybrid transfer learning method [15]. It is crucial to perform correct data preparation in leaf disease research. This improves plant disease pattern recognition, forecasting, and model performance.

A hybrid model based on SVM and RF for Cassava leaf disease detection is presented in [16]. The proposed model utilizes multiple feature selection processes, including selecting image type, association in parameters, quality, and uniformity. The proposed classification model achieved more than 90% accuracy compared to the existing model.

The SVM and Naive Bayes machine-learning-based model is presented in [17] to detect plant diseases. The researcher suggested that a massive data history and machine-learning methods play an essential role in plant disease analysis. The machine-learning method [18] provides a valuable contribution to evaluate a considerable volume of leaf image data. Another research [19] presented a deep-learning-based model with ImageNet for Cassava leaf disease detection.

2.2. Leaf Shape, Colour, and Texture Based

Leaf disease detection based on leaf properties is discussed in research [20]. The proposed model utilized complex geometries and segmentation-based methods for feature extraction. After feature extraction, the SVM classification method was applied to classify leaf diseases. A shape- and texture-based classification for Cassava leaf disease identification is discussed in research [21]. The proposed model achieved more than 84% accuracy and 88% detection rate.

A region-based detection method is discussed in research [22]. This work mainly focused on retrieving Cassava leaf properties using a cluster center method. A bacterial and viral infection detection algorithm is introduced in research [23]. The proposed method first detects leaf image texture and shape features, enhancing disease classification outcomes and improving overall precision and accuracy.

An innovative procedure for categorizing plant leaf disease is discussed in research [24]. Often, these plants have distinctive leaves that vary by features, such as margin, color, shape, and texture. A shape-, color-, and texture-based leaf disease classification are discussed in research [25]. This research classified diseases using combinations of two and more characteristics, such as shape, size, color, and texture. In the proposed method, a shape-based technique first extracts the curve receipt using leaf stem and afterward determines the inconsistencies using a Jeffrey divergence estimate method. Leaf disease detection based on computer vision and leaf feature analysis method was discussed in research [26].

2.3. Neural Network Based

A deep-learning-based model to analyze Cassava leaf diseases is presented in research [27]. This proposed model firstly performs a subdivision method and later applies a classification approach to diagnose Cassava leaf disease. GoogleNet- and AlexNet-based convolutional neural network structures were discussed in research [28] to analyze and identify distinct CNN leaf diseases.

A neural-network-based Cassava leaf disease prediction model is described in research [29]. This research utilizes various neural network models on different crops to analyze diseases and infections. Experimental results show the strength of the proposed model through higher recognition rates. A deep-learning-based model is described in research [30] to predict leaf disease. This research utilizes a feature selection method to recognize thirteen particular crop diseases. Researchers have trained CNN architecture by utilizing the Caffe deep-learning approach.

An improved deep-learning-based model is described in research [31] to predict leaf disease classification. This research work also covers the limitation of existing works. A nine-layer-based convolutional neural network model is presented in [32] to characterize Cassava diseases in plants.

A NASNet-based fully convolutional architecture is described in research [33]. This model applied a feature selection model to recognize fungal leaf infection. The proposed model achieved an accuracy rate of 94.1% compared to an existing model. A superficial CNN model is presented in research [34] to identify and characterize plant leaf diseases. In the initial phase, researchers retrieved the leaf features using the feature extraction method and then categorized them using a feature selection method with random forest classification methods.

2.4. Comparative Analysis

Table 1 represents the comparative analysis of various existing methods used in plant leaf disease detection and analysis.

Table 1. A Comparative Analysis of Various Existing Research Works.

Reference	Dataset	Technique/Model	Outcomes
[35]	Online Cassava Leaf disease dataset	DRN (Deep Residual Neural) Network	Precision 94.24% and AUC 90.1%
[36]	Online Cassava Leaf disease dataset	Random Forest, SVM and SCNN (Shallow CNN)	Detection rate 91.7% and Time 89.6%
[37]	Online Cassava Leaf disease dataset	9-Layered CNN Model	Accuracy 90.48%
[38]	Online Cassava Leaf disease dataset	FR-CNN (Faster Recurrence CNN)	Specificity rate 77.8%, Precision rate 91.8%, and Sensitivity rate 73.26%
[39]	Online Cassava Leaf disease dataset	SSD (Single Sot Multi-box Method)	Precision rate 90.8%

Table 1. Cont.

Reference	Dataset	Technique/Model	Outcomes
[40]	Online Cassava Leaf disease dataset	MNet (Mobile Net Detector) Model	Accuracy 89.41% and Sensitivity rate 76.96%
[41]	Online Cassava Leaf disease dataset	GoogleNet and AlexNet CNN Model	Precision 87.9, Recall 86.58, and F-measure 81.47%
[42]	Online Cassava Leaf disease dataset	Machine-learning methods SVM, Naïve Bayes	Sensitivity rate 0.798, Specificity rate 0.756, and AUC rate 0.875
[43]	Online Cassava Leaf disease dataset	CNN model	Accuracy 93.5, Precision 91.9

3. Materials and Methods

This section covers the proposed model architecture and working steps.

3.1. Proposed ECNN Architecture

This research provides a comprehensive learning method for real-time Cassava leaf disease detection based on an enhanced CNN model (ECNN). The existing Standard CNN model is based on extensive features and a massive computational process that increases the computational overhead. We present an enhanced CNN model (ECNN) for Cassava leaf disease detection and an analysis for overcoming these issues. The existing Standard CNN model is improved by adding new features and properties.

In the proposed ECNN model, a depth-wise layer separation feature is introduced, minimizing the feature count and computational overhead. Additionally, a global average election polling layer replaces the fully connected layer and decreases the variable count. Then, a batch normalization layer is applied to adjust computational efficiency. The proposed ECNN model utilizes a distinct block processing feature to deal with data imbalance. The next phase utilizes de-correlation stretching with Gamma correction feature, which improves color segregation with high band-to-band correlation features on the image dataset.

The architecture of the proposed ECNN model involves three convolutional layers and four fully integrated layers in the head. The first layer contains 32 (5×5) convolutions, in order to know and understand more significant characteristics of workflow normalization. This layer also contains batch sizes of (3×3) for the max-pooling feature. The subsequent two and three layers consist of two main pairs of convolution layers. They mainly contain 64 features, with size (3×3) batch normalization features. They also contain 128 features of size (3×3) for max pooling, respectively. The layers are arranged in a particular manner to facilitate the entire learning system to learn broader and deeper characteristics by applying the stacking of two pairs of convolution layers. Figure 1 shows the architectural features of the proposed ECNN framework.

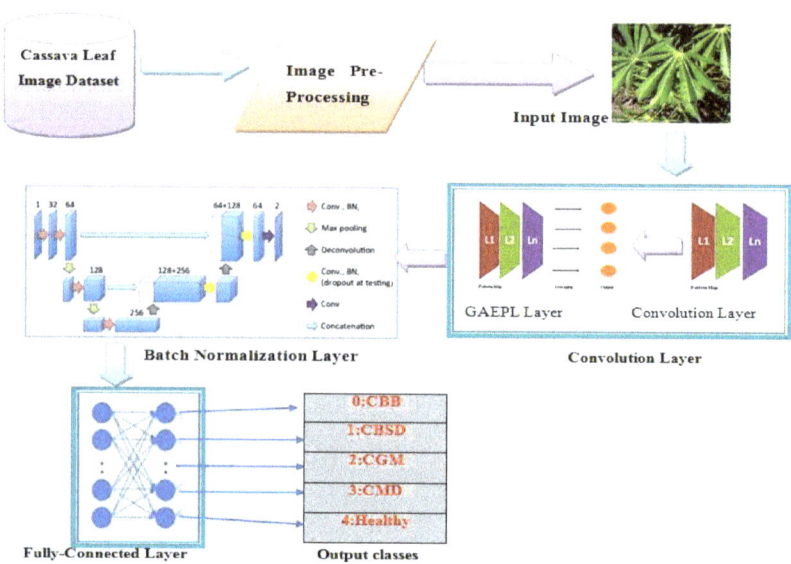

Figure 1. Architecture of Proposed ECNN Model.

3.1.1. Global Average Election Polling Layer (GAEPL)

GAEPL's objective is to standardize the entire network structure and minimize the dimensionality from three-dimensional to one-dimensional, which minimizes the overfitting issues. The proposed ECNN model utilizes the pattern map feature within the last CNN layer to aggregate all the outputs into a sequence of one-dimensional form. After applying a GAEPL, the number of variables is considerably reduced because the advancement of pattern maps in matrices is not required, as described in Figure 2.

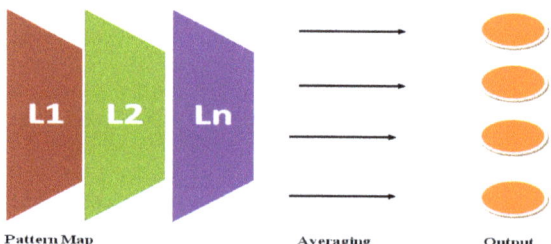

Figure 2. Global Election Polling Layer.

The advantage of a GAEPL over the convolutional layers is that it can effectively maintain the multilayer architecture by improving the connection between the pattern maps and analogies. It also provides more convincing features and well-understood pattern map classifications [44].

A pooling function includes sliding a two-dimensional filtration system across each link of its feature space. It also aggregates all the features within the filter's communication range. For a convolution layer feature space composed of parameters (Nw: width of feature space, Nh: height of feature space and Nc: Total number of channels/links in a feature space, f: filter size, and s: length of stride), the measurement of results acquired straight after a pooling layer can be defined as

$$[(N_h - (f+1)/S) \times (N_w - (f+1)/s) \times N_c] \tag{1}$$

Each link in the feature space is combined into a single value using the global pooling layer function. As a result, the (Nh × Nw × Nc) feature space is adjusted to (1 × 1 × Nc). It is the same as using only a filter with aspects (Nh × Nw), i.e., the feature map's elements.

3.1.2. Batch Normalization Layer (BNL)

BNL is a training method for complex CNN architecture. It standardizes the number of parameters at each level in small batches. It also improves the teaching methods and significantly minimizes the training epochs needed to build deep convolutional networks. Figure 3 shows the working of BNL [45].

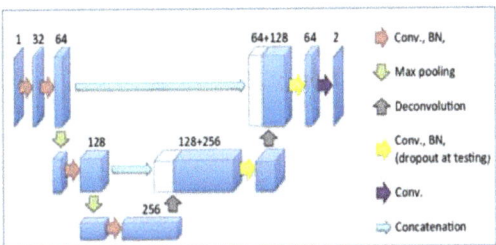

Figure 3. Batch Normalization Layer in ECNN.

In CNN, the quantity of neurons in each layer is often expansive. If data transmission at a specific layer starts shifting from one layer to another, the network size also grows, enhancing the modeling risks. Consequently, a batch normalization process mainly aims to relieve the above issues. A batch normalization process splits the population into small clusters and fixes each cluster's variables [46]. A record inside one cluster collectively depends on the direction of the differential and minimizes unpredictability when the value decreases. A CNN group requires fewer items than a complete dataset during the process, which dramatically reduces the computation count. An activation function is used in the batch normalization process. Before applying an activation function, the batch normalization layer normalizes the input data toward all the levels and overcomes the problem of addressing the input offset. A batch normalization process transforms the input n as per the following formula given in Equation (2):

$$BN(n) = \beta + \gamma + \frac{n - \mu\beta}{\sigma\beta} + \beta \qquad (2)$$

where $n \in B$ represents an input element toward batch normalization (BN), which is mainly related to a small batch β, γ represents the scale variable, $\sigma\beta$ represents the standard deviation, and $\mu\beta$ represents the sample mean value.

3.1.3. Distinct Block Processing (DBP)

This research utilized an imbalanced Cassava leaf disease dataset. The data are biased against CBSD, CBD, and CGM disease classes, and they also include Cassava leaf images of varying sizes. The imbalanced dataset needs immediate attention, and it should be converted into a balanced dataset for better outcomes. A distinct block technique is used to fix this problem. Therefore, when the resolution of the source image is significantly greater than the neural network's potential, the block processing method is utilized [47].

On the other hand, the block processing method enables the preservation of visual information. It has earlier been utilized effectively in numerous computer-vision-based research works. The input data are filtered from block to block during a distinct block operating condition. The input image is divided further into a rectangular shape, and each block is processed independently to evaluate the correlating block image outcome and define the image pixels. The images are separated into distinct blocks in the top left corner. A zero-padding value is introduced to boost the series of images in less identified classes, and the blocks do not align to a particular object. All Cassava leaf disease class labels contain similar images for all five classes. Different block processing methods boost each class's feature count.

3.2. Working of Proposed ECNN

The Cassava leaf disease detection and analysis using the proposed ECNN model includes various phases. Each phase has its distinct features. The max-pooling layer's goal is to decrease the geographic capacity dimensions of all image pixels. After parameter selection and improvement with the grid search process, the network's head comprises four fully linked layers of 512 neurons. The first, second, and third layers contain 1024 neurons in this process, and the fourth layer contains 256 neurons. There is a neuron for each classification in the output-based convolutional layers correlating to five Cassava leaf disease classes. The dropout feature is utilized in the fully inter-linked layers to overcome inaccuracy and overfitting issues. In particular, the fully connected layers obtain essential information from the object through the fully connected components. To utilize these selected features to identify and classify all the healthy and unhealthy classes from the leaf images, the convolution layer value can be measured as Equation (3)

$$x_k^l = f\left(\sum_{i \in M_k}^n x_j^{l-1} \binom{n}{k} * x_{jk}^l + a_k^l\right) \qquad (3)$$

where x_j^{l-1} represents the feature map value of the last layer used as an output, x_k^l represents the channel output value, n represents the layer number, a_k^l represents the offset value related to channel, M_k represent the subset data for input.

3.2.1. Phase 1

The first phase performs image transformation, including mask segment, deskew, gray, thresh, rnoise, canny, and sharpen. Then, to remove image imbalance, we apply a pre-processing data phase based on Contrast Limited Adaptive Histogram Equalization (CLAHE) method [48]. Figure 4 shows image transformation. Here, one to ten transformations are performed by various methods. In Figure 4: (1): original, (2): mask, (3): segment, (4): deskew, (5): gray, (7): thresh, (8): rnoise, (9): canny, and (10): sharpen.

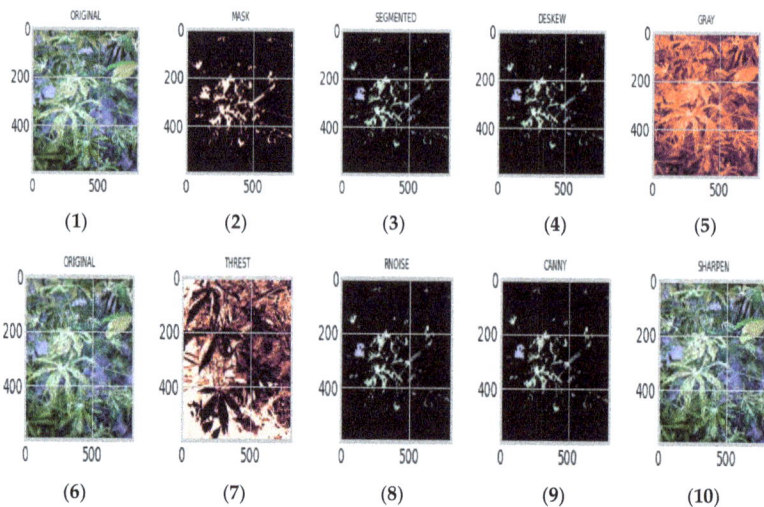

Figure 4. Image Transformation (Image (**1,6**): Original, (**2**): Mask, (**3**): Segment, (**4**): Deskew, (**5**): Gray, (**7**): Thresh, (**8**): Rnoise, (**9**): Canny, and (**10**): Sharpen).

Figure 5 shows the image pre-processing by using the CLAHE method. The CLAHE method improves the performance of image processing methods in low-resolution and low-contrast environments. The initial color image is transferred from RGB to Y.I.Q. and H.S.I. shared spaces. In the next phase, a CLAHE method is utilized in the Y.I.Q. and H.S.I. color spaces to produce two improved image datasets. Then, the Y.I.Q. and H.S.I. improved images are subsequently converted to RGB color space.

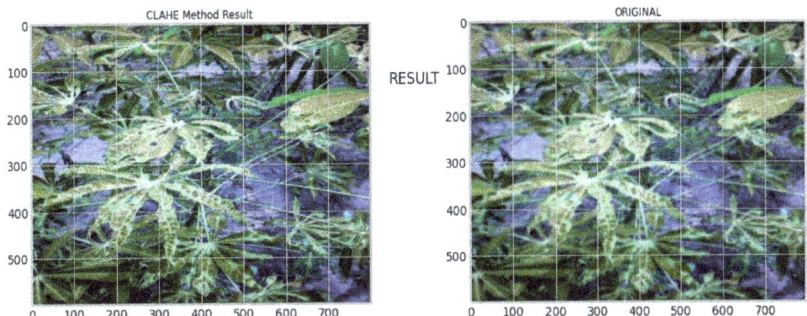

Figure 5. Image Pre-Processing Model Based on CLAHE.

3.2.2. Phase 2

In this phase, we applied the SMOTE method for resampling purposes [49]. The first phase mainly removes the skewness from the images. As discussed, the Cassava leaf disease dataset [50] that we are using for this research is highly imbalanced. The second phase utilized a perfect combination of existing methods: SMOTE (Synthetic Minority Oversampling Technique), class-weight, and focal loss techniques, to enhance the volume of the training dataset, which led to improvements in high precision. SMOTE is a method for oversampling that generates data samples only for class labels. This method mainly overcame the overfitting issue caused by arbitrary data.

The SMOTE method creates unique Cassava leaf disease data samples based on actual results to remove the skewness. The SMOTE approach selects samples in the feature space closest to them, makes a clear distinction between them in the subspace, and draws a new sample once at the position along each path.

3.2.3. Phase 3

Phase three is mainly applied to enhance the size of the Cassava leaf image dataset. To address the issue of a limited dataset, this phase utilizes dataset enhancement techniques, such as random shearing, image flipping, center zooming, random scaling, height/width shift, and random cropping. This phase also utilizes an image-flipping method, which increases the dataset volume. It helps in the testing and training process and provides better precision, accuracy, and performance.

4. Results and Discussion

This section covers the implementation, dataset description, result comparison, and discussion. The python programming language implements existing Standard CNN [2] and proposed ECNN methods. The proposed ECNN model is compared with the existing Standard CNN architecture-based model. To implement these models, we are using a similar type of feature. Various performance measuring parameters are calculated, i.e., precision, recall, f-measures, and accuracy.

4.1. Dataset

The Cassava leaf dataset is collected from the online Kaggle dataset [50]. The original data contain 6256 Cassava leaf images with imbalanced occurrences of 316 healthy Cassava leaves. The dataset also contains the four types of unhealthy infected Cassava leaf classes.

Figure 6 shows the various disease classes of Cassava leaf (0: CBB, 1: CBSD, 2: CGM, 3: CMD, and 4: Healthy).

Figure 6. Healthy and Unhealthy Cassava Images.

Different parameters are calculated to examine the performance of the proposed ECNN model, i.e., dropout, batch size, other numbers of epochs and precision, recall, f-measure, accuracy.

4.2. Data Pre-Processing

In the pre-processing phase, the raw Cassava images are normalized. An imbalance is also removed from the images. The image set is classified into two main categories: standard (healthy) and abnormal (unhealthy). These natural-color images are divided into five binary classes, from 0 to 4. The unhealthy Cassava images are classified into distinct classes. The complete normalization process in data pre-processing for a data sample is described in the Equations (4)–(6):

$$(\gamma)^n = \frac{1}{n} * \sum_{k=0}^{n} N_k \quad (4)$$

$$(\mu)^2 = \frac{1}{n} * \sum_{k=0}^{n} (N_k - \gamma) \quad (5)$$

In Equations (4) and (5), N_k shows the data for a pixel, which is stored at position k, and n shows the pixel samples. γ shows the mean data value, and $(\mu)^2$ shows the variance. Based on Equations (4) and (5), a normalization process can be defined by Equation (6) as follows:

$$N^| = \frac{N_k - \gamma}{(\mu)^2 + \varepsilon} \quad (6)$$

In Equation (6), the $N^|$ represents the normalization value for an ith pixel, and ε is some small random value, where $\varepsilon > 0$.

In Cassava leaf image data pre-processing, the images' R, G, and B components are decreased from their mean values in the normalization progressive enhancement de-averaging. Moreover, there are a variety of issues with the Cassava leaf dataset. The first is the small dataset size, and the next is the poor contrast and resolution images. Another challenge is associated with the skewness in the class label. The top class contains 39.4% of this dataset, and the minor class contains 2.89% magnitude variations [51].

We focused on enhancing Cassava image contrast using the CLAHE method. The CLAHE method can significantly improve the performance of image processing methods in low-resolution and low-contrast environments. To increase the size of the database, various image enhancement methods, i.e., random shearing, image flipping, central zooming, random cropping, random scaling, shifting of image height and width, are used. An image flipping method that helps to enhance the size of the database helps in training and validation for testing results.

In the next phase, all the Cassava leaf images are restructured into (224 × 224) by adjusting the width and length of the images. The images of leaf categories are restructured further into vertically and horizontally flipped components. The Cassava image dataset includes CMD: 2808, CGM: 923, CBB: 166, and CBSD: 1593 images. As shown in Figure 7, these images are completely unbalanced, with a heavy bias toward CBSD and CMD Cassava disease classes.

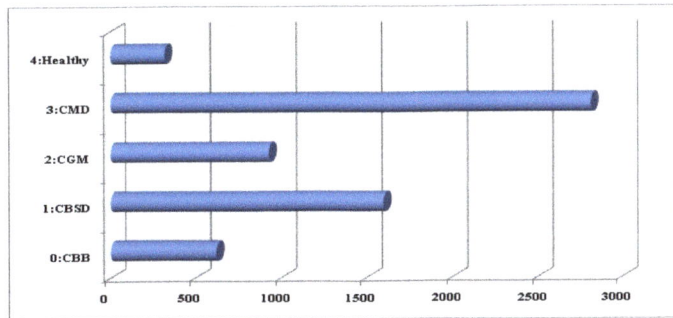

Figure 7. Cassava Leaf Dataset.

4.3. Visualization of Proposed ECNN Model

The proposed ECNN model generates 239 NN layers. Figure 8 represents the visualization outcomes of the first five layers (layer 1 to layer 5) of the proposed ECNN model. Layer 1 represents the input image; layer 2 represents the rescaling process; layer 3 represents normalization; layer 4 represents the stem_conv_pad; and layer 5 represents the stem_conv. The proposed ECNN model's structure consisted of three convolution operations and a core of four fully linked layers.

Layer 1 contains 32 cores (5 × 5) for learning higher batch normalization characteristics, with max pooling of (3 × 3) pool capacity. Layers 2 and 3 contain two fully connected layers with 64 (3 × 3) and 128 (3 × 3) feature selection, batch normalization, and max pooling. A batch normalization process enables the creation of the batches for two different sets of convolution layers. Before completing the max-pooling process, all the layers are structured to enhance the learning of the entire model. In the ECNN layer architecture, layer 4 shows the "stem_conv_pad", which describes the Keras Zero Padding 2D normalization process outcomes, and similar layer 5 shows the "stem_conv", which describes the Conv2D in Keras outcomes [52].

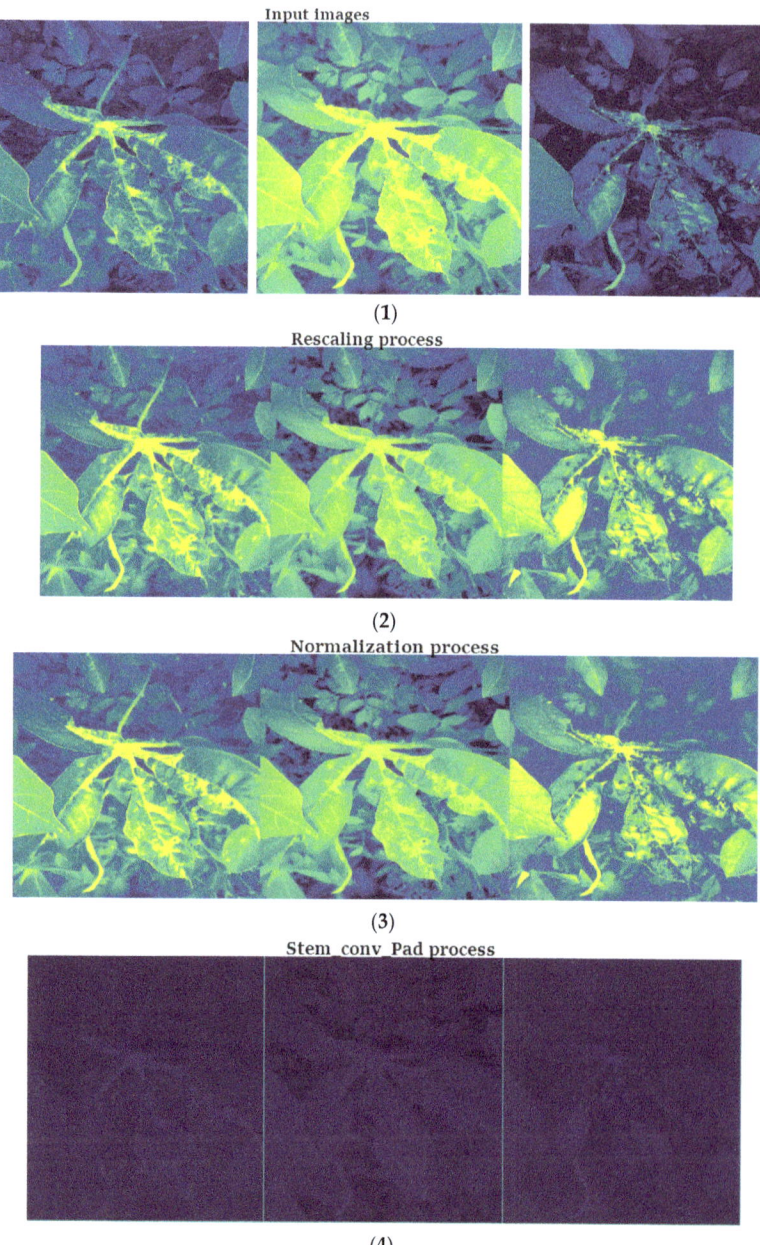

Figure 8. Cont.

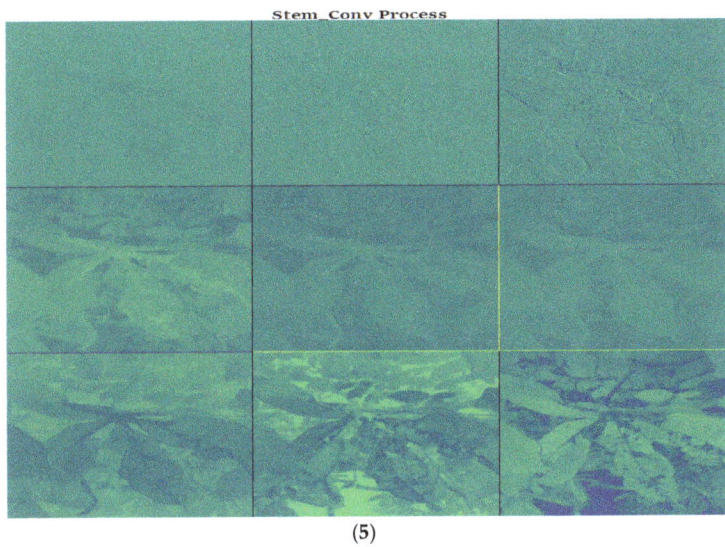

Figure 8. Layered Visualization of Proposed ECNN Model ((**1**) Layer 1: Input, (**2**) Layer 2: Rescaling, (**3**) Layer 3: Normalization, (**4**) Layer 4: stem_conv_pad, and (**5**) Layer 5: stem_conv).

4.4. Experimental Outcomes

The existing Standard CNN model and Proposed ECNN methods are implemented using python and Anaconda distribution in this research. The online Kaggle Cassava leaf dataset is used for analysis. The dataset is divided into training and testing sets.

Following performance measuring, the parameters are calculated to measure the performance of the proposed ECNN method given in Equations (7)–(11) [53–56]:

$$\text{Accuracy} = (TP + TN)/[(TP + TN + FN + FP)] \tag{7}$$

$$\text{Precision} = [TP/(FP + TP)] \tag{8}$$

$$\text{Recall} = [TP/(FN + TP)] \tag{9}$$

$$\text{F-Measure} = 2 \times [(\text{Recall} \times \text{Precision})/(\text{Recall} + \text{Precision})] \tag{10}$$

$$\text{Confusion Matrix (CM)} = \text{the total of true and false forecasts is summarized with score values divided by class. It is the main factor here for a CM.} \tag{11}$$

where TP = True positive rate, FP = False positive rate, FN = False Negative, TN = True Negative.

In this experiment, we used two scenarios for Cassava leaf disease analysis. In Scenario 1, experimental analysis is performed on the imbalanced dataset, and in Scenario 2, experimental analysis was performed on a balanced dataset. Accuracy rate, precision, recall, and F-measure parameters are calculated to evaluate the training and test competitiveness of the CNN and proposed ECNN models.

4.4.1. Scenario 1

The first scenario performs experimental analysis on an imbalanced Cassava leaf disease dataset. The dataset is divided into 60% for training and 40% for testing purposes. K-fold cross-validation is applied with k = 3 for training and testing to achieve a higher precision.

Figure 9 represents the experimental outcome of the proposed ECNN and CNN model for training and validation accuracy, and training and validation loss for imbalanced datasets. The experimental results demonstrate that the proposed ECNN model achieved training and validation accuracy of 94.689% and a loss of 24.547%, which is better than the existing Standard CNN model results, showing training and validation accuracy of 89.754% and a loss of 36.414%.

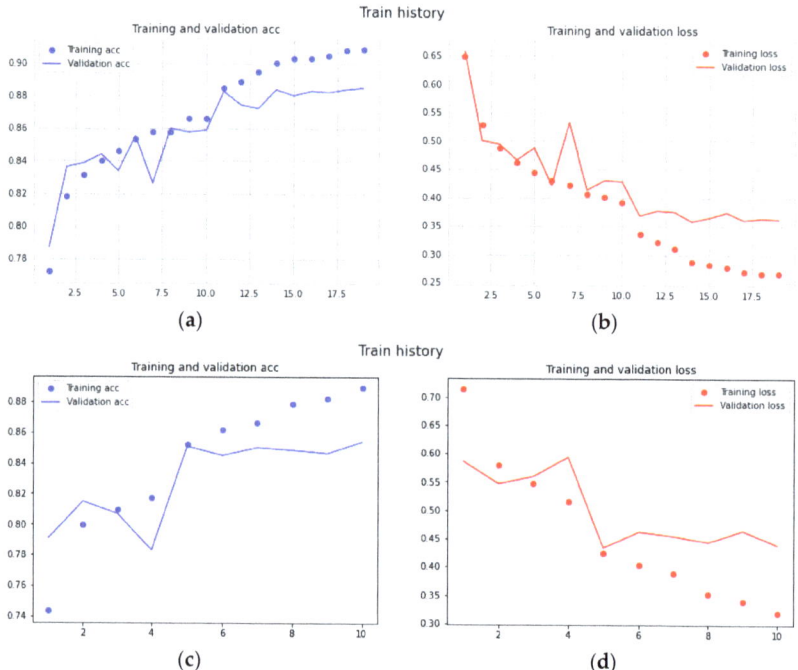

Figure 9. Experimental Outcome of Proposed ECNN and CNN Model on the Imbalanced Dataset ((**a**) ECNN Training and Validation Accuracy, (**b**) ECNN Training and Validation Loss, (**c**) CNN Training and Validation Accuracy, and (**d**) CNN Training and Validation Loss).

Figure 10 represents the confusion matrix of the proposed ECNN model for various Cassava leaf disease classes. This matrix shows the results of actual vs. predicted data. The healthy class shows an accuracy of 99.64%, which is better than the other classes. The CMD disease class is showing poor outcomes, at 94.69%.

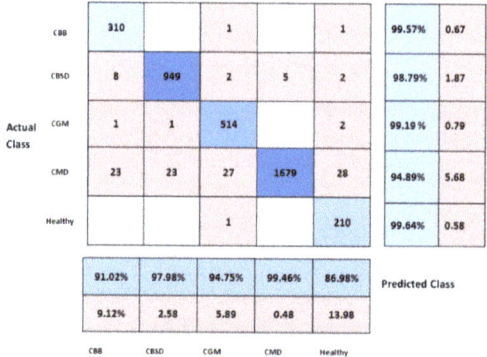

Figure 10. Confusion Matrix of Proposed ECNN Model for Imbalanced Dataset.

Figure 11 represents the experimental results of the existing Standard CNN model and the proposed ECNN model. This graph is plotted between accuracy% and epoch for training and testing. The proposed ECNN method shows better training and testing accuracy for all the epoch cycles, and at epoch 300, it shows more than 99% accuracy.

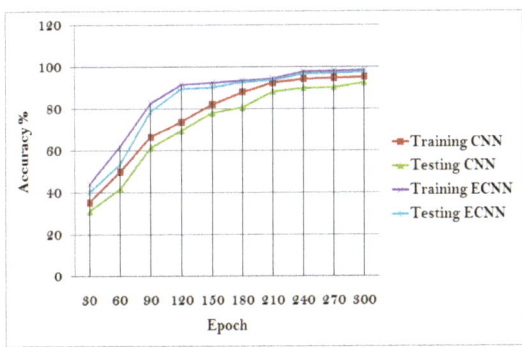

Figure 11. Accuracy Results for ECNN vs. CNN.

Tables 2 and 3 show the experimental outcomes for various Cassava leaf disease classes (0 to 4) for the proposed ECNN and CNN for the imbalanced dataset. These experimental results show that the proposed ECNN model performs better in accuracy, precision, recall, and f-measure than the existing Standard CNN model.

Table 2. Experimental Results for CNN Model for Imbalanced Dataset.

Class Type	Precision%	Accuracy%	Recall%	F-Measure%
CBB	81.256	83.659	82.224	82.154
CBSD	92.454	90.891	91.265	82.656
CGM	80.147	72.651	72.665	77.841
CMD	95.451	95.654	95.669	96.561
Healthy	70.981	68.961	69.781	69.874

Table 3. Experimental Results for ECNN Model for Imbalanced Dataset.

Class Type	Precision%	Accuracy%	Recall%	F-Measure%
CBB	91.021	92.568	84.565	84.998
CBSD	97.989	97.989	93.651	84.665
CGM	94.989	95.648	74.558	78.988
CMD	99.465	99.565	96.336	97.447
Healthy	96.981	97.778	90.145	91.407

4.4.2. Scenario 2

In the second scenario, the balanced dataset of the Cassava leaf is used. This dataset is divided into 60% for training and 40% for testing purposes.

Table 4 shows that the proposed ECNN procedure outperformed the existing Standard CNN model in terms of accuracy results for all the classes. The ECNN model shows 99.47% accuracy for CBB class, which is the highest in all the terms. Once we compare the experimental results of Scenarios 1 and 2, we can see that the proposed ECNN method shows better results for a balanced dataset than an imbalanced dataset.

Table 4. Experimental Results for CNN vs. ECNN Model for a Balanced Dataset.

Class Type	Accuracy%	
	CNN Model	Proposed ECNN
CBB	93.214	99.473
CBSD	91.478	98.132
CGM	89.981	99.391
CMD	93.124	98.924
Healthy	90.478	97.692

5. Conclusions and Future Work

Cassava leaf detection is a hot area of research. This research developed an ECNN model for a high imbalance Cassava leaf dataset to predict the disease class. The existing Standard CNN models utilize a higher extensive set of features and a massive computational process that increases the computational overhead. We upgraded the traditional convolution network model by adding enhanced features to overcome this issue. The proposed ECNN model utilizes a depth-wise layer separation, minimizing the feature count and computational overhead. Additionally, to overcome the dataset imbalance factor, this research applied improved data pre-processing methods. It reduces the error rate and improves image quality.

The proposed ECNN model is compared with the existing Standard CNN architecture-based model. To implement these models, we are using a similar type of feature. An experimental analysis was performed on an online Cassava leaf dataset. This dataset contained five classes: 0: CBB, 1: CBSD, 2: CGM, 3: CMD, and 4: Healthy. An experimental analysis clearly shows the strengthening of the proposed ECNN model in terms of better accuracy, precision, recall, and f-measure than the existing Standard CNN model.

In future work, we will try to improve the current research in various aspects: (a) the dataset can be improved in terms of data size and more disease classes; (b) the ECNN model can be improved by adding more CNN models in hybrid form; (c) the experimental analysis can be performed in a real-time environment with more performance measuring parameters.

Author Contributions: U.K.L., S.S., S.K.P. and N.G. were responsible for the conceptualization of the topic; article gathering and sorting were carried out by U.K.L., A.L.I., S.S., S.K.P., N.G. and A.K.; manuscript writing and original drafting and formal analysis were carried out by U.K.L., A.L.I., C.-T.L., S.S., S.K.P, N.G., A.K. and C.-C.L.; writing of reviews and editing were carried out by U.K.L., A.L.I., C.-T.L., S.S., S.K.P., N.G., A.K. and C.-C.L.; and S.K.P. led the overall research activity. All authors have read and agreed to the published version of the manuscript.

Funding: This research received no external funding.

Institutional Review Board Statement: Not applicable.

Informed Consent Statement: Not applicable.

Data Availability Statement: The data that supports the findings of this paper are available from the corresponding author upon reasonable request.

Acknowledgments: The authors would like to thank anonymous reviewers of Mathematics MDPI Journal for their careful and helpful comments. The work of Agbotiname Lucky Imoize is supported by the Nigerian Petroleum Technology Development Fund (PTDF), the German Academic Exchange Service (DAAD) through the Nigerian-German Postgraduate Program under grant 57473408. This work was partially supported by the Ministry of Science and Technology, Taiwan, under grant MOST 110-2410-H-165-001-MY2 and MOST 110-2410-H-030-032.

Conflicts of Interest: The authors declare no conflict of interest related to this work.

Abbreviations

The following are the abbreviations used in this research:

CNN	Convolutional Neural network
ECNN	Enhanced Convolutional Neural network
CBB	Cassava Bacterial Blight
CBSD	Cassava Brown Streak Disease
CGM	Cassava Green Mottle
CMD	Cassava Mosaic Disease
SVM	Support Vector Machines
RF	Random Forest
DRN	Deep Residual Neural Network
SCNN	Shallow CNN
FR-CNN	Faster Recurrence CNN
SSD	Single Sot Multi-box Method
MNet	Mobile Net Detector Model
GAEPL	Global Average Election Polling Layer
BNL	Batch Normalization Layer
DBP	Distinct Block Processing
CLAHE	Contrast Limited Adaptive Histogram Equalization
RGB	Red Green Blue
YIQ	Y (perceived luminance), I, Q (color/luminance information) NTSC color model
SMOTE	Synthetic Minority Oversampling Technique
T.P.	True positive rate
FP	False-positive rate
FN	False Negative
TN	True Negative
NN	Neural Network
stem_conv_pad	Zero Padding 2D normalization
stem_conv	Conv2D

References

1. Mathulaprangsan, S.; Lanthong, K. Cassava Leaf Disease Recognition Using Convolutional Neural Networks. In Proceedings of the 2021 9th International Conference on Orange Technology (ICOT), Tainan, Taiwan, 16–17 December 2021; IEEE: Piscataway, NJ, USA, 2021; pp. 1–5.
2. Priyadharshini, R.A.; Arivazhagan, S.; Arun, M.; Mirnalini, A. Maize leaf disease classification using deep convolutional neural networks. *Neural Comput. Appl.* **2019**, *31*, 8887–8895. [CrossRef]
3. Ali, A.A.; Chramcov, B.; Jasek, R.; Katta, R.; Krayem, S. Classification of plant diseases using convolutional neural networks. In Proceedings of the Computer Science On-line Conference, 16 July 2021; Springer: Cham, Switzerland, 2021; pp. 268–275.
4. Oyewola, D.O.; Dada, E.G.; Misra, S.; Damaševičius, R. Detecting cassava mosaic disease using a deep residual convolutional neural network with distinct block processing. *PeerJ Comput. Sci* **2021**, *7*, e352. [CrossRef] [PubMed]
5. Ravi, V.; Acharya, V.; Pham, T.D. Attention deep learning-based large-scale learning classifier for Cassava leaf disease classification. *Expert Syst.* **2021**, *39*, e12862. [CrossRef]
6. Thai, H.T.; Tran-Van, N.Y.; Le, K.H. Artificial Cognition for Early Leaf Disease Detection using Vision Transformers. In Proceedings of the 2021 International Conference on Advanced Technologies for Communications (ATC), Ho Chi Minh City, Vietnam, 14–16 October 2021; IEEE: Piscataway, NJ, USA, 2021; pp. 33–38.
7. Methil, A.; Agrawal, H.; Kaushik, V. One-vs-All Methodology based Cassava Leaf Disease Detection. In Proceedings of the 2021 12th International Conference on Computing Communication and Networking Technologies (ICCCNT), Kharagpur, India, 6–8 July 2021; IEEE: Piscataway, NJ, USA, 2021; pp. 1–7.
8. Metlek, S. Disease detection from cassava leaf images with deep learning methods in web environment. *Int. J. 3D Print. Technol. Digit. Ind.* **2021**, *5*, 625–644. [CrossRef]
9. Hassan, S.M.; Maji, A.K.; Jasiński, M.; Leonowicz, Z.; Jasińska, E. Identification of Plant-Leaf Diseases Using CNN and Transfer-Learning Approach. *Electronics* **2021**, *10*, 1388. [CrossRef]
10. Maryum, A.; Akram, M.U.; Salam, A.A. Cassava leaf disease classification using deep neural networks. In Proceedings of the 2021 IEEE 18th International Conference on Smart Communities: Improving Quality of Life Using I.C.T., IoT and A.I. (HONET), Karachi, Pakistan, 11–13 October 2021.
11. Loey, M.; ElSawy, A.; Afify, M. Deep learning in plant diseases detection for agricultural crops: A survey. *Int. J. Serv. Sci. Manag. Eng. Technol.* **2020**, *11*, 41–58. [CrossRef]

12. Oresegun, A.; Fagbenro, O.A.; Ilona, P.; Bernard, E. Nutritional and anti-nutritional composition of cassava leaf protein concentrate from six cassava varieties for use in aqua feed. *Cogent Food Agric.* **2016**, *2*, 1147323. [CrossRef]
13. Ravindran, V.; Kornegay, E.T.; Rajaguru, A.S.B.; Potter, L.M.; Cherry, J.A. Cassava leaf meal as a replacement for coconut oil meat in broiler diets. *Poultry Science* **1986**, *65*, 1720–1727. [CrossRef]
14. Uarrota, V.G.; Moresco, R.; Coelho, B.; Nunes, E.D.C.; Peruch, L.A.M.; Neubert, E.D.O.; Rocha, M.; Maraschin, M. Metabolomics combined with chemometric tools (PCA, HCA, PLS-DA and SVM) for screening cassava (Manihot esculenta Crantz) roots during postharvest physiological deterioration. *Food Chem.* **2014**, *161*, 67–78. [CrossRef]
15. Chen, C.-C.; Ba, J.Y.; Li, T.J.; Chan, C.C.K.; Wang, K.C.; Liu, Z. EfficientNet: A low-bandwidth IoT image sensor framework for cassava leaf disease classification. *Sens. Mater.* **2021**, *33*, 4031. [CrossRef]
16. Dhingra, G.; Kumar, V.; Joshi, H.D. Study of digital image processing techniques for leaf disease detection and classification. *Multimed. Tools Appl.* **2018**, *77*, 19951–20000. [CrossRef]
17. Sambasivam, G.; Opiyo, G.D. A predictive machine learning application in agriculture: Cassava disease detection and classification with imbalanced dataset using Convolutional neural networks. *Egypt. Inform. J.* **2021**, *22*, 27–34. [CrossRef]
18. Saxena, D.K.; Jhanwar, D.; Gautam, D. Classification of leaf disease on using triangular thresholding method and machine learning. In *Lecture Notes in Electrical Engineering*; Springer: Singapore, 2022; pp. 77–88.
19. Singh, A.K.; Chaurasia, B. Plant leaf disease detection using Convolutional neural network and random forest classifier. *Int. J. Innov. Eng. Sci.* **2021**, *6*, 204. [CrossRef]
20. Sardogan, M.; Tuncer, A.; Ozen, Y. Plant leaf disease detection and classification based on CNN with L.V.Q. algorithm. In Proceedings of the 2018 3rd International Conference on Computer Science and Engineering (UBMK), Sarajevo, Bosnia and Herzegovina, 20–23 September 2018; IEEE: Piscataway, NJ, USA, 2018; pp. 382–385.
21. Bose, A.; Ghosh, D.; Banerjee, A.; Saha, D.; Ganguly, P.; Chakrabarti, S. Capsnet-VGG16 Architecture for Cassava Plant Disease Detection. In Proceedings of the International Conference on Computational Intelligence, Data Science and Cloud Computing (IEM-ICDC), Kolkata, India, 25–27 September 2020; Springer: Berlin/Heidelberg, Germany, 2021; Volume 62, p. 207.
22. Sangbamrung, I.; Praneetpholkrang, P.; Kanjanawattana, S. A novel automatic method for cassava disease classification using deep learning. *J. Adv. Inf. Technol.* **2020**, *11*, 241–248. [CrossRef]
23. Pinto, L.A.; Mary, L.; Dass, S. The Real-Time Mobile Application for Identification of Diseases in Coffee Leaves using the CNN Model. In Proceedings of the 2021 Second International Conference on Electronics and Sustainable Communication Systems (ICESC), Coimbatore, India, 4–6 August 2021; 2021; pp. 1694–1700.
24. Owomugisha, G.; Melchert, F.; Mwebaze, E.; Quinn, J.A.; Biehl, M. Matrix relevance learning from spectral data for diagnosing cassava diseases. *IEEE Access* **2021**, *9*, 83355–83363. [CrossRef]
25. Latif, S.; Müller, J. Potential of cassava leaves in human nutrition: A review. *Trends Food Sci. Technol.* **2015**, *44*, 147–158. [CrossRef]
26. Maruthi, M.N.; Bouvaine, S.; Tufan, H.A.; Mohammed, I.U.; Hillocks, R.J. Hillocks. Transcriptional response of virus-infected cassava and identification of putative sources of resistance for cassava brown streak disease. *PLoS ONE* **2014**, *9*, e96642. [CrossRef]
27. Emuoyibofarhe, O.; Emuoyibofarhe, J.O.; Adebayo, S.; Ayandiji, A.; Demeji, O.; James, O. Detection and classification of cassava diseases using machine learning. *Int. J. Comput. Sci. Softw. Eng.* **2019**, *8*, 166–176.
28. Mbugua, J.K.; Suksa-Ngiam, W. Predicting suitable areas for growing cassava using remote sensing and machine learning techniques: A study in Nakhon-Phanom Thailand. *Issues Inf. Sci. Inf. Technol.* **2018**, *15*, 43–56. [CrossRef]
29. Ramcharan, A.; Baranowski, K.; McCloskey, P.; Ahmed, B.; Legg, J.; Hughes, D.P. Deep learning for image-based cassava disease detection. *Front. Plant Sci.* **2017**, *8*, 1852. [CrossRef]
30. Zhang, K.; Wu, Q.; Chen, Y. Detecting soybean leaf disease from synthetic image using multi-feature fusion faster R-CNN. *Comput. Electron. Agric.* **2021**, *183*, 106064. [CrossRef]
31. Trivedi, J.; Shamnani, Y.; Gajjar, R. Plant leaf disease detection using machine learning. In *International Conference on Emerging Technology Trends in Electronics Communication and Networking*; Springer: Singapore, 2020; pp. 267–276.
32. Mohameth, F.; Bingcai, C.; Sada, K.A. Plant disease detection with deep learning and feature extraction using plant village. *J. Comput. Commun.* **2020**, *8*, 10–22. [CrossRef]
33. Deepalakshmi, P.; Lavanya, K.; Srinivasu, P.N. Plant Leaf Disease Detection Using CNN Algorithm. *Int. J. Inf. Syst. Modeling Des.* **2021**, *12*, 1–21. [CrossRef]
34. Suma, V.; Shetty, R.A.; Tated, R.F.; Rohan, S.; Pujar, T.S. CNN based leaf disease identification and remedy recommendation system. In Proceedings of the 2019 3rd International Conference on Electronics, Communication and Aerospace Technology (ICECA), Coimbatore, India, 12–14 June 2019; IEEE: Piscataway, NJ, USA, 2019; pp. 395–399.
35. Tusubira, J.F.; Nsumba, S.; Ninsiima, F.; Akera, B.; Acellam, G.; Nakatumba, J.; Mwebaze, E.; Quinn, J.; Oyana, T. Improving In-field Cassava Whitefly Pest Surveillance with Machine Learning. In Proceedings of the IEEE/CVF Conference on Computer Vision and Pattern Recognition Workshops, Seattle, WA, USA, 14–19 June 2020; pp. 68–69.
36. Gao, F.; Sa, J.; Wang, Z.; Zhao, Z. Cassava Disease Detection Method Based on EfficientNet. In Proceedings of the 2021 7th International Conference on Systems and Informatics (ICSAI), Chongqing, China, 13–15 November 2021; IEEE: Piscataway, NJ, USA, 2021; pp. 1–6.
37. Sharma, P.; Berwal, Y.P.S.; Ghai, W. Performance analysis of deep learning CNN models for disease detection in plants using image segmentation. *Inf. Processing Agric.* **2020**, *7*, 566–574. [CrossRef]

38. Choi, H.C.; Hsiao, T.-C. Image classification of cassava leaf disease based on residual network. In Proceedings of the 2021 IEEE 3rd Eurasia Conference on Biomedical Engineering, Healthcare and Sustainability (ECBIOS), Tainan, Taiwan, 28–30 May 2021.
39. Anthony, P.; Davey, M.R.; Power, J.B.; Lowe, K.C. An improved protocol for the culture of cassava leaf protoplasts. *Plant Cell Tissue Organ Cult.* **1995**, *42*, 299–302. [CrossRef]
40. Aravind, S.; Harini, S. Cassava leaf disease classification using Deep Learning. *Nveo-Nat. Volatiles Essent. Oils J. (NVEO)* **2021**, *8*, 9375–9389.
41. Ayu, H.R.; Surtono, A.; Apriyanto, D.K. Deep learning for detection cassava leaf disease. *J. Phys. Conf. Ser.* **2021**, *1751*, 012072. [CrossRef]
42. Ramcharan, A.; McCloskey, P.; Baranowski, K.; Mbilinyi, N.; Mrisho, L.; Ndalahwa, M.; Legg, J.; Hughes, D.P. A mobile-based deep learning model for cassava disease diagnosis. *Front. Plant Sci.* **2019**, *10*, 272. [CrossRef]
43. Surya, R.; Gautama, E. Cassava Leaf Disease Detection Using Convolutional Neural Networks. In Proceedings of the 2020 6th International Conference on Science in Information Technology (ICSITech), Palu, Indonesia, 21–22 October 2020; IEEE: Piscataway, NJ, USA, 2020; pp. 97–102.
44. Atanbori, J.; Montoya-P, M.E.; Selvaraj, M.G.; French, A.P.; Pridmore, T.P. Convolutional neural net-based cassava storage root counting using real and synthetic images. *Front. Plant Sci.* **2019**, *10*, 1516. [CrossRef]
45. Abayomi-Alli, O.O.; Damaševičius, R.; Misra, S.; Maskeliūnas, R. Cassava disease recognition from low-quality images using enhanced data augmentation model and deep learning. *Expert Syst.* **2021**, *38*, e12746. [CrossRef]
46. Gajjar, R.; Gajjar, N.; Thakor, V.J.; Patel, N.P.; Ruparelia, S. Real-time detection and identification of plant leaf diseases using convolutional neural networks on an embedded platform. *Vis. Comput.* **2021**, 1–16. [CrossRef]
47. Arivazhagan, S.; Shebiah, R.N.; Ananthi, S.; Varthini, S.V. Detection of unhealthy region of plant leaves and classification of plant leaf diseases using texture features. *Agric. Eng. Int. CIGR J.* **2013**, *15*, 211–217.
48. Geetharamani, G.; Pandian, A. Identification of plant leaf diseases using a nine-layer deep convolutional neural network. *Comput. Electr. Eng.* **2019**, *76*, 323–338.
49. Amirruddin, A.D.; Muharam, F.M.; Ismail, M.H.; Tan, N.P.; Ismail, M.F. Synthetic Minority Over-sampling TEchnique (SMOTE) and Logistic Model Tree (LMT)-Adaptive Boosting algorithms for classifying imbalanced datasets of nutrient and chlorophyll sufficiency levels of oil palm (*Elaeis guineensis*) using spectroradiometers and unmanned aerial vehicles. *Comput. Electron. Agric.* **2022**, *193*, 106646.
50. Kaggle Online Dataset, Cassava Leaf Disease. Available online: https://www.kaggle.com/c/cassava-leaf-disease-classification (accessed on 14 December 2021).
51. Zhang, X.; Qiao, Y.; Meng, F.; Fan, C.; Zhang, M. Identification of maize leaf diseases using improved deep convolutional neural networks. *IEEE Access* **2018**, *6*, 30370–30377. [CrossRef]
52. Moolayil, J. An introduction to deep learning and Keras. In *Learn Keras for Deep Neural Networks*; Apress: Berkeley, CA, USA, 2019; pp. 1–16.
53. Trivedi, N.K.; Simaiya, S.; Lilhore, U.K.; Sharma, S.K. COVID-19 Pandemic: Role of Machine Learning & Deep Learning Methods in Diagnosis. *Int. J. Cur. Res. Rev.* **2021**, *13*, 150–155.
54. Lilhore, U.K.; Simaiya, S.; Kaur, A.; Prasad, D.; Khurana, M.; Verma, D.K.; Hassan, A. Impact of Deep Learning and Machine Learning in Industry 4.0: Impact of Deep Learning. In *Cyber-Physical, IoT, and Autonomous Systems in Industry 4.0*; CRC Press: Boca Raton, FL, USA, 2021; pp. 179–197.
55. Guleria, K.; Sharma, A.; Lilhore, U.K.; Prasad, D. Breast Cancer Prediction and Classification Using Supervised Learning Techniques. *J. Comput. Theor. Nanosci.* **2020**, *17*, 2519–2522. [CrossRef]
56. Lilhore, U.K.; Simaiya, S.; Prasad, D.; Guleria, K. A Hybrid Tumour Detection and Classification Based on Machine Learning. *J. Comput. Theor. Nanosci.* **2020**, *17*, 2539–2544. [CrossRef]

Article

A Class-Incremental Learning Method Based on Preserving the Learned Feature Space for EEG-Based Emotion Recognition

Magdiel Jiménez-Guarneros * and Roberto Alejo-Eleuterio

Division of Postgraduate Studies and Research, National Technological of Mexico, Technological Institute of Toluca, Metepec 52149, Mexico; ralejoe@toluca.tecnm.mx
* Correspondence: mjmnzg@gmail.com

Abstract: Deep learning-based models have shown to be one of the main active research topics in emotion recognition systems from Electroencephalogram (EEG) signals. However, a significant challenge is to effectively recognize new emotions that are incorporated sequentially, as current models must perform retraining from scratch. In this paper, we propose a Class-Incremental Learning (CIL) method, named Incremental Learning preserving the Learned Feature Space (IL2FS), in order to enable deep learning models to incorporate new emotions (classes) into the already known. IL2FS performs a weight aligning to correct the bias on new classes, while it incorporates margin ranking loss and triplet loss to preserve the inter-class separation and feature space alignment on known classes. We evaluated IL2FS over two public datasets (DREAMER and DEAP) for emotion recognition and compared it with other recent and popular CIL methods reported in computer vision. Experimental results show that IL2FS outperforms other CIL methods by obtaining an average accuracy of $59.08 \pm 08.26\%$ and $79.36 \pm 04.68\%$ on DREAMER and DEAP, recognizing data from new emotions that are incorporated sequentially.

Keywords: class-incremental learning; deep learning; catastrophic forgetting; emotion recognition; electroencephalogram

Citation: Jiménez-Guarneros, M.; Alejo-Eleuterio, R. A Class-Incremental Learning Method Based on Preserving the Learned Feature Space for EEG-Based Emotion Recognition. *Mathematics* **2022**, *10*, 598. https://doi.org/10.3390/math10040598

Academic Editors: Ezequiel López-Rubio, Esteban Palomo and Enrique Domínguez

Received: 13 January 2022
Accepted: 11 February 2022
Published: 15 February 2022

Publisher's Note: MDPI stays neutral with regard to jurisdictional claims in published maps and institutional affiliations.

Copyright: © 2022 by the authors. Licensee MDPI, Basel, Switzerland. This article is an open access article distributed under the terms and conditions of the Creative Commons Attribution (CC BY) license (https://creativecommons.org/licenses/by/4.0/).

1. Introduction

Emotion analysis has shown to be an important part of research fields such as human–computer interaction and health care, in order to improve the interactive experience and understand the behavior of patients [1,2]. Existing approaches in emotion recognition characterize the responses of emotions in two main modalities [3,4]: behavioral and physiological signals. The first type of modality includes those approaches based on facial expression [5,6], speech emotion recognition [7] and body language. Unlike this type of modality, the physiological signals provide a reliable way to recognize emotions since these signals are produced by the human body that may not be susceptible to subjective approaches based on behavioral signals [8]. In this sense, Electrocardiogram (ECG) [9], Electromyography (EMG) [10], Electroencephalogram (EEG) [4] or even a combination of them [11,12], have been used for emotion recognition. Among these physiological-signal-based approaches, EEG has provided a reliable and promising indicator to identify different emotional states, as it directly reflects brain activity [12]. Furthermore, EEG is a non-invasive device, easy to use, and has a low cost [4,13]. Thus, EEG has been widely used in emotion recognition systems in the last years [3,8,13–18].

Reported works have been mainly focused on extracting discriminative EEG emotional features and building more effective emotion recognition systems. The collected EEG signals are usually analyzed in three categories to extract discriminative features: time domain (e.g., statistics of signal), frequency domain (e.g., differential entropy), and time-frequency domain (e.g., Fourier transform). In this direction, many methods have been proposed via machine learning to leverage the features extracted from EEG signals [17–19]. Recently, several methods are gradually moving towards the deep learning-based approaches, becoming dominant in EEG-based emotion recognition [3,8,13–16,20,21]. For example, different deep learning methods have been proposed to consider the spatial information, such as convolutional neural networks (CNNs) [3,14,16], capsule networks (CapsNets) [21] and graph neural networks (GNN) [8,13]. Likewise, attention mechanisms and recurrent networks [15] have been used to extract spatial and temporal information as emotion features.

Although remarkable progress has been achieved, there is a growing demand for adaptive, scalable, and responsive deep learning methods for emotion recognition tasks. Reported works are focused on recognizing emotions with fixed models while being unable to incorporate other emotions into their knowledge. New emotions may be recorded over time so that devices with pre-installed emotion recognition models may fail to recognize this new knowledge. Whenever samples from a new emotion become available, deep neural network models require retraining the whole model from scratch. This issue may be infeasible both in time or storage while using all training data or when the size of the main memory is limited [22]. Instead, the knowledge learned by a trained model should only be modified by using samples from a new emotion. In this sense, Class-incremental learning (CIL) provides a solution when new samples emerge, updating the knowledge of the model according to samples from new classes, avoiding re-configure the entire system [23].

CIL methods have been widely studied in computer vision [22] since several works have shown that deep learning models suffer from catastrophic forgetting when they are trained incrementally [24]. The catastrophic forgetting is the performance degradation of a neural network model affecting previously learned concepts whenever new ones are incorporated sequentially [25]. Different approaches have rapidly emerged to alleviate catastrophic forgetting. A first approach extends the model capacity to accommodate the latest knowledge as new data are integrated [26,27]. Although no sample is retained during incremental stages, these works may not scale well in specific scenarios since new weights are added each time. A second approach [28–31] uses a fixed model to generate feature representations across different incremental stages while multiple classifiers are trained for new classes. Although the retraining of the entire model is avoided, the performance of these methods depends on the quality of an initial representation, producing sub-optimal classification results in some cases [22]. Moreover, a third approach [25,32–40], named memory replay, stores a small set of representative samples from old classes and updates deep learning models via Fine-tuning (FT) across different incremental stages. The memory replay-based approach has shown better performance than previous approaches [35], but certainly the catastrophic forgetting is still under-studied. Mainly, in EEG-based signal recognition, Lee et al. [41] explored CIL for the imagined speech recognition task, but the authors used one of the most straightforward memory replay-based methods under an undemanding evaluation, as only a single incremental stage was tested for CIL. On the other hand, no work has been reported to study the dynamic changes in class for the EEG-based emotion recognition task. Thus, this research focuses on studying CIL for emotion recognition from EEG signals to enable deep learning models to incorporate new emotions into already known.

In this paper, we introduce *Incremental Learning preserving the Learned Feature Space* (IL2FS), a CIL method to address the catastrophic forgetting in EEG-based emotion recognition. The proposed method aims to preserve the feature space learned over past incremental stages, performing a bias correction on new classes, as well as encouraging the inter-class separation and feature space alignment over old classes. Firstly, we use Weighting Aligning (WA) [36] for bias correction on the weights at the output layer since class imbalance is present. Secondly, we use margin ranking loss to set a margin between scores of the ground-truth from old classes and their nearest score from any class (old or new), instead of only ensuring a separation between old and new classes, as reported in [33]. Finally, unlike previous CIL works for embedding networks [42–44], we propose to use triplet loss [45] to maintain the feature space alignment of old classes. IL2FS was implemented on a Capsule Network (CapsNet) architecture, which presents one of the best performances in terms of accuracy for emotion recognition [21]. We evaluate and validate our proposal on incremental learning tasks over two public datasets, DREAMER [46] and DEAP [11], using a reduced set of samples from old classes and the maximum number of incremental stages that may be built for each dataset.

The main contributions of this work are:

1. We present a Class-incremental Learning method, named IL2FS, for emotion recognition from EEG signals, addressing the catastrophic forgetting problem.
2. IL2FS incorporates a strategy based on bias correction of the new classes while ensuring an inter-class separation and feature alignment of the old classes. This strategy allows better preservation of the learned knowledge for a greater number of incremental stages and a reduced number of reserved samples in memory.
3. We conduct experiments on two benchmarks, DEAP and DREAMER, for emotion recognition research. The proposed method achieves a significant improvement when compared with existing CIL methods.

The rest of this paper is organized as follows: in Section 2, we review previous works on class-incremental learning. Section 3 describes the proposed method in detail. Section 4 presents datasets, preprocessing procedure, neural network architecture and experimental setup. The corresponding results are reported in Section 5. Finally, the discussion and conclusions are reported in Sections 6 and 7.

2. Related Work

Existing works in EEG-based emotion recognition have focused on dynamic data distribution changes, but dynamic changes in class have not been studied yet. In [41], the authors explored CIL using a memory replay-based approach for the imagined speech task. Even so, a simple method [47] based on fine-tuning and the nearest neighbor classifier was adopted. Likewise, an undemanding evaluation was performed since only a single new class was tested, while a considerable percentage of data from old classes is reserved in memory when a new class is added. On the other hand, several CIL methods are available in computer vision to address the catastrophic forgetting problem. Among different approaches, reported in [22], we are interested in memory replay-based methods since they have shown superior performance in terms of accuracy. Thus, we describe several methods based on memory replay to deal with the catastrophic forgetting problem. We group these methods according to the problem they address.

Less forgetting. Knowledge distillation [48] was introduced as a regularizer on the outputs of a reference network and a new network in [49], in order to preserve the predictions of classes learned at previous CIL stages. For this, knowledge distillation aims to keep the new network weights close to the weights of the reference network. Moreover, Hou et al. [33] presented *Learning a Unified Classifier Incrementally via Rebalancing* (LUCIR), which introduces a less-forget constraint through the cosine distance, considering the local geometric structures of old classes in their feature space. More recently, Simon et al. [25] proposed a distillation loss, named *Geodesic*, by adopting the concept of geodesic flow between two tasks, that is, the gradual changes between tasks projected in intermediate subspaces.

Bias correction. In this group, CIL methods focus on updating the neural network weights in order to calibrate the bias produced by the class imbalance of representative samples. Wu et al. [50] proposed *Bias correction* (BiC) to rectify the weights of the model output, but a validation set is still required. In [33], authors observed that magnitudes of the weight vectors for new classes are higher than those of old classes, then, cosine normalization is used over the output layer to reduce the impact of imbalanced data. In this sense, *Incremental Learning with Dual Memory (LI2M)* [47] corrects scores of old classes storing their statistical information in an additional memory. *Classifier Weights Scaling for Class Incremental Learning* (ScaIL) [51] rectifies the weights of old classes to make them more comparable to those of new classes. Zhao et al. [36] proposed *Weight Aligning* (WA) to correct the biased weights at the output layer once the training process has ended. For this, only weight vectors of new classes are aligned to those of old classes using normalization.

Inter-class separation. The knowledge distillation loss has proven to be useful while producing more discriminative results within old classes when a bias correction is performed [36]. However, distillation loss may not be sufficient to ensure an inter-class separation between old and new classes since decision boundaries are re-configured during training over new classes. Thus, authors in [33] introduced margin ranking loss to encourage a margin that separates old and new classes. Chaudhry et al. [37] used bilevel optimization to update the model with new classes, keeping predictions intact on anchor points of old classes that lie close to the class decision boundaries.

Representative samples. Some strategies have been reported to select representative samples of old classes in order to avoid the model from overfitting to new classes. The baseline method, named Herding [32,52], selects the closest samples as most representative of a class, based on a histogram of the distances to the mean sample of that class. Authors in [53] introduced a more complex solution, named *Mnemonics*, which uses a strategy based on meta-learning to update the memory via gradient descent, selecting those samples located on boundary decisions. Generative solutions may also be found in [54,55], where artificial samples are drawn from each incremental stage, using generative adversarial networks (GANs). However, since GANs have proven to be difficult to optimize, they present scalability issues.

3. Proposed Method

In this section, we introduce the proposed method in detail. First, the Class-incremental learning setting is described. Then, we introduce an overview of the proposed method and its components. Finally, the training algorithm of the proposed method is presented.

3.1. Class Incremental Learning Setting

This research is focused on Class-Incremental Learning (CIL) based on the memory replay approach [22,32], where the neural network model complexity is maintained constant through S incremental stages, while new emotions are sequentially incorporated. In each incremental stage, samples from new emotions and a few samples from old emotions are available to retrain an existing neural network model.

Let $\mathcal{X}$ be a feature space with a label space $\mathcal{Y}$ belonging to classes (emotions) in $\mathcal{C}$. A labeled dataset is defined as $\mathcal{D} = \{(\mathbf{x}, \mathbf{y}) | \mathbf{x} \in \mathcal{X}, \mathbf{y} \in \mathcal{Y}\}$. We assume one initial stage and S incremental stages, where $\mathcal{C}$ is split into $S+1$ sets $\mathcal{C}^0, \mathcal{C}^1 ..., \mathcal{C}^S$ with $\mathcal{C} = \mathcal{C}^0 \cup \mathcal{C}^1 \cup ... \cup \mathcal{C}^S$ and $\mathcal{C}^i \cap \mathcal{C}^j = \emptyset$ for $i \neq j$. A budget is determined for the memory $\mathcal{M} = \{(\mathbf{x}, \mathbf{y}) | \mathbf{x} \in \mathcal{X}, \mathbf{y} \in \mathcal{Y}\}$, which is used to store a limited amount of representative samples from old classes. In the initial stage, a deep neural network model is trained on a labeled dataset $\mathcal{D}_0$. Next, a representative set of samples $\mathcal{E}_0$ is selected and stored in memory $\mathcal{M}$ as a replacement of $\mathcal{D}_0$, with $|\mathcal{E}_0| \ll |\mathcal{D}_0|$. In the incremental stage s, a deep network model is updated using the labeled dataset $\mathcal{D}_s$ and memory $\mathcal{M}$, that is, $\mathcal{D}_s \cup \mathcal{M}$. Notice that $\mathcal{M}$ now contains representative samples of old classes $\mathcal{E}_{0:s-1}$ from incremental stage 0 to $s-1$. We assume all training samples in $\mathcal{D}_s$ are available to train a neural network. In CIL, the main objective is to use a deep network model and $\mathcal{D}_s \cup \mathcal{M}$ to accurately classify samples belonging to old and new classes in each incremental stage s, avoiding catastrophic forgetting.

A deep neural network model is usually denoted as a labeling function f with trainable weights Φ, such that $\hat{\mathbf{y}} = f(\mathbf{x}; \Phi)$. The function f may be represented as composite of two functions, $f_{\text{enc}} \circ f_{\text{cls}}$. Here, f_{enc} represents the part of network that encodes an input $\mathbf{x}$ into a latent feature representation $\mathbf{z}$, that is, $\mathbf{z} = f_{\text{enc}}(\mathbf{x}; \theta)$; θ is the set of trainable weights. Then, latent features $\mathbf{z}$ are fed to a feature labeling function f_{cls} with weights ϕ, in order to produce a classification score $\hat{\mathbf{y}}$, i.e., $\hat{\mathbf{y}} = f_{\text{cls}}(\mathbf{z}; \phi)$. In CIL, the number of classes of the model output increases at each incremental stage. Thus, the network model f is expected to classify $|\mathcal{C}^s|$ more classes at incremental stage s than at stage $s-1$.

3.2. Overview of the Proposed Method

The proposed method, named *Incremental Learning preserving the Learned Feature Space* (IL2FS), faces the catastrophic forgetting problem aiming to preserve the learned feature space from old classes. For this, IL2FS performs a bias correction of new classes, while the inter-class separation and feature space alignment of old classes are ensured. Firstly, a bias correction is performed on the weights at the output layer via Weight Aligning [36], as imbalanced data are present when trained over a reduced set of representative samples of old classes. Then, an inter-class separation is encouraged between scores from old classes and their nearest class (old or new) via margin ranking loss, instead of only encouraging a separation between old and new classes, as reported in [33]. Finally, since that new knowledge may modify the learned feature space at previous CIL stages, we propose to use triplet loss [45] to preserve the feature space alignment of old classes.

The complete flowchart is shown in Figure 1 and the overall objective can be written as follows

$$\mathcal{L}_{\text{inc}}(\mathcal{D}_s, \mathcal{M}, f_{(s-1)}; \Phi) = \beta \cdot \mathcal{L}_{\text{tri}} + \mathcal{L}_{\text{cls}} + \alpha \cdot \mathcal{L}_{\text{mr}}, \quad (1)$$

where $\mathcal{L}_{\text{tri}}$ is the triplet loss, $\mathcal{L}_{\text{cls}}$ is a classification loss, and $\mathcal{L}_{\text{mr}}$ is the margin ranking loss. λ, α, β are the trade-off hyper-parameters.

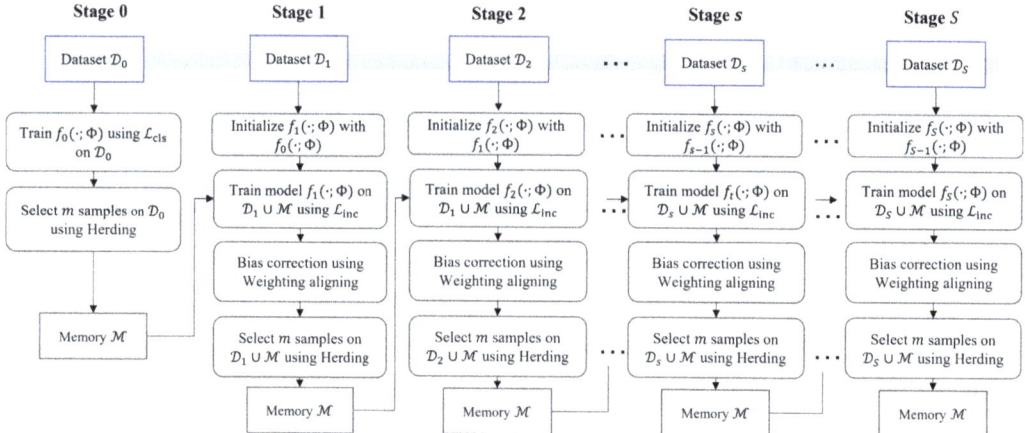

Figure 1. Flowchart of the proposed method throughout S incremental stages.

As shown in Figure 1, the network model f_0 is trained at stage 0 on $\mathcal{D}_0$, using the classification loss. Next, the Herding method [32,52] is employed to select m representative samples to be stored in memory $\mathcal{M}$. At the incremental stage s, weights Φ are initialized using those learned at stage $s-1$. Then, the network model f_s is retrained on $\mathcal{D}_s \cup \mathcal{M}$, using loss function $\mathcal{L}_{\text{inc}}$. Exponential Moving Average (EMA) [56] is also incorporated into IL2FS in order to stabilize the training of f_s over n training steps:

$$\Phi_{\text{EMA}}^{(n)} = (1 - \lambda_{\text{EMA}}) \cdot \Phi_{\text{EMA}}^{(n-1)} + \lambda_{\text{EMA}} \cdot \Phi^{(n)}, \quad (2)$$

where $\Phi_{\text{EMA}}^{(n)}$ is the EMA of successive Φ weights over n and λ_{EMA} is the decay rate or momentum. Then, at the end of the model's training, Weighting Aligning is used to align the norms of the weight vectors between old and new classes at the output layer. Likewise, m representative samples are selected on $\mathcal{D}_s \cup \mathcal{M}$, considering a balanced selection. This procedure is repeated every time new classes emerge, which must be incorporated into an existing model.

3.3. Bias Correction

Weight Aligning (WA) [36] has been used for bias correction, given that a class imbalance is produced by using a reduced set of representative samples of old classes in new incremental stages. Thus, WA rectifies the weight vectors at the output layer of a network model, aligning the norms of the weight vectors between old and new classes.

The output layer is rewritten as

$$\mathbf{W} = (\mathbf{W}_{\text{old}}, \mathbf{W}_{\text{new}}), \qquad (3)$$

where

$$\begin{aligned}\mathbf{W}_{\text{old}} &= (\mathbf{w}_1, \mathbf{w}_2, ..., \mathbf{w}_{C_{\text{old}}}) \in \mathbb{R}^{d \times C_{\text{old}}}, \\ \mathbf{W}_{\text{new}} &= (\mathbf{w}_{C_{\text{old}}+1}, ..., \mathbf{w}_{C_{\text{new}}}) \in \mathbb{R}^{d \times C},\end{aligned} \qquad (4)$$

while the norms of the weight vectors are expressed as follows

$$\begin{aligned}\|\mathbf{W}_{\text{old}}\| &= (\|\mathbf{w}_1\|, \|\mathbf{w}_2\|, ..., \|\mathbf{w}_{C_{\text{old}}}\|), \\ \|\mathbf{W}_{\text{new}}\| &= (\|\mathbf{w}_{C_{\text{old}}+1}\|, ..., \|\mathbf{w}_{C_{\text{new}}}\|).\end{aligned} \qquad (5)$$

Then, the weights of new classes are normalized by using

$$\bar{\mathbf{W}}_{\text{new}} = \gamma \cdot \mathbf{W}_{\text{new}}, \qquad (6)$$

where

$$\gamma = \frac{M(\|\mathbf{W}_{\text{old}}\|)}{M(\|\mathbf{W}_{\text{new}}\|)}. \qquad (7)$$

Here, $M(\cdot)$ computes the mean value using these weight vectors.

3.4. Inter-Class Separation

We assume that decision regions of old classes may change during model retraining, as representative samples of old classes are used for this process. Then, an inter-class separation is ensured by setting a margin over class scores throughout the different incremental learning stages.

Margin ranking loss was introduced in [33] to ensure a separation between old and new classes (see Section 2). Unlike previous work, we use a variant of the margin ranking loss to encourage an inter-class separation between the ground-truth score of an old class and its nearest score coming from any class, old or new.

For each sample $\mathbf{x}$ in memory $\mathcal{M}$, a separation is encouraged between the ground-truth old classes and their nearest class (old or new). For each sample $\mathbf{x}$ in memory $\mathcal{M}$, the score $\bar{\omega}(\mathbf{x})$ of the ground-truth old class is considered positive, while the maximum score $\bar{\omega}^k(\mathbf{x})$ among the remaining classes is considered hard negative. We have:

$$\mathcal{L}_{\text{mr}} = \sum_{\mathbf{x} \sim \{\mathcal{M}\}} \sum_{k=1}^{K} \max(b - \bar{\omega}(\mathbf{x}) + \bar{\omega}^k(\mathbf{x}), 0), \qquad (8)$$

where b is the margin, $\bar{\omega}(\mathbf{x})$ is the score of the ground-truth class for the sample $\mathbf{x}$, and $\bar{\omega}^k(\mathbf{x})$ is the nearest class score for $\mathbf{x}$.

3.5. Feature Space Alignment

We incorporate triplet loss [45] to leverage the less forgetting, preserving the alignment of the feature space of classes learned at previous incremental stages. Note that existing strategies are mainly focused on maintaining the same output predictions of old classes (see Section 2). On the other hand, previous works in CIL [42–44] have mainly used triplet loss to train embedding networks and ensure an inter-class separation. However, unlike previous works, we incorporate triplet loss to preserve the feature space alignment of old samples, producing near feature representations from $f_{\text{enc}_{(s-1)}}$ and $f_{\text{enc}_{(s)}}$ for the same processed sample. Here, $f_{\text{enc}_{(s-1)}}$ is the model learned at the last incremental stage $(s-1)$ and $f_{\text{enc}_{(s)}}$ is the new model to train in the current stage s. Representations from different samples, processed by $f_{\text{enc}_{(s-1)}}$ and $f_{\text{enc}_{(s)}}$, are pushed away from each other by a small margin. Note that class labels for the processed samples are not used in our proposal, as an inter-class separation is not pursued.

More specifically, we use triplet loss to push latent feature representations $\mathbf{z}_{s-1} = f_{\text{enc}_{(S-1)}}(\mathbf{x}_1)$ and $\mathbf{z}_s = f_{\text{enc}_{(S)}}(\mathbf{x}_1)$ close to each other for the same sample $\mathbf{x}_1$. Meanwhile, the latent features $\mathbf{z}_{s-1}$ and $\mathbf{z}_s$, produced by $f_{\text{enc}_{(S-1)}}$ and $f_{\text{enc}_{(S)}}$, but coming from samples $\mathbf{x}_1$ and $\mathbf{x}_2$, are pushed away from each other by a margin.

The triplet loss is defined as follows

$$\mathcal{L}_{\text{tri}} = \sum_{\mathbf{x} \sim \{\mathcal{M}\}} \max(d(\mathbf{z}^a, \mathbf{z}^p) - d(\mathbf{z}^a, \mathbf{z}^n) + a, 0), \qquad (9)$$

where $\mathbf{z}^a$ is the anchor input, $\mathbf{z}^p$ is a positive input of the same label as $\mathbf{z}^a$, while $\mathbf{z}^n$ is a negative input of a different label as $\mathbf{z}^a$; a is the margin and d is the cosine dissimilarity measure. Anchor-positive pairs are formed by latent features generated by $f_{\text{enc}_{(S-1)}}$ and $f_{\text{enc}_{(S)}}$ for the same sample, while anchor-negative pairs are formed by latent features generated by $f_{\text{enc}_{(s-1)}}$ and $f_{\text{enc}_{(S)}}$ for a pair of different samples. $f_{\text{enc}_{(S-1)}}$ processes all samples within the current batch to generate their respective latent feature representations. After, each featured sample is labeled according to its index into the batch of samples. This procedure is repeated for all samples but using $f_{\text{enc}_{(S)}}$; later, featured samples are concatenated with those obtained by $f_{\text{enc}_{(S-1)}}$. Then, the multi-similarity miner [57] is used to generate anchor-positive pairs $(\mathbf{z}^a, \mathbf{z}^p)$ and anchor-negative pairs $(\mathbf{z}^a, \mathbf{z}^n)$ over labeled feature representations in order to preserve the feature alignment of old classes.

3.6. Training of IL2FS

Algorithm 1 presents the training procedure of IL2FS at incremental stage s. First, the set of weights Φ is initialized using weights $\Phi_{(s-1)}$ (line 1). Next, we compute latent features for $\mathbf{x}$ using the reference model and current model (lines 7–8). Featured samples are labeled according to their indices into the dataset (lines 9–10). Anchor-positive and anchor-negative pairs are generated using the Multi-similarity miner (line 11) to be employed in triplet loss $\mathcal{L}_{\text{tri}}$. Then, scores for ground-truth old classes and their nearest classes are computed in order to be used in margin ranking loss $\mathcal{L}_{\text{mr}}$ (lines 12–14). After, neural network model f_s is trained using the loss function $\mathcal{L}_{\text{inc}}$ (line 15). Note that $\mathcal{L}_{\text{inc}}$ is composed of classification loss $\mathcal{L}_{\text{cls}}$, triplet loss $\mathcal{L}_{\text{tri}}$ and margin ranking loss $\mathcal{L}_{\text{mr}}$. The EMA weights $\Phi_{\text{EMA}}^{(n)}$ are computed from $\Phi^{(n)}$ (line 16). After training f_s, weight vectors of the output layer are rectified employing the Weighting Aligning method (line 18). Finally, the memory $\mathcal{M}$ is updated by selecting m representative samples on $\mathcal{D}_s \cup \mathcal{M}$ by means of the Herding method (line 19).

Algorithm 1 Training algorithm of IL2FS at incremental stage s.

Inputs: $\mathcal{D}_s$ – training labeled dataset from new classes; $\mathcal{M}$ – memory containing representative samples from old classes; $f_{(s-1)}(\cdot;\Phi_{s-1})$ – reference model trained at incremental stage $s-1$; $\lambda_{\mathrm{mr}}, \alpha, \beta$ – trade-off hyperparameters; λ_{EMA} – decay rate; η – learning rate; n – number of epochs.

Output: $f_s(\cdot;\Phi_{\mathrm{EMA}})$ – a trained neural network model; $\mathcal{M}$ – updated memory with representative samples from old classes.

1: Initialize Φ_s with $\Phi_{(s-1)}$.
2: $\mathbf{x}_{old}, \mathbf{y}_{old} \leftarrow \mathcal{M}$
3: $\mathbf{x}_{new}, \mathbf{y}_{new} \leftarrow \mathcal{D}_s$
4: $\mathbf{x} \leftarrow \mathbf{x}_{old} \cup \mathbf{x}_{new}$
5: $\mathbf{y} \leftarrow \mathbf{y}_{old} \cup \mathbf{y}_{new}$
6: **repeat**
7:    $\mathbf{z}_{ref} \leftarrow f_{\mathrm{enc}_{(S-1)}}(\mathbf{x})$ ▷ Compute features for samples using the reference model
8:    $\mathbf{z}_{cur} \leftarrow f_{\mathrm{enc}_{(S)}}(\mathbf{x})$ ▷ Compute features for samples using the current model
9:    $\mathbf{v}_{ref} \leftarrow \mathrm{GenerateLabels}(\mathbf{z}_{ref})$ ▷ Assign labels based on indices into the dataset
10:    $\mathbf{v}_{cur} \leftarrow \mathrm{GenerateLabels}(\mathbf{z}_{cur})$
11:    $\mathbf{z}^a, \mathbf{z}^p, \mathbf{z}^n \leftarrow \mathrm{MultiSimilartyMiner}(\mathbf{z}_{ref} \cup \mathbf{z}_{cur}, \mathbf{v}_{ref} \cup \mathbf{v}_{cur})$ ▷ Generate anchor-positive and anchor-negative pairs
12:    $\bar{\omega}(\mathbf{x}) \leftarrow f_{(s-1)}(\mathbf{x}_{old})$ ▷ Compute scores for samples from old classes using the reference model
13:    $\bar{\omega}_a(\mathbf{x}) \leftarrow f_s(\mathbf{x})$ ▷ Compute scores for all samples using the current model
14:    $\bar{\omega}^k(\mathbf{x}) \leftarrow \mathrm{NearestClass}(\bar{\omega}(\mathbf{x}), \bar{\omega}_a(\mathbf{x}))$ ▷ Obtain scores from the nearest classes to old classes
15:    $\Phi^{(i)} \leftarrow \Phi^{(i-1)} - \eta \cdot \nabla[\beta \cdot \mathcal{L}_{\mathrm{tri}}(\mathbf{z}^a, \mathbf{z}^p, \mathbf{z}^n; \Phi^{(i-1)}) + \mathcal{L}_{\mathrm{cls}}(f_s(\mathbf{x}), \mathbf{y}; \Phi^{(i-1)}) + \alpha \cdot \mathcal{L}_{\mathrm{mr}}(\bar{\omega}(\mathbf{x}), \bar{\omega}^k(\mathbf{x}); \Phi^{(i-1)})]$
16:    $\Phi_{\mathrm{EMA}}^{(i)} = (1 - \lambda_{\mathrm{EMA}}) \cdot \Phi_{\mathrm{EMA}}^{(i-1)} + \lambda_{\mathrm{EMA}} \cdot \Phi^{(i)}$
17: **until** n epochs are reached
18: $\Phi_{\mathrm{EMA}} \leftarrow \mathrm{WeightingAligning}(\Phi_{\mathrm{EMA}})$ ▷ Bias correction
19: $\mathcal{M} \leftarrow \mathrm{Herding}(\mathcal{D}_s \cup \mathcal{M})$.   ▷ memory is updated using the Herding method
20: **return** $f_s(\cdot;\Phi_{\mathrm{EMA}}), \mathcal{M}$

4. Experimental Design

This section first describes two public datasets used in our experiments. Then, the neural network architecture, comparison methods and implementation details are introduced. (Code is available at https://github.com/mjmnzg/IL2FS. Accessed on 11 January 2022).

4.1. Datasets

Experiments were performed on two public datasets, DREAMER [46] and DEAP [11], since they are benchmarks for emotion recognition research [3,14,15,21]. DREAMER is a multi-channel dataset containing records of nine emotions from EEG signals per subject. Likewise, DEAP is a large-scale dataset containing EEG signals with different emotional evaluations. More importantly, both datasets were selected since a high number of classes may be obtained from EEG data, making it useful for the analysis of the catastrophic forgetting problem in emotion recognition.

The DREAMER dataset comprises EEG data from 23 subjects (14 male and nine female). EEG data were collected while the subjects watched 18 film clips, which contain cut-out scenes to evoke nine emotions: calmness, surprise, amusement, fear, excitement, disgust, happiness, anger, and sadness. The length of each film clip is between 65 to 393 s (M = 199 s). EEG signals were recorded at a sampling rate of 128 Hz using an Emotiv EPOC system that uses 16 electrodes, following locations according to the International 10–20 systems: AF3, F7, F3, FC5, T7, P7, O1, O2, P8, T8, FC6, F4, F8, AF4, M1, and M2. Sensor M1 acts as a ground reference, while M2 is a feed-forward reference; then, the remaining 14 electrodes were recorded and used for feature extraction. EEG data from all subjects have 18 experimental EEG trials, two per elicited emotion. Each EEG trial begins with a neural film to help the subjects return to the neutral emotion state, while data serve as a baseline. EEG signals of each trial were filtered with Hamming bandpass linear phase FIR filters to extract frequencies inside the ranges of interest (4–30 Hz). Likewise, artifacts were removed by using artifact subspace reconstruction (ASR) [58]. At the final step, the Common Average Reference (CAR) method [59] was applied to compute the average value over all electrodes and subtracts it from each sample of each electrode. In our experiments, we adopt a discrete categorization instead of a dimensional categorization, with nine classes available.

The DEAP dataset contains EEG and peripheral physiological signals from 32 subjects while watching 40 music videos. EEG signals were collected using a cap of 32 electrodes, placed according to the international 10–20 system [60]. For this, a sampling rate of 512 Hz was used, then downsampled to 128 Hz. We used the pre-processed data (https://www.eecs.qmul.ac.uk/mmv/datasets/deap/readme.html. Accessed on 1 June 2021), where each trial contains 60 s of recorded signals under stimulation and 3 s of baseline signals in a relaxed state. A bandpass filter from 4.0–45.0 Hz was applied over EEG signals, and eye artifacts were removed as in [11] using independent component analysis (ICA). EEG data were averaged to the common reference. Subjects rate their levels of arousal, valence, linking, and dominance from 1 to 9 for each music video. In our experiments, we adopt a multi-class categorization scheme, combining discrete ratings of valence, arousal and dominance. Firstly, we divide each emotion dimension into two categories using a rating of 5 as threshold: low/high valence, low/high arousal and low/high dominance. Secondly, we label each EEG trial used as a combination of binary categorization in three dimensions. For instance, its label is 0 when the rating is low for the three dimensions, while the label is 1 when the rating for valence and arousal is low, but the rating for dominance is high. Finally, the recognition task is a multi-class classification composed of a maximum of 8 classes, given that not all subjects rate for every level of arousal, valence and dominance.

4.2. Preprocessing

We applied the preprocessing procedure of baseline removal on EEG signals as in the works reported by [3,15,21,61] since this method highlights the effects of stimulated emotions. We begin by using a non-overlapping window to slice baseline signals into N segments of 1 s for each trial and C electrodes. From the set of N segments, we obtain the mean segment, which represents the base emotional state without stimulation. Next, the mean segment is subtracted from the EEG signals under stimulation. The obtained differences represent the electrical changes in the brain under stimulation. Following this pre-processing, 1080 EEG samples are obtained for each subject in DREAMER, where 60 segments are obtained from each experimental trial; 18 experimental trials per subject. In this direction, each trial in DEAP is divided into 60 segments, each one containing 128 sampling points. Then, we obtain 2400 EEG samples for each subject since there are 40 trials per subject. Finally, each EEG sample in DREAMER and DEAP is a 32×128 matrix and 14×128 matrix, composed of the number of electrodes and sampling points, respectively.

4.3. Neural Network Architecture

We adopted a Capsule Network (CapsNet) architecture [21], which showed one of the best accuracy performances for EEG-based emotion recognition research. Figure 2 presents the CapsNet architecture and Table 1 describes the implementation details. Unlike the original CapsNet architecture, we add a module based on an attention mechanism, which includes a Channel-Attention block [62] into the modules from Convolutional to PrimaryCaps. In addition, the bottleneck layer proposed in [21] was removed since it dramatically increases the resources used in memory. To train CapsNet, the classification loss $\mathcal{L}_{cls}$ uses the margin and reconstruction losses, as suggested in [63]. For this purpose, CapsNet employs a separated margin loss $\mathcal{L}_k$ for each class k. On the other hand, reconstruction loss $\mathcal{L}_{rec}$ uses the sum of squared differences between the outputs of a decoder and the input EEG signal values. This decoder consists of 3 fully-connected layers that model the EEG signals.

Table 1. Specifications of the Capsule Network architecture. We include a Channel-Attention block before the PrimaryCaps module. The decoder setting for reconstruction loss is shown at the bottom.

Id	Modules	Layers (Input ID)	Hyperparameters	Output Shape
I1	Input	–	–	DREAMER: 14×128 DEAP: 32×128
C2	Convolutional	Convolution-2D (I1)	DREAMER: 64 filters, size = 6, stride = 1, activation = ReLU DEAP: 64 filters, size = 9, stride = 2, activation = ReLU	DREAMER: $64 \times 123 \times 9$ DEAP: $64 \times 60 \times 12$
A3		Average pooling (C2)	Size = 1, stride = 1	
C4		Convolution-2D (A3)	32 filters, size = 1, stride = 1, activation = ReLU	
C5	Channel-Attention	Convolution-2D (C4)	64 filters, size = 1, stride = 1	
M6		Maxpooling (C2)	size=1, stride=1	
C7		Convolution-2D (M6)	32 filters, size = 1, stride = 1, activation = ReLU	
C8		Convolution-2D (C7)	64 filters, size = 1, stride = 1	
S9		Sum (C5, C8)	–	
A10		Activation (S9)	Sigmoid	DREAMER: $64 \times 123 \times 9$ DEAP: $64 \times 60 \times 12$
C11	PrimaryCaps	Convolution-2D (A10)	DREAMER: 8×16 filters, size = 6, stride = 2 DEAP: 8×16 filters, size = 9, stride = 2	
R12		Reshape (C11)	–	DREAMER: 1088×8 DEAP: 832×8
E13	EmotionCaps	Dynamic routing (R12)	16 units	16×16
N14	Norm	Normalization (E13)	–	16
O15	FC	Fully connected (N14)	Dynamic outputs	DREAMER: 9 DEAP: 8
Decoder				
F1	FC1	Fully connected (O15)	256 units	256
F2	FC2	Fully connected (F1)	512 units	512
F3	FC3	Fully connected (F2)	DREAMER: 14×128 units DEAP: 32×128 units	DREAMER: 14×128 DEAP: 32×128

4.4. Comparison Methods

We compared IL2FS with eight popular and recent CIL methods based on memory replay: Fine-tuning (FT) [51], Fine-tuning+Nearest Centroid Classifier (FT+NCC) [41,51], Less without Forgetting (LwF) [49], Incremental Classifier and Representation Learning (iCARL) [32], Mnemonics [53], ScaIL [51], Weighting Aligning (WA) [36], and Geodesic+LUCIR [25]. We selected such CIL methods in our comparison since they arise as promising solutions to address the catastrophic forgetting problem in emotion recognition. All comparison methods were downloaded from repositories of original authors and then adapted for our experiments, except FT and FT+NCC, which do not represent a challenge to implement as they are basic methods. Note that all CIL methods use the same preprocessing procedure and the CapsNet architecture described in the previous sections.

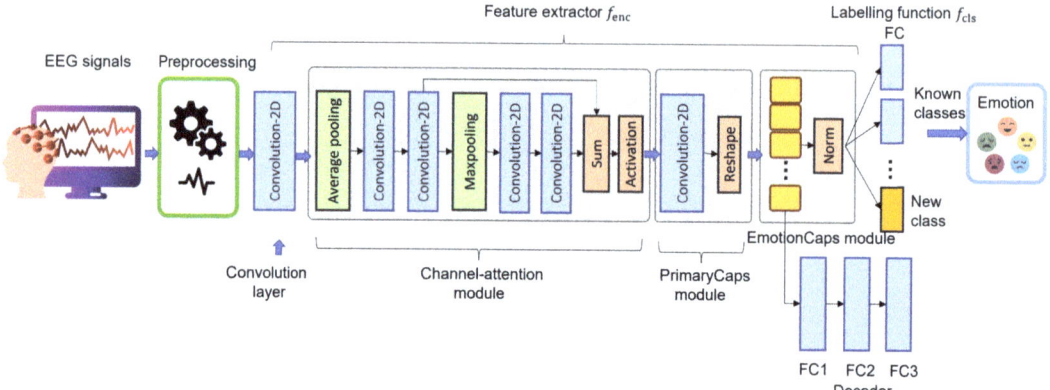

Figure 2. Diagram of the Capsule Network architecture.

4.5. Implementation Details

We first configured the hyper-parameters for the classification loss of the CapsNet architecture. Thus, the margins m^+ and m^- for the separated margin loss $\mathcal{L}_{cls}$ were set to 0.9 and 0.1, as suggested in [21,63]. Likewise, the reconstruction loss $\mathcal{L}_{rec}$ was scaled by 0.3 during training; this value was selected from {0.01, 0.1, 0.2, 0.3, and 0.5}.

Concerning the specific configuration of our proposed method, we adopted a mean layer instead of a normalization layer (N14) in the CapsNet architecture. For $\mathcal{L}_{tri}$, we used a margin $a = 0.1$ since a feature space alignment is pursued between extracted features from a reference network model and a new network model; a larger margin showed to affect the classification results negatively. To ensure an inter-class separation via margin ranking loss $\mathcal{L}_{mr}$, we used a margin b equal to 5, which was selected from {1, 3, 5, 8, and 10}. Finally, for trade-off hyper-parameters, we used $\alpha = 1$ and $\beta = 0.1$, which were selected from {0.01, 0.1, 1, and 2}. We use a momentum $\lambda_{EMA} = 0.995$ to place a greater significance on the most recent values.

Table 2 describes the specific hyper-parameters of CIL methods used in our comparison. Similar to our proposal, all hyperparameters were selected via grid search in combination with coordinated descent [64] in order to ensure the best configuration. Specifically, we select a small finite list of values for each hyper-parameter and each value is changed at a time while the rest of the hyper-parameters remains fixed.

Table 2. Hyper-parameter setting. a,b are margins; $\lambda, \lambda_o, \lambda_{dis}, \lambda_{mr}$, are the trade-off hyperparameters for each CIL method.

Methods	Hyper-Parameters
FT, FT+NCC, ScaIL	-
LwF, iCARL	$T = 2, \lambda_o = 1$
Mnemonics	$\lambda_{dis} = 0.5, \lambda_{mr} = 1, b = 5$
WA	$T = 2, \lambda = 0.4$
Geodesic+LUCIR	$\lambda_{dis} = 1, \lambda_{mr} = 1, b = 5$

Regarding the training algorithm of the CIL methods, we used Adam optimizer employing a mini-batch size of 10; a larger size showed to reduce the classification results using an incremental learning evaluation. For DREAMER, we set a learning rate of 0.001 up to epoch 30, when it decays to 0.0001, keeping this value until epoch 50 when the training concludes. For DEAP, we set an initial learning rate of 0.001 up to epoch 15, when it also decays by a factor of 10, and then holds this value until the end of epoch 20. Other learning rates (0.1, 0.01, 0.001, 0.0001) were evaluated, but they did not improve the accuracy performance. An L1 regularizer was incorporated to CapsNet with a weight decay of 0.0004 for the Adam algorithm.

Our proposal and the comparison methods were implemented with PyTorch and trained on an Intel(R) Core (TM) i7 PC with an Nvidia GTX 1080 graphics card and Ubuntu v20.04 LTS.

4.6. Evaluation

As reported in [22,32], we follow the standard evaluation protocol used for the CIL setting based on the memory replay approach. The Holdout method is applied for a given dataset to build the training and testing data for each available class. Likewise, classes are arranged in a fixed random order. Each method is trained in a class-incremental way on available training data, as described in Section 3.1. At the end of each incremental stage, the resulting classifier is evaluated on testing data for already trained classes. Note that the testing dataset is not revealed to the CIL methods during training in each incremental stage to avoid overfitting. At the end of S incremental stages, we obtain S classification accuracies, averaged and reported as the final result.

We adopted an instantiation of the above protocol for each subject's data on the DREAMER and DEAP datasets, considering the most challenging scenario possible. Firstly, we start from a model trained on two classes, while remaining classes in DREAMER and DEAP come in 7 and at most six incremental stages, respectively. Secondly, we set the memory size $\mathcal{M}$ to approximately 1% of the full training set from each subject in order to store representative samples from old classes. We used 90% of the data of each class for training, while the rest of the data was used for testing. Thus, about ten samples can be stored in memory for DREAMER through 7 incremental stages, while at least 28 samples can be stored for DEAP during six stages. Note that not all subjects in DEAP rate the same levels of arousal, valence and dominance, producing an imbalanced dataset; an oversampling was applied using a random selection. Classes from incremental stages are arranged in sequence with a fixed random order. We performed five repetitions with different partitions of data and different classes, using different random seeds; a stratified sampling was performed with respect to the classes. From accuracy results by training in a class-incremental way, we compute the average and standard deviation over the incremental stages as final results. We assumed that training and testing datasets are independent and identically distributed, i.e., both datasets were drawn from the same distribution. Thus, we did not consider any change of distribution.

5. Results

Table 3 shows the average accuracy and standard deviation for all methods over DREAMER. We observed that IL2FS achieved the best average accuracy (59.08%) with one of the lowest standard deviations (8.26). Notice that IL2FS outperformed the second-best method (Mnemonics) by 8.96 percentage points (pp). Statistical differences were computed among the evaluated methods on the average accuracy of the 23 subjects. The Friedman test was applied, followed by Wilcoxon signed-rank as post hoc with the Finner correction. Friedman's test showed significant differences among CIL methods ($\chi^2(8) = 169.99$, $p = 0.0$). The Wilcoxon test indicated that the difference between IL2FS and CIL methods was statistically significant ($p < 0.05$).

Table 4 shows the average accuracy and standard deviation for all methods on DEAP. We can see that IL2FS achieved the best average accuracy (79.36%) with the lowest standard deviation (4.68). The second-best method was Geodesic+LUCIR, obtaining an average accuracy of 8.94 percentage points shorter than IL2FS. Friedman's test indicated significant differences among compared methods ($\chi^2(8) = 230.03$, $p = 0.0$). Wilcoxon signed-rank test revealed that differences between IL2FS and CIL methods are statistically significant ($p < 0.05$) for the given dataset.

Table 3. Accuracy and standard deviation for CIL methods on the DREAMER dataset using approximately 1% of the training size. The best results are in bold.

Subj.	FT	FT+NCC	LwF	iCARL	Mnemonics	ScaIL	WA	Geodesic +LUCIR	IL2FS
1	44.08 ± 13.86	48.63 ± 13.37	44.78 ± 10.25	48.26 ± 09.95	51.94 ± 14.00	40.09 ± 11.21	47.65 ± 14.92	53.29 ± 16.29	**64.58 ± 12.02**
2	35.82 ± 13.87	38.31 ± 14.31	37.27 ± 15.84	39.95 ± 16.19	47.86 ± 17.64	30.56 ± 11.64	39.83 ± 19.94	42.54 ± 14.50	**53.64 ± 11.78**
3	32.51 ± 11.59	34.93 ± 09.87	33.32 ± 12.91	37.31 ± 13.34	42.54 ± 12.50	29.96 ± 11.96	35.33 ± 14.45	44.37 ± 14.46	**54.43 ± 11.12**
4	53.96 ± 11.88	56.55 ± 11.41	54.23 ± 14.23	56.84 ± 14.47	60.72 ± 15.30	40.09 ± 08.64	55.13 ± 16.93	60.16 ± 13.10	**64.08 ± 09.19**
5	38.76 ± 14.35	41.65 ± 13.52	35.65 ± 15.67	37.73 ± 16.52	51.42 ± 16.95	29.24 ± 10.62	39.87 ± 17.65	51.13 ± 17.09	**60.74 ± 12.52**
6	35.80 ± 13.39	38.47 ± 13.38	36.38 ± 15.31	40.12 ± 15.06	44.35 ± 14.42	34.98 ± 09.59	37.01 ± 16.35	42.08 ± 12.74	**53.31 ± 12.94**
7	32.77 ± 11.33	35.89 ± 11.14	31.71 ± 11.98	35.87 ± 13.15	42.01 ± 13.49	27.76 ± 08.13	34.81 ± 14.29	45.17 ± 14.06	**56.34 ± 10.35**
8	33.77 ± 11.41	36.90 ± 11.63	31.03 ± 11.29	33.39 ± 11.84	41.25 ± 12.33	27.18 ± 10.71	34.57 ± 12.06	43.31 ± 13.65	**49.98 ± 10.66**
9	28.69 ± 08.12	32.11 ± 09.09	28.75 ± 11.89	32.67 ± 11.03	37.97 ± 13.07	25.95 ± 09.10	30.72 ± 14.50	39.73 ± 13.10	**49.07 ± 12.59**
10	35.62 ± 13.81	38.06 ± 14.24	36.46 ± 15.85	38.56 ± 15.54	40.70 ± 13.61	28.70 ± 08.46	38.47 ± 13.67	40.54 ± 12.53	**51.48 ± 11.21**
11	35.91 ± 10.19	39.53 ± 10.20	33.02 ± 13.70	36.61 ± 12.86	41.62 ± 12.32	34.08 ± 13.04	36.83 ± 12.10	46.29 ± 13.24	**56.08 ± 14.38**
12	45.95 ± 09.95	50.54 ± 10.42	46.08 ± 12.05	49.81 ± 12.10	56.21 ± 14.50	37.23 ± 09.55	51.48 ± 15.69	57.70 ± 13.65	**66.81 ± 09.14**
13	46.41 ± 15.88	48.24 ± 16.25	45.25 ± 16.26	48.39 ± 15.22	57.09 ± 14.84	39.42 ± 09.57	52.48 ± 16.78	55.51 ± 15.10	**68.07 ± 11.11**
14	45.27 ± 12.84	48.52 ± 11.64	46.56 ± 18.02	49.50 ± 17.38	54.18 ± 16.59	38.57 ± 14.70	50.10 ± 21.21	51.96 ± 17.24	**60.94 ± 13.67**
15	64.27 ± 11.47	66.17 ± 11.13	66.48 ± 10.64	69.18 ± 09.85	72.71 ± 12.81	56.49 ± 09.08	69.19 ± 11.46	71.30 ± 11.16	**81.16 ± 07.11**
16	34.37 ± 14.03	37.87 ± 13.67	32.26 ± 11.43	35.40 ± 09.38	42.87 ± 12.67	29.04 ± 08.59	35.41 ± 14.72	43.04 ± 15.06	**50.80 ± 12.11**
17	37.99 ± 12.40	41.80 ± 11.50	38.42 ± 12.16	42.11 ± 11.88	45.49 ± 14.32	31.50 ± 11.78	40.99 ± 13.49	46.73 ± 13.16	**53.91 ± 09.47**
18	50.14 ± 16.92	52.06 ± 17.31	48.56 ± 15.28	51.88 ± 15.45	57.97 ± 17.41	41.17 ± 13.13	52.66 ± 17.81	56.76 ± 15.63	**62.78 ± 11.35**
19	57.42 ± 12.95	61.90 ± 11.30	56.79 ± 15.52	59.20 ± 15.40	65.67 ± 11.72	50.43 ± 10.23	61.13 ± 16.25	66.94 ± 10.98	**71.56 ± 09.73**
20	27.09 ± 13.44	28.79 ± 12.87	29.47 ± 15.63	31.08 ± 14.62	35.81 ± 13.15	23.91 ± 09.11	32.62 ± 15.21	35.83 ± 13.98	**49.75 ± 14.18**
21	41.34 ± 10.87	43.63 ± 10.44	39.95 ± 13.04	42.68 ± 12.74	48.10 ± 12.20	31.82 ± 07.02	42.34 ± 15.87	48.22 ± 10.99	**54.25 ± 12.23**
22	57.39 ± 12.71	61.14 ± 11.34	55.15 ± 14.11	57.58 ± 13.71	66.89 ± 10.40	47.36 ± 08.72	57.42 ± 16.16	64.07 ± 10.88	**68.49 ± 13.69**
23	43.66 ± 15.63	45.99 ± 14.33	38.93 ± 16.62	41.39 ± 16.67	47.38 ± 16.08	32.77 ± 10.21	40.98 ± 17.76	45.17 ± 16.29	**56.66 ± 12.17**
Avg.	41.69 ± 09.80	44.68 ± 09.91	41.15 ± 09.85	44.15 ± 09.85	50.12 ± 09.31	35.14 ± 08.20	44.22 ± 10.22	50.08 ± 09.31	**59.08 ± 08.26**

Table 4. Accuracy and standard deviation for CIL methods on the DEAP dataset using approximately 1% of the training size. The best results are in bold.

Subj.	FT	FT+NCC	LwF	iCARL	Mnemonics	ScaIL	WA	Geodesic +LUCIR	IL2FS
1	57.65 ± 13.84	64.62 ± 11.95	55.14 ± 12.12	62.57 ± 12.48	74.60 ± 17.04	53.14 ± 11.94	61.80 ± 17.93	75.06 ± 13.42	**86.47 ± 06.85**
2	56.83 ± 16.68	61.35 ± 15.75	56.30 ± 18.12	58.82 ± 18.08	64.09 ± 17.77	54.10 ± 05.81	59.24 ± 19.92	62.53 ± 16.90	**74.33 ± 10.94**
3	56.23 ± 09.27	60.40 ± 08.77	59.29 ± 12.84	63.56 ± 12.33	63.78 ± 15.90	52.40 ± 06.23	62.50 ± 12.58	67.24 ± 14.66	**74.31 ± 09.64**
4	58.44 ± 15.77	63.74 ± 15.60	60.47 ± 15.14	65.21 ± 16.46	62.51 ± 18.69	57.31 ± 03.44	60.78 ± 17.60	69.60 ± 14.88	**75.91 ± 12.26**
5	57.34 ± 13.39	63.42 ± 12.05	55.10 ± 11.90	59.98 ± 11.68	66.71 ± 17.31	51.64 ± 09.14	60.28 ± 14.03	69.12 ± 12.86	**78.55 ± 08.14**
6	55.84 ± 14.10	63.04 ± 12.13	56.09 ± 15.08	63.04 ± 14.71	72.35 ± 15.76	51.28 ± 08.98	60.66 ± 17.94	72.20 ± 16.01	**83.16 ± 06.61**
7	64.44 ± 16.04	70.54 ± 14.46	62.59 ± 17.69	69.65 ± 14.68	75.40 ± 15.97	59.38 ± 04.19	67.31 ± 19.10	79.58 ± 14.97	**85.28 ± 06.72**
8	60.46 ± 14.56	67.00 ± 12.39	60.82 ± 14.35	66.61 ± 13.25	70.96 ± 16.66	53.71 ± 03.99	64.64 ± 15.48	71.79 ± 12.41	**82.59 ± 06.95**
9	52.65 ± 15.77	59.46 ± 16.01	52.85 ± 15.62	59.02 ± 15.60	65.73 ± 17.89	48.87 ± 04.24	55.72 ± 16.74	64.45 ± 13.76	**78.22 ± 10.15**
10	72.54 ± 11.89	78.08 ± 10.06	70.43 ± 11.95	74.33 ± 11.30	72.70 ± 13.22	62.91 ± 04.42	74.19 ± 12.94	82.04 ± 09.11	**85.71 ± 05.15**
11	52.94 ± 19.03	59.58 ± 17.35	55.42 ± 18.49	63.22 ± 18.36	64.73 ± 21.20	52.12 ± 07.23	57.57 ± 20.20	66.36 ± 19.73	**77.96 ± 10.11**
12	68.06 ± 16.98	72.76 ± 15.16	68.35 ± 16.77	74.88 ± 15.33	71.02 ± 17.65	69.16 ± 09.76	70.10 ± 15.46	76.61 ± 14.52	**79.11 ± 11.29**
13	46.32 ± 12.19	52.48 ± 11.53	45.36 ± 13.13	50.33 ± 12.75	64.25 ± 16.59	38.55 ± 02.58	48.49 ± 17.13	59.71 ± 15.87	**74.74 ± 12.02**
14	51.04 ± 15.11	58.49 ± 13.71	49.41 ± 16.74	55.65 ± 16.96	64.15 ± 14.57	45.08 ± 03.87	51.73 ± 15.93	63.48 ± 15.68	**75.37 ± 10.65**
15	51.02 ± 13.96	57.96 ± 13.57	53.10 ± 15.41	59.35 ± 15.51	71.36 ± 15.69	53.49 ± 04.22	54.30 ± 16.34	63.75 ± 15.15	**80.50 ± 08.37**
16	61.86 ± 09.81	67.57 ± 09.20	62.10 ± 09.96	67.35 ± 09.11	61.78 ± 19.88	54.16 ± 05.12	63.79 ± 11.46	70.24 ± 13.35	**82.10 ± 10.33**
17	49.18 ± 10.97	55.58 ± 11.15	49.45 ± 13.83	55.88 ± 12.93	61.75 ± 16.90	42.52 ± 04.61	50.79 ± 13.57	62.45 ± 12.58	**68.84 ± 10.02**
18	63.45 ± 09.97	69.54 ± 09.27	61.68 ± 08.82	67.09 ± 08.02	76.78 ± 15.31	66.03 ± 07.85	67.34 ± 14.30	74.56 ± 13.68	**79.82 ± 06.34**
19	61.31 ± 12.87	66.52 ± 12.27	62.42 ± 13.15	67.44 ± 10.48	71.57 ± 17.28	59.35 ± 04.81	66.83 ± 13.87	71.54 ± 16.72	**82.06 ± 08.84**
20	68.44 ± 15.69	73.53 ± 13.52	66.13 ± 17.82	70.82 ± 15.53	67.01 ± 19.20	61.15 ± 05.18	70.73 ± 16.44	74.44 ± 15.08	**82.96 ± 09.52**
21	69.70 ± 14.88	74.58 ± 13.07	69.10 ± 13.62	73.16 ± 13.39	70.00 ± 21.43	67.61 ± 07.90	72.44 ± 16.90	77.39 ± 15.35	**79.11 ± 10.35**
22	66.38 ± 09.98	73.02 ± 10.07	64.10 ± 12.25	69.00 ± 11.38	70.31 ± 13.68	58.79 ± 06.31	69.03 ± 14.77	72.83 ± 09.96	**80.14 ± 08.90**
23	47.61 ± 12.34	55.60 ± 11.60	47.39 ± 09.88	56.89 ± 12.95	77.79 ± 15.13	48.54 ± 05.05	55.51 ± 17.85	69.97 ± 09.84	**83.30 ± 06.33**
24	66.44 ± 15.95	71.95 ± 13.35	68.02 ± 18.04	73.78 ± 16.02	72.32 ± 18.86	66.30 ± 09.06	70.66 ± 18.62	74.67 ± 15.46	**84.28 ± 07.59**

Table 4. *Cont.*

Subj.	FT	FT+NCC	LwF	iCARL	Mnemonics	ScaIL	WA	Geodesic +LUCIR	IL2FS
25	49.94 ± 12.30	57.68 ± 10.63	52.73 ± 10.53	60.48 ± 09.41	63.30 ± 16.39	47.68 ± 04.95	52.64 ± 13.20	62.91 ± 12.41	**76.20** ± 10.29
26	48.79 ± 08.93	54.62 ± 09.74	47.65 ± 08.71	52.85 ± 08.86	60.39 ± 15.62	48.20 ± 08.45	51.76 ± 09.78	59.99 ± 11.23	**66.78** ± 10.25
27	54.70 ± 11.18	64.47 ± 09.56	49.45 ± 07.82	66.25 ± 08.30	80.64 ± 12.15	54.49 ± 10.94	60.36 ± 15.18	74.16 ± 11.72	**80.90** ± 06.87
28	57.35 ± 10.50	64.41 ± 09.25	57.00 ± 11.46	64.69 ± 10.14	69.88 ± 14.89	55.19 ± 07.71	60.71 ± 16.05	71.67 ± 11.63	**77.46** ± 09.02
29	73.05 ± 07.99	77.94 ± 06.10	72.27 ± 07.88	77.25 ± 08.10	78.84 ± 11.28	73.64 ± 08.85	74.40 ± 08.67	82.36 ± 09.38	**85.87** ± 05.34
30	69.05 ± 13.69	74.11 ± 11.48	69.88 ± 13.77	74.64 ± 12.90	75.45 ± 15.11	67.46 ± 03.91	72.50 ± 12.96	80.69 ± 11.56	**83.45** ± 08.12
31	61.55 ± 14.27	66.49 ± 13.00	62.38 ± 12.17	66.14 ± 11.69	67.71 ± 17.99	57.06 ± 04.07	64.61 ± 14.79	69.30 ± 13.98	**77.63** ± 09.48
32	47.53 ± 09.34	54.37 ± 09.16	46.70 ± 10.90	55.44 ± 12.88	71.31 ± 14.29	46.57 ± 06.33	50.94 ± 15.02	60.83 ± 10.50	**76.49** ± 09.43
Avg.	58.69 ± 07.83	64.84 ± 07.24	58.41 ± 07.76	64.56 ± 07.00	69.41 ± 05.48	55.56 ± 08.20	62.01 ± 07.60	70.42 ± 06.50	**79.36** ± 04.68

Comparison with baseline. Figure 3 presents a comparison of IL2FS and existing CIL methods concerning the baseline approach (CapsNet-wo-memory), that is, when CapsNet did not include any data from old classes in a CIL training. In addition, we also included the average accuracy when CapsNet is trained using all training samples from old classes (CapsNet-Full) in each incremental stage. We observed that CapsNet-wo-memory obtained the worst accuracy results when samples of old classes are not available in the memory, suggesting the presence of catastrophic forgetting. However, CapsNet improved its accuracy performance when samples of old classes were employed during Fine-tuning (FT). Note that IL2FS and advanced CIL methods improved the average accuracy of FT by incorporating a specific strategy to address the catastrophic forgetting problem, except ScaIL and LwF. Finally, we observed that IL2FS is still exposed to catastrophic forgetting as CapsNet-Full achieved 90.63% and 98.17% on DEAP and DREAMER.

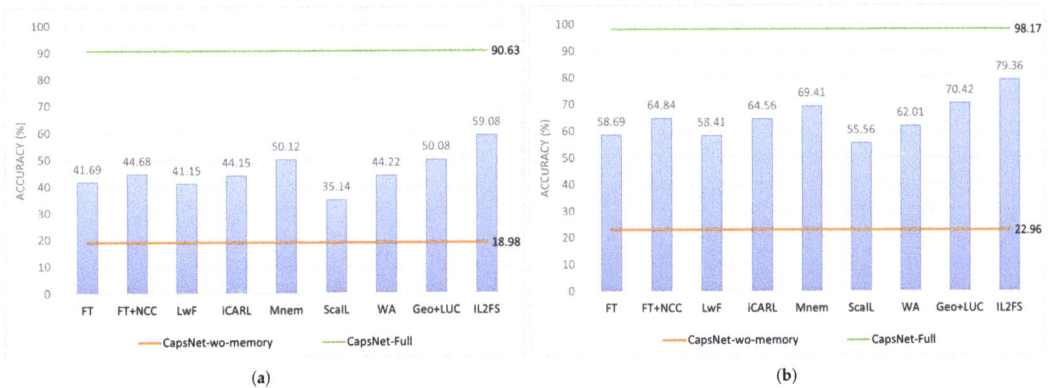

Figure 3. Comparison of CIL methods with baseline approaches on (**a**) DREAMER and (**b**) DEAP. CapsNet-wo-memory represents the average accuracy obtained by CapsNet when data from old classes are not included in the memory during the CIL training. CapsNet-Full indicates the average accuracy using all training samples from old classes in each incremental stage. Mnem and Geo+LUC indicate Mnemonics and Geodesic+LUCIR, respectively.

5.1. Ablation Studies

In this section, we present an analysis with respect to the number of reserved samples from old classes. After, we study the impact of the number of new emotions incorporated into the neural network model. Finally, we analyze the impact of each component of IL2FS.

5.1.1. Effect of the Number of Reserved Samples

Figure 4 shows the comparison of IL2FS with CIL methods, when the memory of old samples has a size close to 1%, 2%, and 5% of the size of the full training set for each subject on DREAMER and DEAP. As expected, CIL methods improved their accuracy performance when more samples were stored in the memory. However, we can see that IL2FS still maintains the best average accuracy for different sizes of the reserved samples. For DREAMER, 66.73% and 75.06% were obtained by IL2FS when the memory is close to 2% and 5% of the size of the full training set. For DEAP, IL2FS achieved average accuracies of 85.35% and 90.73% using memory sizes of 2% and 5%, respectively. Note that our proposal obtained a greater gain in average accuracy than the comparison methods when a smaller number of samples from old classes is reserved in the memory.

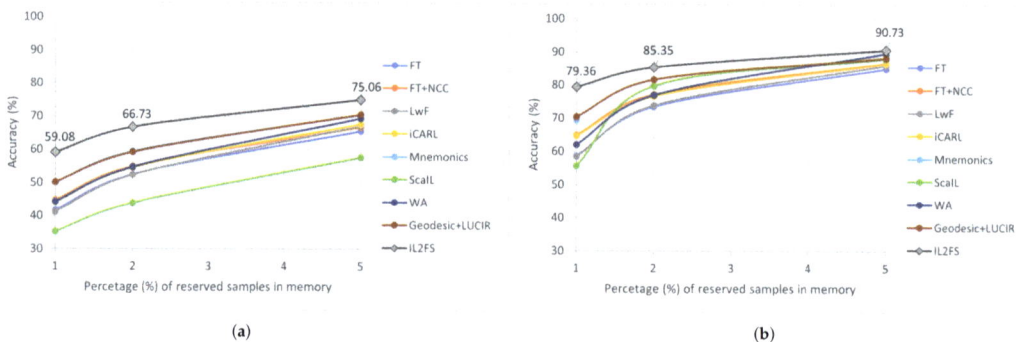

Figure 4. Effect of the number of reserved samples in memory: (**a**) DREAMER and (**b**) DEAP.

5.1.2. Effect of the Number of Incremental Stages

Figure 5 shows the average accuracy of IL2FS for each incremental stage in comparison to CIL methods on DREAMER. We reported the average accuracy of CIL methods over all subjects, employing memory sizes of 1% and 5% of the size of the full training dataset. Accuracy results for CapsNet-wo-memory and CapsNet-Full were also included as baselines. We observed that a CIL strategy helps reduce catastrophic forgetting by improving the accuracy performance of CapsNet-wo-memory. However, note that CIL methods decrease their accuracy performance when the number of stages is increased. It is worth mentioning that IL2FS achieved the best average accuracies throughout different incremental stages. In addition, IL2FS obtained a greater gain than existing methods during the last incremental stages because fewer samples from old classes can be stored in the memory.

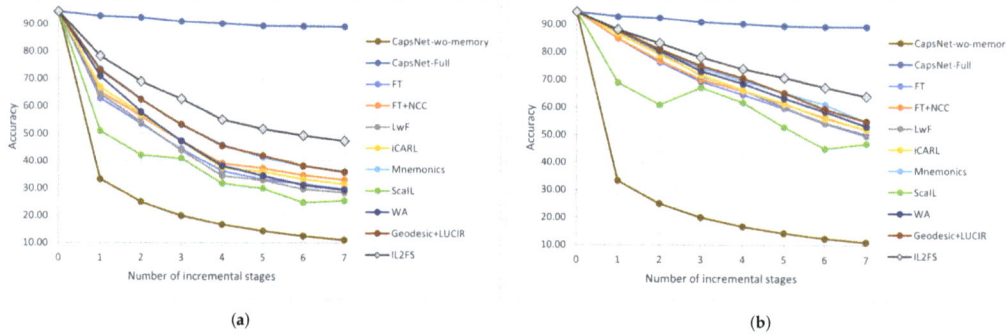

Figure 5. Effect of the number of incremental stages on the DREAMER dataset, using memory sizes of (**a**) 1% and (**b**) 5% of the full training dataset of each subject. We reported average accuracy in each incremental stage over all subjects.

5.1.3. Effect of Each Component of IL2FS

The proposed method comprises three main strategies: weight aligning for bias correction, margin ranking loss for inter-class separation and triplet loss for a feature space alignment of old classes. Table 5 shows the average accuracy over all subjects for each evaluated dataset. Note that Fine-tuning achieved an average accuracy of 41.69% and 58.69% over DREAMER and DEAP, respectively. By using weight aligning for bias correction, the average accuracy is improved by 4.86 and 3.99 percentage points over the DREAMER and DEAP datasets. A variant of margin ranking loss was incorporated to encourage a separation between each ground-truth old class and its nearest class (old or new). This modification allowed IL2FS to outperform Fine-tuning+Weight aligning by 10.22 and 15.33 percentage points over DREAMER and DEAP, respectively. In addition, triplet loss was used to keep a similar alignment of the feature space of old classes. From experiments, we found that by encouraging such alignment, an improvement of 2.31 and 1.35 percentage points is observed in average accuracy on DREAMER and DEAP, respectively.

Table 5. Effect of each component of IL2FS on DREAMER and DEAP. The best results are in bold.

Method	DREAMER	DEAP
Fine-tuning (FT)	41.69 ± 09.80	58.69 ± 07.83
FT+Weight Aligning	46.55 ± 09.01	62.68 ± 07.29
FT+Weight Aligning+Margin ranking loss	56.77 ± 08.47	78.01 ± 04.25
FT+Weight Aligning+Margin ranking loss+Triplet loss (IL2FS)	**59.08 ± 08.26**	**79.36 ± 04.68**

6. Discussion

Experiments showed that a standard deep learning model for emotion recognition (CapsNet) degrades its accuracy performance when trained in a class-incremental way over only samples from new emotions. This problem, known as catastrophic forgetting, is presented because previously learned emotions are negatively affected when new ones are incorporated into the classifier model. Thus, unlike previous works as reported in [3,8,13–16,20,21], this research is focused on studying the catastrophic forgetting problem in EEG-based emotion recognition.

By incorporating existing CIL methods to CapsNet, we showed that classification results of the baseline approach (CapsNet-wo-memory) can be improved, suggesting that CIL methods can help mitigate the catastrophic forgetting in EEG-based emotion recognition. However, experimental results on two public datasets showed that existing CIL methods do not ensure high average accuracies. Thus, a CIL method was developed and validated to address the catastrophic forgetting problem.

Previously, Lee et al. [41] studied the CIL over the imagined speech task from EEG signals. Authors used fine-tuning and the nearest neighbor classifier to address the catastrophic forgetting, however, they stored 20% of the full data of every old class in each incremental stage. Furthermore, only one incremental stage was used for CIL evaluation, while more stages are needed to observe the negative impact of catastrophic forgetting. On the other hand, our experiments consider a rigorous evaluation over two datasets for emotion recognition, including popular and recent CIL methods in our comparison. Based on our results, we found that IL2FS outperformed existing CIL methods on two public datasets: DREAMER and DEAP. Note that we integrated a weighting aligning as the WA method for bias correction, but an inter-class separation and a feature space alignment were also considered by IL2FS, outperforming WA by 14.28 pp and 17.35 pp on DREAMER and DEAP, respectively. Like IL2FS, the Mnemonics and Geodesic+LUCIR methods ensure an inter-class separation via margin ranking loss, but IL2FS encourages the separation between old classes and their nearest one, including old or new, instead of only ensuring a separation between old and new classes. Although Mnemonics and Geodesic+LUCIR also consider strategies for bias correction and an alignment of output predictions, our proposal outperformed Mnemonics by 8.96 pp and 9.95 pp on DREAMER and DEAP, while Geodesic+LUCIR was outperformed by 9 pp and 8.94 pp, respectively. In addition, note that comparison methods, such as LwF, iCARL, WA, Mnemonics, and Geodesic+LUCIR, use different strategies to align the output predictions of old classes to leverage the less forgetting. Unlike these works, IL2FS incorporates triplet loss to preserve the feature space alignment of old classes instead of the output predictions.

Regarding the evaluation which varies the number of reserved samples and the number of incremental stages, IL2FS showed a clear advantage compared to existing methods when the number of reserved samples in the memory is reduced. This issue is also observed when a greater number of CIL stages are achieved since a lower number of samples per class may be stored in memory. The above indicates that IL2FS preserves the learned knowledge better than compared methods throughout different incremental stages on the most challenging scenario possible for the evaluated datasets. On the other hand, as expected, every evaluated method improved its accuracy performance whenever the number of reserved samples in the memory is increased. However, by using a memory size near 5%, IL2FS still obtained the best average accuracy on the DREAMER, while it is similar with respect to the existing CIL methods for the DEAP dataset.

Concerning the effect of each component of IL2FS, weight aligning improved the average accuracy over the Fine-tuning method, which indicates that performing a bias correction is important to reduce the catastrophic forgetting problem in EEG-based emotion recognition. Then, margin ranking loss was incorporated to ensure an inter-class separation between each old class and its nearest class (old or new). Previous work in [33] showed that a separation between old and new classes might be sufficient to help reduce the catastrophic forgetting. However, we found that this strategy [33] on IL2FS obtained a similar average accuracy on DREAMER ($58.55 \pm 7.33\%$ vs. $58.74 \pm 07.56\%$), but the accuracy performance is drastically reduced on DEAP ($53.36 \pm 08.84\%$ vs. $79.36 \pm 04.68\%$). These results suggest that it is preferable to encourage an inter-class separation between each old class and its nearest class (old or new) instead of only ensuring a separation between old and new classes. Finally, unlike previous CIL works [42–44] where triplet loss is mainly used to train embedding networks and provide an inter-class separation, we used such loss function to maintain the same aligning of the feature space learned at previous incremental stages. For this, IL2FS aims to produce near feature representations coming from a reference model and a new model for the same processed sample, while features from different samples are pushed away from each other by a small margin. This strategy showed to be beneficial for the CIL task in two emotion recognition datasets.

The presented study may contribute to designing and building more adaptive and scalable classifiers, as our study showed a first Class-incremental Learning solution to avoid reconfiguring the entire system when new emotions are incorporated sequentially. For this, we consider an evaluation of the most challenging scenario that may be built over the two public datasets for emotion recognition. However, our study did not consider other CIL settings and evaluation protocols. Furthermore, other preprocessing procedures and neural network architectures were also not explored.

7. Conclusions

In this paper, we presented IL2FS, a CIL method to address the catastrophic forgetting in EEG-based emotion recognition from EEG signals. IL2FS aims to preserve the feature space learned over previous incremental stages, performing a bias correction of new classes and ensuring the inter-class separation and feature space alignment from classes learned at previous incremental stages. The proposed method was incorporated into a Capsule Network architecture for EEG-based emotion recognition. Our experiments showed that IL2FS achieved the best average accuracy over two public emotion datasets, outperforming popular and recent CIL methods under different memory sizes. Furthermore, Friedman and Wilcoxon's tests showed that IL2FS significantly outperformed existing CIL methods over the evaluated datasets, using the standard protocol for CIL methods based on memory replay. By using IL2FS, better preservation of the learned knowledge is possible when presented with a greater number of incremental stages and a reduced number of reserved samples in memory. In this direction, new emotions may be incorporated into an existing deep neural network classifier without retraining from scratch, employing a set of representative samples of emotions previously learned in a sequential way. However, the presented results suggest that the proposed solution is still exposed to catastrophic forgetting for a high number of incremental stages and limited memory size.

As future work, we are interested in studying the negative effect of batch normalization layers since a bias may be produced over learned statistics from old classes by training over imbalanced data.

Author Contributions: Conceptualization, M.J.-G.; formal analysis, M.J.-G.; investigation, M.J.-G.; methodology, M.J.-G.; project administration, M.J.-G. and R.A.-E.; software, M.J.-G.; supervision, R.A.-E.; writing—original draft preparation, M.J.-G. and R.A.-E.; writing—review and editing, M.J.-G. and R.A.-E. All authors have read and agreed to the published version of the manuscript.

Funding: This research was funded by the Mexican Council of Science and Technology (COMECYT), grant number CAT2021-0193.

Institutional Review Board Statement: Not applicable.

Informed Consent Statement: Not applicable.

Data Availability Statement: Not applicable.

Conflicts of Interest: The authors declare no conflicts of interest.

Abbreviations

The following abbreviations are used in this manuscript:

BiC	Bias correction
CapsNet	Capsule Network
CIL	Class-incremental Learning
CNN	Convolutional Neural Network
DBN	Deep Belief Network
EEG	Electroencephalogram
FT	Fine-tuning
NCC	Nearest Centroid Classifier
GAN	Generative adversarial network
GNN	Graph Neural Network
iCARL	Incremental Classifier and Representation Learning
IL2FS	Incremental Learning preserving the Learned Feature Space
LI2M	Incremental Learning with Dual Memory
LUCIR	Learning a Unified Classifier Incrementally via Rebalancing
LwF	Learning without Forgetting
ScaIL	Classifier Weights Scaling for Class Incremental Learning
WA	Weight Aligning

References

1. Deng, J.J.; Leung, C.H.C.; Milani, A.; Chen, L. Emotional States Associated with Music: Classification, Prediction of Changes, and Consideration in Recommendation. *ACM Trans. Interact. Intell. Syst.* **2015**, *5*, 1–36. [CrossRef]
2. Ali, M.; Mosa, A.H.; Al Machot, F.; Kyamakya, K. EEG-based emotion recognition approach for e-healthcare applications. In Proceedings of the 2016 Eighth International Conference on Ubiquitous and Future Networks (ICUFN), Vienna, Austria, 5–8 July 2016; pp. 946–950.
3. Huang, D.; Chen, S.; Liu, C.; Zheng, L.; Tian, Z.; Jiang, D. Differences first in asymmetric brain: A bi-hemisphere discrepancy convolutional neural network for EEG emotion recognition. *Neurocomputing* **2021**, *448*, 140–151. [CrossRef]
4. Alarcão, S.M.; Fonseca, M.J. Emotions Recognition Using EEG Signals: A Survey. *IEEE Trans. Affect. Comput.* **2019**, *10*, 374–393. [CrossRef]
5. Kim, J.H.; Poulose, A.; Han, D.S. The Extensive Usage of the Facial Image Threshing Machine for Facial Emotion Recognition Performance. *Sensors* **2021**, *21*, 2026. [CrossRef]
6. Poulose, A.; Reddy, C.S.; Kim, J.H.; Han, D.S. Foreground Extraction Based Facial Emotion Recognition Using Deep Learning Xception Model. In Proceedings of the 2021 Twelfth International Conference on Ubiquitous and Future Networks (ICUFN), Barcelona, Spain, 5–8 July 2021; pp. 356–360.

7. Han, K.; Yu, D.; Tashev, I. Speech Emotion Recognition Using Deep Neural Network and Extreme Learning Machine. *Interspeech* **2014**, 223–227.
8. Song, T.; Liu, S.; Zheng, W.; Zong, Y.; Cui, Z. Instance-adaptive graph for EEG emotion recognition. In Proceedings of the AAAI Conference on Artificial Intelligence, New York, NY, USA, 2–12 February 2020; Volume 34, pp. 2701–2708.
9. Agrafioti, F.; Hatzinakos, D.; Anderson, A.K. ECG pattern analysis for emotion detection. *IEEE Trans. Affect. Comput.* **2011**, *3*, 102–115. [CrossRef]
10. Cheng, B.; Liu, G. Emotion Recognition from Surface EMG Signal Using Wavelet Transform and Neural Network. In Proceedings of the 2008 2nd International Conference on Bioinformatics and Biomedical Engineering, Shanghai, China, 16–18 May 2008; pp. 1363–1366. [CrossRef]
11. Koelstra, S.; Muhl, C.; Soleymani, M.; Lee, J.S.; Yazdani, A.; Ebrahimi, T.; Pun, T.; Nijholt, A.; Patras, I. DEAP: A Database for Emotion Analysis ;Using Physiological Signals. *IEEE Trans. Affect. Comput.* **2012**, *3*, 18–31. [CrossRef]
12. Lan, Y.T.; Liu, W.; Lu, B.L. Multimodal Emotion Recognition Using Deep Generalized Canonical Correlation Analysis with an Attention Mechanism. In Proceedings of the 2020 International Joint Conference on Neural Networks (IJCNN), Anchorage, AK, USA, 19–24 July 2020; pp. 1–6.
13. Zhong, P.; Wang, D.; Miao, C. EEG-based emotion recognition using regularized graph neural networks. *IEEE Trans. Affect. Comput.* **2020**, 1–12. [CrossRef]
14. Shen, L.; Zhao, W.; Shi, Y.; Qin, T.; Liu, B. Parallel Sequence-Channel Projection Convolutional Neural Network for EEG-Based Emotion Recognition. *IEEE Access* **2020**, *8*, 222966–222976. [CrossRef]
15. Tao, W.; Li, C.; Song, R.; Cheng, J.; Liu, Y.; Wan, F.; Chen, X. EEG-based Emotion Recognition via Channel-wise Attention and Self Attention. *IEEE Trans. Affect. Comput.* **2020**, 1–12. [CrossRef]
16. Topic, A.; Russo, M. Emotion recognition based on EEG feature maps through deep learning network. *Eng. Sci. Technol. Int. J.* **2021**, *24*, 1442–1454. [CrossRef]
17. Salankar, N.; Mishra, P.; Garg, L. Emotion recognition from EEG signals using empirical mode decomposition and second-order difference plot. *Biomed. Signal Process. Control* **2021**, *65*, 102389. [CrossRef]
18. Shen, F.; Peng, Y.; Kong, W.; Dai, G. Multi-Scale Frequency Bands Ensemble Learning for EEG-Based Emotion Recognition. *Sensors* **2021**, *21*, 1262. [CrossRef] [PubMed]
19. Xu, X.; Zhang, Y.; Tang, M.; Gu, H.; Yan, S.; Yang, J. Emotion Recognition Based on Double Tree Complex Wavelet Transform and Machine Learning in Internet of Things. *IEEE Access* **2019**, *7*, 154114–154120. [CrossRef]
20. Chao, H.; Liu, Y. Emotion Recognition From Multi-Channel EEG Signals by Exploiting the Deep Belief-Conditional Random Field Framework. *IEEE Access* **2020**, *8*, 33002–33012. [CrossRef]
21. Liu, Y.; Ding, Y.; Li, C.; Cheng, J.; Song, R.; Wan, F.; Chen, X. Multi-channel EEG-based emotion recognition via a multi-level features guided capsule network. *Comput. Biol. Med.* **2020**, *123*, 103927. [CrossRef] [PubMed]
22. Belouadah, E.; Popescu, A.; Kanellos, I. A comprehensive study of class incremental learning algorithms for visual tasks. *Neural Netw.* **2021**, *135*, 38–54. [CrossRef]
23. Geng, X.; Smith-Miles, K. *Incremental Learning*; Springer: Berlin/Heidelberg, Germany, 2009.
24. Kirkpatrick, J.; Pascanu, R.; Rabinowitz, N.; Veness, J.; Desjardins, G.; Rusu, A.A.; Milan, K.; Quan, J.; Ramalho, T.; Grabska-Barwinska, A.; et al. Overcoming catastrophic forgetting in neural networks. *Proc. Natl. Acad. Sci. USA* **2017**, *114*, 3521–3526. [CrossRef]
25. Simon, C.; Koniusz, P.; Harandi, M. On learning the geodesic path for incremental learning. In Proceedings of the IEEE/CVF Conference on Computer Vision and Pattern Recognition, Nashville, TN, USA, 20–25 June 2021; pp. 1591–1600.
26. Liu, Y.; Schiele, B.; Sun, Q. Adaptive aggregation networks for class-incremental learning. In Proceedings of the IEEE/CVF Conference on Computer Vision and Pattern Recognition, Nashville, TN, USA, 20–25 June 2021; pp. 2544–2553.
27. Yan, S.; Xie, J.; He, X. DER: Dynamically Expandable Representation for Class Incremental Learning. In Proceedings of the IEEE/CVF Conference on Computer Vision and Pattern Recognition, Nashville, TN, USA, 20–25 June 2021; pp. 3014–3023.
28. Hayes, T.L.; Kafle, K.; Shrestha, R.; Acharya, M.; Kanan, C. Remind your neural network to prevent catastrophic forgetting. In Proceedings of the European Conference on Computer Vision, Glasgow, UK, 23–28 August 2020; pp. 466–483.
29. Liu, Y.; Parisot, S.; Slabaugh, G.; Jia, X.; Leonardis, A.; Tuytelaars, T. More classifiers, less forgetting: A generic multi-classifier paradigm for incremental learning. In Proceedings of the Computer Vision–ECCV 2020: 16th European Conference, Glasgow, UK, 23–28 August 2020; pp. 699–716.
30. Rajasegaran, J.; Khan, S.; Hayat, M.; Khan, F.S.; Shah, M. Itaml: An incremental task-agnostic meta-learning approach. In Proceedings of the IEEE/CVF Conference on Computer Vision and Pattern Recognition, Seattle, WA, USA, 14–19 June 2020; pp. 13588–13597.
31. Hu, W.; Qin, Q.; Wang, M.; Ma, J.; Liu, B. Continual Learning by Using Information of Each Class Holistically. In Proceedings of the AAAI Conference on Artificial Intelligence, Virtual Event, 2–9 February 2021; Volume 35, pp. 7797–7805. Available online: https://ojs.aaai.org/index.php/AAAI/article/view/16952 (accessed on 12 January 2022).
32. Rebuffi, S.A.; Kolesnikov, A.; Sperl, G.; Lampert, C.H. Icarl: Incremental classifier and representation learning. In Proceedings of the IEEE conference on Computer Vision and Pattern Recognition, Honolulu, HI, USA, 21–26 July 2017; pp. 2001–2010.
33. Hou, S.; Pan, X.; Loy, C.C.; Wang, Z.; Lin, D. Learning a unified classifier incrementally via rebalancing. In Proceedings of the IEEE/CVF Conference on Computer Vision and Pattern Recognition, Long Beach, CA, USA, 16–17 June 2019; pp. 831–839.

34. Iscen, A.; Zhang, J.; Lazebnik, S.; Schmid, C. Memory-efficient incremental learning through feature adaptation. In Proceedings of the European Conference on Computer Vision, Glasgow, UK, 23–28 August 2020; pp. 699–715.
35. Prabhu, A.; Torr, P.H.; Dokania, P.K. Gdumb: A simple approach that questions our progress in continual learning. In Proceedings of the European Conference on Computer Vision, Glasgow, UK, 23–28 August 2020; pp. 524–540.
36. Zhao, B.; Xiao, X.; Gan, G.; Zhang, B.; Xia, S.T. Maintaining discrimination and fairness in class incremental learning. In Proceedings of the IEEE/CVF Conference on Computer Vision and Pattern Recognition, Seattle, WA, USA, 13–19 June 2020; pp. 13208–13217.
37. Chaudhry, A.; Gordo, A.; Dokania, P.K.; Torr, P.H.S.; Lopez-Paz, D. Using Hindsight to Anchor Past Knowledge in Continual Learning. In Proceedings of the Thirty-Fifth AAAI Conference on Artificial Intelligence, AAAI 2021, Virtual Event, 2–9 February 2021; pp. 6993–7001. Available online: https://ojs.aaai.org/index.php/AAAI/article/view/16861 (accessed on 12 January 2022).
38. Bang, J.; Kim, H.; Yoo, Y.; Ha, J.W.; Choi, J. Rainbow Memory: Continual Learning with a Memory of Diverse Samples. In Proceedings of the IEEE/CVF Conference on Computer Vision and Pattern Recognition, Nashville, TN, USA, 20–25 June 2021; pp. 8218–8227.
39. Kurmi, V.K.; Patro, B.N.; Subramanian, V.K.; Namboodiri, V.P. Do not Forget to Attend to Uncertainty while Mitigating Catastrophic Forgetting. In Proceedings of the IEEE/CVF Winter Conference on Applications of Computer Vision, Waikola, HI, USA, 5–9 January 2021; pp. 736–745.
40. Tang, S.; Chen, D.; Zhu, J.; Yu, S.; Ouyang, W. Layerwise optimization by gradient decomposition for continual learning. In Proceedings of the IEEE/CVF Conference on Computer Vision and Pattern Recognition, Nashville, TN, USA, 20–25 June 2021; pp. 9634–9643.
41. Lee, D.Y.; Lee, M.; Lee, S.W. Decoding Imagined Speech Based on Deep Metric Learning for Intuitive BCI Communication. *IEEE Trans. Neural Syst. Rehabil. Eng.* **2021**, *29*, 1363–1374. [CrossRef]
42. Huo, J.; Zyl, T.L.v. Comparative Analysis of Catastrophic Forgetting in Metric Learning. In Proceedings of the 2020 7th International Conference on Soft Computing Machine Intelligence (ISCMI), Stockholm, Sweden, 14–15 November 2020; pp. 68–72. [CrossRef]
43. Yu, L.; Twardowski, B.; Liu, X.; Herranz, L.; Wang, K.; Cheng, Y.; Jui, S.; Weijer, J.V.d. Semantic drift compensation for class-incremental learning. In Proceedings of the IEEE/CVF Conference on Computer Vision and Pattern Recognition, Seattle, WA, USA, 14–19 June 2020; pp. 6982–6991.
44. Zhao, H.; Fu, Y.; Kang, M.; Tian, Q.; Wu, F.; Li, X. Mgsvf: Multi-grained slow vs. fast framework for few-shot class-incremental learning. *arXiv* **2021**, arXiv:2006.15524.
45. Schroff, F.; Kalenichenko, D.; Philbin, J. Facenet: A unified embedding for face recognition and clustering. In Proceedings of the IEEE Conference on Computer Vision and Pattern Recognition, Boston, MA, USA, 7–12 June 2015; pp. 815–823.
46. Katsigiannis, S.; Ramzan, N. DREAMER: A Database for Emotion Recognition Through EEG and ECG Signals From Wireless Low-cost Off-the-Shelf Devices. *IEEE J. Biomed. Health Inform.* **2018**, *22*, 98–107. [CrossRef] [PubMed]
47. Belouadah, E.; Popescu, A. Il2m: Class incremental learning with dual memory. In Proceedings of the IEEE/CVF International Conference on Computer Vision, Seoul, Korea, 27–28 October 2019; pp. 583–592.
48. Hinton, G.; Vinyals, O.; Dean, J. Distilling the knowledge in a neural network. *arXiv* **2015**, arXiv:1503.02531.
49. Li, Z.; Hoiem, D. Learning without forgetting. *IEEE Trans. Pattern Anal. Mach. Intell.* **2017**, *40*, 2935–2947. [CrossRef] [PubMed]
50. Wu, Y.; Chen, Y.; Wang, L.; Ye, Y.; Liu, Z.; Guo, Y.; Fu, Y. Large scale incremental learning. In Proceedings of the IEEE/CVF Conference on Computer Vision and Pattern Recognition, Long Beach, CA, USA, 16–17 June 2019; pp. 374–382.
51. Belouadah, E.; Popescu, A. ScaIL: Classifier Weights Scaling for Class Incremental Learning. In Proceedings of the 2020 IEEE Winter Conference on Applications of Computer Vision (WACV), Snowmass Village, CO, USA, 1–5 March 2020.
52. Welling, M. Herding Dynamic Weights for Partially Observed Random Field Models. In Proceedings of the Twenty-Fifth Conference on Uncertainty in Artificial Intelligence, UAI 2009, Montreal, QC, Canada, 18–21 June 2009; pp. 599–606.
53. Liu, Y.; Su, Y.; Liu, A.A.; Schiele, B.; Sun, Q. Mnemonics training: Multi-class incremental learning without forgetting. In Proceedings of the IEEE/CVF conference on Computer Vision and Pattern Recognition, Seattle, WA, USA, 14–19 June 2020; pp. 12245–12254.
54. Wu, C.; Herranz, L.; Liu, X.; van de Weijer, J.; Raducanu, B. Memory replay gans: Learning to generate new categories without forgetting. *Adv. Neural Inf. Process. Syst.* **2018**, *31*, 5962–5972.
55. van de Ven, G.M.; Siegelmann, H.T.; Tolias, A.S. Brain-inspired replay for continual learning with artificial neural networks. *Nat. Commun.* **2020**, *11*, 4069. [CrossRef]
56. Tarvainen, A.; Valpola, H. Mean teachers are better role models: Weight-averaged consistency targets improve semi-supervised deep learning results. In Proceedings of the Advances in Neural Information Processing Systems 30, Long Beach, CA, USA, 4–9 December 2017; pp. 1195–1204.
57. Wang, X.; Han, X.; Huang, W.; Dong, D.; Scott, M.R. Multi-Similarity Loss with General Pair Weighting for Deep Metric Learning. In Proceedings of the IEEE Conference on Computer Vision and Pattern Recognition, Long Beach, CA, USA, 16–17 June 2019; pp. 5022–5030.
58. Mullen, T.R.; Kothe, C.A.; Chi, Y.M.; Ojeda, A.; Kerth, T.; Makeig, S.; Jung, T.P.; Cauwenberghs, G. Real-time neuroimaging and cognitive monitoring using wearable dry EEG. *IEEE Trans. Biomed. Eng.* **2015**, *62*, 2553–2567. [CrossRef] [PubMed]
59. Davidson, R.J. Affective neuroscience and psychophysiology: Toward a synthesis. *Psychophysiology* **2003**, *40*, 655–665. [CrossRef]
60. Sanei, S.; Chambers, J.A. *EEG Signal Processing*; John Wiley & Sons: Hoboken, NJ, USA, 2013.

61. Yang, Y.; Wu, Q.; Fu, Y.; Chen, X. Continuous Convolutional Neural Network with 3D Input for EEG-Based Emotion Recognition. In *Information Processing*; Cheng, L., Leung, A.C.S., Ozawa, S., Eds.; Springer International Publishing: Cham, Switzerland, 2018; pp. 433–443.
62. Woo, S.; Park, J.; Lee, J.Y.; Kweon, I.S. CBAM: Convolutional Block Attention Module. In Proceedings of the Computer Vision–ECCV 2018, Munich, Germany, 8–14 September 2018; Springer International Publishing: Cham, Switzerland, 2018; pp. 3–19.
63. Sabour, S.; Frosst, N.; Hinton, G.E. Dynamic Routing Between Capsules. In *Advances in Neural Information Processing Systems*; Guyon, I., Luxburg, U.V., Bengio, S., Wallach, H., Fergus, R., Vishwanathan, S., Garnett, R., Eds.; Curran Associates, Inc.: New York, NY, USA, 2017; Volume 30.
64. Montavon, G.; Orr, G.B.; Müller, K. (Eds.) *Neural Networks: Tricks of the Trade*, 2nd ed.; Lecture Notes in Computer Science; Springer: Berlin/Heidelberg, Germany, 2012; Volume 7700.

Article

Infrared Small Target Detection Based on Partial Sum Minimization and Total Variation

Sur Singh Rawat [1,*], Saleh Alghamdi [2], Gyanendra Kumar [3], Youseef Alotaibi [4], Osamah Ibrahim Khalaf [5] and Lal Pratap Verma [6]

1. JSS Academy of Technical Education, Noida 201301, India
2. Department of Information Technology, College of Computers and Information Technology, Taif University, Taif 21944, Saudi Arabia; s.algamedi@tu.edu.sa
3. School of Computing Sciences and Engineering, Galgotias University, Greater Noida 201306, India; gyanendrakumar@galgotiasuniversity.edu.in
4. Department of Computer Science, College of Computer and Information Systems, Umm Al-Qura University, Makkah 21955, Saudi Arabia; yaotaibi@uqu.edu.sa
5. Al-Nahrain Nano-Renewable Energy Research Center, Al-Nahrain University, Baghdad 10001, Iraq; usama81818@nahrainuniv.edu.iq
6. Department of Computer and Communication Engineering, Manipal University Jaipur, Jaipur 302004, India; lalpratap.verma@jaipur.manipal.edu
* Correspondence: sur.rawat@jssaten.ac.in

Abstract: In the advanced applications, based on infrared detection systems, the precise detection of small targets has become a tough work today. This becomes even more difficult when the background is highly dense in addition to the nature of small targets. The problem raised above is solved in various ways, including infrared patch image (IPI) based methods which are considered to have the best performance. In addition, the greater shrinkage of singular values in the methods based on IPI leads to the problem of nuclear norm minimization (NNM), which leads to the problem of incorrectly recognizing small targets in a highly complex background. Hence, this paper proposed a new method for infrared small target detection (ISTD) via total variation and partial sum minimization (TV-PSMSV). The proposed TV-PSMVS in this work basically replaces the IPI's NNM with partial sum minimization (PSM) of singular values and, additionally, the total variance (TV) regularization term is inducted to the background patch image (BPI) to suppress the complex background and enhance the target object of interest. The mathematical solution of the proposed TV-PSMSV approach was performed using alternating direction multiplier (ADMM) to verify the proposed solution. The experimental evaluation using real and synthetic data set was performed, and the result revealed that the proposed TV-PSMSV outperformed existing referenced methods in the terms of background suppression factor (*BSF*) and the signal to gain ratio (*SCRG*).

Keywords: infrared search and (IRST) track system; infrared patch (IPI) image; signal to clutter ratio (SCR) gain (*SCRG*); robust principal component analysis (RPCA); nuclear norm minimization (NNM); total variation (TV)

MSC: 65D18

1. Introduction

Early warning systems, video surveillance systems, military services and infrared search and track systems (IRST) are all examples of applications that use infrared small target detection (ISTD) technology. The object of interest usually remains in the complex background and is tough to detect due to the low noise ratio [1,2]. In general, ISTD approaches can be classified into two categories: sequential detection (SD) methods and single-frame detection (SFD) methods. To estimate the precise location of small targets, SD approaches such as 3-D matching filters [3,4] use both spatial and temporal information in the image. On the other hand, SFD algorithms are more reliable and efficient. TDMMS (two-dimensional least-mean squares) [5] max-mean and max-mean filters [6,7], and other SFD algorithms are the common examples. A human visual system (HVS) [8,9] based on ISTD has been recently introduced where the target is considered to be the most prominent object. Local contrast measure (LCM) [2] and its extended version are the highly researched saliency-based approaches.

Another type of technique treats the detection of small targets as a binary classification issue. Some of the well-known approaches in this class [10,11] are principal component analysis (PCA) [12] and its extended version [13]. Wang et al. [14] built a large sea-sky background dictionary to overcome the dictionary sample difficulties. Wang et al. [15] employed the parameter of study weight to bifurcate the object of interest from the background. The first work using patch image was coined by Gao et. al. and gave an IPI model to handle the problem of ISTD [1]. This IPI based model assumes that the background patch image has the non-local self-correlation characteristic. Continuing this work, Y. He et al. [16] presented a method based on sparse and low-rank representations for ISTD. Inspired by this, Zhang et al. [17] proposed a block-diagonal adaptive target-constrained representation method for sparse target separation and low-rank backgrounds.

The current IPI-based methods are affected by a difficult problem called l_1-norm sparsity issue, as a result of which these methods cannot accurately detect the background and sometimes fail to classify the target component in the target image. Dai et al. [18] has proposed a new method using the structural information of the background image, which has better performance than other methods. However, this method requires calculating the weight of the column, which is a difficult task. Dai et al. [19] again created a new non-negative IPI model that uses the partial sum of the least sum of the singular values to correctly and accurately estimate the background and preserve the large singular values.

The main drawback of this strategy is the difficulty in determining the energy constraint ratio as well as the ranking of the metrics. To overcome which Gao et al. [20] Reweighted IPI (ReWIPI) was proposed to restrict the background patch image while preserving the background edge information, which is based on the work of [21]. Similar work was proposed in [22] However, even this may result in incorrect singular value decomposition (SVD) calculations due to poor weight adjustment.

In [23], a proposal that used *TV* regularization and principal component pursuit (TV-PCP) to provide intrinsic smoothness to the background patch image and another method [24] based on the LP norm and *TV* was also proposed. Work on small target detection method based on the *TV* norm is mentioned in [25]. Some recent developments in IPI based approaches are also available in the literature, including reweighted IPI and tensor model with both nonlocal and local prior information [26] and non-convex rank approximation minimization [27,28]. Due to the small size of the target and the fact that the background seems to be highly diversified in character, the small target recognition task is extremely tough. However, current IPI approaches have had a lot of success in recent years. Nonetheless, our findings revealed significant flaws that may have hampered the performance of these cutting-edge approaches.

The initial flaw with these approaches was the improper estimate of background patch images (BPI) using NNM, due to l1-norm-based sparsity issues. Another difficulty was the constant weighting option, which controls the background versus target patch image trade-off. Inconsistency is caused by both the low rank qualities of the background and the sparsity property of the small target image. Such a result, having a global constant weighting parameter, as in [19], is not a smart idea. Taking these problems into account, Dai et al. [18] provided a proposal based on an adaptive column-wise weight parameter. However, the performance of this method suffers due to additional processing required for calculation of column-wise weights. As the present IPI approach uses NNM to restrict the background patch image, edges in a highly varied background might be falsely recognised as a target point owing to excessive shrinking of singular values. To solve this issue, the PSMSV has been substituted for the NNM in the current IPI model, since it preserves the important features present in the background scene. The reason for using PSMSV is that it preserves the large singular values and only minimize variance in the residual rank, which basically minimize the noise variance of observed data and not the whole data matrix. Second, the TV regularisation term was used to the IPI model's background patch image in order to keep strong edges while enhancing the small target.

In this study, a TV-PSMSV-based approach is proposed, which combines TV regularisation with PSMSV. Further, the mathematical solution of transformation optimization using ADMM of the proposed method is presented and, finally, experimental evaluation was used for the verification of performance.

The following is a summary of the research work's main contribution:

1. An ISTD method called TV-PSMSV has been introduced in which a TV term was inducted to the BPI model to obtain more detailed features in the scene. Moreover, the PSMSV was adopted to limit BPI.
2. The suggested TV-PSMSV model used an ADMM-based method to address image transformation optimization.
3. The suggested model was experimentally evaluated using standard data sets; the findings revealed that it outperforms the referred state-of-the-art technique [1,18–20].

The remainder of the paper is laid out as follows. The technique of the suggested method is detailed in depth in Section 2. Section 3 describes the proposed method's experimental findings using the original, noisy, and synthetic images of infrared image sequences, as well as its comparison to existing baseline approaches. In Section 4, the final conclusion is outlined.

2. Materials and Methods

This section presents the proposed TV-PSMSV method, the second part of the section outlines the TV-PSMSV model, the last subsection introduces mathematical transformation and optimization of the image using ADMM technology.

2.1. Total Variation (TV)

An approach based on total variation regularisation was introduced by Rudin et al. [29] is used in numerous applications of image processing. The TV model demonstrated how the TV standard may preserve the edges and corners of an image without sacrificing any details. Let $U \in R^{x \times y}$ indicate an image, and Equations (1) and (2) define the discretised anisotropic TV^A and isotropic TV^I of an image, respectively (2).

$$TV^A(U) = \sum_{i=1}^{x} \sum_{j=1}^{y-1} |U_{i,j} - U_{i,j+1}| + \sum_{i=1}^{x-1} \sum_{j=1}^{y} \quad (1)$$

$$TV^I = \sum_{i=1}^{x-1} \sum_{j=1}^{y-1} \left(\begin{array}{c} |U_{i,j} - U_{i,j+1}|^2 + \\ |U_{i,j} - U_{i+1,j}|^2 \end{array} \right)^{\frac{1}{2}} + \sum_{j=1}^{y-1} |U_{x,j} - U_{x,j+1}| + \sum_{i=1}^{x-1} |U_{i,y} - U_{i+1,y}| \quad (2)$$

Let, $D_i U \in R^2$ represent the discrete gradient of U at pixel I; image U is vectorized as a column vector and D_i represents the gradient operator of image. Then $TV(U)$ can be finally represented as given in Equation (3):

$$TV(U) = \sum_{i} \|D_i(U)\|_2. \quad (3)$$

2.2. TV-PSMSV Model

Single frame images are represented in the following way:

$$f_o(x,y) = f_B(x,y) + f_T(x,y) + f_N(x,y) \quad (4)$$

where f_O, f_B, f_T, f_N are the original, background, target, noise image, and (x,y) is position of pixels in the image sequentially. Gao et al. [1], firstly, adopted (Equation (4)) in the (IPI) model-formulated target background method as below:

$$D = T + B + N, \tag{5}$$

where, D, B, T, and N are the input patch-image, BPI, and the target patch-image (TPI) and the noise patch-image (NPI), respectively. The low-rank BPI matrix B and the sparse TPI matrix T are decomposed from the matrix D. (Equation (5)) can be transformed into an optimization problem as stated below, and this is inspired by the method in [30].

$$\min_{B,T} \|B\|_* + \lambda \|T\|_1, \quad \text{s.t} \ \|D - T - B\|_F \leq \delta \tag{6}$$

Here, symbol $\|.\|_*$ represents the NN of the matrix which can be calculated as the sum of singular values, symbol $\|.\|_1$ represents the l_1-norm and it is calculated by formula $\|X\|_1 = \sum_{ij}|X_{ij}|$, the symbol $\|.\|_F$ represents the Frobenius norm, which is calculated using the formula $\|X\|_F = \sqrt{\sum_{ij} X^2_{ij}}$, symbol λ stands the weighting parameter and δ is the noise level of images.

2.2.1. Background Patch Image (BPI)

The BPI is derived from a combination of low-rank subspace clusters as described in [1], and NNM is used to calculate the BPI. Current target-background separation approaches, such as IPI [1], WIPI [18], and [19], use NNM to restrict the BPI. Because NNM treats all singular values the same, it shrinks them with the same threshold. As a result, instead of using NNM, the proposed method used PSMSV [31] to estimate background owing to inadequate samples. This is because PSMSV retains the larger singular values and minimises noise.

Using PSMSV, the BPI matrix B may be defined as:

$$\begin{cases} \|\|B\|_* - \|P_N B\|_*\| = \left|\sum_{i=1}^{min(m,n)} \sigma_i B - \sum_{i=1}^{N} \sigma_i B\right| \\ \quad = \sum_{i=N+1}^{min(m,n)} \sigma_i B = \|B\|_{*,\leq r} \\ \quad = \|B\|_{p=N}, \end{cases} \tag{7}$$

where symbols representation as follows:

$\sigma_i B$—the ith singular value of B (arranged in descending order), r—the upper limit ratio of $\sigma_N(B)$ and $\sigma_1(B)$ is equal to $\frac{\sigma_N(B)}{\sigma_1(B)}$, $\|B\|_{p=N}$—the target rank of B.

2.2.2. Target Patch-Image (TPI)

Infrared images do not have a defined size for the small target. As a result, the detection system may consider the TPI to be a sparse matrix. The l_1-norm may be used to calculate TPI in an infrared image, as demonstrated below in Equation (8).

$$\|T\|_1 = \left(\sum_{ij}|T_{ij}|\right) \tag{8}$$

2.2.3. Noise Patch-Image (NPI)

It is reasonable to consider that the NPI follows the Gaussian noise distribution as described in Equation (9).

$$\|D - T - B\|_F \leq \delta \tag{9}$$

Here, $\|.\|_F$ stands for Frobenius Norm, and δ values varied depending on the image.

Finally, in addition to PSMSV, the TV regularisation term was included with the BPI. The following is the formulation of the suggested PSMSV-TV model:

$$\min_{B,T} \|B\|_{*,\leq r} + \lambda_1 TV(B) + \lambda_2 \|T\|_1, \quad (10)$$
$$s.t \quad D = B + T + N, \ \|N\|_F \leq \delta$$

where $TV(.)$ represents the TV norm and λ_1, λ_2 are the constant parameter. The Equation (9) can be written as below:

$$\min_{B,T} \|B\|_{*,\leq r} + \lambda_2 \|T\|_1 + \lambda_1 \sum_i \|D_i B\|_2, \quad (11)$$
$$s.t \quad D = T + N + B, \ \|N\|_F \leq \delta$$

Here, D_i is the gradient operator.

Finally, the proposed model applied a post-processing method on the TPI, to detect the object effectively.

2.3. Mathematical Solution of the PSMSV-TV Model Using ADMM

We may further reformulate the aforementioned minimization issue given in Equation (11) by breaking it into sub-problems by using splitting variables as given below:

$$\min_{Z_1, Z_2, Z_3} \|Z_1\|_{*,\leq r} + \lambda_2 \|Z_3\|_1 + \lambda_1 \sum_i \|z_i\|_2$$
$$s.t \quad Z_1 = B, Z_2 = [z_1; z_2; z_3 \ldots ; z_{mn}], z_i = D_i B, \quad (12)$$
$$Z_3 = T, D = N + T + B, \|N\|_F \leq \delta$$

The formulation of augmented Lagrangian function of above Equation (12) is derived in Equation (13).

$$L_A = \min_{P_1, P_2, P_3} \|P_1\|_{*,\leq r} + \lambda_1 \sum_i \|p_i\|_2 + \lambda_2 \|P_3\|_1 + \langle L_1, Z_1 B \rangle + \frac{\beta}{2} \|P_1 - B\|_F^2$$
$$+ \sum_i \langle l_i, p_i - D_i B \rangle + \frac{\beta_i}{2} \|p_i - D_i B\|_F^2 + \langle L_3, P_3 T \rangle + \frac{\beta}{2} \|P_3 - T\|_F^2 + \quad (13)$$
$$\langle L_4, D - N - T - B \rangle + \frac{\beta}{2} \|D - N - T - B\|_F^2$$

The standard trace inner product for the matrix of vectors is denoted by. The Lagrange multipliers are L_1, L_2, L_3 and L_4 and the penalty parameter is >0. Each variable T, B, P_1, P_2, and P_3 in Equation (13) are vectorized to column vectors for simplicity. The optimization problem of image matrix is mathematically solved using the ADMM [30,32]; it is solved in every iteration by minimising each of the T, B, P_1, P_2, and P_3 variables while leaving the other variables constant. Lastly, the Lagrange multipliers have been modified as follows:

$$\begin{cases} L_1^{k+1} \leftarrow L_1^k + \gamma\beta\left(P_1^{k+1} - B^{k+1}\right) \\ L_2^{k+1} \leftarrow L_2^k + \gamma\beta\left(P_2^{k+1} - DB^{k+1}\right) \\ L_3^{k+1} \leftarrow L_3^k + \gamma\beta\left(P_3^{k+1} - T^{k+1}\right) \\ L_4^{k+1} \leftarrow L_4^k + \gamma\beta\left(P_4^{k+1} - B^{k+1} - T^{k+1} - N^{k+1}\right) \end{cases} \quad (14)$$

Here $\gamma > 0$ represent step length.

The P_1 sub-problem can be represented using given below Equation (15)

$$P_1^{k+1} \arg\min_{Z_1} L_A\left(P_1, P_2^k, P_3^k, B^k, T^k\right)$$
$$= \arg\min_{Z_1} \|Z_1\|_{*,\leq r} + \langle L_1, P_1 - B \rangle + \frac{\beta}{2} \|P_1 - B\|_F^2 \quad (15)$$
$$= \arg\min_{Z_1} \|P_1\|_{*,\leq r} + \frac{\beta}{2} \|P_1 - \left(B^k - \frac{L_1^k}{\beta}\right)\|_F^2$$

This sub-problem can be solved by applying the Theorem 1 as given below:

Theorem 1. *Let us consider $X, L \in R^{m \times n}$, $\tau > 0$, and $l = min(m, n)$, which can be decomposed by SVD. L can be considered as two matrices, $L = L_1 + L_2 = U_{L_1} D_{L_1} V_{l_1}^T + U_{L_2} D_{l_2} V_{L_2}^T$; here, U_{L_1}, V_{L_1} are singular value matrices corresponding to N highest singular values by SVD, and U_{L_2}, V_{L_2} from $(N+1)^{th}$ to the last singular values. Finally, the PSVM problem for singular values may be described as shown in Equation (16):*

$$\arg\min_{X} \frac{1}{2}\|X - L\|_F^2 + \tau\|X\|_{p=N} \tag{16}$$

The partial singular value thresholding operator may be used to describe the optimal solution of Equation (15), which is defined as:

$$P_{N,\tau}[Y] = U_Y(D_{Y_1} + S_\tau[D_{Y_2}]V_Y^T) = Y_1 + U_{Y_2} S_\tau[D_{Y_2}]V_{Y_2}^T. \tag{17}$$

Here

$$\begin{aligned} D_{Y1} \text{ is equal to } \text{diag}(\sigma_1, \ldots, \sigma_N, 0, \ldots, 0), \\ D_{Y2} \text{ is equal to } \text{diag}(0, \ldots, 0, \sigma_{N+1}, \ldots, \sigma_l,) \end{aligned} \tag{18}$$

In addition, $S_\tau[x] = \text{sign}(x).\max(|x| - \tau, 0)$ is the thresholding operator [33–35]. It may be phrased as follows for the P_2 sub-problem:

$$\begin{cases} P_2^{k+1} \leftarrow \arg\min_{Z_2} L_A\left(P_1^k, P_2, P_3^k, B^k, T^k\right) \\ = \arg\min_{P_2} \sum_i \left(\begin{array}{c} \|p_i\|_2 + \langle l_i^K, z_i - D_i B^K \rangle \\ +\frac{\beta_i}{2}\|p_i - D_i B^K\|_F^2 \end{array} \right) \end{cases} \tag{19}$$

Because it is a l_2 optimization problem, the sub-problem (19) may be mathematically solved using a 2-D shrinkage-like formula [36].

$$\left\{ p_i = \max\left\{\|D_iB - \frac{l_i}{\beta_i}\|_2 - \frac{1}{\beta_i}, 0\right\} \cdot \frac{\left(D_iB - \frac{l_i}{\beta_i}\right)}{\|D_iB - \frac{l_i}{\beta_i}\|_2}, \right. \tag{20}$$

The reformulation for the P_3 sub-problem can be solved using the Equation (21):

$$\begin{cases} P_3^{k+1} \leftarrow \arg\min L_A\left(P_1^k, P_2^k, P_3, P_2^k, B^k, T^k\right) \\ = \arg\min \lambda_2 \|P_3\|_1, + \langle L_3, P_3 - T\rangle + \frac{\beta}{2}\|P_3 - T\|_F^2 \\ = \arg\min_{Z_3} \lambda_2 \|P_3\|_1 + \frac{\beta}{2}\|P_3 - \left(T^k - \frac{L_3^k}{\beta}\right)\|_F^2 \end{cases} \tag{21}$$

The Equation (21) can be further solved by given below Equations (22) and (23).

$$P_3^{k+1} = Th_{\frac{\lambda_2}{\beta}}\left(T^k - \frac{L_3^k}{\beta}\right) \tag{22}$$

$$Th_\varepsilon(W) = \begin{cases} w - \varepsilon & w > \varepsilon \\ w - \varepsilon & w < -\varepsilon \\ 0 & \text{otherwise} \end{cases} \tag{23}$$

where $Th_\varepsilon(.)$ represent the thresholding.

For N sub-problem, the solutions may be represented as given in Equation (24)

$$\begin{cases} N^{k+1} \leftarrow \arg\min_{N} \langle L^k{}_4, D - B^k - T^k - N \rangle \\ \quad + \frac{\beta}{2} \| D - B - T^k - N \|_F^2 \\ = \| N - \left(D - T^k - B^k + \frac{L_4{}^k}{\beta} \right) \|_F^2 \\ \text{s.t. } \| N \|_F \leq \delta \end{cases} \quad (24)$$

The Equation (24) can be further solved by given below Equation (25).

$$N^{k+1} = P_\Omega \left(D - T^k - B^k + \frac{L_4{}^k}{\beta} \right) \quad (25)$$

where Ω denotes the sphere of the $\|.\|_F \leq \delta$, and the P_Ω is the projection onto the matching sphere.

For the B sub-problem, the solutions may be represented as given in Equation (26)

$$B^{k+1} \leftarrow \frac{\partial L_A}{\partial B} = 0 \quad (26)$$

Equation (26), for example, may be rewritten as:

$$-\frac{\partial L_A}{\partial B} = L_1{}^k + \beta \left(P_1{}^{k+1} - B \right) + \sum_i \left[D_i{}^T l_i + \beta_i D_i{}^T (p_i - D_i B) \right] + L_4{}^k + \beta \left(D - T^{k+1} \right) \quad (27)$$

$$B^{k+1} = \left(\sum_i \beta D_i{}^T D_i + 2\beta \right)^{-1} \left[L_1{}^k + L_4{}^k + \left(\sum_i [\beta_i D_i{}^T (p_i - D_i B) + D_i{}^T l_i] \right) + \beta \left(P_1{}^{k+1} - T + D \right) \right] \quad (28)$$

Sub-problem may be handled in the same way as B sub-problem:

$$T^{k+1} \leftarrow \frac{\partial L_A}{\partial T} = 0 \quad (29)$$

$$T^{k+1} = \frac{L^k + \beta \left(D - B^{k+1} \right) + \beta p_3{}^{k+1} + L_4{}^k}{2\beta} \quad (30)$$

2.4. Modelling for Small Target Extraction from Background Image

The entire target-background extraction process using the PSMSV-TV paradigm is depicted by Figure 1 and is described as given below steps:

A: **Creation of patch image from Input:**

This is the initial phase, when an infrared patch image called D was created using the original image f_D from the image sequence. A sliding window moved from left to right first and then moved down from top to bottom to create the patch-images.

B: **Target background separation:**

In the second phase, the input patch image was processed using Algorithm 1 to fragment it into two matrices; the first one was a B and the second was a T.

C: **Regeneration of the target and background image:**

In the third phase, the proposed method reconstructed the f_T, and the f_B from the target patch images and the background. The whole process could be accomplished using the technique outlined in [1].

D: Segmentation process:

Now the final touch was initiated, where some final-processing to enhance the quality of target image was performed for the adaptive thresholding scheme was run as described in [1] and it was calculated using given Equation (31):

$$t_{up} = max\left(v_{min}, \overline{f_T} + k\sigma\right) \tag{31}$$

Here σ, $\overline{f_T}$ is the standard deviation and the average of the k and f_T respectively, and v_{min} is taken as an empirical constant value.

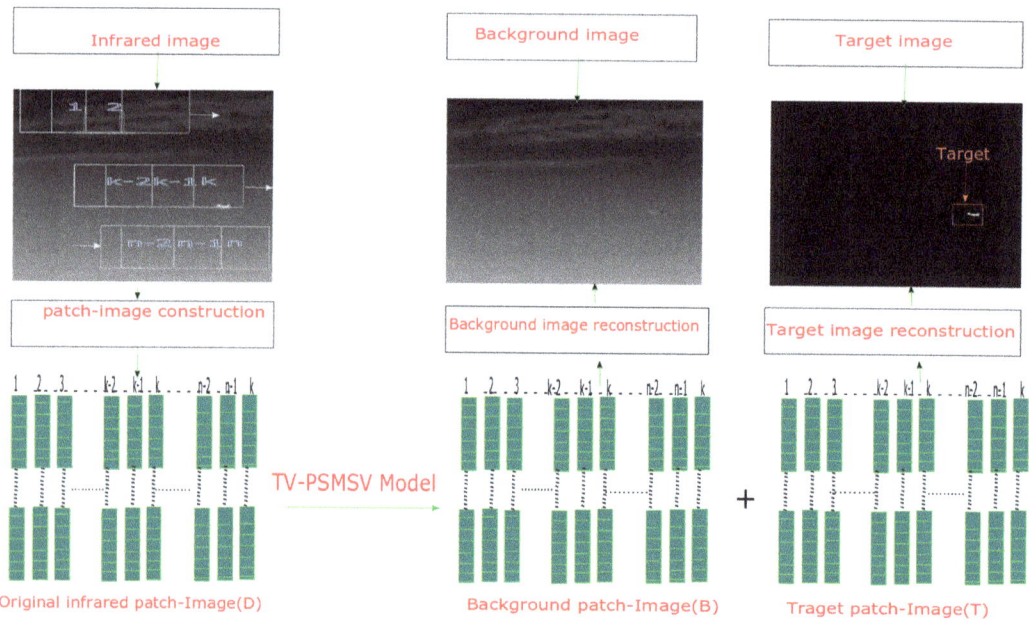

Figure 1. The proposed TV-PSMSV process.

Algorithm 1: The PSMSV-TV Method.

Input: Input is the original IPI $D, \beta, \gamma, \lambda_1, \lambda_2$, ratio r, tol
Output: T^k, B^k

1:   Initialize: $B^k = zeros(m,n)$, $T^k = zeros(m,n)$, $P_1 = P_3 = zeros(m,n)$, $L_1 = L_3 = zeros(m,n)$, $L_2 = zeros(2, mn)$, $P_2 = zeros(mn, 2)$, $\gamma = 1.5$, $tol = 10^{-5}$,
2:   while (*not converged*) do:
3:     $P_1^{k+1} = P_{N,\beta^{-1}}\left(B^k - \frac{L_1^k}{\beta}\right)$
4:     P_2^{k+1} is calculated using Equation (19)
5:     $P_3^{k+1} = Th_{\frac{\lambda_2}{\beta}}\left(T^k - \frac{L_3^k}{\beta}\right)$
6:     B^{k+1} is solved by Equation (28)
7:     T^{k+1} is solved by Equation (30)
8:     $N^{k+1} = P_\Omega\left(D - T^k - B^k + \frac{L_4^k}{\beta}\right)$
9:     Update $L_i(i = 1, 2, 3, 4)$ according to Equation (14)
10:   Convergence checking $\frac{\|D - T^k - B^k\|_F^2}{\|D\|_F} < tol$
11:   k++
12:   end while.

3. Experimental Result Analysis

In the experimental analysis, the performance of the proposed TV-PSMSV was evaluated against the referenced existing methods. This involved standard dataset preparation and comprehensive experimentation on real, noisy, and synthetic image sequences in a variety of background environments.

3.1. Dataset Preparation

The dataset for experimental evaluation consisted of 1080 infrared images with various backgrounds such as sea, sky, cloud, and ground; dataset description was presented in Table 1. We began by experimenting with single item infrared pictures. Second, the suppression capacity of the proposed technique was proven using picture sequences with Gaussian noise. We employed synthetic image sequences to assess the robustness of the proposed technique. In addition, we addressed how characteristics such as image patch size and sliding step size affected the outcomes. The proposed strategy has been compared with eight baseline approaches: max-mean filter [6], max-median filter [6], top-hat filter [37], IPI [1], RPCA [18], NIPPS [19], RIPT [26] and TV-PCP [23] on six distinct original infrared images. The parameter settings for all of the baseline techniques are listed in Table 2. The ADMM was used here to solve the procedure. All of the algorithms were implemented in MATLAB 2015a on a PC with a configuration of 2.2 GHz processor, and 4GB of RAM.

Table 1. Summery of taken dataset.

Infrared Real Sequences #	Image Size	No of Frames	Target Characteristics	Target Type	Background Characteristics
# 1	256 × 200	30	The target is small in size, yet it has a great imaging range.	A small ship	Blurred sea-sky backgrounds.
# 2	256 × 200	250	The target is small in size, yet it has a great imaging range.	An airplane	High dense clouds with less local contrast
# 3	256 × 200	250	The target is small in size, yet it has a great imaging range and SRC value is low.	An airplane	With varying background
# 4	128 × 128	100	The target is small in size, yet it has a great imaging range and SRC value is low	A Helicopter	Changing background
# 5	128 × 128	200	Small size with 1 or 2 target	A ship	Changing background
# 6	280 × 228	250	The target is small in size, yet it has a great imaging range and SRC value is low	A man walking through the forest	Background with heavy clouds.

Table 2. Summery of parameter settings for evaluation.

No.	Methods	Parameter Values
1	Max-Mean Filter [5]	Filter size 5 × 5
2	Max-Median Filter [5]	Filter size 5 × 5
3	Top-Hat filter [37]	Structure shape is 3 × 3
4	NIPPS [19]	Patch size = 50 × 50, sliding step = 10, $\rho = 1.5$, $\lambda = \frac{L}{\sqrt{min(m,n)}}$, $r = 10^{-3}$, $L = 2$, tolerance error, $\varepsilon = 10^{-7}$,
5	RPCA [18]	sliding step = 10, Patch size = 50 × 50, tolerance error $\varepsilon = 10^{-7}$, $\lambda = \frac{1}{\sqrt{m}}$

Table 2. Cont.

No.	Methods	Parameter Values
6	IPI model [1]	sliding step = 10, Patch size = 50 × 50, tolerance error $\varepsilon = 10^{-7}$, $\lambda = \frac{1}{\sqrt{m}}$,
7	RIPT [26]	Patch size is 50 × 50, sliding step is 10, $\lambda = \frac{L}{\sqrt{min(m,n)}}$, $L = 1, h = 1$, $\varepsilon = 10^{-7}$
8	TV-PCP [23]	Patch size is 50 × 50, sliding step is 14, lambda = 0.005, maxIter = 250, Tol = 5 × 10^6, beta = 0.025, gama = 1.5, lambda2 = $1/(sqrt(min(mm, nn))$, $\rho = 1.5$
9	ISTD based on TV-PSMSV	sliding step = 14, Patch size = 50 × 50, $\beta = 0.025$, $\lambda_1 = 0.005$, $\lambda_2 = \frac{L}{\sqrt{min(m,n)}}$, $r = 10^{-3}$, $L = 2$, $\gamma = 1.5$, tolerance error $\varepsilon = 10^{-5}$

3.2. Experimental Evaluation Using Real Image Sequence

3.2.1. Evaluation of Background Suppression of Images Sequences

This section shows the experimental results of each strategy on taken dataset of six different image sequences with different complex backgrounds. In Figures 2 and 3, the suggested TV-PSMSV technique is displayed alongside the max-mean filter, max-median filter [6], top-hat filter [37], IPI [1], RPCA [16], NIPPS [20], RIPT [27] and TV-PCP [23] approaches. In the Figure 2 the experimental results of Max-mean, Max-median, Top-hat and IPI methods are presented. The top hat, max-mean, and max-median methods are simple and easy to implement. Due to this reason, these methods demonstrated strong detecting skills when the background was moderately sluggish and smooth. However, they exhibited poor capability when the background was quite strong and dense.

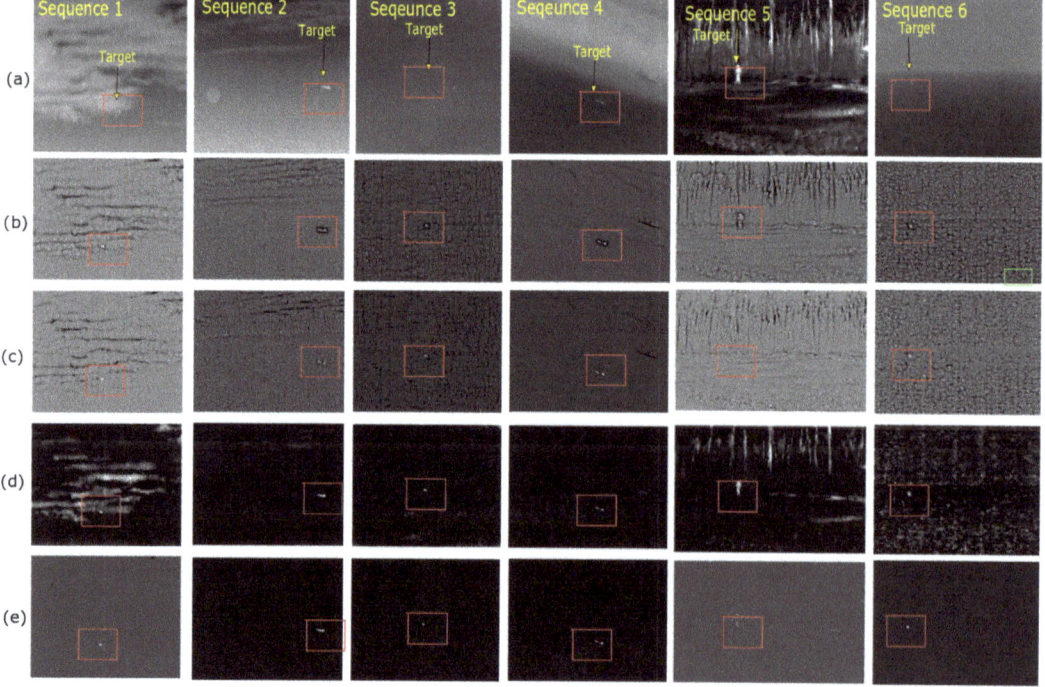

Figure 2. Following rows (**a**–**e**) depicts the background suppression result on six original image sequences: (**a**) Original six image sequences (**b**) Max-mean (**c**) Max-median and (**d**) Top-hat (**e**) IPI.

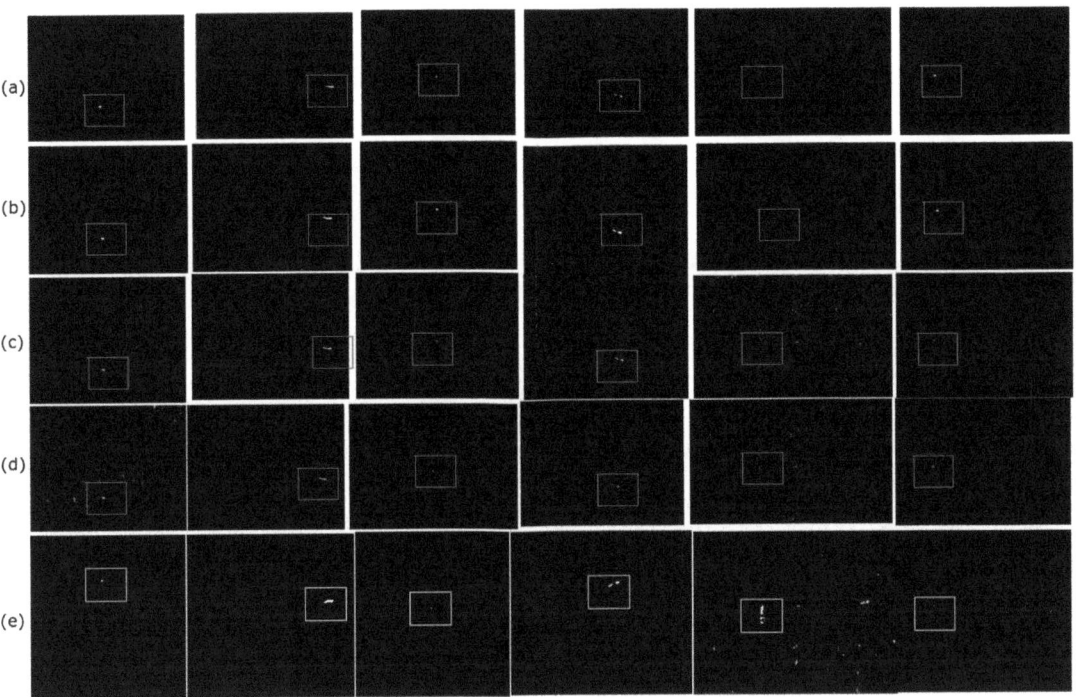

Figure 3. Following rows (**a–e**) depicts the Background suppression result on six original image sequences: (**a**) RPCA, (**b**) NIPPS, (**c**) RIPT, (**d**) TV-PCP, (**e**) PSMSV-TV.

As it can be observed from the Figure 3 that, the RPCA approach has shown good performance, but its shortcoming is that it had a fixed regulating value, making background prediction problematic at times.. The NIPPS approach utilises the partial sum minimization of singular values in place of the NNM in the IPI to contrain the background. Due to this, this method was also capable of suppressing background effectively. In addition to this, the model just minimised the noise variance without taking into account the entire data matrix, which makes this model different from the others. Although the IPI method could detect the target object quite well, this method lacked its performance due to the presence of heavy noise and l1 norm sparsity. Thus, the detection of a non-target object may be seen in the target image.

The RIPT method has impressed well in terms of target detection and background suppression ability. RIPT did not do well in the presence of noise. Although the TV-PCP method performed well, it still had issues in non-smooth background. Motivated by the work in TV-PCP [23], the inner smoothness and the sharp edges information of the background could be extracted by introducing the *TV* norm. Therefore, the suggested approach could smooth the background beautifully, allowing strong edges and buildings to be very easily predicted, allowing the true target to be identified smoothly. Furthermore, there may be clutter in the background of the image whose grey level was comparable to the potential target, making it harder to recognize the target object. As a result, the 3D grey map in Figure 4 could better assist in predicting the position of the small target in the image.

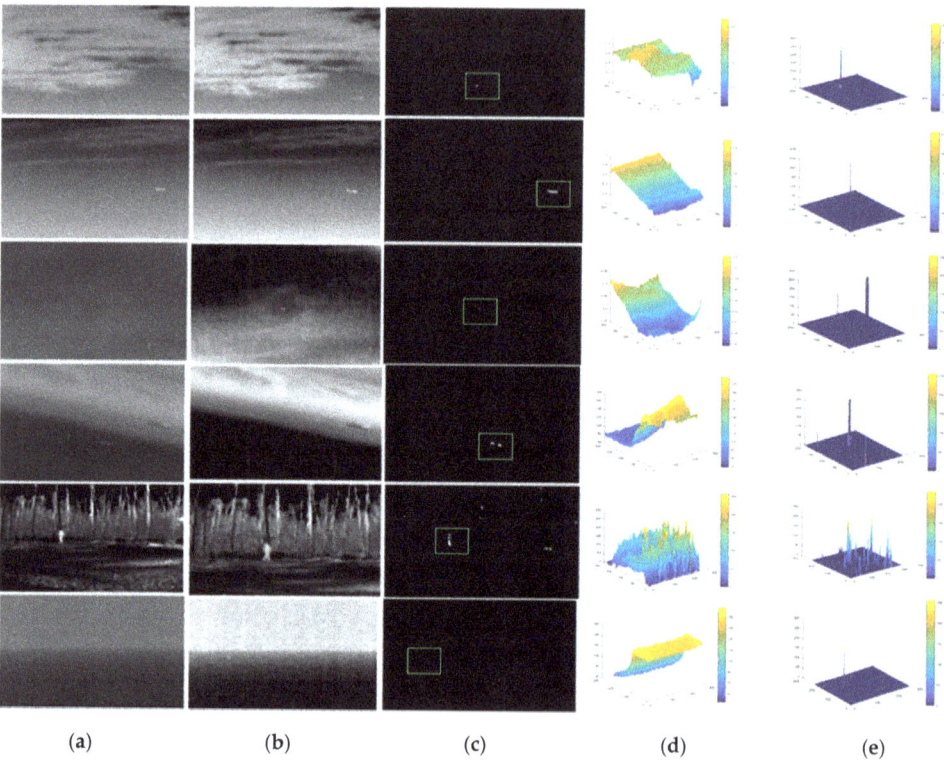

Figure 4. Target background separation result is presented in column (**a**–**e**). (**a**) original images (**b**) Low rank background (**c**) sparse target (**d**) 3-D mesh of (**a**,**e**) 3-D mesh of (**c**).

3.2.2. Evaluation of Background Suppression for Noisy Images Sequences

The next experiment was conducted in the context of noisy images. Figure 5a depicts the original image sequences, whereas Figure 5b,c depict images with Gaussian noise of 10 and 20 standard deviations (sd.), respectively. It can be seen from the findings in Figure 5d,e that the suggested technique performed better than the mentioned methods in terms of background suppression and small target detection in noisy images.

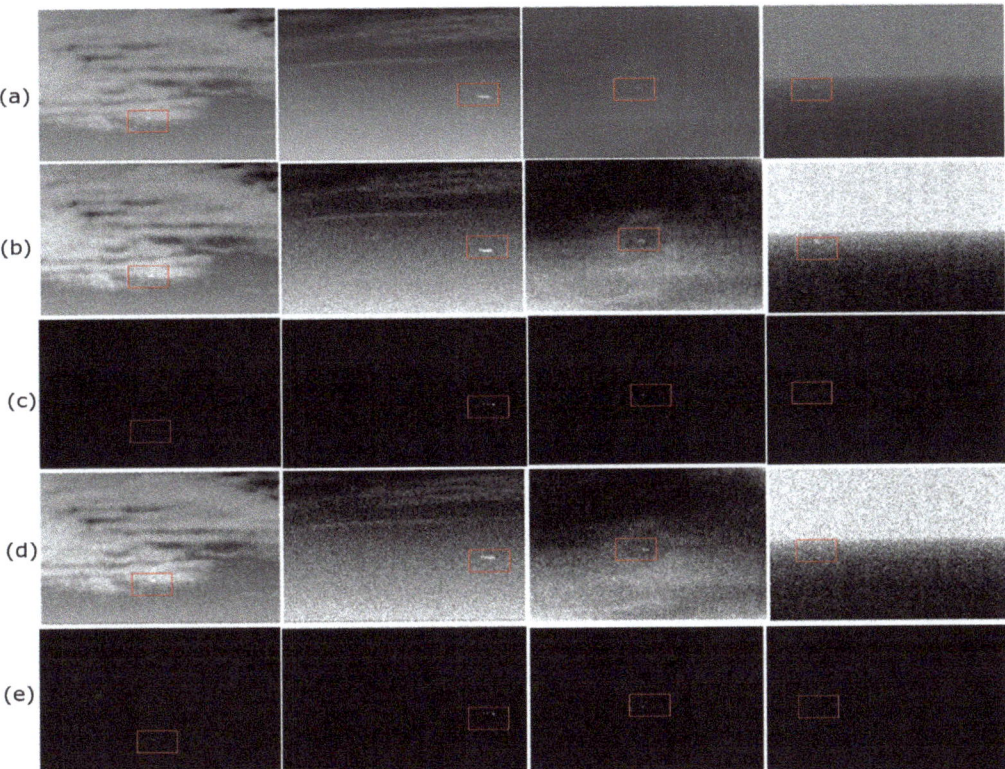

Figure 5. Experimental result in case of noisy images, (**a**) Real images, (**b**) Noisy images with standard deviation (sd.) of 10, (**c**) Background suppression Figure 4b, (**d**) Noisy images with standard deviation (sd.) of 20, and (**e**) Background suppression Figure 4d.

3.2.3. Experimental Evaluation on a Synthetic Image Sequences

In the third evaluation, the performance of the proposed TV-PSMSV method is validated against the synthetic image sequences. A dataset of synthetic image sequences was prepared with varied backgrounds applying real infrared images. The small targets with variable size were embedded into the background at different random locations. The synthetic dataset preparation process was clearly defined in [1]. During the experiment evaluation, one and four target image sequences were identified. In addition, the proposed TV-PSMSV's ability to decrease background noise was evaluated; results are shown into the Figure 6.

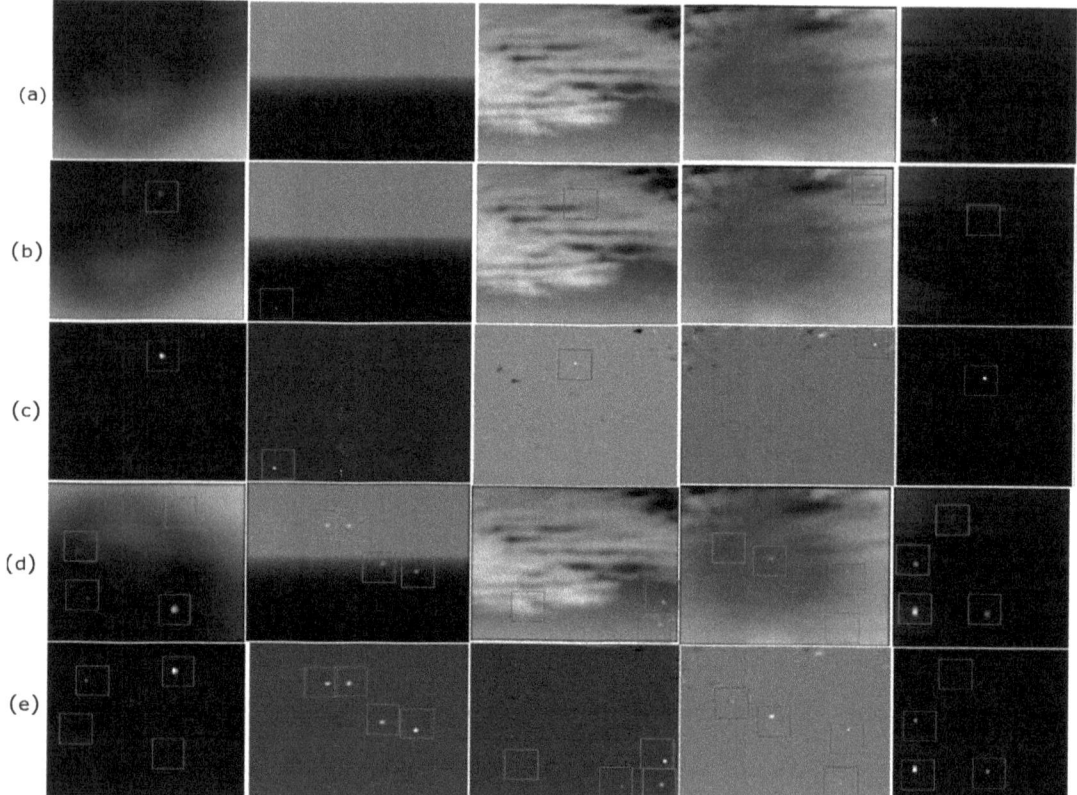

Figure 6. Experimental result in case of synthetic images, (**a**) Background, (**b**) One Target, (**c**) Result of Figure 5b, (**d**) Four targets, and (**e**) Result of Figure 5d.

3.3. Evaluation Metrics Indicators

In order to assess the outcome of the presented TV-PSMSV approach, two standard classical evaluation metrics were considered, namely: SCRG and background suppression factor (BSF). Detailed description of these indicators is outlined in [38] and can be represented as shown in Equation (32):

$$BSF = \frac{C_{in}}{C_{out}}, \quad SCRG = \frac{\left(\frac{S}{C}\right)_{out}}{\left(\frac{S}{C}\right)_{in}} \tag{32}$$

Here, C and S denote the clutter standard deviation and signal amplitude, and the original input and the output target image are represented by in and out, respectively. The experimental results values of BSF and SCRG are shown in Table 3 for all referenced methods along with TV-PSMSV on six different image sequences. The largest and second largest value of these indicators is shown in the table with red and blue colour. From the indicator mentioned in the table, it can be observed that the proposed TV-PSMSV method had the best result of BSF for the sequences 1 to 4 and 6 and second-highest value for the 5th sequence.

Table 3. Observed values of BSF and SCRG.

ISTD	Evaluation Indicators	Seq1	Seq2	Seq3	Seq4	Seq5	Seq6
Top Hat	BSF	0.488	2.339	0.512	2.354	0.923	0.923
	SCRG	1.281	5.733	7.376	53.302	3.081	24.651
Max-Median	BSF	1.296	3.895	0.747	3.249	1.167	1.195
	SCRG	1.608	1.708	5.415	36.456	2.117	17.393
Max-Mean	BSF	1.383	3.387	0.863	3.816	1.861	1.255
	SCRG	1.529	1.580	6.461	51.109	3.117	17.867
IPI	BSF	5.025	4.057	1.481	13.778	29.862	10.410
	SCRG	0.047	3.450	5.665	263.310	125.505	195.948
RPCA	BSF	3.799	25.882	3.073	6.468	0.494	3.790
	SCRG	10.739	60.950	36.166	76.236	0.683	90.559
NIPPS	BSF	4.604	6.169	2.687	6.726	7.413	7.576
	SCRG	2.792	6.298	23.787	168.042	30.018	4.700
RIPT	BSF	3.507	7.124	3.101	2.874	0.896	14.874
	SCRG	2.122	4.835	9.308	1.233	0.062	0.038
TV-PCP	BSF	1.403	4.948	1.776	3.002	1.477	3.026
	SCRG	0.857	2.694	6.726	27.870	0.033	14.284
TV-PSMSV	BSF	12.043	25.905	15.147	21.218	19.065	24.915
	SCRG	14.384	62.224	95.985	189.954	2.061	218.774

Similarly, for the sequences 1 to 6, the suggested method's SCRG value was the greatest. Therefore, it can be concluded that the suggested strategy of TV-PSMSV outperformed the mentioned current methods in terms of enhancement as well as background suppression.

The receiver operation curve (ROC) is a second statistic that may be used for the experimental evaluation of various approaches. The connection between the probability detection P_d as well as false alarm rate P_f is represented by this curve [39] which may be expressed by using Equations (33) and (34)

$$P_d = \frac{Number\ of\ detected\ pixels}{Number\ of\ real\ target\ pixels}, \quad (33)$$

$$P_f = \frac{Number\ of\ false\ alarms}{Total\ number\ of\ pixels\ in\ the\ whole\ image} \quad (34)$$

All of the aforementioned metrics were evaluated in a small local region with a rectangular size of dimensions $a \times b$, background rectangle size of dimensions $(a + 2d) \times (b + 2d)$, and here, d is taken as a constant equal to 20 pixels.

The output of the presented technique against the baseline approaches can be seen in Figure 6, which is represented by an ROC curve. Figure 7a shows that the IPI and RPCA methods produced better results than the proposed method. The suggested methods improved detection ability because of TV term introduced in the BPI, which smooths the background and successfully detects the target. In addition, NIPPS did not get a decent outcome for sequence 1. Figure 7b shows that the TV-PSMSV did not produce good results when related with the RPCA method. Figure 7c shows that the TV-PSMSV technique had the highest performance, followed by IPI, and that the rest of the other methods performed poorly. Figure 8a shows that the suggested TV-PSMSV method, when compared to other methods, produced good results; however, NIPPS had weak detection ability. The suggested TV-PSMSV approach had the best detection rate, followed by IPI, as shown in Figure 8b. Finally, because of adding the TV term with the input scene, it can be observed from Figure 8c that the suggested technique had strong detection ability.

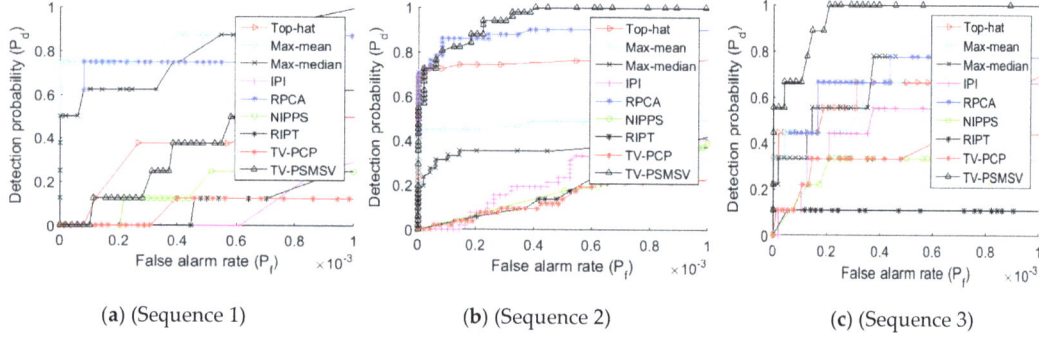

(a) (Sequence 1) (b) (Sequence 2) (c) (Sequence 3)

Figure 7. ROC graph of dataset image sequences (a–c).

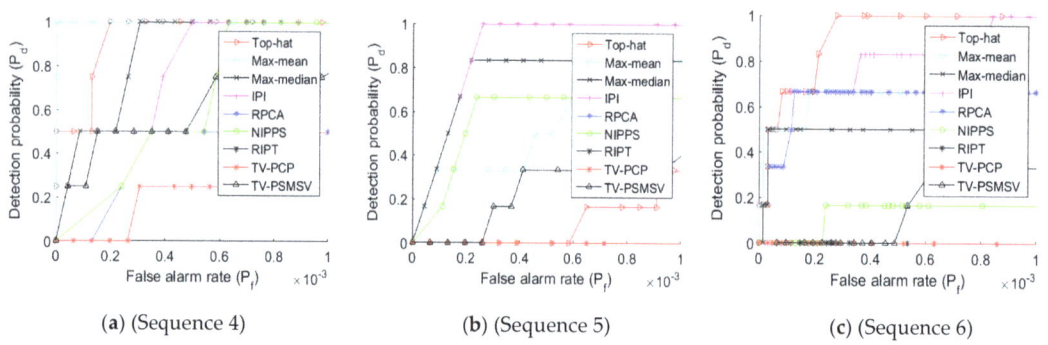

(a) (Sequence 4) (b) (Sequence 5) (c) (Sequence 6)

Figure 8. ROC graph of dataset image sequences (a–c).

3.4. Parameter Analysis

This section evaluates three critical characteristics that is mainly used to test the robustness of the proposed TV-PSMSV technique under various background scenarios are discussed in the next section. These characteristics are patch size, step size, and regulating parameter. We must use these parameters to achieve greater performance, as they may not provide the global best solution. Evaluation results of Figure 9 shows the ROC curves for four separate images with 4 varying characteristics.

3.4.1. Image Patch-Size

Patch size is thought to be a crucial factor in detection of performance. We know that fine-tuning the patch parameter increases the sparsity of the target. However, this will very certainly increase the computational cost of the method. In the experiment, we tested patch sizes of 20, 30, 40, 50, and 60 and generated the ROC curve for the four image sequences, which can be seen in Figure 9a. The ROC curve shows that adjusting the image patch size had an impact on both detection performance and computational complexity. Patch size 30 is thought to be ideal in the method.

3.4.2. Step-Size

Similarly, the step size must be adjusted properly. In the experiment, the patch size was set to 30×30, and then step sizes of 6, 8, 10, and 12 were explored. The ROC curve on step size shows that adopting a small step increases computation time and reduces the algorithm's detection performance. Reduce calculation time by increasing the step size to a large amount. Figure 9b indicates that a step size of 10 is the optimum option.

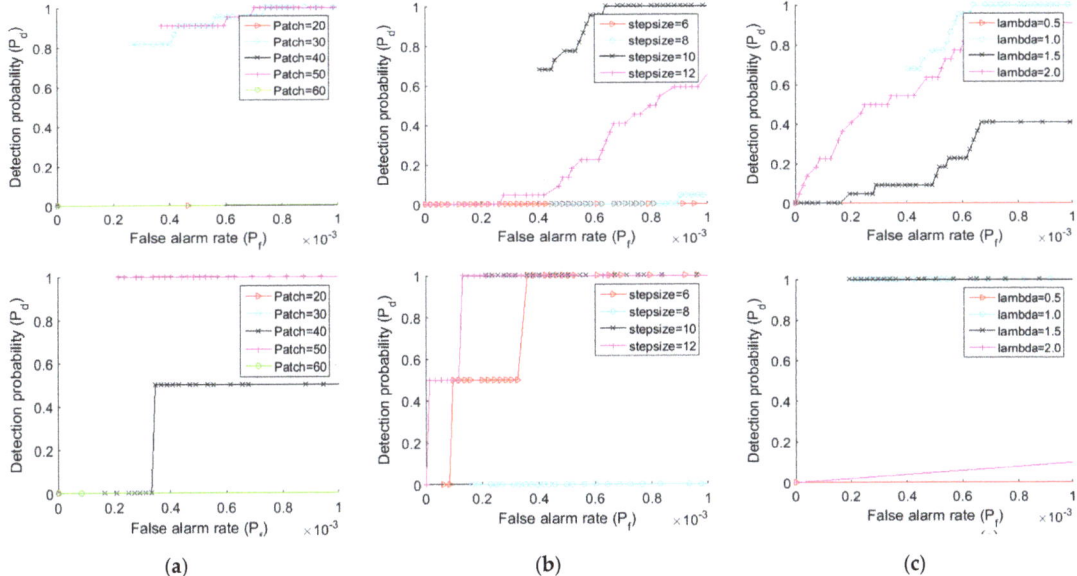

Figure 9. Experimental result of ROC curve for infrared image sequences 1–4 (**a**) Results under different patch size (**b**) Results under different step size. (**c**) Results under different controlling parameter.

3.4.3. Controlling Parameter λ

The controlling parameter $\lambda = \frac{L}{\sqrt{min(m,n)}}$ is another key parameter that helps to balance the BPI and TPI. A larger λ value would over-shrink the small target, while a small value would leave residue in the complex background image, thereby increasing the number of false alarms. $L = 0.5$, $L = 1$, $L = 1.5$, and $L = 2$ are the four values we chose for L. Figure 9c shows the experimental results for various L values (c). When compared to various L values, the ideal value at $L = 1$ yields an excellent performance.

3.4.4. Computational or Running Complexity

Table 4 depicts the running time along with the execution cost of one scene out of the whole dataset as in Figure 2a. The total computation cost of the top-hat method with the size of the structure element as K^2 and the size of the image as M × N is O ($K^2 \log K^2 MN$), whereas the execution cost of the max-mean and max-mean methods here is O (M × N × K^2). The execution cost of all competing approaches based on the IPI model is O (M × N^2), where the patch image size is M × N and it depends on the cost of the SVD of each step in the algorithm.

Table 4. Comparative summary of time and computing cost.

Method	Top-Hat	Max-Median	Max-Mean	RPCA	NIPPS	IPI	RIPT	TV-PCP	TV-PSMSV
Time (s)	0.868	6.65	7.69	8.77	4.11	11.51	1.93	392.77	242.69
Computational Cost	O (K^2 M × N log K)	O (M × N × K^2)	O (M × N × K^2)	O (M × N^2)	O (M × N^2)	O (M × N^2)	O (M × N^2)	O (K × M × N^2)	O (K × M × N^2)

The cost for the NIPPS, RPCA, RIPT and IPI is O (m × n^2) and for TV-PCP and the finally for proposed TV-PSMSV method, the cost of ADMM to updating every sub problem and the multipliers for running patch size of m × n is O (m × n). In addition, the cost of executing a 2-D TV regularisation is O (m × n log (m × n), while the cost of running a full SVD is O (m × n^2). As a result, the total calculation cost is O ((m × n) + (m × n log (m × n)

+ $(m \times n)^2)$; in the worst case, the cost will be $O(m \times n^2 \times k)$, where k denotes the number of time running the process. Because of the induction of TV regularisation, the suggested TV-PSMSV has a substantially higher cost of running per image than the other baseline approaches due to the introduction of TV regularization.

4. Conclusions

In the present work a model, namely, TV-PSMSV is presented, which is used in the ISTD system. This model addressed the issue of employing NNM for restricting the BPI in existing IPI-based approaches. In TV-PSMSV, NNM was substituted with PSMSV to constrain the BPI due to over-shrinkage of singular values. Secondly, to take care of the strong edges in the background of the input scene and to improve the object of interest, a TV regularisation term was inducted into the BPI. Finally, the ADMM approach was used to solve the target-background separation procedure. Experimental outcome demonstrate that the presented TV-PSMSV method yielded better results in stronger background suppression and detection ability than previous baseline approaches. In the near future, this work can be extended into more robust tensor-patch images-based models to improve existing IPI-based approaches.

Author Contributions: Conceptualization: S.A. and S.S.R.; Methodology: S.A. and S.S.R.; Validation: Y.A. and G.K.; Formal Analysis: Y.A. and G.K.; Investigation: O.I.K. and L.P.V. Resources: S.A. and S.S.R.; Data Curation: S.A. and S.S.R.; Writing original draft preparation: S.A. and S.S.R.; Writing review and editing: Y.A. and O.I.K.; Visualization: G.K. and L.P.V.; Supervision: Y.A. and O.I.K.; Project Administration: S.A., Y.A. and S.S.R.; Funding Acquisition: S.A. All authors have read and agreed to the published version of the manuscript.

Funding: This research is funded by Taif University, TURSP-2020/313.

Data Availability Statement: Not applicable.

Acknowledgments: We are grateful to Taif University, Taif, Saudi Arabia, for funding this research under Taif University Researchers Supporting Project Number (TURSP-2020/313).

Conflicts of Interest: There are no conflict of interest declared by the authors.

References

1. Gao, C.; Meng, D.; Yang, Y.; Wang, Y.; Zhou, X.; Hauptmann, A.G. Infrared Patch-Image Model for Small Target Detection in a Single Image. *IEEE Trans. Image Process.* **2013**, *22*, 4996–5009. [CrossRef] [PubMed]
2. Chen, C.L.P.; Li, H.; Wei, Y.; Xia, T.; Tang, Y.Y. A Local Contrast Method for Small Infrared Target Detection. *IEEE Trans. Geosci. Remote Sens.* **2014**, *52*, 574–581. [CrossRef]
3. Reed, I.S.; Gagliardi, R.M.; Stotts, L.B. Optical moving target detection with 3-D matched filtering. *IEEE Trans. Aerosp. Electron. Syst.* **1988**, *24*, 327–336. [CrossRef]
4. Rawat, S.; Verma, S.K.; Kumar, Y. Review on recent development in infrared small target detection algorithms. *Procedia Comput. Sci.* **2020**, *167*, 2496–2505. [CrossRef]
5. Bae, T.-W.; Kim, Y.-C.; Ahn, S.-H.; Sohng, K.-I. A novel Two-Dimensional LMS (TDLMS) using sub-sampling mask and step-size index for small target detection. *IEICE Electron. Express* **2010**, *7*, 112–117. [CrossRef]
6. Deshpande, S.D.; Er, M.H.; Venkateswarlu, R.; Chan, P. Max-mean and max-median filters for detection of small targets. In *Signal and Data Processing of Small Targets*; SPIE: Denver, CO, USA, 1999; Volume 3809, pp. 74–84. [CrossRef]
7. Rawat, S.; Verma, S.K.; Kumar, Y. Infrared small target detection based on Non-convexTriple Tensor Factorization. *IET Image Process.* **2021**, *15*, 556–570. [CrossRef]
8. Itti, L.; Koch, C.; Niebur, E. A model of saliency-based visual attention for rapid scene analysis. *IEEE Trans. Pattern Anal. Mach. Intell.* **1998**, *20*, 1254–1259. [CrossRef]
9. Li, G.; Liu, F.; Sharma, A.; Khalaf, O.I.; Alotaibi, Y.; Alsufyani, A.; Alghamdi, S. Research on the Natural Language Recognition Method Based on Cluster Analysis Using Neural Network. *Math. Probl. Eng.* **2021**, *9982305*. [CrossRef]
10. Alotaibi, Y. A New Database Intrusion Detection Approach Based on Hybrid Meta-heuristics. *Comput. Mater. Contin.* **2021**, *66*, 1879–1895. [CrossRef]
11. Suryanarayana, G.; Chandran, K.; Khalaf, O.I.; Alotaibi, Y.; Alsufyani, A.; Alghamdi, S.A. Accurate Magnetic Resonance Image Super-Resolution Using Deep Networks and Gaussian Filtering in the Stationary Wavelet Domain. *IEEE Access* **2021**, *9*, 71406–71417. [CrossRef]

12. Hu, T.; Zhao, J.J.; Cao, Y.; Wang, F.L.; Yang, J. Infrared small target detection based on saliency and principle component analysis. *J. Infrared Millim. Waves* **2010**, *29*, 303–306.
13. Gao, C.; Su, H.; Li, L.; Li, Q.; Huang, S. Small infrared target detection based on kernel principal component analysis. In Proceedings of the 2012 5th International Congress on Image and Signal Processing, Chongqing, China, 16–18 October 2012; pp. 1335–1339.
14. Wang, X.; Shen, S.; Ning, C.; Xu, M.; Yan, X. A sparse representation-based method for infrared dim target detection under sea–sky background. *Infrared Phys. Technol.* **2015**, *71*, 347–355. [CrossRef]
15. Wang, C.; Qin, S. Adaptive detection method of infrared small target based on target-background separation via robust principal component analysis. *Infrared Phys. Technol.* **2015**, *69*, 123–135. [CrossRef]
16. He, Y.; Li, M.; Zhang, J.; An, Q. Small infrared target detection based on low-rank and sparse representation. *Infrared Phys. Technol.* **2015**, *68*, 98–109. [CrossRef]
17. Zhang, Z.; Ren, J.; Li, S.; Hong, R.; Zha, Z.; Wang, M. Robust Subspace Discovery by Block-diagonal Adaptive Locality-constrained Representation. In Proceedings of the 27th ACM International Conference on Multimedia, Association for Computing Machinery (ACM), Nice, France, 21–25 October 2019; pp. 1569–1577.
18. Dai, Y.; Wu, Y.; Song, Y. Infrared small target and background separation via column-wise weighted robust principal component analysis. *Infrared Phys. Technol.* **2016**, *77*, 421–430. [CrossRef]
19. Dai, Y.; Wu, Y.; Song, Y.; Gao, J. Non-negative infrared patch-image model: Robust target-background separation via partial sum minimization of singular values. *Infrared Phys. Technol.* **2017**, *81*, 182–194. [CrossRef]
20. Guo, J.; Wu, Y.; Dai, Y. Small target detection based on reweighted infrared patch–image model. *IET Image Process.* **2017**, *12*, 70–79. [CrossRef]
21. Gu, S.; Xie, Q.; Meng, D.; Zuo, W.; Feng, X.; Zhang, L. Weighted Nuclear Norm Minimization and Its Applications to Low Level Vision. *Int. J. Comput. Vis.* **2017**, *121*, 183–208. [CrossRef]
22. Zhang, L.; Li, M.; Qiu, X.; Zhu, Y. Infrared Small Target Detection Based on Four-Direction Overlapping Group Sparse Total Variation. *Trait. Signal* **2020**, *37*, 367–377. [CrossRef]
23. Wang, X.; Zhenming, P.; Dehui, K.; Zhang, P.; He, Y. Infrared dim target detection based on total variation regularization and principal component pursuit. *Image Vis. Comput.* **2017**, *63*, 1–9. [CrossRef]
24. Rawat, S.; Verma, S.K.; Kumar, Y. Reweighted infrared patch image model for small target detection based on non-convex $\mathcal{L}_p$-norm minimisation and TV regularization. *IET Image Process.* **2020**, *14*, 1937–1947. [CrossRef]
25. Wan, M.; Gu, G.; Xu, Y.; Qian, W.; Ren, K.; Chen, Q. Total Variation-Based Interframe Infrared Patch-Image Model for Small Target Detection. *IEEE Geosci. Remote Sens. Lett.* **2022**, *19*, 1–5. [CrossRef]
26. Dai, Y.; Wu, Y. Reweighted Infrared Patch-Tensor Model with Both Nonlocal and Local Priors for Single-Frame Small Target Detection. *IEEE J. Sel. Top. Appl. Earth Obs. Remote Sens.* **2017**, *10*, 3752–3767. [CrossRef]
27. Zhang, L.; Peng, L.; Zhang, T.; Cao, S.; Peng, Z. Infrared small target detection via non-convex rank approximation minimization joint $l_{2,1}$ norm. *Remote Sens.* **2018**, *10*, 1821. [CrossRef]
28. Zhang, L.; Peng, Z. Infrared Small Target Detection Based on Partial Sum of the Tensor Nuclear Norm. *Remote Sens.* **2019**, *11*, 382. [CrossRef]
29. Rudin, L.I.; Osher, S.; Fatemi, E. Nonlinear total variation based noise removal algorithms. *Phys. D Nonlinear Phenom.* **1992**, *60*, 259–268. [CrossRef]
30. Chen, G.; Zhang, J.; Li, D.; Chen, H. Robust Kronecker product video denoising based on fractional-order total variation model. *Signal Process.* **2016**, *119*, 1–20. [CrossRef]
31. Oh, T.-H.; Tai, Y.-W.; Bazin, J.-C.; Kim, H.; Kweon, I.S. Partial Sum Minimization of Singular Values in Robust PCA: Algorithm and Applications. *IEEE Trans. Pattern Anal. Mach. Intell.* **2016**, *38*, 744–758. [CrossRef]
32. Wang, Z.; Li, H.; Ling, Q.; Li, W. Robust Temporal-Spatial Decomposition and Its Applications in Video Processing. *IEEE Trans. Circuits Syst. Video Technol.* **2013**, *23*, 387–400. [CrossRef]
33. Donoho, D.L.; Johnstone, I.M. Adapting to Unknown Smoothness via Wavelet Shrinkage. *J. Am. Stat. Assoc.* **1995**, *90*, 1200. [CrossRef]
34. Hale, E.T.; Yin, W.; Zhang, Y. Fixed-Point Continuation for $\ell_1\ell_1$-Minimization: Methodology and Convergence. *SIAM J. Optim.* **2008**, *19*, 1107–1130. [CrossRef]
35. Li, C. *An Efficient Algorithm for Total Variation Regularization with Applications to the Single Pixel Camera and Compressive Sensing*; Rice University: Houston, TX, USA, 2010.
36. Lin, Z.; Chen, M.; Ma, Y. The augmented Lagrange multiplier method for exact recovery of corrupted low-rank matrices. *arXiv* **2010**, arXiv:1009.5055.
37. Bai, X.; Zhou, F. Analysis of new top-hat transformation and the application for infrared dim small target detection. *Pattern Recognit.* **2010**, *43*, 2145–2156. [CrossRef]
38. Hilliard, C.I. Selection of a clutter rejection algorithm for real-time target detection from an airborne platform. In Proceedings of the SPIE Proceedings, Orlando, FL, USA, 13 July 2000; Volume 4048, pp. 74–84.
39. Gu, Y.; Wang, C.; Liu, B.; Zhang, Y. A Kernel-Based Nonparametric Regression Method for Clutter Removal in Infrared Small-Target Detection Applications. *IEEE Geosci. Remote Sens. Lett.* **2010**, *7*, 469–473. [CrossRef]

Article

SVseg: Stacked Sparse Autoencoder-Based Patch Classification Modeling for Vertebrae Segmentation

Syed Furqan Qadri [1,2], Linlin Shen [1,2,*], Mubashir Ahmad [3], Salman Qadri [4], Syeda Shamaila Zareen [5] and Muhammad Azeem Akbar [6]

1. Computer Vision Institute, College of Computer Science and Software Engineering, Shenzhen University, Shenzhen 518060, China; furqangillani79@szu.edu.cn
2. AI Research Center for Medical Image Analysis and Diagnosis, Shenzhen University, Shenzhen 518060, China
3. Department of Computer Science and IT, The University of Lahore, Sargodha Campus, Sargodha 40100, Pakistan; mubashir_bit@yahoo.com
4. Department of Computer Science, MNS-University of Agriculture, Multan 60650, Pakistan; salman.qadri@mnsuam.edu.pk
5. Faculty of Information Technology, Beijing University of Technology, Beijing 100124, China; syedashumailzareen.11@gmail.com
6. Department of Information Technology, Lappeenranta University of Technology, 53851 Lappeenranta, Finland; azeem.akbar@lut.fi
* Correspondence: llshen@szu.edu.cn

Citation: Qadri, S.F.; Shen, L.; Ahmad, M.; Qadri, S.; Zareen, S.S.; Akbar, M.A. SVseg: Stacked Sparse Autoencoder-Based Patch Classification Modeling for Vertebrae Segmentation. *Mathematics* 2022, 10, 796. https://doi.org/10.3390/math10050796

Academic Editors: Ezequiel López-Rubio, Esteban Palomo and Enrique Domínguez

Received: 29 January 2022
Accepted: 25 February 2022
Published: 2 March 2022

Publisher's Note: MDPI stays neutral with regard to jurisdictional claims in published maps and institutional affiliations.

Copyright: © 2022 by the authors. Licensee MDPI, Basel, Switzerland. This article is an open access article distributed under the terms and conditions of the Creative Commons Attribution (CC BY) license (https://creativecommons.org/licenses/by/4.0/).

Abstract: Precise vertebrae segmentation is essential for the image-related analysis of spine pathologies such as vertebral compression fractures and other abnormalities, as well as for clinical diagnostic treatment and surgical planning. An automatic and objective system for vertebra segmentation is required, but its development is likely to run into difficulties such as low segmentation accuracy and the requirement of prior knowledge or human intervention. Recently, vertebral segmentation methods have focused on deep learning-based techniques. To mitigate the challenges involved, we propose deep learning primitives and stacked Sparse autoencoder-based patch classification modeling for Vertebrae segmentation (SVseg) from Computed Tomography (CT) images. After data preprocessing, we extract overlapping patches from CT images as input to train the model. The stacked sparse autoencoder learns high-level features from unlabeled image patches in an unsupervised way. Furthermore, we employ supervised learning to refine the feature representation to improve the discriminability of learned features. These high-level features are fed into a logistic regression classifier to fine-tune the model. A sigmoid classifier is added to the network to discriminate the vertebrae patches from non-vertebrae patches by selecting the class with the highest probabilities. We validated our proposed SVseg model on the publicly available MICCAI Computational Spine Imaging (CSI) dataset. After configuration optimization, our proposed SVseg model achieved impressive performance, with 87.39% in Dice Similarity Coefficient (DSC), 77.60% in Jaccard Similarity Coefficient (JSC), 91.53% in precision (PRE), and 90.88% in sensitivity (SEN). The experimental results demonstrated the method's efficiency and significant potential for diagnosing and treating clinical spinal diseases.

Keywords: stacked sparse autoencoder; deep learning; unsupervised learning; CT images; vertebrae segmentation; SVseg; image patch; MICCAI-CSI dataset; sigmoid classifier

1. Introduction

Vertebrae segmentation is an essential step for spine image analysis and modeling such as spinal abnormalities identification, image-based biomechanical model analysis, vertebrae fracture detection [1], intervertebral disc labeling, and image-guided spine intervention [2]. Spine analysis requires precise vertebral segmentation; for example, image-guided vertebrae intervention often involves precision to the submillimeter level. Manual segmentation of vertebrae is a subjective and time-consuming process, so fully automatic or semi-automatic techniques are needed for many clinical applications. In the diagnosis and treatment of spinal diseases, medical imaging techniques have been used extensively [3]. When assessing spinal health, computer tomography (CT) and magnetic resonance imaging (MRI) are usually the first option to give better spinal anatomy views. However, segmenting individual vertebrae from 3D scans is a tedious and time-consuming process. Computational techniques can be used for automatic quantitative analysis of spine images to enhance physicians' capability to improve spinal healthcare. Recently, many vertebrae segmentation methods for computed tomography (CT) have been proposed [4]. However, it remains a challenging task due to the architectural variation of the spine across the population, the complex shape and pathology, the same structures being in close vicinity, and the spatial relationships between the ribs and vertebrae.

To handle this challenge, several approaches for segmenting vertebrae have been proposed. For example, vertebrae segmentations were obtained by many methods of unsupervised learning, such as region-based segmentation like a watershed, graph-cut, and boundary adjustment, region growing, and adaptive threshold. Level set techniques have been used to deal with the topologically merging complexity and break in the vertebrae. Willmore flow [5] is included in a level set method in guiding surface modeling evolution. The combination of region and edge-based level set functions for CT vertebrae segmentation is proposed in [6]. The authors of [7] used the watershed algorithm, curved reformation, a vertebral template, and a directed graph to segment the spinal column. Another approach [8] employed watershed and mathematical morphology for vertebrae segmentation. Kim and Kim [9] presented a fully automatic method based on 3D fence construction to separate vertebrae. Then a final segmentation was obtained by applying a region-growing algorithm within a constructed 3D fence. Many methods incorporated prior knowledge about vertebrae anatomies like geometric models, a probabilistic atlas, and statistical shape models that estimate the vertebrae mean shape and variation from a segmented training set. These approaches are often sensitive at calculating the initial pose, which is performed either automatically or manually. Automatic initialization has been presented via detecting the vertebrae and intervertebral disk in [7]. The manual initialization is achieved by pacing seeds within the vertebral body [10] or drawing a bounding box to confine the searching range [11]. A single framework has also been proposed integrating the vertebrae's identification, detection, and segmentation [12]. The technique in [13] was based on the detection of the edge and fair registration methodology of a deformed surface for the vertebrae in the thoracic region. The method in [14] was proposed to incorporate statistics on shape and pose in a multivertebrae model for lumbar segmentation. Kadoury et al. [15] presented an articulated spine model of each vertebra using high-order Markov random fields. A landmark-based shape representation model was built using transportation theory for CT vertebrae, and alignment to a specific vertebra was obtained using game theory in [16]. Zhang and Wang [17] proposed the vertebrae segmentation method from CT images in three parts: an adaptive threshold filter;, Point++-based single vertebrae segmentation, and edge information based converge segmentation that enhances the segmentation accuracy.

One limitation of the approaches described above is that they were trained using hand-crafted features such as local intensity features, which are incapable of encoding more representative features of vertebrae images. As a result, they may be unable to handle more complicated cases where spine pathologies and curvatures are present. In recent years, deep learning has become a research hotspot in medical image analysis [18] because of its high feature extraction ability [19–24]. Deep neural networks (DNNs) often use successful tools as an extractor of high-level features. Sekuboyina et al. [25] developed a multilabel FCN model for segmentation of lumbar vertebrae. Probability maps are generated using CNN, which indicates the vertebral body's location and then used these maps to guide a deformed model in [26]. A method [27] is proposed to detect the vertebrae centroids by using an FCN to get a probability map for each vertebra, which is the message-passing technique to extract the plausible set of centroids. Chen et al. [28] used CNN to detect vertebrae and trained the model with a technical loss term to distinguish neighboring vertebra. A deep learning-based methodology for spine segmentation from CT images was proposed for thoracic and lumbar segmentation, and features were directly learned from image patches in [29,30]. A statistical model for CT cervical vertebra segmentation was proposed in [31] to reconstruct the boundary between adjacent vertebrae by an intervertebral fence model, and a VGG-Net like convolutional network was used to train the model. Similarly, the segmentation of cervical vertebra was achieved using the FCN in [32]. A deep learning-based method was proposed in [33] to identify and localize vertebrae that used FCNN to extract short-range contextual information and RNN to extract long-range contextual information.

Related Work

Recently, advancements in deep learning (DL) have led to increased use of DL algorithms [34], particularly stacked sparse autoencoders (SSAEs) for automated medical image segmentation, classification [35], and detection [36–41]. The deep-stacked autoencoder (SAE) framework of deep learning was used for liver segmentation in [42]. SSAE was used to develop breast cancer segmentation [43] from histopathological images and prostate segmentation from MRI in [44]. The liver disease diagnosis method was presented from ultrasound images by feature representation with a stacked sparse auto-encoder (SSAE) in [45]. Although state-of-the-art approaches have produced acceptable results in vertebrae segmentation, they have complicated network designs that are computationally expensive [46]. So, we need to further improve vertebrae segmentation results by reducing complex network architecture. In this study, we propose a stacked sparse autoencoder-based Vertebrae segmentation (SVseg) model from CT images. We extract overlapping patches from CT images as input to train the model. The stacked sparse autoencoder learned high-level features from unlabeled image patches in an unsupervised way. To enhance the learned features' discriminability, we further refined the feature representation in a supervised learning fashion. These high-level features were fed into a logistic regression classifier to fine-tune the model. A sigmoid classifier was added to the network to discriminate the vertebrae patches from nonvertebrae patches by selecting the class with the highest probabilities. To summarize the abovementioned works, unsupervised pretraining and supervised fine-tuning optimize deep-learned features for a specific task, such as vertebrae segmentation, thereby improving final performance.

To the best of our knowledge, our proposed SVseg Model was used here for the first time to segment CT vertebrae images. Transfer learning (TL) [47] can be used to analyze medical images. Pretraining a deep learning network on the source domain [48] and fine-tuning it based on the target domain's instances is a common transfer learning strategy. Transfer learning, on the other hand, requires a sufficient amount of training data to avoid overfitting. Additionally, transfer learning cannot substitute for the necessary data collection, which may be ineffective at improving the performance of a classification task. Hence, SSAE + sigmoid classifier-based modeling is the best choice in our work. Unlike convolutional neural net (CNN)-based feature representation, which contains subsampling and convolutional tasks for feature extraction, our proposed SVseg method has a full connection model to learn high-level features. The method has an encoder–decoder architectural structure, where the encoder network presents pixels' intensity as modeled through lower dimensionality attributes, while the decoder portion reconstructs the intensity of the original pixel by using lower-dimensional features. SSAE is a full connection methodology that extracts a single global weight matrix for feature representations, while CNN is a partial connection technique to stress the importance of locality. For our application, the size of vertebrae and nonvertebrae patches was set to 32×32 pixels—useful for building a full connection model. We used SSAE rather than CNN for our classification-based vertebrae segmentation modeling. The method is evaluated using a dataset from the CSI MICCAI workshop on spine and vertebrae segmentation [49]. The experimental performance shows that the proposed method is more efficient and accurate than earlier presented methods.

The main contributions of our paper are:

- To create the overlapping patches, spine CT images are divided into square patches of the same size. To address the issue of class imbalance, we generated a balanced training set using a random undersampling function for negative samples (nonvertebrae patches).
- Image patches are transformed into the matrix. The SVseg model is capable of learning high-level structural information from a large number of unlabeled image patches in an unsupervised way by SSAE. Thus, SSAE is capable of converting input pixel intensities to structured vertebrae or nonvertebrae representations.
- We constructed a four-layer SSAE architecture with a logistic regression classifier to fine-tune the model in a supervised manner. The results were produced in the form of a matrix containing values of 1 and 0, indicating whether or not the associated patches are vertebrae.
- We validated our proposed SVseg model on the publicly available MICCAI CSI dataset, which achieved the highest performance of 87.39% in DSC, 77.60% in JSC, 91.53% in PRE, and 90.88% in SEN, compared with classical segmentation approaches and well-known vertebral segmentation methods.

The remainder of this paper is structured as follows. Section 2 presents a brief description of the proposed methodology, composed of four procedures. Section 3 describes the experimental setup, dataset, and evaluation metrics. Section 4 contains the experimental results and a discussion. Finally, Section 5 concludes the work and gives suggestions for future work.

2. Methodology

As shown in Figure 1, the proposed method is composed of four procedures: (i) data preprocessing; (ii) SVseg model pretraining; (iii) SSAE + SC for supervised SVseg model designing; and (iv) testing.

2.1. Data Preprocessing

In the data preprocessing, the noise of the whole CT volume was filtered out by applying a rough threshold window. On the dataset, a slice-by-slice process was performed. The vertebrae have higher intensities in images than other tissues but are similar to different bone structures like ribs, so the algorithm learned the difference between vertebrae structures from other bony structures. A Gaussian filter with a sigma value of 1.5 was applied to control CT images' smoothness as a preprocessing step for obtaining accurate segmentation and attenuating the effects of noisy pixels. The CT images of the spine were divided into 32×32 pixel overlapped patches. To create the overlapping patches, we used certain stride pixels. An image patch contains a total of 1024 pixels, and if these pixels are equal to or greater than 50%, then the patch is labeled 1 (vertebra patch); otherwise, it is labeled 0 (nonvertebra patch). There was an imbalance in the number of training patches between the two classes used for classification. Most training patches are labeled "0" because the vertebrae area in the images is smaller than the background area, which can lead to background bias. To solve this dilemma, it is necessary to strike a balance between the sizes of the positive and negative training image patches. We generated a balanced training set using a random undersampling function for negative samples (nonvertebrae patches). This improves the network's accuracy and convergence rate during model training [50]. Figure 2 illustrates the data preprocessing.

2.2. SVseg Model Pretraining

In this work, we introduced a stacked sparse autoencoder [51] (SSAE) for high-level feature learning from overlapping image patches during training. An SSAE is an unsupervised technique of deep learning that contains basic layers for feature learning. In the following section, we first discuss the basic feature learning algorithm by sparse autoencoder and then introduce the stacking of sparse autoencoder; finally, we used a sigmoid classifier layer with unsupervised SSAE for fine-tuning the SVseg model.

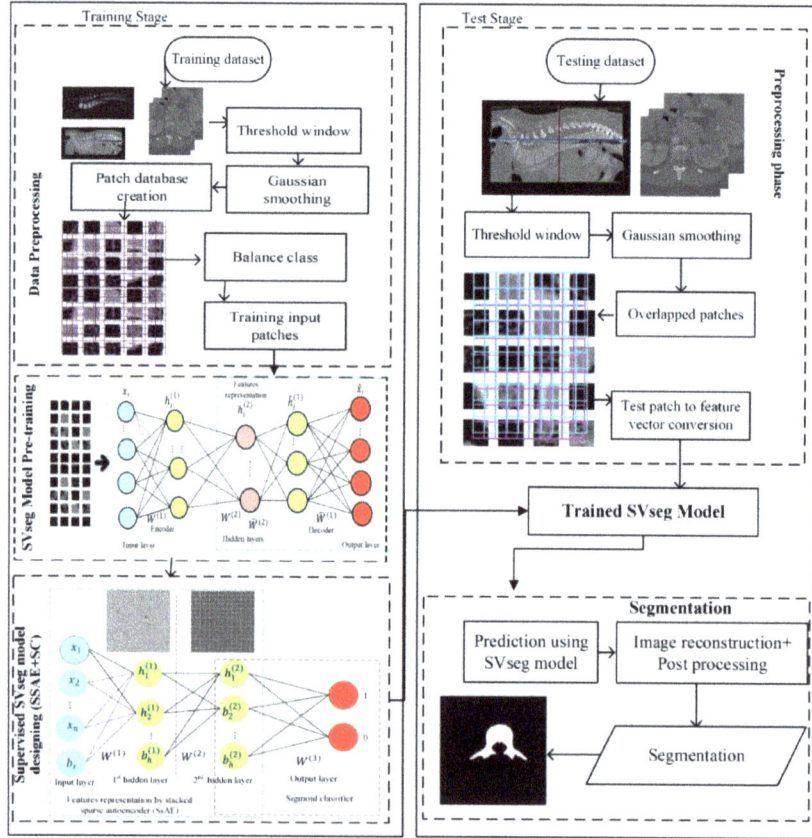

Figure 1. The flowchart of the proposed SVseg model (training stage and testing stage): SVseg consists of four steps: (i) data preprocessing; (ii) SVseg model pretraining; (iii) SSAE + SC for supervised SVseg model designing; and (iv) testing.

The fundamental unit for SSAE, autoencoder (AE) works for feedforward nonlinear neural network training. It is composed of three fundamental layers: an input, a hidden layer, and an output layer structure. There are a number of nodes that make up each layer of AE; these nodes establish full connections between the nodes of adjacent layers. Basically, the autoencoder consists of the encoder–decoder processing step, as shown in Figure 3. The input vector presentation is encoded in the encoding stage to link the input layer and the autoencoder's hidden layer. In contrast, the autoencoder implies the input vector reconstruction from encoded features learning in the hidden layers in the decoding stage. The autoencoder's purpose is to determine the input data representation that could be used to create the best reconstruction. A concatenated vector feature of an image patch was fed into AE in our method. Input image patches x_i were given to AE in the training, and reducing the error factor for all network connection weights was performed as follows:

$$\text{ArgMin}_{W,b,\hat{W},\hat{b}} \sum_{i=1}^{N} \left| x_i - (\hat{W}(\sigma(Wx_i + b)) + \hat{b}) \right|_2^2 . \quad (1)$$

In Equation (1), w, b, and σ are the weights, biases, and activation function of autoencoder parameters. Given an input vector x_i, the autoencoder first encodes this input into the representation $h_i = \sigma(Wx_i + b)$, where h_i is the x_i responses of hidden-layer neurons and h is the dimension that corresponds to the number of neurons in the hidden layer. The autoencoder decodes the original input from the encoding learning throughout the decoding process, $\hat{W}h_i + \hat{b}$. For effective feature extraction from input image patches, the autoencoder requires that the hidden layer dimension be less than the input layer's dimensions; otherwise, error minimization would lead to a trivial solution. The authors of [52] determined that the feature learning of the autoencoder is similar to that of PCA.

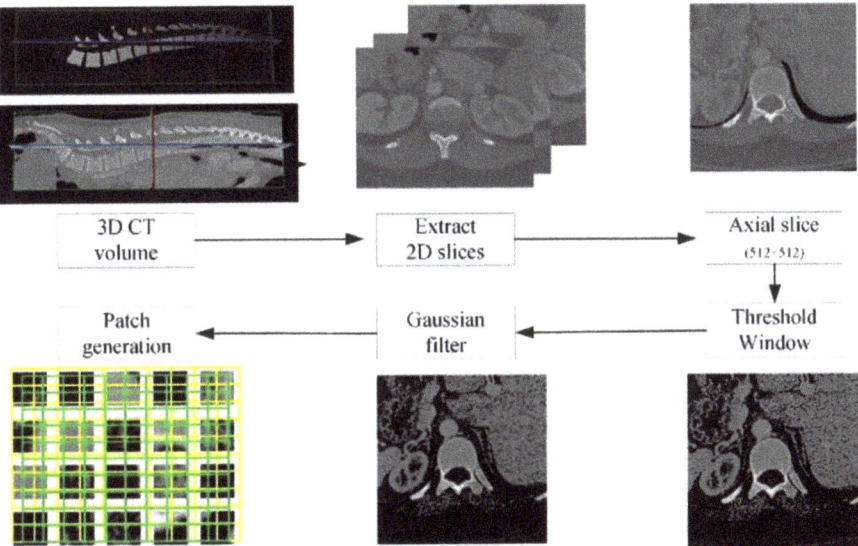

Figure 2. Examples of data preprocessing: 2D axial (512 × 512 pixels) slices are extracted from the 3D CT volume, a threshold window is applied, and a Gaussian smoothing filter is used on these slices; then images are divided into 32 × 32-pixel square patches (vertebrae and nonvertebrae patches).

Rather than a limitation of hidden layer dimension, an alternate approach called sparse autoencoder (SAE) imposed sparsity regularization on the autoencoder's hidden layers. SAE implements the regularization of the hidden layer's responses to avoid trivial solutions that the basic autoencoders tend towards. Those basic autoencoders required the hidden layer's dimension to be less than the input layer's dimension. Precisely, to make infinitesimal, the sparsity regularization is imposed on the autoencoder. To create a balance between the hidden layer's sparsity and reconstruction power, for every input node, only the most suitable hidden nodes responses that drive the SAE to represent the training set in sparse features. It can be stated as follows:

$$\text{ArgMin}_{W,b,\hat{W},\hat{b}} \sum_{i=1}^{N} \left| x_i - (\hat{W}(\sigma(Wx_i - b)) + \hat{b}) \right|_2^2 + \delta \sum_{j=1}^{M} KL(\rho|\rho^j) \tag{2}$$

$$KL(\rho|\rho^j) = \rho \log \frac{\rho}{\rho^j} + (1-\rho) \log \frac{1-\rho}{1-\rho^j}, \tag{3}$$

where δ shows the balancing parameter between sparsity and reconstruction and the dimensions of the hidden layer are defined by M. The term $KL(\rho|\rho^j)$, known as the Kullback–Leibler equation [53] (Equation (3)), shows the divergence in two Bernoulli distributions that have the probability ρ and ρ^j. The sparsity is minimized when ρ^j is close to ρ for each hidden neuron j. From the image patches of vertebrae, the low-level features can be learned by SAE. However, due to variations in the appearance of vertebrae, low-level feature learning is insufficient. In contrast, abstract high-features are more robust to CT images' inhomogeneity. Based on human perception, we applied SSAE for high-level feature learning based on low-level feature representation. The stacking of multiple SAEs, known as SSAE, contracts deep hierarchies. To learn abstract high-level features from input images patch, we stacked the SAE to feed the low-level SAE output layer as an input layer for the high-level SAE. This SSAE network uses an unsupervised method for pretraining the SVseg model. From input overlapping patches, the SSAE was trained without utilizing the label data.

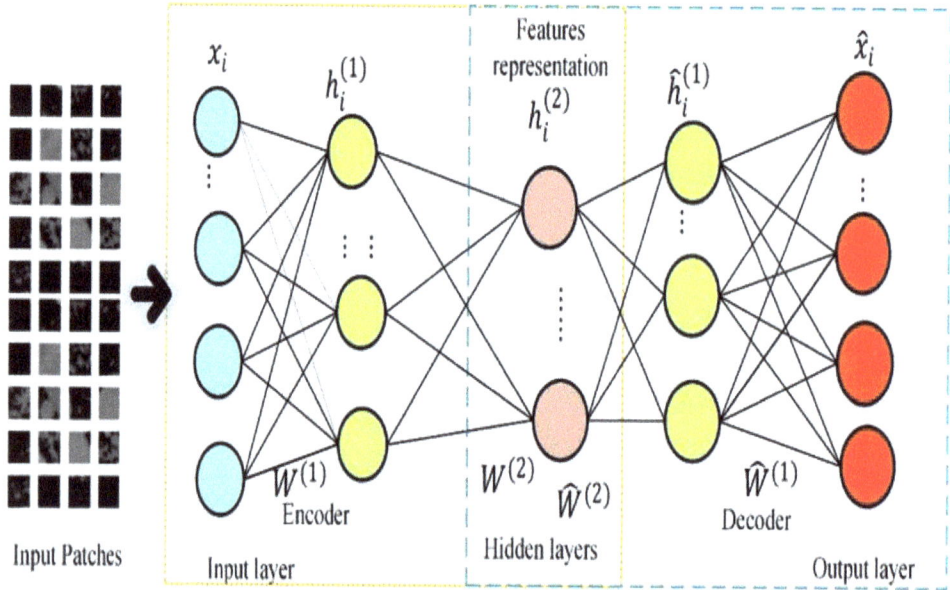

Figure 3. Architecture illustration of high-level feature learning of vertebral input image patches using an autoencoder with encoder and decoder networks.

2.3. SSAE + SC for Supervised SVseg Model Designing

Since SSAE is trained in an unsupervised manner, the high-level feature representation is only data-adaptive, and not necessarily discriminative enough for separating the vertebra from background patches. To discriminate learned features [54,55], a supervised fine-tuned approach SSAE+SC (sigmoid classifier) [56] was used, as shown in Figure 4.

The proposed SVseg model contains four network layers: one input layer, two hidden layers, and one sigmoid layer. The training procedure consists of different stages. Firstly, a sparse autoencoder (SAE) was imposed on the overlapped patches in training data for primary feature learning $h^{(1)}(x)$ by the adjustment of weight W^1. After that, input pixels were given to this trained SAE for representation activations $h^{(1)}(x)$. The secondary presentation $h^{(2)}(x)$ learning was obtained by using the primary representation as an input to the other SAE by the adjustment of the W^2 weight. These secondary representations $h^{(2)}(x)$ were used for the sigmoid layer as input and to learn the mapping of $h^{(2)}(x)$ to labels by the adjustment of the W^3 weight. Finally, one input and two hidden layers were stacked for making SSAE and a final sigmoid layer was added an output layer capable of detecting the vertebrae from the background. The SVseg model included the bottom-up training of SSAE in an unsupervised way, followed by a sigmoid classifier that used supervised learning for top layer training and fine-tuned the entire deep framework.

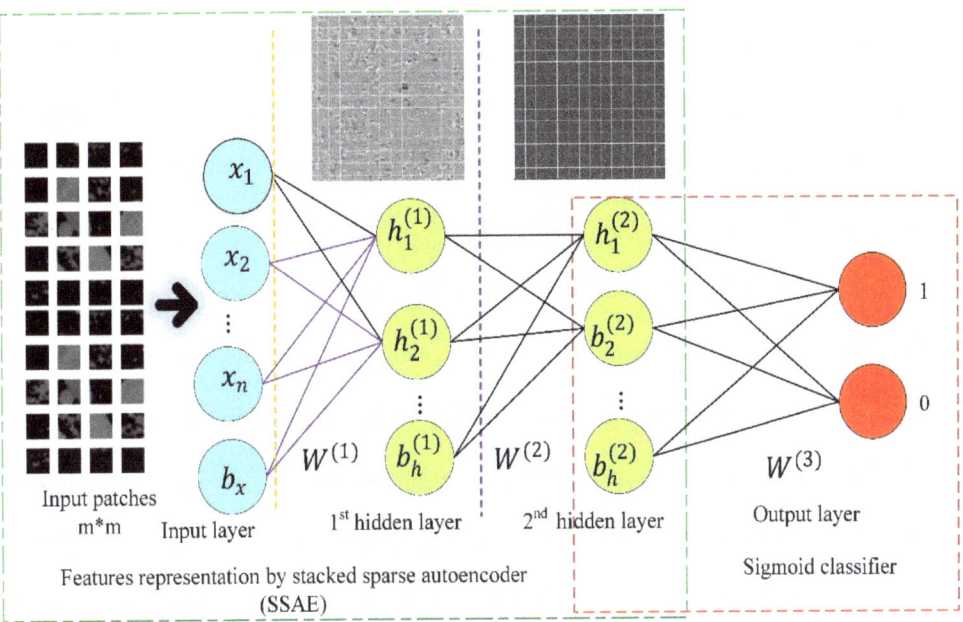

Figure 4. Illustration of unsupervised SSAE fine-tuned by adding a sigmoid classifier (output layer) for the supervised SVseg model design to classify the image patches into vertebrae or nonvertebrae.

The number of nodes in the sigmoid layer was determined to be equal to the number of labels. The sigmoid layer in our method had two nodes, one for vertebra and the other for the background. The sigmoid layer predicts the likelihood of the label of the input data x_i based on learned features, the second hidden layer representation $h_i^{(2)}$. Other classifiers such as SVM and MLP can also be used. The SVM classifier calculates a posterior probability score for a pixel belonging to the target or background class. A probability image was created by reconstructing the score vector, which requires a high degree of generalization. On the other hand, a multilayer perceptron (MLP) is a feedforward neural network with a large number of layers and many nodes in each layer that cannot overcome the problem of overfitting and are stuck in local minima. However, sigmoid logistic regression allowed us to optimize the whole deep framework jointly through fine-tuning. The sigmoid classifier that generalizes logistic regression is shown in the below equation:

$$\sigma(x) = \frac{1}{1 + e^{-x}}, \qquad (4)$$

where x is the input and σ is the sigmoid output function [56] in Equation (4). For fine-tuning, the weights and biases of the sigmoid layer and SSAEs were optimized together, and the sigmoid layer was used for classification. The cost function can be minimized using a gradient descent-based model [51]. For every input x_i, the two output values are calculated and these values are the classification probability of the input. This paper considers two class classification problems, and the label of the patch is {0, 1}, where 1 and 0 refer to vertebrae and nonvertebrae patches, respectively. It should be noted that the label information is not used in the SSAE learning procedure because SSAE learning is a method of unsupervised learning. After the high-level feature learning, the sigmoid layer (output layer) is fed the learned high-level representation of vertebrae structures along with its label (Figure 4). The trained model is then fed test patches, which return a 0 or 1 value indicating whether the input image patch represents a vertebra or not.

2.4. Testing

After training, the SVseg model is ready to test unseen vertebrae patches for model validation. Test image patches were fed to the SVseg model and produced a predicted value of one or zero, interpreted as the probability of corresponding to vertebra or background. Based on these results, a binary segmented image was obtained after reconstruction of the predicted patches. Due to the high contrast between vertebra, ribs, and other skeletal structural tissues, some background pixels were misclassified as vertebrae, while some vertebrae pixels were misclassified as background. Thus, these outliers were removed by applying morphological operations [57] such as dilation, erosion, and hole filling to improve the segmentation accuracy in postprocessing.

3. Experimental Setup

We intended to compare our proposed SVseg model with other segmentation algorithms. Our model's performance was evaluated on the public dataset of segmentation challenge in MICCAI Computational Spine Imaging (CSI) 2014 [49].

3.1. Dataset

The datasets were collected at the Medical Center at the University of California, Irvine (Orange, CA, USA) [49]. The dataset contained a total of 15 CT images, 10 CT images (5595 slices) for the training, and five CT images (3418 slices) for the testing. Each CT scan covered the whole lumbar and thoracic spine and included complete vertebrae segmentation masks. The scanning settings were: slice thickness of 0.7–2.0 mm, voltage of 120 kVp, a kernel for soft tissue reconstruction, and intravenous contrast. The axial in-plane resolution varied between 0.3125 and 0.3613 mm^2.

3.2. Experiments

A given set of hyperparameters initialized the SSAE network. These parameters included framework parameters, weights of the sigmoid layer, number of layer's hidden neurons, target activation ρ for hidden neurons, sparsity penalty β, and L2 regularization λ. A random search [58] was used to find the optimal network structure in terms of performance. First, we tried to define the spectrum of hyperparameters, and then we selected the values randomly. We trained our framework with these selected values and repeated this process until we found the best productivity. For evaluation, the dataset was split into three subgroups I_{train}, I_{valid}, and I_{test}. From the 20 training CT images, we generated 651,712 overlapping image patches (325,856 vertebrae patches + 325,856 nonvertebrae patches). We randomly selected 80% of the patches for I_train and 20% for I_valid. The size of each slice was about 512 × 512 pixels. Training set I_train and I_valid contained 525,568 and 126,144 sample patches, respectively, which were used to train the SVseg model. The mini-batch size was set to 64 for efficient training, and I_train was divided into 8212 mini-batches and I_valid into 1971 mini-batches. The proposed method contained four network layers: one input layer with 1024 neurons; two hidden layers with 729 and 196 hidden neurons, respectively; and one sigmoid layer consisting of two neurons corresponding to the number of classes. Many experiments were conducted to determine the SVSeg model's number of hidden layers and the number of nodes in each hidden layer. The performance of the models was monitored in each experiment until the SVseg model achieved its optimal performance (two hidden layers, the first with 729 nodes and the second with 196 nodes).

Figure 5 shows the visualization of the first and second hidden layers' feature presentations by the four-layered SSAE based on the visualization model [59]. These features demonstrate that the model is capable of revealing vertebrae and nonvertebral structures from training patches. The learned feature representation in the first hidden layer (with 729 (27 × 27) nodes) indicates the vertebrae's detailed boundary features and other structures as shown in Figure 5a, while feature representation in the second hidden layer (with 196 (14 × 14) nodes) expresses the high-level feature learning of vertebrae as shown in Figure 5b. The 6 × 6 zoomed image of the SSAE's first hidden layer indicates weights at the left side, and the boundary and corner of vertebrae at the right side in Figure 6. Each square represents the weight between a single hidden node and the corresponding pixel in the original image. In the weight matrix, a gray pixel represents zero, whereas a white pixel represents a positive value. According to these findings, SVseg appears to be capable of learning useful high-level features that can be used to better describe vertebrae structures. The hyperparameters were selected to minimize the discrepancy between input and its reconstructions. In our work, this disparity was calculated as the mean square error (MSE). MSE is calculated between the input and reconstructed input from the AE decoder. Its gradually decreasing values relate to its saturation with respect to the number of epochs during the training phase.

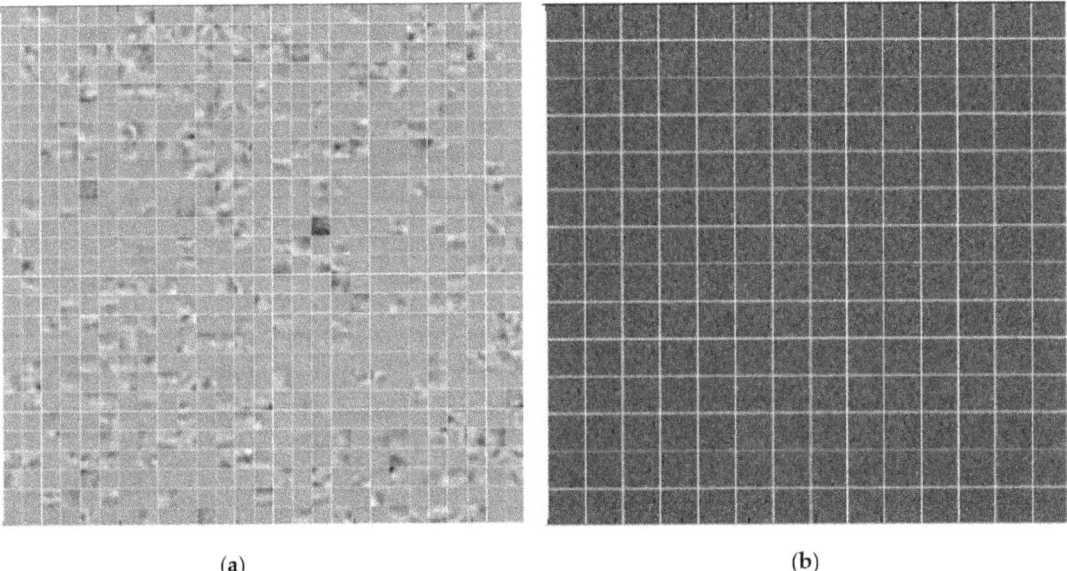

(a) (b)

Figure 5. Visualization of high-level feature presentation extracted from input pixel intensities of our proposed two-hidden-layer SVseg model with sparsity constraint of 0.15 and sparsity regularization of 0.20. (**a**) The learned feature representation in the first hidden layer with 729 nodes. The learned high-level feature representation in the second hidden layer with 196 nodes is shown in (**b**). As anticipated, (**a**) illustrates detailed border features of vertebrae and other tissue, whereas (**b**) illustrates high-level vertebral features.

Figure 7 shows the SVseg model pretraining learning curve in an unsupervised fashion, where 100 epochs are used and no label data are provided. After the pretraining, the supervised SVseg model learning curve, MSE of training, and validation corresponding to a number of epochs are shown in Figure 8. Figure 8a shows the best fit curve for our model training with MSE of 0.034 for training and MSE of 0.038 for validation. The learning curve diverges rapidly before 700 epochs and then stabilizes after 2500 epochs. Figure 8b depicts the problem of overfitting caused by a deviation in the validation curve from the training curve. Figure 8c,d shows the poor training MSE graph with a low learning rate and small batch size, respectively. The heuristic approach was used to obtain the correct training curve, as illustrated in Figure 8a. Therefore, initialization of weight is important in deep learning.

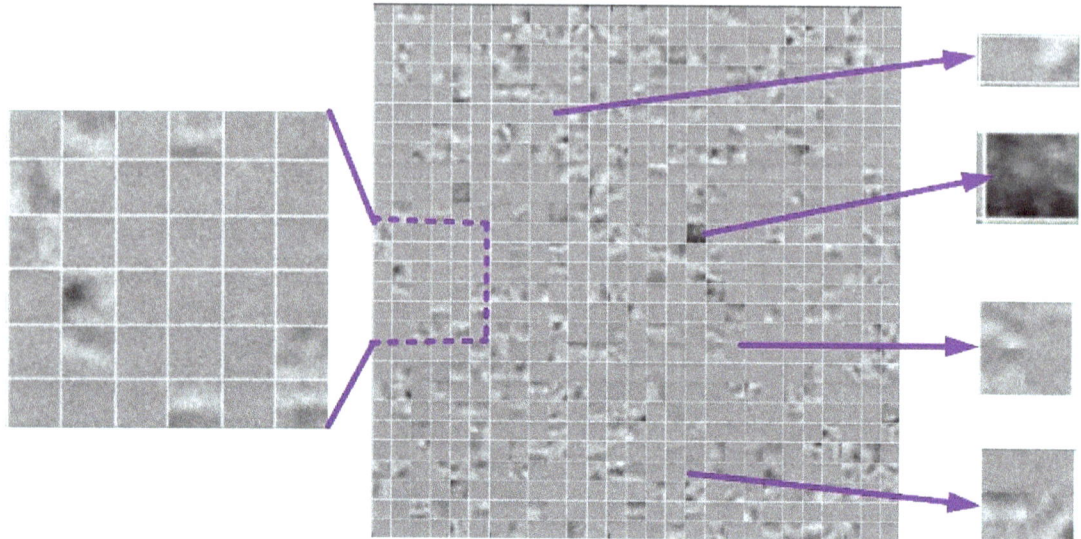

Figure 6. The visualizations of SSAE's first hidden layer expresses the learned feature representation (**center** image). The 6 × 6 zoomed image shows the weights of first hidden layer (**left** image), and four random weights from the 729-node hidden layer (**right** images).

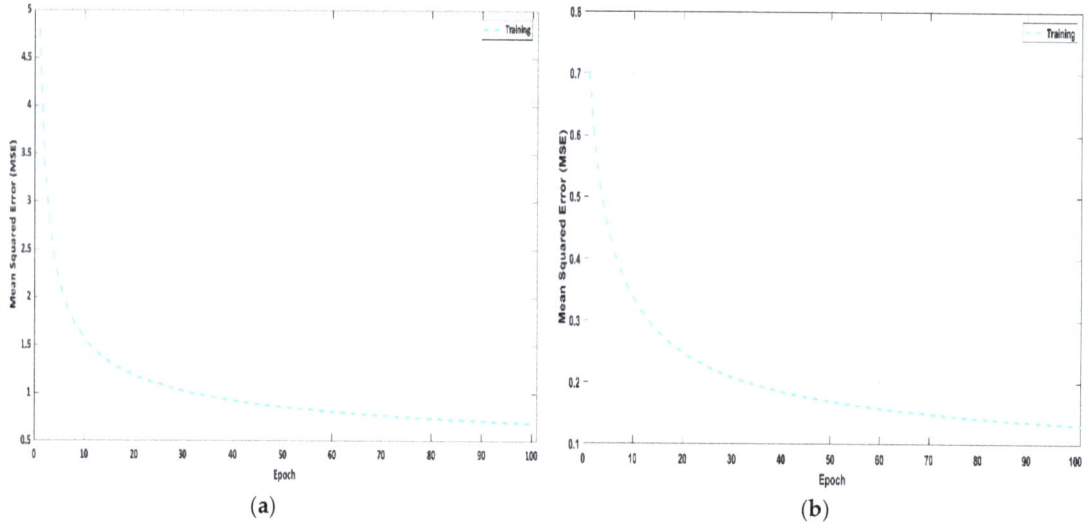

Figure 7. Pretraining graph of SSAE for the unsupervised analysis of two hidden layers: (**a**) first hidden layer with 729 nodes; (**b**) second hidden layer with 196 nodes; 100 epochs are used.

3.3. Evaluation Metrics

In this study, the Dice similarity coefficient (DSC) [60], Jaccard similarity coefficient (JSC) [61], precision (PRE), and sensitivity (SEN) were used as quantitative assessment metrics to evaluate segmentation performance [20,29]. We evaluated true positives (TP), true negatives (TN), false positives (FP), and false negatives (FN) by comparing the true labels with predicted labels:

$$DSC = \frac{2|A \cap B|}{|A| + |B|} = \frac{2TP}{2TP + FP + FN} \tag{5}$$

$$JSC = \frac{|A \cap B|}{|A \cup B|} = \frac{TP}{TP + FP + FN} \tag{6}$$

$$\text{Precision} = \frac{TP}{TP + FP} \tag{7}$$

$$\text{Sensitivity} = \frac{TP}{TP + FN}. \tag{8}$$

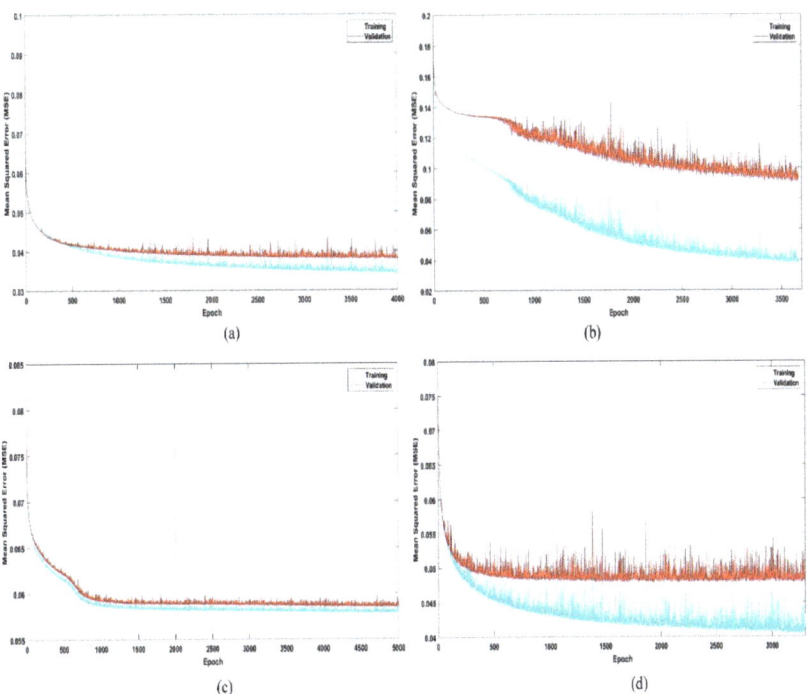

Figure 8. Learning curves of SSAEs model during different experiments. (**a**) Best fit curve for our model training with MSE of 0.034 for training and MSE of 0.038 for validation; 4000 epochs were used and the mini-batch size was set to 64 for efficient model training. The learning curve diverged rapidly before 700 epochs and then stabilized after 2500 epochs; (**b**) depicts the problem of overfitting caused by a deviation in the validation curve from the training curve; (**c**,**d**) show poor training MSE graphs with a low learning rate and small batch size, respectively.

4. Results and Discussion

To demonstrate the efficiency of the SVseg model, the model was compared to five other state-of-the-art models. We, therefore, compared the SVseg to other models to evaluate the segmentation efficiency. The training procedures of AE + SC, StAE + SC, SAE + SC, 3SAE + SC, and 4SAE + SC were similar to the techniques used for SVseg, as shown in Figure 4.

(i) Autoencoder plus sigmoid classifier (AE + SC): The sparsity constraint on the hidden layer of AE as controlled by the parameter σ in Equation (2). If the sparsity constraint was removed by σ = 0 in Equation (2), the sparse AE was transformed into a single-layered AE. The input x of the sigmoid classifier in Equation (4) was learned via single-layer AE, and the SC was trained for model fine-tuning. Then, SC was used with AE to determine if a vertebra was present or absent inside each image patch.

(ii) Stacked Autoencoder plus sigmoid classifier (StAE + SC) is a neural network composed of many layers of basic AE with each layer's outputs connected to the inputs of the subsequent layer. StAE is a two-layered fundamental AEs model. SC's input x in Equation (4) is a feature learned from the pixel intensities of an image patch using a two-layer AEs.

(iii) Sparse autoencoder plus sigmoid classifier (SAE + SC): In this approach, the input x of SC in Equation (4) is a feature learned from the pixel intensities of an image patch using a single layer of Sparse AE.

(iv) Three-layer sparse autoencoder plus sigmoid classifier (3SAE + SC): This model is composed of three Sparse AE layers, with the outputs of each layer connected to the inputs of the subsequent layer. The first and second hidden layers have the same nodes as in our SVseg, and the third layer has 49 hidden nodes.

(v) Four-layer sparse autoencoder plus sigmoid classifier (4SAE + SC): This network is composed of four sparse AE layers and has the same parametric settings as the SVseg model but the third and fourth layers have 49 and 16 hidden nodes, respectively. An SC layer is attached at the end of network for fine-tuning. The 4SAE + SC model uses the same method for training as shown in Figure 4.

The quantitative performance of SVseg and different models was analyzed using the metrics in Equations (5)–(8), respectively. Table 1 indicates the means of DSC, JSC, PRE, and SEN of SVseg and comparative models. Table 1 shows that the SVseg model results give superior segmentation performance compared to the other models in all metrics. While the results tend to favor "deeper" architecture over "shallow" architecture in encoding high-level features from pixel intensities, the 3SAE + SC and 4SAE + SC models' poor performance compared to the SVseg model suggests that adding more layers may cause an overfitting problem. Figure 9 shows the visualization of vertebrae segmentation results, randomly selected from five test cases based on our SVseg model.

Table 1. Performance evaluation metrics (DSC, JSC, PRE, and SEN) of SVseg with various models AE + SC, StAE + SC, SAE+SC, 3SAE + SC, and 4SAE for vertebrae segmentation on MACCAI CSI dataset.

Methods	DSC (%)	JSC (%)	PRE (%)	SEN (%)
AE + SC	78.91	65.17	82.57	79.61
StAE + SC	83.39	71.51	88.17	85.71
SAE + SC	81.41	69.65	85.83	78.63
3SAE + SC	85.12	74.09	90.59	88.41
4SAE + SC	84.73	73.51	85.33	90.13
SVseg (proposed)	**87.39**	**77.60**	**91.53**	**90.88**

4.1. Computational Cost

The experiments were carried out on a 1.80 GHz i7 CPU, 32 GB RAM, NVIDIA GeForce MX250 GPU using MATLAB 2018a environment. In this study, we compared SVseg's computational efficiency to that of five other state-of-the-art approaches. Table 2 shows the execution times for each model. Regarding training time, the two autoencoder-based models that do not include sparsity required less training time than the three models with sparsity. In addition, as the number of layers in the architecture increased, more time was needed for training. In terms of run-time execution, our proposed SVseg model was more efficient than the other five models.

Figure 9. Visualization of vertebrae segmentation results, randomly selected from five test cases of the thoracolumbar spine database (mid-axial slices). The first row shows the segmentation superimposed on the image, the second row shows segmented images, and the last row shows ground truths.

Table 2. The execution time of AE + SC, StAE + SC, SAE + SC, 3SAE + SC, and 4SAE + SC trained on the training dataset and the time required to evaluate them on a test image of 512 × 512 pixels.

Methods	Training Time (h)	Segmentation Time (s)
AE + SC	21.05	16
StAE + SC	22.16	19
SAE + SC	23.07	13
3SAE + SC	26.47	23
4SAE + SC	37.22	23
SVseg Model	22.35	12

4.2. Discussion

As shown in Table 3, we also compared our SVseg model with classical segmentation algorithms including U-Net [62], DeepLabv3+ [63], MultiResUNet [64], Densely-UNet [65], and other well-known vertebrae segmentation methods. Table 3 indicates that the proposed SVseg model outperformed all the other models in terms of DSC and JSC. Compared with the classical U-Net [62], DeepLabv3+ [63], MultiResUNet [64], Densely-UNet [65], SpineParseNet [20], Mask R-CNN [66], and multiscale CNN [67] our SVseg model was significantly better by (3.79, 5.78), (13.86, 19.46), (1.90, 3.05), (4.23, 6.43), (0.07, 0.11), (18.19, 24.45), (0.89, 2.93) on average (DSC%, JSC%), respectively.

The SVseg model also achieved the best results compared with well-known vertebrae segmentation methods. For example, a mean 86.17% DICE score was reported for vertebrae segmentation using (D-TVNet) based on U-Net [68]. The experimental results showed that D-TVNet was unable to determine the critical points for measuring the spine curve angle using segmented bones. Additionally, when the noise was significant, and the bones not sharp, this method was ineffective at identifying them. While the D-TVNet method is capable of removing some noise from images, it can also accidentally remove relevant bones in some cases. In [29], a deep learning approach was proposed for automatic CT vertebra segmentation and achieved a 86.1% DICE score. The starting thoracic vertebrae have a lower DICE due to the influence of the ribs and intervertebral discs. This method segmented several bones not seen in the label annotations, resulting in misclassification and a low DICE score. These variables contributed to error segmentations. A deep learning patch-based technique for cervical vertebra segmentation in X-ray images was proposed in [32] with a DICE score of 84%, but this framework has a number of flaws. By eliminating outlier centers away from the vertebral curve, the center localization structure can be strengthened even further. The current framework for center localization was limited by the fact that it does not know which center belongs to which vertebra. In another paper [69], a DICE score of 87% was obtained using a deep learning approach on the thoracolumbar spine from CT images, but this approach omits information about a spine's structural consistency. The result is odd behavior in which this method fails to segment parts of a vertebra, or, in some cases, entire vertebrae at the beginning or end of a spine. It should be investigated how such global systemic regularity can be imposed during the training phase. Table 3 shows that SVseg achieved the highest mean DSC and JSC for segmentation of vertebrae compared to all methods.

Table 3. The SVseg model achieved the highest mean DSC (%) and JSC (%) compared with classical segmentation algorithms and also other vertebrae segmentation methods.

Methods	Backbone	DSC (%)	(JSC) (%)
Classical U-Net [62]	U-Net	83.60	71.82
DeepLabv3+ [63]	DeepLabv3+	73.53	58.14
MultiResUNet [64]	U-Net	85.42	74.55
Densely-UNet [65]	3DU-Net	83.16	71.17
SpineParseNet [20]	3D-GCSN, 2DResUNet	87.32	77.49
Mask R-CNN [66]	ResNet 101	69.20	53.15
Multiscale CNN [67]	FCN	86.50	74.67
D-TVNet [68]	U-Net	86.68	76.49
PaDBN [29]	DBN	86.10	75.59
S. Al Arif et al. [32]	U-Net	84.00	72.41
A. Sekuboyina et al. [69]	U-Net	87.00	76.99
SVseg Model (**proposed**)	SSAE	**87.39**	**77.60**

The above results and discussion prove that our proposed approach has the benefits of automatically learning high-level features from data images, rather than relying on handcrafted feature extraction, which often necessitates advanced engineering skills. SSAE differs from an autoencoder (AE) because it imposes sparsity on the mapped features, preventing the problem of trivial solutions when the dimensionality of hidden features exceeds the dimensions of input features. After stacking, SSAE can learn high-level features, similar to other deep learning techniques. Our SVseg model has the ability of high-level feature extraction by unsupervised learning, followed by training the sigmoid classifier in a supervised manner. The model was evaluated on a publicly CSI MICCAI dataset for training and testing.

As a result, the SVseg model achieved excellent segmentation of the vertebrae from CT images. To avoid potential issues caused by the limited amount of training data, we pretrained the model layer-by-layer, which allowed it to learn the hierarchy of features one layer at a time. Specifically, the previous layer's learned features were fed into the next layer during each layer's training. Secondly, the entire model was refined by only a few iterations during the fine-tuning stage, which is important for mitigating the overfitting problem.

Thus, our model enhanced the accuracy and practicality of segmentation findings, enabling spine clinical diagnosis to be supported without relying on a complex network design.

We can also use transfer learning to avoid overfitting problems [47,70]. We can use other human organs' CT images to initialize our model in the unsupervised pretraining process, obtaining a more general CT image appearance. We believe that, by performing this initialization, we will be able to improve the fine-tuning process and, as a result, overcome the small sample problem. In the fields of machine learning and computer vision, similar methods have been commonly used [47,70]. However, our model takes a long time to segment the vertebrae since it is implemented in MATLAB. Using Keras with a TensorFlow backend in Python is an option to improve the time efficiency of our approach. This will result in a decrease in computational time.

5. Conclusions

In conclusion, we proposed the SVseg model for CT image-based vertebrae segmentation. To overcome the difficulties of robust feature presentation caused by the large diversity of vertebra appearance, we proposed deep feature extraction by the SSAE architecture. The supervised sigmoid classifier fine-tunes the learned features from pretraining to estimate the target image's vertebrae likelihood map. In this study, we found that the supervised fine-tuning step was positively impacted by sparsity regularization during training. The sparsity target forced the filters to collect more distinct features from image patches during the training phase. Our proposed method was tested on the publicly available CSI MICCAI dataset. When compared to other classical segmentation algorithms and well-known vertebrae segmentation methods, our model performed better in terms of segmentation accuracy. Finally, the SVseg model outperformed a variety of state-of-the-art methods in terms of vertebrae segmentation accuracy, both qualitatively and quantitatively. To better characterize vertebrae, we intend to extend our proposed model to other imaging modalities in the future and incorporate it with other deep learning feature extraction methods. Additionally, further validation, improvement, and implementation of our approach for additional applications like 3D medical image segmentation and multiclass classification will be our future focus.

Author Contributions: Conceptualization, S.F.Q. and L.S.; methodology, S.F.Q.; software, S.F.Q. and M.A.; validation, S.F.Q., L.S. and S.Q.; formal analysis, M.A., S.Q., S.S.Z. and M.A.A.; investigation, L.S.; resources, L.S.; data curation, S.F.Q.; writing—original draft preparation, S.F.Q. and L.S.; writing—review and editing, S.F.Q., L.S.; visualization, M.A., S.Q., S.S.Z. and M.A.A; supervision, L.S.; project administration, S.F.Q. and L.S.; funding acquisition, L.S. All authors have read and agreed to the published version of the manuscript.

Funding: This work was supported in part by the Natural Science Foundation of China through grant 91959108.

Institutional Review Board Statement: Not applicable.

Informed Consent Statement: Not applicable.

Data Availability Statement: The authors confirm that the data supporting the findings of this study are available within the article.

Conflicts of Interest: The authors declare no conflict of interest.

References

1. Muñoz, H.E.; Yao, J.; Burns, J.E.; Summers, R.M. Detection of vertebral degenerative disc disease based on cortical shell unwrapping. In Proceedings of the International Conference on Medical Image Computing and Computer-Assisted Intervention, Novak, CL, USA, 29 March 2013; Aylward, S., Ed.; Volume 15, p. 86700C.
2. Bourgeois, A.C.; Faulkner, A.R.; Pasciak, A.S.; Bradley, Y.C. The evolution of image-guided lumbosacral spine surgery. *Ann. Transl. Med.* **2015**, *3*, 69. [PubMed]
3. Kim, G.-U.; Chang, M.C.; Kim, T.U.; Lee, G.W. Diagnostic modality in spine disease: A review. *Asian Spine J.* **2020**, *14*, 910. [CrossRef] [PubMed]

4. Qadri, S.F.; Shen, L.; Ahmad, M.; Qadri, S.; Shamaila, S.; Khan, S. OP-convNet: A patch classification based framework for CT vertebrae segmentation. *IEEE Access* **2021**, *9*, 158227–158240. [CrossRef]
5. Lim, P.H.; Bagci, U.; Bai, L. Introducing willmore flow into level set segmentation of spinal vertebrae. *IEEE Trans. Biomed. Eng.* **2013**, *60*, 115–122. [CrossRef]
6. Huang, J.; Jian, F.; Wu, H.; Li, H. An improved level set method for vertebra CT image segmentation. *Biomed. Eng. Online* **2013**, *12*, 48. [CrossRef] [PubMed]
7. Yao, J.; O'Connor, S.D.; Summers, R.M. Automated spinal column extraction and partitioning. In Proceedings of the Biomedical Imaging: Nano to Macro, Arlington, VA, USA, 6–9 April 2006; pp. 390–393.
8. Naegel, B. Using mathematical morphology for the anatomical labeling of vertebrae from 3D CT-scan images. *Comput. Med. Imaging Graph.* **2007**, *31*, 141–156. [CrossRef]
9. Kim, Y.; Kim, D. A fully automatic vertebra segmentation method using 3D deformable fences. *Comput. Med. Imaging Graph.* **2009**, *33*, 343–352. [CrossRef]
10. Mastmeyer, A.; Engelke, K.; Fuchs, C.; Kalender, W.A. A hierarchical 3D segmentation method and the definition of vertebral body coordinate systems for QCT of the lumbar spine. *Med. Image Anal.* **2006**, *10*, 560–577. [CrossRef]
11. Burnett, S.S.C.; Starkschall, G.; Stevens, C.W.; Liao, Z. A deformable-model approach to semi-automatic segmentation of CT images demonstrated by application to the spinal canal. *Med. Phys.* **2004**, *31*, 251–263. [CrossRef]
12. Klinder, T.; Ostermann, J.; Ehm, M.; Franz, A.; Kneser, R.; Lorenz, C. Automated model-based vertebra detection, identification, and segmentation in CT images. *Med. Image Anal.* **2009**, *13*, 471–482. [CrossRef]
13. Ma, J.; Lu, L.; Zhan, Y.; Zhou, X.; Salganicoff, M.; Krishnan, A. Hierarchical segmentation and identification of thoracic vertebra using learning-based edge detection and coarse-to-fine deformable model. In Proceedings of the International Conference on Medical Image Computing and Computer-Assisted Intervention, Beijing, China, 20–24 September 2010; pp. 19–27.
14. Rasoulian, A.; Rohling, R.; Abolmaesumi, P. Lumbar spine segmentation using a statistical multi-vertebrae anatomical shape+pose model. *IEEE Trans. Med. Imaging* **2013**, *32*, 1890–1900. [CrossRef] [PubMed]
15. Kadoury, S.; Labelle, H.; Paragios, N. Automatic inference of articulated spine models in CT images using high-order Markov Random Fields. *Med. Image Anal.* **2011**, *15*, 426–437. [CrossRef] [PubMed]
16. Ibragimov, B.; Likar, B.; Pernuš, F.; Vrtovec, T. Shape representation for efficient landmark-based segmentation in 3-D. *IEEE Trans. Med. Imaging* **2014**, *33*, 861–874. [CrossRef] [PubMed]
17. Zhang, J.; Wang, H. A novel segmentation method for cervical vertebrae based on PointNet++ and converge segmentation. *Comput. Methods Programs Biomed.* **2021**, *200*, 105798. [CrossRef] [PubMed]
18. Tufail, A.B.; Ma, Y.-K.; Kaabar, M.K.A.; Rehman, A.U.; Khan, R.; Cheikhrouhou, O. Classification of Initial Stages of Alzheimer's Disease through Pet Neuroimaging Modality and Deep Learning: Quantifying the Impact of Image Filtering Approaches. *Mathematics* **2021**, *9*, 3101. [CrossRef]
19. Hirra, I.; Ahmad, M.; Hussain, A.; Usman Ashraf, M.; Saeed, I.A.; Qadri, S.F.; Alghamdi, A.M.; Alfakeeh, A.S. Breast Cancer Classification from Histopathological Images using Patch-based Deep Learning Modeling. *IEEE Access* **2021**, *9*, 24273–24287. [CrossRef]
20. Pang, S.; Pang, C.; Zhao, L.; Chen, Y.; Su, Z.; Zhou, Y.; Huang, M.; Yang, W.; Lu, H.; Feng, Q. SpineParseNet: Spine Parsing for Volumetric MR Image by a Two-Stage Segmentation Framework with Semantic Image Representation. *IEEE Trans. Med. Imaging* **2021**, *40*, 262–273. [CrossRef]
21. Masuzawa, N.; Kitamura, Y.; Nakamura, K.; Iizuka, S.; Simo-Serra, E. Automatic Segmentation, Localization, and Identification of Vertebrae in 3D CT Images Using Cascaded Convolutional Neural Networks. In Proceedings of the Lecture Notes in Computer Science (Including Subseries Lecture Notes in Artificial Intelligence and Lecture Notes in Bioinformatics), Lima, Peru, 4–8 October 2020; Volume 12266 LNCS, pp. 681–690.
22. Chen, Y.; Gao, Y.; Li, K.; Zhao, L.; Zhao, J. Vertebrae Identification and Localization Utilizing Fully Convolutional Networks and a Hidden Markov Model. *IEEE Trans. Med. Imaging* **2020**, *39*, 387–399. [CrossRef]
23. Ahmad, M.; Ai, D.; Xie, G.; Qadri, S.F.; Song, H.; Huang, Y.; Wang, Y.; Yang, J. Deep Belief Network Modeling for Automatic Liver Segmentation. *IEEE Access* **2019**, *7*, 20585–20595. [CrossRef]
24. Ahmad, M.; Ding, Y.; Qadri, S.F.; Yang, J. Convolutional-neural-network-based feature extraction for liver segmentation from CT images. In Proceedings of the Eleventh International Conference on Digital Image Processing (ICDIP 2019), Guangzhou, China, 10–13 May 2019; Jiang, X., Hwang, J.-N., Eds.; Volume 1117934, p. 159.
25. Sekuboyina, A.; Valentinitsch, A.; Kirschke, J.S.; Menze, B.H. A Localisation-Segmentation Approach for Multi-label Annotation of Lumbar Vertebrae using Deep Nets. *arXiv* **2017**, arXiv:1703.04347.
26. Korez, R.; Likar, B.; Pernuš, F.; Vrtovec, T. Model-based segmentation of vertebral bodies from MR images with 3D CNNs. In Proceedings of the International Conference on Medical Image Computing and Computer-Assisted Intervention, Athens, Greece, 17–21 October 2016; pp. 433–441.
27. Yang, D.; Xiong, T.; Xu, D.; Huang, Q.; Liu, D.; Zhou, S.K.; Xu, Z.; Park, J.; Chen, M.; Tran, T.D.; et al. Automatic vertebra labeling in large-scale 3D CT using deep image-to-image network with message passing and sparsity regularization. In Proceedings of the International Conference on Information Processing in Medical Imaging, Boone, NC, USA, 25–30 June 2017; pp. 633–644.

28. Chen, H.; Shen, C.; Qin, J.; Ni, D.; Shi, L.; Cheng, J.C.Y.; Heng, P.-A. Automatic localization and identification of vertebrae in spine CT via a joint learning model with deep neural networks. In Proceedings of the International Conference on Medical Image Computing and Computer-Assisted Intervention, Munich, Germany, 5–9 October 2015; pp. 515–522.
29. Qadri, S.F.; Ai, D.; Hu, G.; Ahmad, M.; Huang, Y.; Wang, Y.; Yang, J. Automatic Deep Feature Learning via Patch-Based Deep Belief Network for Vertebrae Segmentation in CT Images. *Appl. Sci.* **2019**, *9*, 69. [CrossRef]
30. Qadri, S.F.; Ahmad, M.; Ai, D.; Yang, J.; Wang, Y. Deep Belief Network Based Vertebra Segmentation for CT Images. In *Proceedings of the Chinese Conference on Image and Graphics Technologies*; Wang, Y., Wang, S., Liu, Y., Yang, J., Yuan, X., He, R., Duh, H.B.-L., Eds.; Springer: Singapore, 2018; Volume 757, pp. 536–545.
31. Liu, X.; Yang, J.; Song, S.; Cong, W.; Jiao, P.; Song, H.; Ai, D.; Jiang, Y.; Wang, Y. Sparse intervertebral fence composition for 3D cervical vertebra segmentation. *Phys. Med. Biol.* **2018**, *63*, 115010. [CrossRef] [PubMed]
32. Al Arif, S.M.M.R.; Knapp, K.; Slabaugh, G. Fully automatic cervical vertebrae segmentation framework for X-ray images. *Comput. Methods Programs Biomed.* **2018**, *157*, 95–111. [CrossRef] [PubMed]
33. Liao, H.; Mesfin, A.; Luo, J. Joint vertebrae identification and localization in spinal CT images by combining short- and long-range contextual information. *IEEE Trans. Med. Imaging* **2018**, *37*, 1266–1275. [CrossRef]
34. Türk, F.; Lüy, M.; Baricsçi, N. Kidney and Renal Tumor Segmentation Using a Hybrid V-Net-Based Model. *Mathematics* **2020**, *8*, 1772. [CrossRef]
35. Abraham, B.; Nair, M.S. Computer-aided classification of prostate cancer grade groups from MRI images using texture features and stacked sparse autoencoder. *Comput. Med. Imaging Graph.* **2018**, *69*, 60–68. [CrossRef]
36. Li, G.; Han, D.; Wang, C.; Hu, W.; Calhoun, V.D.; Wang, Y.P. Application of deep canonically correlated sparse autoencoder for the classification of schizophrenia. *Comput. Methods Programs Biomed.* **2020**, *183*, 105073. [CrossRef]
37. Hou, L.; Nguyen, V.; Kanevsky, A.B.; Samaras, D.; Kurc, T.M.; Zhao, T.; Gupta, R.R.; Gao, Y.; Chen, W.; Foran, D.; et al. Sparse autoencoder for unsupervised nucleus detection and representation in histopathology images. *Pattern Recognit.* **2019**, *86*, 188–200. [CrossRef]
38. Li, S.; Jiang, H.; Bai, J.; Liu, Y.; Yao, Y.-D. Stacked sparse autoencoder and case-based postprocessing method for nucleus detection. *Neurocomputing* **2019**, *359*, 494–508. [CrossRef]
39. Jia, W.; Muhammad, K.; Wang, S.H.; Zhang, Y.D. Five-category classification of pathological brain images based on deep stacked sparse autoencoder. *Multimed. Tools Appl.* **2019**, *78*, 4045–4064. [CrossRef]
40. Qadri, S.F.; Zhao, Z.; Ai, D.; Ahmad, M.; Wang, Y. Vertebrae segmentation via stacked sparse autoencoder from computed tomography images. In Proceedings of the Eleventh International Conference on Digital Image Processing (ICDIP 2019), Guangzhou, China, 10–13 May 2019; Jiang, X., Hwang, J.-N., Eds.; p. 160.
41. Adem, K.; Kiliçarslan, S.; Cömert, O. Classification and diagnosis of cervical cancer with softmax classification with stacked autoencoder. *Expert Syst. Appl.* **2019**, *115*, 557–564. [CrossRef]
42. Ahmad, M.; Yang, J.; Ai, D.; Qadri, S.F.; Wang, Y. Deep-Stacked Auto Encoder for Liver Segmentation. In Proceedings of the Chinese Conference on Image and Graphics Technologies, Beijing, China, 30 June–1 July 2018; pp. 243–251.
43. Xu, J.; Xiang, L.; Hang, R.; Wu, J. Stacked Sparse Autoencoder (SSAE) based framework for nuclei patch classification on breast cancer histopathology. *IEEE Trans. Med. Imaging* **2016**, *35*, 119–130. [CrossRef] [PubMed]
44. Guo, Y.; Gao, Y.; Shen, D. Deformable MR Prostate Segmentation via Deep Feature Learning and Sparse Patch Matching. *IEEE Trans. Med. Imaging* **2016**, *35*, 1077–1089. [CrossRef] [PubMed]
45. Hassan, T.M.; Elmogy, M.; Sallam, E.-S. Diagnosis of Focal Liver Diseases Based on Deep Learning Technique for Ultrasound Images. *Arab. J. Sci. Eng.* **2017**, *42*, 3127–3140. [CrossRef]
46. Qadri, S.F.; Awan, S.A.; Amjad, M.; Anwar, M.; Shehzad, S. Applications, challenges, security of wireless body area networks (WBANs) and functionality of IEEE 802.15.4/zigbee. *Sci. Int.* **2013**, *25*, 697–702.
47. Pan, S.J.; Yang, Q. A survey on transfer learning. *IEEE Trans. Knowl. Data Eng.* **2009**, *22*, 1345–1359. [CrossRef]
48. Deng, J.; Dong, W.; Socher, R.; Li, L.-J.; Li, K.; Fei-Fei, L. Imagenet: A large-scale hierarchical image database. In Proceedings of the 2009 IEEE Conference on Computer Vision and Pattern Recognition, Miami, FL, USA, 20–25 June 2009; pp. 248–255.
49. Yao, J.; Burns, J.E.; Forsberg, D.; Seitel, A.; Rasoulian, A.; Abolmaesumi, P.; Hammernik, K.; Urschler, M.; Ibragimov, B.; Korez, R.; et al. A multi-center milestone study of clinical vertebral CT segmentation. *Comput. Med. Imaging Graph.* **2016**, *49*, 16–28. [CrossRef]
50. Shin, H.-C.; Roth, H.R.; Gao, M.; Lu, L.; Xu, Z.; Nogues, I.; Yao, J.; Mollura, D.; Summers, R.M. Deep convolutional neural networks for computer-aided detection: CNN architectures, dataset characteristics and transfer learning. *IEEE Trans. Med. Imaging* **2016**, *35*, 1285–1298. [CrossRef]
51. Ng, A. *Sparse Autoencoder*; CS294A Lecture Notes; Stanford Univ.: Stanford, CA, USA, 2011. Available online: https://web.stanford.edu/class/cs294a/sparseAutoencoder_2011new.pdf (accessed on 28 January 2022).
52. Bengio, Y. Deep learning of representations for unsupervised and transfer learning. In Proceedings of the ICML Workshop on Unsupervised and Transfer Learning, Bellevue, WA, USA, 2 July 2012; pp. 17–36.
53. Kullback, S.; Leibler, R.A. On information and sufficiency. *Ann. Math. Stat.* **1951**, *22*, 79–86. [CrossRef]
54. Rota Bulo, S.; Kontschieder, P. Neural decision forests for semantic image labelling. In Proceedings of the IEEE Conference on Computer Vision and Pattern Recognition, Columbus, OH, USA, 23–28 June 2014; pp. 81–88.

55. Suk, H.-I.; Shen, D. Deep learning-based feature representation for AD/MCI classification. In Proceedings of the International Conference on Medical Image Computing and Computer-Assisted Intervention, Berlin/Heidelberg, Germany, 22 September 2013; pp. 583–590.
56. Han, J.; Moraga, C. The influence of the sigmoid function parameters on the speed of backpropagation learning. In Proceedings of the International Workshop on Artificial Neural Networks, Berlin/Heidelberg, Germany, 7 June 1995; pp. 195–201.
57. Kang, Y.; Engelke, K.; Kalender, W.A. A new accurate and precise 3-D segmentation method for skeletal structures in volumetric CT data. *IEEE Trans. Med. Imaging* **2003**, *22*, 586–598. [CrossRef]
58. Bergstra, J.; Bengio, Y. Random search for hyper-parameter optimization. *J. Mach. Learn. Res.* **2012**, *13*, 281–305.
59. Lee, H.; Grosse, R.; Ranganath, R.; Ng, A.Y. Convolutional deep belief networks for scalable unsupervised learning of hierarchical representations. In Proceedings of the 26th Annual International Conference on Machine Learning, Montreal, QC, Canada, 14–18 June 2009; pp. 609–616.
60. Dice, L.R. Measures of the amount of ecologic association between species. *Ecology* **1945**, *26*, 297–302. [CrossRef]
61. Jaccard, P. Étude comparative de la distribution florale dans une portion des Alpes et des Jura. *Bull. Soc. Vaud. Sci. Nat.* **1901**, *37*, 547–579.
62. Ronneberger, O.; Fischer, P.; Brox, T. U-net: Convolutional networks for biomedical image segmentation. In Proceedings of the International Conference on Medical Image Computing and Computer-Assisted Intervention, Munich, Germany, 5–9 October 2015; pp. 234–241.
63. Chen, L.-C.; Zhu, Y.; Papandreou, G.; Schroff, F.; Adam, H. Encoder-decoder with atrous separable convolution for semantic image segmentation. In Proceedings of the European Conference on Computer Vision (ECCV), Munich, Germany, 8–14 September 2018; pp. 801–818.
64. Wang, Z.; Zhang, Z.; Voiculescu, I. RAR-U-NET: A Residual Encoder to Attention Decoder by Residual Connections Framework for Spine Segmentation Under Noisy Labels. In Proceedings of the 2021 IEEE International Conference on Image Processing (ICIP), Anchorage, AK, USA, 19–22 September 2021; pp. 21–25.
65. Kolařík, M.; Burget, R.; Uher, V.; Říha, K.; Dutta, M. Optimized High Resolution 3D Dense-U-Net Network for Brain and Spine Segmentation. *Appl. Sci.* **2019**, *9*, 404. [CrossRef]
66. Wang, R.; Yi Voon, J.H.; Ma, D.; Dabiri, S.; Popuri, K.; Beg, M.F. Vertebra Segmentation for Clinical CT Images Using Mask R-CNN. In *8th European Medical and Biological Engineering Conference, Proceedings of the EMBEC 2020, Portorož, Slovenia, 29 November–3 December 2021*; Springer: Cham, Switzerland, 2021; Volume 80, pp. 1156–1165. ISBN 9783030646097.
67. Whitehead, W.; Moran, S.; Gaonkar, B.; Macyszyn, L.; Iyer, S. A deep learning approach to spine segmentation using a feed-forward chain of pixel-wise convolutional networks. In Proceedings of the 2018 IEEE 15th International Symposium on Biomedical Imaging (ISBI 2018), Washington, DC, USA, 4–7 April 2018; Volume 2018, pp. 868–871.
68. Lyu, J.; Bi, X.; Banerjee, S.; Huang, Z.; Leung, F.H.F.; Lee, T.T.-Y.; Yang, D.-D.; Zheng, Y.-P.; Ling, S.H. Dual-task ultrasound spine transverse vertebrae segmentation network with contour regularization. *Comput. Med. Imaging Graph.* **2021**, *89*, 101896. [CrossRef] [PubMed]
69. Sekuboyina, A.; Kukačka, J.; Kirschke, J.S.; Menze, B.H.; Valentinitsch, A. Attention-driven deep learning for pathological spine segmentation. In Proceedings of the International Workshop and Challenge on Computational Methods and Clinical Applications in Musculoskeletal Imaging, Quebec City, QC, Canada, 10 September 2017; pp. 108–119.
70. Van Opbroek, A.; Ikram, M.A.; Vernooij, M.W.; De Bruijne, M. Transfer learning improves supervised image segmentation across imaging protocols. *IEEE Trans. Med. Imaging* **2015**, *34*, 1018–1030. [CrossRef]

Article

Geodesics in the TPS Space

Valerio Varano [1,*], Stefano Gabriele [1], Franco Milicchio [2], Stefan Shlager [3], Ian Dryden [4] and Paolo Piras [5]

1 Department of Architecture, Roma Tre University, 00184 Rome, Italy; stefano.gabriele@uniroma3.it
2 Department of Engineering, Roma Tre University, 00146 Rome, Italy; franco.milicchio@uniroma3.it
3 Department of Biological Anthropology, University of Freiburg, 79106 Freiburg, Germany; stefan.schlager@anthropologie.uni-freiburg.de
4 School of Mathematical Sciences, University of Nottingham, Nottingham NG7 2RD, UK; ian.dryden@nottingham.ac.uk
5 CPIA3 Roma, 00186 Roma, Italy; paolopiras3@gmail.com
* Correspondence: valerio.varano@uniroma3.it

Abstract: In shape analysis, the interpolation of shapes' trajectories is often performed by means of geodesics in an appropriate Riemannian Shape Space. Over the past several decades, different metrics and shape spaces have been proposed, including Kendall shape space, LDDMM based approaches, and elastic contour, among others. Once a Riemannian space is chosen, geodesics and parallel transports can be used to build splines or piecewise geodesics paths. In a recent paper, we introduced a new Riemannian shape space named *TPS Space* based on the Thin Plate Spline interpolant and characterized by an appropriate metric and parallel transport rule. In the present paper, we further explore the geometry of the TPS Space by characterizing the properties of its geodesics. Several applications show the capability of the proposed formulation to conserve important physical properties of deformation, such as local strains and global elastic energy.

Keywords: shape analysis; geodesics; thin plate spline

MSC: 53Z50

1. Introduction

In shape analysis, the interpolation of shapes' trajectories is often performed by means of geodesics in appropriate Riemannian Shape Spaces. Different proposed metrics and shape spaces include Kendall shape space [1,2], LDDMM-based approaches [3–6], and elastic contour [7]. Once a Riemannian space is chosen, geodesics and parallel transports can be used to build splines or piecewise geodesics paths [1,8,9]. If the torsion of the connection defined on the Riemannian space does not vanish, then a difference can appear between *geodesics* and *autoparallel lines* [10]. In recent papers [11–14], the present authors introduced and developed a new Riemannian shape space named *TPS Space* based on the Thin Plate Spline interpolant and characterized by an appropriate metric and a parallel transport rule, and the efficiency of this TPS parallel transport was compared with other methods in [14]. One of the main features of the TPS connection is its independence from the path. In fact, TPS parallel transport is named Direct Transport. This feature leads to a flat space (vanishing Riemannian Curvature) with torsion. In previous contributions, the geodesics of the TPS Space have never been studied. The present paper aims at studying the characterization of geodesics and parallel lines in the TPS space together with numerical techniques to compute them. Looking for geodesics' computation is of particular importance in a variety of morphological analyses, such as in spline regression, which have applications in a wide range of shape analysis tasks spanning fields from medical/clinical investigations to biological research. As will be clarified in the following pages, in a connection with torsion, geodesics and autoparallel lines can coincide; however, this is not a rule [10,15]. In particular, it happens only if the torsion is completely skew-symmetric. On the other hand, the TPS connection is defined by directly assigning a parallel transport rule without analytically defining the corresponding covariant derivative, ∇. For this reason, it is not possible to calculate the Christoffel symbols of the connection or the components of the torsion to establish whether it is completely skew-symmetric [15]. In the following, we exploit the qualitative definitions of Direct Transport and TPS metric in 2D to build the geodesics and the autoparallel lines of the TPS space numerically. In particular, geodesics are built by minimising the length of the path connecting two given points (the initial and final shapes), while autoparallel lines are calculated via shooting from a point (the initial configuration) and a vector (the initial deformation velocity). Our set of examples allows the geometry of the TPS Space to be explored by characterizing the properties of its geodesics and parallel lines. The paper is organised as follows:

- In Section 2, the general definitions of the two families of curves in Riemannian spaces are summarized.
- In Section 3, the main concept defining the TPS Space are recalled.
- In Section 4, the novel contribution of this paper is presented, that is, the construction of and comparison between autoparallel and geodesic lines in TPS Space.
- In Section 6, the numerical results are shown in order to discuss and compare the main features of autoparallel and geodesic lines in TPS Space.

2. Geodesics in Riemannian Manifolds

In this section, we sketch several concepts in differential geometry, referring to [10,15,16] for details.

In differential geometry, a Riemannian manifold $(\mathcal{M}, g)$ is a smooth manifold $\mathcal{M}$ equipped with a positive-definite inner product g on the tangent space $T_p\mathcal{M}$ at each point p.

A connection on the manifold is a rule allowing for parallel transport vectors along a smooth curve $\gamma(t) \in \mathcal{M}$. This rule allows for the comparison of vectors belonging to different tangent spaces.

To be more precise, any parallel transport rule $\tau_{b,a}$ along a path from a to b has to fulfill the following properties:

$$\tau_{b,a} : T_a\mathcal{M} \to T_b\mathcal{M} \text{, is linear, and non-singular.}$$
$$V_a \mapsto V_b;$$

moreover, for any point c on the path

$$\tau_{b,c} \circ \tau_{c,a} = \tau_{b,a} \tag{1}$$

It follows from this that $\tau_{a,a}$ is the identity on $T_a\mathcal{M}$, and $\tau_{a,b} = (\tau_{b,a})^{-1}$.

This procedure defines the connection, inducing a covariant derivative, ∇, that can be then calculated by the following limit:

$$\nabla_{V_p} U = \lim_{h \to 0} \frac{\tau_{h,0}^{-1} U_{\gamma(h)} - U_{\gamma(0)}}{h} \tag{2}$$

A vector field V is said to be parallel along the curve γ if the following holds:

$$\nabla_{\dot{\gamma}} V = 0. \tag{3}$$

A connection is considered compatible with a metric g if the parallel transport is an isometry, i.e., if $g_a(V_a, W_a) = g_b(\tau_{b,a}(V_a), \tau_{b,a}(W_a))$ for each pair of vectors V_a, W_a along each path.

In terms of connection, this means that:

$$g(\nabla_X Y, Z) + g(\nabla_X Z, Y) = X \cdot g(Y, Z) \tag{4}$$

The *torsion* of the connection ∇ is a tensor field defined as

$$\nabla_V W - \nabla_W V - [V, W], \tag{5}$$

with $[\cdot, \cdot]$ the Lie bracket.

A connection is called symmetric when the torsion is null for all V, W. A fundamental result of Riemannian Geometry is the existence of a unique symmetric connection compatible with the metric g, named the Levi–Civita (LC) connection, which we call ∇^g.

In its more general meaning, a geodesic is a curve $\gamma(t) \in \mathcal{M}$ the tangent field $\dot\gamma(t)$ of which is parallel along the curve itself:

$$\nabla_{\dot\gamma} \dot\gamma = 0. \tag{6}$$

In other terms, a geodesic is the curve on the manifold where one walks, maintaining the same direction, according to the given parallel transport rule. In this general sense, the geodesic can be called an *autoparallel line* [10].

On the other hand, if the connection is the Levi–Civita one, the geodesics acquire an additional property. Given two points, p, q, belonging to a convex neighbourhood of $(\mathcal{M}, g)$, a geodesic from p to q is the shortest path joining p and q according to the metric g. The distance $d(p, q)$ between p and q can be calculated as $\int_p^q \sqrt{g(\dot\gamma(t), \dot\gamma(t))} dt$.

In this paper, following [10], by *geodesics* we mean only those geodesics of the Levi–Civita connection, ∇^g; we refer to the geodesics of a different connection, ∇, as *autoparallel lines*.

In general, the difference between a Levi–Civita connection, ∇^g, and any connection ∇ is a $(2, 1)$ tensor field D [15]:

$$\nabla_X Y = \nabla^g_X Y + D(X, Y) \qquad X, Y \in T\mathcal{M} \tag{7}$$

The symmetric and the antisymmetric part of D have direct geometric meanings:

- A connection ∇ is torsion-free if and only if D is symmetric.
- A connection ∇ has the same geodesics as the Levi–Civita connection ∇^g if and only if D is skew-symmetric.

As a consequence of (4), the connection ∇ is compatible with the metric g if and only if D belongs to the space

$$\mathcal{D}^g := T\mathcal{M} \otimes (\Lambda^2 T\mathcal{M}) = \left\{ D \in \otimes^3 T\mathcal{M} | D(X, V, W) + D(X, W, V) = 0 \right\} \tag{8}$$

Finally, by means of (6)–(8), we find that a connection ∇ on $(\mathcal{M}, g)$ is both metric and geodesic-preserving if and only if its torsion lies in $\Lambda^3 T\mathcal{M}$, i.e., if it is *completely skew-symmetric*. In this case, $2D = T$ and

$$\nabla_X Y = \nabla^g_X Y + \frac{1}{2} T(X, Y, -) \tag{9}$$

3. Geometry of the TPS Space

In the present section, we summarize the formulation of the TPS Space presented and developed in [11–13]. Both the metric g and parallel transport are based on the interpolation function called Thin Plate Spline (TPS). Then, in order to introduce the Riemannian structure of the TPS Space, we need to first summarize the formulation of the TPS. Furthermore, in order to introduce the metric g we need to explain *strain energy*, *bending energy*, and *body bending energy* and how they are used to build g.

3.1. Thin Plate Spline

Let $\mathcal{E}^m$ be the m-dimensional Euclidean space and $\Omega_X, \Omega_{X'} \subset \mathcal{E}^m$ be two regular regions representing the undeformed (source) and deformed (target) configurations of a body (Figure 1), respectively. We label as x the points in Ω_X and as x' the points in $\Omega_{X'}$. The displacement field is represented by the following difference vectors:

$$u(x) = x' - x \tag{10}$$

If the configurations are sampled in k points (landmarks), then Ω_X and $\Omega_{X'}$ are named k-*configurations* and represented by the $k \times m$ matrices X and X', respectively. The displacements experienced by the k landmarks can be collected in the $k \times m$ matrix $U = X' - X$. Because translations do not affect the shape, they are filtered out by *centring* configurations in the origin of $\mathcal{E}^m$. The set of all centred k-configurations is named Centred Configuration Space $\mathcal{CC}_m^k$. Given a configuration X, the corresponding centred configuration can be represented in two different ways: by a $k \times m$ matrix obtained as $X_C = CX$ or, alternatively, by a $(k-1) \times m$ matrix $X_H = HX$, where $C = I_k - \frac{1}{k}1_k1_k^T$, I_k is the $k \times k$ identity matrix and 1_k is a $k \times 1$ column of ones, while H is the Helmert sub-matrix. The jth row of the Helmert sub-matrix H is obtained by

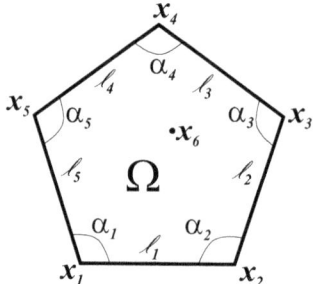

Figure 1. Example of a 2D configuration made by six landmarks, with the first five lying on the boundary and one, x_6, inside the region Ω.

$$(h_j, ..., h_j, -jh_j, 0, ..., 0), \qquad h_j = -(j(j+1))^{-1/2}$$

and thus, the jth row consists of h_j repeated j times followed by jh_j and then $k - j - 1$ zeros, $j = 1, ..., k-1$. The notable property $H^T H = C$ can be used to switch from one parametrization to the other. In the following we use only centred configurations; we therefore remove the subscript, C or H, by specifying, when necessary, which parametrization we are using. Let $X, X' \in \mathcal{CC}_m^k$ be a pair of centred configurations. The Thin Plate Spline (TPS) Φ is a function that interpolates, in $\mathcal{E}^m$, the deformation from X to X'. The TPS is parametrized by the pair (A_X, W_X) where $A_X \in GL(m)$ is a linear transformation of $\mathcal{E}^m$ represented by a $m \times m$ matrix and W_X is a $k \times m$ matrix. Given a point $x \in \mathcal{E}^m$ and a centred configuration $X \in \mathcal{CC}_m^k$, we obtain

$$x' = \Phi(x) = A_X x + W_X^T s(x) \tag{11}$$

where $s(x) = (\sigma(x - x_1), ..., \sigma(x - x_k))^T C$ is a $(k \times 1)$ matrix, $x_i \in X$ is the position of the i-th landmark, and

$$\sigma(h) = \begin{cases} ||h||^2 \log(||h||^2) & \text{if } ||h|| > 0; \\ 0 & \text{if } ||h|| = 0. \end{cases} \quad \text{for } m = 2$$

$$\sigma(h) = \begin{cases} -||h|| & \text{if } ||h|| > 0; \\ 0 & \text{if } ||h|| = 0. \end{cases} \quad \text{for } m = 3$$

Equation (11), applied landmark-wise to X, reads:

$$X' = XA_X^T + S_X W_X, \quad \text{with } (S_X)_{ij} = C_{ik}\sigma(x_k - x_l)C_{lj}. \tag{12}$$

Because X and X' are centred, Equation (12) represents $m \times (k-1)$ interpolation constraints, while the matrices (A_X, W_X) consist of $m \times m + k \times m = (m+k)m$ parameters. In order to solve the interpolation problem we need to introduce $m \times (m+1)$ more constraints on W_X, uncoupling the affine and non-affine parts:

$$1_k^T W_X = 0, \qquad X^T W_X = 0. \tag{13}$$

For a given pair (X, X') there exists a unique set of parameters for the pair (A_X, W_X) that solve the problem (12), constrained with (13):

$$A_X^T = \Gamma_{21X} X', \quad W_X = \Gamma_{11X} X', \tag{14}$$

where

$$\Gamma_{21X} = \left(X^T S_X^{-1} X\right)^{-1} X^T S_X^{-1}$$
$$\Gamma_{11X} = S_X^{-1} - S_X^{-1} X \Gamma_{21X}$$

are a $m \times k$ and a $k \times k$ matrices, respectively, which only depend on the source configuration X. We note that the inverse of the singular matrix S_X is obtained by means of the Helmert matrix as

$$S_X^{-1} = H^T \left(H S_X H^T\right)^{-1} H \tag{15}$$

Finally the target X' can be represented as the deformation of X:

$$X' = X\Gamma_{21X} X' + S_X \Gamma_{11X} X' = XA_X^T + S_X W_X. \tag{16}$$

The $k \times k$ matrix Γ_{11X} is called the *Bending Energy matrix* and is used to extract the non linear part of the deformation. Because it vanishes on affine deformations, its eigenvectors associated with non vanishing eigenvalues are only $(k-1-m)$. These are called *principal warp eigenvectors*, and represent the principal modes of deformation of the shape X [11].

3.2. Energies

It has been proven [17] that TPS is the only interpolating function that minimizes the *bending energy J*, which gauges the second derivative of the displacement field:

$$J = \int_{\mathbb{R}^m} \nabla^2 u \cdot \nabla^2 u \tag{17}$$

Note that the bending energy is defined as an integral on the whole, $\mathbb{R}^m$. In [12], in order to provide a mechanical interpretation of bending energy, the concept of *body-bending energy* was introduced, allowing the integration to be performed entirely inside the body:

$$J_\Omega = \int_\Omega \nabla^2 u \cdot \nabla^2 u \tag{18}$$

The body-bending energy is slightly smaller than the bending energy, and the *decay* $\rho = J/J_\Omega$ can be used to quantify the difference. Both J and J_Ω can be used as pseudo-metrics on TCC_m^k, as they measure the difference between two configurations and vanish in affine deformations. In order to endow $X \in CC_m^k$ with a Riemannian metric we need a non-singular distance. Here, we propose slightly modifying the Dirichlet Energy used in the deformable templates method [18] to obtain the following expression for the *strain energy*, φ, stored by the body:

$$\varphi = \frac{1}{2}\int_\Omega E \cdot E \qquad (19)$$

where

$$E = \frac{\nabla u + (\nabla u)^T}{2} \qquad (20)$$

is the strain tensor (in the case of small displacements). We note that φ vanishes on the rotational part of the local deformation. On the other hand we stress that (19) is a global measure that should be calculated via integration, starting from local measures, by means of a discretization of the whole domain Ω. In [12] it is shown that (19) can be calculated directly as a global quantity starting from landmark displacements, at least for bilinear deformations in 2D. In fact, in that case, when a rectangle bends in a generic trapezoid the deformation can be parametrized as follows:

$$u = (A - I)x + [(\chi \otimes e_1 \otimes e_2)x]x \qquad (21)$$

where $\chi = \chi_1 e_1 + \chi_1 e_2$ are the bending with respect to the two axes, A is a linear transformation, and I is the $(m \times m)$ identity matrix. Then, the strain energy can be calculated as the sum of one contribution depending on the norm of A and a second contribution proportional to the bending energy, J. The proportionality coefficient depends only on geometrical quantities of Ω:

$$\varphi = \frac{1}{2}\mathcal{A}(A - I) \cdot (A - I) + \frac{\mathcal{I}_p}{4\rho\mathcal{A}}J \qquad (22)$$

where $\mathcal{I}_p$ and $\mathcal{A}$ are the polar inertia and the area of Ω, respectively. In the next section, we show that both J and $(A - I) \cdot (A - I)$ can be calculated by means of the TPS parameters Γ_{21X} and Γ_{11X}. Then, the expression (22) can be globally calculated starting from landmark displacements by means of TPS.

3.3. TPS Metric

In [11], it is shown that the value of the bending energy J associated with a displacement, U, of a configuration, X, obtained using the quadratic form

$$J(U) = \nu\pi \text{Tr}(U^T B U). \qquad (23)$$

where $\nu = 16$ for $m = 2$ and is $\nu = 8$ for $m = 3$. For this reason the matrix $B := \Gamma_{11X}$ is called the Bending Energy Matrix of X. This fact allows us to evaluate the bending energy directly by means of a closed form expression, avoiding the need to discretize the configuration in a huge number of triangles. Furthermore we note that the Bending Energy Matrix depends only on X and can be used as a pseudo-metric on TCC_m^k. Let two given configurations, X and $X' = X + U$, related landmark-wise by a bilinear deformation as (21); then, the strain energy (22) can be calculated as

$$\varphi(U) = \frac{1}{2}\mathcal{A}\,\text{Tr}(U^T \Gamma_{21X}^T \Gamma_{21X} U) + \frac{4\pi \mathcal{I}_p}{\rho\mathcal{A}}\text{Tr}(U^T B U) \qquad (24)$$

and the average strain energy on the body can be obtained as

$$\overline{\varphi}(U) = \frac{\varphi(U)}{\mathcal{A}} = \frac{1}{2}\text{Tr}(U^T \Gamma_{21X}^T \Gamma_{21X} U) + \frac{4\pi \mathcal{I}_p}{\rho\mathcal{A}^2}\text{Tr}(U^T B U) \qquad (25)$$

While this expression is valid only for bilinear deformations, it can be generalized by assuming certain approximations concerning, in particular, the decay, ρ. In [13], it is further shown that for the body-bending energy calculation it is possible to define a symmetric matrix, B_Ω, such that the following holds:

$$J_\Omega(U) = \operatorname{Tr}(U^T B_\Omega U) \tag{26}$$

Then, in general, the decay, $\rho(U)$, is not isotropic and can be calculated by means of the Rayleigh quotient:

$$\rho(U) = \frac{J(U)}{J_\Omega(U)} = \frac{16\pi \operatorname{Tr}(U^T B U)}{\operatorname{Tr}(U^T B_\Omega U)} \tag{27}$$

In the two-dimensional case, the BEB matrix B_Ω is defined as follows:

$$B_\Omega = \Gamma_{11X} C_\Omega \Gamma_{11X} + \Gamma_{11X} C_{\partial\Omega} \Gamma_{11X} \tag{28}$$

$$(C_\Omega)_{ij} = 8\alpha_i \sigma(x_i - x_j) \tag{29}$$

$$(C_{\partial\Omega})_{ij} = \sum_{p=1}^{k-q} \int_0^1 \Big[\nabla^2 s_i(x_p + \zeta \ell_p) \nabla s_j(x_p + \zeta \ell_p)$$
$$- s_i(x_p + \zeta \ell_p) \operatorname{div}\left(\nabla^2 s_j(x_p + \zeta \ell_p)\right) \Big] \cdot *(\ell_p) d\zeta$$

where $s(x) = (\sigma(x - x_1), ..., \sigma(x - x_k))^T$ and the values of the angles α_i are

$$\alpha_i = \begin{cases} 2\pi & \text{if } x_i \in \Omega; \\ \arccos(\frac{\ell_i}{\|\ell_i\|} \cdot \frac{\ell_{i+1}}{\|\ell_{i+1}\|}) & \text{if } x_i \in \partial\Omega. \end{cases} \tag{30}$$

while $\ell_i = (x_{i+1} - x_i)$, $*(\ell_p)$ is the vector ℓ_p rotated clockwise by $\pi/2$, q is the number of landmarks that does not lie on the boundary $\partial\Omega$, and $(k - p)$ is the number of landmarks lying on $\partial\Omega$ (see Figure 1). As ρ can assume different values depending on the direction of the deformation, while we need a metric depending only on X, in the following we assume an isotropic decay $\bar\rho$:

$$\bar\rho = \frac{16\pi}{(k - z)} \operatorname{Tr}\left(B B_\Omega^{-1}\right) \tag{31}$$

where $z \geq (m + 1)$ is the number of vanishing eigenvalues of $\left(B B_\Omega^{-1}\right)$. Then, in the following, we approximate the calculus of the BEB by assuming

$$B_\Omega \simeq \bar\rho B \tag{32}$$

Finally, we generalize (25), defining the distance between two generic configurations X and X' (called Γ-Energy), as follows:

$$\Gamma(X, X') := \operatorname{Tr}\left((X' - X)^T G (X' - X)\right) \tag{33}$$

where

$$G := \mu_1 \Gamma_{21X}^T \Gamma_{21X} + \mu_2 \Gamma_{11X} \qquad \mu_1 = \frac{1}{2} \text{ and } \mu_2 = \frac{4\pi \mathcal{I}_p}{\bar\rho \mathcal{A}^2} \tag{34}$$

We note that $\Gamma_{21X}, \Gamma_{11X}, \mu_2$ depend only on the source configuration, X. From a mechanical point of view, we can define the Γ-energy $\Gamma(U)$ as the average strain energy $\bar\varphi(\tilde U)$, evaluated on a more simple deformation $\tilde U$ characterized by the same uniform component $\tilde U_u = U_u$ of U and a bilinear deformation $\tilde U_{nu}$ storing the same body bending energy of U_{nu}, i.e., such that $J_\Omega(\tilde U_{nu}) = J_\Omega(U_{nu})$. In [12], it is shown that the Γ-energy is a good approximation of the strain energy for more general deformations as well as bilinear ones. Then, the TPS Space [11–13] can be defined as the CC_m^k equipped with the TPS metric tensor:

$$g(U, V) := \text{Tr}\left(U^T G V\right) \tag{35}$$

In particular, the *affine* and *non-affine* components of the metric are defined by the sub-metrics

$$g_u(U, V) := \text{Tr}\left(U^T G_u V\right) \qquad g_{nu}(U, V) := \text{Tr}\left(U^T G_b V\right) \tag{36}$$

where

$$G_u := \mu_1 \Gamma_{21X}^T \Gamma_{21X} \qquad G_{nu} = \mu_2 \Gamma_{11X} \tag{37}$$

Alignments: OPA and MOPA Techniques

After the TPS metric tensor G is introduced, we introduce a technique for managing rotations in order to align two configurations, X and Y, based on minimization of the distance, defined as

$$d(X, Y) = \inf_{Q \in SO_m} \sqrt{\text{Tr}((YQ - X)^T G^\alpha (YQ - X))}.$$

The *aligned configuration*, $\hat{Y}$, is obtained by means of an *optimal rotation*, $\hat{Q}$, minimizing d.

$$\hat{Y} = Y\hat{Q}$$

where $\hat{Q} = \text{argmin } g((YQ - X), (YQ - X))$. According to this definition, $\hat{Q}$ turns out to be the rotational component of the polar decomposition of $Y^T G X$. When $\alpha = 0$, we obtain the rotational component of $Y^T X$, the classical Ordinary Procrustes Analysis (OPA). When $\alpha = 1$, then $Y^T G X = A_X$. In the latter case, we define the alignment Modified OPA, or MOPA [11].

3.4. TPS Direct Transport

The connection called the TPS connection was introduced in [11] and developed in [13]. It has the following properties:

1. It is compatible with the TPS metric;
2. It is compatible with the decomposition provided in (12);
3. It is independent of the path.

We assume all the configurations to be centred and represented by Helmertized landmarks; then, if not otherwise specified, each matrix is a $(k-1) \times m$ matrix. Furthermore, deformation vectors have a subscript denoting the starting point, that is, the source configuration; for details, see [11].

Let X and Y be two source configurations and let V_X and V_Y be the two associated deformation vectors, provided by

$$\begin{aligned} V_X &= X' - X = X(A_X^T - I) + S_X W_X, \\ V_Y &= Y' - Y = Y(A_Y^T - I) + S_Y W_Y. \end{aligned} \tag{38}$$

We can then say that V_Y is the parallel transport of a given V_X, that is, $V_Y = \tau_{Y,X}(V_X)$, if and only if the uniform part of V_Y equals that of V_X

$$A_Y = A_X; \tag{39}$$

and the non uniform part W_Y of V_Y solves the linear systems

$$Y^T W_Y = X^T W_X = 0 \qquad Q_Y E_Y^T W_Y = Q_X E_X^T W_X, \tag{40}$$

where the $(k-1) \times (k-1-m)$ *body principal warps matrix* E_X collects all the body principal warps of X and Q_X is a suitable $(k-1-m) \times (k-1-m)$ orthogonal matrix (i.e., $Q_X^T Q_X = I$) defined on each configuration X and representing a rotation or reflection of the principal warps. After being chosen, a configuration P as a Pole for the space Q_X is estimated, minimising the Euclidean distance $\|E_X Q_X^B - E_P\|$ between the rotated principal warps of X and the corresponding basis on the pole, P.

The *principal warps matrix* can be built as follows:

- Perform a TPS analysis on X and find the S_X and Γ_{11X};
- Perform an eigenvalue analysis on Γ_{11X} and obtain $\Gamma_{11X} = \Gamma \Lambda \Gamma^T$, where Γ is the $(k-1) \times (k-1)$ matrix containing the eigenvectors γ_i in column and Λ is the diagonal $(k-1) \times (k-1)$ matrix of the eigenvalues $\lambda_1, \ldots, \lambda_{k-1}$ ordered by increasing magnitude (the first m eigenvalues will be equal to 0);
- Drop the first m columns from Γ by obtaining the $(k-1) \times (k-1-m)$ matrix $\bar{\Gamma}$, containing the principal warp eigenvectors by column;
- Drop the first m rows and the first m columns from Λ by obtaining the $(k-1-m) \times (k-1-m)$ matrix $\bar{\Lambda}$;
- Define the $(k-1) \times (k-1-m)$ matrix $E_X = S_X \bar{\Gamma} \bar{\Lambda}^{1/2}$.

The same steps must be used to build the *principal warps matrix* E_Y on the target configuration.

The first equation of (40) constrains W_b to be orthogonal to the affine part, while the second defines the isometry in the subspace of the non-affine deformations. This last requirement implies the conservation of the total bending energy. The system (40) can be written as

$$\begin{bmatrix} Y^T \\ Q_Y E_Y^T \end{bmatrix} [W_Y] = \begin{bmatrix} X^T \\ Q_X E_X^T \end{bmatrix} [W_X].$$

This can be re-written as

$$W_Y = M_Y^{-1} M_X W_X$$

And so:

$$V_Y = \left(Y \Gamma_{21X} + \sqrt{\frac{\mu_2(X)}{\mu_2(Y)}} S_Y M_Y^{-1} M_X \Gamma_{11X} \right) V_X, \tag{41}$$

It is worth noting that Equation (41), characterizing V_Y as the parallel transport of V_X, depends only on quantities related to the startpoint, X, and endpoint, Y, of the transport, and does not depend on the path. For this reason, the TPS connection is characterized by vanishing curvature and non-vanishing torsion. Moreover, it is easy to check that (41) is compatible with the TPS metric G and with the decomposition provided in (12).

4. Geodesics and Autoparallel Lines in TPS Space

In the present section, we introduce the main contribution of the present paper, that is, to show the most important features of the geodesics and autoparallel lines in the TPS space and compare the two families of lines.

In the previous section, the TPS connection has been defined by directly assigning the parallel transport rule (41) without analytically defining the corresponding covariant derivative ∇. For this reason, it is not immediately necessary to calculate the Christoffel symbols of the connection or the Christoffel symbols of the corresponding Levi–Civita connection ∇^g, nor the components of the torsion for the purpose of establishing whether it is completely skew-symmetric [15] and thus whether or not the autoparallel lines and geodesic lines coincide.

After V_X, V_Y in (41) is substituted with $\dot{X}0, \dot{X}(t)$ and X, Y with $X0, X(t)$, we obtain

$$\dot{X}(t) = \left(X(t) \Gamma_{21X0} + \sqrt{\frac{\mu_2(X0)}{\mu_2(X(t))}} S_{X(t)} M_{X(t)}^{-1} M_{X0} \Gamma_{11X0} \right) \dot{X}0, \tag{42}$$

Equation (42) can be integrated to shoot the autoparallel line starting from $X0$ with initial velocity $\dot{X}0$. In the general case, this integration is not simple because it involves the construction and inversion of the matrix M_Y and alignment with the pole, P. Fortunately, the integration of (42) is not as complicated in the case of purely affine deformations. In the next Section 4.1, we show the analytical solution of geodesic and autoparallel lines for the case of purely affine deformations. Then, in Sections 4.2 and 4.3, we exploit the qualitative definitions of Direct Transport and TPS metrics in 2D to numerically build the geodesics and autoparallel lines of the TPS space, respectively, in the general case. In particular, geodesics are built by minimising the length of the path connecting two given points (initial and final shapes), while autoparallel lines are calculated via shooting from a point (initial configuration) and a vector (initial deformation velocity).

4.1. Analytical Solution for the Affine Subspace

A trajectory of affine transformations of X_0 can be represented as

$$X(t) = X_0 A_{X_0}^T(t) \tag{43}$$

with $A_{X_0}(t) \in SL(m) \forall t$ and $A(0) = I$

$$X_0 = X(t) A_{X_0}^{-T}(t) \tag{44}$$

$$\dot{X}(t) = X_0 \dot{A}_{X_0}^T(t) = X(t) A_{X_0}^{-T}(t) \dot{A}_{X_0}^T(t) \tag{45}$$

$$\dot{X}(0) = X_0 A_{X_0}^{-T}(0) \dot{A}_{X_0}^T(0) = X_0 \dot{A}_{X_0}^T(0) \tag{46}$$

The trajectory is an autoparallel line if and only if

$$\dot{X}(t) = \tau_{X(t), X_0} \dot{X}(0) \forall t \in [0, 1] \tag{47}$$

that is, by means of the (39)

$$\dot{X}(t) = X(t) A_{X_0}^{-T}(t) \dot{A}_{X_0}^T(t) = X(t) \dot{A}_{X_0}^T(0) \tag{48}$$

that is,

$$\dot{A}_{X_0}(t) A_{X_0}^{-1}(t) = \dot{A}_{X_0}(0) \tag{49}$$

we note that this equation is the same as that characterizing the autoparallel lines in $GL(m)$. The solution is as follows:

$$X(t) = X_0 \exp\left[t \dot{A}_{X_0}(0)\right]^T \qquad t \in [0, 1] \tag{50}$$

as is well known, in $GL(m)$ geodesics and autoparallel lines coincide [15,19]; then, this property holds for TPS-geodesics and TPS-autoparallel lines as well in the case of affine deformations. The geodesic from X_0 to X_1 can be calculated as

$$X(t) = X_0 \exp\left[t \log(\Gamma_{21 X_0} X_1)\right] \qquad t \in [0, 1] \tag{51}$$

4.2. Geodesics Calculation: Objective Function Optimisation and Equality Constraints

Given two configurations X_0, X_1, we calculate the geodesics from X_0 to X_1 by exploiting the property of minimizing the Riemannian distance. The geodesic trajectory $\{X(t) | t \in [0, 1], X(0) = X_0, X(1) = X_1\}$ can be calculated by minimizing the functional:

$$d(X_0, X_f) = \int_0^1 \sqrt{g(\dot{X}(t), \dot{X}(t))} dt \tag{52}$$

In addition, we require that the curve has a constant speed, $\left(g(\dot{X}, \dot{X})\right)^{\cdot} = 0$, and we enforce this constraint by adding a Lagrange multiplier, k, to the objective function:

$$f(X(t)) = d(X_0, X_f) + k \int_0^1 \left(g(\dot{X}, \dot{X})\right)^{\cdot} dt = 0 \tag{53}$$

The optimization problem is solved numerically by discretizing $X(t)$ in a finite number n of steps X_i using Algorithm 1, sketched below.

Algorithm 1: geodesic algorithm.

Result: Geodesic path with initial configuration X_0 and final configuration X_f using n discretization steps.

1 initialization: $X_0, X_n = X_f, n$;
2 **for** $i \leftarrow 1$ **to** n **do**
3   Set $V_i = X_{i+1} - X_i$
4   Set $d_i = \sqrt{g(V_i, V_i)}$
5   Set $dd_i = d_i - d_{i-1}$
6 **end**
7 Return $f = \sum_{i=1}^{n-1} d_i + k \sum_{i=1}^{n-1} dd_i^2$;

Then, the objective function is minimized by the R optimizer *Solnp*, R package version 1.16 [20]. The solver is an indirect solver implementing the augmented Lagrange multiplier method with an SQP interior algorithm.

4.3. Autoparallel Lines Calculation Algorithm via Shooting

Autoparallel lines do not minimize any distance, and are built directly by means of the parallel transport rule (41) via shooting. Let $Xo \in \mathcal{M}$ be the initial configuration and $V \in T\mathcal{M}$ be the initial deformation velocity; V can be called *shooting vector* and the path $X(t)$ such that $X(0) = X_0, \dot{X}(0) = V, \nabla_{\dot{X}} \dot{X} = 0 \forall t \in [0,1]$ is called *shooting path* of Xo and V. In order to interpolate between X_0 and X_1 with an autoparallel line, shooting should be used iteratively to find a shooting vector $\overline{V}$ such that a shooting path starting at X_0 and with $\overline{V}$ as shooting vector reaches X_1 in a unit time (see [7]). In the present work, we are interested in comparing the behaviour of geodesics and autoparallel lines; thus, we avoid the iterative procedure by limiting ourselves to implementing a single shooting procedure starting from a configuration X_o and a deformation V_o and then using Algorithm 2, sketched below.

Algorithm 2: shooting algorithm.

Result: Shooting path with initial position X_0 and initial velocity V_0 using n discretization steps.

1 initialization: X_0, V_0, n;
2 **for** $i \leftarrow 1$ **to** n **do**
3   Set $X_i = X_{i-1} + V_{i-1}$ /* update configuration   */
4   Set $V_i = \tau_{X_i, X_{i-1}}(V_{i-1})$ /* update velocity via PT   */
5 **end**
6 Return X;

---

5. Examples

We propose five experiments aimed at finding TPS geodesics and comparing them with original shapes, shapes inputted in the optimizer, and shapes from geodesic shooting. For each experiment, eight shapes were generated.

1. Affine case, spherical: in this simple case, the starting rectangle experiences only a size increase.
2. Affine case, general: in this case, the rectangle undergoes only a pure affine transformation.
3. Non-affine case bending: in this case, the rectangle experiences pure bending parameterized according to the parameters specified below.
4. Non-affine case bending+size: in this case, the rectangle experiences pure bending parameterized according to the parameters specified below, with the addition of a size increase.
5. Non-affine case bending+general affine component: in this case, the rectangle experiences pure bending parameterized according to the parameters specified below, with the addition of the same parameters of affine transformation as in case 2.

5.1. Dataset

A set of parametric shape paths were generated, starting from a rectangle 1×3, by means of the following formula:

$$\begin{pmatrix} x(t) \\ y(t) \end{pmatrix} = \begin{pmatrix} F_{11}(t) & F_{12}(t) \\ F_{21}(t) & F_{22}(t) \end{pmatrix} \left[\begin{pmatrix} 1 + \chi(t) x_o \\ \chi(t) \end{pmatrix} \begin{pmatrix} \sin(\chi(t) y_o) \\ \cos(\chi(t) y_o) - 1 \end{pmatrix} \right]. \qquad (54)$$

where $F_{11}(t), F_{22}(t), F_{12}(t), F_{21}(t)$ parametrize the affine transformations and $\chi(t)$ is the amount of bending. Each experiment is articulated in the following steps:

1. A parametric trajectory $X(t)$ is generated by the mean of the (54). In this way, the initial and final points, $X(0)$ and $X(1)$, are identified.
2. Linear interpolation between $X(0)$ and $X(1)$.
3. The geodesic $Y(t)$, such that $Y(0) = X(0)$ and $Y(1) = X(1)$ are calculated following the procedure sketched in Section 4.2. The distance, $d(X(0), X(1))$, and the initial tangent, $Y'(0)$, are calculated.
4. The autoparallel line $Z(t)$, starting from $X(0)$, is built by shooting $Z'(0) = Y'(0)$ by means of Direct Transport for a distance of $\ell = d(X(0), X(1))$, following the procedure sketched in Section 4.3.

For all cases, we computed the linear interpolation between the first shape (the undeformed rectangle in all cases) and the last shape of any experiment. These linearized shapes (eight shapes) were the input for the optimizer, imposing as equality constraints the maintenance of the first and last shapes in order to force the geodesic to pass between these shapes. Finally, we performed a common Principal Component Analysis (PCA) for each experiment except for the first (which was trivial in terms of pure shape change), including all of the four sets of shapes: original, linearized, optimized, and shooted.

In each one of the experiments, we checked:

- The trend of the Γ-energy.
- The trend of the components of the Γ-energy.

5.2. Affine Case: Spherical

A parametric trajectory of eight configurations was generated by applying (54) to the initial rectangular shape by selecting eight values of the parameters in the following ranges: $F_{11}(t) = F_{22}(t) \in [1, 2]; F_{12}(t) = F_{21}(t) = 0; \chi(t) = 0$. Figure 2 and Table 1 show the results for the size-only case. Geodesic searching via optimization satisfactorily recovers both the size change and the equally spaced Γ-energy steps between consecutive shapes. The non-affine component of the Γ-energy, d_b, is of course equal to zero. Optimized geodesics and shooting quietly coincide. Figure 3 shows scatterplots of Table 1 values.

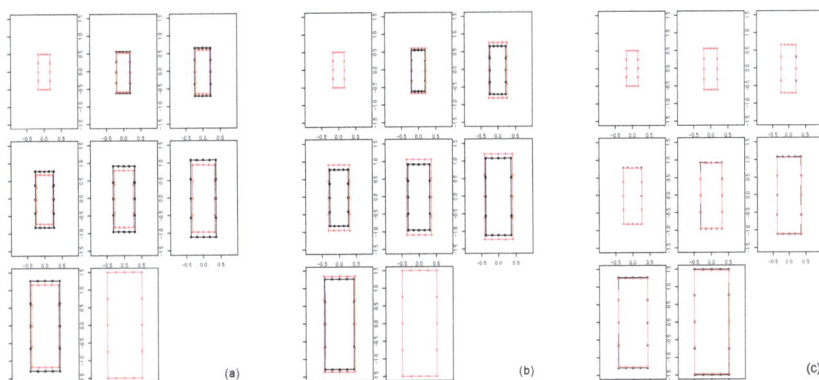

(a) (b) (c)

Figure 2. Affine spherical case results. (**a**) Left panel: geodesic trajectory shapes (black) plotted against the original parametric shapes (red). (**b**) Center panel: geodesic trajectory shapes (black) plotted against the shapes found via linear interpolation between the first and last shapes of the parametric dataset (red). (**c**) Right panel: geodesic trajectory shapes (black) plotted against autoparallel trajectory (red) built via shooting of the first two configurations of the geodesic.

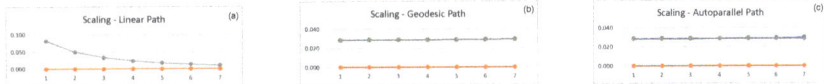

Figure 3. Trend of the energies for different interpolations: (**a**) Left: linear interpolation (**b**) Center: geodesics interpolation. (**c**) Right: autoparallel interpolation. Blue refers to d_u, red to d_b, grey to d_{tot}.

Table 1. Values of the energies for the affine spherical case; d_u represents the affine component of the Γ-energy, d_b the non-affine component and d_{tot} the total Γ-energy.

LINEAR			GEODESIC			A-PARALLEL		
d_u	d_b	d_{tot}	d_u	d_b	d_{tot}	d_u	d_b	d_{tot}
0.082	0.000	0.082	0.029	0.000	0.029	0.029	0.000	0.029
0.049	0.000	0.049	0.029	0.000	0.029	0.029	0.000	0.029
0.033	0.000	0.033	0.029	0.000	0.029	0.029	0.000	0.029
0.024	0.000	0.024	0.029	0.000	0.029	0.029	0.000	0.029
0.018	0.000	0.018	0.029	0.000	0.029	0.029	0.000	0.029
0.014	0.000	0.014	0.029	0.000	0.029	0.029	0.000	0.029
0.011	0.000	0.011	0.030	0.000	0.030	0.029	0.000	0.029

5.3. Affine Case: General Case

A parametric trajectory of eight configurations is generated by applying (54) to the initial rectangular shape by selecting eight values of the parameters in the following ranges:

$$F_{11}(t) \in [-0.2, 1.2]; \quad F_{12}(t) \in [-0.2, 1.2];$$
$$F_{21}(t) \in [-0.2, 1.2]; \quad F_{22}(t) \in [0, 0.6];$$
$$\chi(t) = 0.$$

Figure 4 and Table 2 show the results of the general affine-only case. Optimized geodesics correctly recover the original parameterized deformation, with equally spaced gamma-energy steps between consecutive shapes and db equal to zero. Figure 5 shows scatterplots of Table 2 values. Figure 6 shows the first two PCs resulting from PCA performed on all four types of datasets of the general affine case (parameterized, linearized, optimized geodesic, shooting).

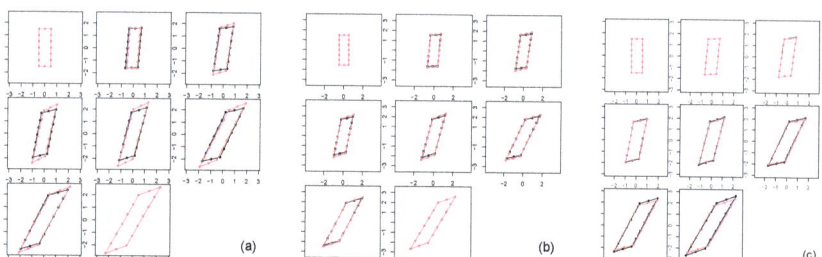

Figure 4. Affine general case results. (**a**) Left panel: geodesic trajectory shapes (black) plotted against the original parametric shapes (red). (**b**) Center panel: geodesic trajectory shapes (black) plotted against the shapes found via linear interpolation between the first and last shapes of the parametric dataset (red). (**c**) Right panel: geodesic trajectory shapes (black) plotted against autoparallel trajectory (red) built via shooting of the first two configurations of the geodesic.

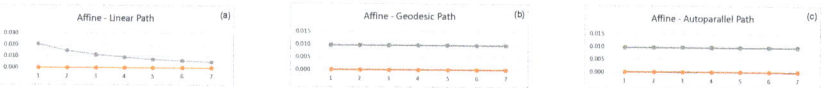

Figure 5. Trend of the energies for different interpolations: (**a**) Left: linear interpolation (**b**) Center: geodesics interpolation. (**c**) Right: autoparallel interpolation. Blue refers to d_u, red to d_b, grey to d_{tot}.

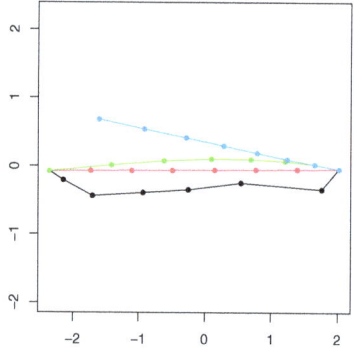

Figure 6. PC1-PC2 scatterplot of the PCA performed on the four set of shapes resulting from the general affine case. PC1 explains 97.2% of total variance, while PC2 explains 2.66%. Black refers to the optimized shapes, red to the linearized, green to the original shapes, and cyan to the shooted shapes.

Table 2. Values of the energies for the affine general case; d_u represents the affine component of the Γ-energy, d_b the non-affine component, and d_{tot} the total Γ-energy.

LINEAR			GEODESIC			A-PARALLEL		
d_u	d_b	d_{tot}	d_u	d_b	d_{tot}	d_u	d_b	d_{tot}
0.020	0.000	0.020	0.010	0.000	0.010	0.010	0.000	0.010
0.015	0.000	0.015	0.010	0.000	0.010	0.010	0.000	0.010
0.011	0.000	0.011	0.010	0.000	0.010	0.010	0.000	0.010
0.009	0.000	0.009	0.010	0.000	0.010	0.010	0.000	0.010
0.007	0.000	0.007	0.010	0.000	0.010	0.010	0.000	0.010
0.006	0.000	0.006	0.010	0.000	0.010	0.010	0.000	0.010
0.005	0.000	0.005	0.010	0.000	0.010	0.010	0.000	0.010

5.4. Non Affine Case: Bending

A parametric trajectory of eight configurations is generated by applying (54) to the initial rectangular shape by selecting eight values of the parameters in the following ranges:

$$F_{11}(t) = 0; \quad F_{12}(t) = 0;$$
$$F_{21}(t) = 0; \quad F_{22}(t) = 0;$$
$$\chi(t) \in [0, 1.5].$$

The results of the general non-affine case are shown in Figures 7–9 and Table 3. This simulation is particularly challenging due to the particular non-affine transformation experienced by the rectangle. Despite this, the geodesic optimization finds shapes characterized by approximately equally spaced steps in terms of both gamma energy and its two components, du and db. The PCA scatterplot in Figure 9 shows coherent behaviour for all datasets except, as expected, for the linearized shapes.

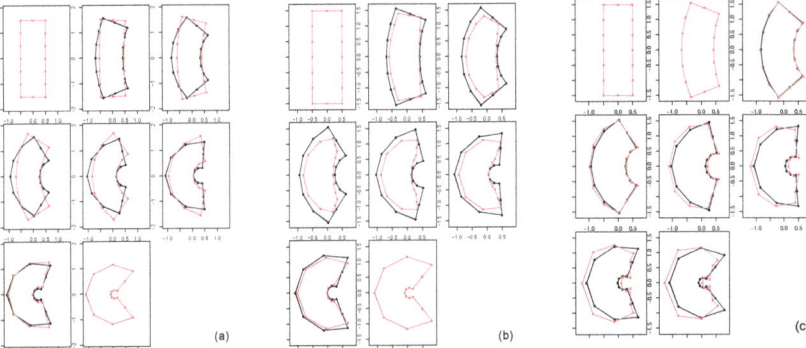

Figure 7. Non-affine case bending-only results. (**a**) Left panel: geodesic trajectory shapes (black) plotted against the original parametric shapes (red). (**b**) Center panel: geodesic trajectory shapes (black) plotted against the shapes found via linear interpolation between the first and last shapes of the parametric dataset (red). (**c**) Right panel: geodesic trajectory shapes (black) plotted against autoparallel trajectory (red) built via shooting of the first two configurations of the geodesic.

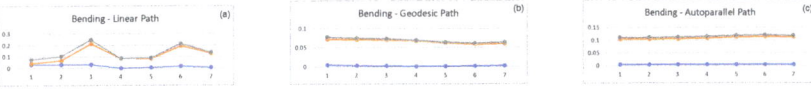

Figure 8. Trend of the energies for different interpolations: (**a**) Left: linear interpolation (**b**) Center: geodesics interpolation. (**c**) Right: autoparallel interpolation. Blue refers to d_u, red to d_b, grey to d_{tot}.

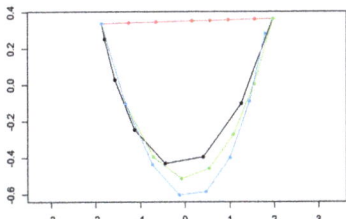

Figure 9. PC1-PC2 scatterplot of the PCA perfomed on the four set of shapes resulting from the pure bending case. PC1 explains 91.11% of total variance, while PC2 explains 6.50%. Black refers to the optimized shapes, red to the linearized, green to the original shapes and cyan to the shooted shapes.

Table 3. Values of the energies for the non-affine case of bending: d_u represents the affine component of the Γ-energy, d_b the non-affine component, and d_{tot} the total Γ-energy.

LINEAR			GEODESIC			A-PARALLEL		
d_u	d_b	d_{tot}	d_u	d_b	d_{tot}	d_u	d_b	d_{tot}
0.033	0.042	0.075	0.005	0.072	0.077	0.005	0.106	0.111
0.034	0.070	0.104	0.003	0.072	0.075	0.005	0.106	0.111
0.033	0.215	0.248	0.002	0.071	0.073	0.005	0.107	0.112
0.001	0.084	0.085	0.001	0.068	0.069	0.005	0.110	0.115
0.006	0.084	0.090	0.001	0.062	0.063	0.005	0.114	0.119
0.020	0.195	0.214	0.002	0.059	0.061	0.005	0.115	0.120
0.008	0.129	0.137	0.003	0.061	0.064	0.005	0.114	0.119

5.5. Non-Affine Case: Bending and Scaling

A parametric trajectory of eight configurations is generated by applying (54) to the initial rectangular shape by selecting eight values of the parameters in the following ranges:

$$F_{11}(t) \in [1,2]; \quad F_{12}(t) = 0;$$
$$F_{21}(t) = 0; \quad F_{22}(t) \in [1,2];$$
$$\chi(t) \in [0,1.5].$$

Adding a significant size change to the previous experiment led to the results shown in Figures 10–12 and Table 4. The equal spacing of the Γ-energy of the optimized geodesics is rather acceptable, while its behaviour in the PCA space behaves more coherently than that of the parametrized or shooted shapes.

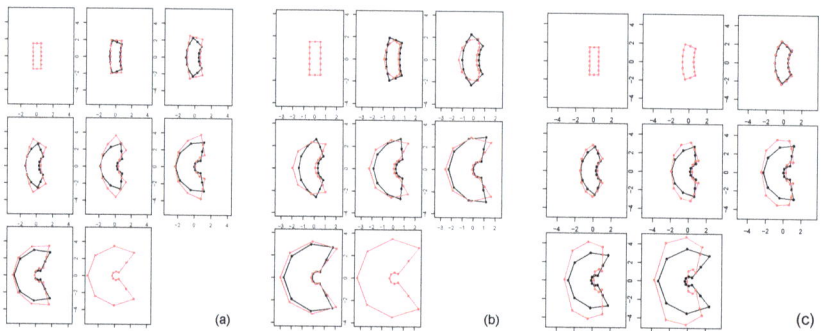

Figure 10. Non-affine case bending+size results. (**a**) Left panel: geodesic trajectory shapes (black) plotted against the original parametric shapes (red). (**b**) Center panel: geodesic trajectory shapes (black) plotted against the shapes found via linear interpolation between the first and last shapes of the parametric dataset (red). (**c**) Right panel: geodesic trajectory shapes (black) plotted against autoparallel trajectory (red) built via shooting of the first two configurations of the geodesic.

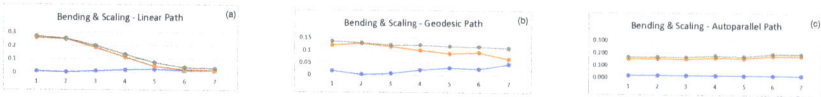

Figure 11. Trend of the energies for different interpolations: (**a**) Left: linear interpolation (**b**) Center: geodesics interpolation. (**c**) Right: autoparallel interpolation. Blue refers to d_u, red to d_b, grey to d_{tot}.

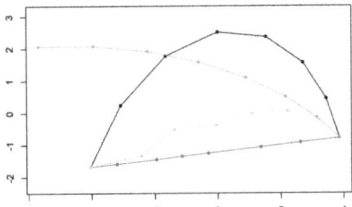

Figure 12. PC1-PC2 scatterplot of the PCA perfomed on the four set of shapes resulting from the bending+size case. PC1 explains 79.36% of total variance, while PC2 explains 17.54%. Black refers to the optimized shapes, red to the linearized, green to the original shapes and cyan to the shooted shapes.

Table 4. Values of the energies for the non-affine case of bending and scaling; d_u represents the affine component of the Γ-energy, d_b the non-affine component, and d_{tot} the total Γ-energy.

LINEAR			GEODESIC			A-PARALLEL		
d_u	d_b	d_{tot}	d_u	d_b	d_{tot}	d_u	d_b	d_{tot}
0.060	0.37	0.431	0.017	0.120	0.137	0.017	0.150	0.167
0.003	0.41	0.412	0.003	0.128	0.131	0.017	0.150	0.167
0.147	0.42	0.571	0.007	0.115	0.122	0.017	0.150	0.168
0.028	0.04	0.073	0.021	0.101	0.122	0.017	0.159	0.177
0.021	0.03	0.056	0.029	0.087	0.116	0.017	0.155	0.172
0.036	0.07	0.104	0.025	0.091	0.115	0.017	0.176	0.193
0.012	0.03	0.040	0.044	0.065	0.110	0.017	0.175	0.193

5.6. Non-Affine Case: Bending and General Affine Component

A parametric trajectory of eight configurations is generated by applying (54) to the initial rectangular shape by selecting eight values of the parameters in the following ranges:

$$F_{11}(t) \in [-0.2, 1.2]; \quad F_{12}(t) \in [-0.2, 1.2];$$
$$F_{21}(t) \in [-0.2, 1.2]; \quad F_{22}(t) \in [0, 0.6];$$
$$\chi(t) \in [0, 1.5].$$

The last experiment is represented by a combination of non-affine and affine components. Results relative to this deformation are shown in Figures 13–15 and Table 5. Optimized geodesics *struggle* to find proper shape at fourth and fifth step of the deformation series; in the end, however, the final series results behave consistently in terms of both equal gamma energy spacing and general morphology.

Table 5. Values of the energies for the non-affine case of bending and general affine deformation; d_u represents the affine component of the Γ-energy, d_b the non-affine component, and d_{tot} the total Γ-energy.

LINEAR			GEODESIC			A-PARALLEL		
d_u	d_b	d_{tot}	d_u	d_b	d_{tot}	d_u	d_b	d_{tot}
0.037	0.196	0.233	0.004	0.096	0.100	0.004	0.110	0.114
0.017	0.453	0.470	0.005	0.097	0.101	0.004	0.110	0.114
0.039	0.689	0.729	0.005	0.100	0.104	0.004	0.113	0.117
0.010	0.158	0.168	0.001	0.108	0.110	0.004	0.120	0.123
0.012	0.152	0.164	0.013	0.101	0.114	0.004	0.114	0.117
0.025	0.289	0.315	0.028	0.089	0.117	0.004	0.115	0.119
0.009	0.124	0.132	0.017	0.103	0.120	0.004	0.128	0.132

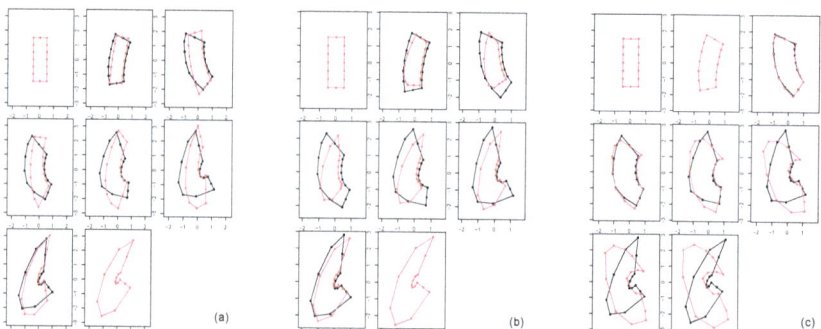

Figure 13. Non-affine case, bending+general affine component, results. (**a**) Left panel: geodesic trajectory shapes (black) plotted against the original parametric shapes (red). (**b**) Center panel: geodesic trajectory shapes (black) plotted against the shapes found via linear interpolation between the first and last shapes of the parametric dataset (red). (**c**) Right panel: geodesic trajectory shapes (black) plotted against autoparallel trajectory (red) built via shooting of the first two configurations of the geodesic.

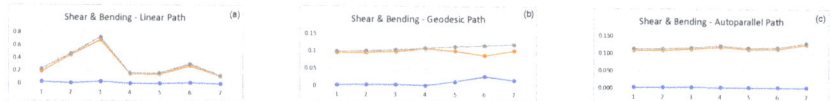

Figure 14. Trend of the energies for different interpolations: (**a**) Left: linear interpolation (**b**) Center: geodesics interpolation. (**c**) Right: autoparallel interpolation. Blue refers to d_u, red to d_b, grey to d_{tot}.

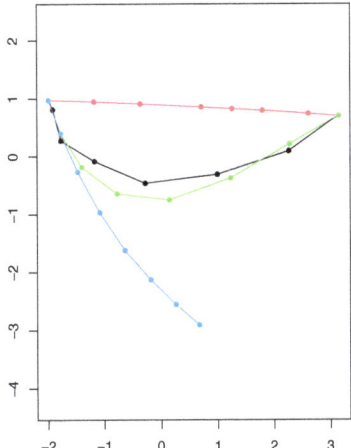

Figure 15. PC1-PC2 scatterplot of the PCA perfomed on the four set of shapes resulting from the bending+general affine component case. PC1 explains 62.61% of total variance, while PC2 explains 25.48%. Black refers to the optimized shapes, red to the linearized, green to the original shapes and cyan to the shooted shapes.

6. Discussion

The set of performed numerical analyses, together with the analytical results of Section 4.1, showed that: The TPS geodesics are able to catch important qualitative behaviours of the parametric deformations. In particular, in each example the horizontal sides of the initial rectangle remain straight for the whole path while the vertical sides bends, exactly as happens in the parametric path. For affine deformations, TPS geodesics coincide with TPS autoparallel lines and both coincide with the LC geodesics of the group GL(m). For non-affine deformations TPS geodesics and TPS autoparallel lines do not coincide. In particular, the autoparallel lines are not very similar, especially in the last steps, to the parametric path. This was expected for the procedure of shooting used here. On the other hand, certain qualitative behaviours are lost, as was expected. TPS Autoparallel lines conserve the percentage of affine and non-affine energies, while this does not happen in optimized geodesic. Future directions of the present work will involve the use of 3D data. This will certainly depend on the possibility of its being independent of the body-bending energy matrix computation. Three-dimensional data offer many practical applications, spanning a wide range of scientific disciplines such as cardiology [11,12], vertebrate paleontology [21,22], and paleoanthropology.

Author Contributions: Conceptualization, V.V., P.P. and I.D.; software, P.P., F.M., S.G., S.S.; original draft preparation, V.V., P.P.; writing, review and editing, V.V. and P.P. All authors have read and agreed to the published version of the manuscript.

Funding: This research received no external funding.

Data Availability Statement: Samples of the compounds are available from the authors.

Conflicts of Interest: The authors declare no conflict of interest.

Abbreviations

The following abbreviations are used in this manuscript:

TPS Thin Plate Spline
PT   Parallel Transport
DT   Direct Transport

References

1. Kim, K.R.; Dryden, I.; Le, H.; Severn, K. Smoothing splines on Riemannian manifolds, with applications to 3D shape space. *J. R. Stat. Society. Ser. B Stat. Methodol.* **2021**, *83*, 108–132. [CrossRef]
2. Huckemann, S.; Hotz, T.; Munk, A. Intrinsic MANOVA for Riemannian manifolds with an application to Kendall's space of planar shapes. *IEEE Trans. Pattern Anal. Mach. Intell.* **2010**, *32*, 593–603. [CrossRef] [PubMed]
3. Trouvé, A. Diffeomorphisms groups and pattern matching in image analysis. *Int. J. Comput. Vis.* **1998**, *28*, 213–221. [CrossRef]
4. Miller, M.I.; Younes, L.; Trouvé, A. Diffeomorphometry and geodesic positioning systems for human anatomy. *Technology* **2014**, *2*, 36–43. [CrossRef] [PubMed]
5. Louis, M.; Charlier, B.; Jusselin, P.; Pal, S.; Durrleman, S. A fanning scheme for the parallel transport along geodesics on Riemannian manifolds. *SIAM J. Numer. Anal.* **2018**, *56*, 2563–2584. [CrossRef]
6. Niethammer M., V.F. Riemannian metrics for statistics on shapes: Parallel transport and scale invariance. In Proceedings of the 4th MICCAI workshop on Mathematical Foundations of Computational Anatomy (MFCA), Nagoya, Japan, 22 September 2013.
7. Xie, Q.; Kurtek, S.; Le, H.; Srivastava, A. Parallel transport of deformations in shape space of elastic surfaces. In Proceedings of the IEEE International Conference on Computer Vision, Sydney, NSW, Australia, 1–8 December 2013; pp. 865–872.
8. Le, H. Unrolling shape curves. *J. Lond. Math. Soc.* **2003**, *68*, 511–526. [CrossRef]
9. Louis, M.; Bône, A.; Charlier, B.; Durrleman, S.; The Alzheimer's Disease Neuroimaging Initiative. Parallel transport in shape analysis: A scalable numerical scheme. In *International Conference on Geometric Science of Information*; Springer: Berlin, Germany, 2017; pp. 29–37.
10. Marsland, S.; Twining, C. Data analysis in Weitzenbock space. In Proceedings of the 2017 International Joint Conference on Neural Networks (IJCNN), Anchorage, AK, USA, 14–19 May 2017; pp. 340–347.
11. Varano, V.; Gabriele, S.; Teresi, L.; Dryden, I.; Puddu, P.; Torromeo, C.; Piras, P. The TPS Direct Transport: A new method for transporting deformations in the Size-and-shape Space. *Int. J. Comput. Vis.* **2017**, *124*, 384–408. [CrossRef]
12. Varano, V.; Piras, P.; Gabriele, S.; Teresi, L.; Nardinocchi, P.; Dryden, I.; Torromeo, C.; Puddu, P. The decomposition of deformation: New metrics to enhance shape analysis in medical imaging. *Med Image Anal.* **2018**, *46*, 35–56. [CrossRef] [PubMed]
13. Varano, V.; Piras, P.; Gabriele, S.; Teresi, L.; Nardinocchi, P.; Dryden, I.; Torromeo, C.; Schiariti, M.; Puddu, P. Local and global energies for shape analysis in medical imaging. *Int. J. Numer. Methods Biomed. Eng.* **2020**, *36*, e3252. [CrossRef] [PubMed]
14. Piras, P.; Varano, V.; Louis, M.; Profico, A.; Durrleman, S.; Charlier, B.; Milicchio, F.; Teresi, L. Transporting Deformations of Face Emotions in the Shape Spaces: A Comparison of Different Approaches. *J. Math. Imaging Vis.* **2021**, *63*, 875–893. [CrossRef]
15. Agricola, I.; Friedrich, T. A note on flat metric connections with antisymmetric torsion. *Differ. Geom. Appl.* **2010**, *28*, 480–487, cited By 18. [CrossRef]
16. Kobayashi, S. 2: *[Foundations of Differential Geometry]/Shoshichi Kobayashi and Katsumi Nomizu*; Interscience Publishers: New York, NY, USA, 1969.
17. Bookstein, F.L. Principal warps: Thin-plate splines and the decomposition of deformations. *IEEE Trans. Pattern Anal. Mach. Intell.* **1989**, *11*, 567–585. [CrossRef]
18. Younes, L. *Shapes and Diffeomorphisms*; Springer: Berlin/Heidelberg, Germany, 2010; Volume 171.
19. Guigui, N.; Pennec, X. A Reduced Parallel Transport Equation on Lie Groups with a Left-Invariant Metric. In Proceedings of the International Conference on Geometric Science of Information, Paris, France, 21–23 July 2021; pp. 119–126.
20. Ghalanos, A.; Theussl, S. Rsolnp: General Non-linear Optimization Using Augmented Lagrange Multiplier Method; R Package Version 1.16; 2015. Available online: https://cran.r-project.org/web/packages/Rsolnp/Rsolnp.pdf (accessed on 15 March 2021).
21. Piras, P.; Sansalone, G.; Teresi, L.; Moscato, M.; Profico, A.; Eng, R.; Cox, T.; Loy, A.; Colange, I.P.; Kotsakis, T. Digging adaptation in insectivorous subterranean eutherians. The enigma of Mesoscalops montanensis unveiled by geometric morphometrics and finite element analysis. *J. Morphol.* **2015**, *276*, 1157–1171. [CrossRef] [PubMed]
22. Piras, P.; Marcolini, F.; Raia, P.; Curcio, M.; Kotsakis, T. Testing evolutionary stasis and trends in first lower molar shape of extinct Italian populations of Terricola savii (Arvicolidae, Rodentia) by means of geometric morphometrics. *J. Evol. Biol.* **2009**, *22*, 179–191. [CrossRef] [PubMed]

Article

Infrared Target-Background Separation Based on Weighted Nuclear Norm Minimization and Robust Principal Component Analysis

Sur Singh Rawat [1,*], Sukhendra Singh [2], Youseef Alotaibi [3], Saleh Alghamdi [4] and Gyanendra Kumar [5,*]

1. Department of Computer Science and Engineering, JSS Academy of Technical Education, Noida 201301, India
2. Department of Information Technology, JSS Academy of Technical Education, Noida 201301, India
3. Department of Computer Science, College of Computer and Information Systems, Umm Al-Qura University, Makkah 21955, Saudi Arabia
4. Department of Information Technology, College of Computers and Information Technology, Taif University, Taif 21944, Saudi Arabia
5. School of Computing Sciences and Engineering, Galgotias University, Greater Noida 201310, India
* Correspondence: sur.rawat@jssaten.ac.in (S.S.R.); gyanendrakumar@galgotiasuniversity.edu.in (G.K.)

Citation: Rawat, S.S.; Singh, S.; Alotaibi, Y.; Alghamdi, S.; Kumar, G. Infrared Target-Background Separation Based on Weighted Nuclear Norm Minimization and Robust Principal Component Analysis. *Mathematics* **2022**, *10*, 2829. https://doi.org/10.3390/math10162829

Academic Editors: Ezequiel López-Rubio, Esteban Palomo and Enrique Domínguez

Received: 5 July 2022
Accepted: 4 August 2022
Published: 9 August 2022

Publisher's Note: MDPI stays neutral with regard to jurisdictional claims in published maps and institutional affiliations.

Copyright: © 2022 by the authors. Licensee MDPI, Basel, Switzerland. This article is an open access article distributed under the terms and conditions of the Creative Commons Attribution (CC BY) license (https://creativecommons.org/licenses/by/4.0/).

Abstract: The target detection ability of an infrared small target detection (ISTD) system is advantageous in many applications. The highly varied nature of the background image and small target characteristics make the detection process extremely difficult. To address this issue, this study proposes an infrared patch model system using non-convex (IPNCWNNM) weighted nuclear norm minimization (WNNM) and robust principal component analysis (RPCA). As observed in the most advanced methods of infrared patch images (IPI), the edges, sometimes in a crowded background, can be detected as targets due to the extreme shrinking of singular values (SV). Therefore, a non-convex WNNM and RPCA have been utilized in this paper, where varying weights are assigned to the SV rather than the same weights for all SV in the existing nuclear norm minimization (NNM) of IPI-based methods. The alternate direction method of multiplier (ADMM) is also employed in the mathematical evaluation of the proposed work. The observed evaluations demonstrated that in terms of background suppression and target detection proficiency, the suggested technique performed better than the cited baseline methods.

Keywords: infrared search (IRST) and track system; RPCA; NNM; IPI; signal to clutter ratio (SCR); SCR gain (SCRG)

MSC: 65D18

1. Introduction

The various target detection applications that exist today are early warning, infrared search and tracking systems (IRST), and medical imaging; all rely heavily on the capability of ISTD. Due to the poor SCR, it is challenging to compute imaging distance, size, and texture [1–3]. Many researchers have performed exceptionally well in the past. So far, algorithms have been in two categories: sequential and single-frame detection [4]. The first category makes use of both spatial and temporal information, which is not easily available in real-time applications, and therefore, performance is lacking for methods based on such approaches. On the other hand, the detection algorithm must be extremely fast and accurate in locating the target.

As a result, the single-frame detection approach plays an important role and is heavily used. The motivation for the proposed approach is the existence of weakness in the existing IPI models. Although the infrared patch-image (IPI) model has proven successful in target background separation due to a quality that allows it to fit with reality, its performance is due to the effectiveness of patch-image dimensionality. The sparsity measure owing to the l_1-norm, on the other hand, shows less responsiveness in the case of a highly complex background with sharp edges than in the case of a smooth background. As a result, these strong edges may be sparse under l_1-norm reduction, implying that the strong edges may appear as targets under the constant global threshold of the IPI model, potentially increasing the false alarm rate. The existing IPI model has a low number of patches with strong edges, and thus, the strong edges could be viewed as an outlier. This is because nuclear NNM shrinks all SV by applying the same threshold and treats them equally. Furthermore, large SVs in a patch image convey more information than small SVs. Hence, we should punish the larger SVs less than the smaller SVs.

WNNM, on the other hand, gives different weights to SV according to importance to retain large SVs, which provide more edge information. In this work, the WNNM has been used in place of the NNM in the existing IPI model to constrain the complex background patch image (BPI) due to l1 norm minimization. The proposed model presented is addressed using the ADMM approach.

This study makes the following contributions:

➢ The infrared patch-image model via IPINCNWNNM–RPCA was proposed and was solved by the ADMM method.
➢ Extensive simulation was carried out that shows that the proposed scheme not only has good detection capabilities but also has good background estimation capabilities.

The structure of the remaining work is as follows: the materials and the procedures are presented in Section 2. In Section 3, the suggested IPNCWNNM–RPCA model is discussed in detail. The experimental evaluation and their interpretation are presented in Section 4, and the study closes in Section 5.

2. Materials and Methods

In the single-frame detection approach, several methods have been presented in the past: background perception, object saliency recognition, pattern classification, and IPI. A detailed summary of these critical methods is presented in Table 1 with their advantages and disadvantages.

2.1. Methods Based on Background Assumptions

This group of algorithms assumes that the background transition is slow and that the local region's pixel correlation is fairly strong. These methods are very simple and easy to execute. The two-dimensional least (TDLMS) mean square [5], max–median, and max–mean [6] algorithms fall into this category, but these are not efficient in dense clouds. Improved approaches such as the edge-directed TDLMS filter [7] have been developed.

TDLMS based on neighborhood analysis [8] and an edge component-based bilateral filter [9] that predicts edge direction and maintains edges have shown better results. Top-hat filter and toggle-contrast filter [10,11], both based on morphological processes, suffer from the same issue discussed above.

2.2. Methods Based on Object Saliency Identification

These approaches use the difference of Gaussian presented by Wang et al. [12] to compute the saliency map. The weighted local coefficient of variation (WLCV) was presented by Rao et al. [13]. Chen et al. [3] presented a local contrast measure (LCM) that computes the saliency map. The improved version (ILCM) was proposed by Han et al. [14]. This category includes methods that consider the target more critical than the background. In addition, these methods are based on human visual phenomena. The work proposed in [15,16] uses the Laplacian of Gaussian (LOG) in target detection. The work proposed in [12] uses difference of Gaussian (DOG) for the saliency map calculation, and in another work, Han et al. [14] proposed the upgraded DOG filter to compute the saliency map. More work is available in the literature that fits this category [17,18].

2.3. Pattern Classification Based Methods

The approaches under this class are binary classification methods where the background and the targets are separated based on the patch information. These methods are inspired by the work of M. Turk and A. Pentland [19] and J. Write at al. [20] and founded on the principle of face recognition using PCA. The leading methods for projection are PCA [21], probabilistic PCA [22], nonlinear PCA [23], and sparse [24,25] representation. From the vast background, Wang et al. [25] constructed a method. The target and the background patch were separated using an adaptive weight in [26]. One distinct problem with these methods is the need for dictionary samples, which take a long time to process, and they also need a large dataset to perform.

2.4. Patch Image-Based Methods

The motivation for this class is the work in BM3D [27] and BM4D [28]. The method of this category creates dataset patches. The first study in this approach for target background separation was by Gao et al. [1]. By applying this technique, low-rank and sparse matrices were recovered by turning the IPI model into an optimization problem. This technique has the benefit of not requiring the usage of substantial dictionary samples.

Although the IPI model produces positive results, it has a serious problem with the l_1-norm sparsity minimization, which involves a trade-off between reducing the dim target and maintaining the strong edges of the image. Y. He et al. [29,30] conducted two other works based on the low-rank and sparse representations paradigm. Dai et al. [31] developed a new non-negative IPI model that estimates the background correctly and precisely while preserving. Similar work was proposed by Rawat et al. in [32], and Dai et al. [33,34] proposed an approach in which the prior structural knowledge is embedded in the background image. This approach leads to the complexity of calculation and has the rank computation issue. To tackle this, Gao et al. [35] suggested reweighted IPI (ReWIPI), which is based on the work in [36] to confine the BPI while keeping the background edge information. However, due to insufficient weight adjustment, this may give inaccurate SVD estimates.

In [37], a suggestion was made to add inherent smoothness to the BPI using TV regularization, and principal component pursuit (TV–PCP) and non-convex rank approximation minimization [38–40] are some recent breakthroughs in IPI-based techniques. Small target recognition is exceedingly difficult due to the object's small size. Current IPI tactics, on the other hand, have performed nicely; however, some issues need to be addressed.

Table 1. Details of the key state-of-the-art target detection methods.

References	Publication Year	Method Name	Advantages	Disadvantages
Methods based on Background spatial consistency				
M.M. Hadhoud and D.W. Thomas [5]	1998	TDLMS	This method is very simple to use for purposes like reducing noise and improving the object of interest.	In a noisy environment, it fails to perform.
S.D. Deshpande et al. [6]	1999	Max–median and max–mean	These methods are very simple to use for purposes like reducing noise and improving the object of interest.	In addition to the targets, these methods also enhance the strong cloud.
T.-W. Bae et al. [7]	2012	TDLMS edge-directional filter	Applies filtering to preserve the edges by estimating the direction.	In a noisy environment, it fails to perform.
Y. Cao et al. [8]	2008	Neighborhood-based analysis of TDLMS filter	The process computes the edge direction and preserves the edge based on neighbor information.	In a noisy environment, it fails to perform.
T.-W. Bae & K.-I. Sohng [9]	2010	Bilateral filter according to edge component	The process estimates the edge information based on bilateral filters.	In a noisy environment, it fails to perform.

Table 1. Cont.

References	Publication Year	Method Name	Advantages	Disadvantages
R. Fortin and J. Rivest M. Zeng et al., X. Bai et al. [10,11,41,42]	1996, 2006, 2012, 2010	Morphological-based methods, top-hat filter, and toggle contrast	These methods are very simple to use.	It is necessary to have a well-designed filter that can meet the desired qualities.
Methods based on Target saliency				
Kim et al. [15] and Shao et al. [16]	2012	LOG	The primary purposes of these methods are to reduce noise and improve the object of interest.	Does not work well with very small or insignificant objects.
Wang et al. [12]	2012	Difference of Gaussian	Improves the target intensity and suppresses the clutter.	Does not work well with very small or insignificant objects.
Han et al. [14]	2016	Gabor filter	Improves the target intensity and suppresses the clutter.	Does not work well with very small or insignificant objects.
Chen et al. [3]	2014	LCM	Utilizes the local contrast information.	Does not work well with very small or insignificant objects.
Rao et al. [13]	2021	WLCV	Utilizes the weighted saliency map information.	Does not work well with very small or insignificant objects.
Yu et al. [17]	2022	Multiscale local contrast learning	Utilizes the local contrast information.	Does not work well with very small or insignificant objects.
Y. Wei et al. [18]	2016	MPCM	Utilizes the multi-patch information and the local contrast information.	Does not work well with very small or insignificant objects.
Small Target detection using patch-level				
T. Hu et. al. [21], Y. Cao, [22], Liu et al. [23] C., Z.-Z. Li et al. and Wang et al. [24,25]	2010, 2008, 2005, 2012, 2014, 2015	PPCA, NLPCA, KPCA, (SR), and sea-sky background dictionary	Perform well when it comes to targeting background classification under noise.	The downsides of these systems include that each overlapped patch must be projected into a dictionary and that reconstructing the object of interest is a time-consuming process.
Small Target detection using patch-image level				
Gao et al. [1], Rawat et al. [31–34] Gao et. [35,37–39]	2013, 2022, 2017, 2017, 2017, 2017, 2017, 2019,	IPI, TV-PSMSV, NIPPS, ReWIPI, RIPT, TV-PCP, NRAM, PSTN	In a complex clutter scene, these approaches display significant target- background suppression.	Compositionality is high in this case. Second, the l_1 norm-based approach is used.

3. The Proposed Method

A single-frame image can be modeled in the following way:

$$f_D(a,b) = f_T(a,b) + f_B(a,b) + f_N(a,b) \qquad (1)$$

where $f_D(a,b)$—real image, $f_B(a,b)$—background image, $f_T(a,b)$—target image, $f_N(a,b)$—noise image, and (a,b)—location of pixels coordinates in the taken image. The performance of RPCA in separating the background and the target image [43] motivated Gao et al. [1] to design an IPI model. The RPCA technique is used to reformulate target and background separation into an optimization problem by dividing the background into a low-rank matrix and the target into a sparse matrix. The sparse target image patch matrix T and the low-rank BPI matrix B are the two matrices that make up the patch-image matrix D in the IPI model. These matrices are then separated using RPCA as follows:

$$\min_{B,T} \|B\|_* + \lambda \|T\|_1, \quad s.t \quad D = B + T \tag{2}$$

where, $\|.\|_*$ is the matrix's nuclear norm, which is calculated by adding SV, and $\|.\|_1$ is the l_1-norm, which is defined by $\|X\|_1 = \sum_{ij} |X_{ij}|$. A method known as accelerated proximal gradient [20] can be used to solve the convex optimization issue described in [1].

Although the IPI model has proven successful in target background separation due to a quality that allows it to fit with reality, its performance is due to the effectiveness of patch-image dimensionality. The sparsity measure owing to the l_1-norm, on the other hand, shows less responsiveness in the case of a highly complex background with sharp edges than in the case of a smooth background. As a result, these strong edges may be sparse under l_1-norm reduction, implying that the strong edges may appear as targets under the constant global threshold of the IPI model, potentially increasing the false alarm rate. We know that the IPI model has a low number of patches with strong edges, and thus, strong edges could be viewed as an outlier, which is a goal. This is because NNM shrinks all singleton values with the same threshold and treats them all equally. Furthermore, large single values in a patch image convey more information than tiny SVs; hence we should punish larger SVs less than small SVs. As previously stated in section two, WNNM is utilized in place of NNM, which assigns various weights to different SVs in order to retain the large SVs, which provide more edge information. As mentioned in Equation (1), the infrared image in the patch domain can be modeled as a linear combination of background and the target image patch as given below; for simplicity, we are neglecting the noise component:

$$D = B + T \tag{3}$$

3.1. Background Patch-Image

Figure 1a, where the SVs of all BPIs trend towards zero, illustrates the BPI's strong association with both local and nonlocal patches, as was already indicated. The BPI is created using the nuclear norm. However, because the nuclear norm handles all SV identically, it is not always viable to anticipate the background patch picture using it. As a result, they shrink at the same rate, and high SVs, which contain more information, are penalized more severely than small SVs. As a result, instead of using the nuclear norm to assign weights to all the SV, we used the weighted SV threshold procedure to obtain the best background patch image.

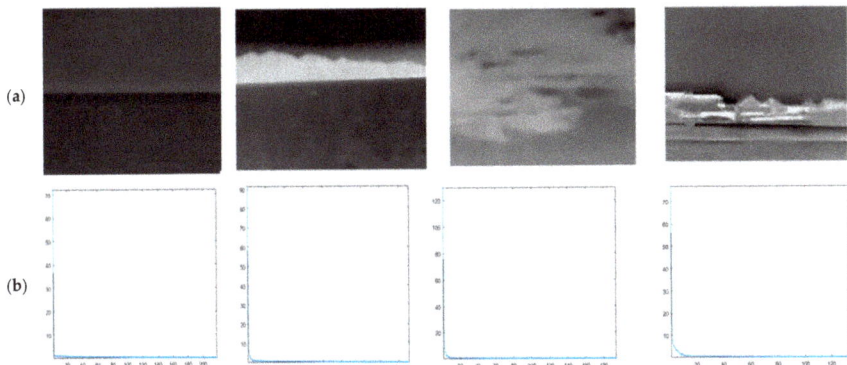

Figure 1. Characteristics of the background patch images with a low rank: (**a**) four different representational background images and (**b**) singular value distribution of corresponding background images.

Background matrix B's weighted nuclear norm is defined as:

$$\|B\|_{w,*} = \sum_i w_i \sigma_i(B) \tag{4}$$

where $w = [w_1 \ldots \ldots w_n]^T$ is a weight that is allocated to i, and $w_i \geq 0$ is a nonnegative weight that is assigned to $\sigma_i(B)$.

3.2. Small Target Patch-Image

The target size changes from 2×2 to 9×9, and its brightness is not fixed as it is with infrared photographs. Because the target is tiny in relation to the total image, we may think of the target patch image as a sparse matrix. The l_1 norm can be used as $\|T\|_1$ and here $\|T\|_1 = \sum_{ij}|T_{ij}|$.

3.3. Background Separation Solution for Small Target

The proposed IPI model employing weighted nuclear norm minimization via resilient principal component analysis can be offered as a result of reformulating Equation (2):

$$\min_{B,T} \|B\|_{w,*} + \lambda \|T\|_1, \quad s.t \quad D = B + T \tag{5}$$

where λ is the parameter for weighting. ADMM is used to solve Equation (6), and its augmented Lagrange function is as follows:

$$\mathcal{L}(B,T,Y,\mu) = \|B\|_{w,*} + \lambda \|T\|_1 + tr\left[Y^T(D-B-T)\right] + \frac{\mu}{2}\|D-B-T\|^2_F \tag{6}$$

Here, Y is the Lagrange multiplier, μ is the scalar quantity, and $tr[.]$ is the trace operator. We can minimize $\mathcal{L}$ with respect to B and T using the inexact augmented Lagrange multiplier (IALM):

$$B^{k+1} = \arg\min_B \mathcal{L}(B^k, T^k, Y^k, \mu_k) \tag{7}$$

$$= \arg\min_B \|B\|_{w,*} + \frac{\mu}{2}\|D + \mu_k^{-1}Y^k - T^{k+1} - B\|^2_F$$

$$T^{k+1} = \arg\min_T \mathcal{L}(B^{k+1}, T, Y^k, \mu_k) \tag{8}$$

$$= \arg\min_T \lambda \|T\|_1 + \frac{\mu}{2}\|D + \mu_k^{-1}Y^k - B^k - T\|^2_F$$

$$Y^{k+1} = Y^k + \mu_k\left(D - B^{k+1} - T^{k+1}\right) \tag{9}$$

The WNNM here can be addressed using the weighed nuclear norm proximal (WNNP) operator by changing it into a quadratic programming form with linear constraints:

$$\begin{cases} \hat{X} = prox_{\|.\|_{w,*}}(Y) \\ = \arg\min_T \|Y - X\|^2_F + \|X\|_{w,*} \end{cases} \tag{10}$$

Theorem 1. *As $Y \in R^{m \times n}$ without loss of generality, assume that $m \gg n$, and let $Y = U\Sigma V^T$ is the evaluated SVD of Y, here $\Sigma = \begin{pmatrix} diag(\sigma_1, \sigma_2, \sigma_3 \ldots \ldots \sigma_n) \\ 0 \end{pmatrix} \in R^{m \times n}$. The global optimum of WNMP problem (11) can be expressed as $\hat{X} = U\hat{D}V^T$ where $D = \begin{pmatrix} diag(d_1, d_2, d_3 \ldots \ldots d_n) \\ 0 \end{pmatrix}$*

is a diagonal non-negetive matrix and $(d_1, d_2, d_3 \ldots \ldots d_n)$ is the ultimate answer to the convex optimization problem in Equation (11):

$$\min_{d_1, d_2, d_3, \ldots \ldots d_n} \sum_{i=1}^{n} (\sigma_i - d_i)^2 + w_i d_i, \quad (11)$$
$$\text{s.t } d_1 \geq d_2 \geq \ldots \ldots d_n \geq 0$$

The closed-form optimum solution of WNNP can be obtained by weighted singular value threshold operation:

$$prox_{\lambda \|.\|_{w,*}} = D(Y) = US_{\frac{w}{2}}(\Sigma) V^T \quad (12)$$

where $Y = U\Sigma V^T$ is the evaluated SVD of Y, $S_{\frac{w}{2}}(\Sigma)$ is the soft threshold operator, and w is a weight vector.

$$S_{\frac{w}{2}}(\Sigma) = S(Y) = \max\left(\Sigma_{ii} - \frac{w_i}{2}, 0\right) \quad (13)$$

$$B^{k+1} = D_{\mu_k^{-1}}\left(D - T^{k+1} + \mu_k^{-1} Y^k\right) \quad (14)$$

$$T^{k+1} = S_{\mu_k^{-1}}\left(D - B^k + \mu_k^{-1} Y^k\right) \quad (15)$$

Theorem 2. *The sequences $\{X^k\}$ and $\{E^k\}$ created by the algorithm below should satisfy the following conditions if the weights are arranged in increasing order:*

(1) $\lim_{n \to \infty} \| X^{k+1} - X^k \|^2_F = 0$
(2) $\lim_{n \to \infty} \| E^{k+1} - E^k \|^2_F = 0$
(3) $\lim_{n \to \infty} \| Y - E^{k+1} - X^{k+1} \|^2_F = 0$

$$\text{where } \min_{X,E} \|X\|_* + \lambda \|E\|_1, \quad (16)$$
$$\text{s.t } Y = X + E$$

The symbol in the algorithm $\|.\|_2$ represents spectrum norm, $vec(.)$ represents the vector operator of the matrix, and $\|.\|_{inf}$ is the infinite norm of a vector.

In this work, we have utilized a reweighting approach as given below and utilized in the algorithm to improve the sparseness:

$$w_i^1 = \frac{C}{\sigma_i(X_1) + \theta} \quad (17)$$

Here, C represents a positive regularization parameter and θ represents a small positive to take care of the dividing by zero problem.

$$\sigma_i(X^*) = \begin{cases} 0 & \text{if } c_2 < 0 \\ \frac{c_1 + \sqrt{c_2}}{2} & \text{if } c_2 \gg 0 \end{cases} \quad (18)$$
$$\text{Where } X^* = U\Sigma V^T$$

3.4. Separation Model for Target-Background Model

Figure 2 above depicts the target-background division paradigm in its entirety. The entire procedure can be summarized as follows:

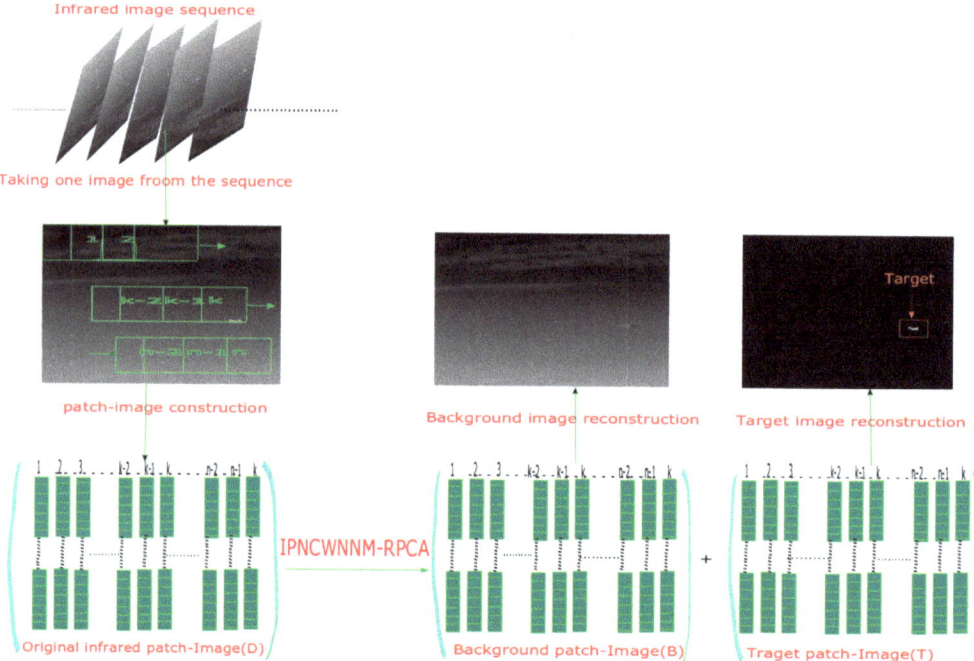

Figure 2. The proposed IPNCWNNM–RPCA model's process.

3.4.1. Creation of the Patch-Image Form Input

This is the initial phase, when an infrared patch image called D is created using the original image f_D from the image sequence. A sliding window moves from left to right first and then moves down from top to bottom to create the patch images.

3.4.2. Target-Background Separation

In the second phase, the input patch image is processed using Algorithm 1 to fragment it into two matrices, first **B** and then **T**.

3.4.3. Regeneration of the Target and Background Images

In the third phase, the proposed method reconstructs f_T, and f_B from the target patch images and the background. The whole process can be accomplished using the technique outlined in [1].

3.4.4. Segmentation Process

Now the final touch is initiated where some final processing to enhance the quality of target image is performed to run the adaptive thresholding scheme as described in [1].

The adaptive threshold evaluation is performed using Equation (19):

$$t_{up} = \max\left(v_{min}, \overline{f_T} + k\sigma\right) \tag{19}$$

where $\overline{f_T}$, σ represents the average and the standard deviation of f_T, and k, respectively, and v_{min} denotes the constant, which is taken as an empirical value. If $f_T(x, y) > t_{up}$, then pixels are part of the target image; otherwise, they are the part of the background image.

Algorithm 1 Solving IPNWNNM-RPCA via ADMM

Input: Real patch image D, weighting parameter λ, w.
Output: (B^k, T^k)
Initialize: $B^0 = T^0 = 0, Y^0 = \frac{D}{\max(\|D\|_2, \|M\| vec(D)\|_{inf})}$,
$\rho = 1.05, \varepsilon = 10^{-7}, k = 0, \theta > 0, \mu_0 = \frac{1}{\|D\|_2}, \mu_{max} = 10^7$;
While (not converged) do

1. Correct the other and Change the **B** by

$$B^{k+1} = D_{\mu_k^{-1}}\left(D - T^{k+1} + \mu_k^{-1} Y^k\right);$$

2. Correct the other and Change the **T** by

$$T^{k+1} = S_{\mu_k^{-1}}\left(D - B^k + \mu_k^{-1} Y^k\right);$$

3. Correct the other and Change the **Y** by

$$Y^k + \mu_k\left(D - B^{k+1} - T^{k+1}\right);$$

4. Update by μ

$$\mu_{k+1} = \rho * \mu_k;$$

5. Check convergence condition

$$\frac{\|D - B^{k+1} - T^{k+1}\|_F^2}{\|D\|_F} < \varepsilon$$

6. Update k

k++;
end

4. Experimental Result Analysis

This section presents a detailed experimental evaluation of the IPNCWNNM–RPCA model and finally compares its performance with that of the referenced state-of-art methods.

4.1. Parameter Settings, Baseline Methods, and Evaluation Indicators Metrics

We analyzed real infrared single images and sequences with a range of backgrounds, including water, sky, cloud, and land, using the proposed IPNCWNNM–RPCA model as well as six additional cutting-edge techniques. Additionally, the approach described in [1] is used to make the synthetic images.

Figure 3 shows representative images from the image sequences, whereas Table 2 provides a detailed description of these images. Table 3 gives the detailed parameters for several baseline approaches. The ADMM is used to solve all of the infrared patch-based approaches. All of the algorithms were developed in MATLAB 2015-a on a computer with a 2.4 GHz processor and 8-GB of RAM.

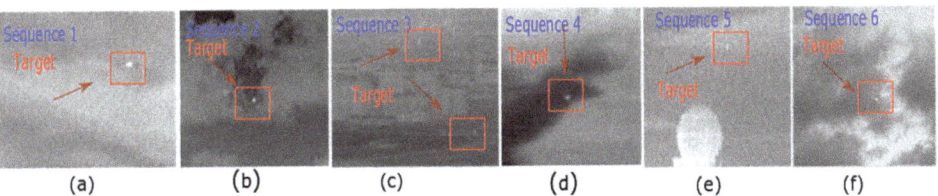

Figure 3. (**a**–**f**) are the six real infrared image sequences.

Table 2. Summary of the real image sequence data.

Sequences	Target Type	Image Size	No of Frames	Background Image Features	Target Image Features
1	Small ship	256 × 200	30	Dense sea-sky	• Small size (SS) • Varying size • Large imaging distance (LID)
2	An airplane	256 × 200	250	High dense clouds with less local contrast	• Small size • Varying size • LID
3	Two target	256 × 200	250	Changing background	• LID • SS • Low SCR
4	Copter	128 × 128	100	Changing background	• LID • Low SCR • SS
5	Ship	128 × 128	200	Changing background	• SS • A one-to-two target
6	An airplane	280 × 228	250	High dense clouds with less local contrast	• LID • SS

Table 3. Summary of the different parameters used in the evaluations.

Sr. No.	Techniques	Parameters
1	Max–median [6]	Filter = 5 × 5
2	Max–mean [6]	Filter = 5 × 5
3	IPI [1]	Sliding step = 10, tolerance error $\varepsilon = 10^{-7}$, Patch size = 50 × 50, $\lambda = \frac{1}{\sqrt{m}}$
4	NIPPS [31]	Sliding step = 10, Patch size = 50 × 50, $r = 10^{-3}$, L = 2, $\varepsilon = 10^{-7}$, $\lambda = \frac{L}{\sqrt{\min(m,n)}}$, $\rho = 1.5$
5	Top-Hat [11]	Filter shape = square, square size = 3 × 3
6	RPCA [26]	sliding step = 10, Patch size = 50 × 50, $\varepsilon = 10^{-7}$, $\lambda = \frac{1}{\sqrt{m}}$
7	RIPT [35]	$\lambda = \frac{L}{\sqrt{\min(m,n)}}$, Patch size = 50 × 50, L = 1, h = 1, $\varepsilon = 10^{-7}$, sliding step = 10
8	PSTN [39]	$\lambda = \frac{L}{\sqrt{(\max(n1,n2)*n3)}}$, Patch size = 40 × 40, L = 0.6, $\rho = 1.05$, sliding step = 40, $\varepsilon = 10^{-7}$
9	Infra small target detection based on nonconvex LP norm minimization (IPCWLP–RPCA [41])	tolerance error $\varepsilon = 10^{-7}$, $C = \sqrt{m}$, $\theta = 0.005$, $\rho = 1.05$, Patch size is 50 × 50, $\lambda = \frac{1}{\sqrt{m}}$, sliding step is 10
10	Our Method	$\lambda = \frac{1}{\sqrt{m}}$, Patch size = 50 × 50, $C = \sqrt{m}$, sliding step = 10, $\varepsilon = 10^{-7}$, $\theta = 0.005$, $\rho = 1.05$

4.2. Evaluation Indicators

This section describes how the background of an image can be suppressed as well as the target in an image can be improved. The suggested method's performance is validated using two standards, namely, SCRG and BSF. These indicators are described in depth in [44] and can be stated as follows:

$$\text{BSF} = \frac{C_{in}}{C_{out}}, \quad \text{SCRG} = \frac{(S/C)_{out}}{(S/C)_{in}} \tag{20}$$

where S and C denote the signal amplitude and clutter standard deviation (SD) and $_{in}$ and $_{out}$ in the formula denote the input original image and output target image, respectively. Before and after the image is analyzed, SCRG reports the signal's amplification result. When no information about the target is available, BSF assigns a level of suppression. As a result, it is expected that both indicators will have a high value in order to improve efficiency. The response of various methods can be validated using a metric known as ROC. The changing connection between the likelihood of target detection Pd and the false alarm rate Pf is shown by this curve [45], and it may be put this way:

$$\begin{cases} P_f = \frac{\text{Number of false alarms}}{\text{Total count of pixels in the complete image}} \\ P_d = \frac{\text{Count of detected pixels}}{\text{Count of original target pixels}} \end{cases} \quad (21)$$

As illustrated in Figure 4, all of the aforementioned indicators are computed in a small local region. If a tiny target's size is a × b, the background rectangle's size is (a + 2d) × (b + 2d), where d is a constant equal to 20 pixels.

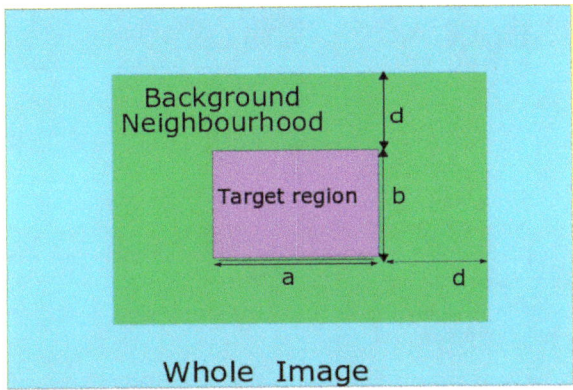

Figure 4. The infrared target and local background area.

4.3. Results of Experiments on Single Infrared Images

In the outcome analysis, we used a dataset containing more than 1500 single infrared images with different backgrounds. Each image has a maximum of two targets, and we used them to demonstrate the background suppression capabilities of different approaches in different background environments. Figure 5a–e show representative images and findings from different perspectives. When the background image is smooth, as in the images shown in Figure 5b–d, the max–mean, max–median, and top-hat approaches can identify the target. However, they fail to enhance the target when the background is complex, as seen in Figure 5e. In addition, the top-hat approach relies on good filter selection to properly detect the target; otherwise, it will fail. Similarly, baseline approaches such as IPI as shown in Figure 5e identify the target pretty effectively. However, when there is much clutter in the background, the methods fall short because they overshrink the image, causing the non-target element to be recognized instead of the genuine target.

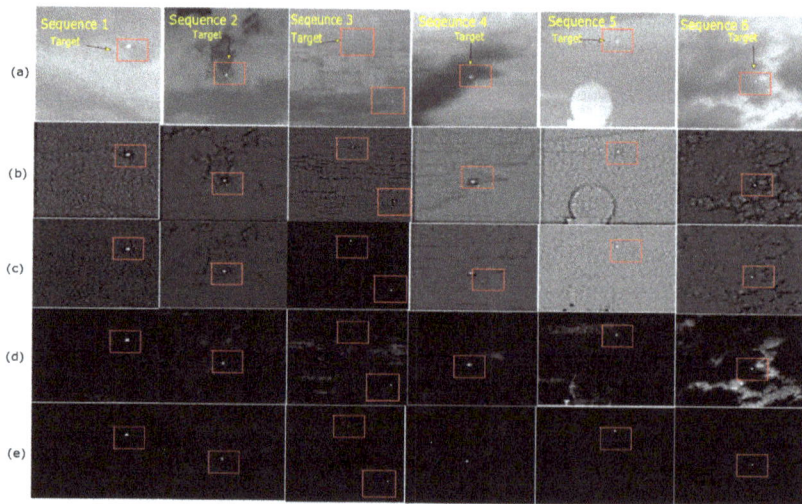

Figure 5. The target detection performances of the various methods on the image sequences presented in rows (**a**–**e**): (**a**) real image sequences; (**b**) max–mean; (**c**) max–median; (**d**) top-hat; (**e**) IPI.

The RPCA method as shown in Figure 6a is capable of detecting the target. However, its performance is hampered by the global threshold-holding parameter. NIPPS shown in Figure 6b outperforms other baseline approaces in terms of compassion. However, it suffers in a complicated background because the rank of the patch image matrix must be predicted accurately. Although RIPT and NRAM, shown in Figure 6c,d, performed very well, these methods fail to perform well in the presence of heavy noise. Moreover, these methods suffer from a matrix rank issue.

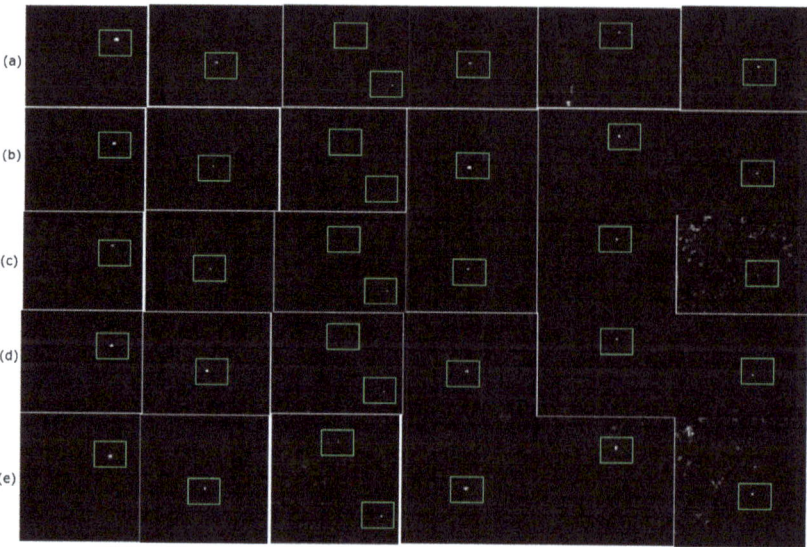

Figure 6. The target detection performance of the various methods on the image sequences presented in rows (**a**–**e**): (**a**) RPCA; (**b**) NIPPS; (**c**) RIPT; (**d**) IPCWLP–RPCA; (**e**) our method.

The suggested IPNCWNNM–RPCA technique as presented in Figure 6e smooths the clutter background by employing weighted nuclear norm singular value minimization, in which each singular value is given a variable weight, and highly informative SVs are shrunk less while less informative single values are shrunk more.

As a result of our method, strong edges such as corners and buildings may be predicted with ease, and the true candidate target can be identified quickly. The receiver operating curves (ROC) for the dataset's single infrared image are presented in Figure 7a–f, indicating that our method has a better response when compared with other referenced methods.

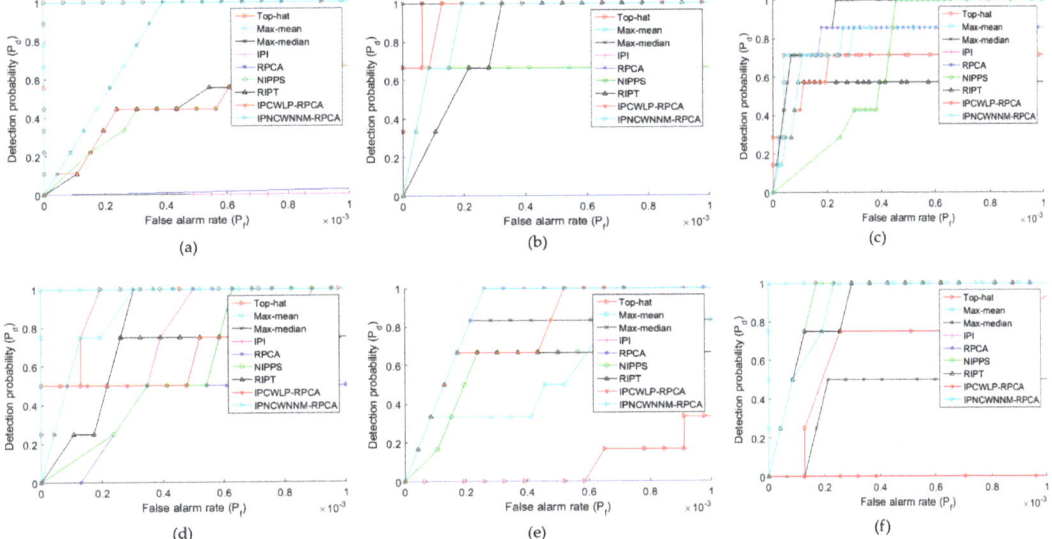

Figure 7. (a–f) are the Receiver operating characteristic curves (ROCs) for the six image sequences from Figure 5a.

In comparison with the other methods, the proposed IPNCWNNM–RPCA has impressive background suppression and target identification capabilities. The highest BSF and SCRG are in bold in Table 4, and the second highest values are in blue. Because time is such an essential component for any technique, IPNCWNNM–RPCA is slower than the other IPI-based methods. This is because a significant amount of time is spent creating patch images and reshaping them. The computing times for each approach are indicated in Table 5. Nonetheless, we will work to reduce this time constraint in the future.

Table 4. BSF and the SCRG values obtained using the various approaches for each of the test images in Figure 4a. The best outcomes are indicated in bold.

Detection Methods	Evaluation Indicators	Image6	Image5	Image4	Image3	Image2	Image1
Max–Median	BSF	1.914	1.861	3.816	1.934	3.404	1.354
	SCRG	1.863	3.117	51.109	16.001	6.358	5.881
Top Hat	BSF	0.528	0.923	2.354	0.882	1.573	1.104
	SCRG	2.938	3.081	53.302	9.440	4.024	6.546
Max–Mean	BSF	1.521	1.167	3.249	1.714	1.795	1.185
	SCRG	6.640	2.117	36.456	10.211	2.532	4.460
RPCA	BSF	0.952	0.494	6.468	7.443	0.681	0.489
	SCRG	2.274	0.683	76.236	73.628	0.279	3.166
IPI	BSF	22.280	29.862	13.778	8.799	13.565	3.219
	SCRG	115.118	**125.505**	**263.310**	113.135	34.854	0.013

Table 4. Cont.

Detection Methods	Evaluation Indicators	Image6	Image5	Image4	Image3	Image2	Image1
NIPPS	BSF	36.604	7.413	6.726	3.898	**39.983**	3.955
	SCRG	182.053	30.018	168.042	55.151	80.137	15.629
RIPT	BSF	13.638	26.180	10.155	10.340	5.210	4.734
	SCRG	71.826	107.088	196.948	87.306	16.036	18.458
IPCWLP—RPCA	BSF	1.60	2.55	1.37	3.23	1.40	1.29
	SCRG	9.31	96.89	**115.04**	74.74	7.69	**188.50**
IPNCWNNM–RPCA	BSF	40.290	101.232	3.226	15.132	2.551	1.600
	SCRG	**194.540**	14.860	**74.835**	**125.127**	**106.124**	21.213

Table 5. Comparative analysis of the costs and time involved in the computations.

Detection Methods	Top Hat	Max–Mean	Max–Median	IPI	RPCA	NIPPS	RIPT	NRAM	PSTN	IPCWLP-RPCA	IPNCWNNM-RPCA
Complexity	$O(k^2 \log k^2 M \times N)$	$O(k^2 M \times N)$	$O(k^2 M \times N)$	$O(m \times n^2)$	$O(m \times n^2)$	$O(m \times n^2)$	$O(m \times n^2)$	$O(m \times n^2)$	$O(d_1 d_2 d_3 (d_1 d_2 + d_2 d_2 + d_1 d_2))$	$O(k \times m \times n^2)$	$O(m \times n^2)$
Time (s)	0.968	7.70	6.84	12.64	10.86	5.15	1.95	3.89	0.35	11.78	10.52

4.4. Computational Complexity

The computational cost of running sequence No. 2 in Figure 5a is given in Table 5. The computing costs for the top-hat approach with a structuring size of k^2 and an image size of $M \times N$ is $(k^2 \log k^2 MN)$, and the max–mean and median are provided as $M \times N \times k^2$, respectively. We can observe that the SVD operations in the algorithm require a significant amount of time in all of the IPI model-based techniques. The cost of IPCWLP–RPCA is $(k \times m \times n^2)$, and for RPCA, IPI, NIPPS, and our technique, it is therefore given by $O(m \times n^2)$ for the image patch size of $m \times n$.

4.5. Infrared Image Sequences Yielded Experimental

The proposed method has been tested on various real infrared image sequences in a variety of environments. The targets in these image sequences are small and monotonous and have poor contrast. Furthermore, the images have sharp edges, which makes detection challenging. Eight state-of-the-art techniques, including max–mean [6], max–median [6], top-hat [11], IPI [1], NIPPS [31], RPCA [26], RIPT [35], and NRAM [38], have been compared with the proposed method in order to validate its efficacy. The Figure 8a displays the initial infrared image sequences, while Figures 8b–e and 9a–e exhibit the results of the various baseline techniques.

Max–mean and max–median can find the small target when there is a smooth background but not when there is a complex background. Similarly, the top-hat technique is effective against a clean background but fails against one that is complex. Second, because the top-hat filter's mask is determined by the target's size, it is difficult hard to create a mask that matches the target's size. IPI-based approaches are very effective at detecting tiny targets. However, they fail to perform better in cluttered backgrounds because they are unable to distinguish between real targets and strong edges, which they may incorrectly recognize as a target due to l_1-minimization.

The global weighting parameter is used in the RPCA method, which makes it difficult to detect small targets in a cluttered background. Furthermore, the NIPPS approach is reliant on knowing the rank of the matrix ahead of time, which is not always easy to predict. The suggested technique used weighted nuclear norm minimization, which gives SVs various weights and penalizes less informative SVs more than more informative SVs. Second, there are no restrictions on rank prediction ahead of time.

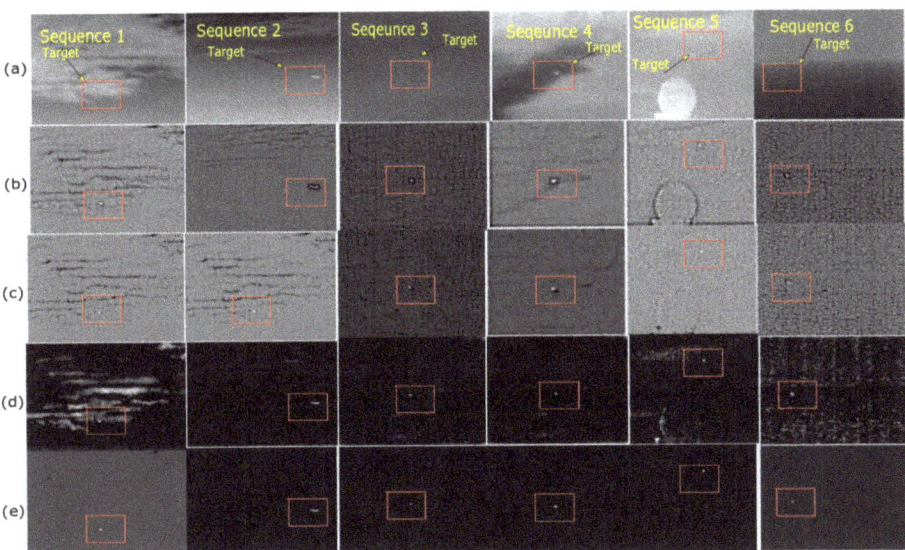

Figure 8. The target detection performances of the various methods on the image sequences presented in rows (**a**–**e**): (**a**) real image sequences; (**b**) max–mean; (**c**) max–median; (**d**) top-hat; (**e**) IPI.

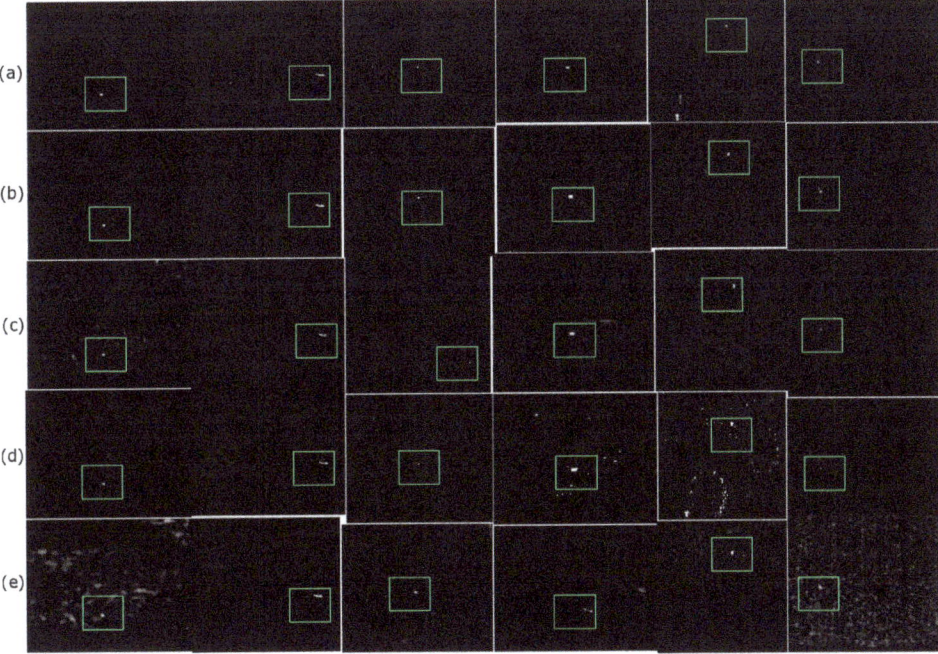

Figure 9. The target detection performances of the various methods on the image sequences presented in rows (**a**–**e**): (**a**) RPCA; (**b**) NIPPS; (**c**) RIPT; (**d**) NRAM; (**e**) our method.

As a result, compared with existing baseline approaches, the suggested method not only suppresses the strong clutter background but it detects the small target better. The different SCRG values for the image sequences from the six state-of-the-art approaches and the suggested method are shown in Table 6.

Table 6. SCRG values for the test images shown in Figure 8a.

Detection Methods	Evaluation Indicators	Image6	Image5	Image4	Image3	Image2	Image1
Max–Median	BSF	1.255	1.861	3.816	0.863	3.387	1.383
	SCRG	17.867	3.117	51.109	6.461	1.580	1.936
Top Hat	BSF	0.923	0.923	2.354	0.512	2.339	0.488
	SCRG	24.651	3.081	53.302	7.376	5.733	1.412
Max–Mean	BSF	1.195	1.167	3.249	0.747	3.895	1.295
	SCRG	17.393	2.117	36.456	5.415	1.708	1.765
RPCA		3.790	0.494	6.468	3.073	25.882	3.701
	SCRG	90.559	0.683	76.236	36.166	60.950	12.672
IPI	BSF	10.410	29.862	13.778	7.680	52.274	8.698
	SCRG	195.948	125.505	263.310	79.869	112.307	17.799
NIPPS	BSF	7.576	7.413	6.726	2.687	6.169	4.453
	SCRG	4.700	30.018	168.042	23.787	6.298	0.621
RIPT	BSF	14.874	0.896	3.125	3.101	7.124	3.440
	SCRG	0.038	0.062	24.799	9.308	4.835	0.476
NRAM	BSF	3.026	1.477	3.002	1.776	4.948	1.401
	SCRG	14.284	0.033	27.870	6.726	2.694	0.404
IPNCWNNM–RPCA	BS	18.138	41.475	14.482	8.678	4.022	5.564
	SCRG	27.860	0.394	134.26	95.494	89.265	18.298

The best SCRG shows that the target can be improved and is easily visualized. The largest SCRG and BSF are bold, while the second highest values are in blue. SCRG and BSF should be high enough for improved detection.

For the different real image sequences, Figure 10 shows the ROCs of the six approaches and the proposed method. Figure 10a shows that the proposed method has performed effectively and has achieved probability 1 for image sequences 1. The NIPPS approach has a low detection rate and has the lowest reaction in Figure 10b, whereas IPI comes in second. Figure 10c shows that the suggested method is late when compared with the IPI method, and again NIPPS has a low detection rate. Finally, we can see in Figure 10d,e the comparison of the proposed approach with the other methods. Moreover, from Figure 10f, it can be seen that our approach has performed nicely, although the IPI approach produces a strong response. In sum, the suggested method has responded nicely in easing the detection of the target object in the image.

Compared with the existing baseline approaches, the suggested method not only suppresses the strong clutter background but detects the small target better. The different SCRG values for the image sequences from the six state-of-the-art approaches and the suggested method are shown in Table 6.

4.6. Simulation Results for the Infrared Image Sequences with Noise

In the presence of noise, the proposed approach was tested on image sequences. Figure 11a depicts the original image sequences, while Figure 11b,c depict images with the noise of 10 and 20 standard deviations, respectively. Figure 11d,e show that in the presence of noise, the suggested technique suppresses the background and correctly detects the small target.

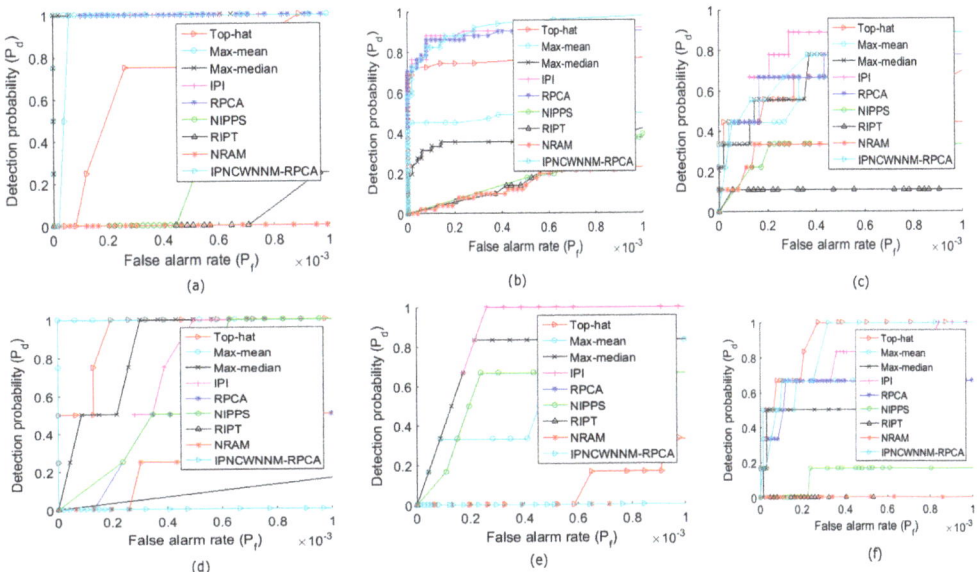

Figure 10. (**a**–**f**) are the ROC curves of the six image sequences from Figure 8a.

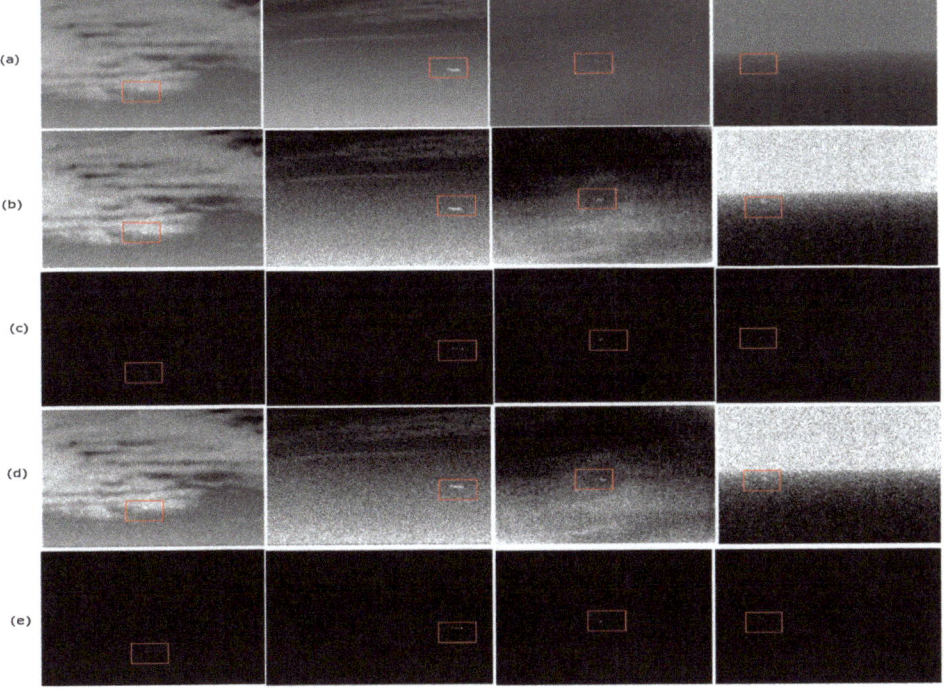

Figure 11. Background suppression results with noise images. (**a**) Original images with noise. (**b**) Noise images with a SD of 10. (**c**) Images after background suppression of Figure 8b. (**d**) Noise images with a SD of 20 (**e**) Images after background suppression of Figure 8c.

4.7. Simulation Results When Infrared Image Sequences Are Synthetic

On test datasets of infrared image sequences, we tested the suggested method's performance. Actual infrared BPIs were used to construct a total of 100 synthetic test image sequences, each with 50 different-sized targets positioned at random locations throughout the background and varying clutter backgrounds. The whole preparation method for synthetic datasets is provided in [1]. In the assessment procedure, one and four target image sequences were employed. The original BPI sequences are shown in Figure 12a. Figure 12b depicts a single target in the original background, while Figure 12c depicts the outcome of the suggested method on a synthetic image. Figure 12d depicts the four targets in the real background, while Figure 12e depicts the outcome of the suggested method on a synthetic image. In the case of synthetic image sequences, we may say that the suggested technique is robust enough to detect the small targets.

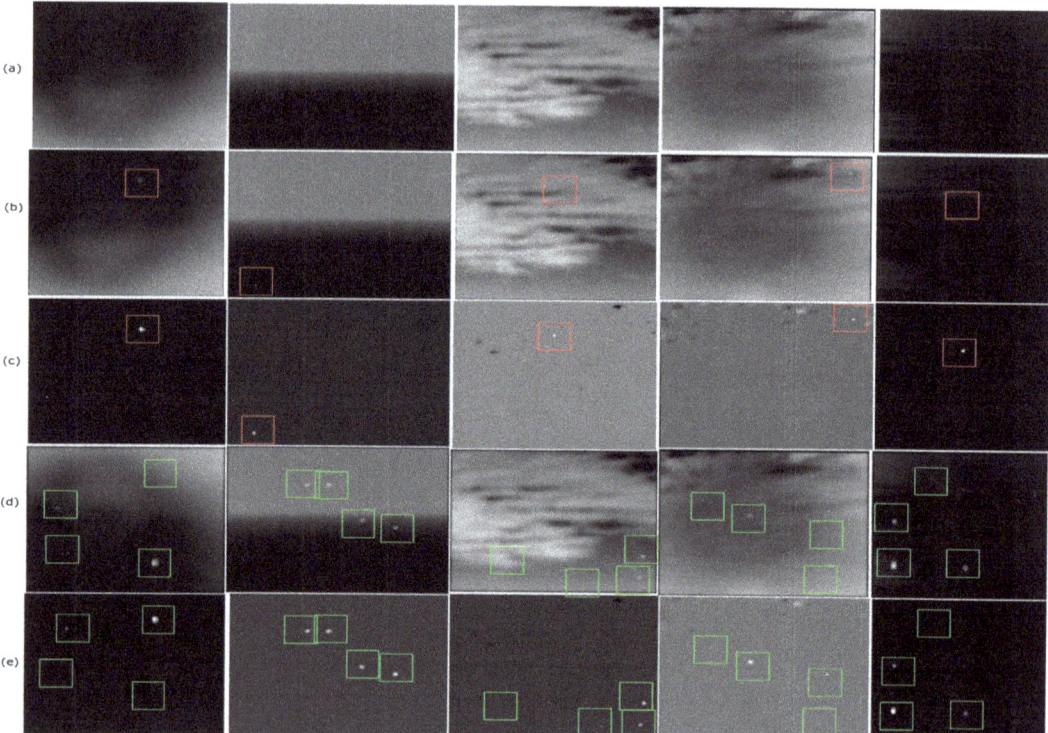

Figure 12. Experimental results for the synthetic image sequences (**a**) Background—synthetic image sequences. (**b**) Images with one target and (**c**) background suppression of Figure 9b. (**d**) Images with four different small targets. (**e**) Background suppression of Figure 9d.

4.8. Parameter Analysis

Three factors that are crucial for the robustness of the recommended technique under various background conditions have been used in this section: step size, patch size, and regulatory parameters. It is essential to make these adjustments in order to achieve the greatest outcomes. It is also crucial to remember that the criteria do not always produce the best overall outcome. ROC curves made for various picture sequences may be used to assess the effectiveness of the proposed approach utilising these parameters, as illustrated in Figure 13 in the section below.

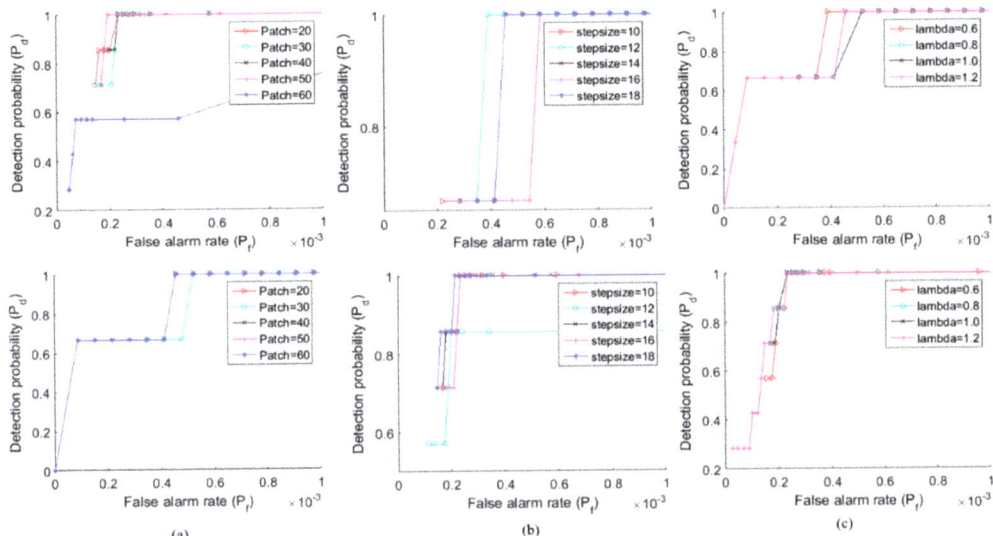

Figure 13. ROC curves of infrared sequence: (**a**) ROC curve of patch size for sequence; (**b**) ROC curve of step size for sequence; (**c**) ROC curve of controlling parameter for sequence.

4.8.1. Patch Size

We used varied patch sizes in the experiment to see how our approach performed, and we discovered that raising the patch size improves the target's sparsity while simultaneously increasing the computation cost. During the experimental observation, we utilised patch sizes of 20, 30, 40, 50, and 60, taking into account the appropriate patch size for an enhanced response of the proposed model. The ROC curves for the two image sequences were produced, as seen in Figure 13a. The ROC curve demonstrates that increasing the image patch size significantly affects both detection effectiveness and computational cost.

Due to the loss of nonlocal information, patch size 60 with the proposed technique has inferior detection performance, which will surely make it more difficult to distinguish between the target and background. This suggests that for optimum performance, a patch size of 40×40 is ideal.

4.8.2. Step Size

The step size has to be tuned in the same manner as the patch size. During the experimental observation, the patch size was set to 40×40, and the step size was changed in increments of two units, yielding step sizes of 10, 12, 14, 16, and 18, respectively. The ROC curve on step size for the two picture sequences shown in Figure 13b indicates that using a small step can increase computation time and also negatively affects the detection performance of the suggested approach. Additionally, increasing the step size helps speed up processing. Our findings have led us to the conclusion that 12 is the ideal step size.

4.8.3. Controlling Parameter λ

For the proposed method, $\lambda = \frac{L}{\sqrt{(\max(n1,n2)*n3)}}$, and lambda, L, is an important regulating parameter that controls both the background patch picture and the target patch image. A large L can cause an issue with overshrinking, but a small value will maintain the residue in the background picture and may even provide a misleading alert. In this experiment, we employed four distinct L values: L = 0.6, L = 0.8, L = 1.0, and L = 1.2. Compared with the other values, L = 0.8 generated superior results, as evidenced by the created ROC curves for two picture sequences utilizing these values shown in Figure 13c.

5. Conclusions

Due to the l_1 norm problem, the IPI model has difficulty constraining the background using the basic nuclear norm minimization. Because of this flaw, the non-target edges in the backdrop are mistaken for target spots. To overcome this problem and properly constrain the background patch image, the existing IPI model has been utilized in this work, which employs WNNM in conjunction with RPCA. In this model, the weights are applied to each singular value, and larger singular values are penalized less than smaller ones.

As a result, the provided model improves target recognition and background suppression. In comparison with the state-of-the-art approaches, the experimental findings show that the current IPNCWNNM–RPCA not only suppresses the clutter background but efficiently detects the object. The proposed model could further be improved in future by using the tensor norm instead of the nuclear norm or the WNN.

Author Contributions: Conceptualization: Y.A. and S.S.R.; Methodology: S.S. and S.S.R.; Validation: Y.A. and G.K.; Formal Analysis: Y.A. and S.S.; Investigation: S.A. and S.S. Resources: S.A. and S.S.R.; Data Curation: S.A. and S.S.R.; Writing original draft preparation: S.A. and S.S.R.; Writing review and editing: Y.A. and S.S.R.; Visualization: G.K. and S.S.; Supervision: Y.A.; Project Administration: S.A., Y.A. and S.S.R.; Funding Acquisition: Y.A. All authors have read and agreed to the published version of the manuscript.

Funding: This research was supported by the Deanship of Scientific Research at Umm Al-Qura University, grant 22UQU4281768DSR06.

Institutional Review Board Statement: Not applicable.

Informed Consent Statement: Not applicable.

Data Availability Statement: The data presented in this study are available upon reasonable request from the corresponding author.

Acknowledgments: The authors would like to thank the Deanship of scientific research at Umm Al-Qura University for supporting this work grant code: (22UQU4281768DSR06).

Conflicts of Interest: The authors declare no conflict of interest.

References

1. Gao, C.; Meng, D.; Yang, Y.; Wang, Y.; Zhao, X.; Hauptmann, A.G. Infrared patch-image model for small target detection in a single image. *IEEE Trans. Image Processing* **2013**, *22*, 4996–5009. [CrossRef]
2. Reed, I.S.; Gagliardi, R.M.; Stotts, L.B. Optical moving target detection with 3-D matched filtering. *IEEE Trans. Aerosp. Electron. Syst.* **1988**, *24*, 327–336. [CrossRef]
3. Chen, C.P.; Li, H.; Wei, Y.; Xia, T.; Tang, Y.Y. A local contrast method for small infrared target detection. *IEEE Trans. Geosci. Remote Sens.* **2014**, *52*, 574–581. [CrossRef]
4. Rawat, S.; Verma, S.K.; Kumar, Y. Review on recent development in infrared small target detection algorithms. *Procedia Comput. Sci.* **2020**, *167*, 2496–2505. [CrossRef]
5. Hadhoud, M.M.; Thomas, D.W. The two-dimensional adaptive LMS (TDLMS) algorithm. *IEEE Trans. Circuits Syst.* **1998**, *35*, 485–494. [CrossRef]
6. Deshpande, S.D.; Meng, H.E.; Venkateswarlu, R.; Chan, P. Max-mean and max-median filters for detection of small targets. *SPIE's Int. Symp. Opt. Sci. Eng. Instrum.* **1999**, *3809*, 74–83.
7. Bae, T.W.; Zhang, F.; Kweon, I.S. Edge directional 2D LMS filter for infrared small target detection. *Infrared Phys. Technol.* **2012**, *55*, 137–145. [CrossRef]
8. Cao, Y.; Liu, R.; Yang, J. Small target detection using two-dimensional least mean square (TDLMS) filter based on neighborhood analysis. *Int. J. Infrared Millim. Waves* **2008**, *29*, 188–200. [CrossRef]
9. Bae, T.W.; Sohng, K.I. Small target detection using bilateral filter based on edge component. *J. Infrared Millim. Terahertz Waves* **2010**, *31*, 735–743. [CrossRef]
10. Bai, X.; Zhou, F.; Xue, B. Infrared dim small target enhancement using toggle contrast operator. *Infrared Phys. Technol.* **2012**, *55*, 177–182. [CrossRef]
11. Bai, X.; Zhou, F. Analysis of new top-hat transformation and the application for infrared dim small target detection. *Pattern Recognit.* **2010**, *43*, 2145–2156. [CrossRef]
12. Wang, X.; Lv, G.; Xu, L. Infrared dim target detection based on visual attention. *Infrared Phys. Technol.* **2012**, *55*, 513–521. [CrossRef]

13. Rao, J.; Mu, J.; Li, F.; Liu, S. Infrared Small Target Detection Based on Weighted Local Coefficient of Variation Measure. *Sensors* **2022**, *22*, 3462. [CrossRef] [PubMed]
14. Alotaibi, Y. A New Database Intrusion Detection Approach Based on Hybrid Meta-heuristics. *Comput. Mater. Contin.* **2021**, *66*, 1879–1895. [CrossRef]
15. Rour, R.; Parida, P.; Alotaibi, Y.; Alghamdi, S.; Khalaf, I.O. Skin Lesion Extraction Using Multiscale Morphological Local Variance Reconstruction Based Watershed Transform and Fast Fuzzy C-Means Clustering. *Symmetry* **2021**, *11*, 2085.
16. Shao, X.; Fan, H.; Lu, G.; Xu, J. An improved infrared dim and small target detection algorithm based on the contrast mechanism of human visual system. *Infrared Phys. Technol.* **2012**, *55*, 403–408. [CrossRef]
17. Yu, C.; Liu, Y.; Wu, S.; Hu, Z.; Xia, X.; Lan, D.; Liu, X. Infrared small target detection based on multiscale local contrast learning networks. *Infrared Phys. Technol.* **2022**, *123*, 104107. [CrossRef]
18. Wei, Y.; You, X.; Li, H. Multiscale patch-based contrast measure for small infrared target detection. *Pattern Recognit.* **2016**, *58*, 216–226. [CrossRef]
19. Turk, M.; Pentland, A. Eigenfaces for recognition. *J. Cogn. Neurosci.* **1991**, *3*, 71–86. [CrossRef] [PubMed]
20. Wright, J.; Ganesh, A.; Rao, S.; Peng, Y.; Ma, Y. Robust principal component analysis: Exact recovery of corrupted low-rank matrices via convex optimization. In Proceedings of the Advances in Neural Information Processing Systems, Vancouver, BC, Canada, 7–10 December 2009; pp. 2080–2088.
21. Hu, T.; Zhou, J.J.; Cao, Y.; Wang, F.L.; Yang, J. Infrared small target detection based on saliency and principle component analysis. *J. Infrared Millim. Waves* **2010**, *29*, 303–306.
22. Suryanarayana, G.; Chandran, K.; Khalaf, O.I.; Alotaibi, Y.; Alsufyani, A.; Alghamdi, S.A. Accurate Magnetic Resonance Image Super-Resolution Using Deep Networks and Gaussian Filtering in the Stationary Wavelet Domain. *IEEE Access* **2021**, *9*, 71406–71417. [CrossRef]
23. Liu, Z.; Chen, C.; Shen, X.; Zou, X. Detection of small objects in image data based on the nonlinear principal component analysis neural network. *Opt. Eng.* **2005**, *44*, 093604. [CrossRef]
24. Li, Z.Z.; Chen, J.; Hou, Q.; Fu, H.X.; Dai, Z.; Jin, G.; Li, R.Z.; Liu, C. Sparse representation for infrared dim target detection via a discriminative over-complete dictionary learned online. *Sensors* **2014**, *14*, 9451–9470. [CrossRef] [PubMed]
25. Wang, X.; Shen, X.; Ning, C.; Xu, M.; Yan, X. A sparse representation-based method for infrared dim target detection under sea–sky background. *Infrared Phys. Technol.* **2015**, *71*, 347–355. [CrossRef]
26. Wang, C.; Qin, S. Adaptive detection method of infrared small target based on target-background separation via robust principal component analysis. *Infrared Phys. Technol.* **2015**, *69*, 123–135. [CrossRef]
27. Dabov, K.; Foi, A.; Katkovnik, V.; Egiazarian, K. Image denoising by sparse 3-D transform-domain collaborative filtering. *IEEE Trans. Image Process.* **2007**, *16*, 2080–2095. [CrossRef]
28. Maggioni, M.; Katkovnik, V.; Egiazarian, K.; Foi, A. Nonlocal transform-domain filter for volumetric data denoising and reconstruction. *IEEE Trans. Image Process.* **2013**, *22*, 119–133. [CrossRef]
29. He, Y.; Li, M.; Zhang, J.; An, Q. Small infrared target detection based on low-rank and sparse representation. *Infrared Phys. Technol.* **2015**, *68*, 98–109. [CrossRef]
30. Kollapudi, P.; Alghamdi, S.; Veeraiah, N.; Alotaibi, Y.; Thotakura, S. A New Method for Scene Classification from the Remote Sensing Images. *CMC-Comput. Mater. Contin.* **2022**, *72*, 1339–1355. [CrossRef]
31. Dai, Y.; Wu, Y.; Song, Y.; Guo, J. Non-negative infrared patch-image model: Robust target-background separation via partial sum minimization of singular values. *Infrared Phys. Technol.* **2017**, *81*, 182–194. [CrossRef]
32. Rawat, S.S.; Saleh, A.; Kumar, G.; Alotaibi, Y.; Khalaf, I.O.; Verma, L.P. Infrared Small Target Detection Based on Partial Sum Minimization and Total Variation. *Mathematics* **2022**, *10*, 671. [CrossRef]
33. Dai, Y.; Wu, Y.; Song, Y. Infrared small target and background separation via column-wise weighted robust principal component analysis. *Infrared Phys. Technol.* **2016**, *77*, 421–430. [CrossRef]
34. Rawat, S.; Verma, S.K.; Kumar, Y. Reweighted infrared patch image model for small target detection based on non-convex L_p-norm minimisation and TV regularization. *IET Image Process.* **2020**, *14*, 1937–1947. [CrossRef]
35. Dai, Y.; Wu, Y. Reweighted infrared patch-tensor model with both nonlocal and local priors for single-frame small target detection. *IEEE J. Sel. Top. Appl. Earth Obs. Remote Sens.* **2017**, *10*, 3752–3767. [CrossRef]
36. Gu, S.; Xie, Q.; Meng, D.; Zuo, W.; Feng, X.; Zhang, L. Weighted nuclear norm minimization and its applications to low level vision. *Int. J. Comput. Vis.* **2017**, *121*, 183–208. [CrossRef]
37. Wang, X.; Zhenming, P.; Dehui, K.; Zhang, P.; He, P. Infrared dim target detection based on total variation regularization and principal component pursuit. *Image Vis. Comput.* **2017**, *63*, 1–9. [CrossRef]
38. Zhang, L.; Peng, L.; Zhang, T.; Cao, S.; Peng, Z. Infrared small target detection via non-convex rank approximation minimization joint l2, 1 norm. *Remote Sens.* **2018**, *10*, 1821. [CrossRef]
39. Zhang, L.; Peng, Z. Infrared small target detection based on partial sum of the tensor nuclear norm. *Remote Sens.* **2019**, *11*, 382. [CrossRef]
40. Gaun, X.; Zhang, L.; Huang, S.; Peng, Z. Infrared small target detection via non-convex tensor rank surrogate joint local contrast energy. *Remote Sens.* **2020**, *12*, 1520. [CrossRef]
41. Rawat, S.S.; Verma, S.K.; Kumar, Y.; Kumar, G. Infrared small target detection based on non-convex Lp-norm minimization. *J. MESA* **2021**, *12*, 929–942.

42. Zeng, M.; Li, J.; Peng, Z. The design of top-hat morphological filter and application to infrared target detection. *Infrared Phys. Technol.* **2006**, *48*, 67–76. [CrossRef]
43. Candes, E.J.; Li, X.; Ma, Y.; Wright, J. Robust principal component analysis? *J. ACM* **2011**, *58*, 1–37. [CrossRef]
44. Hilliard, C.I. Selection of a clutter rejection algorithm for real-time target detection from an airborne platform. In Proceedings of the SPIE, Orlando, FL, USA, 13 July 2000; Volume 4048, pp. 74–84.
45. Gu, Y.; Wang, C.; Liu, B.; Zhang, Y. A kernel-based nonparametric regression method for clutter removal in infrared small-target detection applications. *IEEE Geosci. Remote Sens. Lett.* **2010**, *7*, 469–473. [CrossRef]

Article

VPP: Visual Pollution Prediction Framework Based on a Deep Active Learning Approach Using Public Road Images

Mohammad AlElaiwi [1], Mugahed A. Al-antari [2], Hafiz Farooq Ahmad [1], Areeba Azhar [3], Badar Almarri [1] and Jamil Hussain [4,*]

1. Computer Science Department, College of Computer Sciences and Information Technology (CCSIT), King Faisal University, P.O. Box 400, Al-Ahsa 31982, Saudi Arabia
2. Department of Artificial Intelligence, College of Software & Convergence Technology, Daeyang AI Center, Sejong University, Seoul 05006, Republic of Korea
3. Department of Mathematics, College of Natural & Agricultural Sciences, University of California-Riverside (UCR), Riverside, CA 92521, USA
4. Department of Data Science, College of Software & Convergence Technology, Daeyang AI Center, Sejong University, Seoul 05006, Republic of Korea
* Correspondence: jamil@sejong.ac.kr; Tel.: +82-2-3408-3180

Abstract: Visual pollution (VP) is the deterioration or disruption of natural and man-made landscapes that ruins the aesthetic appeal of an area. It also refers to physical elements that limit the movability of people on public roads, such as excavation barriers, potholes, and dilapidated sidewalks. In this paper, an end-to-end visual pollution prediction (VPP) framework based on a deep active learning (DAL) approach is proposed to simultaneously detect and classify visual pollutants from whole public road images. The proposed framework is architected around the following steps: real VP dataset collection, pre-processing, a DAL approach for automatic data annotation, data splitting as well as augmentation, and simultaneous VP detection and classification. This framework is designed to predict VP localization and classify it into three categories: excavation barriers, potholes, and dilapidated sidewalks. A real dataset with 34,460 VP images was collected from various regions across the Kingdom of Saudi Arabia (KSA) via the Ministry of Municipal and Rural Affairs and Housing (MOMRAH), and this was used to develop and fine-tune the proposed artificial intelligence (AI) framework via the use of five AI predictors: MobileNetSSDv2, EfficientDet, Faster RCNN, Detectron2, and YOLO. The proposed VPP-based YOLO framework outperforms competitor AI predictors with superior prediction performance at **89**% precision, 88% recall, 89% F1-score, and 93% mAP. The DAL approach plays a crucial role in automatically annotating the VP images and supporting the VPP framework to improve prediction performance by 18% precision, 27% recall, and 25% mAP. The proposed VPP framework is able to simultaneously detect and classify distinct visual pollutants from annotated images via the DAL strategy. This technique is applicable for real-time monitoring applications.

Keywords: AI-based visual pollution prediction (VPP); deep active learning (DAL); deep learning; simultaneous VP detection and classification

MSC: 68T45

1. Introduction

In the beginning of 2018, the Kingdom of Saudi Arabia (KSA) launched the Quality of Life (QoL) project under the Saudi Vision 2030 framework, contingent on the usage of advanced AI technology to improve the quality of life of its residents by establishing a more comfortable environment for their contemporary lifestyles. The program aims to increase inhabitant engagement with numerous social and cultural activities based on entertainment, culture, tourism, sports, and other sectors able to nurture an increased quality of life. Heightened participation in such activities is predicted to have a positive economic and social impact by allowing for the establishment of numerous jobs and a diverse range of activities being made available to Saudi residents [1]. As such, the current standing of Saudi cities could be elevated to make them among the world's most livable cities [2]. The community targeted for this program consists of individuals residing within the boundary of Saudi Arabia, including, but not limited to, citizens, residents, visitors, and tourists. As an integral part of the KSA 2030 vision, a strategic economic and social reform framework, municipalities across thirteen provincial regions in Saudi Arabia have launched intensive remedial policies in an effort to secure high living standards for residents of the Kingdom. As we know, the continuation of expansive and invasive anthropogenic influences on the natural environment endangers all living organisms. As defined by the Intergovernmental Science-Policy Platform on Biodiversity and Ecosystem Services (IPBES), the five significant ecosystem propulsors and biodiversity losers in dire need of swift and effective change are (1) climate change, (2) direct exploitation, (3) pollution, (4) biological invasions, and (5) sea-use change [3]. As such, they are reversing the significant environmental damage engendered by man, which is unequivocally the primary source of discussion in influential environmental discourses throughout recent history.

As defined by toxicity-based literature, pollution is an offshoot of industrial and economic progression, with acute consequences for the environment and its inhabitants. Abiotic drivers, or the non-living components of an ecosystem, precipitated through human activity result in inexhaustible levels of pollution released into both untouched and man-made ecosystems. The degree of such drivers is, of course, in direct relation to the distance between natural and urban areas—an interval that continues to diminish as the demand for ecosystem inputs increases in direct correlation with the growth of human populations. Although much research on air, water, and land pollution exists, sensory pollution, or human-induced stimuli that interfere with the senses, is a relatively unevaluated phenomenon with severe repercussions. This pollution of "disconnection" has recently evolved to include visual pollution (VP)—disturbances or obstructions in the natural environment. Visual pollutants are the final benefactors to multimodal environmental deterioration when examined alongside other forms of sensory pollution in urban environments. Visual pollution (VP), as detailed in this study, refers specifically to disruptive presences that limit visual ability on public roads, with an emphasis on excavation barriers, potholes, and dilapidated sidewalks.

Visual pollution appears in digital images with varying irregular shapes, colors, and sizes, as observed in Figure 1. This particular form of pollution is a relatively recent concern when considering the current plethora of contaminants habitually spotlighted in the academic literature [4]. Several factors, however, have driven an upsurge in visual pollutants; the incessant construction of new buildings, the inevitable deterioration of asphalt roads as well as sidewalks, and even weather conditions, for instance, are directly connected to the rise in VP.

It is important to adhere to and follow government rules for the construction of buildings or any other civil works in neighborhoods to minimize the occurrence of visual pollution. In an effort to mitigate the adverse effects of such disagreeable elements, the government of Saudi Arabia has launched several field campaigns that manually inspect the country for visual pollutants and alert all construction protocol violators to swiftly rectify any virulent activities in order to avoid disciplinary action [1]. However, this non-automatic process is highly time-consuming, economically unfeasible, and mentally as well as physically draining for employees. As such, our team endeavors to architect AI technological processes applicable to real-time investigations of three distinct visual pollutants: (1) excavation barriers, (2) potholes, and (3) dilapidated sidewalks. Identifying and predicting VP, in particular, can be achieved by training convolutional neural networks (CNNs) with various layers of artificial neurons in the context of image recognition and vision computing [5]. Prior to You Only Look Once (YOLO) [6], all multi-stage object detectors (R-CNN, Fast R-CNN, Faster R-CNN, and others) that exhibited state-of-the-art

(SOTA) accuracy used regions to localize targets rather than assessing whole input images. The YOLO architecture consists of a single neural network with a neck, a head, and a backbone, with varying numbers of outputs in the head. When applied to real-time data, these algorithms can also trade-off between accuracy and speed, resulting in unreliable models. On the other hand, YOLO is a series of contemporary object detection models that predicts bounding boxes and classification probabilities from complete images in single evaluations. Because of its speed, precision, more robust network architecture, and efficient training method, this model eventually superseded most traditional SOTA algorithms [7]. In recent years the YOLO detection series has been proven to be a great resource for cutting-edge real-time object detection, as well as to have a significant amount of financial potential. To use YOLOv5 for visual pollution detection we would need to train a YOLOv5 model to recognize specific types of visual pollution, such as excavation barriers, potholes, or dilapidated sidewalks. This could be done by collecting a dataset of images that contain these types of visual pollution and using them to train the model. Once the model has been trained, it can be used to detect and classify visual pollution in new images or video frames. One potential application of this approach could be to use YOLOv5 for the automated monitoring of public spaces for visual pollution, such as streets, parks, or sidewalks. This could help identify areas where intervention is needed to address visual pollution and improve an environment's appearance. It could also be used to monitor the effectiveness of efforts to reduce visual pollution over time. Due to its high speed and performance, we employed the YOLO architecture as an objective backbone detector for the current study.

Figure 1. Examples of the three categories central to this study: (**a**,**b**) represent the barrier category, (**c**,**d**) illustrate the sidewalk category, and (**e**,**f**) depict the pothole category. All RGB images were collected from Saudi Arabia.

The objective of this study is to assist government organizations with AI-based technology that automatically predicts and recognizes visual pollution without user intervention. The major contributions of this work are summarized as follows:

- The proposed AI-based real-time visual pollution prediction (VPP) aims to simultaneously detect and categorize visual pollution (VP) from color images.
- An end-to-end AI-based framework is trained and evaluated using a private dataset in a multi-class classification scenario to simultaneously predict various pollutants.
- A new private VP dataset is collected by the Ministry of Municipal and Rural Affairs and Housing (MOMRAH), Saudi Arabia. This dataset has various VP classes and is called the MOMRAH benchmark dataset: excavation barriers, potholes, and dilapidated sidewalks.
- Deep active learning (DAL) supports MOMRAH experts in automatically annotating the VP dataset for multiple tasks: detection with a bounding box and classification with a class label. The annotation process is conducted at an object level, not just at an image level. This is because some images carry multiple and different objects at once.
- A comprehensive training process is conducted to optimize and select the optimal solution for the proposed VPP. We perform various emerging AI predictors, which are MobileNetSSDv2, EfficientDet, Faster RCNN, Detectron2, YOLO-v7, and YOLOv5.
- An ablation or adaptation study is conducted to check the reliability of the proposed AI-based VPP framework when unseen images from different sources are used.

The rest of this paper is organized as follows: A review of the contemporary literature relevant to this study is presented in Section 2. Technical details of the proposed VPP framework are presented in Section 3. The results of the experimental study are reported and discussed in Section 4. Finally, Section 5 presents our conclusions.

2. Related Works

The concept of visual pollution (VP) was identified in the mid-twentieth century, alongside ongoing investigations of the malicious nature of air and water pollution. Contrary to the plethora of academic literature concentrated on air and water pollutants, however, is VP, a relatively unexplored issue essential to providing comfortable living environments in a modernizing world. Initially, researchers defined VP as the impairment of a region's visual quality caused by unnecessary advertisements and signage [8]. Lately, however, this concept has been expanded to include any element that results in landscape-based chaos; a myriad of factors, including perpetual construction, the inevitable demise of asphalt roads, erosion, and even a lack of commitment by residents in following garbage management protocols all coincide with the current interpretation of VP [9]. Exposure to VP has also been proven to beget several adverse mental and physical consequences. According to research on the effect of VP on human physiology and psychology, the absence of VP can reduce the perception of pain by increasing cortisol production in the body [1]. Recent emphasis has been placed on managing visual pollutants via identification-based software, such as a geographic information system (GIS), through which methods of cartographic visualization can be adopted in mapping and, correspondingly, reducing VP [10]. Simultaneously, Delphie and ordering weighing methods have also been used in the academic literature to manipulate a number of visual pollutants [10].

In addition, the analytical hierarchy process (AHP) is considered a multi-criteria decision-making technique for dealing with subjective and numerous contradictory criteria for investigating the effects of VP [8]. Artificial intelligence (AI) technology has recently garnered attention in several research fields, including medicine and healthcare [11–14], weather forecasting [15], energy control systems [16], army studies [17], and air as well as water pollution prediction [10]. The colossal success AI technology has had in such topics makes it highly effective in tackling various practical issues [13,18]. Deep learning feature extraction, in particular, is key in architecting a convolutional neural network (CNN) able to predict any feature-based anomaly. Figure 2 follows a contemporary timeline of advanced AI-based techniques used for object detection mentioned in [19].

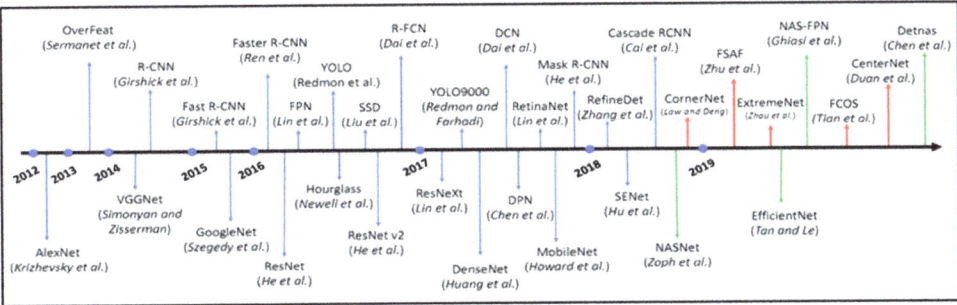

Figure 2. State-of-the-art AI-based object detection techniques [19].

In 2011, Koch et al. presented a two-stage method to detect fissures in images of asphalt roads [20]. Firstly, the image is segmented into two defect and non-defect regions, and any potential pothole shapes are determined via geometric characteristics based on said defect regions. The textural characteristics of the extracted regions are then compared with the textures of the remaining normal regions. If the textures of the defect regions are coarser and grainier than the normal surface, the region is classified as a pothole. An accuracy of 86%, precision of 82%, and recall of 86% were observed. N. Ahmed et al., on the other hand, used a deep convolutional network made up of five convoluting and max-pooling layers to classify VP into four categories: billboards and signage, network and communication towers, telephone and communication wires, and street litter [5]. They collected a dataset of 200 images per category from the Google Images search engine and achieved 95% training accuracy and 85% validation accuracy in their results. Shu et al. adopted a similar deep learning technique via the YOLOv5 model to detect pavement cracks from a dataset of 400 street view images in multiple Chinese cities [21]. A detection accuracy of 70% with a speed detection ability of 152 ms was encountered in identifying cracks in both paved and non-paved street images. Yang et al. proposed a more contemporary detection methodology based around a feature pyramid and hierarchical boosting network (FPHBN) to detect fissures [22]. This method can integrate contextual information from low-level and high-level features in a feature pyramid to generate accurate maps for fissure detection. They achieved an acceptable average intersection over union (AIU) of 0.079, but the execution time for a single image was high—approximately 0.259 s. An ensemble learning methodology was used by Liu et al. to visually detect smoke in an effort to reduce the air pollution produced by industrial factories [10]. Three different CNN architectures with five, eight, and eleven convolutional as well as pooling layers were trained separately using two different visual smoke datasets. Smoke was then detected via the ensemble majority voting strategy. The average detection results over two different datasets were obtained with an overall accuracy of 97.05%, precision of 99.86%, recall of 96.16%, and an F1-measure of 97.97%. Wakil et al. developed a visual pollution assessment (VPA) tool for predicting VP in an urban environment in Pakistan [23]. Their proposed VPA tool has assisted regulators in assessing and charting VP consistently and objectively, while also providing policymakers with an empirical basis for gathering evidence, hence facilitating evidence-based and evidence-driven policies that are likely to have a significant impact, especially in developing countries. In 2021, Wakil et al. presented a web-based spatial decision support system (SDSS) to facilitate stakeholders (i.e., development control authorities, advertisers, billboard owners, and the public) in balancing the optimal positioning of billboards under current governing regulations [24]. The SDSS system has been functional in identifying urban hot spots and exploring suitable sites for new billboards, therefore assisting advertising agencies, urban authorities, and city councils in better planning and managing existing billboard locations to optimize revenue and improve urban aesthetics [24]. Chmielewski et al. proposed a methodological framework for the measurement of VP using tangential view landscape metrics accompanied by statistically significant proofs [9]. The visible area metrics were found to be highly sensitive VP indicators; the maximum visible distance metrics provided evidence for the destructive effect of outdoor advertisements (OAs) on view corridors [9]. In this paper, an end-to-end deep learning predictor is adopted, trained, and evaluated based on real datasets generated from the KSA. The proposed prediction framework aims to simultaneously detect and classify visual pollutants in three categories: excavation barriers, potholes, and dilapidated sidewalks.

3. Materials and Methods

The schematic diagram of the proposed VPP framework is demonstrated in Figure 3. The proposed framework is able to directly predict the VP objects from the whole input image without user interactions and interventions. This is key to developing a rapid framework for real-time predicting purposes. Accurate and rapid object prediction is crucial for real-time AI applications. In this paper, a comprehensive experimental study is conducted and compares the performances of several object detection methods: MobileNetSSDv2 [25], EfficientDet [26], Faster R-CNN [27], Detectron2 [28], and YOLO [6,12–14,29,30]. The best predictor is selected to achieve the best prediction performance in a compact structure, which is determined to be YOLOv5. Thus, the proposed VPP has a compact, lightweight deep structure and could predict even multiple objects at once. Generally, deep learning detectors consist of two main parts: the CNN-based backbone used for deep feature extraction, the head predictor used to predict the class type, and the bounding box coordinators for the objects [6]. Recently, deep learning detectors are developed by inserting some different deep layers between the backbone and the head, and this part is called the neck network [6]. The VPP has a deep learning backbone for extracting deep high-level features based on the concept of deep learning convolutional networks. Indeed, many deep networks in the literature are used and have their capabilities for deep feature extraction proven, such as VGG [31], ResNet [32], DenseNet [33], Swin Transformer [34], CSP with SPP [35], and others.

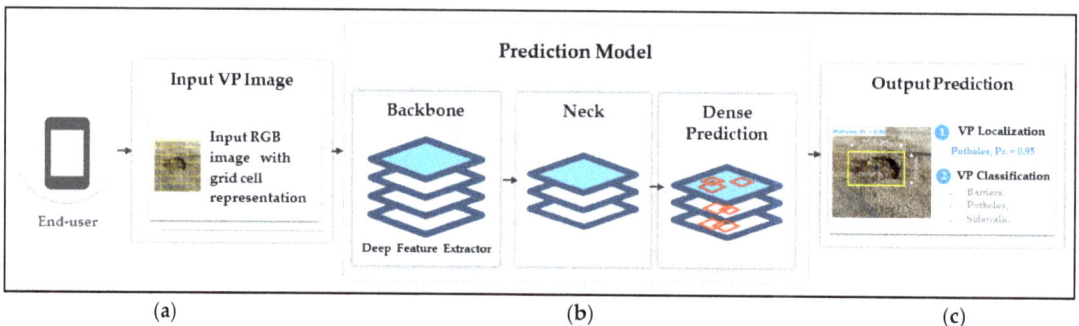

Figure 3. Abstract view of the proposed visual pollution predictor (VPP) framework based on the YOLOv5 predictor. The process consists of three steps: (**a**) feeding an input image, (**b**) using a YOLO prediction model, and (**c**) outputting a prediction with localization and classification.

The neck network is then a key link between the backbone and heads, and is designed to better use the extracted deep features via the backbone network. It includes several bottom-up and top-down deep learning paths for reprocessing and rationally using the extracted features from the backbone network. Here, the output has multiple predictors, or factors, for detection and classification tasks. Afterward, predictor layers are used to predict the object's existing probabilities. For detection, the bounding box predictors are the center coordinators (x,y), width (w), and height (h). For classification, different neurons are assigned to predict a VP object's type to be a barrier, pothole, or sidewalk. All predictors are stored in a tensor of prediction, as shown in Figure 3.

3.1. Visual Pollution Real Dataset: MOMRAH VP Dataset

The dataset is collected from different regions in the Kingdom of Saudi Arabia (KSA) via the Ministry of Municipal and Rural Affairs and Housing (MOMRAH) as a part of a visual pollution campaign to improve Saudi Arabia's urban landscape. To collect this dataset, Saudi citizens and expatriates are requested to take pictures of visual pollutants by using their smartphones and upload them to the government-created Balady mobile application [4]. Our team received official permission from Saudi Arabia's MOMRAH to use the collected data for this study. The VP real dataset is called the MOMRAH VP dataset, and it has 34,460 RGB images for three different classes, which are excavation barriers, potholes, and dilapidated sidewalks. The MOMRAH dataset is publicly published to enrich the research domain with a new VP image dataset [36]. The data distribution over three different classes is shown in Figure 4. Fortunately, some images have more than one object, and this helps to increase the number of training object ROIs. Thus, the total number of object ROIs per class are recorded to be 8417 for excavation barriers, 25,975 for potholes, and 7412 for dilapidated sidewalks. Unfortunately, this dataset lacks annotation labels for both detection and classification tasks since it is collected for the first time as a raw dataset. To annotate all of the images for detection (i.e., bounding box) and classification (i.e., classification label) tasks, a deep active learning strategy is used, where the initial 1200 VP images (i.e., 400 images per class) are manually annotated by four experts. The DAL strategy of the data annotation is presented in Section 3.3.

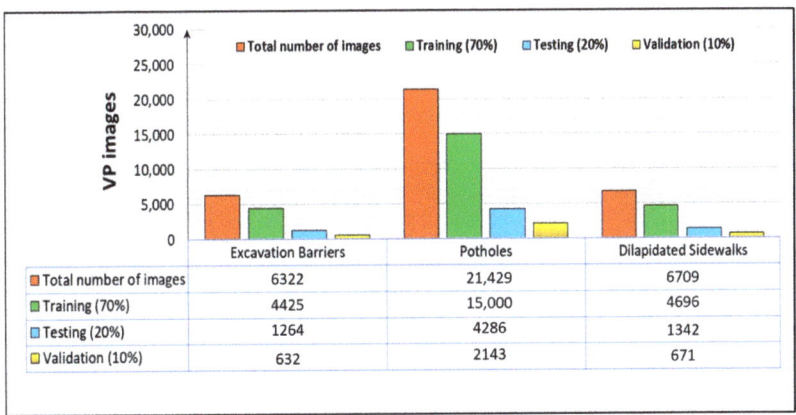

Figure 4. Visual pollution real dataset (i.e., the MOMRAH VP dataset) distribution over three different classes: excavation barriers, potholes, and dilapidated sidewalks. The dataset per class is split into 70% for training, 10% for validation, and 20% for testing.

3.2. Data Pre-Processing

The following pre-processing steps are performed to prepare the dataset for fine-tuning the deep learning models within the proposed framework: irrelevant image removal, normalization, resizing, and data splitting. Experts investigate the raw RGB images in the MOMRAH VP dataset in-depth, and irrelevant, inaccurate, or unreliable images related to the visual pollution topic are immediately excluded. Some examples of irrelevant and excluded images are depicted in Figure 5. Since the normalization process could improve the overall prediction performance, the VP images are normalized to bring their intensity into the range of [0, 255] [13,18]. Meanwhile, all images are resized using bi-cubic interpolation to scale their intensity pixels into the same range of 460×600.

Figure 5. Some examples of the irrelevant images that are excluded during the pre-processing step.

3.3. Deep Active Learning (DAL) for Automatic Data Annotation

Active learning provides an effective method for people to help annotate data, as participants only need to inspect the data they are interested in, while a learning algorithm can automatically adaptively choose and prioritize other data for annotation. Data annotation is especially expensive for object detection tasks. Each object detection frame typically has tens of thousands of pixels, and annotators have to label them manually with boxes around the objects. Annotation can be as simple as drawing a bounding box, but is still highly time-consuming. In addition to the costs, monitoring and controlling the quality of the annotations are more challenging. To summarize, human-in-the-loop may be necessary for general object detection systems, but it is expensive and more difficult in regard to controlling the quality of annotations.

Active learning uses annotated data to reduce the amount of work required to accomplish a target performance. It is used for object classification, image segmentation, and activity recognition. Active learning begins by training a baseline model using a small, labeled dataset, which is then applied to an unlabeled dataset. It estimates, for each unlabeled sample, whether this sample contains essential information that the baseline model has not yet learned by using various query selection strategies (random, uncertainty (entropy), and more). Once the samples containing the most important information have been identified and labeled by the trained model and verified by a human, they can be added to the initial training dataset to train a new model that is anticipated to perform better.

Several different strategies can be used for active learning. One common strategy is called "query by committee," which involves training a committee of multiple models on the available labeled data and then having each model make predictions on the unlabeled data. The model then selects the data points on which the models disagree the most and requests labels for those points in order to resolve the disagreement. This method, query by committee, can be effective because it allows the model to focus on the most informative and uncertain data points, leading to faster and more efficient learning. Another common strategy is "uncertainty sampling", which involves selecting data points for which the model is least certain of the correct label. In this method, data points with the highest entropy (a measure of uncertainty) or data points closest to the model's decision boundary are selected. Other active learning strategies can be used, such as "representative sampling", in which the model selects data points that are representative of the overall distribution of the data, or "variance reduction", in which the model selects data points that are expected to have the most significant impact on reducing the variance in the model's predictions. In this work, we employed the representative sampling technique using the visual similarity algorithm provided by the Voxel51 brain module.

The proposed deep learning VPP framework is developed to detect and classify the VP objects into three classes: excavation barriers, potholes, and dilapidated sidewalks. To train and develop such a VPP framework, all images in the dataset must be annotated for detection and classification tasks. For the classification task, all images are annotated by four experts in the ministry of MOMRAH by providing an associated class label for each image. For the detection task, a detection label must be represented as a bounding box to surround the whole object (i.e., ROI) inside the image with the coordinators of the start point (x_1, y_1), end point (x_2, y_2), width (w), and height (h), as shown in Figure 3a. To perform this labeling, four experts are requested in parallel to manually annotate the best and most clear 400 images from each class by using the CVAT toolbox [37]. Since the labeling process is challenging and time-consuming, the deep active learning (DAL) strategy is mainly involved and used to automatically annotate the rest of the VP images. The primary process of the DAL strategy is depicted in Figure 6. The deep active learning strategy is performed with the following steps: First, we select the best clear 400 images from each class, and four experts become involved to manually annotate the object localization by using the CVAT toolbox. Second, the best deep learning detector model is selected to be trained based on the annotated small dataset (i.e., 400 images per class). Third, the trained DL model is used to test the most relevant and similar images among the remaining unlabeled ones. Fourth, based on the query strategy, the most relevant and exciting samples are selected via the visual similarity approach to be checked by expert-in-the-loop. The selection procedure is usually carried out by checking the high similarity among the initial samples in the first round and the remaining unlabeled ones. The high-similarity instances are selected to be systematically verified and reviewed by an expert. Indeed, the experts interact with machine-in-the-loop to check, modify, and confirm the automated labeling process. The experts have to check that all of the images received some label boxes and manually adjust the boxes' locations and class labels, add some other boxes for the unseeing objects, or even delete the wrong detected boxes. Fifth, after the experts complete the labeling correction process for the first round, the AI model is retrained again using the new trusted labeled images (i.e., 400 + new confirmed subset). Finally, the VP images with lower similarity ratios that could not be labeled in the first round are used as a testing set for the second round of the DAL cycle. This way, the automatic DAL process is repeated until the stopping criteria are satisfied by correctly annotating all of the VP images.

Figure 7 shows some examples of the deep active learning procedure for annotating the images and building a benchmark dataset. Once the DAL process is completed and a benchmark dataset is built, the images per class are randomly split into three different sets: 70% for training, 10% for validation, and 20% for testing. The training and validation sets are used to train and fine-tune the AI models, while the evaluation strategy is performed using the isolated testing set.

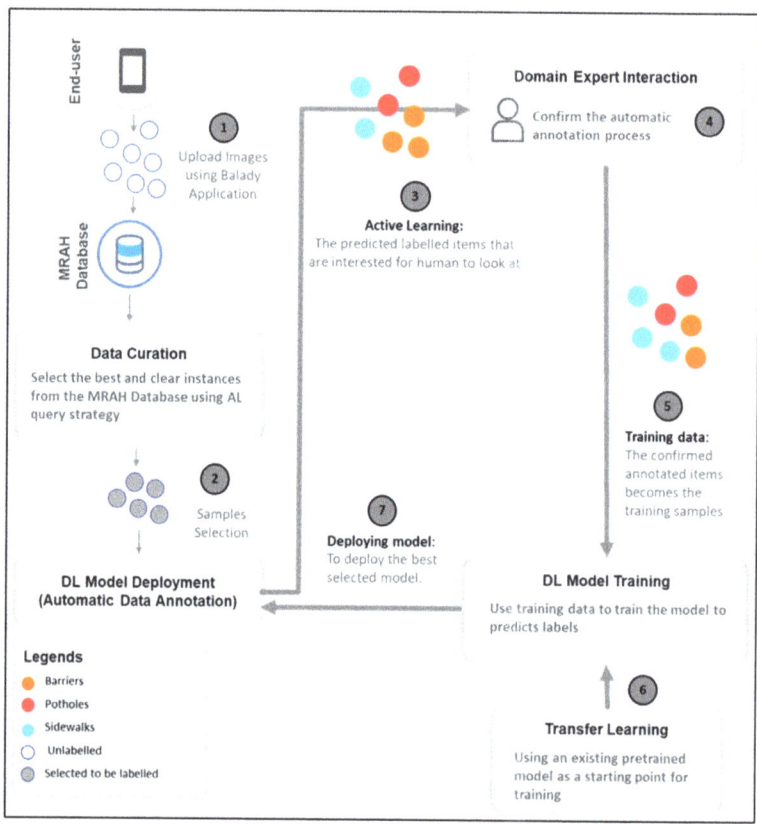

Figure 6. Deep active learning (DAL) strategy for the automatic data annotation process.

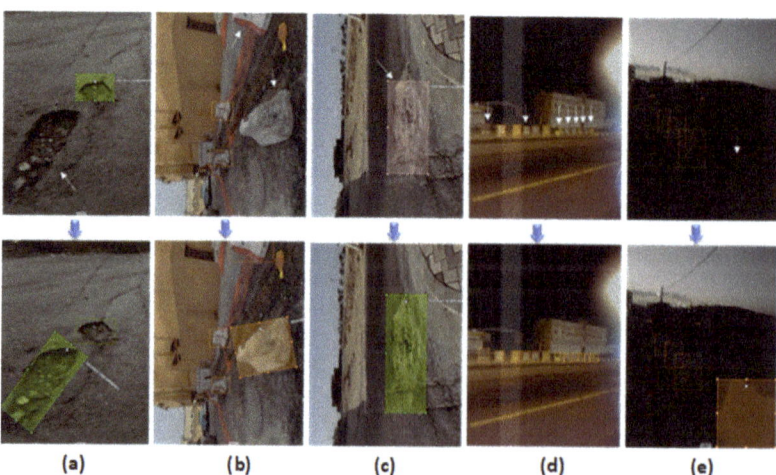

Figure 7. Some examples of the deep active learning (DAL) procedure for image annotation. The first row shows the automatic annotation via a machine during the first round, while the second row depicts the same images but with an expert's interventions and label corrections. Examples from the three categories of excavation barriers, potholes, and dilapidated sidewalks are shown in numbers (**a**–**e**).

3.4. Training Data Enlargement via an Augmentation Strategy

Training data augmentation is a well-proven technique used to enlarge the number of training images for model generalization, avoid over-fitting, and solve the class imbalance problem [38]. To effectively fine-tune deep learning models, a large number of images is required [12,39]. The effectiveness augmentation strategy is mainly used to expand the nature of the dataset. Thus, the deep learning model could be more robust due to the varying image conditions. Augmentation based on the image photometric and/or geometric distortions is recently used to increase the number of training images [6]. For photometric distortion, we imperially adjust the images' hue, saturation, and value by 0.015, 0.7, and 0.4, respectively. For geometric distortion, 0.9 random scaling, 0.1 translation, and 0.5 rotation lift-right are used. Moreover, the recent augmentation methods of Mosaic and MixUp are used with probabilities of 1 and 0.1, respectively [6]. Finally, a total VP training augmented dataset of 41,804 images is generated to fulfill the requirements of deep learning models: 8417 excavation barriers, 25,975 potholes, and 7412 dilapidated sidewalks.

3.5. The Concept of VP Object Detection—VPP-Based YOLO

The AI-based deep learning method "You Only Look Once (YOLO)" has different architectures, such as YOLOv5s, YOLOv5m, YOLOv5l, and YOLOv5x. Basically, all versions of YOLOv5 use the deep learning architecture of the cross-stage partial network (CSP) Darknet with spatial pyramid pooling (SPP) layers [35] as a backbone, a path aggregation network (PANet) [40] as a neck, and head detectors [41]. The difference among these versions basically depends on the number of feature extraction modules and the size as well as number of the convolution kernels at each specific location inside the deep network [6]. The schematic diagram of the YOLOv5 is depicted in Figure 8. We select the YOLO predictor since it has an excellent reputation as a one-stage detector with very high prediction speed [6,13,42]. Indeed, the YOLO predictor is mainly used as a detection method regression methodology. It can handle whole input images and predict both object localization as well as object classification type [41–43]. As shown in Figure 8, YOLOv5 consists of backbone, neck, and detector networks, or head predictors, representing the final prediction output.

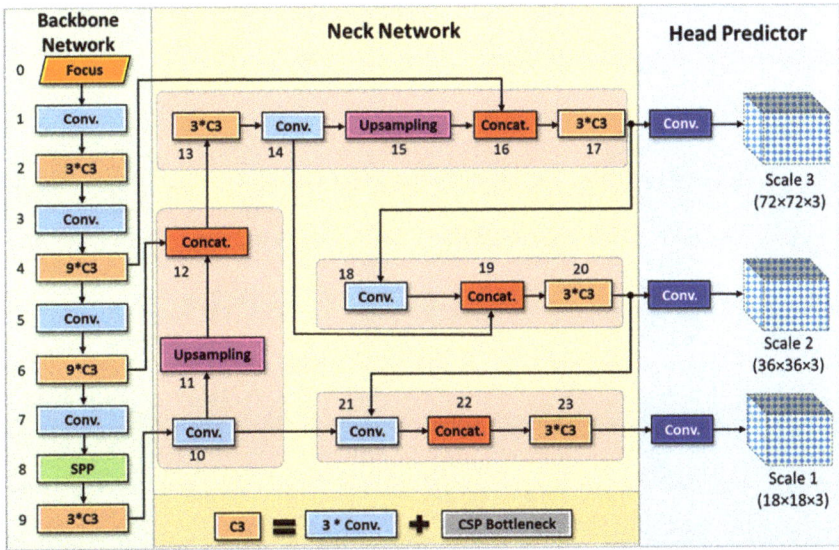

Figure 8. Schematic diagram of VPP-based YOLOv5 to detect and classify the real VP public road images. The * indicates the convolutional process.

In order to adapt to different augmented images, YOLOv5 has the capability to integrate an adaptive anchor frame calculation on the input images. Thus, YOLO could automatically initialize the anchor frame size when the input images are changed and fed to the deep networks [42]. CSP and SPP are utilized for extracting deep feature maps using multiple convolutional and pooling layers for the backbone network. In fact, the CSP network is used to accelerate the learning process, while SPP is used to extract deep features from different scales of the specific feature maps. Both CSP and SPP networks are used to increase the prediction accuracy compared to older versions of YOLO [35]. Indeed, many deep networks in the literature are used and have proven their capabilities for deep feature extraction, such as VGG [31], ResNet [32], DenseNet [33], and Swin Transformer [34]. The feature pyramid deep learning structures of the feature pyramid network (FPN) and the pixel aggregation network (PAN) are consecutively used for the neck network. The FPN conveys the strongest semantic deep features from the top to the lower feature maps. Simultaneously, the PAN is used to convey the strong localization of deep features from lower to higher feature maps. Indeed, both deep learning networks are jointly utilized to strengthen the extracted feature. Thus, the detection performance is increased due to the benefits of both the FPN and PAN. For the final detection procedure, the head predictor is utilized to detect the final target objects with different feature maps' sizes [6]. The head output is mainly designed to detect the final object localization and predict the object type inside the inputted whole image.

3.5.1. Hyperparameters' Evolution

In deep learning, hyperparameters are parameters set prior to formal training. Appropriate hyperparameters could enhance a model's performance. The YOLOv5 algorithm had 23 hyperparameters that were primarily used to set the learning rate, loss function, data enhancement parameters, and others. It was necessary to retrain the appropriate hyperparameters, since all of the data in this study were significantly different from those of the public dataset. YOLOv5 was able to perform hyperparameter optimization by using a genetic algorithm that primarily employed mutation to produce offspring based on the optimal combination of all predecessors, with a probability of 0.90 and a standard deviation of 0.20. In this study, 320 generations of iterative training were set, and the model's F1 and mAP were used to evaluate and determine the optimal hyperparameters. The optimality of the corresponding hyperparameters is denoted by the maximum value of the fitness function in the evolutionary process.

3.5.2. Transfer Learning

Transfer learning, a popular technique in deep learning, could improve the efficiency and robustness of the model training. Typically, external convolutional networks are employed primarily for extracting generic features and concentrating on individual recognition, such as color, shape, and edges. Deeper networks place a greater emphasis on learning task-specific characteristics, primarily for classifying targets. Through the characteristics of transfer learning, the detection algorithm utilized the pre-trained weight during training, eliminating the need for random initialization. This training method could decrease the model's search space and increase training efficiency. The YOLOv5 algorithm utilized the pre-trained weight from the COCO dataset, which contained 1.2 million targets in 80 categories. Although the pre-training weight contained many general features, the COCO dataset differed significantly from this study's recognition target. Therefore, it was necessary to determine if transfer learning could detect potholes, sidewalks, and barrier detection by using the model's mAP.

3.6. Experimental Setting

For training, the strategy of multi-scale training is used to learn prediction across different resolutions of the inputted VP images [40]. Moreover, a mini-batch size of 32 and a number of epochs of 100 are utilized for training and validating the proposed AI models.

A stochastic gradient descent (SGD) optimizer is used with an initial learning rate of 0.01, a final one-cycle learning rate of 0.1, a momentum of 0.937, a weight decay of 5×10^{-4}, warmup epochs of 3, a warmup momentum of 0.8, and a warmup initial bias learning rate of 0.1. The predicted box loss gain, class loss gain, and object loss gain are designed to be 0.05, 0.3, and 0.7, respectively. Moreover, the IoU training threshold and anchor-multiple thresholds are adjusted to be 0.2 and 4, respectively.

3.7. Implementation Environment

The comprehensive experimental study is achieved by using a PC with the following specifications: an Intel(R) Core(TM) i7-10700KF CPU @ 3.80GHz, 32.0 GB of RAM, six CPUs, and one NVIDIA GeForce RTX 3060 GPU.

3.8. Evaluation Strategy

We used the standard evaluation parameters regarding training loss, validation loss, precision, recall, and mean average precision (mAP). The loss of YOLOv5 was used to evaluate the inconsistency between the model prediction results and the ground truths, and it was composed of three components: bounding box loss, object loss, and classification loss. In order to prevent the under-fitting or over-fitting of the VPP model, training loss (loss of the training set) and validation loss (loss of the validation set) would be observed during the training process to obtain the optimal detection model. The mAP metric comprises the product of the accuracy and recall of the detected bounding boxes and ranges from 0 to 1, with higher values denoting superior performance. The mAP may represent the model's global detection performance, especially in comparison to F1. The mAP can be obtained by calculating the area under the corresponding precision–recall curve, which is the standard metric for evaluating an object detection algorithm. In evaluating an object detection algorithm, the mAP is frequently used as the primary performance metric. Based on the principle of IoU, the mAP is an excellent indicator of the network's sensitivity. IoU is the ratio of the overlap area between the ground truth and its predicted areas to the union area. Precision and recall are calculated using true positive (TP), false positive (FP), true negative (TN), and false negative (FN) based on the multi-class confusion matrix. The weighted average of precision and recall are utilized to calculate the F1-score (F1).

4. Experimental Results and Discussion

The experiment of this study is conducted via three evaluation scenarios. First, the dataset initially labeled by experts (i.e., 400 images per class) is used to select the best prediction AI model for our proposed VPP framework. The best AI model is also tested and verified with various activation functions to achieve the best prediction performance. Simultaneously, the trainable hyperparameters of the selected model are carefully optimized via different initialization strategies. Second, once the deep learning model is selected and optimized, the deep active learning (DAL) strategy is used to automatically annotate the remaining raw VP images in our private MOMRAH dataset. Finally, the proposed VPP framework is trained and evaluated using the big data of the labeled VP images over three trails. Meanwhile, the prediction performance of the VPP framework is directly compared with that of other state-of-the-art prediction models using the same MOMRAH dataset.

4.1. The Optimization Results of the Proposed AI-Based VPP Framework

A comprehensive experimental study is conducted to optimize the capability of the proposed AI-based VPP framework for selecting the best solution that leads to optimal prediction performance. To perform this study, the initial curated benchmark dataset (i.e., 400 images per class) annotated by the experts is used. We sequentially investigate three factors that could support the proposed framework, providing better prediction performance. First, various depth and width deep learning networks are investigated using four different YOLO architectures, which are YOLOv5s, YOLOv5m, YOLOv5l, and YOLOv5x. This is to select the optimal version of the YOLO detector that could achieve the best evaluation performance. Second, once the optimal YOLO version is selected, six activation functions are used and investigated: LeakyReLU, ReLU, Sigmoid, Mish, SiLU, and Tanh. Finally, we investigate three different initialization methods for the trainable hyperparameters of the best AI predictor selected in the first step. All of the experimental results regarding this optimization strategy are presented in the following sections.

4.1.1. Evaluation Results Based on the Various YOLO Structures' Depth and Width

By evaluating four various YOLO networks, we find that YOLOv5x achieves the best prediction performance and outperforms the other architectures. This could be due to its largest convolutional deep learning structure compared with the smaller versions (i.e., YOLOv5s, YOLOv5m, and YOLOv5l), since it is known that deeper and wider deep learning models can achieve better performance. To achieve this finding, all deep learning YOLO predictors are separately trained and tuned using the initial curated dataset, which consists of 400 VP images of each class (i.e., excavation barriers, potholes, and dilapidated sidewalks). All models are trained using the same training settings of 250 epochs and the default hyperparameter initialization method. Figure 9 depicts the optimized loss function performance over 250 epochs during the training time of all of the deep learning models. It is shown that all versions of the YOLO detectors could learn well and achieve better loss values by increasing the number of epochs. YOLOv5x is optimized well, achieving the lowest loss function compared with the other YOLO versions, while YOLOv5s is fine-tuned and achieves the lowest performance in terms of all of the loss functions, as shown in Figure 9. Figure 10 shows the evaluation metrics of precision, recall, and mAP, which were recorded for the same training settings of the four versions of the YOLO detectors. It is clearly shown that all of the evaluation metrics during the training time improve with an increase in the training epochs. This means that the deep learning detectors learned well without any over-fitting to the seen training data.

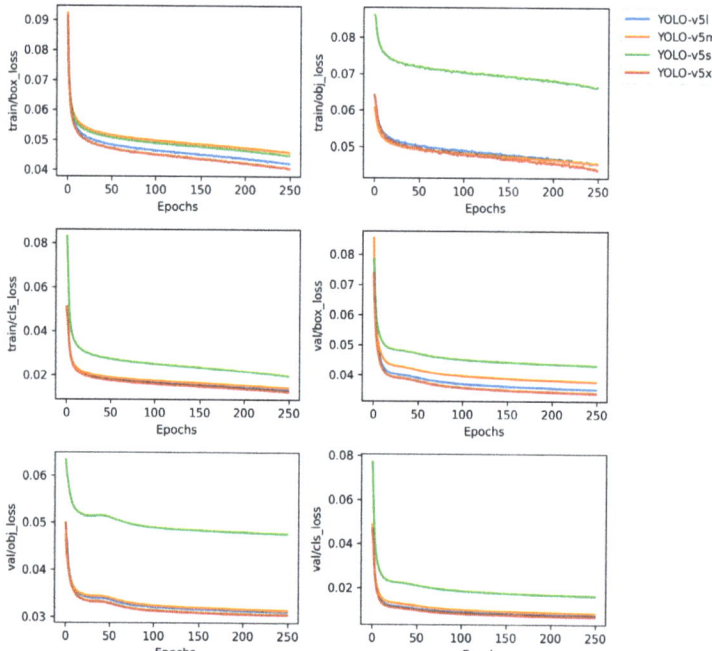

Figure 9. Training parameter optimization results of the proposed VPP framework based on various deep learning YOLO structures (i.e., YOLOv5s, YOLOv5m, or YOLOv5l) in terms of train/valid detected box, object, and cls loss functions.

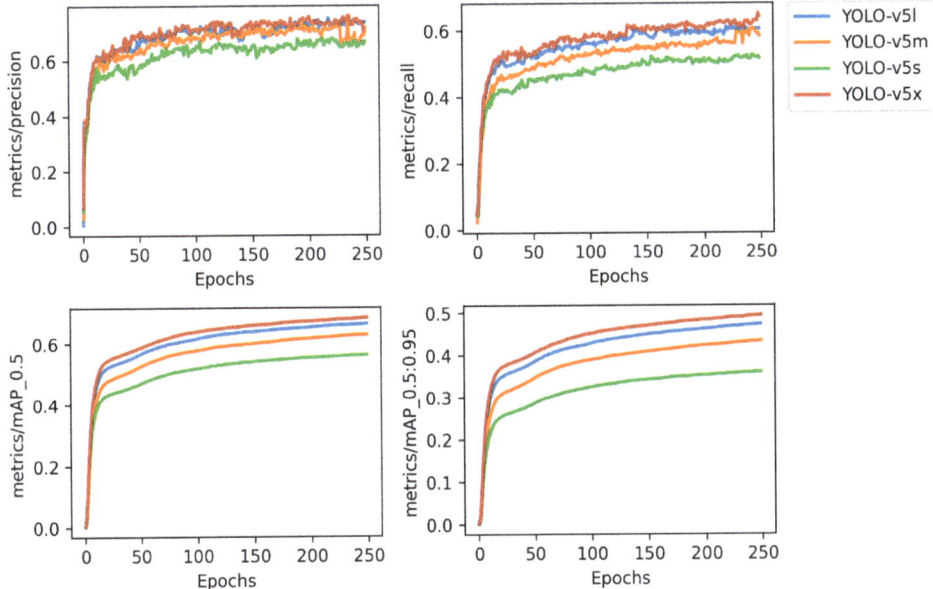

Figure 10. Evaluation performance of the proposed VPP framework based on various deep learning YOLO structures (i.e., YOLOv5s, YOLOv5m, or YOLOv5l) in terms of precision, recall, and mAP.

The best detection performance of all varieties of the YOLO detectors over three trials are presented in Table 1. It is obviously shown that YOLOv5x could achieve the best prediction performance, with 70% precision, 62% recall, an F1-score 66%, and 67% mAP. On the other hand, YOLOv5x is the heaviest deep learning model, with a model size of 169.26 MB and 88,453,800 trainable parameters. This means that its volume and number of parameters could characterize the model's complexity, requiring more GPU memory and a long time for fine-tuning all of the parameters. In contrast, YOLOv5s has the smallest deep learning architecture, with a model size of 14.08 MB and 72,318 parameters. Comparing the aforementioned experiments, it is clear that YOLOv5x is a superior deep-learning model that could achieve the best prediction performance over three classes of potholes, sidewalks, and barrier detection.

Table 1. The evaluation performance of all versions of the YOLO detectors as an average over three trails.

AI Model	Precision	Recall	F1-Score	mAP
YOLOv5s	0.65	0.50	0.57	0.55
YOLOv5m	0.69	0.57	0.62	0.61
YOLOv5l	0.72	0.59	0.65	0.65
YOLOv5x	**0.70**	**0.62**	**0.66**	**0.67**

4.1.2. Evaluation Results of the Best YOLO Candidate with Various Activation Functions

Once YOLOv5x is selected as the best candidate for the proposed VPP framework, we conduct another optimization study to select the optimal activation function that could support YOLOv5x, achieving better prediction results. Six activation functions are used to achieve this goal: LeakyReLU, ReLU, Sigmoid, Mish, SiLU, and Tanh. YOLOv5x is separately trained and evaluated six times according to each activation function. Meanwhile, YOLOv5x is fine-tuned using the initial curated dataset over 250 epochs with the default hyperparameter initialization strategy. The training and evaluation results over 250 epochs using all of the activation functions are compared, as shown in Figures 11 and 12.

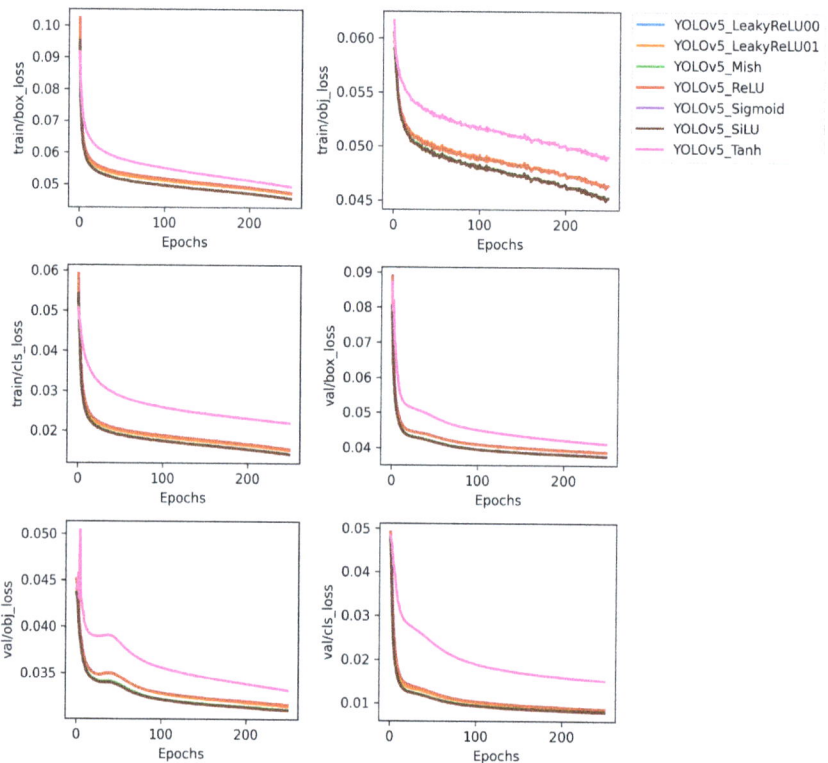

Figure 11. Training and validation loss functions of the proposed VPP framework based on the best candidate of the selected YOLOv5x over 250 epochs. The deep learning YOLOv5x is separately trained using six different activation functions: LeakyReLU, ReLU, Sigmoid, Mish, SiLU, and Tanh.

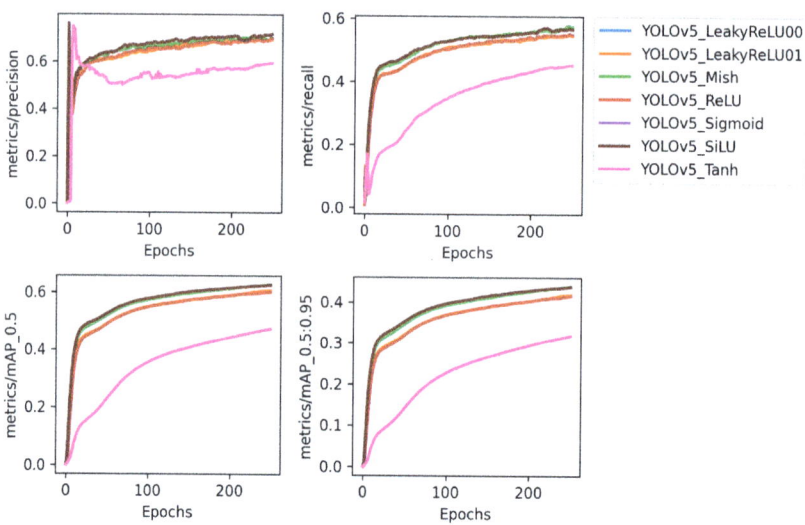

Figure 12. Evaluation prediction performance of the proposed VPP framework using different activation functions of LeakyReLU, ReLU, Sigmoid, Mish, SiLU, and Tanh.

From the empirical results, the selected activation functions of LeakyReLU, Sigmoid, Mish, and SiLU could similarly support the YOLO model to achieve better prediction performance than Tanh and ReLu. The worst evaluation performance is achieved using the Tanh activation function. To conclude, we choose to use the Mish default activation function for conducting the rest of our experiments in this study.

4.1.3. Influence of Hyperparameter Optimization on Prediction Performance

To further improve the prediction performance of YOLOv5x, an additional experimental study is conducted to investigate the most efficient training hyperparameter initialization strategy. The YOLOv5x model is separately trained using three different hyper-parameters and initialization strategies, which are hyp.scratch-low (https://github.com/ultralytics/yolov5/blob/2da2466168116a9fa81f4acab744dc9fe8f90cac/data/hyps/hyp.scratch-low.yaml (accessed on 23 June 2022)), hyp.scratch-med (https://github.com/ultralytics/yolov5/blob/2da2466168116a9fa81f4acab744dc9fe8f90cac/data/hyps/hyp.scratch-med.yaml (accessed on 23 June 2022)), and hyp.scratch-high (https://github.com/ultralytics/yolov5/blob/2da2466168116a9fa81f4acab744dc9fe8f90cac/data/hyps/hyp.scratch-high.yaml (accessed on 23 June 2022)). YOLOv5 has around 30 hyperparameters utilized for a variety of training configurations. These values are specified in *.yaml files located in the/data directory. Better initial predictions will provide better ultimate outcomes; thus, it is essential to establish these parameters correctly before evolving. The same training settings and deep learning YOLOv5x structure are used for each instance of training. By conducting this study, the training and validation loss function values could be reduced with the best evolved hyperparameters that can also support YOLOv5x to achieve better prediction performance results. Figures 13 and 14 depict the training evaluation results of YOLOv5x using various hyperparameters and initialization strategies.

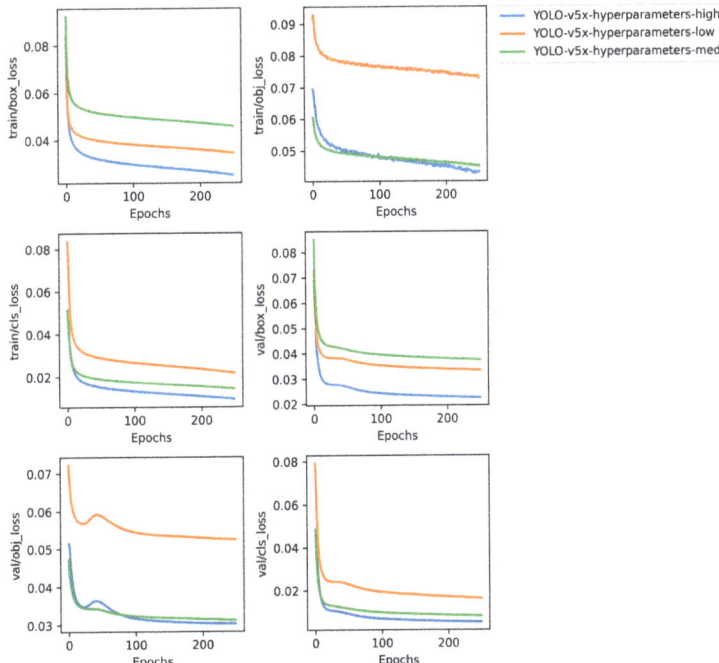

Figure 13. Training and validation loss functions of the proposed VPP framework over 250 epochs. The deep learning YOLOv5x is separately trained using three different hyperparameters and initialization strategies: hyp.scratch-low, hyp.scratch-med, and hyp.scratch-high.

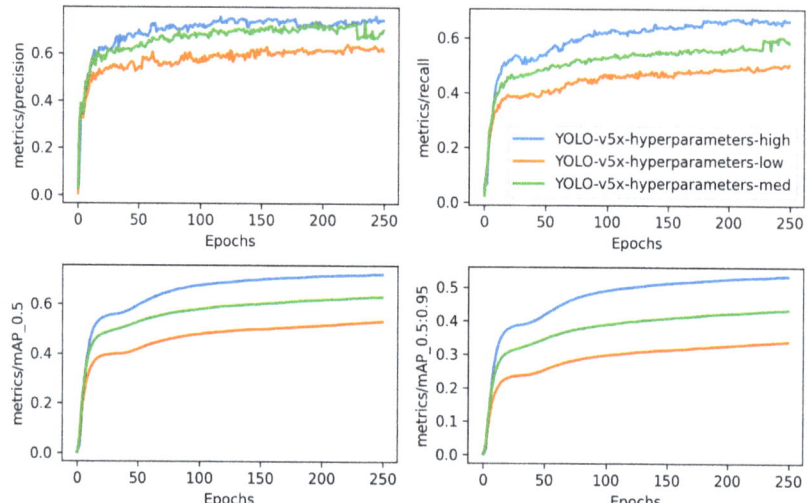

Figure 14. Evaluation prediction performance of the proposed VPP framework using three different hyperparameters and initialization strategies: hyp.scratch-low, hyp.scratch-med, and hyp.scratch-high.

The quantitative average evaluation results of the best YOLO model using three hyperparameters and initialization strategies are summarized in Table 2. As a result of varying training settings, the prediction performance in terms of mAP is increased from 53% using hyp.scratch-low to 71% with hyp.scratch-high. Indeed, the hyperparameter optimization process shows a significant improvement with 18% mAP of the prediction performance. It is important to investigate the multiple factors that could evolve the hyperparameters to boost the model's prediction performance.

Table 2. The evaluation performance of YOLOv5x with three different hyperparameters and initialization strategies.

AI Model	Precision	Recall	F1-Score	mAP_0.5
hyp.scratch-low	0.61	0.50	0.55	0.53
hyp.scratch-med	0.70	0.58	0.63	0.62
hyp.scratch-high	0.74	0.66	0.70	0.71

By using such training remedies and training setting optimization the prediction performance of the proposed VPP framework is significantly improved. Comparing the results in Tables 1 and 2, we can clearly show an improvement in performance by 15% and 5% in terms of F1-score and mAP, respectively.

4.2. Prediction Evaluation Performance during the Deep Active Learning (DAL) Strategy

After selecting the best AI model (i.e., YOLOv5x) and optimizing the model's training activation functions and hyperparameters, the DAL strategy is used to automatically annotate the reset of the unlabeled VP images in our MOMRAH private database. For the DAL query image selection strategy, we use the visual similarity approach of voxel51 brain, which can easily query and sort images to automatically find similar image examples with initial annotated ones through an app's point-and-click interface.

For the first DAL cycle, the new subset of unlabeled images is selected based on higher similarity with the previous labeled set, which is the initial annotated VP images. The new subset of selected images is then automatically labeled via the DAL strategy based on the previous fine-tuned AI model using the initial annotated images. Then, the new and initial labeled image sets are merged and used to fine-tune the deep learning model again for the next DAL cycle. This means that the number of annotated images for the coming DAL cycle will be increased, which makes the prediction results better than those of the previous cycle. For each DAL cycle, we select 500 new images based on high similarity with the previous labeled images. As shown in Figure 15, the prediction performance of the AI model is dramatically increased with an increase in the number of labeled images of each DAL cycle. Indeed, the visual similarity approach is compared with other approaches, such as random sampling and entropy-based sampling for instance selection and finding images or objects within similar examples. For each selection approach the DAL strategy based on YOLOv5x is separately conducted, and the prediction results over all of the cycles are presented in Figure 15. This means that YOLOv5x is fine-tuned for each DAL-based query selection approach using the same deep learning structure and optimized training settings as concluded in Section 4.1. Each point in Figure 15 represents the mean of three trials utilizing different shuffled initial labeled images. In the last active learning cycle, the prediction performance of 89% mAP is achieved using the visual similarity approach, which is better than the random baseline approach by 9.88%. The entropy selection approach achieves prediction performance with mAP of 85.05%, outperforming the random baseline approach with mAP of 80.65%. Indeed, the entropy method could not capture the uncertainty of bounding box regression, which is the essential part of object detection. Thus, we decide to use the annotation results using the visual similarity selection approach to conduct our experimental results in this study. We can conclude that the query selection approach plays a crucial role in improving the final prediction performance of the proposed VPP framework.

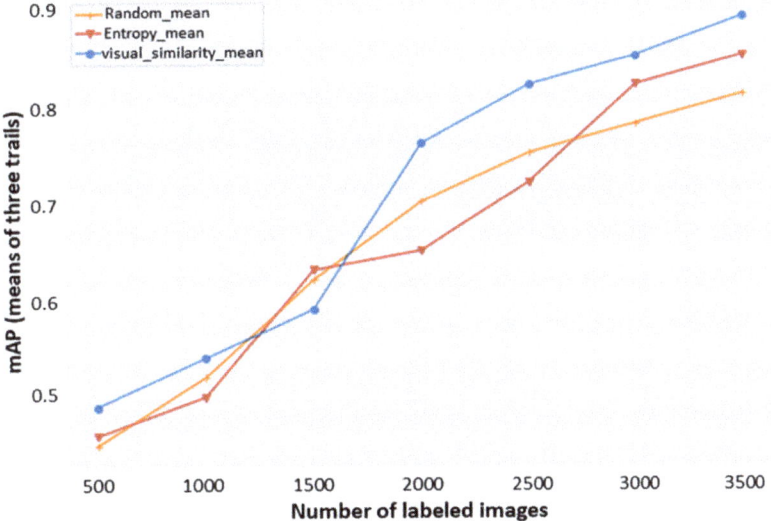

Figure 15. Active learning results of the object detection via the proposed VPP framework used to automatically annotate the VP objects in the VP images in our MOMRAH database.

4.3. Prediction Evaluation Results Using the Whole Annotated Dataset

Another study is conducted after annotating all of the VP images in our MOMRAH database. This is to investigate the capability of the proposed AI-based VPP framework using the manipulated MOMRAH big data and check the prediction performance improvements. Figures 16 and 17 illustrate the prediction behavior of the proposed AI framework using the best AI model (i.e., YOLOv5x). Up to the tenth epoch, the loss values of the box, object, and classification loss functions decrease dramatically for the validation dataset, exhibiting a rapid decline. Meanwhile, the prediction performance reached its peak in terms of evaluation metrics with 88% precision, 89% recall, and 92% mAP. Such performance is achieved as the best training weights, which are fine-tuned at epoch number 50 by using the early stopping strategy. The prediction performance is improved in comparison with the small initial dataset by 18% precision, 27% recall, and 25% mAP. This means that the DAL annotation process of the VP images is a key to achieving such promising evaluation performance.

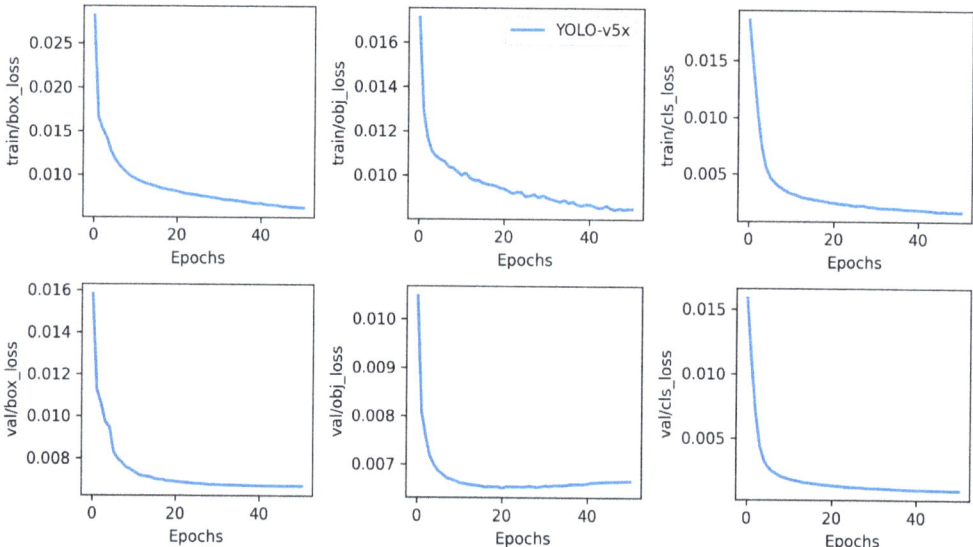

Figure 16. Training and validation loss functions of the proposed VPP framework based on YOLOv5x over 50 epochs using whole DAL-annotated VP images.

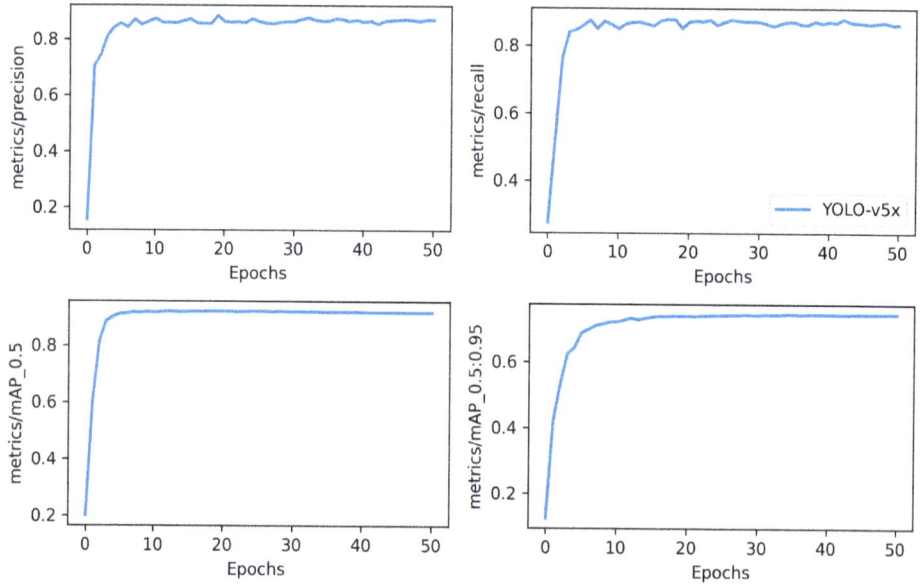

Figure 17. Evaluation prediction performance of the proposed VPP framework based on YOLOv5x using whole DAL-annotated VP images.

4.4. Evaluation Comparison Results

This section presents an evaluation comparison of the proposed VPP framework using various state-of-the-art AI-based object detectors: MobileNetSSDv2 [25], EfficientDet [26], Faster R-CNN [27], Detectron2 [28], and YOLO [6,12,14,29,30]. All of these AI detectors are trained and evaluated using our annotated MOMRAH dataset in a multi-class prediction scenario. Meanwhile, the same training settings are used to fine-tune these deep learning detectors. Such target detection methods are selected to find the optimal prediction performance of the proposed VVP framework applicable for real-time VP applications. Table 3 shows the evaluation comparison results of the proposed VPP framework based on five different AI detectors. It is clearly shown that the optimal prediction performance is achieved using YOLOv5x, with 88% precision, 89% recall, and 92% mAP. Comparing the detection capabilities of several object detection methods, the proposed method achieved the best balance between detection performance and detection speed, while also being hardware-friendly and hence more practical. After optimization, the proposed VPP framework could recognize 319 frames per second (FPS), which is better than other predictors. Recently, YOLOv7 was released after we finalize our methodology and experimental studies; however, we also evaluated it as the most current version of YOLO [7], which provided good performance in terms of mAP and FPS. In the future, YOLOv7 will be considered as the backbone of the suggested framework for more prediction improvements. Such impressive results provide us with evidence that the proposed VPP framework based on the YOLO predictor is the best solution, since it shows an encouraged capability to be applicable for real-time applications.

Table 3. Direct evaluation prediction performance of the proposed VPP framework using our annotated MOMRAH dataset. Different state-of-the-art deep learning object detectors are used for this study: MobileNetSSDv2, EfficientDet, Faster RCNN, Detectron2, and YOLO.

AI Predictor	Precision	Recall	F1-Score	mAP@0.5	Inferencing Time (Msec)	FPS
MobileNetSSDv2	0.70	0.58	0.63	0.62	600	13.2
EfficientDet	0.74	0.66	0.70	0.72	583.1	8.32
Faster R-CNN	0.84	0.77	0.80	0.80	540.2	98.2
Detectron2	0.87	0.86	0.86	0.89	342.0	120.2
YOLOv5x	0.88	0.89	0.88	0.92	22.7	319
YOLOv7	0.89	0.88	0.89	0.93	18.5	325

Moreover, some qualitative evaluation results are demonstrated in Figure 14 to show the performance of the proposed VPP-based framework using different AI predictors. The final model predictor could correctly identify all types of visual pollution. Therefore, such a sophisticated detective system might be used in real-time monitoring applications. As shown in Figure 18 and Table 3, the proposed VPP framework has the best prediction performance using the YOLOv5x perdition model. The lowest evaluation performance is recorded using MobileNetSSDv2, since an average of 62% mAP is achieved. Meanwhile, the predictors YOLOv5x and Detectron2 have almost similar prediction behaviors, with slightly better performance in the case of YOLO by 1% precision, 3% recall, and 3% mAP. As is presented in the last row of Figure 18, the proposed VPP framework has the capability to predict multiple objects in a simultaneous manner regardless of the class type. Both potholes and barriers are perfectly predicted via YOLOv5x with very high confidence scores of 93%, while EfficientDet fails to detect pothole objects. In cases where the input frame has no objects (i.e., not polluted), the VPP framework will still work and tell us that there is no pollution on this image. Therefore, no object bounding box or confidence score will be generated. This is a general aspect of any machine-based learning system (robotics, CAD systems, VP frameworks, and so on).

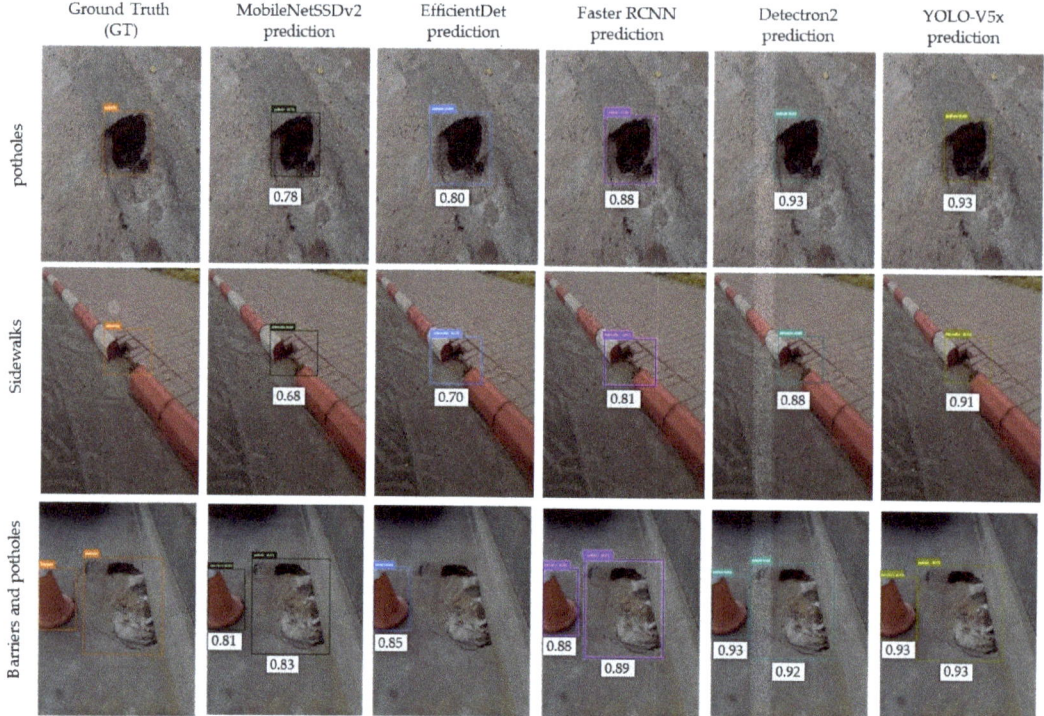

Figure 18. Qualitative evaluation results of the proposed VPP framework for VP detection and classification using AI predictors: MobileNetSSDv2, EfficientDet, Faster RCNN, Detectron2, and YOLO. The prediction object surrounding the box with its confidence score is superimposed on the original image for each AI predictor. The confidence score or classification probability is highlighted inside a small white box besides a detected object.

For indirect comparison with the existing research findings, we summarize in Table 4 some relative studies that have been conducted for VP prediction. Major research studies were conducted to identify solely potholes from road images. For our study, we propose a comprehensive AI-based framework to predict multiple objects simultaneously, such as excavation barriers, potholes, and dilapidated sidewalks. Additionally, we show our performance using precision, recall, and F1-score alongside the impressive mAP evaluation index, which is important for providing us with an impression about model prediction reliability and feasibility. Such an indirect compression always lacks a fair work comparison since the datasets, execution environments, parameter settings, and AI models are totally different. However, our study is compared with recent AI studies to understand the objective of the research area and investigate the work limitations as well as future work.

Table 4. Comparison evaluation results of the proposed VPP framework against the latest works available in the literature.

Reference	Dataset	Target Classes	Methodology	Evaluation Performance (mAP) (%)			
				Precision	Recall	F1-Score	mAP
Aparna et al. (2019) [43]	Road thermal images	Pothole	Classification via CNN-based ResNet	81.15	-	-	-
M. H. Yousaf et al. (2018) [44]	Private dataset: 120 pavement images	Pothole	Classification via SVM	71.59	-	-	-
Ji-Won Baek et al. (2020) [45]	Private road damage images	Pothole	YOLO-based algorithm	83.45	-	-	-
Pham et al. (2020) [28]	2020 IEEE Global Road Damage Cup Challenge	Longitudinal crack, transverse crack, alligator crack, and pothole	Faster-RCNN	-	-	51.40	-
Proposed *	Private MOMRAH Dataset	Excavation barriers, potholes, and dilapidated sidewalks	Simultaneous detection and classification via AI-based VPP framework	89.0	88.0	89.0	93.0

* The evaluation result of the proposed VPP is recorded using YOLOv7.

4.5. Work Limitation and Future Work

The scarcity of annotated VP images in a multi-class manner for both detection and classification tasks is always a challenge for supervised AI models. The deep active learning strategy is used for the automatic labeling process but still needs a lot of labor attention, concentration, and effort, since experts must be involved with the machine to correct the automatic labels. Including more classes in our dataset is another challenge, since the individuals that collect the VP images always have different mobile phones with different camera settings, which leads to diversity in image settings.

We have a future plan to continue improving prediction performance using advanced AI approaches such as explainable AI (XAI) to also provide explainable results besides label predictions. Meanwhile, the latest emerging AI techniques, such as transformer-based and knowledge distillation, could be good candidates for more prediction improvement once they are integrated with YOLO in a hybrid scenario, as in our preliminary study [46]. Another plan is to increase the number of classes of visual pollution (VP) to improve the proposed VPP framework to be able to predict several objects in different environments.

4.6. Ablation Study

Our private dataset is publicly published with three classes of excavation barriers, potholes, and dilapidated sidewalks. Unfortunately, we could not find similarly categorized public datasets from different sources with multiple classes to perform an ablation study using multiple classes. However, to conduct an ablation study using unseen VP images from different resources, we found a public dataset called "Pothole detection dataset" [47] but with a single pothole class with 1482 VP images. The proposed VPP framework is re-tested and verified using all VP pothole images. We achieved 81% precision, 75% recall, and 70% mAP, which is more reasonable and acceptable performance, as shown in Figure 19. Moreover, transfer learning is a recent emerging strategy that is expected to assist in producing better predication evaluation results than those received by training from scratch. As mentioned above, transfer learning is a great technique for rapidly retraining a model on new data while retraining the whole network. The proposed model is initialized with weights from a pretrained COCO model (YOLOv5X), where the backbone layers serve as feature extractors by passing the freeze argument while training. Therefore, the domain adaptations are automatically archived when evaluating the trained model on different datasets.

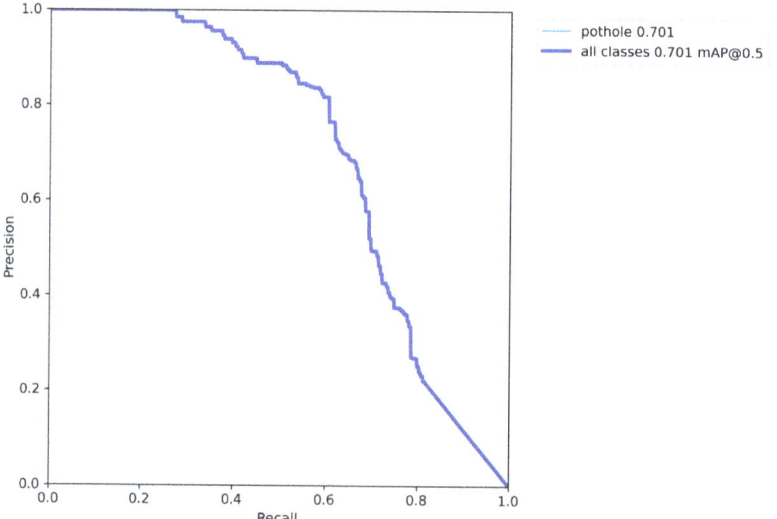

Figure 19. Precision–recall curve on a public dataset which only has images of potholes.

5. Conclusions

This paper proposes an AI-based VPP framework to detect and classify different VP objects in a multi-class simultaneous and classification scenario. To train and evaluate the proposed VPP model, the deep active learning (DAL) approach plays a crucial role in annotating our MOMRAH dataset's VP images. The DAL strategy is applied via three different query image selections: random, entropy-based, and visual similarity, achieving mAP performances of 80.65%, 85.05%, and 89%, respectively. Using annotated big data via DAL, the prediction performance of the proposed VPP framework is improved by 18% precision, 27% recall, and 25% mAP. Indeed, the VPP framework is constructed based on five state-of-the-art AI predictors: MobileNetSSDv2, EfficientDet, Faster RCNN, Detectron2, and YOLO. A comprehensive experimental evaluation study is conducted to select the best AI predictor. The derived evaluation results show that VPP-based YOLO outperforms other predictors, achieving mAP of 92% compared with the figures of 62%, 72%, 80%, and 92% for MobileNetSSDv2, EfficientDet, Faster RCNN, and Detectron2, respectively. Based on the recognition objects, the hyperparameters of the best detector are determined via a comprehensive optimization strategy where transfer learning is used to improve prediction performance. This study compared the backbone of YOLOv5 networks with various widths and depths, and the results demonstrated that, under identical setting conditions, YOLOv5x had superior usability in terms of detection performance, model weight size, and detection speed. This method achieved an optimal balance between detection performance and detection speed while being hardware-friendly, making it more applicable. Over public roads, the optimized YOLOV5x achieved 92 percent mAP in detecting barriers, potholes, and sidewalks.

Author Contributions: Conceptualization, M.A., M.A.A.-a. and J.H.; data curation, M.A., M.A.A.-a. and J.H.; funding acquisition, H.F.A.; investigation, M.A. and J.H.; methodology, M.A., M.A.A.-a. and J.H.; project administration, H.F.A.; software, M.A., M.A.A.-a. and J.H.; supervision, H.F.A.; validation, M.A.A.-a., H.F.A., B.A. and J.H.; visualization, J.H.; writing—original draft, M.A.A.-a.; writing—review and editing, M.A., M.A.A.-a., H.F.A., A.A., B.A. and J.H. All authors have read and agreed to the published version of the manuscript.

Funding: This work was supported through the Annual Funding track by the Deanship of Scientific Research, Vice Presidency for Graduate Studies and Scientific Research, King Faisal University, Saudi Arabia. (Project no. AN000673.)

Data Availability Statement: The private MOMRAH visual pollution (VP) dataset is used under permission number 4400003688 from the Ministry of Municipal and Rural Affairs and Housing, Kingdom of Saudi Arabia (KSA). The MOMRAH dataset is publicly published at the following link: https://data.mendeley.com/datasets/bb7b8vtwry (accessed on 28 October 2022).

Acknowledgments: We would like to acknowledge the project sponsors of the Annual Funding track by the Deanship of Scientific Research, Vice Presidency for Graduate Studies and Scientific Research, King Faisal University, Saudi Arabia. (Project no. AN000673.) We are thankful to the Ministry of Municipal and Rural Affairs and Housing (MOMRAH), Kingdom of Saudi Arabia (KSA), without whose permission for acquiring, using, and publishing the data this project could not have been completed. (Permission letters no. 4300454067 and 4400003688).

Conflicts of Interest: The authors declare no conflict of interest.

References

1. Campaign to Improve Saudi Arabia's Urban Landscape. Available online: https://www.arabnews.com/node/1910761/saudi-arabia (accessed on 26 April 2022).
2. Aqeel, A.B. Quality of Life. Available online: https://www.vision2030.gov.sa/v2030/vrps/qol/ (accessed on 26 April 2022).
3. Models of Drivers of Biodiversity and Ecosystem Change. Available online: https://ipbes.net/models-drivers-biodiversity-ecosystem-change (accessed on 10 December 2022).
4. Visual Pollution, Pollution A to Z. Available online: https://www.encyclopedia.com/environment/educational-magazines/visual-pollution (accessed on 25 April 2022).
5. Ahmed, N.; Islam, M.N.; Tuba, A.S.; Mahdy, M.; Sujauddin, M. Solving visual pollution with deep learning: A new nexus in environmental management. *J. Environ. Manag.* **2019**, *248*, 109253. [CrossRef]
6. Zhu, X.; Lyu, S.; Wang, X.; Zhao, Q. TPH-YOLOv5: Improved yolov5 based on transformer prediction head for object detection on drone-captured scenarios. In Proceedings of the 2021 IEEE/CVF International Conference on Computer Vision Workshops (ICCVW), Montreal, BC, Canada, 11–17 October 2021; pp. 2778–2788.
7. Wang, C.-Y.; Bochkovskiy, A.; Liao, H.-Y.M. YOLOv7: Trainable bag-of-freebies sets new state-of-the-art for real-time object detectors. *arXiv* **2022**, arXiv:2207.02696.
8. Szczepańska, M.; Wilkaniec, A.; Škamlová, L. Visual pollution in natural and landscape protected areas: Case studies from Poland and Slovakia. *Quaest. Geogr.* **2019**, *38*, 133–149. [CrossRef]
9. Chmielewski, S. Chaos in motion: Measuring visual pollution with tangential view landscape metrics. *Land* **2020**, *9*, 515. [CrossRef]
10. Liu, H.; Lei, F.; Tong, C.; Cui, C.; Wu, L. Visual smoke detection based on ensemble deep cnns. *Displays* **2021**, *69*, 102020. [CrossRef]
11. Al-Masni, M.A.; Al-Antari, M.A.; Choi, M.T.; Han, S.M.; Kim, T.S. Skin lesion segmentation in dermoscopy images via deep full resolution convolutional networks. *Comput. Methods Programs Biomed.* **2018**, *162*, 221–231. [CrossRef]
12. Al-Antari, M.A.; Al-Masni, M.A.; Choi, M.T.; Han, S.M.; Kim, T.S. A fully integrated computer-aided diagnosis system for digital X-ray mammograms via deep learning detection, segmentation, and classification. *Int. J. Med. Inform.* **2018**, *117*, 44–54. [CrossRef] [PubMed]
13. Al-antari, M.A.; Hua, C.-H.; Bang, J.; Lee, S. Fast deep learning computer-aided diagnosis of COVID-19 based on digital chest x-ray images. *Appl. Intell.* **2020**, *51*, 2890–2907. [CrossRef] [PubMed]
14. Al-Antari, M.A.; Kim, T.-S. Evaluation of deep learning detection and classification towards computer-aided diagnosis of breast lesions in digital x-ray mammograms. *Comput. Methods Programs Biomed.* **2020**, *196*, 105584. [CrossRef]
15. Salman, A.G.; Kanigoro, B.; Heryadi, Y. Weather forecasting using deep learning techniques. In Proceedings of the 2015 International Conference on Advanced Computer Science and Information Systems (ICACSIS), Depok, Indonesia, 10–11 October 2015; pp. 281–285.
16. Wang, X.; Chen, J.; Quan, S.; Wang, Y.-X.; He, H. Hierarchical model predictive control via deep learning vehicle speed predictions for oxygen stoichiometry regulation of fuel cells. *Appl. Energy* **2020**, *276*, 115460. [CrossRef]
17. Gunning, D.; Aha, D. DARPA's explainable artificial intelligence (XAI) program. *AI Mag.* **2019**, *40*, 44–58.
18. Al-antari, M.A.; Hua, C.-H.; Bang, J.; Choi, D.-J.; Kang, S.M.; Lee, S. A rapid deep learning computer-aided diagnosis to simultaneously detect and classify the novel COVID-19 pandemic. In Proceedings of the 2020 IEEE-EMBS Conference on Biomedical Engineering and Sciences (IECBES), Langkawi Island, Malaysia, 1–3 March 2021; pp. 585–588.
19. Wu, X.; Sahoo, D.; Hoi, S.C. Recent advances in deep learning for object detection. *Neurocomputing* **2020**, *396*, 39–64. [CrossRef]
20. Koch, C.; Brilakis, I. Pothole detection in asphalt pavement images. *Adv. Eng. Inform.* **2011**, *25*, 507–515. [CrossRef]
21. Shu, T.; Yan, Z.; Xu, X. Pavement crack detection method of street view images based on deep learning. *Journal of Physics: Conference Series* **2021**, *1952*, 022043. [CrossRef]
22. Yang, F.; Zhang, L.; Yu, S.; Prokhorov, D.; Mei, X.; Ling, H. Feature pyramid and hierarchical boosting network for pavement crack detection. *IEEE Trans. Intell. Transp. Syst.* **2019**, *21*, 1525–1535. [CrossRef]

23. Wakil, K.; Naeem, M.A.; Anjum, G.A.; Waheed, A.; Thaheem, M.J.; Hussnain, M.Q.u.; Nawaz, R. A hybrid tool for visual pollution Assessment in urban environments. *Sustainability* **2019**, *11*, 2211. [CrossRef]
24. Wakil, K.; Tahir, A.; Hussnain, M.Q.u.; Waheed, A.; Nawaz, R. Mitigating urban visual pollution through a multistakeholder spatial decision support system to optimize locational potential of billboards. *ISPRS Int. J. Geo-Inf.* **2021**, *10*, 60. [CrossRef]
25. Chiu, Y.-C.; Tsai, C.-Y.; Ruan, M.-D.; Shen, G.-Y.; Lee, T.-T. Mobilenet-SSDv2: An improved object detection model for embedded systems. In Proceedings of the 2020 International Conference on System Science and Engineering (ICSSE), Kagawa, Japan, 31 August–3 September 2020; pp. 1–5.
26. Tan, M.; Pang, R.; Le, Q.V. Efficientdet: Scalable and efficient object detection. In Proceedings of the 2020 IEEE/CVF Conference on Computer Vision and Pattern Recognition (CVPR), Seattle, WA, USA, 13–19 June 2020; pp. 10781–10790.
27. Ren, S.; He, K.; Girshick, R.; Sun, J. Faster R-CNN: Towards Real-Time Object Detection with Region Proposal Networks. *IEEE Trans. Pattern Anal. Mach. Intell.* **2017**, *39*, 1137–1149. [CrossRef]
28. Pham, V.; Pham, C.; Dang, T. Road damage detection and classification with detectron2 and faster r-cnn. In Proceedings of the 2020 IEEE International Conference on Big Data (Big Data), Atlanta, GA, USA, 10–13 December 2020; pp. 5592–5601.
29. Dima, T.F.; Ahmed, M.E. Using YOLOV5 algorithm to detect and recognize american sign language. In Proceedings of the 2021 International Conference on Information Technology (ICIT), Amman, Jordan, 14–15 July 2021; pp. 603–607.
30. Al-Masni, M.A.; Al-Antari, M.A.; Park, J.-M.; Gi, G.; Kim, T.-Y.; Rivera, P.; Valarezo, E.; Choi, M.-T.; Han, S.-M.; Kim, T.-S. Simultaneous detection and classification of breast masses in digital mammograms via a deep learning YOLO-based CAD system. *Comput. Methods Programs Biomed.* **2018**, *157*, 85–94. [CrossRef]
31. Simonyan, K.; Zisserman, A. Very deep convolutional networks for large-scale image recognition. *arXiv* **2014**, arXiv:1409.1556.
32. He, K.; Zhang, X.; Ren, S.; Sun, J. Deep residual learning for image recognition. In Proceedings of the 2016 IEEE Conference on Computer Vision and Pattern Recognition (CVPR), Las Vegas, NV, USA, 27–30 June 2016; pp. 770–778.
33. Huang, G.; Liu, Z.; Maaten, L. Densely Connected Convolutional Networks. In Proceedings of the 2017 IEEE Conference on Computer Vision and Pattern Recognition (CVPR), Honolulu, HI, USA, 21–26 July 2017.
34. Liu, Z.; Lin, Y.; Cao, Y.; Hu, H.; Wei, Y.; Zhang, Z.; Lin, S.; Guo, B. Swin transformer: Hierarchical vision transformer using shifted windows. In Proceedings of the 2021 IEEE/CVF International Conference on Computer Vision Workshops (ICCVW), Montreal, BC, Canada, 11–17 October 2021; pp. 10012–10022.
35. He, K.; Zhang, X.; Ren, S.; Sun, J. Spatial pyramid pooling in deep convolutional networks for visual recognition. *IEEE Trans. Pattern Anal. Mach. Intell.* **2015**, *37*, 1904–1916. [CrossRef] [PubMed]
36. Mohammad, A.; Hafiz, A.; Jamil, H.; Mugahed, A.; Bader, A.; Areeba, A. *Saudi Arabia Public Roads Visual Pollution Dataset*; King Faisal University: Hufof, Saudi Arabia, 2022. [CrossRef]
37. Tzutalin, L. LabelImg. Available online: https://github.com/tzutalin/labelImg (accessed on 25 April 2022).
38. Kim, J.-H.; Kim, N.; Park, Y.W.; Won, C.S. Object detection and classification based on YOLO-v5 with improved maritime dataset. *J. Mar. Sci. Eng.* **2022**, *10*, 377. [CrossRef]
39. Redmon, J.; Farhadi, A. YOLO9000: Better, faster, stronger. In Proceedings of the 2017 IEEE Conference on Computer Vision and Pattern Recognition (CVPR), Honolulu, HI, USA, 21–26 July 2017.
40. Liu, S.; Qi, L.; Qin, H.; Shi, J.; Jia, J. Path aggregation network for instance segmentation. In Proceedings of the 2018 IEEE/CVF Conference on Computer Vision and Pattern Recognition Workshops (CVPRW), Salt Lake City, UT, USA, 18–22 June 2018; pp. 8759–8768.
41. Redmon, J.; Divvala, S.; Girshick, R.; Farhadi, A. You only look once: Unified, real-time object detection. In Proceedings of the 2016 IEEE Conference on Computer Vision and Pattern Recognition Workshops (CVPRW), Las Vegas, NV, USA, 26 June 2016–1 July 2016; pp. 779–788.
42. Li, Z.; Tian, X.; Liu, X.; Liu, Y.; Shi, X. A two-stage industrial defect detection framework based on improved-yolov5 and optimized-inception-resnetv2 models. *Appl. Sci.* **2022**, *12*, 834. [CrossRef]
43. Bhatia, Y.; Rai, R.; Gupta, V.; Aggarwal, N.; Akula, A. Convolutional neural networks based potholes detection using thermal imaging. *J. King Saud Univ. -Comput. Inf. Sci.* **2022**, *34*, 578–588.
44. Yousaf, M.H.; Azhar, K.; Murtaza, F.; Hussain, F. Visual analysis of asphalt pavement for detection and localization of potholes. *Adv. Eng. Inform.* **2018**, *38*, 527–537. [CrossRef]
45. Baek, J.-W.; Chung, K. Pothole classification model using edge detection in road image. *Appl. Sci.* **2020**, *10*, 6662. [CrossRef]
46. Al-Tam, R.M.; Al-Hejri, A.M.; Narangale, S.M.; Samee, N.A.; Mahmoud, N.F.; Al-Masni, M.A.; Al-Antari, M.A. A hybrid workflow of residual convolutional transformer encoder for breast cancer classification using digital x-ray mammograms. *Biomedicines* **2022**, *10*, 2971. [CrossRef]
47. Universe, R. Pothole Detection Dataset. Available online: https://universe.roboflow.com/aegis/pothole-detection-i00zy (accessed on 17 December 2022).

Disclaimer/Publisher's Note: The statements, opinions and data contained in all publications are solely those of the individual author(s) and contributor(s) and not of MDPI and/or the editor(s). MDPI and/or the editor(s) disclaim responsibility for any injury to people or property resulting from any ideas, methods, instructions or products referred to in the content.

Article

Breast Abnormality Boundary Extraction in Mammography Image Using Variational Level Set and Self-Organizing Map (SOM)

Noor Ain Syazwani Mohd Ghani [1], Abdul Kadir Jumaat [1,2,*], Rozi Mahmud [3], Mohd Azdi Maasar [4], Farizuwana Akma Zulkifle [5] and Aisyah Mat Jasin [6]

[1] School of Mathematical Sciences, College of Computing, Informatics and Media, Universiti Teknologi MARA (UiTM), Shah Alam 40450, Selangor, Malaysia
[2] Institute for Big Data Analytics and Artificial Intelligence (IBDAAI), Universiti Teknologi MARA (UiTM), Shah Alam 40450, Selangor, Malaysia
[3] Radiology Department, Faculty of Medicine and Health sciences, Universiti Putra Malaysia, Serdang 43400, Selangor, Malaysia
[4] Mathematical Sciences Studies, College of Computing, Informatics and Media, Seremban Campus, Universiti Teknologi MARA (UiTM) Negeri Sembilan Branch, Seremban 70300, Negeri Sembilan, Malaysia
[5] Computing Sciences Studies, College of Computing, Informatics and Media, Kuala Pilah Campus, Universiti Teknologi MARA (UiTM) Negeri Sembilan Branch, Kuala Pilah 72000, Negeri Sembilan, Malaysia
[6] Computing Sciences Studies, College of Computing, Informatics and Media, Pahang Branch, Raub Campus, Universiti Teknologi MARA (UiTM), Raub 27600, Pahang, Malaysia
* Correspondence: abdulkadir@tmsk.uitm.edu.my

Citation: Ghani, N.A.S.M.; Jumaat, A.K.; Mahmud, R.; Maasar, M.A.; Zulkifle, F.A.; Jasin, A.M. Breast Abnormality Boundary Extraction in Mammography Image Using Variational Level Set and Self-Organizing Map (SOM). *Mathematics* 2023, *11*, 976. https://doi.org/10.3390/math11040976

Academic Editors: Ezequiel López-Rubio, Esteban Palomo and Enrique Domínguez

Received: 31 December 2022
Revised: 31 January 2023
Accepted: 11 February 2023
Published: 14 February 2023

Copyright: © 2023 by the authors. Licensee MDPI, Basel, Switzerland. This article is an open access article distributed under the terms and conditions of the Creative Commons Attribution (CC BY) license (https://creativecommons.org/licenses/by/4.0/).

Abstract: A mammography provides a grayscale image of the breast. The main challenge of analyzing mammography images is to extract the region boundary of the breast abnormality for further analysis. In computer vision, this method is also known as image segmentation. The variational level set mathematical model has been proven to be effective for image segmentation. Several selective types of variational level set models have recently been formulated to accurately segment a specific object on images. However, these models are incapable of handling complex intensity inhomogeneity images, and the segmentation process tends to be slow. Therefore, this study formulated a new selective type of the variational level set model to segment mammography images that incorporate a machine learning algorithm known as Self-Organizing Map (SOM). In addition to that, the Gaussian function was applied in the model as a regularizer to speed up the processing time. Then, the accuracy of the segmentation's output was evaluated using the Jaccard, Dice, Accuracy and Error metrics, while the efficiency was assessed by recording the computational time. Experimental results indicated that the new proposed model is able to segment mammography images with the highest segmentation accuracy and fastest computational speed compared to other iterative models.

Keywords: active contour; mammography images; selective segmentation; SOM; variational level set

MSC: 68U10; 00A71

1. Introduction

Nowadays, cancer has become a leading cause of death worldwide. The Ministry of Health [1] stated that breast cancer is a serious disease that primarily affects women. Breast cancer is a type of cancer that is found in the breast tissue and happens when cells in the breast grow in an uncontrolled way. Spreafico et al. [2] stated that this cancer can affect both males and females, however, it is more common among females compared to males. Mammography, MRI and ultrasound are several types of breast cancer diagnostic techniques that function to detect breast abnormalities at an early stage and help to improve the chance of successful treatment [3]. Among all those techniques, mammography, which is a breast cancer screening technology that provides grayscale images of the breast, is the gold standard technique used for early-stage detection of breast abnormalities.

In medicine, segmentation plays an important role and has been widely developed in medical imaging technologies such as mammograms since it is an automated diagnostic system that can extract the boundary of the abnormality region [4]. Segmentation is also known as the process of splitting or extracting an image into several segments or objects that helps to reduce the image's complexity for subsequent analysis. The variational segmentation approaches were normally derived in a level set mathematical framework by minimizing the cost energy function using calculus of variations [5,6], while non-variational segmentation approaches were usually based on the heuristic approach [7]. There is a wide range of literature on the non-variational (non-level set) segmentation method in extracting the abnormality region using mammography images. For instance, the fuzzy technique [6], Intuitionistic Fuzzy Image Processing [8], clustering-based methods [9–12] and neural network [13]. Other than that, deep learning methods such as the U-net model [14] are frequently used for mammogram image segmentation [15]. The non-variational approaches had tremendous use and success in the past and can obtain fast solutions; however, they are too reliant on the amount of data [16], which is hard to implement when the amount of time needed is short, with drawbacks in terms of accuracy since it was based on the heuristic approach [7].

On the other hand, variational level set-based segmentation approaches are more structured and capable of achieving high speeds, accuracy and performance stability according to [7,17]. According to [18], variational level set-based segmentation techniques can be divided into two main categories: level set-based global segmentation (global variational) and level set-based selective segmentation (selective variational). Global segmentation necessitates segmenting the boundary of all objects in an input image. Meanwhile, selective segmentation only segments the desired object from an input image according to specific geometrical restrictions.

In the literature, well-known global variational active contour models were implemented by [19] on grayscale mammography images. Meanwhile, in 2017, Ciecholewski [20] applied the Active Contour Without Edges (ACWE) model [21] but was unable to produce a satisfactory result when faced with a strong intensity inhomogeneity of images. Because of that, the authors in [22] combined the ACWE model with the Fuzzy C means clustering method to handle the intensity inhomogeneity of images and reduce the presence of noise. Other than that, Somroo and Choi [23] introduced a novel shifted Heaviside signed pressure force (SPF) function. However, the SPF function fails to segment the targeted object that is near the neighbor object or the boundary is fuzzy. Two other related works on the level-set global segmentation method using mammography images are [24,25].

Indeed, all the studies mentioned above are for level set-based global segmentation, as all features in an image should be segmented. However, the result produced by global segmentation may have poor segmentation quality when the targeted abnormality regions have almost similar intensities or are very close to healthy tissue boundaries, have fuzzy contours, low contrast and the presence of noise [26]. Therefore, variational level set-based selective image segmentation is more convenient to implement as this method aims to extract a single target object from an image using additional geometric constraint information.

Selective segmentation is concerned with segmenting or extracting a specific object in a given image, depending on minimal user input [27–29]. There is scarce research involving variational level set-based selective segmentation for grayscale mammography images. The related research on level set-based selective models for grayscale images was introduced by [26,30,31]. Other than that, according to [31,32], the state-of-the-art model in selective segmentation is the Interactive Image Segmentation (IIS) model [33]. In [33], they introduced the IIS model with two sets of geometric constraints, namely geometric points for the inside and outside of a targeted object. This model is capable of segmenting both grayscale and vector-valued images. The most recent and effective research on selective segmentation techniques was proposed by [34]. They reformulated the model that was completed by [18] by incorporating an image enhancement technique in the fitting term to segment mammography images. While the result was successful, the total variation

(TV) term used in the formulation is computationally expensive, which will slow down the segmentation process [35]. In addition, their model cannot segment mammography images with complex intensity inhomogeneity.

One effective approach to segment an image with intensity inhomogeneity is to incorporate an unsupervised neural network machine learning algorithm, namely the Self-Organizing Map (SOM), in a variational level set formulation called SOMCV as proposed by Abdelsamea et al. [36]. Although the SOMCV model was formulated in a global segmentation framework, we found that the SOMCV is capable of selectively segmenting a targeted object in an image due to the advantage of using SOM in the formulation. This can be achieved by placing the initial contour relatively close to the targeted object.

Therefore, with these problems and motivations, the aim of this study is to formulate a new selective type of the variational level set model to segment mammography images that incorporates the ideas of selective segmentation from [34] and the idea of using the unsupervised neural network algorithm, SOM, from [36]. The next section of this paper provides a brief overview of the models that are related to this study, followed by formulations of the proposed models. Then, the experimental outcomes of the existing and proposed models are presented.

2. Review of the Existing Models

This section provides a brief review of the models that are significant to this study.

2.1. Chan and Vese (CV) Model

Active Contour Without Edges by [21], which is formulated based on [37], is very important in variational image segmentation. In this model, it is assumed that the image $u_0 = u_0(x,y)$ is constructed using two regions where the intensities of unknown values d_1 and d_2 are approximately piecewise constant, separated by an unknown curve or contour D. Let the image domain be Ω. Assume the detected object is represented by the region Ω_1 with the value d_1 inside the curve D, whereas the intensity of u_0 is approximated by the value d_2 in $\Omega_2 = \Omega \setminus \Omega_1$, outside the curve D.

The level set technique, developed by [38], is applied, in which the unknown curve D is represented by the zero level set of the Lipschitz function φ. Thus, the CV model is defined as:

$$\min_{\varphi, d_1, d_2} CV(\varphi, d_1, d_2),$$
$$CV(\varphi, d_1, d_2) = \mu \int_\Omega |\nabla H(\varphi)| d\Omega + \alpha^+ \int_\Omega (u_0 - d_1)^2 H(\varphi) d\Omega + \alpha^- \int_\Omega (u_0 - d_2)^2 (1 - H(\varphi)) d\Omega \quad (1)$$

Here, the non-negative parameters μ, α^+ and α^- represent the weights of the regularizing term and the fitting term, respectively. They introduce a Heaviside function, $H(\varphi(x,y))$, and a Dirac delta function, $\delta(\varphi(x,y))$, with small (near zero) constant ε for curve stability [39]. Then, keeping d_1 and d_2 consistent in $CV(\varphi, d_1, d_2)$ leads to the following Euler Lagrange (EL) Equation for φ:

$$\begin{cases} \mu \delta(\varphi) \nabla \cdot \left(\frac{\nabla \varphi}{|\nabla \varphi|} \right) - \alpha^+ \delta(\varphi)(u_0 - d_1)^2 + \alpha^- \delta(\varphi)(u_0 - d_2)^2 = 0 & in\ \Omega, \\ \frac{\delta(\varphi)}{|\nabla \varphi|} \frac{\partial u_0}{\partial \vec{n}} = 0 & on\ \partial \Omega. \end{cases} \quad (2)$$

where $|\nabla \varphi|$ is the norm of the gradient of the level set function φ, also known as the TV term. The finite difference method is then applied to solve the EL equation. Nonetheless, the CV model produces unsatisfactory results when segmenting a targeted object in intense inhomogeneity vector-valued images and has a high computational cost due to the existence of a highly non-linear curvature term $\nabla \cdot \left(\frac{\nabla \varphi}{|\nabla \varphi|} \right)$, as shown in Equation (4).

2.2. SOM-Based Chan–Vese (SOMCV) Model

Abdelsamea et al. [36] successfully developed a global segmentation model based on the unsupervised neural network SOM approach, called the SOM-based Chan–Vese model (SOMCV). It works by directly incorporating information from the prototype neurons in a trained SOM to decide whether to shrink or expand the existing contour during the iterative optimization process.

During the training process, the neurons of each SOM are topologically arranged in the corresponding map based on their prototypes (weights), and the neurons at a certain geometric distance from them are moved toward the current input using the classical self-organization learning rule of the SOM, expressed by:

$$s_p(t+1) := s_p(t) + \eta(t)g_{cp}(t)\left[u_0^{(tm)}(x_t, y_t) - s_p(t)\right], \quad (3)$$

where $\eta(t)$ is the learning rate defined as:

$$\eta(t) := \eta_0 \exp\left(-\frac{1}{\kappa_\eta}\right), \quad (4)$$

The intensity $u_0^{(tm)}(x_t, y_t)$ of a randomly-extracted pixel (x_t, y_t) of a training image is applied as the input to the SOM at time $t = 0, 1, 2, \ldots t_{max}^{(tm)} - 1$, where $t_{max}^{(tm)}$ is the number of iterations in the SOM's training. The function $g_{cp}(t)$ is a neighborhood kernel at time t of the neuron p around the Best-Matching Unit (BMU) neuron c defined as

$$g_{cp}(t) := \exp\left(-\frac{||m_b - m_n||^2}{2m^2(t)}\right), \quad (5)$$

where $m_b, m_n \in R^2$ are the location vectors of neurons b and n in the output neural map, and $m(t)$ is a time-decreasing neighborhood radius which is expressed as follows:

$$m(t) := m_0 \exp\left(-\frac{t}{\kappa_m}\right), \quad (6)$$

where $m_0 > 0$ is the initial neighborhood radius of the map and $\kappa_m > 0$ is another time constant. Once the SOM's training has been achieved, the trained network is adapted online in the testing session to estimate and describe globally the foreground and background intensity distributions of an identical test image $u_0(x, y)$ during the evolution of the contour D. For each neuron p, the quantities

$$s_k^+ := \text{argmin}_p |s_p - \text{mean}(u_0(x,y)|(x,y) \in in(D))|, \quad (7)$$

$$s_k^- := \text{argmin}_p |s_p - \text{mean}(u_0(x,y)|(x,y) \in out(D))|, \quad (8)$$

which are the distances of the associated prototype s_p from the mean intensities of the current foreground and background approximations, respectively, are also calculated repeatedly throughout the testing session. Therefore, the energy function of the proposed SOMCV model is defined as:

$$E_{SOMCV}(\varphi) := \alpha^+ \int_\Omega e^+ H(\varphi(x,y))d\Omega + \alpha^- \int_\Omega e^- (1 - H(\varphi(x,y)))d\Omega. \quad (9)$$

where $\alpha^+, \alpha^- \geq 0$, φ is the segmentation curve, H is the Heaviside function, $e^+(x, y, D) := \left(u_0(x,y) - s_k^+(D)\right)^2$ and $e^-(x, y, D) := \left(u_0(x,y) - s_k^-(D)\right)^2$. The model can be iteratively solved using the finite differences method.

2.3. Primal-Dual Selective Segmentation 2 (PD2) Model

Recently, Ghani et al. [34] developed a selective segmentation model, namely the Primal-Dual Selective Segmentation 2 (PD2). This model is an improvement on the prior model proposed by Jumaat and Chen [18], termed the Primal-Dual Selective Segmentation (PD) model. The PD model may yield disappointing results for low-contrast images. Therefore, Ghani et al. [34] modified the PD model by replacing the fitting term with an image enhancement algorithm which can enhance low-contrast images. Now, we will introduce the PD model.

Assume $u_0 = u_0(x,y)$ as the image in domain Ω. Here, the marker set $A = \{m_j = (x_j, y_j) \in \Omega, 1 \leq j \leq n\}$ is introduced to generate the polygon S with marker points $n(\geq 3)$ that will be set close to the targeted object. $R_d(x,y)$ functions as the Euclidean distance of each point $(x,y) \in \Omega$ from its nearest points of $(x_s, y_s) \in S$:

$$R_d(x,y) = \sqrt{(x - x_s)^2 + (y - y_s)^2}. \tag{10}$$

Then, the PD model is defined as:

$$\min_{a,b \in [0,1]} \{PD(a,b) = \mu \int_\Omega |\nabla a|_g d\Omega + \int_\Omega rb\, d\Omega + \theta \int_\Omega R_d b\, d\Omega + \frac{1}{2\tau} \int_\Omega (a-b)^2 d\Omega\} \tag{11}$$

where μ, θ and τ indicate the weightage parameters used to control the TV function, $|\nabla a|_g$, distance function, R_d and penalty term, $(a - b)^2$, respectively. In addition, the function r is defined as the fitting term where $r = (k_1 - u_0)^2 - (k_2 - u_0)^2$, b is a dual variable and $g(x,y)$ is known as the edge detector function. k_1 and k_2 are the unknown constants that specify the average intensity of input image inside and outside the contour a.

Let u_{HS} be the output image by applying the image enhancement approach that will enhance the contrast of an input image so that the hidden information can be revealed for a better segmentation result. The modified PD model, termed PD2, is defined by replacing the fitting term, u_0, in Equation (11) with an image enhancement algorithm (u_{HS}) as follows:

$$PD2(a,b) = \mu \int_\Omega \left(|\nabla a|_g + \left[(k_1 - u_{HS})^2 - (k_2 - u_{HS})^2 \right] b + \theta R_d b + \frac{1}{2\tau}(a-b)^2 \right) d\Omega. \tag{12}$$

Equation (12) is solved using an alternating minimization approach.

3. The Proposed Models

The PD2 model [34] may lead to a slow segmentation process due to the existence of the total variation function. Moreover, this model cannot handle images with complex intensity inhomogeneity. Therefore, the main idea of this study is to formulate a new selective type of the variational level set model to segment mammography images that incorporate the ideas of selective segmentation from [34] and the idea of using SOM from [36].

Thus, the variational energy functional minimization problem of the proposed model, termed the Selective Self-Organizing Map (SSOM), is defined as:

$$E_{SSOM}(D) := \alpha^+ \int_{in(D)} \left(u_0(x,y) - s_k^+(D) \right)^2 dxdy + \alpha^- \int_{out(D)} \left(u_0(x,y) - s_k^-(D) \right)^2 dxdy + \int_{inside(D)} \theta R_d(x,y) dxdy. \tag{13}$$

The functions s_k^+ and s_k^- are similarly defined as given in Equation (7) and (8), respectively. The parameters $\alpha^+, \alpha^- \geq 0$ represent the weights of two image energy terms inside and outside the contour, respectively, while $\theta > 0$ is known as the area of parameter of the distance fitting term. The value of θ in each image changes according to the targeted object. If the area parameter is set to a value that is too large, the outcome will just be the polygon S, which is undesirable. To compute Equation (13) in whole image domain Ω, the contour curve D is then replaced with the level set function φ, obtaining:

$$\min_{\varphi} E_{SSOM}(\varphi) := \alpha^+ \int_\Omega H(\varphi)\big(u_0(x,y) - s_k^+(D)\big)^2 d\Omega$$
$$+\alpha^- \int_\Omega (1 - H(\varphi))\big(u_0(x,y) - s_k^-(D)\big)^2 d\Omega + \int_\Omega \theta H(\varphi) R_d d\Omega, \tag{14}$$

where $\varphi(x,y)$ and $S_d(x,y)$ are replaced with φ and R_d, respectively, for simplicity. The Heaviside step function H and Dirac function δ are defined as

$$H(\varphi(x,y)) = \frac{1}{2}\left[1 + \frac{2}{\pi}\tan^{-1}\left(\frac{\varphi}{\varepsilon}\right)\right] \tag{15}$$

$$\delta(\varphi(x,y)) = H'(\varphi(x,y)) = \frac{\varepsilon}{\pi(\varepsilon^2 + \phi^2)}, \tag{16}$$

where ε is a constant used to avoid values of H and δ that tend to be zero, which potentially leads to the failure of the object to be extracted if it is far from the initial contour.

3.1. Derivation of Euler Lagrange (EL) Equation

The optimization problem of the energy function in Equation (14) can be solved using the Calculus of Variation technique to obtain the EL equation, $\partial E_{SSOM}(\varphi)/\partial \varphi$. The evolution of the level set function $\varphi(x,y)$ should satisfy the EL equation. To derive the EL equation, let the integrand $I_1(\varphi) = H(\varphi)$, $I_2(\varphi) = (1 - H(\varphi))$ and the Taylor expansion equation at $i = 0$ be defined as follows:

$$f(i) = f(0) + f'(0)a + O(i^2)$$
$$= (x^2 + y^2)^q + q(x^2 + y^2)^{q-1}(2xg_1 + 2yg_2)i + O(i^2) \tag{17}$$

Afterwards, by adding the variation ηv to the level set function φ such that $\varphi = \varphi + \eta v$, where v in an arbitrary test function and η is a close-to-zero real parameter, it becomes

$$I_1(\varphi + \eta v) = H(\varphi + \eta v), \quad I_2(\varphi + \eta v) = 1 - H(\varphi + \eta v). \tag{18}$$

Next, we differentiate $I_1(\varphi + \eta v) = H(\varphi + \eta v)$ and $I_2(\varphi + \eta v) = 1 - H(\varphi + \eta v)$ with respect to η as follows:

$$\frac{d}{d\eta} I_1(\varphi + \eta v) = \frac{d}{d\eta} H(\varphi + \eta v) = H'(\varphi + \eta v)v = \delta_\varepsilon(\varphi + \eta v)v, \tag{19}$$

$$\frac{d}{d\eta} I_2(\varphi + \eta v) = \frac{d}{d\eta}(1 - H_\varepsilon(\varphi + \eta v)) = -H_\varepsilon'(\varphi + \eta v)v = -\delta_\varepsilon(\varphi + \eta v)v. \tag{20}$$

Therefore, applying Taylor expansion, which is Equation (17), at $\eta = 0$ will give

$$I_1(\varphi + \eta v) = I(\varphi) + I'(\varphi)\eta + O(\eta^2) = H_\varepsilon(\varphi) + \delta_\varepsilon(\varphi)v\eta + O(\eta^2), \tag{21}$$

and

$$I_2(\varphi + \eta v) = I_2(\varphi) + I_2'(\varphi)\eta + O(\eta^2) = (1 - H_\varepsilon(\varphi)) - \delta_\varepsilon(\varphi)v\eta + O(\eta^2). \tag{22}$$

Now, the first variation of $E_{SSOM}(\varphi)$ in Equation (14) is defined as

$$\frac{\partial E_{SSOM}(\varphi)}{\partial \varphi} = \lim_{\eta \to 0} \frac{E_{SSOM}(\varphi + \eta v) - E_{SSOM}(\varphi)}{\eta} = 0 \tag{23}$$

Before the evaluation of Equation (31), we initially compute

$$\int_\Omega \frac{E_{SSOM}(\varphi+\eta v) - E_{SSOM}(\varphi)}{\eta} d\Omega$$
$$= \frac{1}{\eta} \int_\Omega \left[\alpha^+ \left(u_0(x,y) - s_k^+(D)\right)^2 \left(H_\varepsilon(\varphi) + \delta_\varepsilon(\varphi)v\eta + O(\eta^2) - H_\varepsilon(\varphi)\right) \right.$$
$$+ \alpha^- \left(u_0(x,y) - s_k^-(D)\right)^2 \left(1 - H_\varepsilon(\varphi) - \delta_\varepsilon(\varphi)v\eta + O(\eta^2) - (1 - H_\varepsilon(\varphi))\right)$$
$$\left. + \theta R_d \left(H_\varepsilon(\varphi) + \delta_\varepsilon(\varphi)v\eta + O(\eta^2) - H_\varepsilon(\varphi)\right) \right] d\Omega \quad (24)$$

Simplifying Equation (24), it becomes

$$\int_\Omega \frac{E_{SSOM}(\varphi+\eta v) - E_{SSOM}(\varphi)}{\eta} d\Omega = \frac{1}{\eta} \int_\Omega \left[\alpha^+ \left(u_0(x,y) - s_k^+(D)\right)^2 \left(\delta_\varepsilon(\varphi)v\eta + O(\eta^2)\right) \right.$$
$$+ \alpha^- \left(u_0(x,y) - s_k^-(D)\right)^2 \left(-\delta_\varepsilon(\varphi)v\eta + O(\eta^2)\right)$$
$$\left. + \theta R_d \left(\delta_\varepsilon(\varphi)v\eta + O(\eta^2)\right) \right] d\Omega \quad (25)$$

Next, we evaluate Equation (23) using information from Equation (25):

$$\int_\Omega \left[\delta_\varepsilon(\varphi) v \left(\alpha^+ \left(u_0(x,y) - s_k^+(D)\right)^2 - \alpha^- \left(u_0(x,y) - s_k^-(D)\right)^2 + \theta R_d \right) \right] d\Omega = 0 \quad (26)$$

The integrand in Equation (26) will be zero if

$$\delta_\varepsilon(\varphi) v \left(\alpha^+ \left(u_0(x,y) - s_k^+(D)\right)^2 - \alpha^- \left(u_0(x,y) - s_k^-(D)\right)^2 + \theta R_d \right) = 0 \quad (27)$$

Finally, since it should be satisfied with the arbitrary function v, the EL equation for the SSOM model is

$$-\delta_\varepsilon(\varphi) \left(-\alpha^+ \left(u_0(x,y) - s_k^+(D)\right)^2 + \alpha^- \left(u_0(x,y) - s_k^-(D)\right)^2 - \theta R_d \right) = 0 \quad (28)$$

Hence, applying the gradient descent method will obtain the following gradient descent flow:

$$\frac{\partial \varphi}{\partial t} = -\frac{\partial E_{SSOM}(\varphi)}{\partial \varphi} = \delta_\varepsilon(\varphi) \left(-\alpha^+ \left(u_0(x,y) - s_k^+(D)\right)^2 + \alpha^- \left(u_0(x,y) - s_k^-(D)\right)^2 - \theta R_d \right) \quad (29)$$

Equation (29) is solved and discretized using the forward finite differences method. Here, $\frac{\partial \phi}{\partial t}$ is denoted as the progression of the level set function $\varphi(x,y)$ with respect to artificial time t. Note that the direction of the progression of $\varphi(x,y)$ is in the opposite direction of the EL equation, i.e., $-\partial E_{SSOM}(\varphi)/\partial \phi$, which is the steep descent direction of the energy function $E_{SSOM}(\varphi)$.

In order to preserve the regularity of the function $\varphi(x,y)$, which is essential to produce a smooth segmentation contour, we replaced the traditional TV regularized term used in the PD2 model with the Gaussian function $G_\sigma = e^{-(x^2+y^2)/2\sigma^2}$, where σ is represented as the standard deviation, which controls the smoothness of the contour.

The Gaussian function is convolved with the level set function $\varphi(x,y)$, and the respective output in each iteration is used as the initial condition for the next iteration. As a result, the requirement to solve the highly non-linear curvature term, which is computationally expensive, can be eradicated thus making the evolution of the function $\varphi(x,y)$ in our proposed SSOM model significantly more efficient.

3.2. A New Variant of the SSOM Model

Mammography images are known to be low contrast, which can lead to unsatisfactory segmentation results. Given a grayscale mammography image, its histogram consists of its intensity value, which is a graph indicating the number of times each intensity value occurs in the image. We can deduce a great deal about the appearance of an image from its histogram. For example, Figure 1 indicates a mammography image with its histogram profile.

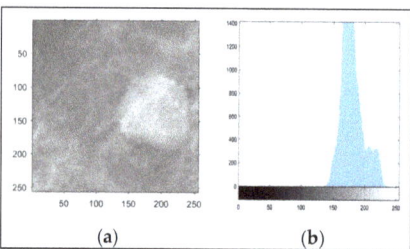

Figure 1. A mammography image (**a**) with its histogram profile (**b**).

Based on Figure 1, the mammography image in Figure 1a has low contrast because its intensity values are clustered at the upper end as indicated in the histogram in Figure 1b. A low-contrast image may affect the segmentation output. In a well-contrasted image, the intensity values would be well spread out over much of the intensity value (gray levels) range.

We can spread out the intensity values in a specified range by applying the piecewise linear function defined as

$$y = \frac{d-c}{b-a}(x-a) + c \tag{30}$$

Based on the function, pixel values less than a are all converted to c, and pixel values greater than b are all converted to d. The output intensity, y between c and d is computed based on the Equation (30). Here, x is the input intensity between a and b. This procedure has the effect of stretching or spreading the intensity values of the input image to the interested output intensity values. In this study, we set a as the bottom 1% of all input intensity values, b as the top 1% of all input intensity values, while c and d equal are 0 and 1, respectively. These settings show satisfactory results as demonstrated in [34].

Figure 2 demonstrates the output intensity, the corresponding histogram of the mammogram image in Figure 1a and the output image after applying the piecewise linear function.

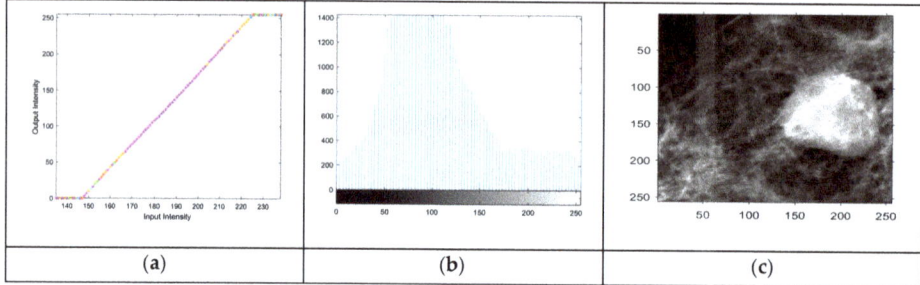

Figure 2. The output intensity (**a**), the corresponding histogram (**b**) and the output image (**c**).

As shown in Figure 2a, the input intensity values of the mammography image in Figure 1a are transformed according to the piecewise linear function. The results of the transformation are indicated as the output intensity in Figure 2a. The corresponding histogram of the transformation is illustrated in Figure 2b. Based on the histogram, we can observe that the intensity values after the transformation are more spread out compared to the original histogram profile in Figure 2b. This indicates that the output image has greater contrast than the original as shown in Figure 2c.

Here, by applying the idea of spreading out the intensity values using the piecewise linear function of Equation (30), we proposed a modified version of SSOM termed the SSOMH (Selective Self-Organizing Map Histogram)-based segmentation model. Let

$u_0 = u_0(x, y)$ be indicated as an input image while u_{HS} is indicated as an output image after applying the piecewise linear function. Then, the modified model is defined as follows:

$$E_{SSOMH}(D) := \alpha^+ \int_{in(D)} \left(u_{HS}(x,y) - s_k^+(D)\right)^2 dxdy + \alpha^- \int_{out(D)} \left(u_{HS}(x,y) - s_k^-(D)\right)^2 dxdy \\ + \int_{inside(D)} \theta R_d(x,y) dxdy, \quad (31)$$

The contour curve D is then replaced with the level set function φ, obtaining:

$$E_{SSOMH}(\varphi) : = \alpha^+ \int_\Omega H(\varphi) \left(u_{HS}(x,y) - s_k^+(D)\right)^2 d\Omega \\ + \alpha^- \int_\Omega (1 - H(\varphi)) \left(u_{HS}(x,y) - s_k^-(D)\right)^2 d\Omega + \int_\Omega \theta H(\varphi) R_d d\Omega. \quad (32)$$

Then, the associated EL equation by calculus of variation is defined as follows:

$$-\delta_\varepsilon(\varphi)\left(-\alpha_1\left(u_{HS}(x,y) - s_k^+(D)\right)^2 + \alpha_2\left(u_{HS}(x,y) - s_k^-(D)\right)^2 - \theta R_d\right) = 0. \quad (33)$$

with the following gradient descent flow:

$$\frac{\partial \varphi}{\partial t} = \delta_\varepsilon(\varphi)\left(-\alpha_1\left(u_{HS}(x,y) - s_k^+(D)\right)^2 + \alpha_2\left(u_{HS}(x,y) - s_k^-(D)\right)^2 - \theta R_d\right) \quad (34)$$

Finally, Equation (34) is solved and discretized using the forward finite differences method.

3.3. Steps of the Algorithm for the Proposed SSOM and SSOMH Models

This algorithm shows the steps involved in implementing the new proposed models, the SSOM model and the SSOMH model, to compute the solution using MATLAB R2017b software with an 11th Gen Intel(R) Core(TM) i5-1155G7 CPU @ 2.5 GHz and 8GB installed memory (RAM). The description of Algorithm 1 will be as follows:

The stopping criteria used for both models are set as the value of tolerance $tol = 1 \times 10^{-5}$ and maximum number of iterations, $t_{max}^{(evol)} = 100$. Next, Algorithm 2 is discussed, which is known as the SSOMH model. All steps in Algorithm 2 are equivalent to Algorithm 1 except for Step 8 and Step 11. The model is minimized based on Equation (32) while in Step 11, the evolving level set function is based on Equation (34). Algorithm 2 is described as follows:

3.4. Convergence Analysis

Based on the proposed SSOM model in Equation (14), let $\Omega = \{\overline{\varphi} | \nabla E_{SSOM}(\overline{\varphi}) = 0\}$ be the solution set. Our method's gradient algorithm can be thought of as a synthetic mapping $A = MP$. Here, $P(\varphi) = (\varphi, -\nabla E_{SSOM}(\varphi))$ is a mapping from R^n to $R^n \times R^n$, while M is a mapping from $R^n \times R^n$ to R^n. Thus, the point φ^k can be obtained as well as its negative gradient by mapping P to a given point φ as follows:

$$-\nabla E_{SSOM}\left(\phi^k\right) = \delta_\varepsilon(\varphi)\left(-\alpha^+\left(u_0(x,y) - s_k^+(D)\right)^2 + \alpha^-\left(u_0(x,y) - s_k^-(D)\right)^2 - \theta R_d\right). \quad (35)$$

To prove the convergence of Algorithm 1, we need to show that these five sufficient conditions are met

1. M is a closed mapping;
2. P is continuous;
3. A is closed at $\varphi(\nabla E_{SSOM}(\varphi) \neq 0)$;
4. $E_{SSOM}(\varphi)$ is a decent function of A and φ;
5. The sequence $\left\{\varphi^{(k)}\right\}$ is contained in a compact set, T.

Algorithm 1: Algorithm for the SSOM Model.

1. **Procedure**
   - Input
     - Training and testing grayscale mammography images.
     - Number of neurons and network topology.
     - Iterations number $t_{\max}^{(tm)}$ for neural map training.
     - Maximum iterations number $t_{\max}^{(evol)}$ for the evolution contour.
     - $\eta_0 > 0$; initial learning rate.
     - $m_0 > 0$; initial neighborhood radius of the map.
     - $\kappa_\eta, \kappa_m > 0$; time constant in learning rate and contour smoothing parameter.
     - $\alpha^+, \alpha^- \geq 0$, weights of the image energy terms inside and outside the contour, respectively.
     - $\sigma > 0$; Gaussian contour of the smoothing parameter.
     - $\beta > 0$; binary approximation constant of the level set function.
   - Output
     - Segmentation result.

   TRAINING SESSION
2. Initialize the weights of the neurons in the output layer at random.
3. **Repeat**
4.   Choose a pixel x_t at random in the image domain Ω and determine the winner neuron to the input intensity $J^{(tm)}(x_t)$.
5.   Update the weights of neuron s_p using Equations (3)–(6).
6. **Until** the learning of weights (prototypes) is complete (i.e., reached the iterations number $t_{\max}^{(tm)}$).

   TESTING SESSION
7. Choose a subset Ω_0 (e.g., square) in the image domain Ω with boundary Ω_0'. Then, initialize the level set function as:
$$\varphi(x,y) = \begin{cases} \beta, & (x,y) \in \Omega_0 \setminus \Omega_0', \\ 0, & (x,y) \in \Omega_0', \\ -\beta, & (x,y) \in \Omega \setminus (\Omega_0 \cup \Omega_0'). \end{cases}$$
8. Minimize the functional *SSOM* based on Equation (14).
9. **Repeat**
10.   Calculate s_k^+ and s_k^- from Equations (7) and (8).
11.   Evolve the level set function φ based on the finite difference of Equation (29).
12.   Perform the update at each iteration of the finite difference framework to reinitialize the current level set function to be binary.
$$\varphi \leftarrow \beta(H(\varphi) - H(-\varphi)),$$
Then, regularize the obtained level set function via convolution:
$$\varphi \leftarrow G_\sigma * \varphi,$$
13. **Until** the evolution of the curve converges (i.e., a sufficient stopping criterion is met, $\|\varphi^{n+1} - \varphi^n\| / \|\varphi^n\| \leq tol$ or reaches maximum iterations number, $t_{\max}^{(evol)}$).
14. **End procedure.**

Algorithm 2: Algorithm for SSOMH Model.

1. Step 1 to Step 7 is identical to Algorithm 1.
2. For Step 8, minimize the functional *SSOMH* based on Equation (32).
3. Then, follow Step 9 and Step 10 from Algorithm 1.
4. Next, evolve the level set function φ based on the finite difference approximation of Equation (34).
5. For Step 12 to Step 14, the flow is similar to Algorithm 1.

We now verify these conditions. Firstly, through mapping M, given a current point φ^k and a direction $d = -\nabla E_{SSOM}(\varphi^k)$, we can obtain an updated solution: $\varphi^{k+1} = \varphi^k + d\Delta t$, where the energy $E_{SSOM}(\varphi^{k+1})$ is lower than the point φ^k from the previous iteration. When $\nabla E_{SSOM}(\varphi) \neq 0$, M is a closed mapping by Lemma 1 from [40].

Next, the mapping P is continuous because the energy function $E_{SSOM}(\varphi)$ is continuous and differentiable. The mapping A is closed at $\varphi(\nabla E_{SSOM}(\phi) \neq 0)$, according to Inference 1 from [40]. When $\varphi \notin \Omega$, we obtain $d = -\nabla E_{SSOM}(\varphi) \neq 0$ and $\nabla E_{SSOM}(\varphi)^T d < 0$, indicating that $E_{SSOM}(\varphi)$ is a decent function of A and φ.

Furthermore, the evolution of our algorithm's level set function can be described in the following limits:

$$\varphi(x,y) = \begin{cases} \varphi(x,y) & if \; |\varphi(x,y)| < L \\ -L & if \; \varphi(x,y) < -L \\ L & if \; \varphi(x,y) > L \end{cases},$$

where L is a positive number. As a result, we can define a compact set:

$$T: \left\{ \varphi(\varphi_1, \ldots, \varphi_N) : \varphi \in R^N, |\varphi_i| \leq L \forall i \in [1, N] \right\},$$

where N denotes the number of pixels in the input image. The sequence $\left\{ \varphi^{(k)} \right\}$ is obviously contained in T. Thus, Algorithm 1 is convergent according to Lemma 3 from [40]. To prove the convergence of Algorithm 2, a similar approach is taken. The differences are only: (1) the term E_{SSOM} is changed to E_{SSOMH} and (2) Equation (35) is replaced by the following Equation (36):

$$-\nabla E_{SSOMH}\left(\phi^k\right) = \delta_\varepsilon(\varphi)\left(-\alpha^+ \left(u_{HS}(x,y) - s_k^+(D)\right)^2 + \alpha^- \left(u_{HS}(x,y) - s_k^-(D)\right)^2 - \theta R_d\right). \tag{36}$$

The proof is completed. □

4. Experimental Results

In this section, the accuracy and efficiency of the SSOM model and the SSOMH model will be compared with the iterative models and deep learning-based method. The iterative models are the SOMCV model, the PD2 model and the state-of-the-art IIS model, while the deep learning method is U-Net. The SSOM, SSOMH, PD2, and U-Net algorithms are implemented using MATLAB, while the IIS model is implemented using software provided by the authors [33].

To test the performances of all methods, two experiments were conducted. The first experiment was on segmenting the region of interest (ROI) images from the INbreast database, while the second experiment was on segmenting ROI images from the CBIS-DDSM database. Both datasets are publicly available datasets of breast cancer abnormalities with ground-truth annotations from [41,42], respectively. Due to the limited number of ROI in each dataset, we have augmented the original ROIs by applying the Contrast Enhancement method and rotating them with the angles $\Delta = \{0°, 90°, 180°, 270°\}$. Thus, a total of 500 ROIs for each database were prepared. There were 400 ROIs (80%) used for training, 50 ROIs (10%) used for testing and 50 ROIs (10%) used for validation.

In each experiment, the parameter's value, $\eta_0 = 0.1$, $\sigma = 1$, and the parameter's weight, $\alpha^+ = \alpha^- = 1$ are fixed for all problems. In addition, $r_0 := \max(J, K)/2$, where J and K are the numbers of the row and column of the neural map, $t_{max}^{(tm)} = 100$, $t_{max}^{(evol)} = 100$, $\kappa_m := t_{max}^{(tm)}/\ln(m_0)$ and $\beta = 1$. A 1-dimensional neural map is preferable and has been chosen for the SOM network of grayscale images (i.e., $J = 5$, $N = 1$). These settings are suggested by [36] to produce a good result. In addition, the same parameter values are used for all models to avoid bias.

For the selective segmentation models, the value of the parameter θ that functions to restrict only the target object will be different for each trial. In this study, the value of θ varies between 18 and 10,000. The third experiment in this study was conducted to demonstrate the sensitivity of this parameter to our proposed model.

4.1. Segmentation Results of Test Images from the INbreast Database

In this first experiment, the segmentation performance for all models was compared using two methods. The first method is a qualitative method in which the performances are evaluated using visual observation, while the second method is a quantitative method in which the computation time, Dice similarity coefficients (DSCs), Jaccard similarity coefficients (JSCs), also known as IoU, Accuracy and Error metrics of the output images in the models are calculated using the following formulas:

$$DSC = \frac{2 \times TP}{(2 \times TP + FP + FN)}, \quad JSC = \frac{DSC}{2 - DSC}$$
$$Accuracy = \frac{(TP + TN)}{(FN + FP + TP + TN)}, \quad Error = \frac{(FP + FN)}{(TP + FN + FP + TN)} \tag{37}$$

where TP is true positive (foreground pixels of the segmented image are completely extracted), FP is false positive (background pixels of the segmented image are wrongly retrieved as foreground), FN is false negative (foreground pixels of the segmented image have been mistakenly erased), and TN is true negative (background pixels of the segmented image have been completely removed).

Basically, a low value of computing time indicates efficient processing time. For the metrics evaluations, high values of JSC, DSC and Accuracy approaching to 1 indicate that the model is accurate at segmenting the input images, while smaller values of Error approaching to 0 show better segmentation results of the test images. The DSC and JSC coefficients are known as an overlapping metric between two data sets, while the Accuracy and Error metrics are determined by the closeness and the wrong predictions of the segmentation results, respectively [43]. The result was scaled from 0 to 1.

Figure 3 demonstrates the results of the segmentation performed using each model for 4 chosen image samples out of 50 test images from the INbreast database. To remove unnecessary information and speed up the segmentation process, the images are cropped to the ROI with a size of 256 × 256 pixels.

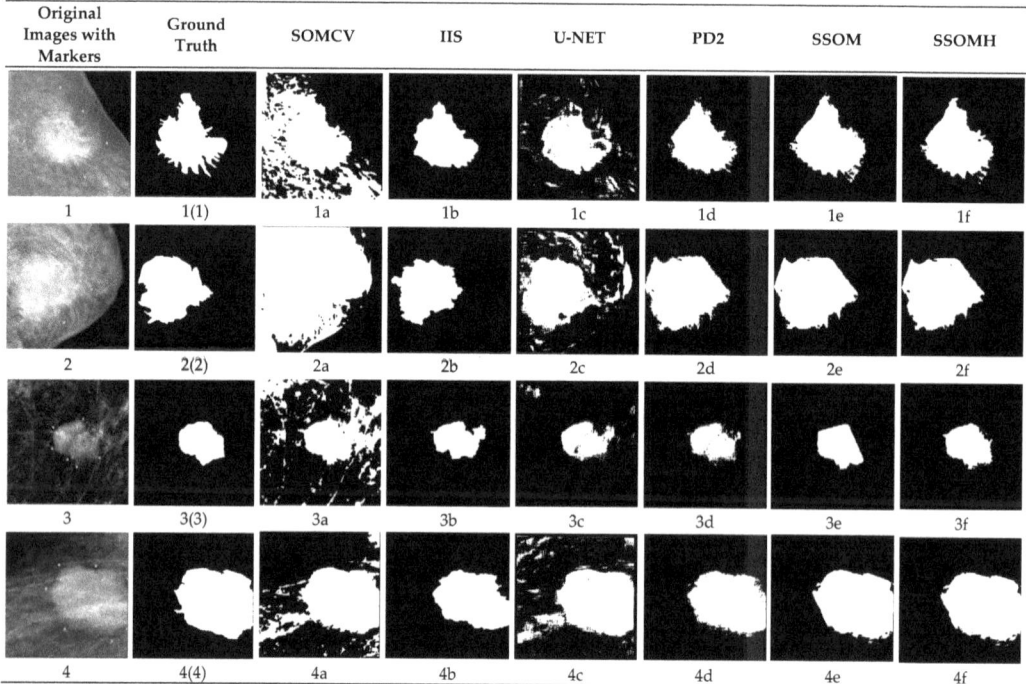

Figure 3. Segmentation Results of Four Samples of Test Images (INbreast Database) for the SOMCV, IIS, U-NET, PD2, SSOM and SSOMH Models.

Based on Figure 3, the first column demonstrates the original images with green markers indicating the targeted object. The second column shows the ground-truth images as benchmarks for the segmentation output. The results for the SOMCV, IIS, U-NET, PD2, SSOM and SSOMH models are indicated in the third, fourth, fifth, sixth, seventh and eighth columns, respectively. The findings were presented in the form of binary images. As we can see, the result for SOMCV was over-segmented mainly because the targeted region is too close to the surrounding healthy breast tissues. The result generated using U-Net is better than SOMCV; however, we lack the large dataset required to produce the impressive results that deep learning approaches typically produce.

The IIS produces a smooth result, but some regions are under-segmented due to inhomogeneous intensity. The segmentation region generated using the PD2 model has many small particles and is less smooth compared to SSOM and SSOMH due to intensity inhomogeneity of the mammography images. Note that the segmentation result of the SSOM model is almost identical to the SSOMH model thanks to the unsupervised neural network, SOM and distance fitting term in the variational level set formulations in the SSOM and SSOMH models, which is vital to segment an image with intensity inhomogeneity and to capture the boundary of abnormality region, respectively.

In addition, we also provide a quantitative evaluation of the segmentation accuracy based on the JSC, DSC, Accuracy and Error metrics. Table 1 shows the average values of JSC, DSC, Accuracy and Error of the segmentation results for each model using the INbreast Database. The data in Table 1 are visualized in Figure 4.

Table 1. Average Values of JSC, DSC, Accuracy and Error for All Models.

Model	JSC	DSC	Accuracy	Error
SOMCV	0.434	0.584	0.735	0.265
IIS	0.801	0.887	0.961	0.040
U-NET	0.519	0.674	0.847	0.153
PD2	0.819	0.899	0.962	0.038
SSOM	0.883	0.937	0.976	0.024
SSOMH	0.884	0.938	0.977	0.023

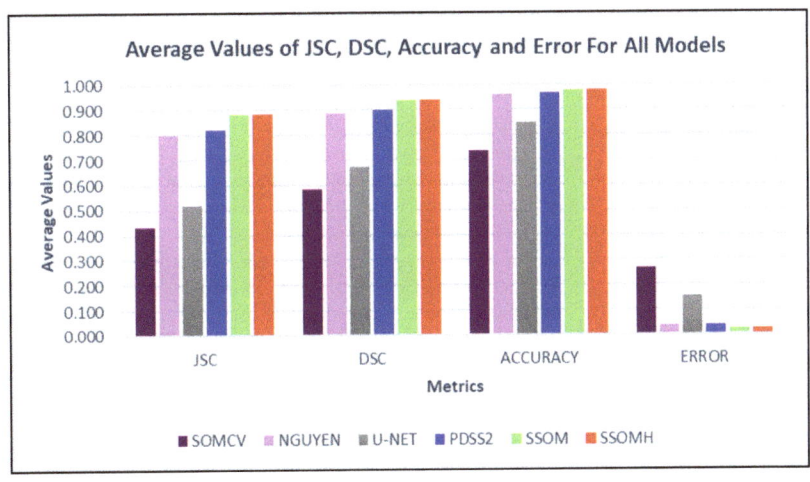

Figure 4. Average Values of JSC, DSC, Accuracy and Error for All Models.

Based on Table 1 and Figure 4, the JSC, DSC and Accuracy metrics of the SSOMH model achieved the highest values with the lowest value of the Error metric, which indicates the highest segmentation accuracy in segmenting the targeted objects compared to the SOMCV, IIS, U-NET, PD2 and SSOM. Again, this is evidence of the advantage of using the combination of SOM-based machine learning approach, distance fitting term and the idea of spreading out the intensity values using a piecewise linear function as applied in this model.

In addition, a quantitative analysis of the segmentation speed is also performed in this experiment. We clarify that the efficiency comparison on IIS cannot be performed because the interactive software provided by the authors [33] used for implementing the IIS model does not have any built-in functions or tools for recording time processing. Table 2 illustrates the computation speed of segmentation results for each model.

Table 2. Average Computation Time for All Models.

Model	Computation Time (Seconds)	
	Training	Testing
SOMCV	0.05	1.67
U-NET	327.00	0.76
PD2	Not Related	71.03
SSOM	0.05	1.42
SSOMH	0.05	1.39

Based on Table 2, the U-Net method achieved the fastest computational speed in the testing phase but the slowest speed during the training phase. Note that the computation time for SOMCV, SSOM and SSOMH during training are the same, while the testing speeds are almost similar because the Gaussian function was used in the models to efficiently speed up the computation time. In addition, the PD2 model has the slowest testing speed in segmenting the region, which is due to the computationally expensive TV term in the model that slows down the segmentation process.

Therefore, based on the experiments above, the proposed SSOMH model is more recommended than the SSOM model due to its efficiency and effectiveness in segmenting breast abnormality with inhomogeneous intensity. The SSOMH model is able to increase the contrast of the test images to reveal detailed information about hidden abnormalities present in the given images for better segmentation. Thus, the SSOMH is chosen to be compared with the SOMCV, IIS, U-Net and PD2 models in the next experiment.

4.2. Segmentation Results of Test Images from the CBIS-DDSM Database

In this second experiment, 50 mammography images of size 256 × 256 pixels from the CBIS-DDSM database were tested. The SSOMH is compared with SOMCV, IIS, U-Net and PD2 models. Figure 5 demonstrates 4 samples of input images (out of 50 test images) with green markers indicating the targeted object and the ground truth images as benchmarks for the segmentation. The results were presented in the form of binary images.

By visual observation, the result of the SOMCV model was over-segmented while the U-Net and IIS were under-segmented for test images 2, 3 and 4. The PD2 and SSOMH models could selectively segment the targeted region; however, the result delivered using SSOMH is smoother compared to PD2. In addition, the quantitative evaluation of the segmentation result based on the JSC, DSC, Accuracy and Error metrics are also provided. Table 3 below shows the average values of JSC, DSC, Accuracy, and Error of the segmentation results for each model using the CBIS-DDSM database, which are visualized in Figure 6.

From Table 3 and Figure 6, the SSOMH model achieved the highest values of the JSC, DSC and Accuracy metrics and the lowest value of Error, which indicate the highest segmentation accuracy in segmenting the targeted objects compared to the SOMCV, IIS, U-NET and PD2 models. The lowest values of JSC, DSC and Accuracy are obtained with the SOMCV model.

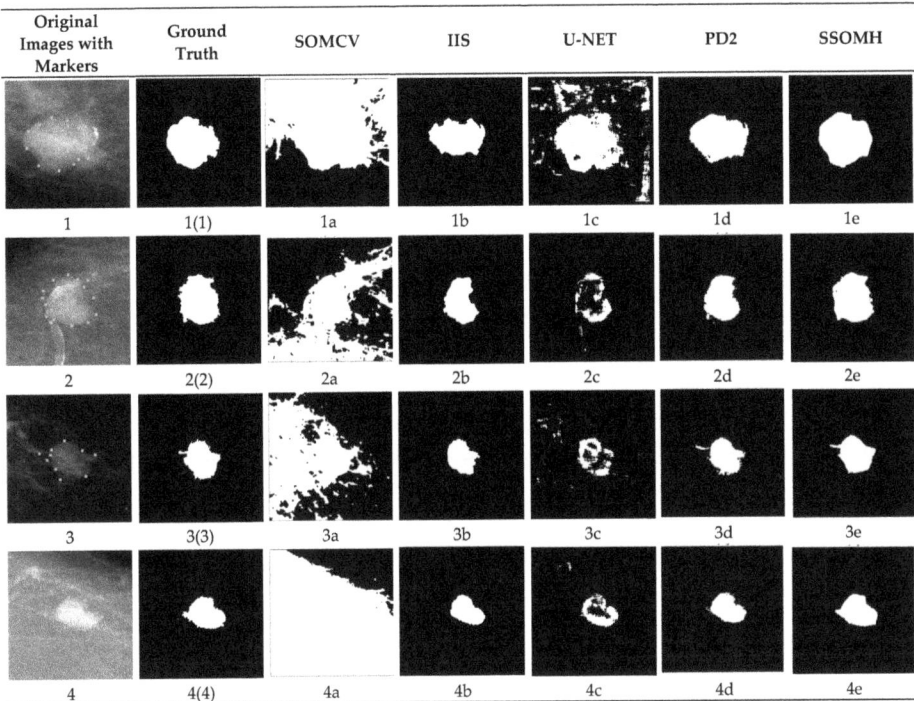

Figure 5. Segmentation Results of Four Samples of Test Images (CBIS-DDSM Database) for the SOMCV, IIS, U-NET, PD2, SSOM and SSOMH Models.

Table 3. Average Values of JSC, DSC, Accuracy and Error for All Models.

Model	JSC	DSC	Accuracy	Error
SOMCV	0.425	0.576	0.695	0.304
IIS	0.449	0.616	0.778	0.222
U-NET	0.569	0.712	0.893	0.107
PD2	0.768	0.867	0.945	0.055
SSOMH	0.856	0.920	0.964	0.036

Similar to the first experiment on the INbreast Database, a quantitative analysis on the segmentation speed is also performed in this experiment for all tested models, except the IIS model, when segmenting test images using the CBIS-DDSM database, as illustrated in the following Table 4.

Based on Table 4, the result for U-Net is consistent with the previous experiment 1 where the method achieved the fastest testing time but was slower during the training phase compared to the other models. On the other hand, the computation time of the testing phase for SOMCV and SSMOH is comparable to U-Net. The segmentation time for PD2 is slower compared to the other models.

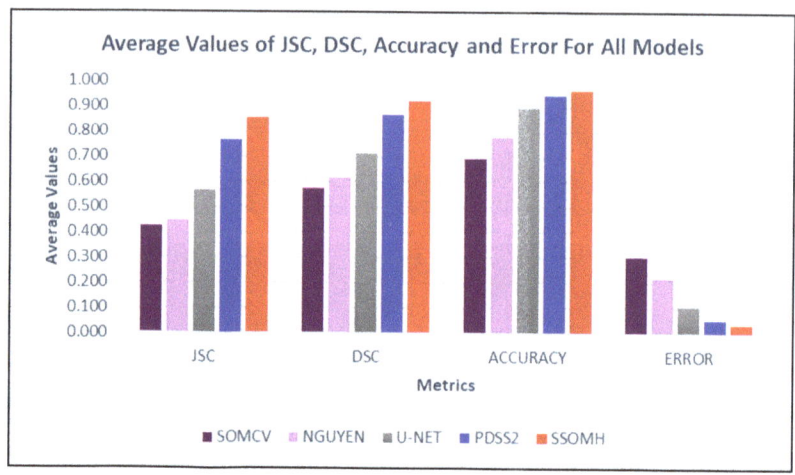

Figure 6. Average Values of JSC, DSC, Accuracy and Error for All Models.

Table 4. Average Computation Time for All Models.

Model	Computation Time (Seconds)	
	Training	Testing
SOMCV	0.05	1.79
U-NET	307.00	0.73
PD2	Not Related	98.54
SSOMH	0.05	0.8

4.3. Results of SSOMH Model with Different Values of Area Parameter θ

In this final experiment, the important area parameter θ is tested to determine how it affects the segmentation accuracy of the recommended SSOMH model. Figure 7 demonstrates the segmentation results of the SSOMH model for test image 3 from Figure 3 with different values of θ.

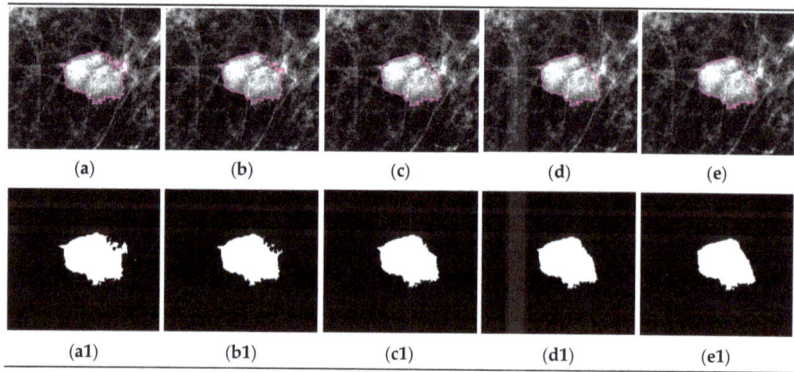

Figure 7. Segmentation Results for SSOMH Model with Different Values of θ.

We set the values of parameter θ for (**a–e**) to 100, 300, 1000, 2000 and 4000, respectively. The respective results are indicated in (**a1–e1**). By visual observation, (**c1**) with θ = 1000 shows a better segmentation result compared with (**a1,b1,d1,e1**) according to the benchmark in Figure 3. In addition, the quantitative evaluation of the segmentation accuracy is also provided based on the JSC, DSC, Accuracy and Error metrics. Figure 8 illustrates the values of JSC, DSC, Accuracy and Error for different values of θ.

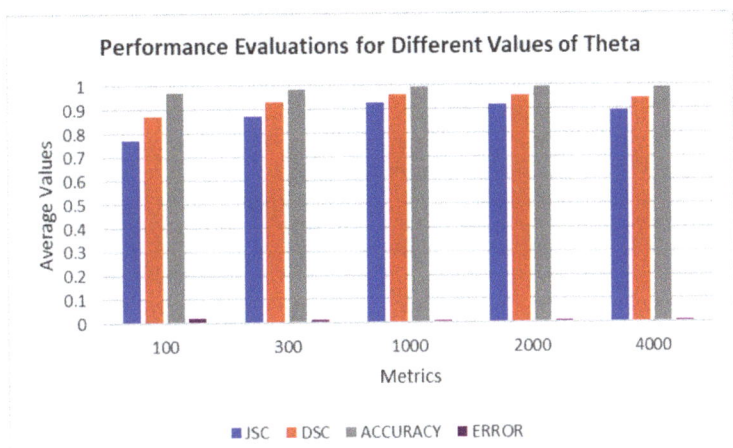

Figure 8. Performance Evaluations of the SSOMH Model with Different Values of θ.

Figure 8 shows the JSC, DSC, Accuracy and Error metrics for different values of θ. It can be observed that the image with $\theta = 1000$ has the highest JSC, DSC and Accuracy values with the lowest Error values, indicating more accurate segmentation results compared to the images with the other θ values shown above. Thus, the values of θ should be controlled using trial and error to achieve accurate segmentation, which is the main limitation of the proposed model. As a general guide, the value of θ should be large when the targeted object is too close to the normal tissue, while a smaller value of θ s required for a clearly separated object.

5. Conclusions

In this research work, we focused on the extraction of the abnormality region in mammography images using the selective segmentation technique. Two models were proposed, namely SSOM and SSOMH. Both models adopted the idea of using distance fitting terms to capture the targeted region, the SOM machine learning-based approach to segment images with intensity inhomogeneity and a Gaussian function for curve regularization in the formulations. In the SSOMH model, the idea of spreading out the intensity values using a piecewise linear function is applied to increase the contrast of the mammography images. To minimize the energy functions of the SSOM and SSOMH models, the Euler–Lagrange equations were established using calculus of variations. Then, the equations were solved in MATLAB software using the gradient descent algorithm. The efficiency of each model was evaluated in terms of computational time, and segmentation accuracy was measured by evaluating the JSC, DSC, Accuracy and Error values for each image.

Based on the first experiment using the INbreast database, it is recommended to use the SSOMH model to segment mammography images due to its efficiency and high accuracy compared to the SSOM model. In the same experiment, SSOMH outperformed the SOMCV, IIS, U-Net and PD2 models in terms of Accuracy. Similar observation can be made in the second experiment using the CBIS-DDSM database. Based on both experiments, we found that U-Net has faster testing time but a slower training time compared to SSOMH. However, the segmentation process of SSOMH was faster than the other iterative models (SSOM, SOMCV and PD2).

As demonstrated in the last experiment, this study has the drawback that the parameter of θ must be manually set because each image requires a distinct set of values. The parameter must be adjusted one at a time using a process of trial and error until the targeted segmented image is achieved.

For future research, it is recommended to investigate how to choose a suitable value of the parameter θ. On the other hand, the recommended model, i.e., the SSOMH model, can be extended into a vector-valued (color) framework and a three-dimensional (3D) framework for segmentation of color and 3D mammography images, respectively. The reason is that vector-valued (color) and 3D images provide more significant details that are beneficial in the evaluation of medical and non-medical images. Moreover, as the SSOMH model is non-convex, it may be sensitive to initialization. Future directions will try to formulate a convex formulation of the model.

Author Contributions: Conceptualization, N.A.S.M.G., A.K.J. and R.M.; methodology, N.A.S.M.G., A.K.J. and R.M.; investigation, N.A.S.M.G.; validation, N.A.S.M.G., A.K.J., R.M., M.A.M., F.A.Z. and A.M.J.; formal analysis, N.A.S.M.G.; writing—original draft preparation, N.A.S.M.G.; writing —review and editing, N.A.S.M.G., A.K.J., R.M., M.A.M., F.A.Z. and A.M.J.; visualization, N.A.S.M.G.; supervision, A.K.J., R.M., M.A.M., F.A.Z. and A.M.J. All authors have read and agreed to the published version of the manuscript.

Funding: This research was funded by the Ministry of Higher Education (MOHE) and Universiti Teknologi MARA, Shah Alam, grant number FRGS/1/2021/STG06/UITM/02/3.

Data Availability Statement: Not applicable.

Conflicts of Interest: The authors declare no conflict of interest.

References

1. Ministry of Health. *Malaysia National Cancer Registry 2012–2016*; Ministry of Health: Putrajaya, Malaysia, 2019. Available online: https://drive.google.com/file/d/1BuPWrb05N2Jez6sEP8VM5r6JtJtlPN5W/view (accessed on 1 November 2021).
2. Spreafico, F.S.; Cardoso-filho, C.; Cabello, C.; Sarian, L.O.; Zeferino, L.C.; Vale, D.B. Breast Cancer in Men: Clinical and Pathological Analysis of 817 Cases. *Am. J. Men's Health* **2020**, *14*, 1–6. [CrossRef] [PubMed]
3. Shamsi, M.; Islamian, J.P. Breast cancer: Early diagnosis and effective treatment by drug delivery tracing. *Nucl. Med. Rev.* **2017**, *20*, 45–48. [CrossRef]
4. Yasiran, S.S.; Jumaat, A.K.; Manaf, M.; Ibrahim, A.; Wan Eny Zarina, W.A.R.; Malek, A.; Laham, M.F.; Mahmud, R. Comparison between GVF Snake and ED Snake in Segmenting Microcalcifications. In Proceedings of the 2011 IEEE International Conference on Computer Applications and Industrial Electronics (ICCAIE), Penang, Malaysia, 4–7 December 2011; pp. 597–601.
5. Chen, K. Introduction to variational image-processing models and applications. *Int. J. Comput. Math.* **2013**, *90*, 1–8. [CrossRef]
6. Rick, A.; Bothorel, S.; Bouchon-Meunier, B.; Muller, S.; Rifqi, M. Fuzzy techniques in mammographic image processing. In *Fuzzy Techniques in Image Processing*; Physica: Heidelberg, Germany, 2000; pp. 308–336.
7. Yearwood, A.B. A Brief Survey on Variational Methods for Image Segmentation. 2010, pp. 1–7. Available online: researchgate.net/profile/Abdu-Badru-Yearwood/publication/323971382_A_Brief_Survey_on_Variational_Methods_for_Image_Segmentation/links/5abd38e8a6fdcccda6581b05/A-Brief-Survey-on-Variational-Methods-for-Image-Segmentation.pdf (accessed on 1 November 2021).
8. Vlachos, I.K.; Sergiadis, G.D. Intuitionistic Fuzzy Image Processing. In *Soft Computing in Image Processing*; Springer: Berlin/Heidelberg, Germany, 2007; pp. 383–414.
9. Chowdhary, C.L.; Acharjya, D.P. Segmentation of mammograms using a novel intuitionistic possibilistic fuzzy c-mean clustering algorithm. In *Nature Inspired Computing*; Advances in Intelligent Systems and Computing; Springer: Singapore, 2018; pp. 75–82. [CrossRef]
10. Ghosh, S.K.; Mitra, A.; Ghosh, A. A novel intuitionistic fuzzy soft set entrenched mammogram segmentation under Multigranulation approximation for breast cancer detection in early stages. *Expert Syst. Appl.* **2021**, *169*, 114329. [CrossRef]
11. Chowdhary, C.L.; Mittal, M.; P., K.; Pattanaik, P.A.; Marszalek, Z. An efficient segmentation and classification system in medical images using intuitionist possibilistic fuzzy C-mean clustering and fuzzy SVM algorithm. *Sensors* **2020**, *20*, 3903. [CrossRef] [PubMed]
12. Chaira, T. An Intuitionistic Fuzzy Clustering Approach for Detection of Abnormal Regions in Mammogram Images. *J. Digit. Imaging* **2021**, *34*, 428–439. [CrossRef]
13. Atiqah, N.; Zaman, K.; Eny, W.; Wan, Z.; Rahman, A.; Jumaat, A.K.; Yasiran, S.S. Classification of Breast Abnormalities Using Artificial Neural Network. *AIP Conf. Proc.* **2015**, *1660*, 050038. [CrossRef]
14. Ronneberger, O.; Fischer, P.; Brox, T. U-net: Convolutional networks for biomedical image segmentation. In Proceedings of the International Conference on Medical Image Computing and Computer-Assisted Intervention: 2015 18th International Conference, Munich, Germany, 5–9 October 2015; Part III. pp. 234–241.

15. Michael, E.; Ma, H.; Li, H.; Kulwa, F.; Li, J. Breast Cancer Segmentation Methods Current Status and Future Potentials. *Biomed Res. Int.* **2021**, *2021*, 9962109. [CrossRef] [PubMed]
16. Saravanan, R.; Sujatha, P. A State of Art Techniques on Machine Learning Algorithms: A Perspective of Supervised Learning Approaches in Data Classification. In Proceedings of the 2018 Second International Conference on Intelligent Computing and Control Systems (ICICCS), Madurai, India, 14–15 June 2018; pp. 945–949.
17. Barbu, T.; Marinoschi, G.; Moroanu, C.; Munteanu, I. Advances in Variational and Partial Differential Equation-Based Models for Image Processing and Computer Vision. *Math. Probl. Eng.* **2018**, *2018*, 1701052. [CrossRef]
18. Jumaat, A.K.; Chen, K. A Reformulated Convex and Selective Variational Image Segmentation Model and its Fast Multilevel Algorithm. *Numer. Math. Theory Methods Appl.* **2019**, *12*, 403–437.
19. Rahmati, P.; Adler, A.; Hamarneh, G. Mammography segmentation with maximum likelihood active contours. *Med. Image Anal.* **2012**, *16*, 1167–1186. [CrossRef] [PubMed]
20. Ciecholewski, M. Malignant and benign mass segmentation in mammograms using active contour methods. *Symmetry* **2017**, *9*, 277. [CrossRef]
21. Chan, T.F.; Vese, L.A. Active contours without edges. *IEEE Trans. Image Process.* **2001**, *10*, 266–277. [CrossRef] [PubMed]
22. Saraswathi, D.; Srinivasan, E.; Ranjitha, P. An Efficient Level Set Mammographic Image Segmentation using Fuzzy C Means Clustering. *Asian J. Appl. Sci. Technol.* **2017**, *1*, 7–11.
23. Somroo, S.; Choi, K.N. Robust active contours for mammogram image segmentation. In Proceedings of the 2017 IEEE International Conference on Image Processing (ICIP), Beijing, China, 17–20 September 2017; pp. 2149–2153.
24. Hmida, M.; Hamrouni, K.; Solaiman, B.; Boussetta, S. Mammographic mass segmentation using fuzzy contours. *Comput. Methods Programs Biomed.* **2018**, *164*, 131–142. [CrossRef]
25. Radhi, E.A.; Kamil, M.Y. Segmentation of breast mammogram images using level set method. *AIP Conf. Proc.* **2022**, *2398*, 020071.
26. Badshah, N.; Atta, H.; Ali Shah, S.I.; Attaullah, S.; Minallah, N.; Ullah, M. New local region based model for the segmentation of medical images. *IEEE Access* **2020**, *8*, 175035–175053. [CrossRef]
27. Jumaat, A.K.; Chen, K.E. An optimization-based multilevel algorithm for variational image segmentation models. *Electron. Trans. Numer. Anal.* **2017**, *46*, 474–504.
28. Jumaat, A.K.; Chen, K. Three-Dimensional Convex and Selective Variational Image Segmentation Model. *Malays. J. Math. Sci.* **2020**, *14*, 81–92.
29. Jumaat, A.K.; Chen, K. A fast multilevel method for selective segmentation model of 3-D digital images. *Adv. Stud. Math. J.* **2022**, 127–152. Available online: https://tcms.org.ge/Journals/ASETMJ/Special%20issue/10/PDF/asetmj_SpIssue_10_9.pdf (accessed on 1 November 2021).
30. Acho, S.N.; Rae, W.I.D. Interactive breast mass segmentation using a convex active contour model with optimal threshold values. *Phys. Med.* **2016**, *32*, 1352–1359. [CrossRef]
31. Ali, H.; Faisal, S.; Chen, K.; Rada, L. Image-selective segmentation model for multi-regions within the object of interest with application to medical disease. *Vis. Comput.* **2020**, *37*, 939–955. [CrossRef]
32. Ghani, N.A.S.M.; Jumaat, A.K. Selective Segmentation Model for Vector-Valued Images. *J. Inf. Commun. Technol.* **2022**, *5*, 149–173. Available online: http://e-journal.uum.edu.my/index.php/jict/article/view/8062 (accessed on 1 November 2021).
33. Nguyen, T.N.A.; Cai, J.; Zhang, J.; Zheng, J. Robust Interactive Image Segmentation Using Convex Active Contours. *IEEE Trans. Image Process.* **2012**, *21*, 3734–3743. [CrossRef] [PubMed]
34. Ghani, N.A.S.M.; Jumaat, A.K.; Mahmud, R. Boundary Extraction of Abnormality Region in Breast Mammography Image using Active Contours. *ESTEEM Acad. J.* **2022**, *18*, 115–127.
35. Zhang, K.; Song, H.; Zhang, L. Active contours driven by local image fitting energy. *Pattern Recognit.* **2010**, *43*, 1199–1206. [CrossRef]
36. Abdelsamea, M.M.; Gnecco, G.; Gaber, M.M. A SOM-based Chan-Vese model for unsupervised image segmentation. *Soft Comput.* **2017**, *21*, 2047–2067. [CrossRef]
37. Mumford, D.; Shah, J. Optimal approximations by piecewise smooth functions and associated variational problems. *Commun. Pure Appl. Math.* **1989**, *42*, 577–685. [CrossRef]
38. Osher, S.; Sethian, J.A. Fronts propagating with curvature-dependent speed: Algorithms based on Hamilton-Jacobi formulations. *J. Comput. Phys.* **1988**, *79*, 12–49. [CrossRef]
39. Altarawneh, N.M.; Luo, S.; Regan, B.; Sun, C.; Jia, F. Global Threshold and Region-Based Active Contour Model For Accurate Image Segmentation. *Signal Image Process.* **2014**, *5*, 1–11. [CrossRef]
40. Chen, B.L. *Optimization Theory and Algorithms*, 2nd ed.; Tsinghua University Press: Beijing, China, 1989.
41. Moreira, I.C.; Amaral, I.; Domingues, I.; Cardoso, A.; Cardoso, M.J.; Cardoso, J.S. INbreast: Toward a Full-field Digital Mammographic Database. *Acad. Radiol.* **2012**, *19*, 236–248. [CrossRef] [PubMed]

42. Lee, R.S.; Gimenez, F.; Hoogi, A.; Miyake, K.K.; Gorovoy, M.; Rubin, D.L. Data Descriptor: A curated mammography data set for use in computer-aided detection and diagnosis research. *Sci. Data* **2017**, *4*, 170177. [CrossRef] [PubMed]
43. Azam, A.S.B.; Malek, A.A.; Ramlee, A.S.; Suhaimi, N.D.S.M.; Mohamed, N. Segmentation of Breast Microcalcification Using Hybrid Method of Canny Algorithm with Otsu Thresholding and 2D Wavelet Transform. In Proceedings of the 2020 10th IEEE International Conference on Control System, Computing and Engineering (ICCSCE), Penang, Malaysia, 21–22 August 2020; pp. 91–96. [CrossRef]

Disclaimer/Publisher's Note: The statements, opinions and data contained in all publications are solely those of the individual author(s) and contributor(s) and not of MDPI and/or the editor(s). MDPI and/or the editor(s) disclaim responsibility for any injury to people or property resulting from any ideas, methods, instructions or products referred to in the content.

Article

Analysis and Recognition of Human Gait Activity Based on Multimodal Sensors

Diego Teran-Pineda [1,*], Karl Thurnhofer-Hemsi [1,2] and Enrique Dominguez [1]

1 Department of Computer Languages and Computer Science, University of Málaga, Bulevar Louis Pasteur, 35, 29071 Málaga, Spain; karlkhader@lcc.uma.es (K.T.-H.); enriqued@lcc.uma.es (E.D.)
2 Biomedical Research Institute of Málaga (IBIMA), C/ Doctor Miguel Díaz Recio, 28, 29010 Málaga, Spain
* Correspondence: dfteran@uma.es

Abstract: Remote health monitoring plays a significant role in research areas related to medicine, neurology, rehabilitation, and robotic systems. These applications include Human Activity Recognition (HAR) using wearable sensors, signal processing, mathematical methods, and machine learning to improve the accuracy of remote health monitoring systems. To improve the detection and accuracy of human activity recognition, we create a novel method to reduce the complexities of extracting features using the HuGaDB dataset. Our model extracts power spectra; due to the high dimensionality of features, sliding windows techniques are used to determine frequency bandwidth automatically, where an improved QRS algorithm selects the first dominant spectrum amplitude. In addition, the bandwidth algorithm has been used to reduce the dimensionality of data, remove redundant dimensions, and improve feature extraction. In this work, we have considered widely used machine learning classifiers. Our proposed method was evaluated using the accelerometer angles spectrum installed in six parts of the body and then reducing the bandwidth to know the evolution. Our approach attains an accuracy rate of 95.1% in the HuGaDB dataset with 70% of bandwidth, outperforming others in the human activity recognition accuracy.

Keywords: multimodal sensor; motion classification; computational intelligence; complex feature extraction; activity recognition; QRS algorithm

MSC: 68T10

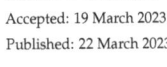

1. Introduction

Human gait is a natural activity that people do every time to move from one point to another, involving muscles, nerves and brain activities. Human joints are a fundamental part of human movement, and therefore, a gait analysis is needed to study kinetics and kinematics [1,2], which are examined by physiotherapists, orthopedists, and neurologists to analyze and assess the status, treatment, and rehabilitation of patients [3]. Extrinsic and intrinsic factors (both psychological and physical) influence daily human activities; hence, determining normal gait parameters is very difficult [4]. In addition, there are a wide range of applications in different fields, such as neurology for monitoring neurological symptoms [5], or rehabilitation and physical therapy for the detection of gait disorders [6,7].

Physical activity monitoring via body-worn devices has recently been increased by sensor technologies (multimodal fusion sensors). They help vulnerable people maintain or increase the quality of individual and social lives through activity tracking [8]. The development of automatic information systems and improved methods to analyze biosignals with AI in this area is a way to contribute to more efficient health care.

The devices used to acquire body signals are classified into three approaches: non-wearable sensor (NWS), wearable sensor (WS), and hybrid system [2]. Nevertheless, WS is most commonly used due to its low cost, small dimensions, and high precision. These sensors are installed in the body to acquire the gait biosignal information during personal daily activities. WS includes force sensors, accelerometers, gyroscopes, extensometers, inclinometers, goniometers, active markers, electromyography, etc. To optimize the functionalities of such sensors (accelerometers, gyroscopes, and magnetometers), they are fused into a single unit called Inertial Measurement Units (IMUs) with multimodal fusion sensors technologies.

Extensive research has used body-worn inertial sensors and fortified the development of original Human Activity Recognition (HAR) applications. These applications include health rehabilitation, well-being assistance [9], smart homes and biofeedback systems [8], gait analysis [10–13], motion symmetry study [14], or for monitoring human activities [15,16]. Each of these applications requires continuous monitoring and tracking [17–21].

Feature extraction and selection algorithms are meant to sort pertinent features or suppress redundant information to increase activity recognition accurately and efficiently. These relevant features are commonly based on time-domain, wavelet and statistical analysis, with several IMU sensors installed in the body [22]. The frequency spectral of accelerometers has helped researchers predict vibrations in building structures [23] or turbines [24] and recognize the running path of dogs [25]. In addition, selection techniques to identify the most relevant features in datasets are needed to simplify the learned models and decrease the computational complexity and improve the model's efficiency for recognition tasks. Using expensive industrial IMU sensors and extracting more complex features such as entropy [26,27] or frequency measures [20,28] brings promising results.

In this paper, we propose a novel methodology based on the frequency domain and bandwidth reduction of IMU accelerometer signals for HAR applications. The main objective is to analyze the minimum amount of features necessary to obtain good performance in the model training and decrease the computational time of the signal processing and classification. For that purpose, a new signal preprocessing methodology is presented based on the frequency domain analysis, and functional transforms are included to reduce the computational complexity due to the high dimensionality of features. Only accelerometer signals are considered, since it is the most relevant feature that allows distinguishing between activities, but also, we want to demonstrate the effectiveness of our proposal with less information, which could be of interest in some treatments where a simple sensor is needed to be implanted for a treatment. The proposed method is applied successfully to a public benchmark dataset named the Human Gait Database (HuGaDB) for performance evaluation.

The rest of the paper is organized as follows. Section 2 addresses briefly a literature review. In Section 3, our proposed methodology is presented. Section 4 analyzes and discusses the experimental results. Finally, the conclusion and future research are presented in Section 5.

2. Related Work

Wearable sensors (WS) are used in recent advances because researchers have successfully implemented body-worn devices to monitor personal locomotion behaviors and recognize human activity. The most common WS uses an accelerometer and gyroscope integrated into one wearable inertial mobile unit (IMU). Another type of WS based on the electrical current associated with muscular actions is also used in combination with IMUs for HAR [22]. These WS named electromyography (EMG) measure the myoelectric signals produced by muscular actions, hence their importance in activity recognition. A study on the fusion of EMG and IMU sensors for HAR is presented in [22], showing the potential of incorporating EMG signals in activity recognition.

A motoring real-time personal locomotion is introduced in [8], wielding three inertial sensors at different body locations (wrist, thigh, and chest). Data were processed through Gaussian and zero-phase filters. A hierarchical feature-based technique is used to extract features based on stochastic gradient descent optimization methods, achieving an accuracy rate of 92.50% in their experiments using the HuGaDB dataset. In [5], a technique to extract features using Discrete Fourier Transforms is proposed to estimate the mean power in selected frequency bands for ataxic gait assessment recognition. The accelerometric data were acquired by 31 time-synchronized sensors (perception neuron system) located at different body parts. Different classifiers were used for evaluation, such as support vector machines, Bayesian, nearest neighbors, and neural network methods, with the highest accuracy of 98.5%. The data comprised 13 normal and 12 ataxic individuals, and the entire study was conducted in a clinical environment. Deep learning techniques were applied to predict falls in older adults [9]. Data were collected on fall risk factors in the elderly using WS (accelerometers), questionnaires, and physical tests. The dataset consisted of 296 older adults wearing a triaxial accelerometer on their lower back for a week and the following six months in which fall incidences and descriptions were obtained. Researchers used the raw accelerometer data (without making the preprocessing step) as input to an LSTM classifier, obtaining a time reduction and an AUC (Area Under the Curve) of 0.75.

In summary, most of the works conclude that the more sensors and extracted features from data, the better the accuracy of the computer classification algorithm. Nevertheless, sensors installed on the human body produce less comfort for the patient (ergonomic), make it more challenging to perform human activities, increase noise, and require more time to (pre/post)process data and analyze the activities in real time [29].

3. Methodology

This section presents the mathematical techniques we propose to classify human gait signals. Figure 1 illustrates the proposed method workflow. The first step is collecting the raw data to preprocess it, removing noise and undesired signals, then extracting relevant features, and finally training and testing a human activity classifier.

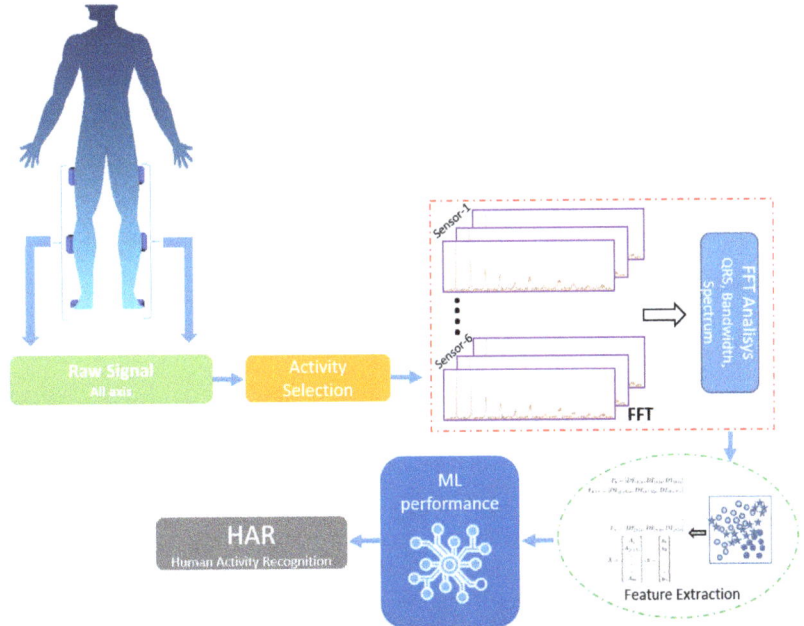

Figure 1. Flow chart of the proposed methodology.

This work intends to start from the raw accelerometer signal in our proposed methodology. This approach was used by other works, such as in [9], where they obtained good results in processing time, or in [30], where nuances could be unintentionally removed from the raw features when the parameters are extracted. We intend to model a classifier with less data and less processing time. For instance, Figure 2a illustrates a raw signal containing two activities, and Figure 2b presents only one signal corresponding to the walking activity from the right shin. As in [9], we use the raw acceleration data directly as input to study and transform the signal.

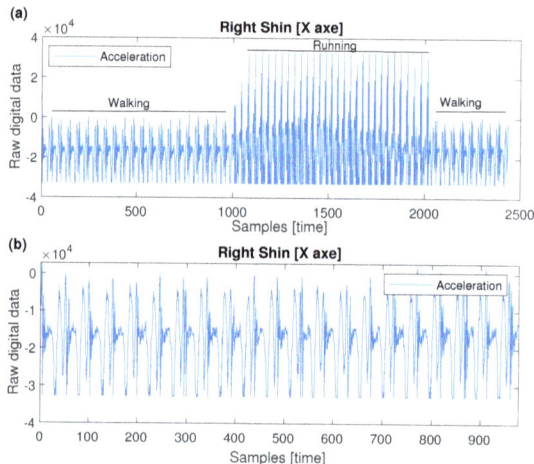

Figure 2. Raw signal from X-axis accelerometer of the right shin: (**a**) whole raw data, (**b**) walking subsample.

Feature extraction is a commonly used technique to clear data and focus only on the relevant features by reducing the dimensionality. Several methods proposed in the literature focused on extracting signal features, such as those based on time–frequency domain, and many other techniques that allow the reduction of data dimensionality [31].

In this work, a total of six sensors were installed on different parts (feet, shins, and thighs) of the legs, each containing a 3-axis accelerometer X, Y and Z (18 total signals). All information of the signals is converted into the frequency domain using FFT to reduce the size, eliminate useless data, and facilitate the training process of the classifiers.

3.1. Signal Preprocessing

There are methods for feature extraction based on the time, frequency, and time-frequency domain, which are usually applied to the raw data. In this work, we propose a set of signal processing steps to obtain relevant features, which are summarized in Algorithm 1.

Algorithm 1 Features extraction from acceleration signal

Input: acc = acceleration data (x,y,z) from each part of the body
f_{c2} = max bandwidth frequency
Output: Feature vector of the selected frequency bandwidth
Method: IMU_features(x,y,x)

1: raw_data ← acc
2: **while** iteration=1,2,..., $N_{patients}$ **do**
3:     filtered_data ← Highpass_filter(raw_data)
4:     angle_data ← Resultant_angle(filtered_data)
5:     fft_data ← ExtractFFT(angle_data)
6:     norm_data ← Normalize(fft_data)
7:     extrap_data ← Freq_norm(norm_data)
8:     f_{c1} ← QRS(extrap_data)
9:     feature_vector ← get(extrap_data,f_{c1},f_{c2})
10: **end while**
11: **return:** feature_vector

3.1.1. Noise Filtering

First, the high-pass Chebyshev filter filters the direct current (DC) noise. The approximation of the gain response as a function of angular frequency w is indicated in Equation (1). The high-pass filter of eighth order, cutoff frequency of 0.4 Hz, and attenuation of 80 are applied.

$$G_n(\omega) = \frac{1}{\sqrt{1 + \frac{1}{\varepsilon^2 T_n^2(\omega_0/\omega)}}} \qquad (1)$$

where ε is the ripple factor, ω_0 is the cutoff frequency and T_n is a Chebyshev polynomial of the n-th order.

As an example, in Figure 3a, we can see the signal spectrum with one pulse at 0 Hz (DC noise), and the pass-high filter removes the noise (Figure 3b).

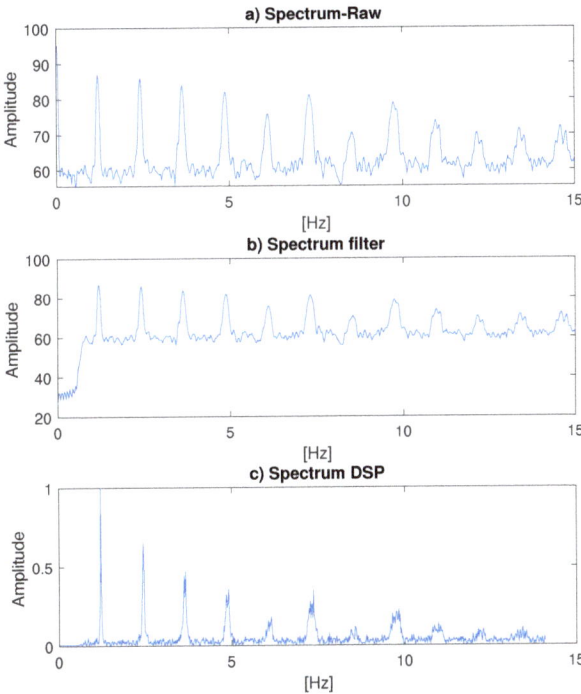

Figure 3. Signal in the frequency domain of X-axis accelerometer in right foot (walk activity). (**a**) Raw data. (**b**) Spectrum after pass-band filter. (**c**) Spectrum after FFT and normalization.

3.1.2. Resultant Angle

The number of features is a crucial stage of feature selection, where the information in the feature matrix will influence the discrimination ability of the deep features. If the signal is considerably large, then a data reduction technique is helpful to simplify the input while preserving the properties of the signal. In those cases, besides complicated data analysis, the proposed method may be incompatible with the dataset, and the proposed classifier may be generalized to a limited dataset.

As was denoted at the beginning of the Section, we have 18 signals, 3 axes for each of the 6 sensors. A common practice is to create the feature vector F^k containing the filtered signal for the 3 axes:

$$F^k = [f_X^k, f_Y^k, f_Z^k], \quad k = 1, \ldots, 6. \qquad (2)$$

However, there is much redundant information that slows down the training of the classification model. For that reason, we computed the resultant angle of the accelerometer's specific forces [32]:

$$Angle_X = \arctan\left(\sqrt{\frac{f_X^2}{f_Y^2 + f_Z^2}}\right) \quad (3)$$

where f_X, f_Y, f_Z are the gravity forces, i.e., the accelerometer signals. f_X is in the numerator since the principal signal would be the X-axis.

Applying Equation (3) to our filtered signals and translating into Equation (2), we reduce the size of the feature vector of each body accelerometer.

$$F^k = Angle_X^k \quad (4)$$

3.1.3. Frequency Domain Analysis

In this research, the Fast Fourier Transform (FFT) has been used to convert the received resultant signals into the frequency domain. Specifically, the Discrete Fourier Transform (DFT) [31,33,34] is applied to improve the computational complexity. The frequency content of the input signal x is then extracted using the following transformation:

$$X(k) = \sum_{n=0}^{N-1} x_n exp\left[-i2\pi\frac{nk}{N}\right] \quad (5)$$

where $X = FFT(x)$, x_n is the n-th element of an input signal, k is the frequency sample, and N is the transformation length.

FFT's performance depends on the signal's length, and to improve its speed, the Cooley/Tukey algorithm is used through the Matlab *fft* function, which exploits the symmetries to reduce a large DFT into smaller DFTs. This process helps reduce computational complexity from $O(N^2)$ to $O(NlogN)$, improving speed [33]. Our research used the entire IMU signal for the FFT operation and transformed it separately for each patient.

3.1.4. Power and Bandwidth Normalization

After applying the FFT, the signal is normalized in the range [0,1] by applying

$$X_{power\_norm} = \frac{|X_{fft}|}{\max(|X_{fft}|)} \quad (6)$$

Figure 3c depicts the resulting signal.

In the same way, the signal was normalized in the power spectrum, and it is convenient to equalize the signal in the frequency axis. This way, all samples fall into the power spectrum, helping the classifier have homogeneous training. For that purpose, the maximum frequency for all the data samples is found, and then, linear extrapolation is computed:

$$\mathcal{F}_{MAX} = \max(\{\mathcal{F}_j, \quad j = 1, \ldots, M\})$$
$$X_{freq\_norm} = \text{linear\_extrap}(X_{power\_norm}, \mathcal{F}_{MAX}) \quad (7)$$

where $\mathcal{F}$ represents the set of frequency values of a sample, and M represents the total number of samples.

Figures 4 and 5 present a detailed spectral analysis (evolution of spectral components) as the relative power along the frequency. This figure shows an example of the processed accelerometer signal of the walking activity.

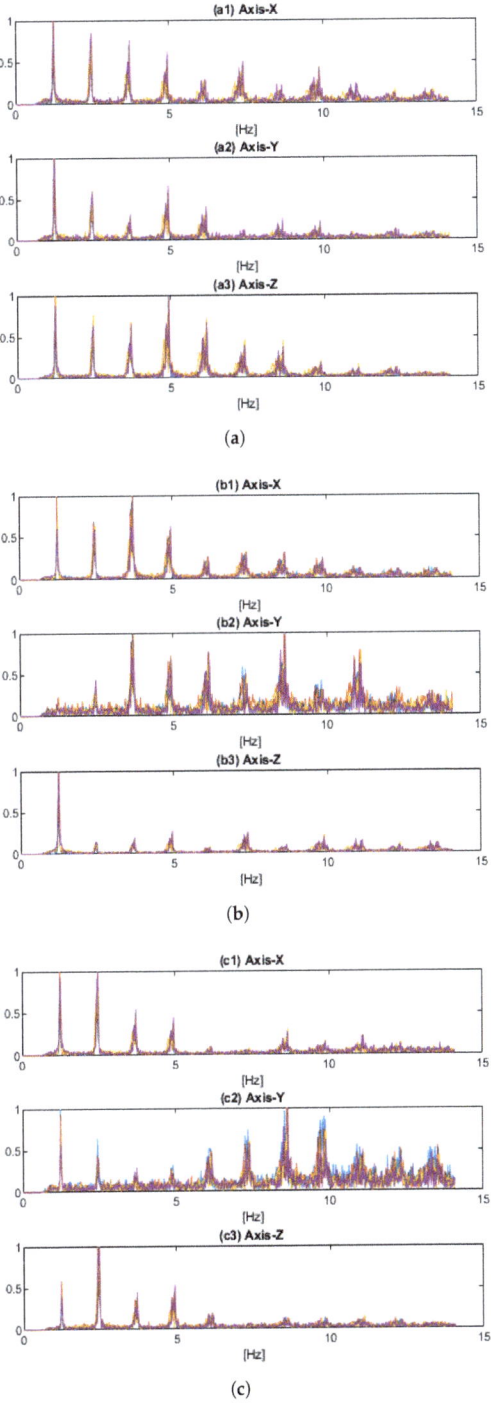

Figure 4. Right Walk Activity Spectrum. (**a**) Foot Spectrum. (**b**) Shin Spectrum. (**c**) Thigh Spectrum.

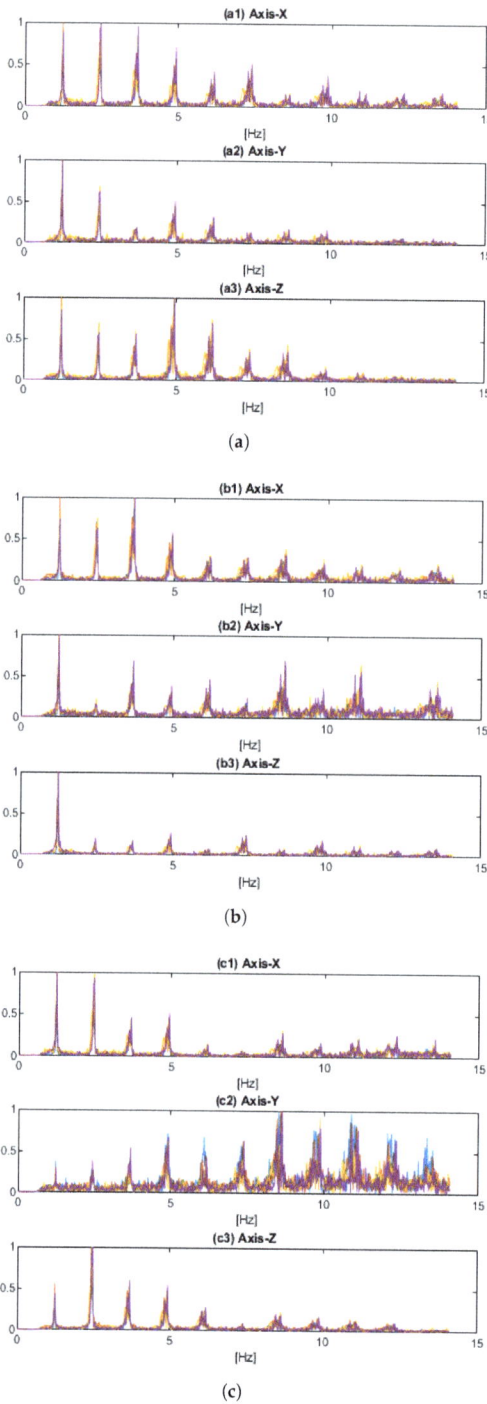

Figure 5. Left Walk Activity Spectrum. (**a**) Foot Spectrum. (**b**) Shin Spectrum. (**c**) Thigh Spectrum.

3.1.5. Mean Relative Power QRS Detection

As it was exposed in [31], the first and second dominant frequency amplitudes hold the most information about the signal, so we propose a method to extract those amplitudes based on QRS complexes and use them as the inputs of the classification models.

The key element of extracting these frequency amplitudes is setting, and appropriate threshold tolerance, which is used by the QRS algorithm [35]. This technique is used in spectrum analysis to recognize QRS complexes, reducing false detections caused by interferences in ECG signals. Figure 6 shows an example of the QRS detection, where R is the peak of the principal spectrum, Q is the start of the peak signal, and S is the end of the peak signal, which will be unnecessary for our application, as explained later.

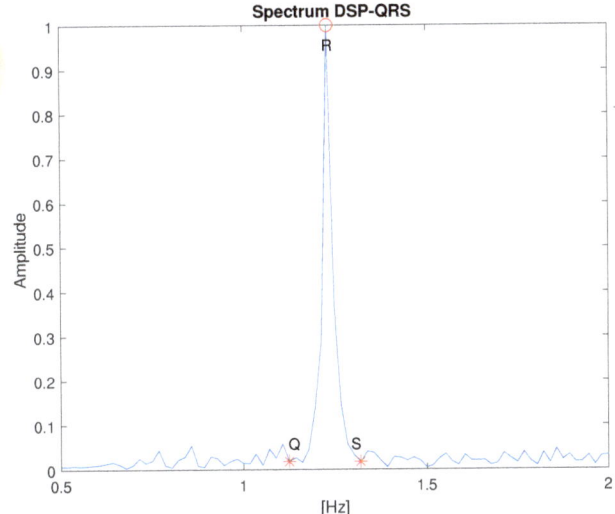

Figure 6. Example of the QRS calculation in the first spectrum.

However, peak detection is a very critical step, since information can be lost if an adequate threshold is not set up correctly. For instance, in [36], a modified version of the QRS algorithm with an adaptative threshold is presented, defining two kinds of peaks: signal and noise peak. If a peak value is larger than the threshold, it is marked as a QRS complex, and then, the signal peak is updated.

This solution has a problem with the noise peak because it detects some spectra as noise, and the signal amplitude is not constant, such as the ECG signal. For instance, a threshold of 0.257 when calculated with the data in Figure 7 loses the information of other spectrums.

The Pan and Tompkins algorithm inspires our proposal to detect the QRS complex [35]. First, a differentiation provides complex slope information, and then, an amplitude squaring function and a moving window integrator are applied. The following paragraphs will describe the process in detail:

1. Differentiation. After filtering and normalizing, the signal is differentiated as follows:

$$y(nT) = \frac{1}{8}[-x(nT-2T) - 2x(nT-T) + 2x(nT+T) + x(nT+2T)] \quad (8)$$

where T is the sampling period.

2. Squaring. It amplifies the slope of the frequency response.

$$y(nT) = [x(nT)]^2 \quad (9)$$

3. Moving-Windows Integration. To obtain waveform feature information:

$$y(nT) = \frac{1}{N}[x(nT - (N-1)T) + x(nT - (N-2)T) + \cdots + x(nT)] \qquad (10)$$

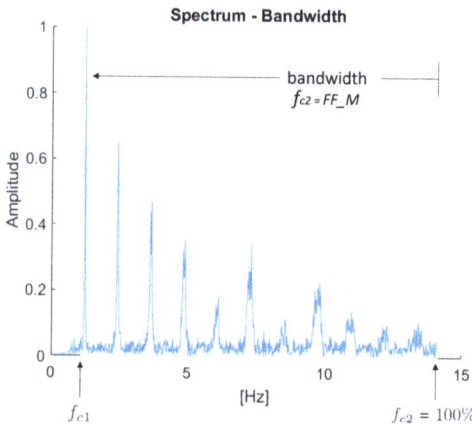

Figure 7. Example of the selected bandwidth, where f_{c1} = Q and f_{c2} = 100%.

After that, the Mean Relative Power signal is used to initialize the threshold. This measure aims to vary the bandwidth of our spectral signal so that only the desired signal information is considered. Equation (11) calculates the average power in a window selected by the desired frequencies:

$$P_w = \int_{-f}^{f} |X(f)|^2 \, df \qquad (11)$$

As shown in [5], each of the selected spectral features of a signal segment of N samples is evaluated and divided by the first half-part signal ($N/2$ samples) in order to keep the most significant information. Equation (12) computes the discrete Mean Relative Power in a specified frequency band:

$$MP_{rel} = \frac{\sum_{k \in \phi} |X(k)|^2}{\sum_{k=0}^{N/2} |X(k)|^2} \qquad (12)$$

where ϕ is the set of indices for which the frequency values $f_k = \frac{k}{N} f_s \in [f_{c1}, f_{c2}]$. In the given case, we study the accelerometric spectral features in the [0%, 100%] range.

Therefore, the MP_{rel} is used as signal peaks instead of using both the integration waveform signal peak and the noise-filtered signal peak for the threshold initialization as in [35].

$$M_{VAL} = MP_{rel}(signal)$$
$$SPKI = 0.13 * M_{VAL} \qquad (13)$$
$$THRESHOLD = 0.25 * SPKI + 0.75 * NPKI$$

where *signal* refers to the integration waveform and filtered signal, respectively; $SPKI$ is the estimate of the signal peak, $NPKI$ is the noise peak, and $THRESHOLD$ is the applied threshold.

The rest of the detection procedure follows the original QRS algorithm. Once the peaks are detected, the initial frequency f_{c1} is set, and the rest of the bandwidth is the signal extracted to be used for the next step:

$$f_{c1} = Q \qquad (14)$$

where Q is the Q-element of the QRS complex of the first peak. As an example, in Figure 6, the point Q is automatically found by the proposed methodology, and we set the value to f_{c1}. On the other hand, f_{c2} will define the last point of the bandwidth frequency. Figure 7 shows a f_{c2} reaching 100% bandwidth.

3.2. Sliding Bandwidth Analysis

The selected frequency range is varied to reduce the number of features and sensors. The bandwidth is located within the range f_{c1} to f_{c2} of each frequency analysis, as shown in Figure 7, and these sets are expressed in Equation (15):

$$BW = f_{c2} - f_{c1} \quad for \quad f_{c1} \leq f_{c2} \leq 100\% \tag{15}$$

Therefore, the power spectra analyzed vary according to the length of BW:

$$PS = [X(k)]_\theta \tag{16}$$

where $\theta \in [f_{c1}, f_{c2}]$ is the set of indices for which the frequency values vary within the bandwidth.

4. Experimental Results

4.1. Dataset Description

The Human Gait Database [37] is commonly used in research for human activity recognition (HAR), gesture recognition (GR), and gait analysis (GA). This dataset has been used in many works because they represent the inertial movement of a person and help to develop models before installing them in wearable sensor systems. The dataset comprises 18 healthy participants who were split into two groups: 15 participants to create and validate the model and 3 participants to test the model. This way, the information the classification models test will be completely independent of the one used for training, assuring a fair comparison.

In total, six inertial sensors (IMU) (each IMU sensor has a three-axis accelerometer and three-axis gyroscope) and electromyography (sEMG) sensors were placed on the right and left thighs, shins, and feet. The total number of signals collected is 38:36 from the IMU sensor and 2 from the sEMG sensor. This database contains 12 activities: Walking with ID (1), Running with ID (2), Going up with ID (3), Going down with ID (4), Sitting with ID (5), Sitting down with ID (6), Standing up with ID (7), Standing with ID (8), Bicycling with ID (9), Up by elevator with ID (10), Down by elevator with ID (11), and Sitting in the car with ID (12).

4.2. Classification Experiments

The proposed method was applied to accelerometric raw data on the HuGaDB dataset. After the initial spectral preprocessing, we set the frequency f_{c2} to 100% to check the performance of the classifiers with the total bandwidth. For the experiments, Discriminant Analysis (DA), Support Vector Machine (SVM) and Neural Network (NN) classification models were employed. The code was written in Matlab (R2021b). The method was applied on each axis, receiving signals from the right and left legs.

As mentioned, the dataset contains information on six different sensors, which is summarized in Table 1.

Table 1. Acceleromether used in the body.

	Left			Right		
Data	Feet	Shins	Thighs	Feet	Shins	Thighs
k	1	2	3	4	5	6

In order to carry out the classification experiments, all preprocessed accelerometer signals are concatenated into an activity vector.

$$A_j = [\{F^k\}]_j, \quad k = 1, \ldots, 6. \tag{17}$$

where j represents the number of sample activities, the training data comprises a set of signals for $N = 15$ persons that carried out several activities. These activities are previously identified in the whole signal and separated into different M samples. The set of samples $\{A_j\}_{j=1,\ldots,M}$ and their respective true class labels will form the training data. After preprocessing the dataset, the total number of training samples after preprocessing the dataset is 152, where $M = 122$ (from 15 participants) will be used for training and 30 will be used for testing (from 3 participants).

First, the performance achieved using the maximum bandwidth was compared. Here, 10-fold cross-validation was carried out to train the models and make a preliminary selection among several classifiers, using 75% of the data for training and 25% for testing (from 15 participants, as indicated in Section 4.1). After that, the unseen test set (from three participants) was used to compute the real performance. Each instance is represented by the patient, for a total of 18 patients within each activity, meaning that each class keeps the same amount of class instances for both the train and test sets.

The results of the different classifiers are compared in Table 2. In addition, we compared our performance with a state-of-art method that used a similar sensor and data configurations to our experiments [8] to have a fair comparison. We did not compare our approach with other published work on a combination of sensor signals. Hence, our methodology yielded an accuracy of 95.10% using NN and 91% using SVM compared to the 5% and 4% less accuracy, respectively, obtained by the competing method. In addition, our method was applied with a Discriminant Analysis classifier, achieving 95.5% accuracy, being chosen as the best for our proposal. The methodology proposed in [8] is still worse with 92.5% accuracy.

Table 2. Accuracy Experiments using HuGaDB and Frequency Features.

Method	DA (%)	SVM (%)	NN (%)
Gochoo et al. [8]	-	85.68	91.23
Ours	95.50	91.00	95.10

The rest of the experiments will focus on modifying the bandwidth to analyze the impact of applying the proposed method with less information.

4.3. Bandwith Analysis

This analysis aims to reduce the sample data (8022 features per sample) used to train the classifiers. Each activity contains 56.35 samples per second, and the acquisition time varies. We study the accelerometric power spectral in $[f_{c1}, f_{c2}]$, where f_{c1} is detected automatically and f_{c2} will vary for training. The bandwidth extension has been studied in these three classifiers, reducing the bandwidth by 10% each time, starting from the endpoint of the spectrum, $f_{c2} = 100\%$.

Figure 8 summarizes the accuracy obtained for each bandwidth. It can be observed that the precision of the DA classifier does not change up to a bandwidth of 70%. In addition, it can be observed that the NN classifier has good precision in the range of 90% to 50%, although it slowly decreases when the bandwidth is shortened. Lastly, the SVM classifier presents the worst overall performance, although it is quite robust to the reduction of training data, having even better performance with only 30–50% of the bandwidth. From these results, we can extract that using 70% of the bandwidth with the DA classifier produces the same accuracy as if 100% bandwidth is used. Therefore, data can be reduced to 5615 features to improve the training time of the classifiers, obtaining the same outcomes.

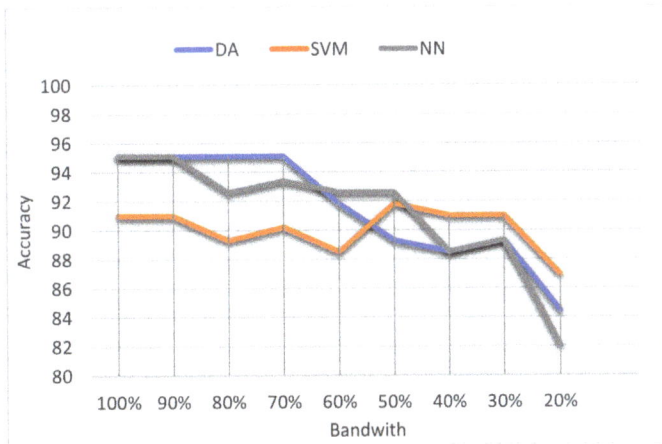

Figure 8. Evolution of accuracy over different bandwidths.

Figure 9 depicts the behavior of the classifiers when changing the bandwidth for each type of activity. Each of the classifiers has obtained excellent performances for most of the activities. For instance, walking, going up the stairs, and going up with the elevator only needed a primary spectrum in the 20% window of bandwidth, independently of the classifier; however, other activities need a wider bandwidth to be recognized. However, to obtain excellent general performance, more data are required. The DA classifier, shown in Figure 9a, can perfectly recognize up to nine activities with 70% bandwidth. SVM and NN (Figure 9b,c) reflected similar performances except for the elevator and going downstairs. However, they improve the recognition of the car-sitting activity, reaching 100% accuracy with 40% and 50% bandwidth, respectively.

Focusing on the type of activity, the elevator is the most critical one. It is interesting to see that for the SVM, 60% of the bandwidth is necessary to reach 80% accuracy, but for NN, 70% of the data is needed. The DA cannot detect this activity properly, but the action of sitting has a perfect detection with only 30% of the bandwidth. On the other hand, the run and bicycle are better classified by the NN, which means that it works better with complex signals.

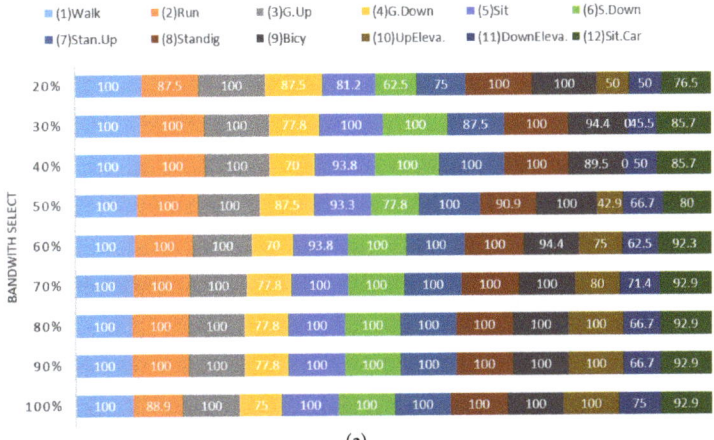

(a)

Figure 9. *Cont.*

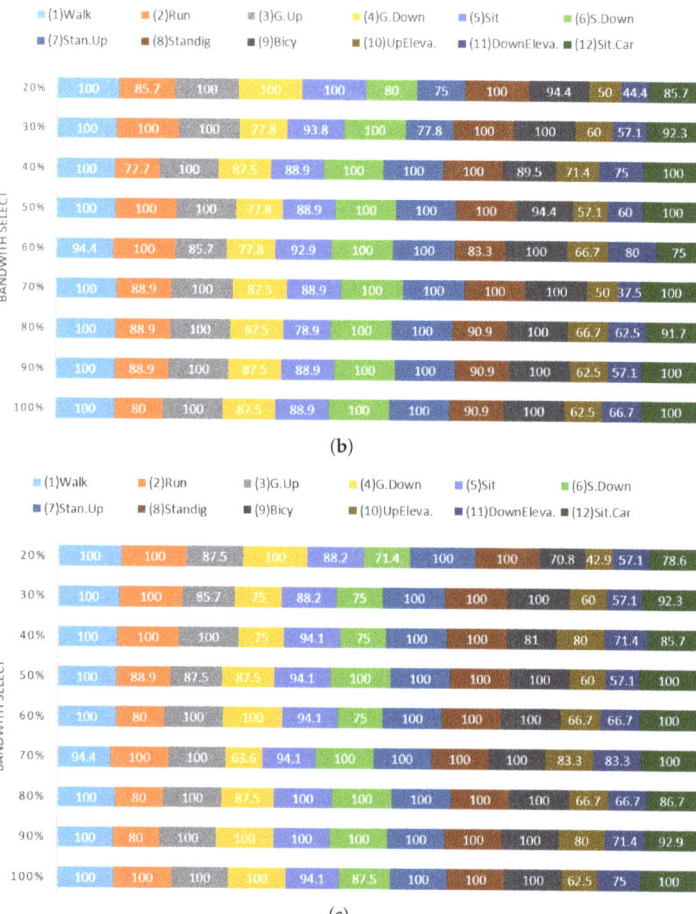

Figure 9. Human Activities Accuracy with Bandwidth Select. (**a**) DA—Discriminant Analysis Classification. (**b**) SVM—Support Vector Machine Classification. (**c**) NN—Neural Network Classification.

5. Conclusions

This paper presents a new methodology based on the frequency domain. Features were extracted from the raw data of IMUs by varying the frequency window to optimize the number of relevant features. All the information provided by the raw accelerometer signals was optimized and transformed using the proposed methodology. In addition, a modified QRS algorithm is proposed to automatically find the first frequency and the beginning of the bandwidth.

The standard HuGaDB dataset was used with the best classifiers found in the literature for HAR problems (DA, SVM, and NN). Experimental results show the improved accuracies achieved (Table 2) when the proposed methodology is applied. These results were achieved using the whole frequency spectrum. Additionally, the performance of our proposal was analyzed for reduced bandwidths and studied in detail for the different activities to be recognized. SVM is the most robust classifier, producing a similar performance for reduced bandwidths, although DA achieves the best accuracy for reduced bandwidths (up to 70%). Regarding the recognition of the different activities, both Up Elevator and Down Elevator are the activities with the worst accuracy. In the end, activity recognition varies depending on the bandwidth used due to where the most significant information is placed in the frequency spectrum. For instance, Walking and Running activities are easily recognized, even with 20% of the bandwidth, because the relevant information of these activities is in the first power spectrum.

Future works will include more types of signals as part of the input for training by creating an adequate methodology to preprocess and join the signals to achieve better outcomes than state-of-art methods. In addition, another important study to carry out is the reduction of the number of sensors, determining which positions and how many of them are enough to provide good classification results.

Author Contributions: Conceptualization, D.T.-P. and E.D.; methodology, D.T.-P.; software, D.T.-P.; validation, D.T.-P. and K.T.-H.; formal analysis, K.T.-H.; investigation, D.T.-P.; writing—original draft preparation, D.T.-P.; writing—review and editing, K.T.-H. and E.D.; supervision, K.T.-H. and E.D. All authors have read and agreed to the published version of the manuscript.

Funding: This research was partially funded by the Autonomous Government of Andalusia (Spain), grant number UMA20-FEDERJA-108. It is also partially supported by the University of Málaga (Spain), grant numbers B1-2019_01, B1-2019_02, B1-2021_20, and B4-2022. Partial funding for open access charge: Universidad de Málaga.

Data Availability Statement: HuGaDB https://github.com/romanchereshnev/HuGaDB (accessed on 13 November 2021).

Acknowledgments: The authors thankfully acknowledge the computer resources, technical expertise and assistance provided by the SCBI (Supercomputing and Bioinformatics) center of the University of Málaga. They also gratefully acknowledge the support of NVIDIA Corporation with the donation of a RTX A6000 GPU with 48Gb. The authors also thankfully acknowledge the grant of the Universidad de Málaga and the Instituto de Investigación Biomédica de Málaga y Plataforma en Nanomedicina-IBIMA Plataforma BIONAND.

Conflicts of Interest: The authors declare no conflict of interest. The funders had no role in the design of the study; in the collection, analyses, or interpretation of data; in the writing of the manuscript; or in the decision to publish the results.

Abbreviations

The following abbreviations are used in this manuscript:

HuGaDB	Human Gait Database
NWS	Non-Wearable Sensor
WS	Wearable Sensor
IMU	Inertial Measurement Units
HAR	Human Activity Recognition
EMG	Electromyigraphy
PAMAP2	Physical Activity Monitoring for Aging People
SGD	Stochastic Gradient Descent
FARAO	Fall Risk Assessment in Older Adults
AUC	Area Under the Curve
GR	Gesture Recognition
GA	Gait Analysis
FFT	Fast Fourier Transform
DFT	Discrete Fourier Transform
DSP	Digital Signal Process
DC	Direct Courrient
PS	Power Spectral
BW	Bandwidth
DT	Data Transform
DA	Discriminant Analysis
SVM	Support Vector Machine
NN	Neural Network

References

1. Senanayake, C.; Senanayake, S. Human assisted tools for gait analysis and intelligent gait phase detection. In Proceedings of the 2009 Innovative Technologies in Intelligent Systems and Industrial Applications, Kuala Lumpur, Malaysia, 25–26 July 2009; IEEE: Piscataway, NJ, USA, 2009; pp. 230–235.
2. Teran, P.D.; Dominguez, E. Human gait model based on a machine learning and filtering noisy signals with recursive algorithm. In Proceedings of the 2020 IEEE International Conference on Bioinformatics and Biomedicine (BIBM), Seoul, Republic of Korea, 16–19 December 2020; IEEE: Piscataway, NJ, USA, 2020; pp. 1142–1145.
3. Prakash, C.; Kumar, R.; Mittal, N. Recent developments in human gait research: parameters, approaches, applications, machine learning techniques, datasets and challenges. *Artif. Intell. Rev.* **2018**, *49*, 1–40. [CrossRef]
4. Song, Y.; Zhang, J.; Cao, L.; Sangeux, M. On discovering the correlated relationship between static and dynamic data in clinical gait analysis. In Proceedings of the Joint European Conference on Machine Learning and Knowledge Discovery in Databases, Prague, Czech Republic, 23–27 September 2013; Springer: Berlin/Heidelberg, Germany, 2013; pp. 563–578.
5. Dostál, O.; Procházka, A.; Vyšata, O.; Ťupa, O.; Cejnar, P.; Vališ, M. Recognition of motion patterns using accelerometers for ataxic gait assessment. *Neural Comput. Appl.* **2021**, *33*, 2207–2215. [CrossRef]
6. Buckley, E.; Mazzà, C.; McNeill, A. A systematic review of the gait characteristics associated with Cerebellar Ataxia. *Gait Posture* **2018**, *60*, 154–163. [CrossRef] [PubMed]
7. Joukov, V.; Bonnet, V.; Karg, M.; Venture, G.; Kulić, D. Rhythmic extended Kalman filter for gait rehabilitation motion estimation and segmentation. *IEEE Trans. Neural Syst. Rehabil. Eng.* **2017**, *26*, 407–418. [CrossRef] [PubMed]
8. Gochoo, M.; Tahir, S.B.U.D.; Jalal, A.; Kim, K. Monitoring real-time personal locomotion behaviors over smart indoor-outdoor environments via body-worn sensors. *IEEE Access* **2021**, *9*, 70556–70570. [CrossRef]
9. Nait Aicha, A.; Englebienne, G.; Van Schooten, K.S.; Pijnappels, M.; Kröse, B. Deep learning to predict falls in older adults based on daily-life trunk accelerometry. *Sensors* **2018**, *18*, 1654. [CrossRef] [PubMed]
10. Allseits, E.; Kim, K.J.; Bennett, C.; Gailey, R.; Gaunaurd, I.; Agrawal, V. A novel method for estimating knee angle using two leg-mounted gyroscopes for continuous monitoring with mobile health devices. *Sensors* **2018**, *18*, 2759. [CrossRef]
11. Del Din, S.; Hickey, A.; Hurwitz, N.; Mathers, J.C.; Rochester, L.; Godfrey, A. Measuring gait with an accelerometer-based wearable: influence of device location, testing protocol and age. *Physiol. Meas.* **2016**, *37*, 1785–1797. [CrossRef]
12. Staab, W.; Hottowitz, R.; Sohns, C.; Sohns, J.M.; Gilbert, F.; Menke, J.; Niklas, A.; Lotz, J. Accelerometer and gyroscope based gait analysis using spectral analysis of patients with osteoarthritis of the knee. *J. Phys. Ther. Sci.* **2014**, *26*, 997–1002. [CrossRef]
13. Zilani, T.A.; Al-Turjman, F.; Khan, M.B.; Zhao, N.; Yang, X. Monitoring movements of ataxia patient by using UWB technology. *Sensors* **2020**, *20*, 931. [CrossRef]
14. Procházka, A.; Vyšata, O.; Charvátová, H.; Vališ, M. Motion symmetry evaluation using accelerometers and energy distribution. *Symmetry* **2019**, *11*, 871. [CrossRef]
15. Ebara, T.; Azuma, R.; Shoji, N.; Matsukawa, T.; Yamada, Y.; Akiyama, T.; Kurihara, T.; Yamada, S. Reliability of smartphone-based gait measurements for quantification of physical activity/inactivity levels. *J. Occup. Health* **2017**, *59*, 17–0101. [CrossRef] [PubMed]
16. Voicu, R.A.; Dobre, C.; Bajenaru, L.; Ciobanu, R.I. Human physical activity recognition using smartphone sensors. *Sensors* **2019**, *19*, 458. [CrossRef]
17. Castillejo, P.; Martinez, J.F.; Rodriguez-Molina, J.; Cuerva, A. Integration of wearable devices in a wireless sensor network for an E-health application. *IEEE Wirel. Commun.* **2013**, *20*, 38–49. [CrossRef]
18. Chatterjee, R.; Maitra, T.; Islam, S.H.; Hassan, M.M.; Alamri, A.; Fortino, G. A novel machine learning based feature selection for motor imagery EEG signal classification in Internet of medical things environment. *Future Gener. Comput. Syst.* **2019**, *98*, 419–434. [CrossRef]
19. Gravina, R.; Alinia, P.; Ghasemzadeh, H.; Fortino, G. Multi-sensor fusion in body sensor networks: State-of-the-art and research challenges. *Inf. Fusion* **2017**, *35*, 68–80. [CrossRef]
20. Uddin, M.Z.; Hassan, M.M. Activity recognition for cognitive assistance using body sensors data and deep convolutional neural network. *IEEE Sensors J.* **2018**, *19*, 8413–8419. [CrossRef]
21. Fortino, G.; Giannantonio, R.; Gravina, R.; Kuryloski, P.; Jafari, R. Enabling effective programming and flexible management of efficient body sensor network applications. *IEEE Trans. -Hum.-Mach. Syst.* **2012**, *43*, 115–133. [CrossRef]
22. Badawi, A.A.; Al-Kabbany, A.; Shaban, H.A. Sensor type, axis, and position-based fusion and feature selection for multimodal human daily activity recognition in wearable body sensor networks. *J. Healthc. Eng.* **2020**, *2020*, 7914649 [CrossRef]
23. Beltran-Carbajal, F.; Abundis-Fong, H.F.; Trujillo-Franco, L.G.; Yañez-Badillo, H.; Favela-Contreras, A.; Campos-Mercado, E. Online frequency estimation on a building-like structure using a nonlinear flexible dynamic vibration absorber. *Mathematics* **2022**, *10*, 708. [CrossRef]
24. Kuo, J.Y.; You, S.Y.; Lin, H.C.; Hsu, C.Y.; Lei, B. Constructing Condition Monitoring Model of Wind Turbine Blades. *Mathematics* **2022**, *10*, 972. [CrossRef]
25. Hayati, H.; Mahdavi, F.; Eager, D. Analysis of agile canine gait characteristics using accelerometry. *Sensors* **2019**, *19*, 4379. [CrossRef] [PubMed]
26. Nguyen, N.; Phan, D.; Pathirana, P.N.; Horne, M.; Power, L.; Szmulewicz, D. Quantification of axial abnormality due to cerebellar ataxia with inertial measurements. *Sensors* **2018**, *18*, 2791. [CrossRef]

27. Phan, D.; Nguyen, N.; Pathirana, P.N.; Horne, M.; Power, L.; Szmulewicz, D. Quantitative assessment of ataxic gait using inertial sensing at different walking speeds. In Proceedings of the 2019 41st Annual International Conference of the IEEE Engineering in Medicine and Biology Society (EMBC), Berlin, Germany, 23–27 July 2019; IEEE: Piscataway, NJ, USA, 2019; pp. 4600–4603.
28. Caliandro, P.; Conte, C.; Iacovelli, C.; Tatarelli, A.; Castiglia, S.F.; Reale, G.; Serrao, M. Exploring risk of falls and dynamic unbalance in cerebellar ataxia by inertial sensor assessment. *Sensors* **2019**, *19*, 5571. [CrossRef] [PubMed]
29. Antoniades, A.; Spyrou, L.; Martin-Lopez, D.; Valentin, A.; Alarcon, G.; Sanei, S.; Took, C.C. Detection of interictal discharges with convolutional neural networks using discrete ordered multichannel intracranial EEG. *IEEE Trans. Neural Syst. Rehabil. Eng.* **2017**, *25*, 2285–2294. [CrossRef]
30. Tunca, C.; Salur, G.; Ersoy, C. Deep learning for fall risk assessment with inertial sensors: Utilizing domain knowledge in spatio-temporal gait parameters. *IEEE J. Biomed. Health Informatics* **2019**, *24*, 1994–2005. [CrossRef]
31. Taylan, O.; Sattari, M.A.; Elhachfi Essoussi, I.; Nazemi, E. Frequency Domain Feature Extraction Investigation to Increase the Accuracy of an Intelligent Nondestructive System for Volume Fraction and Regime Determination of Gas-Water-Oil Three-Phase Flows. *Mathematics* **2021**, *9*, 2091. [CrossRef]
32. Tjhai, C.; O'Keefe, K. Using step size and lower limb segment orientation from multiple low-cost wearable inertial/magnetic sensors for pedestrian navigation. *Sensors* **2019**, *19*, 3140. [CrossRef]
33. Kang, H.; Lee, J.; Kim, D. Hi-fft: Heterogeneous parallel in-place algorithm for large-scale 2D-fft. *IEEE Access* **2021**, *9*, 120261–120273. [CrossRef]
34. Adámek, K.; Novotný, J.; Thiyagalingam, J.; Armour, W. Efficiency near the edge: Increasing the energy efficiency of FFTs on GPUs for real-time edge computing. *IEEE Access* **2021**, *9*, 18167–18182. [CrossRef]
35. Pan, J.; Tompkins, W.J. A Real-Time QRS Detection Algorithm. *IEEE Trans. Biomed. Eng.* **1985**, *BME-32*, 230–236. [CrossRef] [PubMed]
36. Lu, X.; Pan, M.; Yu, Y. QRS detection based on improved adaptive threshold. *J. Healthc. Eng.* **2018**, *2018*, 5694595. [CrossRef] [PubMed]
37. Chereshnev, R.; Kertész-Farkas, A. Hugadb: Human gait database for activity recognition from wearable inertial sensor networks. In Proceedings of the International Conference on Analysis of Images, Social Networks and Texts, Moscow, Russia, 5–7 July 2018; Springer: Berlin/Heidelberg, Germany, 2018; pp. 131–141.

Disclaimer/Publisher's Note: The statements, opinions and data contained in all publications are solely those of the individual author(s) and contributor(s) and not of MDPI and/or the editor(s). MDPI and/or the editor(s) disclaim responsibility for any injury to people or property resulting from any ideas, methods, instructions or products referred to in the content.

Review

Auto-Encoders in Deep Learning—A Review with New Perspectives

Shuangshuang Chen [1,2,*] and Wei Guo [2]

1. Jiangsu Provincial Key Constructive Laboratory for Big Data of Psychology and Cognitive Science, Yancheng Teachers University, Yancheng 224002, China
2. College of Information Engineering, Yancheng Teachers University, Yancheng 224002, China
* Correspondence: chenss@yctu.edu.cn; Tel.: +86-13851344541

Abstract: Deep learning, which is a subfield of machine learning, has opened a new era for the development of neural networks. The auto-encoder is a key component of deep structure, which can be used to realize transfer learning and plays an important role in both unsupervised learning and non-linear feature extraction. By highlighting the contributions and challenges of recent research papers, this work aims to review state-of-the-art auto-encoder algorithms. Firstly, we introduce the basic auto-encoder as well as its basic concept and structure. Secondly, we present a comprehensive summarization of different variants of the auto-encoder. Thirdly, we analyze and study auto-encoders from three different perspectives. We also discuss the relationships between auto-encoders, shallow models and other deep learning models. The auto-encoder and its variants have successfully been applied in a wide range of fields, such as pattern recognition, computer vision, data generation, recommender systems, etc. Then, we focus on the available toolkits for auto-encoders. Finally, this paper summarizes the future trends and challenges in designing and training auto-encoders. We hope that this survey will provide a good reference when using and designing AE models.

Keywords: auto-encoder; deep learning; artificial intelligence; survey

MSC: 68V99

1. Introduction

Deep neural networks (DNNs), usually referred to as deep learning [1], are a cutting-edge area of machine learning on the forefront of artificial intelligence (AI). They are based on algorithms for learning multiple levels of representation in order to model complex relationships among data. Higher-level concepts and features are thus defined in terms of lower-level ones. Neural networks had traditionally been trained with the back-propagation (BP) algorithm, which is so named because this algorithm propagates the error in the neural network's estimate backward from the output layer towards the input layer [2]. We can use BP to adjust the model parameters along the way. Unfortunately, there were several weaknesses with the BP algorithm which did not work well for DNNs. These included the tendency for the algorithm to fall into poor local minima when the DNNs were initialized with random weights. This is mainly because local optima and other optimization challenges are widespread in the non-convex objective function of the DNNs [3]. The severity will increase essentially as the depth of the network increases. The requirement for labeled datasets is another problem because most data are unlabeled. In 2006, the optimization difficulty associated with DNNs was empirically alleviated when Ref. [4] proposed the Deep Belief Network (DBN), which was a significant advance in deep learning (DL). This class of deep generative models, with a new learning algorithm that greedily trains one layer at a time, exploits an unsupervised learning algorithm for each layer called the Restricted Boltzmann Machine (RBM) [5]. Meanwhile, Ref. [6] exploited the same principle to pre-train the network, and then the RBMs were "unrolled" to create a deep auto-encoder (AE).

Specifically, an AE is one of the basic building blocks, which can be stacked to form hierarchical deep models to organize, compress, and extract high-level features without any labeled training data. It allows for unsupervised learning and non-linear feature extraction. There are some historical contexts of the AE. In the 1980s, the AE was also called an "auto-associator" as described by Ref. [7]. They proposed that the optimal parameter values can be obtained by applying the usual BP or can be derived using standard linear algebra. Then, in 2006, Ref. [8] verified that the principle of the layer-wise greedy unsupervised pre-training can be applied when an AE is used as the layer building block instead of the RBM. In 2008, Ref. [9] showed a straightforward variation of ordinary AEs—the denoising auto-encoder (DAE)—that is trained locally to denoise corrupted versions of the inputs. Ref. [10] introduced a sparse auto-encoder (SAE), which is another variant of the AE. Sparsity is a useful constraint when the number of hidden units is large. In Ref. [11], Rifai et al. presented a novel method for training a deterministic AE. They show that by adding a well-chosen penalty term to the traditional reconstruction cost function, they can achieve results that equal or surpass those attained using DAE as well as other regularized AEs on a range of datasets. This penalty term corresponds to the Frobenius norm of the Jacobian matrix of the encoder activations with respect to the input. Lately, various approaches for AEs have been extensively studied and discussed [12–16]. Among those, Ref. [16] proposed the "k sparse auto-encoder (kSA)", which is an AE with a linear activation function, where in hidden layers only the k highest activities are kept. Based on Ref. [16], two novel feature aggregation algorithms, called Database-adaptive kSA aggregation and Per-data adaptive kSA aggregation, realize more accurate local feature aggregation. The two algorithms have jointly optimized codebook learning and feature encoding. The AE and its various variants have been widely applied in AI, such as image classification [17–19], saliency estimation [20,21], medical image analysis [22], and many more.

- Importance of this survey. There are plenty of studies that have been performed in the field of deep learning-based AEs. However, as far as we know, there are very few reviews that have shaped this area well by positioning the existing works and current progress. Although some Refs. [23,24] have attempted to formalize this research field, but few try to summarize the current efforts in depth or elaborate on the outstanding problems in this field. This survey will seek to provide a comprehensive summary of the current research on deep learning based on AEs and to point out future directions along this dimension. Because of the rising popularity and potential of AEs in deep learning, this survey will be of high scientific and practical value. We have analyzed these works based on AEs from different perspectives and put forward some new insights in this area. To this end, nearly 300 studies are shortlisted and studied in this survey.

- How were the papers collected? In this survey, we collected over three hundred related papers. We used Google Scholar as the main search engine. Additionally, we used the database, Web of Science, as an important tool to discover related papers. We also focused on some high-quality academic conferences such as NIPS, ECCV, ICML, ICLR, CVPR, IJCAI, ICCV, AAAI, etc., to find recent works. The major keywords we used included auto-encoder, deep learning, neural networks, overview, etc.

- Contributions of this survey. This survey provides an overview of various AE methods and their applications; particularly, these can be applied in the computer vision domain. It is intended to be useful for computer vision and general neural computing researchers who are interested in state-of-the-art DL. In addition, one of our main goals is to thoroughly review the literature, clarify less understood challenges, and offer learned lessons from existing works. To summarize, there are three key contributions of this survey: (1) we conducted a literature review of AE models and highlighted many influential research prototypes; (2) we provided an overview and summary of the state of the art; and (3) we discussed promising future extensions in this research field to highlight the vision and expand the horizons of research on AEs.

- Paper Organization. The basic AE and its variants will be discussed in Section 2. In this section, we have introduced the basic AE as well as its basic concept and structure. Additionally, different variants as well as their developments were listed. In Section 3, we analyze and study AEs from three different perspectives. In Section 4, the relationships between AEs, shallow models, and other DL models are described. Section 5 discusses the basic AE and its variants that have successfully been applied in a wide range of fields, such as pattern recognition, computer vision, data generation, recommender systems, etc. In Section 6, we focus on the available toolkits for AEs. Finally, this paper summarizes the future trends and challenges in designing and training AEs.

2. Methods and Recent Developments

In recent years, AEs have been extensively studied in the field of AI. Therefore, a large number of related works have emerged. In this section, we divide these models into two major categories: the basic AE and its variants. In addition, we will further review each technology of these models and their recent developments.

2.1. The Basic AE

The idea of AEs has been part of the historical landscape of neural networks for decades. So, what is an AE? The basic AE is an auto-associative neural network, and it derives from the multi-layer perceptron, which attempts to reproduce its input, i.e., the target output is the input [7]. Ref. [25] proposed another explanation: an AE network can convert an input vector into a code vector using a set of recognition weights. Then, a set of generative weights are used to convert the code vector into an approximate reconstruction of the input vector. We can use the basic AE as a building block to train deep networks. Being associated with a basic AE, each level of a deep network can be trained separately.

2.1.1. Structure and Objectives

The basic AE is composed of an input layer, a hidden layer, and an output layer (see Figure 1).

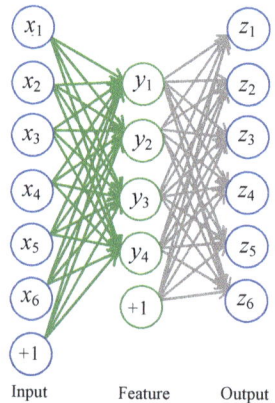

Figure 1. An example of the basic AE with 6 input units and 4 hidden units (features). From left to right, respectively, the input layer, the hidden layer, and the output layer. x_i is an input unit, y_j is a hidden unit, and z_i is an output unit. The number "1" denotes bias. Connections are exclusively drawn between different layers.

An AE takes an input vector and then maps it to the hidden representation $y \in \mathbb{R}^{d'}$ using the deterministic mapping $y = f_\Theta(x) = s_f(Wx + b)$. W is a $d' \times d$ weight matrix, b is a bias vector, and s_f is the encoder activation function (typically the element-wise sigmoid or hyperbolic tangent non-linearity or the identity function, if staying linear). The latent representation y, or the hidden representation, is then mapped back (with a decoder) into a reconstruction vector $z \in \mathbb{R}^d$ (z is the same shape as x). The mapping is performed using a similar transformation, e.g., $z = g_\Theta(y) = s_g(W'y + b')$, where $\theta = \{W, b, W', b'\}$ and s_g is the decoder activation function. In addition, z can be seen as a prediction of x given the hidden representation y. This process can be summarized as follows: each input x_i is thus mapped to a corresponding y_j which is then mapped to a reconstruction z_i, such that $z_i \approx x_i$. It is a good approach for the weight matrix W' to be optionally constrained by $W' = W^T$. In this way, the number of free parameters is reduced, which simplifies the training [26]. This is referred to as tied weights.

The set of parameters θ of such a model is optimized so that the loss function is minimized, as shown in Equation (1):

$$\theta^* = \underset{\theta}{\operatorname{argmin}} \sum L(x, z) \tag{1}$$

where L is a loss function. The method for choosing s_g and L depends largely on the input domain range and nature [27]. L can be chosen as the traditional mean squared error (MSE), which can be expressed as Equation (2). This, coupled with a linear decoder (i.e., $s_g(a) = a$), is a natural choice for an unbounded domain. Conversely, if inputs are bounded between 0 and 1, using s_g (sigmoid) can ensure a similarly bounded reconstruction. In addition, if the input x is interpreted as either a sequence of bits or a sequence of bit probabilities (i.e., they are Bernoulli probability vectors), then the cross-entropy (CE) can be used [8], as defined in Equation (3).

$$L(x, z) = \frac{1}{2} \sum_i (x_i - z_i)^2 \tag{2}$$

$$L(x, z) = -\sum_i x_i \log z_i + (1 - x_i) \log(1 - z_i) \tag{3}$$

In particular, there are two properties that make it reasonable to interpret the CE as a cost function [28]. First, it is non-negative, that is, $L(x, z) > 0$. Second, the CE tends toward zero as the neuron becomes better at computing the desired output, z, for all training inputs, x. Provided the output neurons are sigmoid neurons, the CE is nearly always the better choice. However, if the output neurons are linear neurons, then the MSE will not give rise to any problems with a learning slowdown. In this case, the MSE is, in fact, an appropriate cost function to use [28].

Recent Refs. [29,30] use another kind of cost function called exponential (EXP) cost, which is inspired by the error entropy concept. This is a parameterized function, which holds an extra parameter (tau), namely,

$$L(x, z) = \tau \exp(\frac{1}{\tau} \sum_i (x_i - z_i)^2) \tag{4}$$

This cost can be flexible enough to emulate the behavior of the classic costs mentioned above and to exhibit properties that are preferable in particular types of problems, such as good robustness to the presence of outliers [29]. In these works, the authors compare the performances of MSE, CE, and EXP costs when used for the pre-training of deep networks whose hidden layers are regarded as stacked AEs. Additionally, Ref. [29] also uses the three costs in the supervised fine-tuning of deep networks. Various combinations of pre-training and fine-tuning costs are compared in terms of their impact on classification performance.

In 1994, Hinton and Zemel applied the Minimum Description Length (MDL) principle to derive an energy-based objective function for training an AE [25]. They developed a stochastic Vector Quantization (VQ) method, which is very similar to a mixture of Gaussians, where each input vector is encoded with:

$$E_i = -\log \pi_i - k \log t + \frac{k}{2} \log 2\pi\sigma^2 + \frac{d^2}{2\sigma^2} \tag{5}$$

where π_i is the weight of the ith Gaussian; k is the dimensionality of the input vector; t is the quantization width; d is the Mahalanobis distance to the mean of the Gaussian; and σ^2 is the variance in the fixed Gaussian used for encoding the reconstruction errors. They define E_i to be the energy of the code. Using only this scheme to encode wastes bits because, for example, there may be vectors that are equally distant from two Gaussians. The amount wasted is:

$$H = -\sum p_i \log p_i \tag{6}$$

where p_i is the probability that the code will be assigned to the ith Gaussian. So, the true expected cost is obtained as:

$$F = \sum_i p_i E_i - H \tag{7}$$

Note that F has exactly the form of Helmholtz free energy. The probability distribution that minimizes F is:

$$p_i = \frac{e^{-E_i}}{\sum_j e^{-E_j}} \tag{8}$$

This study also demonstrates that an AE can learn factorial codes using non-equilibrium Helmholtz free energy as an objective function. More details can be found in [25]. We argue that the loss functions mentioned above are based on a common underlying principle. At a high level, they can be viewed as a scalar-valued energy function $E(x, t)$ (t is the model parameters) that operates on input data vectors x. The function $E(x, t)$ is designed to produce low energy values when x is similar to some training data vectors and high energy values when x is dissimilar to any training data vector.

2.1.2. Training

'Training' is the learning process in artificial neural networks (ANNs); it is usually implemented using examples and achieved with iteratively adjusting the connection weights. Training algorithms for ANNs fall into two major categories—gradient-based and non-gradient-based. AEs may be thought of as being a special case of feed-forward networks and can be trained with all of the same techniques. In this section, we will focus on gradient-based methods as they are more commonly used in recent times and usually converge much faster as well [31,32].

As mentioned in Section 2.1.1, our discussion has centered on implementing the functions that compute $L(\theta; x)$ with the parameters set θ. Therefore, the goal of the training process is to find a θ such that $L(\theta; x)$ approximates the function we are trying to model. Let $\nabla L(\theta; x)$ denote the gradient of $L(\theta; x)$ with the parameters θ. The gradient does not have a closed form solution. Instead, it can be efficiently implemented using the BP algorithm, which is the workhorse of learning in neural networks. The parameters θ of an AE can be most commonly trained with the optimization algorithms following the gradient computed using BP. In Ref. [33], the authors introduce three BP-based optimizers—Stochastic Gradient Descent (SGD), limited-memory Broyden–Fletcher–Goldfarb–Shanno (L-BFGS), and Conjugate Gradient (CG), which can be used to optimize AEs.

A widely used heuristic for training neural networks relies on a framework called SGD [34]. In neural networks, the loss function is highly non-convex; however, we can still implement the SGD algorithms and find a reasonable solution. The insight of the SGD is that the gradient is an expectation, which may be approximately estimated using a small set of samples [35]. Specifically, during each step of the algorithm, we can pick out a small number of examples $D = \{x_1, \ldots, x_m\}$ drawn uniformly from the training set. We refer to them as a mini-batch. Additionally, we usually choose m as a relatively small number of examples, which ranges from one to a few hundred (according to the value of m, a recent work [36] divides SGD methods into two types: single and mini-batch). Additionally, m usually stays the same as the training set size M grows. We may fit a training set with billions of examples using updates computed on only a hundred examples. This step is repeated for many small sets of examples from the training set until the average of the loss function stops decreasing. In recent years, several algorithms have been most commonly used for optimizing SGD including Momentum, Adam, Adagrad, Adamax, Nadam, Nesterov Accelerated Gradient Descent, and RMSprop [37]. These algorithms can further improve the empirical performance of SGD [38].

In Ref. [39], the loss function of AE is optimized with the L-BFGS algorithm [40], which is also called the SQN method. It is almost identical in its implementation to the BFGS method. The only difference is in the matrix update: the BFGS corrections are stored separately, and when the available storage is used up, the oldest correction is deleted to make space for the new one. All subsequent iterations are in this form: one correction is deleted and a new one is inserted [41]. It is a variant of BFGS; however, it reduces the computational cost of BFGS from $O(n^2)$ to $O(mn)$ space and time per iteration (where n denotes the number of variables in a system and m is the number of updates allowed in L-BFGS). In this case, m is specified by the user [42]. In practice, we rarely want to use m greater than 15 and always take the empirical value of m as 5, 7, or 9 [41]. m is much smaller compared to a very large number of variables about n. The computational cost of L-BFGS reduces to linear complexity $O(n)$. We now turn to an analysis of an alternative optimization algorithm—Conjugate Gradient (CG)—that is one of the most widely used methods in optimization. In 1952, Ref. [43] developed the linear CG for solving large systems of linear equations. It is the most popular iterative method that is effective for a system of the form:

$$Ax = b \qquad (9)$$

where A is a symmetric and positive definite matrix, x is an unknown vector, and b is a known vector. If A is positive-definite as well as symmetric, the problem of solving Equation (1) can be stated equivalently as the following minimization problem:

$$\min_{x} \frac{1}{2} x^T A x - b^T x \qquad (10)$$

Based on this, the work in [43] can also be regarded as a method for finding the minimum of the quadratic function. Then, the authors in [44] extended the linear CG to solve the minimum of general functions and hence, nonlinear optimization was achieved. Later, some important global convergence results for CG methods were given by Polak and Ribiere [45], Zoutendijk [46], Powell [47], and Albaali [48]. CG methods comprise a class of unconstrained optimization algorithms that are characterized by simplicity, modest demands on memory required, and strong local and global convergence properties [49].

We will now analyze the different strengths and weaknesses of these three types of optimization methods in detail. SGD methods have the merits of easy implementation; however, they have many disadvantages [31,50]. One key disadvantage is that they require much manual tuning of optimization parameters such as convergence criteria and learning rates. Another weakness of SGD is that they are inherently sequential. Hence, it is very difficult to parallelize them using GPUs or distribute them using computer clusters. Comparatively, L-BFGS and CG methods can only work with batch leaning, which use the full training set to compute the next update to parameters at each iteration. As available datasets grow ever larger, such batch optimizers are conventionally considered to become increasingly inefficient. Thanks to the availability of fast network hardware, such as large amounts of RAMs, multi-core CPUs, GPUs and computer clusters, these batch methods can be fast [31]. In addition, when the dataset is large, we can use mini-batch training to solve the weakness of batch methods. L-BFGS and CG methods with the presence of a line search procedure are usually much more stable to train and easier to check for convergence [50]. This has already been shown in DL. Here, the authors present experiments carried out on training the basic AE and sparse auto-encoder (SAE) [31]. Mini-batch L-BFGS and CG with line search converge faster than carefully tuned plain SGDs. Compared to L-BFGS, CG performs better because computing the conjugate information can be less expensive than estimating the Hessian. They also reported the performance of different optimization methods on a sparse AE. The results also show that L-BFGS and CG are much faster than SGDs. However, the difference is more significant than in the case of standard AEs. This is because L-BFGS/CG prefers larger mini-batch sizes, and hence, it is easier to estimate the expected value of the hidden activation [31].

In the preceding paragraphs, we have discussed many BP-based optimization techniques commonly used in AEs. Unlike general feed-forward networks, AEs may also be trained using recirculation [51]: a learning algorithm measures the gradient by measuring the effect of a small difference in the input. Although recirculation is regarded as more biologically plausible than BP, it is rarely used for machine-learning applications.

In the past, many genetic algorithms (GAs) have been successfully applied to training neural networks [52–55]. Specifically, GAs have been used as a substitute for the BP-based optimization algorithm or used in conjunction with BP to improve overall performance. In [56], David et al. extend previous works and propose a GA-assisted method for a deep AE. The experimental results indicate that this GA-assisted approach improves performance. The improved performance in the GA-assisted AE could arise from a similar principle of dropout [57] and dropconnect [58] since mutation randomly disables some of the weights during training. Learning rules are the heart of ANN training algorithms. In traditional ANN training, learning rules are previously assigned, such as the generalized chain rule of the BP network. When using GA, we can apply it to design the learning rules of ANNs. Because AEs are feed-forward ANNs, these learning rules also can be applied to AEs.

2.1.3. Taxonomy of the Basic AE

As discussed in Section 2.1.1, the general structure of a basic AE consists of three layers: an input layer, a hidden layer forming the encoding, and an output layer whose units correspond to the input layer. Since the outputs are equal to the input, this amounts to learning an approximation of the identity function. However, copying the input to the output may sound pointless, and we are generally not interested in the output of the decoder. Instead, training the AE is completed to perform the input copying task to make the hidden representation y take on useful properties [33]. For that reason, we can place various constraints on the network, as described below in more detail, and we call these regularized AEs. One constraint is to limit the number of units in the hidden layer, which forces the network to learn a compressed representation of the input. An AE whose hidden dimension is less than the input dimension is called under-complete [33] (also dubbed "narrow" [59] or "bottleneck" [60]). This method allows for the discovery of the most salient features from the dataset that rely on fewer hidden layer units. In the case of a linear AE (linear encoder and decoder) with a traditional MSE function, minimizing Equation (1) learns the same subspace as Principal Component Analysis (PCA) [61,62]. The same is true when using a nonlinear function (such as sigmoid) in the encoder, but it is not true if the weights W and W' are tied, since W cannot be forced to be small and W' large to achieve a linear encoder [27] (Section 4.1.1 describes the relationship of dimension reduction between AE and PCA in more detail). This AE can obtain a more powerful nonlinear generalization of PCA when equipped with nonlinear encoder functions f and nonlinear decoder functions g. Regrettably, if the encoder and decoder are allowed too much capacity, this AE will fail to learn anything useful other than the ability to copy its input to its output [33].

If the hidden code is allowed to have dimensions equal to the input, or in the over-complete case (or so-called "wide AE") where the hidden units have dimensions greater than the input, a similar problem will occur. In these cases, rather than limiting the number of hidden units, regularized AEs can provide alternative constraints. These include sparsity in the representation, robustness to noise, or to missing inputs and smallness in the derivative of the representation. Recent research has demonstrated that these alternative constraints are very successful, even when the network is over-complete [27]. In summary, using comparisons of the size of the hidden layer and the input layer, the basic AE structure can be divided into two categories: the narrow AE and wide AE (also known as under-complete and over-complete, respectively). Using various means in the different forms, we can achieve regularized AEs. In addition to the old bottleneck AEs with fewer hidden units than input, there are other forms of regularize AEs, which will be discussed next.

2.2. Regularized AEs

As described in the previous section, using various regularizers in different forms, we can achieve regularized AEs (also called "variants of the AE" [63]). These regularizers include: a sparsity regularizer, a contractive regularizer, or a denoising form of regularization, etc. In an AE network, inputs x can be mapped to an internal representation $f(x)$ using the encoder function f, and then $f(x)$ is mappeds back to the input space using a decoding function g (detailed above). The regularizer basically attempts to force f to throw away some information present in x or at least represent it with less precision. This means that the r (or f) has to be as simple as possible, i.e., as unresponsive to x as possible, and as constant as possible. In regularized AEs, the derivatives of $f(x)$ or $r(x)$ along the manifold in the x-directions must remain large, while the derivatives of $f(x)$ or $r(x)$ in the x-directions orthogonal to the manifold can be very small. Since a regularized AE with a non-linear encoder is allowed to choose different principal directions, it can capture non-linear manifolds [64].

In Table 1, we list the well-known regularized AEs along with some representative works and briefly summarize their characteristics and advantages. In the next sections, we will describe each of these variants and their most recent developments.

Table 1. Various regularized AEs.

Method	Remark	References
Sparse Auto-encoder	1. Imposes a sparsity constraint on the hidden units 2. Learns useful representations/features for images/audio domains	[65]
k-sparse Auto-encoder	In hidden layers, only the k highest activities are kept, and the others are set to zero	[16,66]
FC-WTA Auto-encoder	Using mini-batch statistics to directly enforce a lifetime sparsity in the activations of the hidden units	[67]
Denoising Auto-encoder	An explicit denoising criterion helps to capture interesting structure in the input	[68,69]
Variational Auto-encoder	Elegant theory, but tends to generate blurry samples when applied to natural images	[70,71]
Ladder Variational Auto-encoder	Providing advanced predictive log-likelihood and a tighter lower bound on the true log-likelihood	[72]
Triplet-based Variational Auto-encoder	Incorporating deep metric learning to learn latent embedding in VAE	[73]
Conditional Variational Auto-encoder	A VAE architecture conditioning on another description of the data, y	[74–76]
Wasserstein Auto-encoder	Using the optimal transport cost between the model distribution and the target distribution	[77–79]
Contractive Auto-encoder	Adding the Froenius norm of the Jacobian matrix of the encoder activations to the reconstruction cost	[80,81]
What and Where Auto-encoder	Providing a unified approach to unsupervised, semi-supervised, and supervised learning	[82]
Convolutional Auto-encoder	Extending the AE using convolution operation	[83–86]
Adversarial Auto-encoder	Training an auto-encoder with an adversarial loss to match the distribution in the latent space to an arbitrary prior	[87,88]
Sequence-to-sequence Auto-encoder	1. Based on Recurrent Neural Networks (RNNs) 2. Learn fixed-length representations of variable-length input	[89–91]

2.2.1. Sparse Auto-Encoder

Sparsity has become an interesting concept recently. It is a useful and desirable constraint when the number of hidden units is large (even larger than the number of input values), allowing the discovery of interesting structures in the dataset and avoiding simply learning the identity function of the encoder–decoder architecture [92,93]. Why use a sparse representation ("representation" is also known as the feature vector or the code)? It has presented several potential advantages in a number of recent studies [94–96]. Particularly, they are robust to noise. In addition, they are advantageous for classifiers because classification is more likely to be easier in higher dimensional spaces. Furthermore, this may explain why biology seems to follow sparse representations. Interest in sparse representations is inspired in part by evidence that neural activity in the brain seems to be sparse. Hence, this has burgeoned the seminal work on sparse coding [97]. Sparsity is a special regularization. SAE introduces sparsity regularization into AE by penalizing either the hidden unit biases or the activations of the hidden units to be sparse [27,98]. The former is completed to make these additive offset parameters more negative, whereas the latter is completed to make them closer to their saturating value at 0 [27]. These two sparse regularization methods can also be called parameterization sparsity and representational sparsity, respectively, which are ascribed to parameter regularization and representational regularization, respectively. With respect to parameter regularization, we can add a parameter norm penalty $\Omega(\theta)$ to the objective function L. We denote the regularized objective function by $\tilde{L}$:

$$\tilde{L}(\theta; x, y) = L(\theta; x, y) + \alpha \Omega(\theta) \tag{11}$$

where $\alpha \in [0, \infty)$ is a hyper-parameter that weights the relative contribution of the norm penalty term. Setting α to 0 means no regularization. Larger values about α will result in more regularization. When the regularized objective function $\tilde{L}$ is minimized, both the original objective L on the training data and some measure about the size of parameters θ (or some subset of the parameters) will be reduced. In Refs. [28,33], the authors put forward a different view from Refs. [27,98]—a parameter norm penalty Ω is usually chosen. In this way, only the weights of the affine transformation at each layer are penalized, and the biases are left to be unregularized. Therefore, the vector w is used to denote all of the weights that should be affected by a norm penalty. If there is no bias parameter, then θ is just w. L_2 regularization and L_1 regularization are two common methods to penalize the size of the model parameters. In comparison to L_2 regularization, L_1 regularization results in a solution that is sparser. It induces parameterization sparsity—meaning that many of the parameters become zero (or close to zero) [33]. Formally, L_1 regularization on the model parameter can be defined as:

$$\Omega(\theta) = \|w\|_1 = \sum_i |w_i| \tag{12}$$

Representational sparsity, on the other hand, describes a representation in which many elements in the representation are zero (or close to it). Representational regularization is finished with the same types of mechanisms that are used in parameter regularization [33]. When the activations about hidden units are directly penalized, we can add a penalty on the representation to the loss function L, which is expressed as $\Omega(y)$. As mentioned before, we use L to represent the regularized loss function. As mentioned before, we use $\tilde{L}$ to represent the regularized loss function:

$$\tilde{L}(\theta; x, y) = L(\theta; x, y) + \alpha \Omega(y) \tag{13}$$

where $\alpha \in [0, \infty)$ weights the relative contribution of the penalty term and the larger value α corresponds to more regularization. Here, an L_1 penalty also can be used on the elements of the representation to induce representational sparsity: $\Omega(y) = \|y\|_1 = \sum_i |y_i|$. In addition to the L_1 penalty, Kullback–Leibler (KL) divergence penalties are also useful for representations with elements constrained to lie on the unit interval. It can be computed as:

$$KL(\rho \| \hat{\rho}_j) = \rho \log \frac{\rho}{\hat{\rho}_j} + (1 - \rho) \log \frac{1 - \rho}{1 - \hat{\rho}_j} \tag{14}$$

where $KL(\rho\|\hat{\rho}_j)$ is the *KL* divergence between a Bernoulli random variable with mean ρ and a Bernoulli random variable with mean $\hat{\rho}_j$. Further, let $\hat{\rho}_j = \frac{1}{n}\sum_{k=1}^{n}\left[y_j(x^{(k)})\right]$ $\forall j = 1\ldots S$ be the average activation of hidden unit j averaged over the training set. Hereinto, $y_j(x)$ denotes the activation of this hidden unit when the network is given a specific input x and S is the number of hidden notes. We would like to enforce the constraint $\hat{\rho}_j = \rho$, where ρ is a sparsity parameter. By setting ρ to be a small value near zero, the activations of many hidden units can be close to or equal to zero, resulting in sparse connections between layers. In Refs. [10,99], the authors depict a kind of sparse AE which comprises parameterization sparsity and representational sparsity. The overall cost function is now:

$$\widetilde{L}(\theta;x) = \frac{1}{M}\sum_{k=1}^{M}L(x^{(k)},z^{(k)}) + \alpha\sum_{j=1}^{S}KL(\rho\|\hat{\rho}_j) + \beta\|W\|_2^2 \tag{15}$$

Recall that the first term describes the discrepancy between the input $x^{(k)}$ and reconstruction $z^{(k)}$ over the entire data. In the second term, $KL(\rho\|\hat{\rho}_j)$ is used to induce representational sparsity. The third term is a parameter regularization term (also called a weight decay term) that tends to decrease the magnitude of the weight and helps preventing overfitting. Here:

$$\|W\|_2^2 = \sum_{l=1}^{n_l}\sum_{i}^{s_{l-1}}\sum_{j}^{s_l}\left(w_{i,j}^{(l)}\right)^2 \tag{16}$$

where n_l is the number of layers and S_l is the number of neurons in layer l. $w_{i,j}^{(l)}$ represents the connection between the i-th neuron in layer l-1 and the j-th neuron in layer l.

From the above, and after noting that in order to learn sparse representations, a term about enforcing sparsity can be added to the loss. This term usually penalizes those active code units and aims to make the distribution of their activities reach a high peak at zero and have heavy tails. One disadvantage of these methods is that some measures may need to be taken in order to prevent the model from always activating the same several units and collapsing all other units to zero [94].

An alternative approach is to place a non-linear module (dubbed the "Sparsifying Logistic") between the encoder and decoder [94]. We can understand this non-linearity in two different ways. Let us consider the k-th training sample and the i-th component of the code $z_i(k)$ with $i \in [1\ldots\tau]$. τ is the number used to represent the components of the code vector. Let $\bar{z}_i(k)$ be its corresponding output after this non-linear module. The transformation performed with this non-linearity is given by:

$$\bar{z}_i(k) = \frac{\eta e^{\beta z_i(k)}}{\varsigma_i(k)}, i \in [1\ldots\tau] \text{ with } \varsigma_i(k) = \eta e^{\beta z_i(k)} + (1-\eta)\varsigma_i(k-1) \tag{17}$$

Let us assume that $\eta \in [0,1]$ and $\beta > 0$. Additionally, $\varsigma_i(k)$ is the weighted sum of values of $e^{\beta z_i(\varphi)}$ corresponding to the previous training samples φ with $\varphi \leq k$. In this sum, the weights are exponentially decaying, which can be seen by unrolling the recursive expression of the denominator in Equation (16). This non-linearity can be seen as a kind of weighted "softmax" function over consecutive samples of the same code unit. The sparseness of the code is controlled by the parameter η. By dividing the right-hand side of Equation (16) by $\eta e^{\beta z_i(k)}$, we have:

$$\bar{z}_i(k) = \left[1 + e^{-\beta(z_i(k) - \frac{1}{\beta}\log(\frac{1-\eta}{\eta}\varsigma_i(k-1)))}\right]^{-1}, i \in [1\ldots\tau] \tag{18}$$

At this point, the Sparsifying Logistic that tracks the average input can be viewed as a logistic function with an adaptive bias. A larger β will turn the non-linearity into a step function and make $\bar{z}_i(k)$ a binary code vector. In this non-linear module, sparsity is a "temporal" property that characterizes every single unit in the code rather than a "spatial" property that is shared by all the units in a code. Spatial sparsity often requires some type of special normalization to ensure that the "on" components of the code are not always the same. In contrast to spatial sparsity methods, this framework tackles the problem in a different way—when encoding different samples, each unit must be sparse independently from the activities of the other components in the code vector.

In the following, we use the feature distribution view to analyze the sparsity of an AE. Ref. [100] analyzes two desirable properties of the feature distribution: population sparsity and lifetime sparsity. The first describes codes in which few neurons are active at any time, and the later describes codes in which each neuron's lifetime response distribution has high kurtosis [101]. To investigate the effectiveness of sparsity by itself, Makhzani et al. [16] propose the "k-sparse auto-encoder", which is an AE with a linear activation function, where in hidden layers, only the k highest activities are kept, and the others are set to zero. This is performed by sorting the activities or by using ReLU hidden units with adaptively adjusted thresholds until the k largest activities are identified. This is different from the traditional methods [10,99] that reconstruct the input from all of the hidden units. This algorithm is also typically seen as enforcing population sparsity.

A "lifetime sparsity" penalty function proportional to the KL divergence between the target sparsity probability (ρ) and the hidden unit marginals ($\hat{\rho}$) is added to the cost function: $\lambda KL(\rho \| \hat{\rho})$. A major drawback of this algorithm is that it only works for certain target sparsity, and the tuning of the λ parameter is a laborious task that requires expert knowledge. In addition, KL divergence was originally proposed for sigmoidal AEs, and it is not clear how to apply it to ReLU AEs where $\hat{\rho}$ could be larger than one (in which case, the KL divergence cannot be evaluated) [67]. For this reason, Ref. [67] proposes a Fully Connected Winner-Take-All (FC-WTA) AE, which aims for any target sparsity rate and has no hyper-parameter to be tuned (except the target sparsity rate). This approach uses mini-batch statistics to directly enforce a lifetime sparsity in the activations of the hidden units. FC-WTA imposes sparsity (lifetime sparsity) across training examples, whereas k-sparse AEs impose sparsity (population sparsity) across different channels. When low sparsity levels are the goal, the latter uses a scheduling technique to avoid the problem of a dead dictionary atom. However, FC-WTA will not encounter this problem because no matter how aggressive the sparsity rate is (no scheduling required), all the hidden units will be updated when visiting every mini-batch.

Earlier, we discussed and analyzed the sparsity of AEs from different views. In summary, sparse over-complete representations can be regarded as an alternative "compressed" representation. Because there are a large number of zeros, it has implicit direct compressibility. This is different from an explicit lower dimensionality [96]. If the representation learned by an AE is sparse, then the AE cannot reconstruct every possible input pattern well. The reason for this is that the number of sparse configurations is necessarily smaller than the number of dense configurations. In addition, the number of configurations in sparse vectors is much less than when less sparsity (or no sparsity at all) is applied, so the entropy of sparser codes is smaller [102].

2.2.2. Denoising Auto-Encoder

As previously mentioned, one strategy to avoid simply copying the input is to constrain the representation: the traditional bottleneck and sparse representations. Ref. [96] has explored and proposed a very different strategy, which is a both more interesting and more challenging objective. The authors change the reconstruction criterion by cleaning partially corrupted input or, in short, "denoising". Denoising is advocated and investigated as a training criterion for learning to extract useful features. This conception leads to a very simple variant of the basic AE. Denoising auto-encoders (DAEs) are trained to reconstruct clean "repaired" input from corrupted versions. First, we need to corrupt the initial input vector x into $\tilde{x}$ using stochastic mapping $\tilde{x} \sim q_D(\tilde{x}|x)$, where q_D denotes a stochastically corrupted process. Each time a training example x is presented, a different corrupted version $\tilde{x}$ is generated according to $q_D(\tilde{x}|x)$. With the basic AE, the corrupted input $\tilde{x}$ is then mapped to hidden representation $y = f_\theta(\tilde{x}) = s_f(W\tilde{x} + b)$ from which we reconstruct $z = g_\theta(y) = s_g(W'y + b')$. Just as in the case of the basic AE, the weight matrix may also optionally be tied to weights. In Ref. [103], the authors justified the use of tied weights between the encoder and decoder within the Score Matching (SM) framework presented. Parameters θ are trained to force z as close as possible to the uncorrupted input x. As previously mentioned, the considered reconstruction error $L(x, z)$ can be MSE, with an affine decoder, or the cross-entropy loss, equipped with an affine+sigmoid decoder. Ref. [96] also claims that denoising, that is, restoring the values of corrupted elements, is only possible due to the dependencies between dimensions in high dimensional distributions. In addition, it is probably less suitable for very low dimensional problems. It has been proven that DAEs can be viewed as an empirically successful alternative to Restricted Boltzmann Machines (RBMs) trained with contrastive divergence for pre-training deep networks [9,96,104].

In the corruption process, there are several types of noise such as salt-and-pepper noise for gray-scale images, additive isotropic Gaussian noise, and masking noise (salt or pepper only). The last type of noise has been used in most simulations [105]. Noise injection, which can be much more powerful than simply shrinking the parameters, is a way to improve the robustness of neural networks. Injecting noise in the input to a neural network can also be seen as a form of data augmentation, which is a particularly effective technique for a specific classification problem—object recognition [33]. This well-known data augmentation method uses stochastically "transformed" patterns to augment the training data, such as transforming original bitmaps using small rotations, scalings, and translations to augment a training set [106,107]. However, the difference between this technique and noise injection in DAE lies in the fact that the latter does not produce extra labeled examples for supervised training, nor does it use any prior knowledge of image topology.

Noise injection in the input data is the key ingredient of a DAE. We can extend this idea to apply noise to the hidden units and visible units of a neural network. This creats a computationally inexpensive but powerful regularization—dropout [108,109]. The term "dropout" means dropping out units (visible and hidden) in a neural network. Dropping a unit out means temporarily removing it from the network together with all its incoming and outgoing connections. The choice of which units to drop is random. Similar to the DAE, it also can be considered as a process of constructing new inputs by multiplying with noise. As noise is applied to the hidden units, dropout can be seen as performing dataset augmentation at multiple levels of abstraction [33].

DAEs also can be analyzed from the following theoretical points of view: the manifold learning perspective, information-theoretic perspective, and stochastic operator perspective [97]. Recently, Ref. [110] proposed a different probabilistic interpretation of the DAE, which is valid for any data type, any corruption process, and any reconstruction loss (so long as it can be viewed as a log-likelihood). In addition, Ref. [104] relates the DAE to energy-based models (EBMs), which are a rich class of probabilistic models. These models define a probability distribution using an exponentiated energy function. Using linear reconstruction and squared error to train a DAE is equivalent to learning an energy-based model, and its energy function is very close to that of a Gaussian RBM. The training uses a regularized variant of the score-matching parameter estimation technique [111], which is called denoising score matching. Finally, Ref. [62] summarized and extended the existing results from Vincent [104]. They further proved that a DAE with arbitrary parametrization with small Gaussian corruption noise is a general estimator of the score. Meanwhile, we also can demonstrate denoising as a learning criterion that can be seen as a dynamical system from the view of the AE [112].

2.2.3. Variational Auto-Encoder

In just four years, the variational auto-encoder (VAE), which is proposed by Ref. [113], has been a slightly more modern and interesting work. So, what is a VAE? It is a model with added constraints on the encoded representations being learned. More precisely, it can learn a latent variable model for its input data. Ref. [33] has also demonstrated that "besides SAE and DAE, VAE is the most naturally interpreted as regularized AE. Almost any generative model with latent variables and equipped with an inference procedure to compute latent representations of a given input may be considered as a particular form of AE". Moreover, VAE is built on top of neural networks, which are appealing and can also be trained with SGD [114]. Instead of letting these neural networks learn an arbitrary function, we can learn the parameters of a complicated distribution modeling its input data. By sampling points from this distribution, we can generate new input data samples: a VAE is also a generative model, which emphasizes the connection with the AE. Additionally, a VAE is the descendant of the Helmholtz machine [33].

How does a VAE work? The underlying process can be divided into four steps, which are shown schematically in Figure 2. Let us consider a high-dimensional dataset $X = \{x^{(i)}\}_{i=1}^{N}$ considering of N i.i.d. samples of some continuous or discrete variable x. First, an encoder network $q_\phi(z|x)$ (also dubbed a "recognition model") turns a given data point x into two parameters in a latent space, which we note as z_mean and z_log_sigma. Here, the unobserved variables z have an interpretation as a code or latent representation, and $q_\phi(z|x)$ is an approximation to the intractable true posterior $p_\theta(z|x)$. $\emptyset$ and θ are, respectively, the recognition model parameters and generative model parameters. Then, we randomly sample similar points z from the latent normal distribution that is assumed to generate the data using:

$$z = z\_mean + \exp(z\_log\_sigma/2) * \varepsilon \qquad (19)$$

where $\varepsilon \sim \mathbb{N}(0, I)$. This operation is called the "reparameterization trick", which can further improve the efficiency in the variational inference of a Gaussian posterior over model parameters [115]. It is a popular regularization method that provides a Bayesian perspective of dropout [116]. Lastly, a decoder network $p_\theta(x|z)$ maps these latent space points back to the original input data. By context, we can learn that VAE can be understood from two perspectives: neural networks and graphical models.

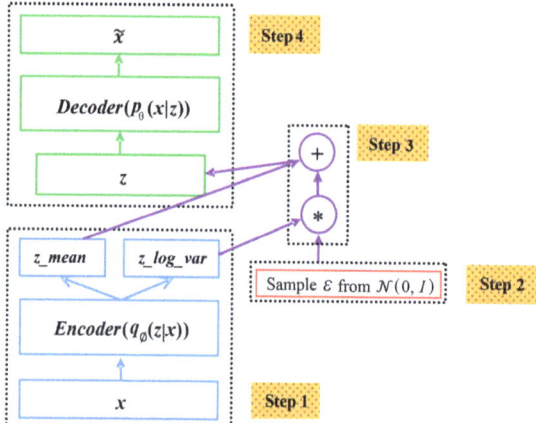

Figure 2. The architecture and operation flows of a VAE.

As previously discussed above, the VAE is a type of AE. However, there remain some differences between a VAE and an AE. The traditional AE learn an arbitrary function to encode and decode the input data, whereas the VAE learn the parameters of a probability distribution modeling the data. Hence, the VAE is a modern version of the AE [82,117]. Recently, some descendants of VAE have been proposed. Ref. [72] proposed the Ladder

Variational Auto-encoder, which can recursively correct the generative distribution using a data dependent approximate likelihood in a process. Compared to the purely bottom-up inference in a VAE, it provides advanced predictive log-likelihood and a tighter lower bound on the true log-likelihood. A novel integrated framework called the Triplet based Variational Auto-encoder (TVAE) was proposed in [73]. In this model, the authors constructed a new loss function (as shown in Equation (20)) that combines a triplet loss and standard evidence lower bound (ELBO) of plain a VAE. In Equation (20), L_{rec} and L_{KL} are the reconstruction loss and the KL Divergence loss, respectively. Thereinto, $L_{triplet}$ denotes the triplet loss. Compared to the traditional VAE, TVAEs are better at encoding more semantic structural information in the latent embedding.

$$L_{TVAE} = L_{rec} + L_{KL} + L_{triplet} \tag{20}$$

In addition to these varieties, there is another extension of the VAE called the Conditional Variational Auto-encoder (CVAE) [75]. Compared to the traditional VAE, it is a more advanced model capable of modeling the distribution of high dimensional output space as a generative model conditioned on the input observation. Taking image generation as an example, the CVAE can generate diverse human faces given skin color.

2.2.4. Wasserstein Auto-Encoder

Ref. [77] proposed a new family of regularized auto-encoders called the Wasserstein auto-encoder (WAE). There are some similarities and differences between the WAE and VAE depicted in the last section. Similar to the VAE, the loss function of the WAE is composed of two terms: the reconstruction cost and a regularizer. The first reconstruction term aligns the encoder–decoder pair so that the decoder can accurately reconstruct the encoded image based on the measurement of the cost function. The second regularization term forces the aggregated posterior $q(z)$ to match the prior distribution $p(z)$ instead of requiring point-wise posteriors $q(z \mid x = x^{(i)})$ to match $p(z)$ for all data points $x^{(i)}$ at the same time. This point is different from the VAE. The authors have proposed two different regularizers. When the reconstruction cost is the squared cost and the regularizer is the GAN objective, the WAE coincides with the adversarial auto-encoder (AAE) [13], which we will more formally introduce in Section 2.2.8. Unlike the VAE, the WAE aims at minimizing optimal transport (OT) between the probabilistic latent variable model distribution and the unknown data distribution. The WAE shares many of the properties of the VAE, such as the encoder–decoder architecture, stable training, and good latent manifold structure. However, the WAE can generate samples with better quality.

Ref. [78] has applied a WAE to the problem of disentangled representation learning. With satisfactory results on a benchmark disentanglement task, the potential of the WAE is demonstrated and proven. Ref. [79] also studied the role of latent space dimensionality in WAE. Using experimentation on synthetic and real datasets, it was demonstrated that random encoders are better than deterministic encoders.

2.2.5. Contractive Auto-Encoder

Another breakthrough development in the AE field was the contractive auto-encoder (CAE^1) proposed by Refs. [11,118]. We can achieve this model by adding a well-chosen penalty term to the traditional reconstruction cost function. Further, this penalty term corresponds to the Frobenius norm of the Jacobian matrix of the encoder activations with respect to the input. The resulting CAE^1 can then be expressed as:

$$J_{CAE}(\theta) = \sum_{x \in D} L(x, g(f(x))) + \lambda \|J_f(x)\|_F^2 \tag{21}$$

where L is the reconstruction error, which can be chosen as MSE or CE loss (see Section 2.1 for a longer discussion). $J_f(x) = \frac{\partial y}{\partial x}(x)$ is the regularization term that corresponds to the Jacobian of the hidden representation y with respect to the input x. Additionally, λ is a hyper-parameter controlling the strength of the regularization. In Ref. [27], the authors listed several core differences between the CAE^1 and DAE. First, CAE^1 only contract the encoder function $f(\cdot)$ rather than the whole reconstruction function. From another point of view, a DAE is actually a particular kind of CAE^1 with very small Gaussian corruption and MSE loss [62]. Second, the hyper-parameter λ controls the norm of the Jacobian penalized; it adjusts the trade-off between reconstruction and robustness (while in the DAE, the two are mingled). Additionally, the CAE^1 and VAE also have certain features in common. These two kinds of models impose constraints on the output of hidden neurons.

Ref. [80] proposed a simple and computationally efficient method to extend the CAE^1 method. This improved method not only penalizes the first order derivative (Jacobian) of the mapping but also the second order (Hessian). This improvement can help to stabilize the learned representation around training points.

2.2.6. What-Where Auto-Encoder

In 2016, Ref. [82] presented a novel architecture called the "stacked what-where auto-encoder" (SWWAE). The idea of "what" and "where" has been proposed previously in cognitive neuroscience. The "what" pathway is involved with object and visual identification. The "where" pathway is used to process the object's spatial location relative to the viewer. The authors have put the idea of "what" and "where" into the model of the SWWAE. In this model, each pooling layer produces two sets of variables, namely, "what" and "where". The former is fed to the next layer. Its complementary variable, the "where", is fed to the corresponding layer in the decoder. The SWWAE integrates discriminative and generative pathways and provides a unified approach for supervised, semi-supervised, and unsupervised learning. The loss function of the SWWAE depicted in Equation (22) is composed of three parts:

$$L = \lambda_{NLL}L_{NLL} + \lambda_{L2rec}L_{L2rec} + \lambda_{L2M}L_{L2M} \tag{22}$$

where L_{NLL} denotes the classification loss, L_{L2rec} is the reconstruction loss at the input level, and L_{L2M} is intermediate reconstruction terms. λ weights the losses against each other.

Contrary to the traditional AE, SAE, and DAE mentioned above, this model includes a supervised loss, which can help factorize the data into semantically relevant factors of variation. Additionally, the SWWAE uses the reconstruction term as a regularizer.

2.2.7. What-Where Auto-Encoder

In the previous section, we depicted the loss function of the SWWAE using Equation (22). If we set $L_{NLL} = 0$, then the SWWAE is equivalent to a deep convolutional auto-encoder (CAE^2). So, what kind of structure is the CAE^2? It equips the convolutional neural network (CNN) as encoders and decoders. Ref. [84] developed the CAE^2 with logistic sigmoid units for feature learning. However, the learning properties of this model were not fully studied, and the connections to other related models were not mentioned. Hence, Ref. [119] proposed a convolutional sparse auto-encoder (CSAE) and built its connections to convolutional sparse coding (CSC). The proposed CSAE includes three basic modules: encoder, sparsifying, and decoder. Contrary to Ref. [84], this model has added a sparsifying module, which can quickly predict the sparse feature maps. Additionally, they also built connections between the CSAE and CSC. In Ref. [85], the authors developed several deep CAE^2 models using the Caffe deep learning framework and evaluated their experiments with MNIST.

Comparing the CAE^2 with the well-known SAE and DAE, there are some advantages. First, this model can scale well to realistic-sized high-dimensional inputs. Both the SAE and DAE, however, are common fully connected deep networks. Hence, these two models introduce computational complexity and force each feature to be global. Additionally, the CAE^2 is different from the traditional AE as it can preserve spatial locality because the weights are shared among all locations in the input.

2.2.8. Adversarial Auto-Encoder

In Section 2.2.4, we referred to the AAE proposed by Ref. [13]. The AAE is a probabilistic AE that incorporates adversarial training [120] to match the aggregated posterior $q(z)$ of the hidden code vector z with an arbitrary prior distribution $p(z)$, such as a multivariate standard normal distribution. Hence, this probabilistic AE is trained with dual objectives: a traditional reconstruction error criterion and an adversarial training criterion. The architecture of the AAE is shown in Figure 3. AAE is trained with SGD in two phases: the reconstruction phase and the regularization phase. In the former phase, the encoder and decoder are updated to minimize the reconstruction error of the inputs. In the latter phase, the adversarial network firstly updates its discriminative network to discriminate the positive samples (generated using the prior distribution $p(z)$) from the negative samples $q(z)$. The generator of an AAE (which is also the encoder of AE) is updated to confuse the discriminative network. Once the training procedure is complete, the decoder of the AE will act as a generative model mapping the imposed prior $p(z)$ to the data distribution.

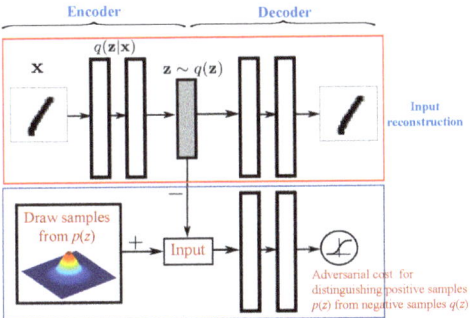

Figure 3. The architecture of an AAE [13]. The red rectangle is a standard AE with an encoder and decoder to reconstruct an image x from a latent code z. The encoder of the AE $q(z \mid x)$ is also a generator of the adversarial network. The blue rectangle describes the discriminative network, which is used to predict whether a sample arises from the hidden code of the AE or from a sampled distribution $p(z)$.

Variation and adversarial are the two key methods for regularizing the encoding space. The AAE is similar to the VAE. The latter uses a KL divergence to impose a prior distribution on the hidden code vector, while the former uses adversarial training to match the aggregated posterior of the hidden code vector to an arbitrary prior. Compared with the VAE, the AAE has the following characteristics. We must have access to the functional form of the prior distribution $p(z)$ to backprop through the KL divergence. While in an AAE, we only need to be able to draw a sample from the prior to induce the latent distribution to match the prior. Further, the adversarial method allows the encoder to be more expressive than the variational method [88]. In Section 2.2.2, we analyzed the benefits of the denoising criterion [96], but no corruption process was introduced for the AAE. Hence, Ref. [87] combined regularization and denoising and used adversarial training to shape the distribution of latent space. They incorporated denoising into the training and sampling of an AAE, thus formulating two improved versions of the denoising AAE: iDAAE and DAAE.

2.2.9. Sequence-to-Sequence Auto-Encoder

In the above sections, we described several types of regularized AEs. The input of these AEs are vectors or 2D images. If our inputs are sequences, how can we complete the task? A general framework has been proposed to encode a sequence using a sequence-to-sequence auto-encoder (SA), in which a Recurrent Neural Network (RNN) is used to encode the input sequence into a fixed-length representation and then another RNN to decode this representation out of that input sequence. This network is trained to minimize the root mean squared error (RMSE) between the input sequence and the reconstruction [89]. In Ref. [90], the authors proposed the use of a SA to represent variable-length audio segments with vectors of fixed dimensionality. To learn more robust representations, they further apply the denoising criterion to SA learning. The input acoustic feature sequence x is randomly added with some noise to yield a corrupted version $\tilde{x}$. Here, the input to SA is $\tilde{x}$, and SA is expected to generate the output y closest to the original x based on $\tilde{x}$. The SA incorporated into this denoising criterion is referred to as the denoising sequence-to-sequence auto-encoder (DSA).

Ref. [121] presented the AUDEEP, which is the first Python toolkit based on TensorFlow for deep unsupervised representation learning from acoustic data. This toolkit used a deep recurrent SA approach built of long short-term memory cells or gated recurrent units. Further, Bowman et al. [122] drew the ideology of "variation" into the SA and trained a sequence-to-sequence VAE successfully. This model can generate sentences from a continuous latent space. When applying attention mechanisms [123] to sequence-to-sequence VAE, however, "bypassing" has arisen. In Ref. [91], the authors proposed a variational attention mechanism to address this problem. In the future, we can further integrate other deep representation learning algorithms to extend SAs.

3. Analyses of AEs
3.1. Energy Perspective

AEs not only have a variety of forms but also can be analyzed and studied from different perspectives. Now, we will analyze AEs from the energy point of view. What does "energy" mean here? Ref. [124] proposed that the essence of the energy-based model is to build a function that maps each point of an input space to a single scalar, which is called "energy". Many unsupervised models can be viewed as a scalar-valued energy function $E(X)$ that operates on input data vectors X [59]. As a kind of unsupervised learning method, AEs also can be regarded as the energy function $E(X)$. This function $E(X)$ associates low energies to input points X that are similar to training samples and high energies to dissimilar points. AEs can extract representations Z (or codes) from which the training samples can be reconstructed. In the energy function, Z can be seen as a deterministic latent variable. From the perspective of energy, AEs can be seen as using an energy function of the following form:

$$E(X) = \min_{Z \in \zeta} E(X, Z) \tag{23}$$

There are several common activation functions (sigmoid, hyperbolic tangent, linear activation, square activation, rectified linear, and modulus activation) for AEs. According to each activation function, Ref. [125] derived the respective energy functions.

3.2. Manifold Perspective

A manifold is a connected region. Mathematically, it is a set of points associated with a neighborhood around each point. From any given point, the manifold locally appears to be a Euclidean space [35]. Manifold learning is capable of finding a low-dimension basis for describing high-dimension data. Additionally, it can uncover the intrinsic dimensionality of high-dimension data. Many machine learning algorithms exploit the idea of a manifold. As one of the machine learning algorithms, AEs are no exception. If you have an AE, it will be trained in a manifold fashion such that similar input data results in output neuron values that are at a low distance from each other. The space spanned by the output neuron variables can be considered to be a learned manifold for the input data space.

Similar to the traditional AE, it takes an input and the input goes through an encoder, which gives a low dimensional output y (more details can be found in Section 2.1). This output y can be interpreted as coordinates of the manifold. How does y denote the coordinates of a dimensional manifold? Ref. [81] introduces a sensitivity penalization term in the objective function, measured as the Frobenius norm of Jacobian of the non-linear mapping of the inputs: $\|J_f(x)\|_F^2$. The Jacobian $J_f(x) = \frac{\partial y}{\partial x}(x)$ measures the sensitivity of y locally around x. It encourages the model to be invariant to local changes in x, except for the changes following tangent vectors. In practice, it is easier to train a DAE, which inserts noise before the inputs are fed into the encoder. The corrupted inputs will be much more likely to be outside and farther from the manifold than the uncorrupted ones, generally on or near the manifold. The purpose of the DAE is that the stochastic operator $p(x|\tilde{x})$ learns a map tending to go from lower probability points $\tilde{x}$ to high probability points x. While $\tilde{x}$ is farther from this manifold, $p(x|\tilde{x})$ will learn to make bigger steps to reach the manifold. That way, the DAE can learn features that are more robust to small perturbations of the input.

Further, Ref. [126] has taken advantage of the manifold learning perspective of the VAE to analyze brain MRI images. Different from other AEs, this proposed method inherently has generative properties. The author has taken advantage of this capability to construct brain images given manifold coordinates.

3.3. Information Theoretic Perspective

Despite the great success of DNNs in practical application, there is still a lack of theoretical and systematic methods for their analysis. As a special type of DL architecture, the idea of AEs is similar to the idea of encoding information in information theory [127]. In this section, we will illustrate an advanced information-theoretic methodology to understand the design of AEs. In order to define a measure of the efficiency and reliability of the signal, Shannon first invented information theory [128]. In this theory, Mutual Information I and Kullback–Leibler (KL) divergence play a very important role. The former is used to measure the information shared between two variables (the original message and the received one) in the signal transmission case. The latter is used to evaluate the difference between two different probability distributions. Ref. [96] provide a description of AEs from the view of information theory. The authors observed that minimizing the expected reconstruction error of an AE is equivalent to maximizing a lower bound on mutual information $I(x; y)$, where x, y denote the input and hidden representation, respectively. Equally, the objective of the DAE is that y captures as much information about x as possible, even if x is a result of corrupted input. As described in the last section, this output y lives in a manifold embedded in a subspace of the input space x. The purpose of this projection from the input dimension space to the hidden manifold is to preserve as much information as possible.

Additionally, we also can analyze the CAE from an information theory perspective. In the case of a sigmoid nonlinearity, the penalty on the Jacobian norm can be expressed in the following simple form:

$$\|J_f(x)\|_F^2 = \sum_{i=1}^{d'} \left(y_i(1-y_i) \right)^2 \sum_{j=1}^{d} W_{ij}^2 \qquad (24)$$

We observe that the Froebenius norm is an approximation of the absolute value of the determinant, and the CAE[1] representation can be described as low entropy. Indeed, by changing variables in Equation (24), in the case of a complete representation, the entropy of the representation y is a linear function of the log-determinant of the Jacobian of W [129]. Meanwhile, Ref. [114] listed the core equation of the VAE (as shown in Equation (25)) and gave the information-theoretic interpretation:

$$log\ p(x) - KL\left[q(z|x)\ ||\ p(z|x)\right] = E_{z\sim q}[log p(x|z)] - KL[q(z|x)||p(z)] \qquad (25)$$

where p, q, x, and z have the same meaning as in Section 2.2.3. We can regard $log\ p(x)$ as the total number of bits required to construct x. Viewing the r.h.s of Equation (25), there are two steps to construct x. In the first step, we use some bits to construct z. The bits required to construct z are measured using a $KL[q(z|x) |\ |p(z)]$. In the second step, we use $p(x|z)$ to measure the amount of information required to reconstruct x from z under an ideal encoding. Accordingly, the total number of bits ($log\ p(x)$) is the sum of these two steps minus a penalty we pay for q being a sub-optimal encoding ($KL[q(z\mid x)\mid\mid p(z\mid x)]$).

4. Relationships with Other Models

There is a connection between AEs and other machine learning algorithms. Here, we will summarize the existing relationships by analyzing the relationship with shallow models and deep models.

4.1. Relationship with Shallow Models

Until recently, shallow structured architectures have been exploited in many fields. Examples of shallow architectures are linear or nonlinear dynamical systems, support vector machine (SVM), logistic regression, principal components analysis (PCA), restricted Boltzmann machine (RBM), independent component correlation algorithm (ICA), etc. In this section, we will analyze the relationships between AEs and shallow architectures.

4.1.1. Relationships with PCA

In this subsection, we will present the connection between PCA and the traditional AE, which is closely related to PCA but much more flexible. Early in 1982, Ref. [130] illustrated the connection between PCA and neural network representations. They showed that a simplified neural network with a linear activation function could be seen as a principal component analyzer. PCA, formalized by Hotelling [131], is a traditional feature extraction method. We can use PCA to learn a linear transformation $h = f(x) = W^T x + b$ of the original data $x \in \mathbb{R}^{d_x}$, the matrix W ($d_x \times d_h$) forms an orthogonal basis for the d_h orthogonal directions of greatest variance in the training data. These uncorrelated d_h features are the components of representation h.

We will analyze traditional AE and PCA from the following points. Firstly, like PCA, traditional AE is also an unsupervised learning algorithm. Secondly, when used with linear neurons and MSE, a narrow AE can learn the same subspace as PCA. This is also true for another kind of narrow AE, which has a single sigmoidal hidden layer, linear output neurons with squared loss, and untied weights [27,132]. Although these AEs will not learn the exact same basis as PCA, their weight matrix W will span the same subspace. In 2006, Ref. [6] described a nonlinear AE using an adaptive and multilayer encoder network to learn a low-dimensional code and a similar decoder network to recover data from the code. It is a nonlinear generalization of PCA that works much better than PCA. Additionally, this nonlinear AE takes advantage of learning non-linear manifolds, while PCA only learns a linear manifold in a higher-dimensional space. Thirdly, although PCA and the narrow AE differ in the specifics of architecture, both of them can be viewed in light of the energy-based framework. PCA is an encoder–decoder architecture that minimizes the energy loss (mean square reconstruction error), without requiring an explicit contrastive term to pull up the energies of unobserved patterns. The energy of the narrow AE is simply described as $E(x) = \mid Dec(Enc(x) - x)\mid^2$. Because of the limitation in the entropy of the code, we can simply pull down on the energy of the training samples without having to pull up on the unobserved points again [59]. Additionally, Ref. [133] and Ref. [134] further used experiments to visualize the comparison results on reducing the dimensionality between AE and PCA. Both PCA and AE mentioned above for dimensionality reduction ignore considering any data relations. Hence, a Generalized Auto-encoder (GAE) has been proposed, which extends the traditional AE to take full advantage of data relations and uses the relations to pursue the manifold structure [135]. They also have derived a variant called GAE-PCA, which is the formulation of traditional PCA with a zero mean.

Recently, many research teams have begun to use a combination of AEs and PCA for a field of application. Ref. [136] has proposed a feature learning method that combines an SAE with a CNN and multiple layers of PCA to form a hierarchical model for American sign language (ASL) finger-spelling recognition. Ref. [137] investigated initializing deep AEs using PCA and further studied the stability of the features. Experimental evaluations further shows the impact of PCA-based initialization for classification tasks. Additionally, an SSAE-based network with SVM and PCA is proposed to improve the accuracy of fault diagnosis in power systems [138].

4.1.2. Relationships with RBM

RBM was initially introduced as Harmonium by Paul Smolensky in 1986 [139]. It is a variant of Boltzmann machines and can learn a probability distribution over a set of inputs, which plays an important role in DL. It only has an input and hidden layer, as shown in Figure 4. Due to this restriction, their neurons must form a bipartite graph: there are no connections between nodes within the visible neurons or hidden neurons.

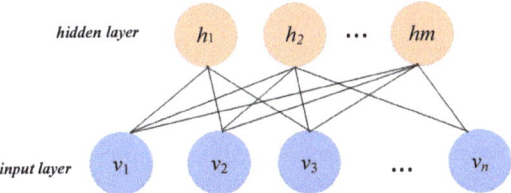

Figure 4. The network structure of the RBM.

There are some relationships between AE and RBM. The latter is an especially popular AE in DL [140]. Overall, these two kind of models are identical because they learn a good model based on the training data [125]. For an AE with sigmoid hidden units, the energy function is identical to the free energy of an RBM. These two kinds of models are both unsupervised learning methods. Both can be understood in terms of encoder and decoder architectures but with different constraints on the code and learning algorithms. Ref. [35] also analyzed the other existing connections between AE and RBM. When applying score matching to RBM, its cost function is identical to the reconstruction error combined with a regularization term, which is similar to the contractive penalty of the CAE. The authors also have illustrated that the gradient in the reconstruction error used in training AEs provides an approximation to the contrastive divergence training of RBMs. As a variant of the AE, the DAE shares this property with RBMs, and they are closely related to each other [141]. Firstly, the DAE is a simple and competitive alternative to the RBM used by Hinton [6] for pre-training deep networks [104]. Secondly, using Gaussian noise and MSE as the reconstruction cost to train a DAE (sigmoidal hidden units and linear reconstruction units) is equivalent to training an RBM with Gaussian visible units [103]. Thirdly, with denoising, the DAE features performed similarly or better than those of the RBM [27].

4.1.3. ICA

Independent component analysis (ICA) is a computational and statistical technique used to reveal hidden factors that underlie sets of random variables, measurements, or signals. It can be interpreted as a form of the feed-forward neural network [142]. Like AE, ICA also can be used as a generative model for the observed multivariate data, which are typically given as a large database of samples. In this generative model, it is assumed that the data variables are linear mixtures of some unknown latent variables, which are supposed non-Gaussian and mutually independent. They are also called the independent components of the observed data [143]. Additionally, similar to AE, ICA and its variants have also been successfully used for unsupervised feature learning. ICA is not only sensitive to whitening but also difficult to learn an over-complete basis set. Ref. [144] proposed Reconstruction ICA (RICA) that not only addresses these shortcomings but also reveals strong connections with the AE. If adding a regularization term in the form $\sum_t \sum_j g(W_j x^{(t)})$ to an AE (with a linear activation and tied weights), where g is a nonlinear convex function, an efficient algorithm for learning RICA will be obtained.

4.1.4. PSD

Predictive sparse decomposition (PSD) is a practically successful model that is a hybrid of sparse coding and an AE [145]. When computing the learned features, PSD uses a fast non-iterative approximation to replace costly and highly non-linear encoding steps in sparse coding. PSD can also be seen as a kind of AE. This model consists of an encoder $f(x)$ and a decoder $g(h)$ that are both parametric. The training process of PSD is to minimize:

$$\|x - g(h)\|^2 + \lambda |h|_1 + \gamma \|h - f(x)\|^2 \tag{26}$$

where h is controlled by the optimization algorithm. Meanwhile, the parametric encoder f is used to compute the learned features, which is a differentiable parametric function. Like the AE, PSD can be stacked and used to initialize a deep network [35]. Additionally, it is also an unsupervised feature learning method, which can be applied to object recognition in images and videos [146,147].

4.2. Relationship with Shallow Models

The stacked auto-encoder (SAE^2), DBN, and CNN are the three main networks used in DL [8]. These models have been applied to fields such as computer vision, automatic speech recognition, natural language processing, bioinformatics, and audio recognition where they have been proven to produce the most advanced results in a variety of tasks. In this section, we will analyze the relationship between the SAE^2, DBN, and CNN.

4.2.1. Relation to DBN

Lately, the RBM and AE have been largely used as building blocks in DL architectures that are called DBN and SAE^2, respectively. Prior to the introduction of DBN in 2006 [148], deep models were considered too difficult to optimize. Refs. [8,148] introduced a greedy layer-wise unsupervised training algorithm that can be applied to the DBN. This algorithm can be simply described as follows [26]: Firstly, train the first layer as an RBM. Secondly, use the first layer's internal representation as input data for the second layer. Thirdly, iterate the second step for the desired number of layers. Lastly, after adding a further layer (e.g., a simple linear classifier), we can fine-tune all the parameters in the deep network using a supervising training criterion.

Similar to the DBN, the layer-wise training criterion is also applicable to the SAE^2. After the first k layers are trained, we can use the internal representation of the k-th layer to train the $(k + 1)$-th layer. Once all the layers are pre-trained, a classification layer is added, and SAE^2 can be fine-tuned using exactly the same method as for the DBN. Additionally, both the DBN and SAE^2 are unsupervised learning methods, and they both belong to the generative model.

4.2.2. Relation to CNN

CNNs have achieved breakthrough performance in many computer vision and machine learning tasks. Many excellent papers [107,149–151] have been published on this topic. In addition, many high-quality open-source CNN software packages have been made available. In the following sections, we will discuss this powerful architecture in detail.

As shown in Figure 5, a CNN is typically composed of multiple alternating convolutional and pooling layers, followed by one or several fully connected layers. This hierarchical structure allows the CNN to extract more and more abstract representations from the lower layer to the higher layer. Convolution and pooling are the key components of CNNs. Many researchers have added these two modules into an AE to construct the CAE^2 mentioned in Section 2.2.7. The type of CAE^2 is not unique. Ref. [152] proposes a CAE^2 to support unsupervised image feature learning for lung nodules using unlabeled data. This proposed structure adds a reconstruction input for the convolution operation. The procedure of the convolutional conversion from the input on feature maps to the output is called the convolutional decoder. Then, the output values are reconstructed using the inverse convolutional operation, which is called a convolutional encoder. Moreover, using the standard unsupervised greedy training for AE, the parameters of the encoder and decoder operation can be calculated. Refs. [84,119,153] also used this kind of CAE² similar to [152].

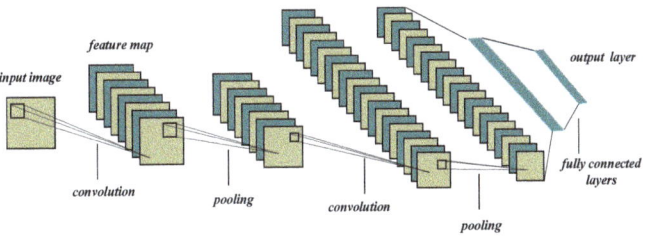

Figure 5. The typical architecture of a CNN.

Another mechanism for the CAE² is to extract random image patches from input images, and then use these patches to train an AE. Once the training is complete, we can use the filters in a convolutional fashion to obtain representations of images. The works [19,154,155] utilized this kind of architecture. As discussed in Ref. [67], the key problem with this architecture is that if the receptive field selection is small, it will not be able to capture relevant features (imagine the extreme of 1×1 patches). If we increase the size of the receptive field, a very large number of features are needed to explain all the position-specific variations within the receptive field.

4.3. Relationship with Matrix Factorization

In this section, the relationship between matrix factorization (MF) and AE will be analyzed. Firstly, we will describe the relationship between the non-negative matrix factorization (NMF) and AE. Secondly, the relationship between the truncated Singular Value Decomposition (TSVD) and AE will be analyzed.

4.3.1. Relation to NMF

MF and AEs are among the most successful approaches to unsupervised learning [156]. The goal of MF is to decompose a matrix into several matrices. There are several matrix factorization methods, such as triangular factorization, full rank factorization, QR factorization, NMF, and singular value decomposition (SVD). Consider a data matrix $V \in \mathbb{R}^{m \times n}$ with only non-negative elements and m dimensions and n data points. If defining two matrices, $W \in \mathbb{R}^{m \times r}$ and $H \in \mathbb{R}^{r \times n}$, they also have only non-negative elements. NMF can reduce the dimensionality of V using the approximation $V \approx WH$. r is a preset dimension reduction parameter (m and n are much larger than r). A one-hidden layer AE can be used to perform NMF. Both NMF and AE can produce a lower dimensional representation of some input data [157]. Additionally, the authors of [157] have proposed an architecture called PAE-NMF, which utilizes the ideas behind the VAE to perform NMF. The model proposed in this paper provides advantages both to the VAE and NMF. For the VAE, by forcing a non-negative latent space, many of the beneficial properties of NMF can be inherited. For NMF, a probabilistic representation of the vectors h is used to model the uncertainty in the parameters of the model due to the limited data.

4.3.2. Relation to tSVD

tSVD is another matrix factorization method that produces a low-rank approximation to a matrix. We need to compute the SVD of the matrix A and then truncate the less-significant singular values. The SVD of the matrix A is given by:

$$A = UDV^T \qquad (27)$$

Suppose that A is an $m \times n$ matrix. Then, U is defined to be an $m \times m$ unitary matrix (i.e., $U^T U = I$), D to be an $m \times n$ matrix, and V^T to be an $n \times n$ unitary matrix (i.e., $V^T V = I$). Conventionally, the entries along the diagonal of D (the singular values) are sorted in non-increasing order. Pick the k largest singular values and then define the tSVD matrix as:

$$\widetilde{A} = U_k D_k V_k^T \tag{28}$$

where $U_k(V_k^T)$ is the first k columns of U (V^T) and D_k is our k by k matrix of top eigenvalues. If x_i ($i = 1, 2, \ldots, m$) is a row of A, $z_i = x_i V_k^T$ can be deemed as the encoding of x_i, and $\widetilde{x}_i = z_i V_k$ corresponds to the decoder function. Analyzing from this point, tSVD and a traditional AE (with linear activation and only one hidden layer) are identical [158]. In other words, the tSVD is a degenerate form or a special linear case of a traditional AE [159].

5. Application Domains

AEs are often used for effective encoding of the original data or learning a representation, in the form of input vectors, at the hidden layers. Additionally, AE is an unsupervised feature extraction method. In this section, we will demonstrate a plethora of applications for AEs in various real-world domains, such as computer vision, speech recognition, fault diagnosis, anomaly detection, etc. To do so, Figure 6 summarizes the taxonomy of the application domains of AEs, which will be described in this section.

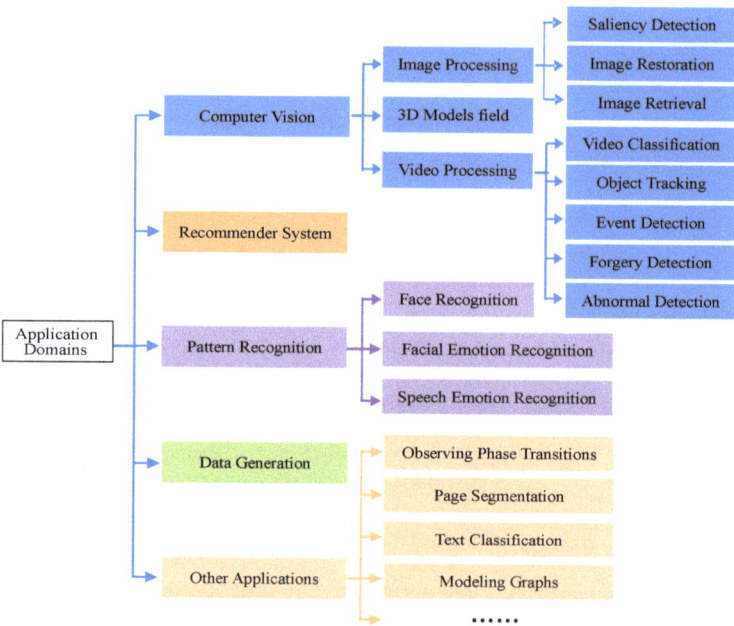

Figure 6. The taxonomy of the application domains of AEs.

5.1. Computer Vision

Computer vision is the science and technology that makes computers accurately understand and efficiently process visual data such as videos and images. As a scientific discipline, computer vision is concerned with the theory for building artificial systems that obtain information from real-world, high-dimensional data. The ultimate goal of computer vision is to give machines the perceptual capability of humans [160]. In the following section, we will provide a general review of several application domains of computer vision for AEs including image processing, video processing, and the 3D model field.

5.1.1. Image Processing

(1) Image classification

Image classification is one of the most important and widely used research directions in the field of computer vision and AI. Its research goal is to classify images into different pre-defined categories according to their attributes. Image representation is the basis of image classification. In order to better represent images and realize automatic classification, it is very important to extract a good feature description for the images. As AEs are effective feature-learning methods, they are widely used in image classification. Ref. [133] used a traditional AE with a single hidden layer to reduce the dimensionality and further used it for the classification of the MNIST and Olivetti face datasets. Both these two datasets contain gray-scale images. Because the traditional AE is a fully connected network, the authors resized the images of the Olivetti face dataset from 64×64 to 28×28 (the same size as MNIST) to reduce the computational complexity. As described before, an AE can be stacked to build a deep network to obtain high-level features. Refs. [64,161] presented a stacked SAE[1] for the classification of nuclei patches in breast cancer histopathology. They extracted two categories of 34×34 patches from the histopathology images: nuclei and non-nuclei patches. The authors used these two kinds of patches to construct the training set and testing set. Similarly, Ref. [162] also used the stacked SAE[1] to train with unsupervised learning for extracting features of halftone images. The halftone image classification phase consists of three modules: effective image patch extraction, feature extraction with a stacked SAE[1,] and majority voting for halftone image classification. In order to reduce the run-time of training and improve the image-correct classification rate, they proposed an effective patch extraction method. Each halftone image in the training set is segmented sequentially into patches with a size of 16×16. Another research team proposed a method called the stacked DAE, which is a direct variant of the stacked basic AE [96]. Further, the stacked DAE was tested on MINIST. Being similar to the method based on the stacked SAE, the training and testing datasets fed into the models are relatively low in resolution, such as small image patches and low-resolution images (e.g., hand-written digits). The AE, SAE, and DAE used in papers [64,96,133,161] are common fully connected networks, which learn features by first encoding the vector-form input data and then reconstructing it, and cannot scale well to realistically sized high-dimensional inputs (e.g., 256×256 images) in terms of computational complexity [84]. Additionally, they both ignore the 2D image structure.

To solve this problem, Ref. [163] proposed a kind of CAE[2] that first extracted patches from the input images and used patch-wise training to optimize the weights of a basic SAE in place of convolutional training to learn weights. The weights are then reorganized as convolutional kernels, which are used to convolve the RGB input images for more abstract feature maps, thus still reserving the local relevance of images. At that time, this research achieved state-of-the-art performance on benchmark datasets such as CIFAR-10 and NORB using only a single layer of features (73.4% and 97.2%, respectively). Ref. [35] utilized this CAE[2] with a single layer of features for natural scene classification. This idea is analogous to Coates et al.'s work [163]. A similar method is used for remote sensing image classification as reported in [19]. While these works [19,35,163] only adopted a single layer of features, the authors of [154] stacked DAEs in a convolutional way to generate a hierarchical model. This stacked convolutional DAE achieved superior classification performance to state-of-the-art unsupervised networks. Due to the depth structure, this model outperforms the single-layer model of [163] on the CIFAR-10 dataset (ranging from 73.4% to 80.4%).

In addition to using a single type of feature to classify image data mentioned above, multiple features can be combined for more comprehensive information. Feature fusion aims to combine the strengths of complementary cues such as local and holistic features, which can be combined at the feature or rank level. These attempts can be used for both natural images and medical images. Inspired by this, Ref. [164] extracted both holistic architecture features and high-dimensional local appearance features from detected cells using a stacked SAE[1]. Then, a graph-based, query-specific fusion approach was used to integrate the strengths of local or holistic features. This fusion of heterogeneous features significantly improves the accuracy by around 10%, i.e., achieving 91.67% overall accuracy on a histopathological image-guided diagnosis of intraductal breast lesions. Similarly, considering that hyperspectral imagery (HSI) is intrinsically defined in both the spectral and spatial domains, Ref. [165] further established two stacked SAE-based feature learning approaches for sparse spectral feature learning and multi-scale spatial feature learning, respectively. Compared to traditional handcraft features, this learned spectral–spatial feature representation is highly discriminative and has more potential turns for HSI classification. Similar to Ref. [165], the method introduced by Ref. [166] also used spatial and spectral information, which was merged using the SAE^2. Unlike Ref. [165], this architecture mixed the traditional feature extraction method and DL architecture. PCA is introduced to condense the whole image, reduce the data dimension to a reasonable scale, and reserve spatial information simultaneously. A series of SAE^2s with different depths were trained, which further proves that the depth of the features affects classification accuracies. There are many studies [167–170] that have combined traditional feature extraction methods (such as HOG, ICA, the Gobor filter, and so on) with the AE. At the same time, a growing number of scholars have integrated other DL methods into AEs. In Ref. [171], the authors proposed a novel approach based on convolutional features and SAE for scene-level land use (LU) classification. This approach first generated an initial feature representation of the scenes under analysis from a CNN, which was pre-learned on a large amount of labeled data from an auxiliary domain. Then, these convolutional features are input into a SAE^1 for learning a new suitable representation in an unsupervised manner. In another work, a novel VAE was developed using the Deep Generative Deconvolutional Network (DGDN) as a decoder of the latent image features and using a CNN as an image encoder. A CNN was used to approximate a distribution for the latent DGDN features [172].

In addition to integrating the theories of CNNs into AEs, another branch of research has emerged. Extreme Learning Machine (ELM) theories and learning mechanisms have been used in more and more AE algorithms. Ref. [173] originally proposed the Extreme Learning Machine Auto-encoder (ELM-AE) and Sparse Extreme Learning Machine Auto-encoder (SELM-AE) with orthogonal and sparse random hidden neurons. Unlike the tied weight auto-encoder (TAE), the hidden neurons in ELM-AE and SELM-AE do not need to be tuned. Additionally, the input weights and biases in additive neurons are initialized using orthogonal and sparse random weights, respectively, which were used to retain the Euclidean information in the data of the hidden layer. Due to only calculating output weights, the proposed linear and nonlinear ELM-AE and SELM-AE have lower computational complexity. The performance comparison of classification on the USPS, CIFAR-10, and NORB Datasets shows that ELM-AE and SELM-AE learn features that are discriminative and sparse. In Ref. [174], the authors presented a method that used ELMs as a stacked supervised AE. In the process of implementing the algorithm, the authors randomly project the 'label pixel' outputs from an ELM module to an independent set of hidden units in the next ELM module. Furthermore, the ELM is known to be relatively fast to train compared to iterative training methods such as the AE. For the reasons above, this work gained the best of both worlds: fast implementation and lower error rates. This method used standard benchmark datasets for multi-class image classification (MNIST, CIFAR-10, and SVHN). In the field of remote sensing image classification, Ref. [175] proposed a method called SAE-ELM that was based on the ELM. Different from Ref. [173] and Ref. [174], the authors chose ELM as a base classifier to improve the learning speed of the algorithm. Finally, the Q statistic is adopted to determine the final ensemble-based classifier. The common feature of these three papers is that they all take advantage of the fast-learning speed of ELM. Different from the single-task AE listed above, Ref. [176] developed a multi-task AE architecture consisting of three layers with multiple separated outputs. Each output corresponds to one task. This multi-task AE can learn features that are robust to the variability in real-world images, so it can be well generalized in various fields. Comparing the classification performance with several single-task AE models, this multi-task AE provides better performance.

In this subsection, we have analyzed the literature based on AEs for image classification (e.g., natural images, medical images, natural scene images, and remotely sensed scene images). We can conclude the following rules:

1. Compared with traditional hand-crafted features, these networks based on AEs provide an automatic method to learn discriminative features from the image and overcome the weaknesses of some traditional feature extraction methods.
2. A series of AE models with different depths have proved that the depth of the network also plays an important role in classification accuracies.
3. The fusion of various features is widely used in image classification. Similarly, image features extracted using AE models can not only be fused with those extracted using traditional methods but also can be combined with those extracted using other DL methods. Feature fusion can further improve the accuracy of image classification.
4. It is very important to study the architecture design of an AE according to different classification tasks.

(2) Saliency detection

Traditional saliency detection methods, relying on contrast inference and hand-designed features, have been categorized into two sub-fields: ① eye fixation prediction and ② salient object detection [21]. Eye fixation prediction focuses on human fixation locations compared to salient object detection, which tends to extract whole meaningful objects. With the rise of DL, many novel frameworks have used deep networks to learn saliency detection models from raw image data, and some of the works have used AEs. Ref. [21] adapted the stacked denoising auto-encoder (SDAE) for learning both optimal features and contrast inference mechanisms from image data to predict human eye fixations. In the first learning stage, they developed a layer-wise unsupervised learning scheme to train the SDAE for obtaining robust representative features. In the second learning stage, the contrast inference component and contrast integration component were embedded in another unified SDAE network, while these two components were processed separately in the traditional methods. Ref. [21] focused on saliency fixation prediction. However, this model cannot be directly applied to saliency object detection. Again, this research team developed the SDAE for saliency object detection by first modeling the background and then separating salient objects from the background [177]. Different from the previous works focusing on the way to calculate the similarity or distinctiveness between a certain image patch and the image boundary, this work pays more attention to exploring the background prior using the SDAE. Rather than using the shallow reconstruction residual, they used the deep reconstruction residual generated with the SDAE to measure the saliency. The similarity between these two papers [21,177] is that the SDAE is used to learn optimal image features rather than to design hand-crafted features. Additionally, the SDAE is not only used for feature extraction but also for contrast inference, contrast integration, and the background prior. Additionally, sparsity is considered when training SDAE models, and the effectiveness of the KL divergence used in the sparsity constraint was also demonstrated in [177]. Compared to Ref. [177], Ref. [178] developed two individual SAE^2 models for adaptive background search and foreground estimation, respectively. One model was called the background search stacked auto-encoder (BS-SAE), which could adaptively extract the rough background region of an image. Using the trained BS-SAE model, one can obtain the feature representation of each image patch, and using softmax regression (SR), one can measure the probability of each image patch being background. Hence, this trained BS-SAE model can infer the background region from the holistic view rather than the regional view or local view. Another model was described as the foreground estimation stacked AE (FE-SAE), where the residual information was also inspired by [177]. This FE-SAE model was constructed by the background superpixels, which had a low reconstruction residual, while these belong to the background. Those belonging to the foreground would have a high reconstruction residual. Further, utilizing the capacity of data reconstruction for AEs, the saliency map can be generated using this FE-SAE. In Ref. [20], the authors were also inspired by the powerful data reconstruction ability and feature learning of the SAE^2. Hence, they constructed a stacked AE-based center–surround (C-S) inference network to model the human visual perception process and to estimate bottom-up saliency.

To obtain a unified reconstruction pattern for the current image, this model was trained with the data sampled randomly from the entire image to obtain a unified reconstruction pattern. Because global competition in sampling and learning processes are integrated into the nonlocal reconstruction and saliency estimation of each pixel, this model can achieve better detection results in comparison to those models with separate consideration of local and global rarity. This C-S inference network also used the relation between reconstruction residual and saliency. Different from Refs. [21,177,178], an extra inference layer was added on the top of the AE to provide ways to explore the C–S contrast relationship. Additionally, the authors have trained RBMs to initialize this SAE^2.

AEs can be used not only for conventional saliency detection but also for an interesting and emerging topic, co-saliency detection. It aims at simultaneously extracting common salient objects in multiple related images. The authors of Ref. [179] proposed a novel co-saliency detection approach using two individual SDAE models. The SDAE not only has the advantage of learning more abstract feature representations based on its deep architecture but also has the advantage of out-of-distribution data for knowledge transferring. So, one SDAE is built as a transfer learning framework, which can be effective for predicting intrasaliency. They first attempted to leverage the deep reconstruction residual obtained in the highest hidden layer of another SDAE to discover the deep intersaliency. Compared with the previous works in this subsection, SDAEs used in this paper are not only for the generation of the robust intrasaliency prior but also for mining deep intersaliency patterns.

In this subsection, we analyzed the literature based on AEs for image saliency detection. From these analyses, we can draw the following conclusions: 1. AEs have multiple merits: the ability to learn more abstract feature representations with the deep architecture, the ability of data reconstruction, and the advantage of out-of-distribution data for knowledge transfer. Hence, they can be applied to the saliency detection model. 2. Multiple independent AEs can be constituted into a whole saliency detection model. 3. In the process of designing a saliency detection model, the reconstruction residual of AEs is an important factor to be considered.

(3) Image restoration

Observed image signals are often corrupted by acquisition channels or artificial editing. The goal of image restoration techniques is to restore the original image from a noisy version. Image restoration is a well-studied problem in computer vision and image processing, including image denoising, inpainting, super resolution, and so on. Image denoising methods can be utilized for an image corrupted by additive white Gaussian noise, which is a common result of many acquisition channels. When some pixel values are missing or when we want to remove more sophisticated patterns, such as superimposed text or other objects from an image, image inpainting methods can be put to use. In reference [39], the authors took advantage of the DAE for image denoising and blind inpainting. They proposed a new training scheme for the DAE, which improved the DAE performance in the tasks of unsupervised feature learning. After training the first layer, the hidden layer activations of both the clean input and the noisy input are calculated to serve as the training data for the second layer. Compared to traditional linear sparse coding algorithms on the denoising task additive white Gaussian noise, this non-linear method achieves better performance. In addition, this approach is capable of tackling the complex blind inpainting problem. Furthermore, the denoising performance can be improved by adding more hidden layers of the DAE, especially when the level of noise is high. When there is no prior information on the target image and only the noise image is available, a DAE also can perform blind image denoising well [180]. Based on Ref. [39], Ref. [181] proposed a simple sparsification of the latent representation found by the encoder. This proposed method gives the advantages of both denoising a small image patch and denoising a larger image consisting of those patches. When test samples are corrupted with noise, this method improves even the classification performance. Different from the Refs. [39,180,181] listed above, Ref. [182] demonstrated that a convolutional denoising auto-encoder (CDAE) could also be used for the efficient denoising of medical images. In Ref. [183], the authors proposed a CAE^2 for image restoration, which was unlike the network architecture of [182]. It is an encoding–decoding framework with symmetric convolutional–deconvolutional layers. Considering that deeper networks tend to be more difficult to train, multiple skip-layer connections were proposed to symmetrically link convolutional and deconvolutional layers. Hence, the training converges became much faster, and better performance was achieved. Compared with the previous works in this subsection, this work has more powerful multi-functions. It achieved better performance than state-of-the-art methods for image denoising, image super-resolution, JPEG deblocking, and image inpainting. Ref. [184] argue that conventional neural networks do not consider that similar visual cues in the human brain can stimulate the same neuron to induce similar neurological signals. As a result, these models are unstable regarding their internal propagation. The stacked non-local AE, which exploited self-similar information in natural images for stability, were constructed. Further, this proposed model was applied to image denoising and image super-resolution. Experiment results revealed that this model outperforms the plain SAE^2.

(4) Image retrieval

Content-based image retrieval has been the subject of growing concern in the multimedia field for over two decades. The traditional image retrieval framework is involved with multiple modules, including feature extraction, codebook learning, feature quantization, image indexing, etc. Those modules are individually designed and independently optimized for the retrieval task. Before image retrieval, users need to express their imaginary intention into some concrete visual query. The quality of the query has a significant impact on the retrieval results [185]. Generally, there are several kinds of query formation, such as sketch map by query, example image by query, context map by query, color map by query, etc. Ref. [186] proposed deep conditional generative models based on AAEs and VAEs for the zero-shot sketch-based image retrieval task. The workflow of the network is first taking the sketch feature vector as an input and then making full use of deep conditional generative models to generate a number of possible image vectors by filling the missing information stochastically. Lastly, they take advantage of these generated image feature vectors to retrieve images from the database. In Ref. [186], the authors made full use of the advantages of VAEs as a powerful generative model. However, the traditional VAEs are prone to the phenomenon of "posterior collapse". Hence, Ref. [187] studied the use of the Vector-Quantized Variational Auto-encoder (VQ-VAE) for representation learning in image retrieval. The VQ-VAE provides an unsupervised model for learning discrete representations by combining vector quantization and the AE. They further modified the VQ-VAE by introducing a product quantizer (PQ) into the bottleneck stage such that an end-to-end unsupervised learning model could be formed for the image retrieval task. This "end-to-end" mechanism is an improvement compared with the traditional image retrieval framework. Compared with directly matching real-valued codes or pixel intensities, binary codes had a lot of advantages for content-based image retrieval [188]. Hence, the authors used very deep AEs initialized with DBNs to map small color images to short binary codes. The above references focus on plain RGB images retrieval, an unsupervised feature learning framework based on AE is proposed to learn sparse feature representations for content-based remote-sensing imagery retrieval (CBRSIR) in [189]. Using the ReLU function and the soft threshold function to realize sparsity, the authors argued that this proposed framework requires fewer parameters than the SAE^1. They also demonstrated that this proposed framework was more effective than traditional BOVW using several performance metrics. Both Refs. [188,189] utilized the basic AE. The authors of Ref. [190] proposed a multiple input multiple task deep auto-encoder (MIMT-DAE), which was combined with the wavelet transformation. For this proposed method, the image is first processed using wavelet transform and decomposed into wavelet coefficients. The wavelet coefficients then become the input for the MIMT-DAE. The result of retrieval performance shows that this combination of wavelet transformation and MIMT-DAE increases the performance of image retrieval for shape and texture compared to a traditional single input single task deep AE with far fewer training parameters required.

5.1.2. Video Process

In the field of computer vision, various AE models have been widely used in the video field, including video classification, video object tracking, video abnormal detection, etc. Table 2 lists the specific application field of AEs for video, the characters, and the areas for improvement. With the rapid progress of storage devices, the internet, and social network, a great deal of video data are generated. To bridge the semantic gap between low-level features and high-level semantics, automatic video annotation and classification technology have become an important technology to improve the efficiency of video retrieval [191]. In Ref. [192], the authors considered three modalities in videos, i.e., image, audio, and text. Hence, they proposed a multimodal feature learning mechanism based on the stacked CAE^1 for video classification. One stacked CAE^1 was built for each single modality, whose outputs would be joint together and fed into another multimodal stacked CAE^1. Compared to other deep and shallow models, the experimental results showed multimodal integration playing important role in video semantics classification. Similarly, Ref. [193] also combined both audio and visual features and learned two separate models trained on audio and visual data of the video. The difference is that three unsupervised feature learning algorithms (RBM, ISA, and deep SAE^1) have been used. A deep convolutional RBM was used to model the audio data and a stacked ISA network was used to extract features from visual data. Finally, they jointly trained audio and visual features using a deep-stacked SAE^1 with discriminative fine-tuning. This confirms the conclusion made in [192] that combining multi-features can obtain better accuracy (97.22% with 40 training examples) as compared to a single type of feature (92.65% with audio only and 88.86% with visual feature only). Fusing multiple modalities also can be used for video event detection [194]. Further, the authors argued that the conventional video representation methods extracted each modality ineffectively. Based on unconstrained minimization and using the conjugate gradient method with a linear search for optimization, a regularized multi-modality AE was developed for video event detection. The superiority of considering multi-modality in the task of video event detection also exists. Compared with traditional reconstruct Independent Components Analysis (RICA), this method is a significant improvement as it captures the relationships between audio and visual modalities from the same category of videos. Because modern editing software provides powerful and easy-to-use tools to manipulate videos, video forgery detection is becoming an important issue in recent years. In Ref. [195], the authors proposed a method to perform forgery detection using an AE and RNN. In this work, the AE can be used not only for image-based salient object detection (SOD) but also for video-based SOD. Ref. [196] considered some inherent correlations between image-based and video-based SOD, and then proposed an unsupervised baseline approach for video-based SOD using saliency guided stacked AEs. There are many forms of feature information present in video data. Above, we discussed the image, text, and audio features in video data. Beyond that, it also has object identity information which is largely static across multiple video frames, object pose, and style information which continuously transforms from frame to frame. Recently, there is a rising interest in disentangled representations. For video sequence modeling, an ideal disentangled representation would be able to separate time-independent concepts (e.g., the identity of the object in the scene) from dynamical information (e.g., the time-varying position and the orientation or pose of that object). Hence, Ref. [197] leveraged a hierarchical VAE for disentangling the object identity and pose information of unsupervised video data. Differing from the conventional VAE, a prior over latent frame features was defined for entire frame sequences, not just individual frames. This prior includes two parts: information that remains relatively constant in the whole video and information that changes temporally. This work could be extended to use a prior with multiple factors, so each factor changes at varying rates from fast to slow to static. Ref. [198] also argue that a VAE model can learn a latent representation of the data, which is split into a static and dynamic part, allowing us to approximately disentangle feature representations. The previous approaches designed the probabilistic graphical model carefully to achieve a disentangled representation. In Ref. [198], the authors explicitly used a latent variable to represent the invariant information through the sequence and a series of latent variables associated with each frame to represent dynamical information. A VAE was used to focus on learning the distribution of the video content and dynamics to generate future sequences without conditioning on the observed sequences. In this work, predicting future frames without conditioning is also different from the traditional method.

There are some other researchers working hard on video object tracking. Visual tracking refers to the automatic estimation of the trajectory of an object as it moves around in a video. Wang and Yeung used the merits of DAE that robust features are learned [199]. An SDAE was trained offline to learn generic image features from a large image dataset as auxiliary data. The knowledge learned was transferred from the offline to the online tracking process. During the online tracking process, adding an additional classification layer to the encoder part of the trained SDAE resulted in a classification neural network. This network achieved very encouraging results with low computational costs. However, only a linear classifier for simplicity was utilized in this current tracker. As in other discriminative trackers, classifiers can be extended to be more powerful for further performance improvement. Inspired by the success of the SDAE and online AdaBoost, a novel object-tracking approach was proposed by combining a family of DNN classifiers using online AdaBoost [200]. Similar to [199], this work also used an SDAE to learn multi-level feature descriptors from an auxiliary image dataset. The difference is that each layer of the SDAE represents a different level of feature space, which is subsequently transformed into a discriminative object/background DNN classifier by adding an additional classification layer. Then, an online AdaBoost feature selection framework is proposed to combine these layered classifiers for online updating to robustly distinguish the target from the background. This approach has two advantages. First, the SDAE is used to automatically learn useful generic image features at different levels. Second, boosting further automatically determined the most suitable level of features for appearance modeling.

Ref. [201] also presented an SAE^2 to learn generic invariant features offline for visual object tracking. In addition, a logistic regression classifier was used to distinguish the object from the background. Unlike [199], this work adopted tracked image patches as training data instead of an auxiliary image dataset. Different from the traditional SAE^1, which enforces sparsity in the hidden layer, this proposed SAE performed subspace pooling on the hidden layer activations and enforced sparsity in the pooling layer, in a way identical to ISA. Then, it trains a second AE with the convolved activations of the first AE just mentioned to learn more complex invariance on larger image patches. Additionally, a temporal slowness constraint is incorporated to the proposed AE for learning generic invariant representations.

Different from those generic object trackers mentioned above, the authors considered motion blur in real videos and proposed a blur invariant object tracker [202]. The SDAE was adopted to learn a robust appearance model. However, compared with some real-time trackers, it is still a bit slow, and there is still a large space to speed up the tracker by optimizing the appearance model. Ref. [203] introduced a new tracking framework based on a context-aware correlation filter. This tracker can achieve high computational speed. The main contribution to high computational speed was the proposed deep feature compression, which was achieved using multiple expert AEs. In the pre-training phase, an expert AE was trained for each category. During the tracking phase, selecting the best expert AE for a given target, only this AE was used. In order to obtain high tracking performance, an external denoising process and a new orthogonality loss term for the pre-training and fine-tuning of expert AEs were used. The framework not only achieved high computing speed but also could run in real-time with a fast speed of over 100 fps. Additionally, this work also considered the solution to the blurriness problem. Generally speaking, as an excellent unsupervised feature extraction model, the theory of the AE is intuitive and graceful. Hence, it has been widely used in video processing and achieved performance results.

Video abnormal detection is one of the key components in video surveillance applications. It has gained more and more attention and became an important research topic in computer vision. The methods for abnormal detection can be divided into the unsupervised method and the supervised method. Due to the lack of human supervision, it is challenging to learn a normal distribution when only normal data samples are given and then identify the samples that do not conform to the normal distribution as anomalies. The AE is a powerful unsupervised learning tool due to its great fitting ability and high-dimensional data modeling ability. It is widely used in video abnormal detection. In [204], the optical flow of the original video sequence is firstly calculated and visualized as an optical flow image, which is then fed into a deep AE. Then, the deep AE extracts the features from the training samples and compresses them into three vectors, which are drawn in a 3-dimension coordinate axis. Finally, the normal and abnormal samples are collected, respectively, on this coordinate axis. Different from Ref. [204], Ref. [205] used a different video reprocessing strategy that was used to generate cubic patches. This method used different feature descriptors for local and global anomalies. They first generated local descriptors and used sparse DAE for global descriptors. Gaussian classifiers were used to classify the local and global descriptors separately, and a fusion technique was used to aggregate the results of both. There is a criterion for AE to identify anomalies. The AE is expected to produce higher reconstruction errors for the abnormal inputs than the normal ones. However, this assumption is not always valid in practice because sometimes the AE "generalizes" very well and can reconstruct the anomaly well, resulting in the omission of anomaly detection.

To alleviate the disadvantage of anomaly detection based on AE, Ref. [206] have developed an improved AE called memory-augmented AE (MemAE) by adding a storage module to the original AE. Given an input, this suggested MemAE first used an encoder to obtain the encoded representation and then used the encoding as a query to retrieve the most relevant patterns in memory for reconstruction. Because of the memory training of the typical normal mode, the normal sample could be reconstructed well, and the error in the abnormal reconstruction could be increased, so that the reconstruction error could be used as the standard of abnormal detection. Ref. [207] also agree that in the testing phase, a well-trained AE has more reconstruction error on an anomaly patch than on a normal patch. However, more than this, if a sparse AE is learned based on normal training patches, it is expected that the representation of the given patch to the AE is sparse. If it is not sparse enough, it is considered a good candidate for an exception. The authors took into account two factors about the reconstruction error and sparse representation, and they introduced two novel cubic patch-based anomaly detectors where one runs based on reconstituting an input video patch and another one was based on the sparse representation of an input video patch. In order to be faster, the two detectors are combined into a cascade classifier. Similar to Ref. [207], Ref. [208] also trained multiple AEs for feature learning. One AE took the cropped images containing objects as input, and it could inherently learn latent appearance features. The other two AEs took the gradients as the input that capture how the object moved before and after the detection moment, respectively. These AEs learn latent motion features. Because most existing approaches lack prior information regarding abnormal events, they are not fully equipped to differentiate between normal and abnormal events. Different from these existing methods, this work formalized abnormal event detection as a one-versus-rest binary classification problem. In the inference phase, each test sample x

was classified with the *k* binary SVM models. The highest classification score was used as the abnormality score s for the respective test sample x:

$$s(x) = -\max_i \{g_i(x)\}, \forall i \in \{1, 2, \ldots, k\} \tag{29}$$

where $g_i(x)$ denoted the score of an independent binary classifier. Equally, Ref. [209] used two Gaussian Mixture Fully Convolutional Variational Auto-encoders (GMFC-VAEs) to formulate a two-stream network to combine the appearance and motion anomalies. They used RGB frames for the appearance anomaly and dynamic flow images for the motion anomaly, respectively. Different from those methods mentioned above, this network was trained exclusively on the normal samples that could be associated with at least one Gaussian component of the GMM. Then, if a test sample could not be associated with any Gaussian component, it would be identified as anomaly. Their method was based on the Gaussian Mixture VAE, which was a model for probabilistic clustering within the framework of the VAE. Based on that, a fully convolutional network (FCN) without a fully connected layer was used for the encoder–decoder structure. Therefore, the GMFC-VAE has been formed. Both the qualitative and quantitative results on two challenging datasets showed the superiority of this method. Ref. [210] also used multiple AEs and the idea of high reconstruction error of abnormal patches. In the training phase, this method adaptively learnt multiple AEs to reconstruct normal patterns at local regions. Given an unknown patch x in the test phase, with the learned AEs $M = \{M_1, \ldots, M_K\}$, the reconstruction errors with each model in M were computed. If there existed a model M_i in the M fitted reconstruction error upper bound, this patch x was regarded as normality. We have analyzed that AEs have been widely used in video abnormal detection as described above. Multiple AEs can be used in a framework to improve the detection performance. Additionally, we can carefully analyze the characteristics of existing video anomaly detection methods to improve present AEs.

Table 2. Various AE models used in video field.

Reference	Method	Task	Characters
Ref. [192]	Stacked CAE[2]	Video classification	Multimodal integration
Ref. [193]	RBM, ISA, deep SAE[1]	Sport Video classification	Combining multiple DL architectures
Ref. [194]	Regularized multi-modality AE	Video event detection	Multimodal integration
Ref. [195]	AE, RNN	Video forgery detection	Combination of AE and RNN
Ref. [196]	Saliency guided SAE[2]	Video-based salient object detection	A video-based SOD dataset was built
Ref. [197]	Hierarchical VAE	Disentangling space and time in video	Using VAE to decompose the static and temporally varying semantic information in video
Ref. [198]	VAE, RNN	Structured sequence modeling	Using VAE for learning disentangled representations of high-dimensional time series
Ref. [199]	SDAE	Video Object tracking	Offline training+online tuning
Ref. [200]	SDAE	Video Object tracking	Using an online AdaBoost feature selection framework to update the ensemble of the DNN classifiers
Ref. [201]	SAE, CAE[2]	Object tracking	Temporal slowness constraint is incorporated to an AE to facilitate representation learning
Ref. [202]	SDAE	Severely blurred object tracking	Proposing a blur invariant object tracker without deblurring image sequences
Ref. [203]	AE	Object tracking	Utilizing multiple expert AEs
Ref. [204]	Deep AE	Abnormal detection	Using optical flow and deep AE
Ref. [205]	Sparse denoising AE	Abnormal detection	1. Using the descriptors to model Gaussian classifiers 2. Using the Mahalanobis distance metric to learn the minimum threshold to define abnormality
Ref. [206]	Memory-augmented AE	Abnormal detection	Adding a storage module on the original AE
Ref. [207]	AE, SAE[1]	Abnormal detection	Presenting a cascade classifier with two stages
Ref. [208]	Object-centric CAE[2]	Abnormal detection	Formalizing abnormal event detection as a multi-class problem
Ref. [209]	Gaussian mixture VAE	Anomaly Detection and Localization	Building upon a two-stream network framework to employ RGB frames and dynamic flows, respectively
Ref. [210]	Adaptive multiple AE	Anomaly Detection	Adaptive multiple AE is used to handle the inter-class variation in normal events

5.1.3. The 3D Model Field

In computer vision and pattern recognition, sometimes we need to build and process 3D models. The AE and its variants, with various characters, also can be used in the 3D model field. In Ref. [211], a novel 3D object retrieval method was proposed based on the stacked local convolutional auto-encoder (SLCAE). This approach applied the greedy layer-wise strategy to train SLCAE and used a gradient descent method for training each layer. It only needed the depth image of 2D views projected from 3D objects. It was view-based and shared the benefits of view-based 3D object analysis: flexible and easy implemented. Ref. [15] proposed a new method to learn the DL representation for 3D shape retrieval using a DBN-initialized AE. By combining the global DL representation achieved with the AE with traditional local descriptor representation, this method obtained state-of-the-art 3D shape retrieval performance. While Ref. [15] used feature fusion strategy, Ref. [212] proposed a rapid 3D feature learning method named the convolutional auto-encoder extreme learning machine (CAE-ELM), which combined the advantages of the CNN, AE, and ELM. This designed architecture performed better and faster than other methods. Complex geometric variations of 3D models often bring great challenges in 3D shape retrieval. Ref. [213] developed a novel 3D shape feature learning method based on a discriminative deep AE, which were insensitive to geometric deformations of shapes. The Fisher discrimination criterion was utilized on the neurons in the hidden layer to develop a deep discriminative AE. A multi-scale shape distribution was computed to input into this network. Finally, concatenating the outputs from the hidden layers of the network at different scales, a global shape descriptor for retrieval was formed. Differing from all the methods stated above in terms of using the unsupervised property of the AE, a new supervised deep AE for depth image-based 3D model retrieval was investigated [214]. This supervised deep AE was achieved by combining the supervised classification information with the reconstruction error for joint optimization. The objective function of this supervised AE was defined as follows:

$$E_s = \alpha E_1 + \beta E_2 \qquad (30)$$

where the reconstruction error term E_1 is the sigmoid cross entropy loss function from the AE and the classification loss term E_2 is the softmax loss function from the classifier. Appropriate supervision in back-propagation provided by the AE can help the retrieval performance. All the papers listed above in this subsection used the AE as a feature extraction tool. Ref. [12] argued that the traditional feature aggregation algorithms (such as Bag-of-Features [215], Locality-constrained Linear coding [216], or Fisher Vector coding [217]) were not necessarily optimal in terms of accuracy because their codebook learning and the feature encoding steps were processed separately. Hence, they proposed two feature aggregation algorithms based on k-Sparse AE: DkSA and PkSA. Multiple local features and benchmark datasets were provided for 3D model retrieval to evaluate DkSA and PkSA quantitatively. AEs also can be used for 3D face generation and reconstruction. The learned 3D representations of human faces are very useful for computer vision problems, such as 3D face tracking and reconstruction from images [218]. Traditional models use higher-order tensor generalizations or linear subspaces to learn a latent representation of a face. Because of this linearity, they are unable to capture extreme deformations and non-linear expressions. To address this, Ref. [218] introduced convolutional Mesh AE (CoMA) combining the convolutions and mesh sampling operations to learn a non-linear representation. The experiments demonstrated that CoMA was significantly better than the latest model in the application of 3D face reconstruction, and the model parameters used were reduced by 75%. Because a 3D face provides more semantic information than a 2D image, 3D face reconstruction from a 2D face image is of great significance for the applications of face detection and recognition. Ref. [219] developed a deep learning framework for 3D face reconstruction. A CAE adds smoothness to the original AE, which makes the learned features robust to minor variations in data such as illumination changes and complex surface shapes unrelated to salient facial features. The authors took advantage of this advantage and stacked a CAE to form two deep AEs for learning the subspace from both the 2D image set and the 3D face set. Then, a one-layer neural network was exploited to model the mapping from the 2D subspace to the 3D subspace. The experiments showed that the proposed method yielded the best quantitative and qualitative results.

5.2. Recommender System

With more and more access to the internet, personalization trends, and changes in computer users' habits, recommender systems (RS) have became prevalent and effective tools of information filtering [220]. They have been widely used to provide users with personalized products and services. Although existing RSs can produce proper recommendations successfully, they still face challenges when dealing with the complexity, huge volume, and dynamics of information. In order to address the problem, many recent researchers have improved RSs by integrating DL models. As a typical DL method, AEs have been widely used for their excellent performance in data dimensionality reduction, feature extraction, and data reconstruction. At the same time, integrating AEs into RSs can understand the needs of users and the characteristics of the project better, so as to improve the recommendation quality [221]. The growing number of studies on AE-based RSs shows the important role about AEs in RS research. These existing studies can be mainly divided into two categories: models that rely solely on AE and integration models. Integration models can be further divided into two subcategories: integrated AEs with traditional RSs and integrated AEs with other DL models. The former can be further divided into loosely coupled models and tightly coupled models.

Following this classification scheme mentioned above, we have elaborated on some important research prototypes of AE-based RSs and summarized their contributions and characteristics.

- Models that rely solely on AEs. Ref. [222] proposed an Auto-encoder-based Collaborative Filtering (ACF), which is the first collaborative recommendation model based on an AE. Instead of directly using the original partially observed vector r_{ui} as input data, r_{ui} is first converted into a vector only represented by 0 and 1, and then this vector is used as input data. ACF uses RBM to pre-train the model to prevent local optimum. However, there are some disadvantages to ACF. First, it is good at handling integer ratings instead of non-integer ratings. Second, the decomposition of some observed vectors increases the sparsity of input data, resulting in lower prediction accuracy. Different from ACF, AutoRec [223] directly takes user rating vectors $r^{(u)}$ or item rating vectors $r^{(i)}$ as input data to obtain the reconstructed rating at the output layer. Because of two types of inputs, AutoRec has two types of variants: item-based AutoRec (I-AutoRec) and user-based AutoRec (U-AutoRec). A partially observed vector $r^{(i)} = (R_{1i}, \ldots, R_{mi}) \in \mathbb{R}^m$ denotes the ratings of item i given by users. Each user $u \in U = \{1 \ldots m\}$ can be represented by a partially observed vector. AutoRec takes each partially observed vector $r^{(i)}$ (or $r^{(u)}$) as input, projects it into a low-dimensional latent space, and then reconstructs $r^{(i)}$ (or $r^{(u)}$) in the output space to predict missing ratings for recommendations. The reconstruction of input is:

$$h(r^{(i)}; \theta) = f(W \cdot g(V \cdot r^{(i)} + \mu) + b) \tag{31}$$

where $f(\cdot)$ and $g(\cdot)$ are activation functions. $\theta = \{W, V, \mu, b\}$ are the parameters of the model. AutoRec has used an AE with a single, k-dimensional hidden layer. The parameters θ are learned by optimizing the objective function (see Equation (32)) for I-AutoRec:

$$\min_\theta \sum_{i=1}^n \left\| r^{(i)} - h(r^i - h(r^i; \theta)) \right\|_2^2 + \frac{\lambda}{2} \cdot (\|W\|_F^2 + \|V\|_F^2) \tag{32}$$

This objective function can be optimized by resilient propagation or L-BFGS. The experiment further illustrated the impact of different combinations of activation functions on the performance of AutoRec. Increasing the number of hidden neurons would improve the result. This is because expanding the dimension of the hidden layer allows this model to have greater ability to simulate the input features [224]. Both these two models are mainly used for rating and learning a non-linear representation of the user-item matrix, and then reconstructed it by determining the missing values. Different from these two models, Ref. [225] proposed collaborative DAE, which was mainly used for ranking prediction. Similar to the standard DAE, the collaborative DAE consists of three layers: input layer, hidden layer, and output layer. The input of collaborative DAE is a user partial observed implicit feedback y_u, where $y_u = \{y_{u1}, y_{u2}, \ldots y_{ul}\}$ is the I-dimensional feedback vector of user u on all the item. The main difference between the collaborative DAE and standard DAE is the user-specific input between the input layer and the hidden layer. This input has been corrupted by Gaussian noise forming $\widetilde{y}_u$, and then collaborative DAE maps the input into a latent representations z_u. SGD is applied to learn the parameters of this model. Different from the above three studies, Zhuang et al. [226] proposed the dual-AE, which is a new representation learning framework. In this framework, the new hidden representations of users and items are simultaneously learned using AEs. Additionally, the deviations in the training data are minimized by the learned representations of users and items. Considering that the optimization problem based on this framework is an unconstrained optimization, a new gradient descent method was developed to learn hidden representations.

- Integrated AEs with traditional RSs. In order to improve the recommendation performance, many researchers are trying to combine AEs with traditional RSs. In this subsection, we will focus on analyzing several important research prototypes for integrating AE with traditional recommendation models. There are many traditional recommendation methods, such as MF, SVD, probability matrix factorization (PMF), factorization machine (FM), and Latent Factor Model (LFM). MF is most widely used in integration models therein. Ref. [227] proposed the Stacked Discriminative denoising auto-encoder-based recommender system, which integrated the SDAE with an MF-based recommender system to incorporate side information with rating information effectively. The previous works have shown that by learning the corrupted versions of training data, the SDAE can improve the performance of the models. The authors of [228] have stacked multiple block models of marginalized DAEs to form a DL architecture. Compared to the conventional DAE, the marginalized DAE has a lower computational cost. A basic block model of this method consists of the input, hidden and output layers, and the matrix factorization of the user-item matrix X. This proposed method coupled the user latent factor matrix with the deepest hidden layer in the marginalized DAE, thus it can correctly capture the complex relationships between the selections made by social friends and those made by the user. Different from Refs. [227,228], Ref. [229] used AE and PCA to extract potential contexts from original data for a potential context-aware recommendation system. These explicit contexts are then integrated into MF process to generate recommendations. Ref. [230] combined an LFM and DAE to form a new architecture, which could recommend multi-items more accurately than traditional methods. In this hybrid recommender system, extended LFM and DAE were utilized to deal with user behavior features and to process visual features, respectively. In addition, some researchers also combined AEs with PMF for RSs [231–233].

- Integrated AE with other DL methods. The flexibility of the AE makes it possible to combine multiple neural building blocks to form a more powerful hybrid model. In Ref. [234], the authors proposed a Collaborative Knowledge Base Embedding (CKE) model for jointly learning the latent representations in collaborative filtering (CF) and the items' semantic representations from the knowledge base. The textual knowledge, structural knowledge, and visual knowledge in the knowledge base were fully exploited. In this hybrid RS, the SDAE and SCAE were used to extract items' textual representations and to find the latent representation from the visual knowledge, respectively. Unlike Ref. [234], Ref. [235] utilized deep generative modeling (DGM) to construct a new set of model-based CF. CF always faces sparse information because of the limited user responses and the vast combinations of users and items. Additionally, VAE is known to find a richer representation, which can meaningfully improve the performance on the task of CF with auxiliary information. They have applied VAE with GAN-style learning and conditional VAE with the ladder structures for collaborative filtering to deal with auxiliary information. This method shows that GAN-style learning can be also applied to a CF field in addition to the image processing field. There will be more possible combinations of AEs and other DL methods but not all have been exploited.

AEs have a straightforward structure, and they are appropriate for feature engineering, dimensionality reduction, and missing value estimation. Among all DL models, AEs are more popular in RS, especially for handling with sparsity and scalability [236]. Based on Ref. [237] and the above references in this subsection, we have summarized the architecture of AE-based RSs, as shown in Figure 7.

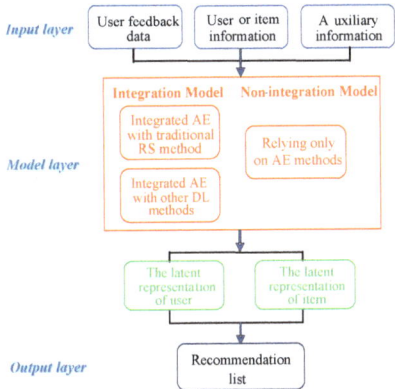

Figure 7. The architecture of AE-based RSs.

5.3. Pattern Recognition

Pattern recognition (PR) refers to the process of processing and analyzing various forms of information, which is an important part of information science and AI. Patterns can also be divided into abstract and concrete forms. The former belongs to the category of concept recognition, such as consciousness, thought, and discussion. It is another branch of AI. The latter is to classify and identify the specific pattern objects such as voice waveform, seismic wave, EEG, ECG, photo, picture, text, symbol, and biological sensors. With the rapid industrial development, ever increasing requirements on the capability of information retrieval and processing has brought new challenges for PR. In recent years, the development in DL architectures has provided novel approaches for solving the problems of PR. In this subsection, we will mostly analyze how to apply AEs to solve the multiple problems in PR field.

5.3.1. Face Recognition

In the face recognition community, one sample per person (OSPP) face recognition is a challenging and opening problem. Because only one sample is available for each subject, lacking samples is the key reason for the failure of most algorithms in OSPP. In Ref. [238], Zhang et al. proposed a new algorithm based on deep AE to generalize intra-class variations of multi-sample subjects to single-sample subjects and reconstructed new samples. Specifically, a generalized deep AE (GDA) is first trained with all images in the gallery, and then a class-specific deep AE (CDA) is fine-tuned for each single-sample subject with its single sample. Samples of the multi-sample subject, which is most like the single-sample subject, are input to the corresponding CDA to reconstruct new samples.

Additionally, the minimum L_2 distance, PCA, sparse represented-based classifier, and SR are used for classification. Inspired by the DAE, Ref. [239] have proposed a supervised AE to build the deep neural network for OSPP. The formulation about this supervised AE is as follows:

$$\min_{W, b_f, b_g} \frac{1}{N} \sum_i (\|x_i - g(f(\tilde{x}_i))\|_2^2 + \lambda \|f(x_i) - f(\tilde{x}_i)\|_2^2) + \alpha (KL(\rho_x \| \rho_0) + KL(\rho_{\tilde{x}} \| \rho_0)) \quad (33)$$

where $\tilde{x}_i$ and x_i denote each probe image in this dataset and its corresponding gallery image, respectively. Additionally,

$$\rho_x = \frac{1}{N} \sum_i \frac{1}{2}(f(x_i) + 1) \quad (34)$$

$$\rho_{\tilde{x}} = \frac{1}{N} \sum_i \frac{1}{2}(f(\tilde{x}_i) + 1) \quad (35)$$

$$KL(\rho \| \rho_0) = \sum_i (\rho_0 \log(\frac{\rho_0}{\rho_j}) + (1 - \rho_0) \log(\frac{1 - \rho_0}{1 - \rho_j})) \quad (36)$$

The activation functions utilized here are the hyperbolic tangent, i.e., $h = f(x) = \tanh(Wx + b_f)$, and $g(h) = \tanh(W^T h + b_g)$. Compared to the basic AE, there are two differences. First, all the faces with variances are forced to be mapped with the canonical face of the person. This strategy is conducive to remove the variances in face recognition. Second, the supervised AE can impose the similarity preservation constraints on the extracted features. Hence, the features corresponding to the same person are made to be similar. It can extract more robust features for face representation. Based on Ref. [239], Ref. [240] has applied the performance of stacked supervised AEs (SSAE) for OSPP from video sequences. In this architecture, a single image sample or its descriptor in the gallery can represent each enrolled person. Conversely, the probe may consist of multiple samples per person (MSPP) collected along the video sequence. Compared to other OSPP methods, this method combining SSAE and MSPP probes has better performance. In the face recognition field, age-invariant face recognition is a challenge and difficult problem because a person shows different appearances at different ages. At the same time, it has become more and more important. It has a wide range of applications, such as finding missing children, identifying criminals, and verifying passports. Based on the fact that age variation is a non-linear but smooth transformation and the powerful ability of AE to learn latent representation from input data, Ref. [241] proposed a new neural network called the coupled AE network. This model has configured two identical AEs and two single-hidden-layer neural networks as a bi-directional bridge. Given the training facial images of different persons, $T = \{x^i{}_1, x^i{}_2\}(x^i{}_1, x^i{}_2 \in R^n, i = 1, 2, 3, \ldots, N)$, N is the total number of training image pairs. x_1 and x_2 represent the younger and older facial image inputs of the same person. These two images were input to these two AEs, respectively. Then, two shallow neural networks as a bridge were adopted to connect these two AEs. Because any neural network with a single hidden layer can complete any complex smooth function, these two shallow neural networks have been used to complete the aging and de-aging process. Further, a nonlinear factor analysis method (see Equation (37)) is applied to the hidden layers:

$$x = \sigma(I, A, \xi) \quad (37)$$

where x denotes inputs and $\sigma(\cdot)$ is a nonlinear function. The representation of a face image can be decomposed into three components nonlinearly using Equation (37): I, A and ξ. I denotes an age-invariant identity feature, A represents the identity-independent age feature, and ξ represents noise which could be any factors deviate from this model. Using this method, we can nonlinearly separate identity features to be age-invariant from one given face image. The experimental results show that it can deal with the age-invariant face recognition effectively. The position variation in face recognition is mainly considered and analyzed in Ref. [242]. The authors argue that the facial appearance variations caused by poses are even larger than that caused by identities. Pose variation is one of the largest challenges in face recognition. Similar to age variation, pose variations change non-linearly but smoothly. Inspired by the impressive ability to handle the non-linearity of AE, the authors proposed a progressive deep structure called the Stacked Progressive Auto-Encoders (SPAE). Each shallow progressive AE in this stacked network is designed to achieve part of the global non-linearity. To be specific, each shallow progressive AE is expected to map the face images at large poses to a virtual view at smaller ones. At the same time, these images are kept unchanged at smaller poses. Then, stacking multiple shallow AEs can convert non-frontal face images to frontal ones progressively. This process makes the pose variations narrow down to zero step by step. Finally, the outputs of the topmost hidden layers in this stacked network are the pose-robust features, which contain very small pose variations. These features can be combined with fisher linear discriminate analysis for face recognition.

Based on the analysis of above the literature, it can be seen that: firstly, modules different from the basic AE can be constructed. Then, these modules can be stacked to form a depth network for face recognition. Secondly, this constructed depth network can aim at one aspect of lighting, expression, disguise, and pose in face recognition only. Similarly, these factors can also be considered comprehensively.

5.3.2. Speech Emotion Recognition

Automatic emotion recognition from speech is a typical problem of wide interest with implications on understanding human behavior and interaction. A classical emotion recognition system involves using high dimensional features on a dataset. These methods have the disadvantages of a limited dataset and difficult analysis in the high dimensional feature space. Ref. [243] solved these issues using the AAE framework. There are two reasons why they used AAE. Firstly, the code vectors learned with AAE can be obtained in a low-dimensional subspace. However, these code vectors do not lose the class discriminability, which can be obtained in the higher dimensional feature space. Secondly, the method using AAE to generate samples synthetically is proven to be promising for improving the classification of data from the real world. Different from Ref. [243], which used AAE to generate samples for the scarcity of emotional speech data, the authors of Ref. [244] proposed another way to alleviate this issue. They used unsupervised feature learning techniques, such as DAE, VAE, AAE, and AVB, to learn features from widely available general speech and utilized these features to train emotion classifiers. These unsupervised methods just mentioned can capture the intrinsic structure of the data distribution in the learned feature representation. Hence, this work designed a CNN-based automatic speech emotion recognition (SER) system. The authors first made the systematic exploration of the four kinds of unsupervised learning techniques just mentioned to improve recognition accuracy. Ref. [245] also focused on the problem of the relatively small emotional speech datasets. They argued that prior works on representation learning for SER did not take full advantage of additional unlabeled speech data and the merit of unsupervised learning on the AE. A large dataset and integrating representations generated with an AE into a CNN-based emotion classifier have improved the recognition accuracy of the presented SER model. Although DL algorithms have the capability for more accurate predictions, Ref. [246] argue that there are still two main problems. First, the labelled speech data is scarce, as analyzed in the previous literature. Even if they contain the trustable labelled speech utterance, there still exits some segments with strong emotion express in same emotion utterance. Second is how to balance the short-term characterization at the frame level and long-term aggregation at the utterance level. Inspired by the recent success of the SAE structure with deep semi-supervised learning and the idea of attention mechanisms in neural machine translation, the authors proposed an SAE with an attention mechanism for speech emotion recognition. The purpose of this framework can benefit from labeled and unlabeled data with the SAE and apply the attention mechanism focusing on speech frames with strong emotional information. Other speech frames without carrying emotional content will be ignored. Hence, this SAE can reduce the required amount of effective labeled data. Compared with existing speech emotion recognition algorithms, the experimental results show that it can provide significantly higher accuracy in the prediction of emotion status.

According to the analysis in this subsection, we can see that it is usually relatively difficult to acquire the labeled data for an emotional speech database. Accordingly, we need experts with psychological expertise to solve this problem. This will increase the difficulty level in both expense and time consumption. In this situation, we can make full use of the potential of AEs with unsupervised feature learning. Further, other machine learning methods should be explored to combine existing AE models.

5.3.3. Facial Expression Recognition

Facial expression recognition (FER) is the most important way of human emotion expression. In the past decades, it has been a very important research area in computer vision and image recognition. The main goal of FER is to recognize the human emotional state (such as anger, contempt, fear, disgust, sadness, happiness, and surprise) based on the given facial images. However, it should be pointed out that FER with high accuracy is still a challenging task. This is mainly related to different lights, postures, and environments. In general, FER consists of three main steps. The first step is to use image processing technology to detect a human face from the whole image. In the second step, key features are extracted from the detected face. Finally, the machine learning model is used to classify the images [247]. Recently, many types of DNN-related algorithms have been successfully applied to facial expression recognition tasks. The traditional DNN has the problems of learning difficulty and high computing complexity. However, the AE has the ability to reconstruct data so that data could be better represented, which can improve the efficiency of data learning. Additionally, enforcing sparsity to AE can reduce the computational complexity. Ref. [248] proposed an SR-based deep sparse auto-encoder network to recognize facial expressions. Firstly, the regions of interest (such as eyebrows, eyes, and mouth) are selected for extracting the facial expression image feature. Then, the greedy pre-trained network produces the initial weights layer by layer. Next, it optimizes the sparse parameters, the hidden layer nodes, and the number of hidden layers to determine the best topology of the network. Finally, SR is used to classify expression feature. The main feature of this reference is that the preliminary application experiments are applied in the developing emotional social robot system (ESRS) with two mobile robots, which can recognize emotions such as happiness and anger. Ref. [247] developed a state-of-the-art face detection method for face detection and extraction. Histogram of oriented gradients (HOG) features are computed from the cropped images. Then, the SAE^2 is used to reduce high-dimensional HOG features for lower dimensions. Finally, they applied SVM on these lower dimension features to classify the facial expressions. In this work, the SAE^2 is used as a tool for feature dimension reduction. Similar work has been completed by Ref. [249]. Three different descriptors (HOG, local binary pattern (LBP), and a gray value) are utilized for extracting features, respectively. Then, PCA is used to compress these local features to make them practical and efficient to apply. Finally, the features compressed by PCA are input to the deep SAE^2. Similar to Ref. [247], Ref. [249] also used local descriptors to extract features. The difference is that the role of the deep SAE^2 here is feature encoding. Another interesting work was performed by Ref. [250]. The authors follow the idea that initializing a CNN with filters of a stacked CAE^2 significantly improves the performance of the CNN. As opposed to traditional CNN models, this method proposed here provides better classification performance and has an additional advantage of learning relatively fast. The analysis of references in this subsection demonstrates that AEs can be used for feature extraction, reduction, and encoding in facial expression recognition. Due to the structural characteristic of AEs, they also can be used for pre-training.

5.4. Data Generation

In recent years, the development in DL has promoted the progress of generative models, which can capture the distributions of high-dimensional datasets and generate new samples. Ref. [251] proposed a method that uses a VAE as an encoder and deems GAN as a high-quality generative model. In this model, the feature representations learned in the GAN discriminator are used as basis for the VAE reconstruction objective. Compared to element-wise errors used in the traditional VAE, feature-wise errors can capture the data distribution better while offering invariance towards translation. Thereby, element-wise errors are replaced with feature-wise errors. This method outperforms VAEs with element-wise similarity measures in terms of visual fidelity. To make a VAE generate high quality images, some approaches have been proposed to increase the network depth to improve the capacity of decoder networks. However, deeper networks are difficult to optimize. Thankfully, the deep residual blocks can solve this problem, allowing for increasing the capacity of the decoder. Additionally, a VAE with residual blocks in the decoder network can generate high quality images. However, it still suffers from the effect of L_2 loss. In Ref. [252], the authors proposed framework to generate high quality images. To make the decoder generate better images, this multi-stage VAE concatenates the original decoder network $f_{\theta 1}(\cdot)$ with the residual block network $f_{\theta 2}(\cdot)$ to increase the capacity of model. In the first stage, $f_{\theta 1}(\cdot)$ is computed with a CNN to generate a coarse image using a L_2 loss function. The subsequent stage uses $f_{\theta 2}(\cdot)$ to take the generated blurry image as input and forms a high-quality image. Because $f_{\theta 2}(\cdot)$ is independent of the VAE model, it can use other loss functions to solve the problem of the effect of L_2 loss. $f_{\theta 2}(\cdot)$ can be considered as a super-resolution module.

5.5. Other Applications

In addition to the domains listed above, there exist substantial studies on other domains, which also apply AEs and their variants. Ref. [117] take advantage of VAEs to observe phase transitions. The weights and latent parameters of the VAE can store information about macroscopic and microscopic properties of the underlying systems. Ref. [253] proposed a natural language-based text-instruction intention understanding method using the stacked DAE. A novel variable-wise weighted stacked auto-encoder (VW-SAE), proposed by Ref. [254], exacts hierarchical output-related feature representation layer by layer for soft sensing applications. Moreover, Ref. [255] use the CAE^2 for page segmentation of historical handwritten documents available as color images. In the text classification domain, a semi-supervised sequential variational auto-encoder (SSVAE) has been proposed for the semi-supervised text classification problem. Surprisingly, AEs can also be used for modeling graphs [256]. As a part of the theoretical basis of machine learning and AI, the research of AEs is of great significance. Furthermore, their applications in various fields also have very important practical values. In addition, AEs are also applied to the parallel basic research fields such as clustering. In the last two years, AEs have been applied to some new research fields. Ref. [257] analyzed the flow-based characteristics of the network traffic data and proposed a new intrusion detection method. This method leverages a deep metric learning methodology that originally combines autoencoders and Triplet networks. Ref. [258] proposed a Crystal Diffusion Variational Autoencoder (CDVAE) for the material design community. The CDVAE can capture the physical inductive bias of material stability to generate the periodic structure of stable materials.

6. Available Deep Learning Toolkits

From the analysis and description in Section 5, we can conclude that AEs can dominate many applications of AI. At the same time, with the rapid development in academic research, there are many DL open-source development toolkits. In this section, we will list some popular DL toolkits which are available for AEs. The candidates are listed in alphabetical order: Caffe, CNTK, Deeplearn4J, Keras, MXNet, Pytorch, PaddlePaddle, TensorFlow, Theano, and Torch. It goes beyond the scope of this paper to discuss all these packages in detail. Hence, we only summarize these toolkits from different perspectives (name, developer, language, supporting system, whether supporting multi-cards on single machine, characteristics, and the literature on AEs using the corresponding framework) in Table 3.

Table 3. Summary of deep learning toolkits for AEs.

Name	Developer	Language	Platform	Supporting Multi_Card	Key Features	Website
Caffe	Berkeley Vision and Learning Center	C++, Python, Matlab	Linux, Windows, Mac OS X	✓	Excellent convnet implementation; adding many extensions	http://caffe.berkeleyvision.org/ accessed on 2 April 2023
CNTK	Microsoft Research	C++, Python, BrainScript	Linux, Widows	✓	Known in the speech community; not usable for a variety of tasks	https://docs.microsoft.com/en-us/cognitive-toolkit/ accessed on 2 April 2023
Deeplearning4J	Skymind	Java, Scala, Clojure	Linux, Windows Mac OS X, Android	✓	Applicable to distributed clusters; providing business support	https://deeplearning4j.org/ accessed on 2 April 2023
Keras	François Chollet et al.	Python	Linux, Windows, Mac OS X	×	User friendliness; modularity; easy extensibility	https://keras.io/ accessed on 2 April 2023
MXNet	Distributed Machine Learning Community	C++, Python, Matlab, Julia, Go, R, Scala, JavaScript	Linux, Windows, Mac OS X Android, iOS	✓	Hybrid front-end; distributed training; 8 language bindings	https://mxnet.io accessed on 2 April 2023
PaddlePaddle	Baidu	C++, Python	Linux, Windows, Mac OS X	✓	Agile framework; support ultra-large-scale training	https://www.paddlepaddle.org.cn/ accessed on 2 April 2023
Pytorch	Facebook	Python	Linux, Mac OS X	✓	Scalable distributed training; well supported on major cloud platforms	http://pytorch.org/ accessed on 2 April 2023
Tensorflow	Google	C\C++, Python, Go, R	Linux, Windows, Mac OS X	✓	High degree of flexibility; portability	https://www.tensorflow.org accessed on 2 April 2023
Theano	University of Montreal	Python	Linux, Windows, Mac OS X	×	Tight integration with NumPy; speed and stability optimizations	http://www.deeplearning.net/software/theano/ accessed on 2 April 2023
Torch	Ronan Collobert, Soumith Chintala, Clement Farabet, Koray Kavukcuoglu	Lua, LuaJIT, C	Linux, Windows, Mac OS X, Android, iOS	✓	Amazing interface to C via LuaJIT; a powerful N-dimensional array; embeddable with ports to iOS and Android backends	https://torch.ch/ accessed on 2 April 2023
Matlab	MathWorks Inc	C, FORTRAN, C++, JAVA, Python	Linux, Windows, MacOS	✓	Computational efficiency; easy to use; widely used; graphics processing	https://www.mathworks.com/products/matlab.html accessed on 2 April 2023
OpenCV	Gary Bradski	C++, Python, Java, MATLAB, OCTAVE, C#, Ch, Ruby, GO	Linux, Windows, Android, Mac OS, iOS, Android	✓	Cross-platform; free; fast and easy to use	https://opencv.org/ accessed on 2 April 2023

There is not a single criterion for determining the best toolkit for DL. Each toolkit was designed and built to address the needs perceived by the developer(s) and also reflect their skills and approaches to problems [259]. All of the DL toolkits are in development. We can choose toolkits by comparing the current performance and function, but more importantly, we can compare the development trend in these different toolkits. DL is currently in a vigorous development stage, so we should pay more attention to the activeness of these toolkits in the open source community to select toolkits [260]. Only the toolkits with high community activity can keep up with the development speed of DL itself, so they will not face the risk of being eliminated in the future. Figure 8 compares some indicators of the activity in each of the DL frameworks listed above on GitHub as of March 2023. From the figure, it can be seen that Tensorflow is far more active than other toolkits in terms of the number for Star, Fork, and Watch. It can be seen that there are many people who actually use this toolkit. This is thanks to the full support of a large number of developers and Google.

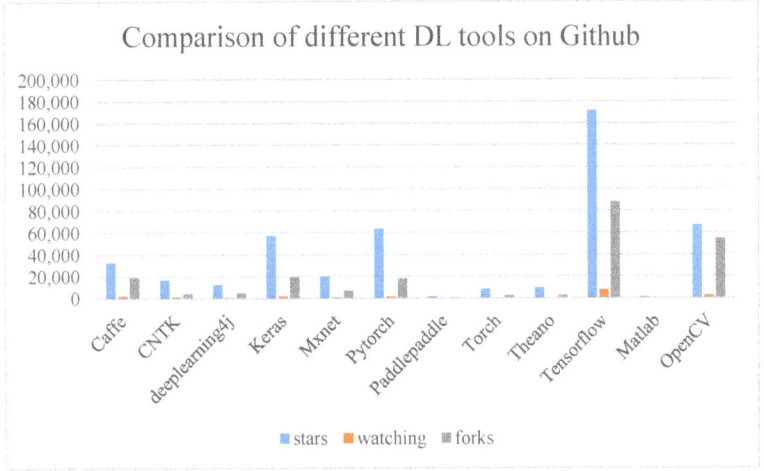

Figure 8. Comparison of different deep learning tools on GitHub.

7. Future Trends

With the deepening in the era of big data, DL is more and more widely used in academia and industry. As a typical model of unsupervised learning in DL, AEs can process a large number of unlabeled data to save human and material resources and provide a good feature learning ability. In this paper, we provide a comprehensive survey of the AE and its variant models. We have mainly introduced the basic theory and features of these various variant models, discussed AEs from different perspectives, and also presented relationships with shallow models and deep models. In particular, we have compared the available DL toolkits for AEs. The various applications show that the research on AEs has become one of the current research hotspots. However, there is still a long way to go in order to fully realize its potential while coping with many unsolved challenges. Now, we will discuss several important open issues and point out the corresponding possible directions for addressing them in the future.

- Constructing a hybrid model based on AEs

Based on the basic AE and its various variants, we can build different hybrid models by combining AEs with other methods. Specifically, there are two main mixing methods. First, the traditional shallow models are integrated with AEs. Although the traditional shallow models depend on the artificial designing feature, they also have the advantages of simplicity and strong interpretability. Therefore, the combination of AE models and these existing shallow models can integrate the advantages of these methods. Although there have some relevant studies [261,262], this direction is still worth researcher's attention. Secondly, other excellent DL models can also be integrated with AEs, such as CNN [263] and GAN [264]. This can improve the overall performance of the model.

- Integrating the attention mechanism into AEs

The human visual attention mechanism is a very important working mechanism in the human visual system, which can greatly improve the working efficiency of the human visual system by allocating different computing resources to different regions in the visual scene [265]. Combining a visual attention mechanism with a DNN can form DL models based on the attention mechanism. At present, the visual attention mechanism has been applied to some DL models, such as RNN, MLP, CNN, etc. Among these models, the RNN based on attention can better model the long-term memory in the sequence data, and CNN based on attention can identify the most relevant information from the input data. At present, integrating the attention mechanism into DL models has had great success in natural language processing, computer vision, and other fields. Applying the attention mechanism to AEs can help AEs learn the most informative features of the dataset. At present, some researchers have applied the attention mechanism to AEs. Ref. [91] put forward a variational attention mechanism for the variational encoder–decoder, where the attention vector is also modeled as Gaussian distributed random variable. Ref. [196] proposed an unsupervised baseline approach for video-based salient object detection using saliency-guided stacked AEs. However, there are few related studies. Hence, more in-depth and extensive studies are needed in the future.

- Integrating a supervised learning mechanism into AEs

AEs can reduce irrelevant and redundant data using unsupervised learning. In other words, it can reduce the dimensions and better process the data with high dimensions. Ref. [266] believes that the more information used in the model, generally speaking, the better performance it can obtain. They found that the use of tag information was often ignored in the frequently used DL methods at home and abroad. The authors have proposed that supervised learning can effectively enhance the discriminability and performance of the model on the basis of making full use of label information. It can obtain better results than unsupervised learning. Ref. [267] constructed a new deep AE model based on supervised learning for image reconstruction. Ref. [268] proposed supervised AE to improve the generalization performance of the model. In order to make up for the limitations of unsupervised learning on feature expression ability and make better use of the efficient feature coding ability of AE, we can combine the advantages of supervised learning to build a new AE model.

- Building AE structures fitting neuroscience and cognitive science

The AE is a kind of artificial neural network. Ref. [269] thinks that compared with the ANN, the local error driven and associated biological realistic algorithm (Leabra) model proposed by O'Reilly and Munakata is more in line with biological neurology. In the Leabra model, the complex neurons make bidirectional connectivity, lateral connectivity, and inhibition mechanisms better implement in one and the same nervous system. In the collected references, there are only two papers [270,271] that use inhibition mechanism in an AE. In the future, this neuroscientific AE will be a very worthy research direction. In addition, in the field of cognitive science, we have seen some preliminary attempts. For example, Ref. [82] proposed the stacked what and where AE. In this model, the filters can focus on learning the shapes (i.e., "what") because the location information (i.e., "where") is encoded into feature maps, which reduces the redundancy among the filters. Hence, this model achieves better results in image classification. Ref. [272] propose that neural computing science is a research method based on research results, hypotheses, or models on neurophysiology and cognitive science. Using mathematical methods to study neural information processing mode will have broad application prospects, so more research content still needs to be further explored.

- Using a better optimization algorithm to adjust the parameters

The method to adjust the parameters in the machine learning field is a new topic in computer science. There are a large number of parameters that need to be adjusted in DNNs. At present, the setting of hyper parameters in AE models mainly depend on manual parameter adjustment. It is necessary to adjust hyper-parameters using trial and error to determine the network performance. When there are many hyper-parameters in the model, the situation becomes more complex. When one single parameter achieves the optimal effect, it cannot guarantee the optimal performance after the combination of multiple parameters. Optimization methods, such as the PSO [273], are therefore required to avoid this problem. According to the statistics of the existing references, only one uses the optimization technique to learn the hyper-parameters automatically [274]. In the future, we can combine the optimization algorithms with AE models to learn the hyper parameters automatically for better performance.

8. Conclusions

This study is first to introduce the basic theory and features of various variant models of AEs. We also provide insight on AEs from various perspectives, including the energy perspective, manifold perspective, and information theoretic perspective. In particular, we also have presented relationships with shallow models and deep models. Additionally, we have summarized its application in various fields and compared available DL toolkits for AEs. Finally, future trends in AEs are analyzed. We hope that this survey can provide a good reference when using and designing AE models.

Author Contributions: Writing—original draft preparation, S.C.; writing—review and editing, S.C. and W.G.; funding acquisition, S.C. and W.G. All authors have read and agreed to the published version of the manuscript.

Funding: This work is supported by the National Natural Science Foundation of China (Grant No. 11971417) and the research fund of Jiangsu Provincial Key Constructive Laboratory for Big Data of Psychology and Cognitive Science (Grant No. 72591862007G).

Data Availability Statement: Not applicable.

Conflicts of Interest: The authors declare no conflict of interest.

References

1. Sze, V.; Chen, Y.H.; Yang, T.J.; Emer, J.S. Efficient processing of deep neural networks: A tutorial and survey. *Proc. IEEE* **2017**, *105*, 2295–2329. [CrossRef]
2. Meyer, D. Introduction to Autoencoders. 2015. Available online: https://davidmeyer.github.io/ (accessed on 26 March 2023).
3. Deng, L.; Yu, D. Deep learning: Methods and applications. *Found. Trends Signal Process.* **2014**, *7*, 197–387. [CrossRef]
4. Hinton, G.E. Deep belief networks. *Scholarpedia* **2009**, *4*, 5947. [CrossRef]
5. Freund, Y.; Haussler, D. Unsupervised learning of distributions on binary vectors using two layer networks. *Adv. Neural Inf. Process. Syst.* **1991**, *4*, 912–919.
6. Hinton, G.E.; Salakhutdinov, R.R. Reducing the dimensionality of data with neural networks. *Science* **2006**, *313*, 504–507. [CrossRef]
7. Bourlard, H.; Kamp, Y. Auto-association by multilayer perceptrons and singular value decomposition. *Biol. Cybern.* **1988**, *59*, 291–294. [CrossRef] [PubMed]
8. Bagnio, Y.; Lamblin, P.; Popovici, D.; Larochelle, H. Greedy layer-wise training of deep networks. In Proceedings of the Advances in Neural Information Processing Systems, Sanur, Indonesia, 8 June 2007; pp. 153–160.
9. Vincent, P.; Larochelle, H.; Bengio, Y.; Manzagol, P.A. Extracting and composing robust features with denoising autoencoders. In Proceedings of the 25th International Conference on Machine Learning, Helsinki, Finland, 5–9 July 2008; pp. 1096–1103.
10. Ng, A. Sparse autoencoder. *CS294A Lect. Notes* **2011**, *72*, 1–19.
11. Rifai, S.; Vincent, P.; Muller, X.; Glorot, X.; Bengio, Y. Contractive auto-encoders: Explicit invariance during feature extraction. In Proceedings of the 28th International Conference on International Conference on Machine Learning, Bellevue, WA, USA, 28 June–2 July 2011.

12. Furuya, T.; Ohbuchi, R. Accurate aggregation of local features by using K-sparse autoencoder for 3D model retrieval. In Proceedings of the 2016 ACM on International Conference on Multimedia Retrieval, New York, NY, USA, 6–9 June 2016; pp. 293–297.
13. Makhzani, A.; Shlens, J.; Jaitly, N.; Goodfellow, I.; Frey, B. Adversarial autoencoders. *arXiv* **2015**, arXiv:1511.05644.
14. Hosseini-Asl, E.; Zurada, J.M.; Nasraoui, O. Deep learning of part-based representation of data using sparse autoencoders with nonnegativity constraints. *IEEE Trans. Neural Netw. Learn. Syst.* **2015**, *27*, 2486–2498. [CrossRef]
15. Zhu, Z.; Wang, X.; Bai, S.; Yao, C.; Bai, X. Deep learning representation using autoencoder for 3D shape retrieval. *Neurocomputing* **2016**, *204*, 41–50. [CrossRef]
16. Makhzani, A.; Frey, B. K-sparse autoencoders. *arXiv* **2013**, arXiv:1312.5663.
17. Xie, G.S.; Zhang, X.Y.; Liu, C.L. Efficient feature coding based on auto-encoder network for image classification. In Proceedings of the Asian Conference on Computer Vision, Singapore, 1–5 November 2014; Springer: Cham, Switzerland, 2014; pp. 628–642.
18. Luo, W.; Yang, J.; Xu, W.; Fu, T. Locality-constrained sparse auto-encoder for image classification. *IEEE Signal Process. Lett.* **2014**, *22*, 1070–1073. [CrossRef]
19. Zhang, F.; Du, B.; Zhang, L. Saliency-guided unsupervised feature learning for scene classification. *IEEE Trans. Geosci. Remote Sens.* **2014**, *53*, 2175–2184. [CrossRef]
20. Xia, C.; Qi, F.; Shi, G. Bottom–up visual saliency estimation with deep autoencoder-based sparse reconstruction. *IEEE Trans. Neural Netw. Learn. Syst.* **2016**, *27*, 1227–1240. [CrossRef]
21. Han, J.; Zhang, D.; Wen, S.; Guo, L.; Liu, T.; Li, X. Two-stage learning to predict human eye fixations via SDAEs. *IEEE Trans. Cybern.* **2015**, *46*, 487–498. [CrossRef] [PubMed]
22. Shin, H.C.; Orton, M.R.; Collins, D.J.; Doran, S.J.; Leach, M.O. Stacked autoencoders for unsupervised feature learning and multiple organ detection in a pilot study using 4D patient data. *IEEE Trans. Pattern Anal. Mach. Intell.* **2012**, *35*, 1930–1943. [CrossRef]
23. Qu, J.L.; Du, C.F.; Di, Y.Z.; Feng, G.A.O.; Chao-ran, G.U.O. Research and prospect of deep auto-encoders. *Comput. Mod.* **2014**, *8*, 128–134.
24. Jia, W.J.; Zhang, Y.D. Survey on theories and methods of autoencoder. *Comput. Syst. Appl.* **2018**, 27. (In Chinese) [CrossRef]
25. Hinton, G.E.; Zemel, R.S. Autoencoders, minimum description length, and Helmholtz free energy. *Adv. Neural Inf. Process. Syst.* **1994**, *6*, 3–10.
26. De Giorgio, A. A Study on the Similarities of Deep Belief Networks and Stacked Autoencoders. 2015. Available online: https://diva-portal.org/ (accessed on 26 March 2023).
27. Bengio, Y.; Courville, A.; Vincent, P. Representation learning: A review and new perspectives. *IEEE Trans. Pattern Anal. Mach. Intell.* **2013**, *35*, 1798–1828. [CrossRef]
28. Nielsen, M.A. *Neural Networks and Deep Learning*; Determination Press: San Francisco, CA, USA, 2015.
29. Amaral, T.; Silva, L.M.; Alexandre, L.A.; Kandaswamy, C.; Santos, J.M.; de Sá, J.M. Using different cost functions to train stacked auto-encoders. In Proceedings of the 2013 12th Mexican International Conference on Artificial Intelligence, Mexico City, Mexico, 24–30 November 2013; IEEE: Piscataway, NJ, USA, 2013; pp. 114–120.
30. Kandaswamy, C.; Amaral, T. *Tuning Parameters of Deep Neural Network Algorithms for Identifying Best Cost Function*; Technical Report 2/2013; Instituto de Engenharia Biomédica/NNIG: Porto, Portugal, 2013.
31. Lai, M. Deep learning for medical image segmentation. *arXiv* **2015**, arXiv:1505.02000.
32. Anitha, R.; Jyothi, S.; Siva, P. Medical image segmentation to diagnosis Alzheimer disease using neural networks. *Int. J. Emerg. Trends Technol. Comput. Sci.* **2016**, *39*, 51–56.
33. Le, Q.V.; Ngiam, J.; Coates, A.; Lahiri, A.; Prochnow, B.; Ng, A.Y. On optimization methods for deep learning. In Proceedings of the 28th International Conference on International Conference on Machine Learning, Bellevue, WA, USA, 28 June–2 July 2011; pp. 265–272.
34. Bottou, L. Stochastic gradient learning in neural networks. *Proc. Neuro-Nımes* **1991**, *91*, 12.
35. Goodfellow, I.; Bengio, Y.; Courville, A. *Deep Learning*; MIT Press: Cambridge, MA, USA, 2016.
36. Ketkar, N.; Santana, E. *Deep Learning with Python*; Apress: Berkeley, CA, USA, 2017.
37. Ruder, S. An overview of gradient descent optimization algorithms. *arXiv* **2016**, arXiv:1609.04747.
38. Zou, F.; Shen, L.; Jie, Z.; Zhang, W.; Liu, W. A sufficient condition for convergences of adam and rmsprop. In Proceedings of the IEEE/CVF Conference on Computer Vision and Pattern Recognition, Long Beach, CA, USA, 15–20 June 2019; pp. 11127–11135.
39. Xie, J.; Xu, L.; Chen, E. Image denoising and inpainting with deep neural networks. *Adv. Neural Inf. Process. Syst.* **2012**, *25*.
40. Nocedal, J. Updating quasi-Newton matrices with limited storage. *Math. Comput.* **1980**, *35*, 773–782. [CrossRef]
41. Liu, D.C.; Nocedal, J. On the limited memory BFGS method for large scale optimization. *Math. Program.* **1989**, *45*, 503–528. [CrossRef]
42. Sainath, T.N.; Horesh, L.; Kingsbury, B.; Aravkin, A.Y.; Ramabhadran, B. Accelerating Hessian-free optimization for deep neural networks by implicit preconditioning and sampling. In Proceedings of the 2013 IEEE Workshop on Automatic Speech Recognition and Understanding, Olomouc, Czech Republic, 8–12 December 2013; IEEE: Piscataway, NJ, USA, 2013; pp. 303–308.
43. Hestenes, M.R.; Stiefel, E. Methods of conjugate gradients for solving. *J. Res. Natl. Bur. Stand.* **1952**, *49*, 409. [CrossRef]
44. Fletcher, R.; Reeves, C.M. Function minimization by conjugate gradients. *Comput. J.* **1964**, *7*, 149–154. [CrossRef]

45. Polak, E.; Ribiere, G. Note sur la convergence de méthodes de directions conjuguées. *Rev. Française D'informatique Rech. Opérationnelle Série Rouge* **1969**, *3*, 35–43. [CrossRef]
46. Zoutendijk, G. Nonlinear programming, computational methods. In *Integer Nonlinear Program*; North-Holland: Amsterdam, The Netherlands, 1970; pp. 37–86.
47. Powell, M.J.D. *Nonconvex Minimization Calculations and the Conjugate Gradient Method*; Numerical Analysis; Springer: Berlin/Heidelberg, Germany, 1984; pp. 122–141.
48. Al-Baali, M. Descent property and global convergence of the Fletcher—Reeves method with inexact line search. *IMA J. Numer. Anal.* **1985**, *5*, 121–124. [CrossRef]
49. Hager, W.W.; Zhang, H. A survey of nonlinear conjugate gradient methods. *Pac. J. Optim.* **2006**, *2*, 35–58.
50. Lyu, Q.; Zhu, J. Revisit long short-term memory: An optimization perspective. In Proceedings of the Advances in Neural Information Processing Systems Workshop on Deep Learning and Representation Learning, Montreal, QC, Canada, 8–13 December 2014; pp. 1–9.
51. Hinton, G.E.; Mcclelland, J.L. Learning Representations by Recirculation. In Proceedings of the Neural Information Processing Systems, Denver, CO, USA, 1 January 1987; MIT Press: Cambridge, MA, USA, 1987.
52. Schaffer, J.D.; Whitley, D.; Eshelman, L.J. Combinations of genetic algorithms and neural networks: A survey of the state of the art. In Proceedings of the International Workshop on Combinations of Genetic Algorithms & Neural Networks, Baltimore, MD, USA, 6 June 1992; IEEE: Piscataway, NJ, USA, 1992.
53. Ding, S.; Li, H.; Su, C.; Yu, J.; Jin, F. Evolutionary artificial neural networks: A review. *Artif. Intell. Rev.* **2013**, *39*, 251–260. [CrossRef]
54. Ijjina, E.P.; Mohan, C.K. Human action recognition using genetic algorithms and convolutional neural networks. *Pattern Recognit.* **2016**, *59*, 199–212. [CrossRef]
55. Montana, D.J.; Davis, L. Training feedforward neural networks using genetic algorithms. In Proceeding of the International Joint Conference on Artificial Intelligence, Detroit, MI, USA, 20–25 August 1989; Volume 89, pp. 762–767.
56. David, O.E.; Greental, I. Genetic algorithms for evolving deep neural networks. In Proceedings of the Companion Publication of the 2014 Annual Conference on Genetic and Evolutionary Computation, Vancouver, BC, Canada, 12–16 July 2014; pp. 1451–1452.
57. Hinton, G.E.; Srivastava, N.; Krizhevsky, A.; Sutskever, I.; Salakhutdinov, R.R. Improving neural networks by preventing co-adaptation of feature detectors. *arXiv* **2012**, arXiv:1207.0580.
58. Wan, L.; Zeiler, M.; Zhang, S.; LeCun, Y.; Fergus, R. Regularization of Neural Networks using DropConnect. In Proceedings of the International Conference on Machine Learning, Atlanta, GA, USA, 16–21 June 2013.
59. Ranzato, M.; Boureau, Y.L.; Chopra, S.; LeCun, Y. A Unified Energy-Based Framework for Unsupervised Learning. In Proceedings of the Conference on Artificial Intelligence and Statistics. PMLR, San Juan, Puerto Rico, 21–24 March 2007; pp. 371–379.
60. Bengio, Y. Deep learning of representations: Looking forward. In Proceedings of the International Conference on Statistical Language and Speech Processing, Tarragona, Spain, 29–31 July 2013; Springer: Berlin/Heidelberg, Germany, 2013; pp. 1–37.
61. Abdi, H.; Williams, L.J. Principal component analysis. *Wiley Interdiscip. Rev. Comput. Stat.* **2010**, *2*, 433–459. [CrossRef]
62. Vidal, R.; Ma, Y.; Sastry, S. Generalized principal component analysis (GPCA). *IEEE Trans. Pattern Anal. Mach. Intell.* **2005**, *27*, 1945–1959. [CrossRef]
63. Guo, Y.; Liu, Y.; Oerlemans, A.; Lao, S.; Wu, S.; Lew, M.S. Deep learning for visual understanding: A review. *Neurocomputing* **2016**, *187*, 27–48. [CrossRef]
64. Alain, G.; Bengio, Y. What regularized auto-encoders learn from the data-generating distribution. *J. Mach. Learn. Res.* **2014**, *15*, 3563–3593.
65. Chen, Z.; Li, W. Multisensor feature fusion for bearing fault diagnosis using sparse autoencoder and deep belief network. *IEEE Trans. Instrum. Meas.* **2017**, *66*, 1693–1702. [CrossRef]
66. Ali, A.; Yangyu, F. k-Sparse autoencoder-based automatic modulation classification with low complexity. *IEEE Commun. Lett.* **2017**, *21*, 2162–2165. [CrossRef]
67. Makhzani, A.; Frey, B.J. Winner-take-all autoencoders. *Adv. Neural Inf. Process. Syst.* **2015**, *28*, 2791–2799.
68. Chen, M.; Weinberger, K.; Sha, F.; Bengio, Y. Marginalized denoising auto-encoders for nonlinear representations. In Proceedings of the 31st International Conference on Machine Learning, Beijing, China, 21–26 June 2014; pp. 1476–1484.
69. Zhao, R.; Mao, K. Cyberbullying detection based on semantic-enhanced marginalized denoising auto-encoder. *IEEE Trans. Affect. Comput.* **2016**, *8*, 328–339. [CrossRef]
70. Lu, G.; Zhao, X.; Yin, J.; Yang, W.; Li, B. Multi-task learning using variational auto-encoder for sentiment classification. *Pattern Recognit. Lett.* **2020**, *132*, 115–122. [CrossRef]
71. Wang, L.; Schwing, A.; Lazebnik, S. Diverse and accurate image description using a variational auto-encoder with an additive gaussian encoding space. In Proceedings of the 31st Conference on Neural Information Processing Systems (NIPS 2017), Long Beach, CA, USA, 4–9 December 2017; Volume 30.
72. Sønderby, C.K.; Raiko, T.; Maaløe, L.; Sønderby, S.K.; Winther, O. Ladder variational autoencoders. In Proceedings of the 30th Conference on Neural Information Processing Systems (NIPS 2016), Barcelona, Spain, 5–10 December 2016; Volume 29.
73. Ishfaq, H.; Hoogi, A.; Rubin, D. TVAE: Triplet-based variational autoencoder using metric learning. *arXiv* **2018**, arXiv:1802.04403.

74. Sohn, K.; Yan, X.; Lee, H.; Yan, X. Learning Structured Output Representation using Deep Conditional Generative Models. In Proceedings of the International Conference on Neural Information Processing Systems, Montreal, QC, Canada, 7–12 December 2015; MIT Press: Cambridge, MA, USA, 2015.
75. Kingma, D.P.; Mohamed, S.; Jimenez Rezende, D.; Welling, M. Semi-supervised learning with deep generative models. *Adv. Neural Inf. Process. Syst.* **2014**, *27*, 1–9.
76. Tang, L.; Xue, Y.; Chen, D.; Gomes, C. Multi-entity dependence learning with rich context via conditional variational auto-encoder. In Proceedings of the AAAI Conference on Artificial Intelligence, New Orleans, LA, USA, 2–7 February 2018; Volume 32.
77. Tolstikhin, I.; Bousquet, O.; Gelly, S.; Schoelkopf, B. Wasserstein auto-encoders. *arXiv* **2017**, arXiv:1711.01558.
78. Rubenstein, P.K.; Schlkopf, B.; Tolstikhin, I.O. Learning Disentangled Representations with Wasserstein Auto-Encoders. In Proceedings of the International Conference on Learning Representations. OpenReview.net, Vancouver, BC, Canada, 30 April–3 May 2018.
79. Rubenstein, P.K.; Schoelkopf, B.; Tolstikhin, I. Wasserstein auto-encoders: Latent dimensionality and random encoders. In Proceedings of the ICLR 2018 Workshop Submission, Vancouver, BC, Canada, 30 April–3 May 2018.
80. Rifai, S.; Mesnil, G.; Vincent, P.; Muller, X.; Bengio, Y.; Dauphin, Y.; Glorot, X. Higher order contractive auto-encoder. In Proceedings of the Joint European Conference on Machine Learning and Knowledge Discovery in Databases, Athens, Greece, 5–9 September 2011; Springer: Berlin/Heidelberg, Germany, 2011; pp. 645–660.
81. Diallo, B.; Hu, J.; Li, T.; Khan, G.A.; Liang, X.; Zhao, Y. Deep embedding clustering based on contractive autoencoder. *Neurocomputing* **2021**, *433*, 96–107. [CrossRef]
82. Zhao, J.; Mathieu, M.; Goroshin, R.; Lecun, Y. Stacked what-where auto-encoders. *arXiv* **2015**, arXiv:1506.02351.
83. Calvo-Zaragoza, J.; Gallego, A.J. A selectional auto-encoder approach for document image binarization. *Pattern Recognit.* **2019**, *86*, 37–47. [CrossRef]
84. Masci, J.; Meier, U.; Cireşan, D.; Schmidhuber, J. Stacked convolutional auto-encoders for hierarchical feature extraction. In Proceedings of the International Conference on Artificial Neural Networks, Espoo, Finland, 14–17 June 2011; Springer: Berlin/Heidelberg, Germany, 2011; pp. 52–59.
85. Turchenko, V.; Chalmers, E.; Luczak, A. A deep convolutional auto-encoder with pooling-unpooling layers in caffe. *arXiv* **2017**, arXiv:1701.04949. [CrossRef]
86. Ribeiro, M.; Lazzaretti, A.E.; Lopes, H.S. A study of deep convolutional auto-encoders for anomaly detection in videos. *Pattern Recognit. Lett.* **2018**, *105*, 13–22. [CrossRef]
87. Creswell, A.; Bharath, A.A. Denoising adversarial autoencoders. *IEEE Trans. Neural Netw. Learn. Syst.* **2018**, *30*, 968–984. [CrossRef] [PubMed]
88. Creswell, A.; Pouplin, A.; Bharath, A.A. Denoising adversarial autoencoders: Classifying skin lesions using limited labelled training data. *IET Comput. Vis.* **2018**, *12*, 1105–1111. [CrossRef]
89. Sutskever, I.; Vinyals, O.; Le, Q.V. Sequence to sequence learning with neural networks. *Adv. Neural Inf. Process. Syst.* **2014**, *27*.
90. Chung, Y.A.; Wu, C.C.; Shen, C.H.; Lee, H.Y.; Lee, L.S. Audio word2vec: Unsupervised learning of audio segment representations using sequence-to-sequence autoencoder. *arXiv* **2016**, arXiv:1603.00982.
91. Bahuleyan, H.; Mou, L.; Vechtomova, O.; Poupart, P. Variational attention for sequence-tosequence models. *arXiv* **2017**, arXiv:1712.08207.
92. Ng, A.; Ngiam, J.; Foo, C.Y.; Mai, Y.; Suen, C.; Coates, A.; Tandon, S. Unsupervised Feature Learning and Deep Learning. 2013. Available online: https://csee.umbc.edu/ (accessed on 26 March 2023).
93. Ranzato, M.A.; Huang, F.J.; Boureau, Y.L.; LeCun, Y. Unsupervised learning of invariant feature hierarchies with applications to object recognition. In Proceedings of the 2007 IEEE Conference on Computer Vision and Pattern Recognition, Minneapolis, MN, USA, 18–23 June 2007; IEEE: Piscataway, NJ, USA, 2007; pp. 1–8.
94. Ranzato, M.A.; Poultney, C.; Chopra, S.; Cun, Y. Efficient learning of sparse representations with an energy-based model. *Adv. Neural Inf. Process. Syst.* **2006**, *19*.
95. Ranzato, M.; Boureau, Y.L.; Lecun, Y. Sparse feature learning for deep belief networks. *Adv. Neural Inf. Process. Syst.* **2008**, *20*, 1185–1192.
96. Vincent, P.; Larochelle, H.; Lajoie, I.; Bengio, Y.; Manzagol, P.A.; Bottou, L. Stacked denoising autoencoders: Learning useful representations in a deep network with a local denoising criterion. *J. Mach. Learn. Res.* **2010**, *11*, 3371–3408.
97. Olshausen, B.A.; Field, D.J. Emergence of simple-cell receptive field properties by learning a sparse code for natural images. *Nature* **1996**, *381*, 607–609. [CrossRef] [PubMed]
98. Liu, W.; Ma, T.; Tao, D.; You, J. HSAE: A Hessian regularized sparse auto-encoders. *Neurocomputing* **2016**, *187*, 59–65. [CrossRef]
99. Witkowski, B. *Autoencoders for Image Classification*; Jagiellonian University: Krakow, Poland, 2013.
100. Ngiam, J.; Chen, Z.; Bhaskar, S.; Koh, P.; Ng, A. Sparse filtering. *Adv. Neural Inf. Process. Syst.* **2011**, *24*.
101. Willmore, B.; Tolhurst, D.J. Characterizing the sparseness of neural codes. *Netw. Comput. Neural Syst.* **2001**, *12*, 255. [CrossRef]
102. Bengio, Y. Learning deep architectures for AI. *Found. Trends Mach. Learn.* **2009**, *2*, 1–127. [CrossRef]
103. Vincent, P. A connection between score matching and denoising autoencoders. *Neural Comput.* **2011**, *23*, 1661–1674. [CrossRef] [PubMed]
104. Erhan, D.; Bengio, Y.; Courville, A.; Vincent, P. Why Does Unsupervised Pre-training Help Deep Learning? *J. Mach. Learn. Res.* **2010**, *11*, 625–660.

105. Tang, Y.; Eliasmith, C. Deep networks for robust visual recognition. In Proceedings of the 27th International Conference on Machine Learning (ICML-10), Haifa, Israel, 21–24 June 2010.
106. Ding, J.; Chen, B.; Liu, H.; Huang, M. Convolutional neural network with data augmentation for SAR target recognition. *IEEE Geosci. Remote Sens. Lett.* **2016**, *13*, 364–368. [CrossRef]
107. Krizhevsky, A.; Sutskever, I.; Hinton, G.E. Imagenet classification with deep convolutional neural networks. *Adv. Neural Inf. Process. Syst.* **2012**, *5*, 1106–1114. [CrossRef]
108. Srivastava, N.; Hinton, G.; Krizhevsky, A.; Sutskever, I.; Salakhutdinov, R. Dropout: A simple way to prevent neural networks from overfitting. *J. Mach. Learn. Res.* **2014**, *15*, 1929–1958.
109. Srivastava, N. Improving neural networks with dropout. *Univ. Tor.* **2013**, *182*, 7.
110. Bengio, Y.; Yao, L.; Alain, G.; Vincent, P. Generalized denoising auto-encoders as generative models. *Adv. Neural Inf. Process. Syst.* **2013**, *26*, 899–907.
111. Hyvärinen, A.; Hurri, J.; Hoyer, P.O. *Estimation of Non-Normalized Statistical Models*; Natural Image Statistics; Springer: London, UK, 2009; pp. 419–426.
112. Seung, H.S. Learning continuous attractors in recurrent networks. In Proceedings of the International Conference on Advances in Neural Information Processing Systems, Denver, CO, USA, 30 November–5 December 1998; MIT Press: Cambridge, MA, USA, 1998.
113. Kingma, D.P.; Welling, M. Auto-encoding variational bayes. *arXiv* **2013**, arXiv:1312.6114.
114. Doersch, C. Tutorial on variational autoencoders. *arXiv* **2016**, arXiv:1606.05908.
115. Kingma, D.P.; Salimans, T.; Welling, M. Variational dropout and the localreparameterization trick. *Adv. Neural Inf. Process. Syst.* **2015**, *28*, 2575–2583.
116. Kingma, D.P. Variational Inference & Deep Learning: A new Synthesis. Ph.D. Thesis, University of Amsterdam, Amsterdam, The Netherlands, 2017.
117. Wetzel, S.J. Unsupervised learning of phase transitions: From principal component analysis to variational autoencoders. *Phys. Rev. E* **2017**, *96*, 022140. [CrossRef] [PubMed]
118. Rifai, S.; Vincent, P.; Muller, X.; Glorot, X.; Bengio, Y. Contracting auto-encoders. In Proceedings of the International Conference on Machine Learning (ICML), Bellevue, WA, USA, 28 June 2011; p. 95.
119. Luo, W.; Li, J.; Yang, J.; Xu, W.; Zhang, J. Convolutional sparse autoencoders for image classification. *IEEE Trans. Neural Netw. Learn. Syst.* **2017**, *29*, 3289–3294. [CrossRef]
120. Goodfellow, I.; Pouget-Abadie, J.; Mirza, M.; Xu, B.; Warde-Farley, D.; Ozair, S.; Bengio, Y. Generative adversarial networks. *Commun. ACM* **2020**, *63*, 139–144. [CrossRef]
121. Freitag, M.; Amiriparian, S.; Pugachevskiy, S.; Cummins, N.; Schuller, B. audeep: Unsupervised learning of representations from audio with deep recurrent neural networks. *J. Mach. Learn. Res.* **2017**, *18*, 6340–6344.
122. Bowman, S.R.; Vilnis, L.; Vinyals, O.; Dai, A.M.; Jozefowicz, R.; Bengio, S. Generating sentences from a continuous space. *arXiv* **2015**, arXiv:1511.06349.
123. Bahdanau, D.; Cho, K.; Bengio, Y. Neural machine translation by jointly learning to align and translate. *arXiv* **2014**, arXiv:1409.0473.
124. LeCun, Y.; Chopra, S.; Hadsell, R.; Ranzato, M.; Huang, F. A tutorial on energy-based learning. In *Predicting Structured Data*; Bakir, G., Hofman, T., Scholkopf, B., Smola, A., Taskar, B., Eds.; MIT Press: Cambridge, MA, USA, 2006.
125. Kamyshanska, H.; Memisevic, R. The potential energy of an autoencoder. *IEEE Trans. Pattern Anal. Mach. Intell.* **2014**, *37*, 1261–1273. [CrossRef] [PubMed]
126. Park, E. *Manifold Learning with Variational Auto-Encoder for Medical Image Analysis*; Technical Report; University of North Carolina at Chapel Hill: Chapel Hill, NC, USA, 2015.
127. Wang, H.L.; Li, Z.H.; Lin, X.M. *Intelligent Question Answering and Deep Learning*; Electronic Industry Press: Beijing, China, 2019. (In Chinese)
128. Shannon, C.E. A mathematical theory of communication. *Bell Syst. Tech. J.* **1948**, *27*, 379–423. [CrossRef]
129. Crescimanna, V.; Graham, B. An information theoretic approach to the autoencoder. In Proceedings of the INNS Big Data and Deep Learning Conference, Sestri Levante, Italy, 16–18 April 2019; Springer: Cham, Switzerland, 2019; pp. 99–108.
130. Oja, E. Simplified neuron model as a principal component analyzer. *J. Math. Biol.* **1982**, *15*, 267–273. [CrossRef]
131. Hotelling, H. Analysis of a complex of statistical variables into principal components. *J. Educ. Psychol.* **1933**, *24*, 417. [CrossRef]
132. Baldi, P.; Hornik, K. Neural networks and principal component analysis: Learning from examples without local minima. *Neural Netw.* **1989**, *2*, 53–58. [CrossRef]
133. Wang, Y.; Yao, H.; Zhao, S. Auto-encoder based dimensionality reduction. *Neurocomputing* **2016**, *184*, 232–242. [CrossRef]
134. Lee, M.K.; Han, D.S. Dimensionality reduction of radio map with nonlinear autoencoder. *Electron. Lett.* **2012**, *48*, 1. [CrossRef]
135. Wang, W.; Huang, Y.; Wang, Y.; Wang, L. Generalized autoencoder: A neural network framework for dimensionality reduction. In Proceedings of the IEEE Conference on Computer Vision and Pattern Recognition Workshops, Columbus, OH, USA, 23–28 June 2014; pp. 490–497.
136. Li, S.Z.; Yu, B.; Wu, W.; Su, S.Z.; Ji, R.R. Feature learning based on SAE–PCA network for human gesture recognition in RGBD images. *Neurocomputing* **2015**, *151*, 565–573. [CrossRef]
137. Seuret, M.; Alberti, M.; Liwicki, M.; Ingold, R. PCA-initialized deep neural networks applied to document image analysis. In Proceedings of the 2017 14th IAPR International Conference on Document Analysis and Recognition (ICDAR), Kyoto, Japan, 9–15 November 2017; IEEE: Piscataway, NJ, USA, 2017; Volume 1, pp. 877–882.

138. Wang, Y.; Liu, M.; Bao, Z.; Zhang, S. Stacked sparse autoencoder with PCA and SVM for data-based line trip fault diagnosis in power systems. *Neural Comput. Appl.* **2019**, *31*, 6719–6731. [CrossRef]
139. Smolensky, P. *Information Processing in Dynamical Systems: Foundations of Harmony Theory*; Colorado University at Boulder Department of Computer Science: Boulder, CO, USA, 1986.
140. Arora, S.; Ge, R.; Moitra, A.; Sachdeva, S. Provable ICA with unknown Gaussian noise, with implications for Gaussian mixtures and autoencoders. *Algorithmica* **2015**, *72*, 215–236. [CrossRef]
141. Zhai, S.; Cheng, Y.; Lu, W.; Zhang, Z. Deep structured energy based models for anomaly detection. In Proceedings of the International Conference on Machine Learning. PMLR, New York, NY, USA, 19–24 June 2016; pp. 1100–1109.
142. Kingma, D.P.; Cun, Y. Regularized estimation of image statistics by score matching. *Adv. Neural Inf. Process. Syst.* **2010**, *23*, 1126–1134.
143. Stone, J.V. *Independent Component Analysis*; A Bradford Book; MIT Press: Cambridge, MA, USA, 2004.
144. Le, Q.; Karpenko, A.; Ngiam, J.; Ng, A. ICA with reconstruction cost for efficient overcomplete feature learning. *Adv. Neural Inf. Process. Syst.* **2011**, *24*, 1017–1025.
145. Kavukcuoglu, K.; Ranzato, M.A.; LeCun, Y. Fast inference in sparse coding algorithms with applications to object recognition. *arXiv* **2010**, arXiv:1010.3467.
146. Jarrett, K.; Kavukcuoglu, K.; Ranzato, M.A.; LeCun, Y. What is the best multi-stage architecture for object recognition? In Proceedings of the 2009 IEEE 12th International Conference on Computer Vision, Kyoto, Japan, 29 September–2 October 2009; IEEE: Piscataway, NJ, USA, 2009; pp. 2146–2153.
147. Kavukcuoglu, K.; Ranzato, M.A.; Fergus, R.; LeCun, Y. Learning invariant features through topographic filter maps. In Proceedings of the 2009 IEEE Conference on Computer Vision and Pattern Recognition, Miami, FL, USA, 20–25 June 2009; IEEE: Piscataway, NJ, USA, 2009; pp. 1605–1612.
148. Hinton, G.E.; Osindero, S.; Teh, Y.W. A fast learning algorithm for deep belief nets. *Neural Comput.* **2006**, *18*, 1527–1554. [CrossRef] [PubMed]
149. Karpathy, A.; Toderici, G.; Shetty, S.; Leung, T.; Sukthankar, R.; Fei-Fei, L. Large-scale video classification with convolutional neural networks. In Proceedings of the IEEE Conference on Computer Vision and Pattern Recognition, Columbus, OH, USA, 23–28 June 2014; pp. 1725–1732.
150. Oquab, M.; Bottou, L.; Laptev, I.; Sivic, J. Learning and transferring mid-level image representations using convolutional neural networks. In Proceedings of the IEEE Conference on Computer Vision and Pattern Recognition, Columbus, OH, USA, 23–28 June 2014; pp. 1717–1724.
151. Gatys, L.A.; Ecker, A.S.; Bethge, M. Image style transfer using convolutional neural networks. In Proceedings of the IEEE Conference on Computer Vision and Pattern Recognition, Las Vegas, NV, USA, 27–30 June 2016; pp. 2414–2423.
152. Chen, M.; Shi, X.; Zhang, Y.; Wu, D.; Guizani, M. Deep feature learning for medical image analysis with convolutional autoencoder neural network. *IEEE Trans. Big Data* **2017**, *7*, 750–758. [CrossRef]
153. Knyaz, V.A.; Vygolov, O.; Kniaz, V.V.; Vizilter, Y.; Gorbatsevich, V.; Luhmann, T.; Conen, N. Deep learning of convolutional auto-encoder for image matching and 3d object reconstruction in the infrared range. In Proceedings of the IEEE International Conference on Computer Vision Workshops, Venice, Italy, 22–29 October 2017; pp. 2155–2164.
154. Du, B.; Xiong, W.; Wu, J.; Zhang, L.; Zhang, L.; Tao, D. Stacked convolutional denoising auto-encoders for feature representation. *IEEE Trans. Cybern.* **2016**, *47*, 1017–1027. [CrossRef]
155. Chen, S.; Liu, H.; Zeng, X.; Qian, S.; Yu, J.; Guo, W. Image classification based on convolutional denoising sparse autoencoder. *Math. Probl. Eng.* **2017**, *2017*, 5218247. [CrossRef]
156. Zhai, S.; Zhang, Z. Dropout training of matrix factorization and autoencoder for link prediction in sparse graphs. In Proceedings of the 2015 SIAM International Conference on Data Mining. Society for Industrial and Applied Mathematics, Vancouver, BC, Canada, 30 April–2 May 2015; pp. 451–459.
157. Squires, S.; Bennett, A.P.; Niranjan, M. A variational autoencoder for probabilistic non-negative matrix factorisation. *arXiv* **2019**, arXiv:1906.05912.
158. Gannon, D. Manifold Learning and Deep Autoencoders in Science. Technical Report. 2017. Available online: https://www.researchgate.net/publication/316658932/ (accessed on 26 March 2023).
159. Chicco, D.; Sadowski, P.; Baldi, P. Deep autoencoder neural networks for gene ontology annotation predictions. In Proceedings of the 5th ACM Conference on Bioinformatics, Computational Biology, and Health Informatics, Newport Beach, CA, USA, 20–23 September 2014; pp. 533–540.
160. Liu, W.; Wang, Z.; Liu, X.; Zeng, N.; Liu, Y.; Alsaadi, F.E. A survey of deep neural network architectures and their applications. *Neurocomputing* **2017**, *234*, 11–26. [CrossRef]
161. Xu, J.; Xiang, L.; Liu, Q.; Gilmore, H.; Wu, J.; Tang, J.; Madabhushi, A. Stacked sparse autoencoder (SSAE) for nuclei detection on breast cancer histopathology images. *IEEE Trans. Med. Imaging* **2015**, *35*, 119–130. [CrossRef]
162. Zhang, Y.; Zhang, E.; Chen, W. Deep neural network for halftone image classification based on sparse auto-encoder. *Eng. Appl. Artif. Intell.* **2016**, *50*, 245–255. [CrossRef]
163. Coates, A.; Ng, A.; Lee, H. An analysis of single-layer networks in unsupervised feature learning. In Proceedings of the Fourteenth International Conference on Artificial Intelligence and Statistics. JMLR Workshop and Conference Proceedings, Lauderdale, FL, USA, 11–13 April 2011; pp. 215–223.

164. Zhang, X.; Dou, H.; Ju, T.; Xu, J.; Zhang, S. Fusing heterogeneous features from stacked sparse autoencoder for histopathological image analysis. *IEEE J. Biomed. Health Inform.* **2015**, *20*, 1377–1383. [CrossRef]
165. Tao, C.; Pan, H.; Li, Y.; Zou, Z. Unsupervised spectral–spatial feature learning with stacked sparse autoencoder for hyperspectral imagery classification. *IEEE Geosci. Remote Sens. Lett.* **2015**, *12*, 2438–2442.
166. Chen, Y.; Lin, Z.; Zhao, X.; Wang, G.; Gu, Y. Deep learning-based classification of hyperspectral data. *IEEE J. Sel. Top. Appl. Earth Obs. Remote Sens.* **2014**, *7*, 2094–2107. [CrossRef]
167. Cheng, G.; Zhou, P.; Han, J.; Guo, L.; Han, J. Auto-encoder-based shared mid-level visual dictionary learning for scene classification using very high resolution remote sensing images. *IET Comput. Vis.* **2015**, *9*, 639–647. [CrossRef]
168. Li, E.; Du, P.; Samat, A.; Meng, Y.; Che, M. Mid-level feature representation via sparse autoencoder for remotely sensed scene classification. *IEEE J. Sel. Top. Appl. Earth Obs. Remote Sens.* **2016**, *10*, 1068–1081. [CrossRef]
169. Geng, J.; Fan, J.; Wang, H.; Ma, X.; Li, B.; Chen, F. High-resolution SAR image classification via deep convolutional autoencoders. *IEEE Geosci. Remote Sens. Lett.* **2015**, *12*, 2351–2355. [CrossRef]
170. Geng, J.; Wang, H.; Fan, J.; Ma, X. Deep supervised and contractive neural network for SAR image classification. *IEEE Trans. Geosci. Remote Sens.* **2017**, *55*, 2442–2459. [CrossRef]
171. Othman, E.; Bazi, Y.; Alajlan, N.; Alhichri, H.; Melgani, F. Using convolutional features and a sparse autoencoder for land-use scene classification. *Int. J. Remote Sens.* **2016**, *37*, 2149–2167. [CrossRef]
172. Pu, Y.; Gan, Z.; Henao, R.; Yuan, X.; Li, C.; Stevens, A.; Carin, L. Variational autoencoder for deep learning of images, labels and captions. *Adv. Neural Inf. Process. Syst.* **2016**, *29*, 2360–2368.
173. Kasun, L.L.C.; Yang, Y.; Huang, G.B.; Zhang, Z. Dimension reduction with extreme learning machine. *IEEE Trans. Image Process.* **2016**, *25*, 3906–3918. [CrossRef] [PubMed]
174. Tissera, M.D.; McDonnell, M.D. Deep extreme learning machines: Supervised autoencoding architecture for classification. *Neurocomputing* **2016**, *174*, 42–49. [CrossRef]
175. Lv, F.; Han, M.; Qiu, T. Remote sensing image classification based on ensemble extreme learning machine with stacked autoencoder. *IEEE Access* **2017**, *5*, 9021–9031. [CrossRef]
176. Ghifary, M.; Kleijn, W.B.; Zhang, M.; Balduzzi, D. Domain generalization for object recognition with multi-task autoencoders. In Proceedings of the IEEE International Conference on Computer Vision, Santiago, Chile, 7–13 December 2015; pp. 2551–2559.
177. Han, J.; Zhang, D.; Hu, X.; Guo, L.; Ren, J.; Wu, F. Background prior-based salient object detection via deep reconstruction residual. *IEEE Trans. Circuits Syst. Video Technol.* **2014**, *25*, 1309–1321.
178. Yan, K.; Li, C.; Wang, X.; Li, A.; Yuan, Y.; Kim, J.; Feng, D. Adaptive background search and foreground estimation for saliency detection via comprehensive autoencoder. In Proceedings of the 2016 IEEE International Conference on Image Processing (ICIP), Phoenix, AZ, USA, 25–28 September 2016; IEEE: Piscataway, NJ, USA, 2016; pp. 2767–2771.
179. Ge, C.; Fu, K.; Liu, F.; Bai, L.; Yang, J. Co-saliency detection via inter and intra saliency propagation. *Signal Process. Image Commun.* **2016**, *44*, 69–83. [CrossRef]
180. Cho, K. Boltzmann machines and denoising autoencoders for image denoising. *arXiv* **2013**, arXiv:1301.3468.
181. Cho, K. Simple sparsification improves sparse denoising autoencoders in denoising highly corrupted images. In Proceedings of the International Conference on Machine Learning. PMLR, Atlanta, GA, USA, 16–21 June 2013; pp. 432–440.
182. Gondara, L. Medical image denoising using convolutional denoising autoencoders. In Proceedings of the 2016 IEEE 16th International Conference on Data Mining Workshops (ICDMW), Barcelona, Spain, 12–15 December 2016; IEEE: Piscataway, NJ, USA, 2016; pp. 241–246.
183. Mao, X.J.; Shen, C.; Yang, Y.B. Image restoration using convolutional auto-encoders with symmetric skip connections. *arXiv* **2016**, arXiv:1606.08921.
184. Wang, R.; Tao, D. Non-local auto-encoder with collaborative stabilization for image restoration. *IEEE Trans. Image Process.* **2016**, *25*, 2117–2129. [CrossRef] [PubMed]
185. Zhou, W.; Li, H.; Tian, Q. Recent advance in content-based image retrieval: A literature survey. *arXiv* **2017**, arXiv:1706.06064.
186. Yelamarthi, S.K.; Reddy, S.K.; Mishra, A.; Mittal, A. A zero-shot framework for sketch based image retrieval. In Proceedings of the European Conference on Computer Vision (ECCV), Munich, Germany, 8–14 September 2018; pp. 300–317.
187. Wu, H.; Flierl, M. Learning product codebooks using vector-quantized autoencoders for image retrieval. In Proceedings of the 2019 IEEE Global Conference on Signal and Information Processing (GlobalSIP), Ottawa, ON, Canada, 11–14 November 2019; IEEE: Piscataway, NJ, USA, 2019; pp. 1–5.
188. Krizhevsky, A.; Hinton, G.E. Using very deep autoencoders for content-based image retrieval. In Proceedings of the European Symposium on Esann, Bruges, Belgium, 27–29 April 2011; Volume 1, p. 2.
189. Zhou, W.; Shao, Z.; Diao, C.; Cheng, Q. High-resolution remote-sensing imagery retrieval using sparse features by auto-encoder. *Remote Sens. Lett.* **2015**, *6*, 775–783. [CrossRef]
190. Zhao, X.; Nutter, B. Content based image retrieval system using Wavelet transformation and multiple input multiple task deep autoencoder. In Proceedings of the 2016 IEEE Southwest Symposium on Image Analysis and Interpretation (SSIAI), Santa Fe, NM, USA, 6–8 March 2016; IEEE: Piscataway, NJ, USA, 2016; pp. 97–100.
191. Wang, M.; Ni, B.; Hua, X.S.; Chua, T.S. Assistive tagging: A survey of multimedia tagging with human-computer joint exploration. *ACM Comput. Surv.* **2012**, *44*, 1–24. [CrossRef]

192. Liu, Y.; Feng, X.; Zhou, Z. Multimodal video classification with stacked contractive autoencoders. *Signal Process.* **2016**, *120*, 761–766. [CrossRef]
193. Sachan, D.S.; Tekwani, U.; Sethi, A. Sports video classification from multimodal information using deep neural networks. In Proceedings of the 2013 AAAI Fall Symposium Series, Arlington, VA, USA, 15–17 November 2013.
194. Jhuo, I.H.; Lee, D.T. Video event detection via multi-modality deep learning. In Proceedings of the 2014 22nd International Conference on Pattern Recognition, Stockholm, Sweden, 24–28 August 2014; IEEE: Piscataway, NJ, USA, 2014; pp. 666–671.
195. D'Avino, D.; Cozzolino, D.; Poggi, G.; Verdoliva, L. Autoencoder with recurrent neural networks for video forgery detection. *arXiv* **2017**, arXiv:1708.08754. [CrossRef]
196. Li, J.; Xia, C.; Chen, X. A benchmark dataset and saliency-guided stacked autoencoders for video-based salient object detection. *IEEE Trans. Image Process.* **2017**, *27*, 349–364. [CrossRef]
197. Grathwohl, W.; Wilson, A. Disentangling space and time in video with hierarchical variational auto-encoders. *arXiv* **2016**, arXiv:1612.04440.
198. Li, Y.; Mandt, S. A deep generative model for disentangled representations of sequential data. *arXiv* **2018**, arXiv:1803.02991.
199. Wang, N.; Yeung, D.Y. Learning a deep compact image representation for visual tracking. *Adv. Neural Inf. Process. Syst.* **2013**, *26*, 809–817.
200. Zhou, X.; Xie, L.; Zhang, P.; Zhang, Y. An ensemble of deep neural networks for object tracking. In Proceedings of the 2014 IEEE International Conference on Image Processing (ICIP), Paris, France, 27–30 October 2014; IEEE: Piscataway, NJ, USA, 2014; pp. 843–847.
201. Kuen, J.; Lim, K.M.; Lee, C.P. Self-taught learning of a deep invariant representation for visual tracking via temporal slowness principle. *Pattern Recognit.* **2015**, *48*, 2964–2982. [CrossRef]
202. Ding, J.; Huang, Y.; Liu, W.; Huang, K. Severely blurred object tracking by learning deep image representations. *IEEE Trans. Circuits Syst. Video Technol.* **2015**, *26*, 319–331. [CrossRef]
203. Choi, J.; Chang, H.J.; Fischer, T.; Yun, S.; Lee, K.; Jeong, J.; Choi, J.Y. Context-aware deep feature compression for high-speed visual tracking. In Proceedings of the IEEE Conference on Computer Vision and Pattern Recognition, Salt Lake City, UT, USA, 18–22 June 2018; pp. 479–488.
204. Qiao, M.; Wang, T.; Li, J.; Li, C.; Lin, Z.; Snoussi, H. Abnormal event detection based on deep autoencoder fusing optical flow. In Proceedings of the 2017 36th Chinese Control Conference (CCC), Dalian, China, 26–28 July 2017; IEEE: Piscataway, NJ, USA, 2017; pp. 11098–11103.
205. Narasimhan, M.G. Dynamic video anomaly detection and localization using sparse denoising autoencoders. *Multimed. Tools Appl.* **2018**, *77*, 13173–13195. [CrossRef]
206. Gong, D.; Liu, L.; Le, V.; Saha, B.; Mansour, M.R.; Venkatesh, S.; Hengel, A.V.D. Memorizing normality to detect anomaly: Memory augmented deep autoencoder for unsupervised anomaly detection. In Proceedings of the IEEE/CVF International Conference on Computer Vision, Seoul, Republic of Korea, 27 October–2 November 2019; pp. 1705–1714.
207. Sabokrou, M.; Fathy, M.; Hoseini, M. Video anomaly detection and localisation based on the sparsity and reconstruction error of auto-encoder. *Electron. Lett.* **2016**, *52*, 1122–1124. [CrossRef]
208. Ionescu, R.T.; Khan, F.S.; Georgescu, M.I.; Shao, L. Object-centric auto-encoders and dummy anomalies for abnormal event detection in video. In Proceedings of the IEEE/CVF Conference on Computer Vision and Pattern Recognition, Long Beach, CA, USA, 15–20 June 2019; pp. 7842–7851.
209. Fan, Y.; Wen, G.; Li, D.; Qiu, S.; Levine, M.D.; Xiao, F. Video anomaly detection and localization via gaussian mixture fully convolutional variational autoencoder. *Comput. Vis. Image Underst.* **2020**, *195*, 102920. [CrossRef]
210. Bao, T.; Ding, C.; Karmoshi, S.; Zhu, M. Video anomaly detection based on adaptive multiple auto-encoders. In Proceedings of the International Symposium on Visual Computing, Las Vegas, NV, USA, 12–14 December 2016; Springer: Cham, Switzerland, 2016; pp. 83–91.
211. Leng, B.; Guo, S.; Zhang, X.; Xiong, Z. 3D object retrieval with stacked local convolutional autoencoder. *Signal Process.* **2015**, *112*, 119–128. [CrossRef]
212. Wang, Y.; Xie, Z.; Xu, K.; Dou, Y.; Lei, Y. An efficient and effective convolutional auto-encoder extreme learning machine network for 3d feature learning. *Neurocomputing* **2016**, *174*, 988–998. [CrossRef]
213. Xie, J.; Dai, G.; Zhu, F.; Wong, E.K.; Fang, Y. Deepshape: Deep-learned shape descriptor for 3d shape retrieval. *IEEE Trans. Pattern Anal. Mach. Intell.* **2016**, *39*, 1335–1345. [CrossRef] [PubMed]
214. Siddiqua, A.; Fan, G. Supervised deep-autoencoder for depth image-based 3d model retrieval. In Proceedings of the 2018 IEEE Winter Conference on Applications of Computer Vision (WACV), Lake Tahoe, NV, USA, 12–15 March 2018; IEEE: Piscataway, NJ, USA, 2018; pp. 939–946.
215. Csurka, G.; Dance, C.; Fan, L.; Willamowski, J.; Bray, C. Visual categorization with bags of keypoints. In Proceedings of the Workshop on Statistical Learning in Computer Vision, ECCV, Prague, Czech Republic, 16 May 2004; Volume 1, pp. 1–2.
216. Wang, J.; Yang, J.; Yu, K.; Lv, F.; Huang, T.; Gong, Y. Locality-constrained linear coding for image classification. In Proceedings of the 2010 IEEE Computer Society Conference on Computer Vision and Pattern Recognition, San Francisco, CA, USA, 13–18 June 2010; IEEE: Piscataway, NJ, USA, 2010; pp. 3360–3367.

217. Perronnin, F.; Sánchez, J.; Mensink, T. Improving the fisher kernel for large-scale image classification. In Proceedings of the European Conference on Computer Vision, Heraklion, Greece, 5–11 September 2010; Springer: Berlin/Heidelberg, Germany, 2010; pp. 143–156.
218. Ranjan, A.; Bolkart, T.; Sanyal, S.; Black, M.J. Generating 3D faces using convolutional mesh autoencoders. In Proceedings of the European Conference on Computer Vision (ECCV), Munich, Germany, 8–14 September 2018; pp. 704–720.
219. Zhang, J.; Li, K.; Liang, Y.; Li, N. Learning 3D faces from 2D images via stacked contractive autoencoder. *Neurocomputing* **2017**, *257*, 67–78. [CrossRef]
220. Batmaz, Z.; Yurekli, A.; Bilge, A.; Kaleli, C. A review on deep learning for recommender systems: Challenges and remedies. *Artif. Intell. Rev.* **2019**, *52*, 1–37. [CrossRef]
221. Zhang, G.; Liu, Y.; Jin, X. A survey of autoencoder-based recommender systems. *Front. Comput. Sci.* **2020**, *14*, 430–450. [CrossRef]
222. Ouyang, Y.; Liu, W.; Rong, W.; Xiong, Z. Autoencoder-based collaborative filtering. In Proceedings of the International Conference on Neural Information Processing, Montreal, QC, Canada, 8–13 December 2014; Springer: Cham, Switzerland, 2014; pp. 284–291.
223. Sedhain, S.; Menon, A.K.; Sanner, S.; Xie, L. Autorec: Autoencoders meet collaborative filtering. In Proceedings of the 24th International Conference on World Wide Web, Florence, Italy, 18–22 May 2015; pp. 111–112.
224. Zhang, S.; Yao, L.; Sun, A.; Tay, Y. Deep learning based recommender system: A survey and new perspectives. *ACM Comput. Surv.* **2019**, *52*, 1–38. [CrossRef]
225. Wu, Y.; DuBois, C.; Zheng, A.X.; Ester, M. Collaborative denoising auto-encoders for top-n recommender systems. In Proceedings of the Ninth ACM International Conference on Web Search and Data Mining, San Francisco, CA, USA, 22–25 February 2016; pp. 153–162.
226. Zhuang, F.; Zhang, Z.; Qian, M.; Shi, C.; Xie, X.; He, Q. Representation learning via dual-autoencoder for recommendation. *Neural Netw.* **2017**, *90*, 83–89. [CrossRef]
227. Wang, K.; Xu, L.; Huang, L.; Wang, C.D.; Lai, J.H. Stacked discriminative denoising auto-encoder based recommender system. In Proceedings of the International Conference on Intelligent Science and Big Data Engineering, Lanzhou, China, 18–19 August 2018; Springer: Cham, Switzerland, 2018; pp. 276–286.
228. Rafailidis, D.; Crestani, F. Recommendation with social relationships via deep learning. In Proceedings of the ACM SIGIR International Conference on Theory of Information Retrieval, Amsterdam, The Netherlands, 1–4 October 2017; pp. 151–158.
229. Unger, M.; Bar, A.; Shapira, B.; Rokach, L. Towards latent context-aware recommendation systems. *Knowl.-Based Syst.* **2016**, *104*, 165–178. [CrossRef]
230. Gu, S.; Liu, X.; Cai, L.; Shen, J. Fashion coordinates recommendation based on user behavior and visual clothing style. In Proceedings of the 3rd International Conference on Communication and Information Processing, Tokyo, Japan, 24–26 November 2017; pp. 185–189.
231. Wang, H.; Shi, X.; Yeung, D.Y. Relational stacked denoising autoencoder for tag recommendation. In Proceedings of the Twenty-Ninth AAAI Conference on Artificial Intelligence, Austin, TX, USA, 25–30 January 2015.
232. Li, S.; Kawale, J.; Fu, Y. Deep collaborative filtering via marginalized denoising auto-encoder. In Proceedings of the 24th ACM International on Conference on Information and Knowledge Management, Melbourne, Australia, 18–23 October 2015; pp. 811–820.
233. Wang, H.; Wang, N.; Yeung, D.Y. Collaborative deep learning for recommender systems. In Proceedings of the 21th ACM SIGKDD International Conference on Knowledge Discovery and Data Mining, Sydney, Australia, 10–13 August 2015; pp. 1235–1244.
234. Zhang, F.; Yuan, N.J.; Lian, D.; Xie, X.; Ma, W.Y. Collaborative knowledge base embedding for recommender systems. In Proceedings of the 22nd ACM SIGKDD International Conference on Knowledge Discovery and Data Mining, San Francisco, CA, USA, 13–17 August 2016; pp. 353–362.
235. Lee, W.; Song, K.; Moon, I.C. Augmented variational autoencoders for collaborative filtering with auxiliary information. In Proceedings of the 2017 ACM on Conference on Information and Knowledge Management, Singapore, 6–10 November 2017; pp. 1139–1148.
236. Liu, Y.; Wang, S.; Khan, M.S.; He, J. A novel deep hybrid recommender system based on auto-encoder with neural collaborative filtering. *Big Data Min. Anal.* **2018**, *1*, 211–221.
237. Mu, R. A survey of recommender systems based on deep learning. *IEEE Access* **2018**, *6*, 69009–69022. [CrossRef]
238. Zhang, Y.; Peng, H. Sample reconstruction with deep autoencoder for one sample per person face recognition. *IET Comput. Vis.* **2017**, *11*, 471–478. [CrossRef]
239. Gao, S.; Zhang, Y.; Jia, K.; Lu, J.; Zhang, Y. Single sample face recognition via learning deep supervised autoencoders. *IEEE Trans. Inf. Forensics Secur.* **2015**, *10*, 2108–2118. [CrossRef]
240. Vega, P.J.S.; Feitosa, R.Q.; Quirita, V.H.A.; Happ, P.N. Single sample face recognition from video via stacked supervised auto-encoder. In Proceedings of the 2016 29th SIBGRAPI Conference on Graphics, Patterns and Images (SIBGRAPI), São Paulo, Brazil, 4–7 October 2016; IEEE: Piscataway, NJ, USA, 2016; pp. 96–103.
241. Xu, C.; Liu, Q.; Ye, M. Age invariant face recognition and retrieval by coupled auto-encoder networks. *Neurocomputing* **2017**, *222*, 62–71. [CrossRef]
242. Kan, M.; Shan, S.; Chang, H.; Chen, X. Stacked progressive auto-encoders (spae) for face recognition across poses. In Proceedings of the IEEE Conference on Computer Vision and Pattern Recognition, Columbus, OH, USA, 23–28 June 2014; pp. 1883–1890.

243. Sahu, S.; Gupta, R.; Sivaraman, G.; AbdAlmageed, W.; Espy-Wilson, C. Adversarial auto-encoders for speech based emotion recognition. *arXiv* **2018**, arXiv:1806.02146.
244. Eskimez, S.E.; Duan, Z.; Heinzelman, W. Unsupervised learning approach to feature analysis for automatic speech emotion recognition. In Proceedings of the 2018 IEEE International Conference on Acoustics, Speech and Signal Processing (ICASSP), Calgary, AB, Canada, 15–20 April 2018; IEEE: Piscataway, NJ, USA, 2018; pp. 5099–5103.
245. Neumann, M.; Vu, N.T. Improving speech emotion recognition with unsupervised representation learning on unlabeled speech. In Proceedings of the ICASSP 2019–2019 IEEE International Conference on Acoustics, Speech and Signal Processing (ICASSP), Brighton, UK, 12–17 May 2019; IEEE: Piscataway, NJ, USA, 2019; pp. 7390–7394.
246. Sun, T.W.; Wu, A.Y.A. Sparse autoencoder with attention mechanism for speech emotion recognition. In Proceedings of the 2019 IEEE International Conference on Artificial Intelligence Circuits and Systems (AICAS), Hsinchu, Taiwan, 18–20 March 2019; IEEE: Piscataway, NJ, USA, 2019; pp. 146–149.
247. Usman, M.; Latif, S.; Qadir, J. Using deep autoencoders for facial expression recognition. In Proceedings of the 2017 13th International Conference on Emerging Technologies (ICET), Islamabad, Pakistan, 27–28 December 2017; IEEE: Piscataway, NJ, USA, 2017; pp. 1–6.
248. Chen, L.; Zhou, M.; Su, W.; Wu, M.; She, J.; Hirota, K. Softmax regression based deep sparse autoencoder network for facial emotion recognition in human-robot interaction. *Inf. Sci.* **2018**, *428*, 49–61. [CrossRef]
249. Zeng, N.; Zhang, H.; Song, B.; Liu, W.; Li, Y.; Dobaie, A.M. Facial expression recognition via learning deep sparse autoencoders. *Neurocomputing* **2018**, *273*, 643–649. [CrossRef]
250. Ruiz-Garcia, A.; Elshaw, M.; Altahhan, A.; Palade, V. Stacked deep convolutional auto-encoders for emotion recognition from facial expressions. In Proceedings of the International Joint Conference on Neural Networks, Anchorage, AK, USA, 14–19 May 2017; IEEE: Piscataway, NJ, USA, 2017.
251. Larsen, A.B.L.; Sønderby, S.K.; Larochelle, H.; Winther, O. Autoencoding beyond pixels using a learned similarity metric. In Proceedings of the International Conference on Machine Learning. PMLR, New York, NY, USA, 20–22 June 2016; pp. 1558–1566.
252. Cai, L.; Gao, H.; Ji, S. Multi-stage variational auto-encoders for coarse-to-fine image generation. In Proceedings of the 2019 SIAM International Conference on Data Mining. Society for Industrial and Applied Mathematics, Calgary, AB, Canada, 2–4 May 2019; pp. 630–638.
253. Li, H.Q.; Fang, N.; Zhao, Q.F.; Xia, Z.Y. Instruction intent understanding method based on Deep Denoising autoencoder. *J. Shanghai Jiaotong Univ.* **2016**, *50*, 1102–1107. (In Chinese)
254. Yuan, X.; Huang, B.; Wang, Y.; Yang, C.; Gui, W. Deep learning-based feature representation and its application for soft sensor modeling with variable-wise weighted SAE. *IEEE Trans. Ind. Inform.* **2018**, *14*, 3235–3243. [CrossRef]
255. Chen, K.; Seuret, M.; Liwicki, M.; Hennebert, J.; Ingold, R. Page segmentation of historical document images with convolutional autoencoders. In Proceedings of the 2015 13th International Conference on Document Analysis and Recognition (ICDAR), Nancy, France, 23–26 August 2015; IEEE: Piscataway, NJ, USA, 2015; pp. 1011–1015.
256. Li, X.; Du, N.; Li, H.; Li, K.; Gao, J.; Zhang, A. A deep learning approach to link prediction in dynamic networks. In Proceedings of the 2014 SIAM International Conference on Data Mining. Society for Industrial and Applied Mathematics, Philadelphia, PA, USA, 24–26 April 2014; pp. 289–297.
257. Xie, T.; Fu, X.; Ganea, O.E.; Barzilay, R.; Jaakkola, T. Crystal diffusion variational autoencoder for periodic material generation. *arXiv* **2021**, arXiv:2110.06197.
258. Andresini, G.; Appice, A.; Malerba, D. Autoencoder-based deep metric learning for network intrusion detection. *Inf. Sci.* **2021**, *569*, 706–727. [CrossRef]
259. Erickson, B.J.; Korfiatis, P.; Akkus, Z.; Kline, T.; Philbrick, K. Toolkits and libraries for deep learning. *J. Digit. Imaging* **2017**, *30*, 400–405. [CrossRef] [PubMed]
260. Zheng, Z.Y.; Gu, S.Y. *TensorFlow: Google Deep Learning Framework in Action*; Publishing House of Electronics Industry: Beijing, China, 2017. (In Chinese)
261. Mohan, J.; Nair, M.S. Domain independent static video summarization using sparse autoencoders and K-means clustering. *J. Intell. Fuzzy Syst.* **2019**, *36*, 1945–1955. [CrossRef]
262. Hammouche, R.; Attia, A.; Akhrouf, S.; Akhtar, Z. Gabor filter bank with deep autoencoder based face recognition system. *Expert Syst. Appl.* **2022**, *197*, 116743. [CrossRef]
263. Wu, N.; Wang, X.; Lin, B.; Zhang, K. A CNN-based end-to-end learning framework toward intelligent communication systems. *IEEE Access* **2019**, *7*, 110197–110204. [CrossRef]
264. Bao, J.; Chen, D.; Wen, F.; Li, H.; Hua, G. CVAE-GAN: Fine-grained image generation through asymmetric training. In Proceedings of the IEEE International Conference on Computer Vision, Venice, Italy, 22–29 October 2017; pp. 2745–2754.
265. Wang, Y. *Research and Application of Neural Network Model Based on Visual Attention Mechanism*; University of Science and Technology of China: Hefei, China, 2017. (In Chinese)
266. Liu, X.; Li, H.Y.; Zhong, B.N.; Du, J.X. Transaudio video speaker tagging combined with supervised joint consistency autoencoder. *J. Electron. Inf. Technol.* **2018**, *40*, 1635–1642. (In Chinese)
267. Zhang, S.; Rui, T.; Ren, T.W.; Yang, C.S.; Zou, J.H. Image reconstruction based on supervised Learning deep autoencoder. *Comput. Sci.* **2018**, *45*, 267–271. (In Chinese)

268. Le, L.; Patterson, A.; White, M. Supervised autoencoders: Improving generalization performance with unsupervised regularizers. *Adv. Neural Inf. Process. Syst.* **2018**, *31*, 107–117.
269. Meng, L.H. *Theory Research and Application of Automatic Encoder*; China University of Mining and Technology: Beijing, China, 2017. (In Chinese)
270. Ni, J.C.; Xu, Y.L.; Ma, S.P.; Li, S. A New Algorithm for Training automatic encoders with Side Suppression Mechanism. *Comput. Appl. Softw.* **2015**, *32*, 157–160. (In Chinese)
271. Rasmus, A.; Valpola, H.; Raiko, T. Lateral connections in denoising autoencoders support supervised learning. *arXiv* **2015**, arXiv:1504.08215.
272. Luo, S.W. *Visual Perception System Information Processing Theory*; Publishing House of Electronics Industry: Beijing, China, 2006. (In Chinese)
273. Zeng, N.; Wang, Z.; Zhang, H.; Alsaadi, F.E. A novel switching delayed PSO algorithm for estimating unknown parameters of lateral flow immunoassay. *Cogn. Comput.* **2016**, *8*, 143–152. [CrossRef]
274. Yuan, F.N.; Zhang, L.; Shi, J.T.; Xia, X.; Li, G. Review on theory and application of self-coding neural networks. *Chin. J. Comput.* **2019**, *42*, 203–230. (In Chinese)

Disclaimer/Publisher's Note: The statements, opinions and data contained in all publications are solely those of the individual author(s) and contributor(s) and not of MDPI and/or the editor(s). MDPI and/or the editor(s) disclaim responsibility for any injury to people or property resulting from any ideas, methods, instructions or products referred to in the content.

MDPI
St. Alban-Anlage 66
4052 Basel
Switzerland
www.mdpi.com

Mathematics Editorial Office
E-mail: mathematics@mdpi.com
www.mdpi.com/journal/mathematics

Disclaimer/Publisher's Note: The statements, opinions and data contained in all publications are solely those of the individual author(s) and contributor(s) and not of MDPI and/or the editor(s). MDPI and/or the editor(s) disclaim responsibility for any injury to people or property resulting from any ideas, methods, instructions or products referred to in the content.

www.ingramcontent.com/pod-product-compliance
Lightning Source LLC
LaVergne TN
LVHW070229100526
838202LV00015B/2110